THEODICY

ANTONIO ROSMINI

THEODICY

Essays on Divine Providence

He was good, and the good can never have any jealousy of anything.*
Plato, in *Timaeus*

Translated by
TERENCE WATSON

ROSMINI HOUSE
DURHAM

Rosmini House, Woodbine Road
Durham DH1 5DR, U.K.

Translated from
Teodicea
Critical Edition, vol. 22, Stresa, 1977

Typeset by Rosmini House, Durham
Printed by Bell & Bain Limited, Glasgow

ISBN 978 1 899093 80 9

Foreword

This translation of Rosmini's *Teodicea* comes late in the series of translations produced and published by Rosmini House, but in Rosmini's output his discussion of the challenging subject of God's Providence preceded his foundational, philosophical work, *A New Essay concerning the Origin of Ideas.*

In this first decade of the 21st. century, a work dedicated totally to the action of the Divine Being in the universe would seem to be also totally irrelevant, if not meaningless, due to rampant agnosticism and growing atheism. There would be those who would say that theodicy has nothing to say to contemporary man. But millions of human beings on this planet still believe in the existence of an uncreated, infinite, eternal and supreme Being; they are not driven by superstition or primitive fear but by an intelligent conviction. For such people this book could have something helpful to offer.

But whether we believe in the existence of such a Being or not, none of us can escape the events of life on this earth, nor guarantee we will not be afflicted by the forces of nature either in our person or in our property. Despite the extraordinary advances of medical science, the problem of personal health remains: while one cure is discovered, a new disease reveals itself, and many known human illnesses still avoid a solution. Similarly, in our battle to defend ourselves against the destructive forces of nature, we make progress and gain a victory here and there. But despite this progress, nature always seems to have something in reserve with which to strike us suddenly and cruelly with consequent massive devastation of property and loss of life. There is also the ever-present tragedy of man's inhumanity to man. Human ingenuity, dedication and intelligence must continue to grapple with the problems that beset us, but they will never find a final, all-encompassing answer. We need some explanation for these cruel events, and this book offers one.

For the person of faith however the matter is different. A believer has a tremendous advantage because he can turn to a higher power, a supreme governor, who has control of all nature and of all human beings and their behaviour, and wishes in fact only good for his intelligent creature. The challenge to the believer is somehow to attain to some understanding of this Provider's government of all things, or at least find some explanations that satisfy the mind and soul so that life can proceed in peace and tranquillity, with complete trust in a 'manager' who knows what he is doing and will certainly obtain his end. Again, *Theodicy* offers the believer thoughts that can strengthen this trust.

Antonio Rosmini was, from his teenage years, a believer who had complete trust in the Providence of God, a trust that would deepen and grow stronger as the years progressed and as misunderstanding, rejection and isolation became the cross he had to carry. At the darkest moment of his life and in reaction to what he was suffering, he wrote: 'As I meditate on it [Providence], I admire it; as I admire it, I extol it; extolling it, I give thanks for it, and giving thanks, I am filled with joy. And how could I do otherwise, if I know through reason and faith and feel in the depth of my spirit that all that is done or wished or permitted by God is done by an eternal, an infinite, an essential love? Indeed, who could be cast down by love?' (1849).

This wonder at, and trust in, divine Providence called forth from him in his younger years (1825) his first publication on the topic. It was a short essay of about ninety pages in which he dealt with the ever-recurring difficulty of evil in the world, a problem that vexes the human mind, resulting sometimes in hopelessness, and even in outright rejection of a loving God.

Continuing his meditation on Providence and the problems it causes for human beings, he composed and published two years later a second essay, again a short work of a hundred pages. In it, he dealt with human weakness relative to the decrees of Providence. He points out that human reason, by the very fact that it is created, cannot ever hope and expect to understand the actions of an infinite Mind.

For twenty years he let the matter rest there. But the experiences of life, his further philosophical meditation and his greater maturity resulted in a third work, this time of more than three hundred pages. Changing the order of the first two essays, he combined them with this third work, called them three 'books' and published them in 1845 as one volume under the title *Theodicy*. In the third longer and more mature work, he presented what for him is the basic law governing all divine actions in the universe: the law of the least means. For him, this law is a natural result of the divine attributes of goodness and wisdom, and as he develops its application, he discusses other laws that result from it.

Philosopher that he was, it was inevitable that wherever it was helpful to his purpose, his philosophical theories found a place in the work. These can cause difficulty, particularly for a reader who knows nothing of Rosmini's philosophical teachings. But this should not be a deterrent to reading the book. Those parts that obviously have a philosophical basis can be omitted without any serious loss to the force of his argument. If the book is read without prejudice, it can go a long way to solving the challenges presented to the human mind and the seeming lack of love and goodness on the part of God in dealing with his creation and intelligent creatures.

TERENCE WATSON

Durham,
July, 2009

Note

The many and long quotations given by the author in their original language have been translated. An *asterisk* indicates that the original language can be found in the section entitled *Original Language References* after the *Appendix*.

Square brackets [ ] indicate notes or additions by the translator or editor of the Critical Edition.

References to this and other works of Rosmini are given by paragraph number unless otherwise stated.

Abbreviations used for Rosmini's quoted works are:

AMS: *Anthropology as an Aid to Moral Science*
CS: *Conscience*
ER: *The Essence of Right* (vol. 1 of *The Philosophy of Right*)
NE: *A New Essay concerning the Origin of Ideas*
PE: *Principles of Ethics*
SC: *The Summary Cause for the Stability or Downfall of Human Societies*
SP: *Society and its Purpose*

Translation of some particular Italian words

Essere (used as a noun) is translated 'being'. *Ente* is translated 'ens' (plural, 'entia'). Rosmini defines *being* as 'the act of every ens and entity', and gives two definitions of *ens*: 'a subject that has being' and 'being, with some of its terms'.

Sensitivo is translated 'sensitive' and sometimes 'feeling' (adjective), describing that which possesses feeling. *Sensibile* is translated 'feelable' and also 'sensible' with the meaning 'feelable', that which can be felt.

The English 'passion' is retained for the Italian *passione* but not with the contemporary meaning of the English word. It simply means that which is experienced passively in feeling, any feeling, any emotion; it is the opposite of *action*.

Rosmini does not use the verb 'realise' with the meaning of 'think' but always with the meaning 'to make real', that is, become or make something *felt* or *sensed*. The same applies to 'reality' and 'real'; they all mean that which is *felt*.

'Goods' means all things that are a good, of whatever nature . Similarly 'evils' refers to all things that are harmful or unpleasant

'Comprehensor' (a theological term) refers to a human being who enjoys the beatific vision of God in heaven, while 'viator' is a human being still 'on the way' on earth.

Rosmini speaks about the 'law of *germ*' instead of the 'law of seed' and does so intentionally, as he explains in the text.

Scripture quotations

These are taken from the Revised Standard Version wherever possible. But in order to follow Rosmini's argument it is sometimes necessary to use the Douai version, indicated by ✝. Finally, where Rosmini has used a version that cannot be found in English, a translation has been made of his Italian; these translations are indicated by [R] in the corresponding footnote.

Contents

BOOK ONE

BOOK TWO

BOOK THREE

TO HIS DEAR SISTER
GIOSEFFA MARGARITA

THE AUTHOR

Some years have passed since you took the place of a mother for some poor orphan girls gathered in a house. At that time I sent you as a gift a book on Christian Education as a sign of the delight that your charitable work caused me. But now that you are bringing to the Church of Trent, which is our common mother, a group of nuns consecrated entirely to serving the Lord in their neighbour, particularly in the sick and needy, you double my first delight and also the gratitude I owe you for such a work. Because your new task is more generous than the first, it brings a more stable and greater good to those who are our brethren through spiritual birth. But the publication of this new book and its dedication to you does not mean I am settling my debt, which is something I cannot do, nor would wish to do even if I could; on the contrary I am fully prepared for my debt to increase. I simply wish to give you a sign that I acknowledge the debt and will do so as long as I live. Indeed, to those who bring us honest joy we must be not only grateful but acknowledge what we have received: we must at least confess all we have received from them. Nor can there be greater pleasures than those we experience at the sight of virtuous actions. The arguments of this book may indeed be demanding and difficult, and for this reason may perhaps not be understood equally by every woman, but they are not beyond your ability because you have already undertaken and persevered in serious study, which you have enjoyed so much in matters of religion and religious philosophy. I trust therefore that you will gladly accept my little gift.

God be with you.

Your affectionate brother,
Antonio

Milan, 14th August 1827

Preface

1. The second of the three books which make up this work was first printed separately, under the title 'Essay',[1] and later published with the first book under the same title 'Essay'. This combined edition was inserted in the collection of *Opuscoli Filosofici* (1827–28) printed at Milan. The third book has not been published.

All three deal with the same subject under a different aspect, but they are connected and perfect each other, and although each can stand on its own and in some way deals fully with its own topic, I thought it fitting to present them to the public as one work under the title *Theodicy.*

No other word expresses more suitably the content of the whole work. *Theodicy* (Θεοῦ δίκη) means 'justice of God', and this treatise has no other object than to justify the equity and goodness of God in the distribution of the goods and evils of the world. Modern authors use the word with less propriety as almost synonymous with natural theology.

2. The connection between the three books is the following:

The first is *logical,* that is, it lays out and prescribes the norms that thought must follow if it wishes to avoid error in its judgments about the dispositions of divine providence. The placing of this book and what it states before the other two was necessary in order to eradicate the first cause of the errors committed by human beings when they judge the supreme dispositions according to which God permits evils and grants goods among his creatures. This cause is *ignorance of logical cognitions* in all who complain against providence and condemn its decrees, impertinently passing sentence on it without first calculating the power of their own reason or investigating whether their understanding is in fact sufficiently capable of solving such challenging and sublime questions. This first book clearly indicates the method of reasoning to be followed in the other two

(1) Printed at Milan by Placido Maria Visai, 1826. — Mendrisio, the Minerva Ticinese Press, 1829.

books; it demonstrates the paths the human mind must take if it wishes to reason securely about such a difficult and important matter.

The second book is *natural*, that is, it is a continual meditation on the laws of nature, the essential limitations of the created world and the chain of causes. Its purpose is also to combat another cause of errors concerning the government of providence: *ignorance of physical cognitions*. People do not advert to the fact that created nature is essentially limited and that the connection between causes and effects follows from the constitution of natures, and produces stupendous order and the beauty of the universe. Consequently, they imagine as possible what in fact is not possible and require God to do absurd things, that is, things which because they are in themselves impossible and null cannot be a term of divine power and wisdom. This explains the foolish complaints against the existence of evil or against its distribution, or against the dispensation of goods. If God accepted these complaints, the whole world would inevitably be thrown into confusion; in fact, as I said, God would have to carry out what is totally impossible. Hence, the purpose of this second book is to demonstrate that creation and everything that can be created is so limited that anyone who might wish to arrange things in another way so that some evils might be avoided would risk incurring much greater evils. The most wise Author of the universe cannot use his supreme goodness to make evil non-existent; he can do no more than ultimately direct his goodness to accomplishing the greatest possible sum of net good, after all the evil and the good have been calculated. It is precisely to this end that the laws governing the dispensation of goods and evils are directed. These laws are made known to us by what the Creator has revealed in order to strengthen our weak understanding and the timidity of our spirit.

Finally the third book is *supernatural*. It combats the third cause of the errors into which the critics of providence fall: *ignorance of theological cognitions*. These critics do not acknowledge the way God carries out actions in nature and also the laws he follows as a result of his divine attributes; they claim that his action should intervene all the time to free them (the critics) from their evils, even from those of which they themselves are the free authors. In their opinion, evils that could not

[2]

be avoided without violating the natural laws should be prevented by miracles; the connection between second causes should be suspended and interrupted at every moment. They claim that it would cost God nothing do all this, and such action would conform to his infinite goodness. In order to correct this error, I have demonstrated that God cannot conform to such nonsensical claims because to do so he would have to operate foolishly and therefore in open opposition to his perfect, absolute goodness, which resides only in wisdom, never in foolishness. Hence, if God wished to halt the course of second causes by his direct action whenever they moved towards evil, he would operate contrary to his own attributes and oppose his own self.

3. In refuting these three errors about providence and giving the teachings relative to it, I have not used a rigorously scientific style in this work. In this way, a wider field is opened to discussion, which becomes more accessible and acceptable to the greatest number of readers. I have also avoided introducing certain very difficult speculations, even though the sublimity of the material drew me almost unwillingly to deal with them. My intention to help the greatest number of people counselled me against their inclusion; I thought the argument would be sufficient without such speculations. If it should please God to grant me the time and strength to publish that part of philosophy that is its crown and summit, natural theology, I will be able to supply all that has been intentionally omitted in this less demanding treatise, which nevertheless can be considered a branch of natural theology.

It is now eighteen years since the second book saw the light for the first time at Milan. Ever since then I have become aware of what was later confirmed by continual experience: not every reader grasped the aim of my thought.(2) They are for the most part people who reprove me sharply for over-clarification of what I write and hence making the work uselessly longer, due to

(2) The observations of an anonymous author (Romagnosi) made in the *Biblioteca Italiana*, p. 146, when the first volume of the *Opuscoli Filosofici* was published, attributed opinions to me that were the opposite of mine. I demonstrated this by the comparison I made between the two, published at the end of the second volume of the *Opuscoli Filosofici*.

an excessive concern of being misunderstood. They prefer to assume the tone of judges and relentless critics, and they do this by using opinions that are not found in my works and have never occurred to my mind. They thus so easily pervert my sentiments, substituting their own imaginings in their place; they use other words with a very different meaning, which they consider synonymous with or the equivalent of what I am saying. I therefore think it appropriate to use this occasion, when I offer a new book to the public, to solemnly declare, for all people of good faith in Italy, that UP TO THE PRESENT TIME NONE OF MY TEACHINGS IS FOUND IN ANY BOOK OF MY ADVERSARIES. I therefore ask honest people who want to know the truth to take my opinions from my works and not from the publications of adversaries, where they will not find my opinions.

DIVINE PROVIDENCE

BOOK ONE

Λογικός **[logical]**

THE LIMITS OF HUMAN REASON IN ITS JUDGMENTS ABOUT DIVINE PROVIDENCE

Forsitan vestigia Dei comprehendas? [Can you find out the deep things of God?]

Job 11: [7]

CHAPTER 1

The study of the ways of divine Providence strengthens us in temptations against virtue

4. If knowledge has no effect on the human heart, if it is like a useless weight on the mind without increasing good or reducing evil, if it does not satisfy or console with at least honest hope our ceaseless yearnings, then such knowledge does not, in my opinion, deserve to be called Wisdom. If however Wisdom is that teaching which improves and strengthens us, and raises our spirit to salutary thoughts, then the only way for us to obtain this knowledge is to contemplate the eternal designs visible in the vicissitudes of created things and make ourselves one with those designs.

5. It seems to me that the sole cause of all the dangers and temptations that entice us to desert the path of virtue is the vexation and difficulty we experience in being constant in the performance of our duties, while at the same time feeling deprived of goods and almost continuously subject to the fascination of evils. Goods arouse our appetite, and to obtain them we forget the laws of righteousness; on the other hand evils depress our spirit, which turns to wrongdoing in the hope of ridding itself of such a heavy burden, or at least of avoiding the extreme vexation of opposition. But the stern voice of conscience suddenly reproaches us for letting ourselves be deceived by our affections, and for violating the irrefutable law that fixes certain limits to the acquisition of goods and to the avoidance of evils. A fierce battle begins between this incorruptible conscience and the inclination of our sense-nature: conscience, this voice from above, ceaselessly promulgates the divine law in our hearts, whereas our sense-nature is blind to the light of truth and struggles only for what is pleasurable and delightful. The final outcome of the combat between these two forces is either we are brought back to Justice or, because temptation is stronger than our virtue, we become hardened in vice.

6. This hardening in vice leads our weak and unhappy spirit

astray, and doubts arise in our mind about the sublime dispositions of divine Providence.

The evils we suffer upset us tremendously; we very much resent the limit imposed on our pleasures. The cause of this dark mood and resentment, which no explanation alleviates, is the God who governs all human things and implants in us the solemn command to do good and avoid evil. But we are wretched people to fall into such a deplorable error: the capacity of our intellect is not sufficient for us to see that the limit imposed on our present pleasures is not a true limit but only appears so. In fact its purpose, ordained by the wisdom of the best lawmaker, is to enable us by very little sacrifice to obtain the unlimited fullness of all we desire.

7. This comforting teaching should be seen as good, and we should embrace it with all our heart, even when we cannot understand and see it as true. But if we also understand it in addition to desiring and believing it, we are fortunate indeed. The wisest of all legislators does not forbid us, granted we are able, to investigate the reasons for the laws he follows in his dispensing good and evil; on the contrary, he actually invites us to investigate them.

8. If however our mind is not capable of this investigation, we have no right to argue arrogantly with God's intelligence about all that happens. Rather, our mind should share in divine Wisdom by faith; we should strengthen our weakness by firmly believing the words of our Creator. His words can persuade us very effectively to be temperate in our use of fleeting pleasures, reminding us of an eternal punishment for their intemperate use. He can persuade us to be patient with momentary sufferings, pointing to an eternal reward as rich recompense. But, as I said, none of us is forbidden to use our mind to learn the sublime reasons for the government of Providence. Providence is totally directed in favour of good people who often sacrifice pleasures and suffer evils for the love of what is just and upright. It is also directed to the confusion of the wicked, to whom nevertheless it does not deny many goods and whom it protects from many evils and leaves free to put upright behaviour before pleasure, and to suffer evils rather than act immorally.

CHAPTER 2

God invites us to study the ways of Providence by putting before us the book of nature and history

9. Whenever I have thought about the way God instructs the human race I have often experienced a sublime feeling. God allows doubts or even difficulties to arise in our mind in order to waken us from our inertia and stimulate us to reflect and to investigate the truth.

We need to have before our mind the whole universe, particularly all that happens in the human race, in its growth, its division into different peoples, the dispersion of these over the face of the earth, their mutual relationships, wars, rivalries and friendships, the union of many into one and the division of one into many. In particular we must note the history of the Hebrew people whom God led by a special providence; they must be a little model of what the whole of humanity was later to be. The whole of this universe, both physical and moral, must be seen as a large sacred book opened by God before the eyes of us all. It contains nothing but problems and difficulties offered to human intelligence so that our search for solutions and answers might increase our knowledge and satisfy our mind. The pages of this large volume turn with the passing of the centuries; the problems written on the first pages are easier to solve than those on the pages that follow, and no page can be turned before answers are found in the human race to the problems that have presented themselves. Apparently, the most wise God was pleased to apply to his human creatures the Socratic method, as it is called. In this method, the most difficult truths are spontaneously drawn from the unformed minds of the uneducated and children, and in my opinion this is what the Eternal Being does. Marvellous things that are totally opposite to our fleeting thoughts are commanded by God to succeed each other before our eyes so that we immediately stop to wonder at such marvels and thus turn our mind to investigate their invisible causes. The unsurpassed Creator of the human race does not wish to say everything, otherwise we would be lazy and inert. On the other hand, he does not like to deprive his beloved creatures of the noble pleasure and merit of teaching themselves and learning many things by their own efforts. To attain this end, he gave us the faculty of knowledge so that we could justly rejoice in developing knowledge for ourselves, and being in some degree our own teacher. God wanted to help us in this task only where our natural knowledge could not suffice. Hence our first human need was that our faculty of knowledge be stimulated and stirred and thus drawn into operation. But our knowledge would not progress in the wisdom we needed if the supreme teacher did not present this faculty with problems or questions. And finally, he had to endow it with some general principles with which it could apply itself to solving the problems it faced. Equipped with these aids, the faculty was able to acquire a knowledge that could only ennoble it. God furnished it with all this, and then, as I said, allowed it to take just and noble pleasure in being a discoverer of a Wisdom.

CHAPTER 3

Those who believe in the existence of God cannot be reasonably disturbed by the apparent difficulties seen in the government of Providence. On the contrary, they willingly study the difficulties in order to know God's greatness better

Si est Deus, utique providens est, ut Deus
[If God is, then as God he is certainly provident]
Lactanctius, *De ira Dei*, c. 9

10. We see therefore that the very objections and difficulties with which we challenge divine Providence, can themselves help us, and should be understood as a sign and gift of Providence. However, if seeing them makes us lose heart — they are after all due merely to our ignorance — we must not consider ourselves defeated and thus become unfaithful to the supreme goodness that wanted to enlighten us by means of the objections.

Indeed, it was by means of similar difficulties that honest people always investigated and discovered the great designs of divine Providence. Because they believed firmly in the existence of a supreme, infinite being, they had no doubts at all about the goodness and wisdom of the one who governs them. Even when the light of their reasoning did not help them solve all the possible difficulties, the difficulties did not affect their faith nor their deep affection for their trustworthy Lord: they pressed on, seeking solutions, because it is precisely by knowing the reasons why God operates so differently from human operation that we come to understand the tremendous distance between divine greatness and human insignificance.

11. The delight felt by wise people when they compel themselves to penetrate God's conduct, which is sublime and far beyond all human thought, closely resembles (and in fact exceeds) the pleasure experienced in the investigation of the conduct of great people who far surpass all their contemporaries in greatness of intelligence and wisdom of counsel. We are impressed by the grand purposes of their enterprises and the new and extraordinary means which enable them to pursue

these ends. The means seem to be such that no one else would think of them and are seen as totally contrary to the end, but the end and enterprise are unexpectedly and happily attained. The more this is true, the more delight we feel in understanding the extraordinary and apparently lonely path these wise people followed, and we are pleased to make our own their far-reaching views. Before the outcome was finally attained, everybody would have criticised and judged the ways as insane. If some people therefore can, through intelligence or character, be greater than others, they often differ from others in the way they think, and sometimes separate themselves by following a way considered false and insane so that no success is seen as possible. Can we wonder then that the most wise God, in the government of his creatures, operates so often in a manner that is difficult for us to conceive and seems mad, in fact in a manner that is totally different from our thinking?

12. We should therefore extend to God the same courtesy we consider worth extending to great people. A great person, an extraordinary, sublime genius, seems to be free of ordinary laws; artists, painters or poets are considered original precisely because they know how to follow a path that no one has yet taken. Such people set aside the ordinary precepts that act as supports for insufficiently secure minds. Their nature is inspired and they pursue a course that at the time is judged impossible or rash. But this does not free them from the eternal rules; all they are freed from is enslavement to the rules followed by people of the world in which they live. People of the world, used to measuring everything by their rules, consider foolish or deformed anything that pertains to a sphere that is inferior to their rules or exceeds them, and they did not see as agreeing with their measure [*App*., no. 1].

CHAPTER 4

The difficulties concerning the government of Providence have their source in the *infinite Wisdom* that presides over that government and in the comparative ignorance of mankind

13. This is the principal reason why, in the midst of troubles, pious people remain firm and sturdy in faith and in the love of the supreme Ens.

No event, no new or difficult and unpleasant experience contrary to the way we think (and apparently contrary also to divine perfections) can cause the least disturbance to a total faith in the divine attributes if the following simple truth is firmly borne in mind: Almighty God, endowed with an intelligence that is infinitely superior to ours, must manifest a conduct different from ours, far exceeding our knowledge, and follow rules that at first sight appear opposed to our limited vision or seem badly suited to his ends. On the other hand, if God followed our human way of thinking, we would have no sign by which to know and admire his wisdom; we would be cut off from every means for rising to the Creator from created things which reflect divine Wisdom.

Because in creatures and events we find nothing more than a ray of wisdom that is uniform and commensurate with human wisdom, we could possibly deduce that a mind governs things but it would be a mind as limited as ours. Thus, we would conceive only the existence of an intelligence as finite as ours but not the existence of a God. We should not be surprised therefore that when viewing events in the universe, our very limited minds are presented with things that at first sight seem totally unintelligible. But the difficulties we encounter in understanding how good and evil are distributed and the universe is governed are necessary but in no way do they harm the truth of a provident God. On the contrary, if they were absent, we would have no grounds for believing we could find any divinity behind the government of human events. Hence, the difficulties themselves are a proof of universal, divine Providence.

14. But there are other reasons to explain why some difficulties arise in our limited human reason when we consider and judge the government of the universe with the little rules we use to judge our own affairs and interests.

The government of a kingdom cannot be subject to the rules that govern the prosperity of a small family. Similarly, the government of the universe cannot be judged with the limited vision natural to us mortal beings. Human thought, in addition to having a natural limitation, is limited by education and habit. We can never rid ourselves of the limitation of education. It is also very difficult to rid ourselves of the limitation of habit, which has become connatural to us and inevitably limited us in nearly all the acts of our life. People show such diversity in their thoughts and judgments that it is hardly possible to find two people who agree on all things. This is certainly not the result of different principles imprinted by nature on their reason, because all human beings, granted they agree on the meaning of words, agree about supreme principles. Nor does it happen because someone with a more powerful mind sees further than another, resulting in their disagreement. This alone does not seem sufficient to explain all their differences. Just because one sees further intellectually than another, this does not necessarily mean they contradict each other: they see different but not contrary things. People with greater vision perceive things not perceived by others but it does not follow that they perceive them in a contrary way.

This opposition in judging the same things or choosing the means to obtain the same end cannot be fully explained except by recourse to the variety of *secondary rules* which people have gradually formed and use to measure the value of things. These diverse secondary rules have come about not only through the different levels of their understanding but through the different affections that guide human attention, and principally through the various experiences people have had of things, and also the greater or lesser volume of business matters they have had to deal with in various ways. The great expenses that a husband believes necessary for the glory of his family or for some important business will perhaps seem a real waste to his hard-working, provident wife who is used to watching the smallest savings in the home. This is not because the two do not

[14]

fully agree about the concept of domestic economy or about the maxim to avoid prodigality, but possibly because the wife has formed a kind of secondary rule for herself from comparing the small sums she is accustomed to dealing with. These rules make her judge as excessive the payments that her husband judges purely moderate and right because he compares them with the total wealth of the house that he administers and of which he has a better knowledge. But it must be carefully noted: secondary rules vary because they are formed by comparisons: the greatness or smallness of an object, its importance or non-importance, its nobility or baseness, usefulness or harmfulness, are things that are often relative in human judgment. Consequently, *secondary rules* differ in practically everyone, which results in different opinions and contrasting views.

14b. Again, when people are involved in some way in the same sphere of affairs, their judgments differ. A mere change of circumstances in the circle of affairs, not to mention the different powers of mind and different attitudes of heart, are sufficient to accustom people to see things from a different point of view and, I would say, in a different light. No matter how wise or prudent a person is in the city, they do not escape every criticism and censure. No one finds himself agreeing in everything with all others of the same state as he. It is not surprising therefore if people of unequal education do not agree. The same is true when someone, accustomed to moving in a wider circle of affairs, does not make the same judgment as another who is used to moving in a narrower circle and therefore thinks things in more limited proportions; we would not be surprised if they disapproved of each other's conduct and considered each other imprudent.

This observation, so obvious and simple, is surely sufficient to silence those who presume to find some defect in the distribution of good and evil in the world? I would ask such people to look at themselves. Do they succeed in avoiding the accusations of others, no matter how they behave? Do they perhaps agree with the whole human race in things that in their own view they do more wisely? The sphere of activity of everyone is so restricted, so narrow when compared with the expanse of the universe. They may indeed find the best in such a small sphere, but why is it they do not agree with others, who are just as much human beings as they are; others have exactly the same origin and the same right as they. We may require God to dispose things according to the way we think, but can't others also require him to dispose things the way they think, which may not agree at all with our thinking, even in the smallest things of life. It seems to me therefore that after a very simple argument like this the blindest person should understand.

15. Let us suppose that the governor of the universe is a human being, or judges in a human way, or that the most brazen detractor of divine Providence has been appointed to rule the world. Would the human race be more satisfied with this arrangement? Would this remove all other detractors? We would be strange people if we did not know that the government of the things of the universe is beyond the mind of every human being and that if God gave impudent human beings the reins of the world for just a single moment, everything would break down in confusion. Evidently the ancients saw this temerity in Clymene's son. His father let him drive the chariot of the sun for one day but, losing his way, he put earth and heaven in danger of being burnt up. Jupiter struck him with lightning just in time and cast him into the river Po. No mortals therefore can sanely presume to know so much that they can undertake such a vast task as the government of the universe. Even if there were such people who were capable and had the approval of everyone else to govern, how could they dare to make themselves judge of the divine Governor? This very difference of opinion alone counsels and teaches them not to make themselves too bold a judge of other human beings.

Therefore no matter how many arguments we present against divine Providence, we can never reasonably uphold them except as products of our own imagination; from them we can deduce nothing against the heavenly dispositions, and much less call into doubt the existence of God or his divine attributes. And I must say, I have at times admired the Germanic goodness of Leibniz for spending so much time answering Bayle's sophistry and defending the conformity of faith with reason.

Moreover, the apparent arguments against divine Providence lose a great deal of their force when we consider that the governing mind of the world must be most wise and infallible, not the mind of mortal, fallible man.

[15]

CHAPTER 5

Every difficulty we solve concerning the government of Providence reduces our ignorance, while adoration of Providence increases our goodness

16. I will leave this consideration for a moment and deal with the other I mentioned, that the *secondary rules* drawn from a narrow sphere of affairs differ from those drawn from a much larger sphere.

Some may say that all such rules, which are so diverse, can be both true and complete. But this would be a contradiction: each rule would be simultaneously true and false. Each will be true when applied to matters within the sphere to which it applies, but false when applied to everything outside that sphere. Secondary rules drawn from a much wider experience and from more wide-ranging matters can be used to judge directly a larger number and greater order of things than more limited, narrower rules. In the end, only those rules will be complete that are drawn from the presence and observation of all the things in the universe and of their mutual connections. If nothing is excluded from this extensive sphere, no experience will be neglected nor be an obstacle to the formation of secondary rules; all accidents and species will, as it were, be experienced, all compared with each other. Consequently, we can see a new and beautiful reason why pious people are moved internally to rejoice rather than be saddened and depressed by the difficulties presented to their minds when they consider the sequence and government of human catastrophes and human happiness. In the present life honest and faithful people encounter things for which they do not straightaway see the reason, or which are totally opposed to their expectation. As a result, God's providence in the matter seems new and strange. Nevertheless they are grateful to God because they see that in something so contrary to their way of thinking, some deep secret of God's wisdom lies hidden. They realise that God perhaps wants to reveal this secret to them. Hence the very darkness and difficulty they encounter become a reminder that in comparison to God they are virtually nothing, and show just how much God is beyond their limited thinking. They are pleased with this ray of light of God's greatness, and meditate on the secret of God's wisdom, investigating the reasons which at the moment they do not see. And if God lets them see the reasons, they will broaden their thinking and use the immense sphere of God's counsels to correct their own puny maxims of human prudence.

[16]

CHAPTER 6

Two paths lead to the solution of the difficulties about Providence: the path of faith and the path of reason

17. God has a special regard for upright, humble people who investigate eternal wisdom in order to share in it and find happiness in it. He shows them the great light present in the sublime reasons that guide him in moderating events. But if he keeps the extreme parts hidden and veiled, he does so solely to enkindle their faith in him and allow them the noble merit of perfect submission to him.

We can therefore distinguish two paths that allow us to avoid all awkwardness and doubts about Providence. One of these paths can be aptly called the 'path of faith', the other 'the path of reasoning'.

18. The first is broad, very straight and open to everyone. Pious people, supported by reason and strengthened to believe truly in what reason tells them about the virtue of steadfast faith, maintain that he who governs the universe is an Infinite Being, full of wisdom, power, justice and goodness. They are content therefore to rest peacefully in him, disturbed by nothing and surprised by nothing. They are fully persuaded that everything that happens, no matter how difficult or unintelligible, is divine work; they need nothing more. All possible objections vanish into nothingness before the word: THERE IS A GOD.

CHAPTER 7

The path of faith is endorsed by reason and strengthens human understanding

19. The proud might disdainfully dismiss faith as a weakness, but it has the gift of bringing peace to the human spirit and, judged in the clear light of calm reason, it is not a weakness.

Reason judges faith worthy of the highest praise, and acknowledges that it makes us much greater than knowledge itself does.

In fact, limiting ourselves to our case, we are simply making effective in the human spirit an undeniable truth taught by reason itself: the existence of God. Our aim is to make people understand this truth in perfect coherence with their thoughts and affections, without any contradiction whatsoever in their reasoning, and without any hesitation or the abandonment of this truth due to a weak mind or spirit. Indeed, if we keep firmly in our hearts that a God of infinite wisdom and goodness exists and provides for the world, we can never doubt that the government of the world could be ever badly directed. On the contrary, if we give in to doubt, there is no greater proof that we are failing in our very reasoning, because we are feebly allowing ourselves to be led away from the truth that reason has presented to us. It is here precisely that faith comes to our aid by strengthening our spirit. Faith — I mean Christian faith — requires and infuses a wonderful strength of spirit, much greater than naked truth can, which is known by reason alone. When reason feels that human strength is weakening in following reason's teachings, it calls in other accessory and particular reasons and even employs flattery.

20. Strength of spirit is great in those people who persistently rule their lives with only one general principle. They need no other supports; they remain coherent with themselves, and overcome all doubts, obstacles and the subtleties and errors of passion. It is an obvious and certain observation that the weaker our understanding and character are, the more we need supports and *accessory reasons* to live a moral life. Women and

children are not too easily governed by the few solid reasons sufficient for a mature man: every little pleasure, sorrow, sensible affection is enough to make them forget reasons which, although certainly listened to, have no effect on the mind. The weak impression made by abstract truth, the incapacity to apply it in a practical way, and the power exercised by sensible things on their sensitive character reduce to almost nothing the effect that their intelligence can have. This is substantially what constitutes the moral weakness of people, and a definite symptom of this weakness is the fact that general principles, although understood at the moment, are seen to have little value in guiding their lives. People need a great many accessory, partial reasons to support their spirit in all directions. To solve at once all the difficulties that come to their spirit does not help them: they need a particular solution for each difficulty and adapted in such a way that it comforts them.

This human pride that gives first place to reason is deplorable. Sophists reason about events in the universe and never finish discussing reason after reason; they display very great ambition, almost challenging the Most High, as if he himself were a sophist like them. But the only thing they display is their weakness. A spirit shows itself to be weak and enfeebled when it does not have enough strength to feel the force of one general reason; instead it needs a great number of very particular reasons to satisfy it. I happily leave to others to judge how such empty spirits should be considered. They ceaselessly argue in unending discussions. Subject to a vanity equal to their weakness, they have assumed the title 'free thinker', but if they should somehow deserve this title, it could be due only to the pride, cruelty and violence with which they act towards the very patient human race.

20a. Thank God therefore that upright, truthful and faithful people conquer the world with a simple faith in God's existence and attributes. The world may consider them simple-minded and poor in good judgment, but they have received a strong spirit and lively mind. One principle alone, the principle of God's existence, and one belief alone, in the divine word, are worth more to them than all trumped-up human knowledge. One principle, splendidly true, totally clear and supreme, suffices for them as a guiding light. By means of this principle their intellect does not hesitate; their spirit causes no conflict; they are guided by their own reason, and even the world itself obeys their will that is in conformity with the will of God.

I have often reflected that the whole difference separating great and extraordinary human beings from ordinary people is simply a greater degree of this strength of spirit I am talking about. Great and enduring enterprises can be conceived only by people governed by few and sublime principles, because the force that these maxims exercise on them raises their whole spirit to a sublime degree and, as if some divinity (so the Greeks expressed themselves) were speaking in their spirit, they abandon themselves to enterprises full of counsel, almost without taking counsel. They do not hesitate: they handle dangers with complete safety, because they feel nothing; the only thing on their minds is the noble purpose on which they have set their sights. They conquer all other people, even nature itself, by greater uniformity and by constancy of action, and by the degree of that feeling that adds such mysterious and irresistible power to the few, universal thoughts they have.

In this way the Christian is constantly ruled by only one great idea whose universality absorbs and includes all other ideas. It is not a Greek dream that the divinity gives them by the light of this idea. The idea is so powerful that it sets them solidly and unshakeably above all other humans who are overwhelmed by an excessive quantity of untrustworthy human ideas, and whose uncertain spirit is tossed to and fro, wavers, often loses heart, and even falls into despair.

CHAPTER 8

The path of *reason* is abused by some, who use it to their own ruin

21. In following the *path of faith* we acquire such great strength of spirit that we adore undisturbed what we do not understand in divine conduct. If this path deserves the reasonable praise we have given it, the path of reason can also prove very helpful to the upright person who follows it.

22. By 'path of reason' I mean our search for the particular reasons that supreme Providence follows in its ordering of creation.

23. Very few people are able to follow this sublime and difficult path safely.

In fact the journey can be undertaken in three ways, which are like three distinct paths, and the profit or harm we experience will be as different as the path we choose to investigate the sublime norms followed by Providence in its government.

24. The first way to use our reason about Providence (the first of these three paths) is followed by people who investigate the divine dispositions with a guilty spirit and with a stubborn and proud mind. They are searching solely for something that will enable them to deny or deform the God whom they do not love and of whom, in their perpetual agitation, they have a great fear.

25. There are people who seem continually to think that it might be possible to show that God does not exist. The sad and fatal outcome of their knowledge is the great darkness of the endless doubts into which they have sunk. Or else, deprived of every joyful ray of truth, their sole consolation is a fleeting moment of dim light provided by a troubled imagination. As the days go by, they understand less and less of the wisdom that moves and gives life to the universe, and they bitterly and fearfully blaspheme the divinity from which that life-giving wisdom emanates.

But the humble, despised believer enjoys a much happier state than these proud know-alls, who are to blame for all the contempt and disdain with which the general public have come to regard both reason, which is such a wonderful good, and knowledge, which is such a great source of consolation.

26. It is neither reason nor knowledge that harm us but the vices of those who foolishly turn the most wonderful and precious of heavenly gifts to their own ruin. As Rousseau said:

> The study of the universe ought to raise man to his Creator... This is true, but all it does is increase human vanity. The philosopher who likes to penetrate divine secrets dares to associate his claimed wisdom with eternal wisdom. He approves, criticises, corrects and prescribes laws for the nature and limitations of the divinity. While he is busy with his vain systems and with making a thousand subtle efforts to correct the machine that is the universe, the farmer who sees the rain and sun fertilise his field at fixed times, is admiring, praising and blessing the hand from which he receives these graces, without giving himself problems about where they came from. The farmer does not use his unbelief to justify his ignorance or his vices; he does not censure the divine works or engage the Lord in battle in order to make his own sufficiency shine forth. Thus, the human spirit will never vulgarise the impious words of Alphonsus X... such a blasphemy is found only on the lips of the learned. While academic Greece abounded with atheists, Helianus observes that not a single barbarian had ever doubted the existence of the divinity. We can observe the same thing today: in the whole of Asia only one nation is educated, and half of them are atheists, and it is the only Asian nation where atheism is known.[1]

27. What deplorable disaster made this man who knew and described so well the influence of useless knowledge, incapable of guarding himself against the same influence? He had excellently demonstrated his knowledge concerning the noble purpose of the study of the universe and how man must raise himself to the knowledge of his Creator. But some misfortune made him abuse this study by denying the divinity or at least distorting it and saying that its Providence did not reach to individual objects of the universe. He had praised the farmer because the farmer, with his heart full of the true purpose of

1 *Réponse au Roi de Pologne*, etc.

wisdom, raises his arms to heaven to thank the Almighty who sends him the rain and sun to fertilise his fields. How then could he write with his own hand: 'We must believe that particular events here below are nothing in the eyes of the master of the universe. His Providence is concerned only with the universal, not the particular; he is content simply with preserving genera and species, presiding over the whole, without bothering about how each individual passes through this fleeting life?'[2] What kind of a man is this who subjects himself to such blatant and fateful contradictions! What kind of human wisdom is it that, blinded by passion, disavows and denies what just a little earlier it saw and professed?

2 *Lettre à M. de Voltaire*, etc.

CHAPTER 9

Those who trust solely in the path of reason put their salvation at risk

28. This way of using human intelligence is dangerous and brings fatal disaster to the unfortunate people who follow it. Scripture says of them, 'I will destroy the wisdom of the wise, and the cleverness of the clever I will thwart. Where is the wise man? Where is the scribe? Where is the debater of this age? Has not God made foolish the wisdom of the world?'[3]

On the other hand, those who are not slaves to passion and vice and have not yet been introduced into the Lord's dwelling, that is, they still do not know about true piety, can learn something about the invisible attributes of their Creator. They can attain the truth through the wisdom visible in creatures, and by following the path of reason.

29. This path however is not safe. Although human reason is the offspring of divine reason, it is short-sighted and liable to error when abandoned to itself. The light of reason as such is infallible, but we who use it are fallible when we apply it. Consequently, those who are forced to make for themselves or, of their own choice have made a law to use only reason as their sole guide can certainly make out the traces imprinted on all things of the wisdom on which they depend. However, they can meet with serious difficulties that disturb them and endanger the good result of their meditation. It is a matter of hazard, a game of chance, where they risk losing everything, subjecting almost everything they possess to the caprice of fortune. Is it therefore pure accident that the difficulties they encounter against divine Providence are commensurate with the level of their intelligence?

30. The degree of mental power we have from nature is certainly totally accidental. So how can we prudently entrust ourselves to be guided by our reason, which is always unknown to us and does not depend on us? We have it exactly as nature gratuitously wished to donate it to us. If the power of the human

[3] Isaiah 29: [14]; 1 Cor 1: 19–20.

mind seems to differ, and does not depend in any way on our will or choice but on the accident by which, unknown to us, we received it, then surely when we abandon ourselves to this reason and submit to its control, we are simply subjecting ourselves to chance? — we are certainly not entrusting ourselves to ourselves, but to something (and this should not surprise us) which does not depend on us at all, something totally unknown. This is a fact, an undeniable fact, no matter how strange it may seem.

31. In the last analysis, the only thing that is always unknown to us is the instrument with which we know everything else, and we cannot measure its power, the power of our reason. Indeed, the only thing that can measure reason is another reason. And if there are two reasons in us (which is absurd), what will measure the second reason?[4] Or do we get into an infinite series of reasons, where the final reason will always be absent, the reason that would measure the power of all the preceding reasons? It is a mistake to think that we rule ourselves by simply ruling our own reason. I repeat: do we know the degree of power of our reason in which we take pride? We did not measure it before we had it or before it was assigned to us by nature. Our opinion was not sought. Before we existed, did we come to the Creator with weighing scales to weigh it and see if the weight was suitable and proportionate to our needs and to the strength of the doubts that would be raised in the life that we would afterwards receive? And when discussing the matter before our birth, did we look at all the difficulties to be encountered in the life destined for us, at all the temptations resulting from these difficulties and what level of intellectual power we needed to solve them and resist the temptations? Hence it is clearly accidental and by no means necessary that

[4] Note, I am discussing here the power of the *individual reason*, not the power of *human reason* considered in itself. To say that the individual reason cannot measure its own level should not cause us to doubt the truth it makes known to us, as I will show later. It is one thing to have the certainty that all we know is true, and another to claim to know *how far our knowledge can go*. We can have the first, and we need it, but the second is beyond the power of individual intelligence. In the case of human reason as such, its limits can certainly be fixed, precisely because the individual reason can, as I said, have certainty about the truth it knows, once it has come to know it.

our reason is able to solve directly the *partial difficulties* which present themselves to us against Providence in the course of our life.

32. I said the difficulties that present themselves to us; I did not mean *all* the difficulties we can encounter relative to the government of the universe. This government is so far-reaching that the human mind can never conceive all the possible problems, all the possible difficulties that present themselves; our mind can never understand the depth of wisdom needed for and present everywhere in such government. It is purely accidental that we apply our mind to undoing the knots and solving the puzzles which our thought encounters; it is also accidental that we are dealing with these particular puzzles and knots rather than others, because this also is not subject to our will. We may find it hard to understand the reason for some event and not know how to reconcile it with divine Wisdom, but there are in nature and in the succession of infinite things other problems much more difficult to solve than those we are aware of, problems and difficulties we do not know nor are we even aware that they exist, because they are so far removed from the profound counsels that direct everything. Consequently, if the problems we encounter are beyond the power of our understanding, what will we do if our only help is such an ignorant guide?

33. Our understanding, in which alone we believe, will in this case cause us to risk deviating from the truth. Strictly speaking, this temptation does not make us give in, but we give in very often through our weakness. When our mind applies itself to the investigation of the causes of things and finds itself held up by the difficulty of discovering them, we experience vexation and discomfort. We make an effort to avoid the discomfort, which is entirely proper to a being endowed with reason, but because we do not find true causes for these things as quickly as we would like, we very often fabricate many imaginary causes. It was precisely this great desire to possess an easy explanation for natural phenomena that led the human race to invent the innumerable deities responsible for every operation of nature and for the great wrong done to this presumptuous and impotent reason. Because we try hard not to be aware of and admit our ignorance, we invent a thousand hypotheses to

persuade ourselves that we know a lot. And the more these hypotheses abounded, the more the world of well-founded truths diminished. People began to accept as certain what at the beginning was taken as an explanation of phenomena and could be proposed with only few degrees of probability at the most; people in general do not keep before them the distinction between probability and certainty. Human nature itself, created for truth, moves from doubt to the *terra firma* of total persuasion. As a result, the hypotheses, now changed into theses and dogmas, had to be different, not because they were more likely in themselves but seemed so to those who were thought wise and who perhaps distinguished themselves from others solely in this: in explaining world events greater difficulties had presented themselves to their mind, and finding themselves incapable of surmounting these difficulties due to ignorance, imagined some false solutions, and presumptuously taught them. This was a source of mythological dreams and philosophical fables.

34. Those people who with this little light of their reason attempt to investigate the designs of divine Providence and put their trust only in chance, do not know to what they are entrusting themselves. They may perhaps discover a part, and this part will be sufficient to satisfy them. But at the same time, it may not be sufficient, and in the end they may remain totally in the dark. The outcome of their effort is uncertain because the instrument they use and the difficulty of the task they are undertaking are unknown. However, if they do obtain the knowledge they seek and also the light they desire to clarify their darkness, their belief in the deity is strengthened more greatly, and they may even bless and honour this deity that has solved their doubts and manifested itself to them in creatures. In this way, reason will lead them directly to faith, and they will be more ready to listen to what this beneficent deity wishes to say more directly to them. They may also co-operate with the divine impulses, his light becoming every day clearer in their hearts that are now so well disposed. It is possible they are led to the possession of the divine word in its entirety and are finally received into the true Church of God. Divine Scripture seems to speak of this when it says: 'A wise man does not hate the commandments and justices', and, 'A man of understanding is faithful to the law of

God.'[5] In other words, our natural reasoning can draw us to faith and to subjection to the divine law, if our reasoning is true and sufficiently complete.

35. But what happens to those who, because their reason is very weak or they are assailed by difficulties that are too much for them, do not know how to reconcile the events of life with the wisdom and goodness of an excellent provider? Will they be in danger of hesitating in their faith in the deity, or tempted to design some system which, with their limited view, facilitates reasoning about events? They could devise an atheistic system, like that of the fatalists or atomists. Such a system strips things of all meaning, leaving them to be driven by blind necessity, and at the same time relieves us (crass as we are for having been able to accept the system) from all further bother to seek reasons and from all the shame of owning up to our ignorance.

36. Nevertheless we must note one thing here. In the ordinary course of both physical and moral events, the wisdom of a provider is very noticeable; we see it everywhere and see it clearly. As Scripture says, it cries aloud in the streets, in the squares, from the rooftops, calling all people to it. We cannot doubt our ability to know and see in the world a mind that disposes all things, a mind whose keen light penetrates even the eyes of those who have shut their eyes. Hence, the difficulties that arise against such a provident mind can be only partial, can be only particular events, which are an exception to the ordinary procedure of things ruled by goodness and wisdom. If this is the case, people can never be excused when particular problems and obstacles cause them to withhold belief in the God who manifests and preaches all things to them. But if the only way human understanding can find objections against the providence that is clearly visible in everything is to concentrate on a tiny part, on an individual event, does this mean that the power of providence is in some danger? Is the outcome perhaps any less uncertain for those who begin by entrusting themselves totally to their own individual reason? It is true that when we cannot explain an event, all we can reasonably deduce from this is our own ignorance. It is equally true that we cannot use our ignorance to argue with certainty to the

[5] Sir 33: 2–3†.

non-existence of the supreme being. But in fact we easily do so: we often exchange what we do not know for what does not exist, particularly when reason alone is our guide and we have already judged in favour of it and shown that we cannot doubt it. We must also add the attractions of the senses, and to these our self-love, a love which is seriously affected by the awareness of our ignorance and is unbearable for any length of time. Those who are unfortunate enough to live a life burdened by misfortunes, not to mention the vexation and problems resulting from their unsuccessful reasonings, are gravely tempted to deny or doubt divine goodness. Calamities, even those of holy people, are called *tests* by divine Scripture, which has high praise for those who remained faithful to the Lord in the depth of suffering, like Job and Tobias. These are the exemplars of faith, possessors of a perfect virtue, whom Scripture places before us. How hard then will the test be for those who put their trust solely in themselves?

37. Sense has a wonderful communication and affinity with human understanding. If something is unpleasant to our feeling, our intellect is immediately inclined to judge badly of the cause of the displeasure. But there can be an excellent and very good cause for every effect that is unpleasant to human feeling; one such most excellent cause is precisely the first cause that moves and disposes all things. If our intellect could see this cause and was not corrupted by the protests of a dissatisfied sense, it would declare it most lovable. But if its attention is drawn to consider only the pain, it forgets the first cause as such, it forgets its beauty and its goodness; it sees and regards it solely in its relationship with the unpleasant sensations. And because it sees it as the cause of these, it represents this cause to itself as lamentable and odious. As a result, it judges the cause darkly, and having made this mistake, it comes to hate it; and later it flees from it altogether, and finally denies it. We see therefore how this way of reasoning sometimes leads people into difficult situations, and sometimes so overwhelms them that it brings them to ruin. This happens when natural reason meets a difficulty that it does not have the power to solve. At the same time we do not find in our spirit sufficient strength to acknowledge our own ignorance and be continually aware of this ignorance. This is particularly the case when we are battling

against the sufferings of nature in its feelings, which disturb us and overwhelm our spirit.

38. St. Paul indicates the punishment God had ready for those who having started on the way of intelligence ended in misfortune. They had indeed seen in a creature of this world traces of the invisible divine attributes, because God himself had posited them there for them to see. But in spite of this, they imprisoned truth in injustice, they did not confess it or make it known; they did not glorify God, nor give him thanks. They debased their own thoughts, and their hearts became so darkened that they changed God's incorruptible glory into some image-likeness of a corrupt human being, or even of birds, four-footed animals, and serpents.[6] Thus, they refused to acknowledge what they nevertheless saw everywhere — they disowned the unity of wisdom shining out in different creatures, the one Providence that manifested one sole provider; they limited, split, multiplied it into fleeting, defective forms drawn from human thought and from the example of human power, and even of animal power.

Consequently, this second way of reasoning, which our natural, good sense uses to scrutinise the dispensation of earthly events, is erroneous and defective; in short, its success is due solely to chance. It should in fact lead us to faith but, through human defect, it frequently leads us astray, and we become lost in the harsh, destructive paths of unbelief.

6 Rom 1: [18–32].

CHAPTER 10

The way of reason is secure when united with the path of faith

39. Although natural reason is short-sighted and liable to error, the cause of our ruin is solely the will, never reason.

Our human will abuses the insufficiency, ignorance and obscurity of reason, and most foolishly and culpably uses these blunt weapons against the supreme Being.

40. Therefore the friend of reason (granted reason is not abused by human weakness or malice) is Christianity. The pastors of the Church always encouraged intelligent people to use their intelligence to help human weakness and ignorance; these make us immature relative to the full reception of revealed doctrines. Leo X, in the eighth session of the Fifth Council of the Lateran, wisely required that the philosophers of his time produce arguments based on pure natural light and refute the errors of the Arabs who at that time were damaging the Church. He said: 'Because truth can never be opposed to truth, all their arguments can be answered by pure reason' [*App.*, no. 2].

41. Although reason leads us only to the threshold of faith, it nevertheless hands us over to faith as a most certain guide and sublime teacher.

But the process does not stop there: faith leads us back to reason, which, when strengthened and supported by faith, becomes a gentle teacher and infallible guide.

We have here the third way of using our intelligence, a way that is far better than the first two. It makes intelligence become a wide, royal road that does not cause us to get lost in a fearful forest of errors, as the first way does that I described. Nor does it lead us, as the second way does, with uncertain and dangerous steps along tortuous, untrustworthy paths, with a very uncertain outcome. Instead, it leads directly to the desired goal for which we are making. This third way therefore, in which we can use our intelligence, is a completely open, clearly visible and straight path that ends in heaven — even on earth it gives us complete rest and a taste of the bright light of truth.

42. Thus, only faith, which comes to strengthen our reason, to help it in its weaknesses, to correct all its errors and bring a remedy to its most obstinate vices, does a service to the human race by bestowing peace. Faith adds to human reason, whether strong or impotent, all that reason lacks; it can in fact be the escort we need. Although the calibre of reason is not the same in all of us, the faith we receive is the same. Moreover, the degree of reason given us by nature is stable and does not increase substantially throughout life; hence it does not always measure up to the needs we meet in life. In contrast, the deposit of faith, like a most precious treasure, is entrusted by God to the human will which, by means of study, merits and prayers, can draw from it all it needs. Whether this deposit increases through use or decreases through neglect is our choice. If we entrust ourselves to it, we can say that we are entrusting ourselves to ourselves, that we know in whose hands we are placing our fortune. This treasure is ours and we can do with it as we wish, and there will always be enough to supply every need of our spirit and mind. It does not matter whether we have little intelligence or great intelligence, revelation and faith can provide what we need to make our intelligence sufficient — they add the light lacking in a weak intelligence, and for the powerful mind unravel the entanglement of specious sophisms in which, by its own action, the mind sometimes gets enmeshed. Revelation and faith give suitable nourishment to both levels of intelligence: to the stronger it gives a more solid, substantial food, to the weaker, pleasant salutary nourishment. We are thus able to give ourselves more calmly to reflection, and faith guides us into far-ranging thoughts that are pleasant and sublime. On the other hand, if our work and occupation give us little time for reflection, faith can satisfy us with just a few, nourishing divine concepts. Such is the comfort that faith gives to human reason. With this third way, we can follow the path of intelligence with a very happy outcome.

43. However, the distinction I made between this way of intelligence and that of faith must be carefully noted. If faith alone, in God and his attributes, is sufficient to solve all human doubts about Providence, or if we live contentedly in our God with faith solely in revelation, I said that we follow the path of faith. But in addition to the existence of the Creator and

revealed dogmas, we can also investigate many other truths, and be content to enter into the marvels of the divine counsels. Provided we never make this journey without faith (on the contrary we maintain faith as an ever-present safeguard of our reason), I say that we are following a path of reasoning which is safe because we are aided by faith; our reasoning is a child of faith. The same clear path was taken by the saints who were intent on investigating the greatest truths. It is the proper path for Christians. Although they do not give up their reason, they are not so utterly simple or so blindly proud as to believe only the words of their individual reason, which does not give, nor can give, proof of being sufficient for their need.

44. Anyone who is not willing to learn from others because he wants to learn everything by himself is blinded by futile pride. If those who lack all education and indeed any association with fellow human beings (association itself can teach us something) cannot in any way step outside the total ignorance in which they are born, and if in order to have some culture we are forced to depend on others, then why should we refuse the help of revealed truths, the teaching of God himself?

CHAPTER 11

Only revelation can reveal the plan of the universe and thus dispel all doubts concerning the perfect goodness of its government

45. In many places of Scripture, faith is described as the begetter of intelligence, as that which strengthens human reason and brings it to the truth, like a teacher that unfolds and consigns the secrets of wisdom to reason. St. Paul, writing to the Hebrews, teaches that only through faith do we know the vast plan God has devised and carries out in the universe.

The whole of this immense chain of events from which the universe results, beginning with the creating word and finishing with the word that judges the world, all these innumerable events are, according to St. Paul, held together by the divine Word and depend on it: 'By faith we understand that the worlds were prepared by the word of God, so that what is seen was made from things that are not visible.'[7] The 'things that are not seen' are the concepts of the Almighty, which subsisted in his mind before the creation of the world; they are the decrees conceived by him from all eternity but remained unseen by creatures because these were not yet formed and the decrees were not yet carried out. These decrees and concepts are the wise architect's plan, according to which the edifice was to be constructed. This plan had never been drawn on any external material, not on paper nor on stone or wood; it existed solely in the architect's mind. Hence, if intellective creatures, before being admitted to the vision of such a mind, are to know where and how to view the great plan of the world, they must first see it externally executed, and only at the end of time will it be completely executed. Thus, the plan, this vast concept, becomes perfectly visible only at the end of the ages. As St. Paul teaches, all ages are contained in it, and all of them, before they begin their course, are planned and disposed in the secret of the great mind. As these ages pass, the majestic edifice corresponding in all its parts to the eternal model is being constructed. But because

[7] Heb 11: 3.

they have not yet passed, and the plan is not totally visible to us who live on earth, only God could positively reveal it in its principal parts and its sublime purpose. Thus, only revelation could put us in touch with the divine concept; only by being told and by faith (which comes from what we hear) could we understand that all the obedient ages are directed by the Eternal Being to the most sublime end of the glory of the humanised Word.

46. God uses this same great reason in the prophet Isaiah to console Israel, his people. Moreover, he demonstrates the feeble support on which the other peoples rely who put their trust in false spirits; he challenges these spirits and all their adorers to explain the great plan of the universe in the way that he can, the one who conceived it and alone carries it out.

This great plan cannot be manifested, nor all the information given that is necessary for the peace of the human spirit which is always worried and concerned about its future destiny, unless the present, past and future are made known. Indeed, all the immensity of time and the whole vastness of space in all their parts are all united and joined in the most complete, perfect unity, and in this unity every atom, every movement depends on one eternally determined end worthy of God, an end that is God himself, the Word. In Isaiah we read: 'I am the first and I am the last; and without me there is no God. Who is like me? Let him call out, announce and explain to me the order in which I have constituted the ancient generation; let him announce to mortals the things to come and contingent things. Do not fear, my servants; do not be disturbed by what the nations can do. From the moment I chose you, I have made you hear and I have announced it to you, you are my witnesses'[8] as if to say: there is no one besides me who can present and reveal to human eyes the great plan that embraces all the things of the world, the length, the breadth, the depth, the past, the present, the future. Nor is there anyone besides me capable of finding and communicating to human beings true consolation in their misfortunes, of giving them the necessary knowledge that explains and justifies the government of the universe, that solves the difficulties of the tormented human mind and calms the anxieties of the

[8] Is 44: 6–8 [R].

human heart. Let those who are far from me tremble therefore in the darkness of their deep ignorance, but those close to me need fear nothing. Let these seek their comfort and put their strength in the revelations I will make to them, and have always made. No matter what external fortune comes to others, they should not be envious of the uncertain and passing lot of such people.

47. Indeed, only God could reveal the moral end of the universe, an end that regulates all the apparent irregularities. Only he, from the beginning, could tell the human beings he had just created how things were drawn from nothing, how the intelligent creature was the end of all other creatures, and finally that intelligent creatures existed because he had created them so that they would find happiness in his service. Only God, when revealing to man the plan he alone had conceived, could make man part of the plan's execution.

This knowledge therefore, which renews to and revives the life of the spirit oppressed by tribulation, reveals the secrets of Providence. It could come only from God, begin only from the word of God; human reason, on its own, could not invent it; it had to be positive. God drew it from the hidden thought of his mind, because the complete realisation and manifestation of the thought would not be made externally except at the end of the world, when the most simple unity will be formed from all things. Hence, without this revelation and because we have only experiential knowledge and are oppressed by evils and confused by the variety of events, it was easy for us to waver or even lose the idea of a beneficent mind governing the world. For this reason God did not leave us without revelation; he began to reveal when our evils began, indeed when we ourselves began to be. We can in fact say that by means of revelation movement was given to human reason that at the beginning had no movement.

48. The existence, wisdom and goodness of God in the government of the universe was truly the fruit-bearing seed sown at the beginning. From it sprang all the good sense, consolation and treasure subsequently possessed by the philosophies of the nations.

Upright people crushed and troubled by painful events, ask of God no other consolation than that he will increase his enlightenment for them and increase the revelation of his secrets in his Providence. A prayer said by the saints in misfortune is: 'To you, O Lord, I lift up my soul. — Make me know your ways, O Lord; teach me your paths. Lead me in your truth, and teach me, for you are the God of my salvation; for you I wait all day long.'[9] Thus, solely through the knowledge of these ways and paths, the person speaking in the Psalm awaited the comfort that his afflicted spirit desired so much. It was a knowledge of Providence's purposes, of the far-reaching views according to which God distributes every good and every evil, as Eusebius and Theodore of Eraclia explain. By communicating a greater abundance of these lights to those who need them, the Lord accomplishes with faithful goodness all that the Apostle says: 'All those who listen to his words are not tempted beyond what they can bear, making sure that with the temptation they also receive light and strength'.[10] Consequently, in suffering and illness, the good suffer only one temptation which St. Paul calls *human*, that is, it is feelable, but this disturbance of their feelings does not arouse doubt in their minds or deflect the consent of their will from true faith.

49. Furthermore, this consoling knowledge which God communicates to his saints does not differ from the body of truths that constitute revealed religion. This religion is therefore very valuable for humanity. Anyone who studies it and judges it fairly, ultimately finds that it is simply a consoling knowledge communicated to mortal beings to comfort and sustain them in their difficulties, to bring them relief in their discouragement, to strengthen them in the truth and in virtue. The noble book of Scripture is therefore a divine letter, a consoling treatise containing the deposit of faith. That this is the purpose and general task of the divine Scriptures was taught by the Apostle to the Romans, comforting them in their troubles: 'For whatever was written in former days was written for our instruction, so that by steadfastness and by the encouragement of the scriptures we might have hope.'[11]

9 Ps 24: 1, 4–5.

10 1 Cor 10: 13 [R].

11 Rom 15: 4.

Chapter 12

In the plan of the universe there is something infinite and mysterious where reason comes to a halt and gives place to faith

50. But if holy people drew the valuable knowledge of consolation from trustworthy, heavenly enlightenment, they did not await this enlightenment in culpable indolence, making no effort themselves. On the contrary they continually meditated on and scrutinised divine Scripture. It was only by reading the Scriptures that the true Israelites obtained relief in their slavery from their evils. The royal Prophet proclaimed: 'When the princes plotted against him and sought his ruin, the only relief he found was applying himself to deep meditation on the justifications of the Lord'.[12] This holy and wise King was persuaded that 'only then will nothing trouble him, nothing disturb him, when his mind has been able to penetrate deeply all the divine precepts.'[13]

51. However, no matter how much we meditate on divine dispositions and diligently study the inspired Scriptures we will never understand all their wisdom and all the laws by which God governs and corrects living and non-living things. We are not capable of seeing the reasons for all events; in short, whatever knowledge we acquire will never render faith entirely useless.

It would be vain to think so. Scripture itself, whose task is to teach us the counsels of Providence, restrains our enthusiasm and the excessive boldness of our desire to know. It instructs us that even as our mind penetrates the highest knowledge, it will in the end always come to the point beyond which it cannot go, yet it will vainly and fruitlessly try to go.

52. This impassable point lies between what is finite and the absolute infinite; it marks a limit for every essentially limited creature. However, the divine thoughts that dictate the universe's path include not only everything on this side of that final

12 Ps 119: 23 [R].

13 Ibid., 6 [R].

point of created intellects but everything stretching beyond it. Thus, the intention of uncreated wisdom reveals itself like light spreading and diffused over all contingent natures. It gradually spread across all the determined ages (like luminous threads joined together to form one cord), became weaker and, over an immeasurable distance, began to disappear from mortal view. Finally, it was totally removed when engulfed by but not confused with the sea of eternal light.

53. Here then we have something extraordinary: on the one hand all finite things are too small for the human mind, and on the other the absolute infinite is too much. Our mind stands midway between two points, each an immense distance from it. It finds itself between too little and too much, between what does not satisfy it and what overwhelms it, between what it infinitely exceeds and what infinitely exceeds it, between what it abandons when seen as too far below it, and what it never succeeds in fully attaining because far too sublime. Something therefore always remains invisible and hidden in the great thought with which God creates and orders the universe. That is why there are mysteries and obscurity of faith. It is from this noble obscurity alone, in which the human mind becomes lost, that we draw the greatest concept and truest feeling possible of the divinity.

54. In this way faith, while helping our understanding, is not destroyed but continually ennobled, deepened and purified. It is nobler, deeper and purer in proportion to the degree that our reason is confused and lost in the interminable spaces of infinity. If we test our strength just a little, if we make even some little effort to scrutinise divine greatness, we can have some hope (which always accompanies superficial knowledge) of understanding later what we do not understand now. But if we are conscious of having already exhausted the power of our understanding, if we know we have reached our limits and the limits of nature — in a word if we come, as it were, to this sacred frontier and adore before it, as before an altar, then human presumption is totally cut from under us. An informed ignorance now begins in us; in our nothingness we sacrifice with greater piety to the infinite object of our faith, as if to that which overcomes not only our accidental ignorance but the very limitation of our nature.

CHAPTER 13

Continuation — We cannot perceive God in this life

55. But this is not the only way by which the path of intelligence is reconciled with the path of faith, and far from destroying each other, both paths provide sympathetic help to human necessity. What I want to say now also demonstrates how human intelligence, no matter how great, continuously needs faith to keep us in perfect peace amid the endless succession of events.

Human intelligence is aroused to its movements solely by the perceptions of the senses. Only the objects of our senses, the things around us, act upon us to give our intelligence the first matter of its concepts. I prescind here from an extraordinary, direct communication of God with the soul. I think all schools of philosophy agree that sensations are the causes, or at least the occasions, of the first operations of our mind; the schools differ only in the way they explain how this happens. I myself keep to what simple experience reveals to us, that in this life things alone are the realities outside of us that act *naturally* on us, and do so in such a way that they arouse in us sensations and images, and our mind directs its attention to these. No reality that differs from us can exercise its action upon us if it does not provide our mind with the matter to which the mind can direct its attention. A thing must stimulate in our feeling some analogous modification and passion that indicates to our mind an ens different from the mind, a term of perception different from the perceiving person.

56. Someone might say that the soul is helped in its operations by another external being, God. I do not deny that the first cause plays a part in all the operations of second causes, but this does not mean that the first being assists the intelligent soul in its acts and gives itself to the soul as matter of its thought. It simply helps every subject to act; it does not constitute the real term for the subject on which the subject acts.

57. Only things therefore provide the human mind with the first matter of its operations, or more accurately, the sensations

or perceptions caused by external things provide the matter. Without these our mind could not even reflect upon itself. This is the constitution of human intelligence, which is simply a power to act by means of a body that serves it as an instrument for obtaining the matter on which it acts. Our body therefore, which shares in life, is midway as it were between the soul, which is life, and external things devoid of life; the body constitutes the communication between these two extremes and for this purpose shares in the nature of both, uniting in itself the corporeal and spiritual substances by means of an exquisite, hidden union.

58. The whole cycle therefore, in which our intellective nature, considered in itself, is enclosed, consists of three parts: 1. an intelligent soul, the subject; 2. a material universe which is perceived together with the feeling of oneself, and which intelligence makes an object to itself, and 3. a body that shares in both the subject and the real object, and is the mediator between these two. In the body the soul receives the forms that compose the universe. Hence it can be aware of itself and exercise on the forms and on itself all the operations to which its activity extends. This is as far as human intelligence naturally develops, and it reduces to two parts: 1. the basic feeling in which intelligence receives the action of things which produces corporeal forms for it, and 2. the exercise of the operations proper to intellectual activity. The operations are carried out on the basic feeling and on the forms, and ultimately reduce to abstractions and syntheses. With human intelligence bound by these terms, it is easy to see that a positive conception of God transcends its power, as the following demonstrates.

59. We find in material creatures, and also in ourselves, perfections really distinct or even separate from each other. From them we can draw the abstract ideas of goodness, wisdom, justice, power and other perfections. But we are not able to conceive all these subsistent perfections in perfect unity; we can never know the most simple perfection that includes all perfections and all the indistinct degrees of entity. Certainly, what is extracted from known objects must in some way exist in those objects, and it is not possible to extract what is not there. Hence, because there is nothing in material substance nor in all limited beings that includes all partial perfections or that is itself

these perfections, we cannot even form an idea of them; we find no example of such a thing or an adequate likeness of it in all the things we know.

60. This fact is further clarified by the following simple observation. The perfections that all creatures possess are predominantly accidental, so that they may or may not have them. For example, intelligent and moral creatures can be wise or unwise, good or bad. But in the concept of the supreme Being it is absolutely impossible for these perfections to be absent; they are substantial and essential to him, they are (to express myself more accurately) his very being. From the examination of all limited nature, therefore, no image or picture of such a Being can be extracted, because such a thing is not found in the whole of nature. Hence, we cannot see *what he is*, although we can see that he is [*App*., no. 3]. The *mode* of the divine nature is totally hidden from our understanding, although our understanding strives to find and see the mode. It remains always an object of our faith, separated from us by a dense, impenetrable curtain. Until this veil is removed by the direct communication that he will make of himself to us, we must adore his inaccessible light with profound humility and trust. Creatures certainly reflect back to us many rays of his glory because he pours out on them his perfections (in so far as these can be communicated) and traces of his wisdom. But his *being* is not seen anywhere or found in creation. According to St. Paul's teaching, the world is only a kind of mirror, an enigma of the divinity, and because the only thing visible is the world, we cannot see the divinity as it is, nor its naturally most real being; all we see are the few rays reflected from this mirror, but reflected with that obscurity which makes them an enigma.

CHAPTER 14

Summary of the four limitations of human reason. The first limitation: reason does not have a positive idea of God

61. It will be helpful to stop for a moment and summarise *the four limitations of human reason* discussed in the previous chapters. I used these limitations and other arguments to show that human intelligence needs the help of revelation and faith to find peace in the ups and downs of human life, and that reason and faith do not in any way exclude or contradict each other; on the contrary, they require each other. After guiding our steps some way forward, one leads sympathetically to the other.

We saw that in the beginning revelation set our human reason in motion and then entrusted us to it.

Reason however, having strayed for a long time from the right path and having forgot the instructions of its first teacher, finally acknowledges by means of its feeling its own insufficiency. It again seeks the help of its teacher and, exhausted by its anxieties, abandons itself to this teacher that is always ready to welcome it.

Faith comes again therefore to help us, enlivening and energising our wayward and almost destroyed reason. Keeping reason always company, faith encourages it to pursue the great path of truth.

Supported in this way, our reason advances and finally reaches the limits posited by its own nature. Here it respectfully halts, readily acknowledges these limits and submits to faith, which alone can pass beyond the limits. Once again, sane reason puts the human spirit into the powerful hands of faith, which raises the spirit above everything created and finally settles it in that most blessed love that never fails. Faith therefore helps, not limits, intelligence, giving it such a strength that by ourselves we may come to know everything we can know. And while it generously allow our reason to enjoy teaching itself as much as it can, it is ready to teach it all that it needs but cannot find on its own, due to its essential limitations.

62. The first of the limitations I discussed, which were not of any particular individual but of the human species as a whole, indeed of all created intelligences, can be stated as:

> CREATED, LIMITED INTELLIGENCES CANNOT HAVE THE POSITIVE CONCEPT OF DIVINE BEING EITHER THROUGH KNOWLEDGE OF THEMSELVES OR THROUGH KNOWLEDGE OF OTHER LIMITED BEINGS, BECAUSE IN NO LIMITED BEING IS BEING IDENTIFIED WITH THE PERFECTION OF BEING. THEREFORE THE NECESSARY LIKENESS TO GOD IS MISSING.

63.We see therefore how true and profound is divine Scripture's description of the searcher after wisdom: 'He who in his heart investigates the ways of wisdom, is like someone in love who contemplates his beloved through the window vents and the cracks in the door, who accommodates himself next to her house and sets his rustic home against the walls and under the same gutter. But he may not pass over the threshold of this sublime dwelling. Nevertheless he is blessed by this alone, to be protected by the same roof against the heat of the sun and the dampness of the rain.'[14]

64. This limitation of human intelligence also seems to be indicated in the book of Job, with the frequent words: 'Is it not perhaps the ear that discerns words, and the jaws that judge flavour?'[15] as if to say that man's judgments are conditioned by the sensations he receives, because the operations of the human mind proceed solely from sensations as from their principles.

65. But perhaps no author of Scripture has written with such great clarity as St. Paul in his first letter to the Corinthians in the passage I referred to above: 'Love never ends. But as for prophecies, they will come to an end; as for tongues, they will cease; as for knowledge, it will come to an end. For we know only in part, and we prophesy only in part; but when the perfect comes, the partial will come to an end. When I was a child, I spoke like a child, I thought like a child, I reasoned like a child; when I became an adult, I put an end to childish things. For now we see in a mirror, dimly, but then we will see face to face. Now I know only in part; then I will know fully, even as I

14 Sir 14: [24–27]; Prov 8 [R].

15 Ibid., 12: 11.

have been fully known.'[16] The Apostle calls created things a mirror of the divinity, and they are the only things we can see with the light our nature naturally enjoys. Created things mirror the divinity only in so far as they have and share in the divine perfections. The level of their participation in these perfections is proportionate to their own perfection, but because they all have a finite nature, they can never participate fully in the perfection of the supreme Being. By this limited participation created things can indicate his existence but cannot give us the positive idea of the immense Being, whose essence is *subsistent perfection itself*, of which there is no copy or example. Note carefully: what creatures lack in perfection is essential to God. The difference therefore between shared perfection and divine perfection is the positive idea of the divinity. His essence remains hidden; not even some likeness has been revealed to us. Our inability to have a concept of this perfection, which creatures lack but is substantial to the divinity, deprives us of what is substantial to God; in other words, we lack the positive idea of God. However we do see the perfections of the supreme Being in tiny quantities and within certain limits. Created things are therefore certainly a large mirror of the divinity but a mirror that presents the image as a puzzle, that is, in a dark, mysterious way, as a kind of code, which has this particular property: it cannot mean any of the things we know or are knowable; it means only one, supreme, most perfect thing which we do not see, but whose necessary existence however is known in the code. Only this particular thing can explain the code, written brilliantly in the whole of nature, shining before us and ceaselessly striking us with its light so that, adoring, we may believe.

66. This explains how some philosophers came to doubt all the truths known by our intelligence. They could not see how we could be certain that these truths were not simply something that our mind, limited by its laws, had generated and hence were a subjective appearance whose objects we could not argue to. They saw that our ideas about the divinity had to be imperfect, and attributed this imperfection and defect to our mind which communicated its own imperfection to the ideas it

[16] [1 Cor] 13: 8–12.

conceived. Consequently, positing the defect of the imperfection of ideas in the organ or faculty of thought, they doubted the truth of every concept of the mind.

67. They failed however, particularly Kant, to note sufficiently the truth that I put forward, following the Apostle. Kant went further than all the others in his speculation, from which, we can in fact say, he extracted the whole of his *critique*. I said that the origin of the imperfection and defect present in our ideas of the divinity (and of every other supra-sensible being) does not arise from the defect of our mind nor from its limitation to a particular form (as they claim), but on the contrary from the process it is constrained to follow, that is, it does not directly see divine things but must extract the concept from sensible, material things by reasoning, or from its own spiritual but still limited substance. This process, imposed on our mind by the external conditions of things, prevents it from naturally acquiring a perfect idea of the supreme Being, or better, prevents it from perceiving him in reality. Creatures do not share in his essence, because it is *incommunicable*, as Scripture so sublimely expresses it. Consequently, no likeness impressed or imprinted on creatures can reveal it to us. We are constrained to guess at it, as it were, from the limited effects of itself that it imposes and imprints on created things. As I have said elsewhere, the human mind receives the truest idea of all things only when it can perceive the things themselves, not when it is constrained to obtain knowledge of them through imperfect and totally inadequate likenesses and relationships. 'When the perfect comes, the partial will come to an end. When I was a child, I spoke like a child, I thought like a child, I reasoned like a child; when I became an adult, I put an end to childish things.'[17] In this case, ideas necessarily retain the imperfections of the likenesses that our mind needed in order to know things.

68. St. Paul explains: when our mind comes to perceive the things themselves, the concepts it acquires are adequate for correcting the imperfections of the ideas it previously possessed. Hence, when we are given the vision of God, we do not need *faith* in order to believe what we do not know: 'Then as for prophecies, they will come to an end; as for tongues, they will

[17] 1 Cor 13: [10–11].

cease; as for knowledge, it will come to an end,’ that is, the knowledge which now makes us proud but will then be childishness. He means that our knowledge here on earth cannot be without obscurity and mystery; it is sufficient to make us know the divine existence, but relative to God’s essence, such knowledge demands faith from us. Once a thing has been shown to exist, we are obliged *by reason* to believe that there is a way it can exist, although we cannot form any concept of it. Hence, ‘we know only in part, and we prophesy only in part’. From the sign which marks everything in the universe we know that there must be the Being indicated by the sign, but what this Being is we cannot clearly make out except, as it were, by guessing it. St. Paul expresses this with the verb ‘to prophesy’, because this is the way the prophets usually speak: they vaguely see future events outlined in their words, and these events are so determined by their own characteristics that no other event can fit the prophecy. Nevertheless, because there is no mention of the many other circumstances of the prophesied event, it remains obscure until the prophecy is fulfilled. But, when the event has happened, the prophecy becomes totally clear and people see that it could not have happened in any way other than that which it had to foretell. This is precisely the case with a perfect puzzle: the only thing that can explain it is precisely the thing it simultaneously characterises and conceals.

69. Prophecies that follow this method show that they do not depart from the very method we have seen employed by the Creator in teaching human beings: he has made the whole of this universe like a puzzle book opened before us all. In this constancy of divine instruction we clearly see the unchangeable truth of the divine word. We see in the nature of this method the wisdom of the one who had previously formed human reason in keeping with such a method. He enclosed our reason in a body endowed with organs so that, upon receiving the impression of feelable things, it could rise from these to intelligible things?

70. It is true therefore that feelable things lead us only to very imperfect concepts of intelligible things, but this also is willed, ordained and benignly guided by God. Two purposes, both sublime, lie behind this imperfection:

1. Relative to us, it gives place to *faith*, that is, produces a

reasonable submission of created intelligence to the divinity, and because intelligence is the noblest part of creation, this submission is the greatest honour that the divinity can receive from his creatures. Furthermore, this greatest honour that creatures render to the Creator forms the greatest merit of creatures, and this greatest merit calls for the greatest reward. Hence, the greatest benefit the Creator could give is to leave us with this obscurity of faith, but much greater is the kindness that shines out here in what he has not given us, a kindness that could not be so resplendent if he had in fact given us the fullness of intelligence. This is the first purpose.

2. Relative to God, the limitation of our knowledge obtains another and very noble gift: it opens up the way to new liberalities. Therefore, later through grace, God gives us everything we lack through nature. According to the expression in the book of Job, he thus 'conquers our knowledge'.[18]

71. We see therefore why God commands the prophet Ezekiel to present the people with enigmas.[19] Scripture, which is always coherent with itself, declares that the Saviour would speak in parables and bring forth from the fullness of his wisdom 'things hidden and unknown from the foundation of the world'.[20]

Eternal goodness thus found a way to bestow knowledge on us without depriving us of the merit of faith. At the same time, we still have the merit of discovering by our own effort and attentiveness many things hidden under those covers. Difficult things no longer constitute an obstacle for people who are unable to understand them, nor have the virtue to put up with ignorance of them, when they become aware of them. Thus the human mind, taught by the same way by which it progresses and develops of itself, experiences less stress and is taught more gently.

72. Hence, it is not surprising that the most ancient wisdom consisted in proposing that the learned compose enigmas for each to solve. This way was considered more in conformity with human nature and with the great example left by the first,

[18] Job 36: [26].

[19] Ezek 27: [2].

[20] Ps.77; Mt 13: [35].

supreme teacher of the human race. We read that Solomon did the same with the king of Tyre.[21] Again, the wise human being is described in Proverbs as 'the one who attentively observes the parable and its interpretation, the words of wise people and their enigmas.[22] Job spoke to his friends about these enigmas, many of which are represented in the order of divine Providence in the dispensation of all good things and all evils. Overwhelmed by his tribulations, he said 'that they should listen to what he said and receive in their ears the enigmas.'[23]

73. The enigmas he proposed, or rather the one enigma, was himself. Although just, he suffered, and was consumed by wounds and vermin. Because his friends did not grasp the explanation of such a great enigma, they were scandalised by his sufferings. Not knowing how to reconcile such harsh afflictions with divine justice, because Job had been just, they took to accusing him of being a sinner rather than leave the matter undecided and confess not to know enough about it.

74. But when they heard Job's mysterious words, they found it still more obscure and difficult to explain the enigma in any other way. He boldly protested that 'he desired to argue with God himself, that he would speak with the Almighty, that if he were judged he knew he would be found just. Call me,' he said trustingly to the Lord, 'call me and I will reply to you, or I will speak and you will reply. How many are my iniquities and sins, my misdeeds and crimes. Come now, show them to me, and why do you hide your face and consider me your enemy?'[24] The only person who could explain these words and the whole prophetic statement, that is, this extraordinary, obscure enigma, was he who had known the key to the whole of the old testament, JESUS Christ, whom Job represented. He was that God-man who, although just, would suffer, and Job was entirely right to speak confidently in the person of JESUS Christ. In the last analysis, it is JESUS Christ who truly explains everything but who himself remains another most sublime enigma, a divine secret, an object of faith. No one can understand Christ

[21] 1 Kings: 3; 2 Chron 9.

[22] [Prov] 1: [6].

[23] [Job] 13: [17].

[24] [Job] 13: [3, 18, 22–26].

fully without understanding the mystery of the Trinity, on which the mystery of the Incarnation depends; to do this, it is necessary to rise to the point that totally exceeds all human intelligence. In dispensing events therefore the ultimate depths of divine counsel can never be penetrated by human counsel.

Job's friend very reasonably said: 'Behold, God is sublime in his strength and there is no one like him among lawmakers. Who can scrutinise his ways? Or who can say to him: You have done an injustice? Remember that you are ignorant of his work, which has been acclaimed by wise men. He indeed sees all people, but each of them sees him only from afar' (this indicates precisely the way we human beings see through the reflection of creatures). This is because 'he, the great God, exceeds our knowledge and the number of his years is incalculable.'[25]

[25] 36: [22–26].

CHAPTER 15

The second limitation of human reason: reason cannot encompass the infinite

75. If no creature, with the power of their natural intelligence, can *perceive* God, who is the beginning and end of the universe, which of us can judge and censure such a being in his government? But that is not all. God cannot be *perceived* or *positively conceived* because none of the creatures we can perceive has what is essential to God, namely, the *identification of essence* with *perfection*. Furthermore, no human being can encompass him because he is actually and in every respect *infinite*.

76. For this reason I posit the following as the second limitation of the human mind: it can never clearly know the last link that suspends, so to speak, the universe in eternity and gives rise to the sublime counsel of Providence that governs it. This limitation can be expressed as:

> FINITE INTELLIGENCE CANNOT KNOW PERFECTLY THE ABSOLUTE INFINITE.

77. We must note that God communicates something of his infinity in some way to all his works so that the infinite is found in the whole of creation: it intermingles with the finite, in space, in time, in substances, in ideas, and in the modifications of things — modifications that are inconceivable without an identical something to form their subject. In short, wherever our thought wishes to penetrate more deeply, it can become lost in limitless regions that stretch to an horizon beyond its gaze and expand into immensity. What mind can make an accurate judgment about the government of such a kingdom whose extent it cannot encompass or fully know its nature?

78. It is precisely in speaking about the way divine Providence distributes good things and evils that the book of Job informs us about the greatness of God and about our own littleness. The book speaks of *the secrets of his wisdom*, and calls

his *law multiple*, composed of countless relationships which only God can know and reveal: 'Will you perhaps understand the traces of God, and find the almighty in a complete, perfect way? Know that he is higher than the heavens and how will you reach them? He is deeper than hell, and how will you know it? His measure outstretches the earth and the breadth of the sea. If he re-arranged everything and compressed it all into one atom, who would contradict him?'[26] as if he were saying: God's power and wisdom are of the same immensity as his nature — his power and his strength exceed the limits of all created natures. No matter how great these natures are, no matter how much they stimulate a feeling of wonder and a concept of sublimity in our limited mind, they can never lead us to an adequate understanding of the being who is beyond every material limit and whose extension is spiritual. His wisdom must not cause us amazement if it overwhelms and exceeds ours. It extends throughout the whole of the universe; it is exceedingly deep in its disposition of human destinies. Hence the Apostle exclaims: 'How inscrutable are his judgments and unsearchable his ways'![27]

[26] 11: [7–10].

[27] Rom 11: [33].

[78]

CHAPTER 16

The third limitation of human reason: the intellectual faculties of every human being have an accidental nature

79. In chapter 9 I mentioned another limit placed by the Creator on human investigation into the secrets of his Providence: the accidental limit that determines the measure of the faculty of knowledge of every human individual. The previous two limits are essential to human reason, indeed to every created intelligence. This third limit, even though accidental, is also equally insuperable for the individual who has received it. It is the following:

> MENTAL POWER IS GIVEN BY GOD TO EACH HUMAN BEING IN SUCH A DETERMINED QUANTITY THAT THOSE WHO POSSESS IT CANNOT MEASURE OR ASCERTAIN THE RELATIONSHIP BETWEEN THEIR POWER AND THE DIFFICULTY OF THE QUESTIONS THAT PRESENT THEMSELVES FOR SOLUTION

80. I said that it is absurd to presume we can solve all questions indifferently with our own direct reason. On the other hand it is reasonable and necessary that we sometimes doubt even the solution which seems correct.

One thing we must constantly do: we must accept as certain that there is always a solution to doubts about divine Providence, even if we cannot always find it, or find the true solution. The ability to show that there must be a solution differs totally from the ability to say what the solution is. We must be satisfied if the following thesis is demonstrated: 'Any event whatsoever that seems contrary to divine goodness or divine wisdom can and must always have a hidden reason which, if revealed to us, would settle every doubt we have, or would show the event to be in accord with divine perfections.' We must not claim more than this or that the reason be always given us. It must be enough to know that there is a reason because there must be a reason.

81. But even if some reason were offered that satisfied us, could we be completely certain that it was the truth? How often are people satisfied with reasons whose strength lies

solely in their way of seeing things? How often does a particular reason satisfy the doubts of some but not of many others? Just as a person will have a difficulty where another does not, so someone can hold as valid a reason that does not convince others. Here I am speaking about what we see happens among human beings, not about the nature of intelligence; I am talking about the reasons we mostly use to satisfy ourselves, not about the reasons that contain a rigorous demonstration and are held by only very few.

82. If this imperfection is accidental, the possibility of its presence in us is nevertheless essential to human nature. In other words, we can on occasion satisfy ourselves with reasons which are not God's but accommodated to our limited views.

83. Let us mentally deprive human nature of all the teaching it has received from God, and let us suppose that the powers of its understanding are totally perfect and complete. Even in this case we would find that it would innocently but imperfectly reason about and justify divine Providence with reasons that in themselves are weak, although powerful relative to itself. Alternatively, when the difficulties returned, it would stop, without producing a particular answer, and trust divine wisdom and goodness.

84. It seems to me therefore that the Lord wishes to humble human nature that proudly vaunts itself and remind it of this essential defect, when he says to man: 'Who is this that darkens counsel by words without knowledge? Gird up your loins like a man, I will question you, and you shall declare to me. Where were you when I laid the foundation of the earth? Tell me, if you have understanding. Who determined its measurements — surely you know! Or who stretched the line upon it?' (that is, who established the connection between its measure and the other measures of the universe?) 'On what were its bases sunk, or who laid its cornerstone when the morning stars sang together and all the sons of God shouted for joy?... Have you commanded the morning since your days began, and caused the dawn to know its place, so that it might take hold of the skirts of the earth, and the wicked be shaken out of it?... Have you entered into the springs of the sea, or walked in the recesses of the deep? Have the gates of death been revealed to you, or have you seen the gates of deep darkness?... Surely you

know, for you were born then, and the number of your days is great! Who has put wisdom in the inward parts, or given understanding to the mind?'[28] In the whole of this sublime chapter God reminds human nature of this limitation which greatly humbles it relative to divine greatness. We ourselves certainly did not give ourselves understanding; we received it from God, and each in the measure God saw fitting. Its power does not depend on us; it is restricted within the terms determined for it and must be satisfied with them.[29] Hence no one can presume to understand the reason for all that happens in the universe. God is indeed justified in addressing the above words to us, as if he were telling each of us: 'If, after your birth, it was you who constructed the world, the task would have conformed to your limited mind from which it came. But you did not create and establish this universe. I made it before you were born, I who created the world and assigned to you a certain level of understanding, which you can indeed use but not increase in the slightest way. I gave it to you as I willed, just as I willed to assign a discernment confined within the limit of feeling to the animals, which lack reason. It was I who determined the relationship between your understanding and what can be known, and you cannot change this relationship. Indeed you

[28] [Job] 38: [2–7, 12–13, 16–17, 21, 36].

[29] Someone might say: if we do not know the power of our mind relative to knowable objects, how can the limitations of human thought be determined. I reply that the power to determine all the limits of the mind is one thing, the power to know some of these limits is another, like the limits I assign to it. We can all say: I know that in this case it is impossible to go any further, just as we can equally say: it is possible to arrive at this particular point. But this does not mean that we can say the same for every case, that we can define how far the mind can go in every case without exception. For example, it is generally possible to show that the mind can perceive truth and is in fact made for this purpose. It can also be demonstrated in particular that a certain truth, for example, that the infinite is absolute, can never be comprehended. But we cannot say the same about innumerable other truths, for example, we can never say whether the innumerable secrets of nature will ever be discovered, nor when they will be discovered; much less can we investigate things whose very existence is unknown. It is at least a gratuitous and rash thesis to maintain, as some do, that 'we can know *all* the truths pertaining to the natural order'. — Finally, in this third limitation I am talking about the reason of the individual person, not the reason of the species.

[84]

cannot know it in any way. To know it, you would have to know all knowable things, because the relationship between two terms cannot be known unless the terms themselves are known. The world does not depend on your mind, nor are the times accommodated to your puniness. In space there are parts you have not seen, like the great depths and the heavens; in time there are things included in the great plan but hidden from you, like those beyond death. If you do not know all the parts of the world that are arranged as I, not you, want them, how can you know how much the sublimity and beauty of my plan surpass and exceed your intelligence? But if you want, you can know that it exceeds it.' Hence it is written: 'He has made all things good in their time, and has delivered the world to their consideration, so that man cannot find out the work which God has made from the beginning to the end.'[30]

[30] Eccles 3: 11†.

CHAPTER 17

The fourth limitation of human reason: the only entia it can know are those that come to it independently of it and are offered for its contemplation

85. To sum up so far. The first *limitation* that human intelligence encounters in its operation arises *from the path it is obliged to follow* if it wants to arrive at the author of the universe. In other words, it must ascend from nature to that craftmanship which exceeds nature and of which the simplicity of essence does not and cannot have an example in anything finite and natural. The second and third limitations come from *the measure of human intelligence relative to its objects*, that is, the second limitation arises from the relationship between intelligence and the *infinite object* that necessarily exceeds human intelligence, and the third from the relationship between intelligence and knowable objects which, although *finite*, are nevertheless *difficult* to reach. Intelligence cannot know if it will or will not obtain clear knowledge of these things by overcoming doubts, solving sophisms and surmounting the difficulty of the questions facing it. These limitations are intrinsic to intelligence and arise from insufficient power of mind to deal with the argument presented to it.

86. We come then to the fourth limitation, essential to the knowing *subject*. I mentioned it in chapter 11; it can be expressed as:

> THE HUMAN MIND CANNOT PRODUCE FOR ITSELF ANY KNOWLEDGE IF THE MATTER OF THE KNOWLEDGE IS NOT GIVEN IT BY A FOREIGN CAUSE.[31]

[31] The four limitations I have assigned to the human faculty of knowledge are not the only ones this faculty has. I posit a fifth in the conditions which restrict it when it passes from its state of potency to that of act. These conditions are the *laws the faculty must follow in all its steps*, laws that result from the nature of the subject who has the faculty. However, because this fifth limitation would require too long a discussion, I have to omit it. Nevertheless, all the limitations and subjective laws which confine and restrict human intelligence do not alter in any way the formal and final objects of the act of knowledge, so that intelligence is a fitting instrument for truth. The efforts

87. A clear observation of human knowledge demonstrates this truth, and we can say that all the philosophical schools generally agree, although they resort to subtleties to explain it and reconcile it with the systems they have accepted. Indeed, all our knowledge supposes an object and supposes that this object, whatever its source, is presented to the gaze of our mind, whether 'knowledge' is understood in common speech to mean what we note with the attention of our understanding or to mean what we retain in our memory after noting it on another occasion. Hence, because the acts of our understanding are distinct from the understanding itself, they presuppose our understanding, on the basis that no potency acts prior to its existence. Consequently, knowledge of things is accidental to human understanding, which therefore can lack knowledge. The result is the double effect of *ignorance* and *error*. But this is not the place to analyse the limitations and defects to which our intellective *acts* are subject. My intention is simply to list the limitations of human understanding.

this sublime power is obliged to make to attain truth and enjoy to the full the divine sight of truth, the tortuous paths it must sometimes follow, the tremendous light in which it is ultimately bathed and by which it is conquered, none of this negates the fact that the only thing we see as a logical necessity is totally pure, most simple truth. This does not prevent us from being certain about it; on the contrary we cannot ultimately be but certain about it. But how do we know the distinction between truth and error? If our intellective faculties had not been meant for the light of truth, who would have taught us that truth exists, who would have caused doubt to arise in us that what we perceive is a lie? If our intellectual powers were not ordered to truth and did not see truth, we would never be concerned whether our concepts were true or false. Scepticism, the most absolute pyrrhonism, is a system that could be invented only by a being created for truth. Scepticism is a witness against itself; it demonstrates that truth exists, that it is the object proper to the human intellective powers, and that these powers can by their nature always discover new truths. Every potency is proportionate to its object, and if it is not damaged by some accidental disorder and is correctly used, attains its object infallibly and naturally.

CHAPTER 18

Continuation. Acts of knowledge that are accidental to understanding. The limited matter of knowledge, given us by the Creator

88. This fourth limitation can be understood more easily by dividing it into the two parts it is composed of according to the ways it can be viewed. The first part can be expressed as:

> HUMAN INTELLIGENCE DOES NOT HAVE AS ESSENTIAL TO IT THE ACTS BY WHICH IT KNOWS SUBSISTENT BEINGS, BUT IS MOVED TO THIS KNOWLEDGE BY THE ACTION OF THE BEINGS THEMSELVES. HENCE, IT CANNOT SPONTANEOUSLY FIX ITS ATTENTION ON ANYTHING ABSTRACT WITHOUT A SIGN. THE ABSTRACT THING, WHEN BOUND TO THIS SIGN, APPEARS AS IF IT WERE SUBSISTENT.

89. It is not unreasonable therefore to liken our intelligence, in the state in which we receive it, to a *tabula rasa*, according to the Aristotelian similitude. It is certainly true that we receive intelligence like a *tabula rasa* or sheet of paper on which nothing is written. What is required, DISTINCT FROM US, is some being who is sufficiently learned, as it were, to write the teachings of wisdom on this blank sheet.

90. If we were abandoned totally to ourselves, to our internal forces that compose our nature, and were not touched or affected by any of the forces outside us, we could never begin to move ourselves and carry out the smallest act of our intelligence. In this state of isolation from other subsistent beings, we would not take one step or conceive one thought, even if the Almighty preserved us for thousands of years. Everything in us would remain at total rest, and the least movement in our mind would be impossible. There would be nothing to move us and no terms to arrive at. It would be a life deprived of motion, so that our existence would be like non-existence. Such a state is the object of an investigative philosophy, and is a key to explain the most wonderful secrets of human study. Hence, without something totally different from us, we would never come to know anything. This original immobility is revealed by observation: human activity, no matter how great

we suppose it to be, never initiates any movement without a stimulus. Once movement has been received, we can maintain, direct and increase it.

91. But what are the external, material beings? Who applies them to our sense organs, and why do we receive the impression of some rather than others? We cannot believe that brute beings are able by their own power to present themselves to us and stimulate our senses, nor can we think that when we are born and find ourselves surrounded and stimulated by certain material beings rather than others, it is the of effect of their own free choice because some of them wanted to be closer to us! We must look outside these external beings for the sufficient reason why some rather than others strike our senses on some occasion and in one way rather than another. We must in fact look for an intelligent, free principle, superior to them, which controls, guides and uses them according to its judgment as instruments for our intellectual development.

To conclude. When we receive existence, we are a totally blank sheet of paper, on which items of knowledge are written. But it is not we ourselves who write them; there is something outside us, some force, some being, whatever it may be, which is certainly superior to material beings and inscribes something on the blank sheet of our understanding.

92. How then can we take pride in our human knowledge? Can a book take pride in itself when its very contents were written by another? We cannot have any knowledge unless we receive from another, from a being outside us, a being that can apply stimuli to our understanding and provide the objects of knowledge. These objects, co-existing with us, are totally independent of us and are given us according to the good pleasure of him who has created us and, together with us, created the universe so that it might become the object and stimulus of human understanding and initiate human activity. In a true sense therefore we are all simply disciples, and one is our teacher, the Lord of all things, God. But because we have naturally the general limitation of knowing nothing if the elements of our knowledge are not presented to us, our knowledge is totally restricted to what another wishes to teach us. Hence abuse of our knowledge is a sad mistake, as if we totally owned it and could use it to battle against our divine teacher and

master, who must surely laugh at the strange know-alls who know precisely nothing more than what the divine master first gives them and what he teaches them and determines for them with firm limits.

93. All human beings therefore receive their knowledge from another. This alone is a humiliation, a dependence that, whether we like it or not, subjects us to the Almighty, and obliges us to glorify him with our existence and with the knowledge we misuse against him.

CHAPTER 19

Continuation. Three objects of our knowledge are given us in a certain determined measure by divine free will

94. Let us look at this dependence, this limitation to which we are subject, and consider its consequences. Instead of considering ourselves in our limited state, as we have just done, we will consider how this state limits our human knowledge. In this way we will have the second of the two parts into which I said the fourth limitation can be divided. The second part states:

> WE KNOW ONLY WHAT GOD IS PLEASED TO REVEAL NATURALLY AND SUPERNATURALLY.

95. The things that God has been pleased to reveal generally to us, that is, the objects of our knowledge, can be reduced to three:

96. First, he has placed before us this universe and offered for our intellectual consideration our own self and all the natural things around us, acting upon our organs. He has thus made a kind of natural revelation. In order to accept this revelation we must use our human faculties, which seems as if we are teaching ourselves. But if we think more deeply, we see that the objects are presented to our human faculties only by God. Hence, to God is due most reasonably the title of teacher, just as the title could be most fittingly given to a person who gave some young people knowledge by explaining to them a series of very fine paintings.

97. Second, God also made a supernatural revelation, a revelation not given to our senses through created things but given, through hearing, to our understanding, a revelation of sublime truths about our end and the means for obtaining this end. These truths let us know the Creator's plan for us and invite us to correspond with that plan.

98. In both these revelations, the natural and the supernatural, divine Wisdom desired that, in these kinds of objects set before our understanding, some things should remain *obscure*

and impenetrable, others should be *difficult* and knowable only after long study, and finally, others should be *clear* and easy to see. He wished that there would be a sufficient quantity of clear things and enough light in obscure things for us to attain the sublime end to which we were destined. But he wanted enough obscurity and impenetrability to make us argue from the experience of this mysterious darkness to the divine greatness and to our own limitation. Finally, he wanted as much difficulty, study and time as was necessary for us to acquire the amount of clear information that suited us. Thus, different people could, without pressure, obtain suitable, intellectual and always sufficient nourishment, and the path of merit was closed to no one in the study and diligence applied to divine things.

99. Third, we had finally to be given a means which would allow us pass from the most sensible perceptions to the highest abstractions of the intellect. Such a means could only be a language. Again therefore, the way was laid open for us to raise our minds from the *first object* to the *second*, that is, from *natural* to *supernatural revelation*. The external revelation of supernatural truths, acting through hearing, also needs its instrument, language. In addition, this revelation presupposes many abstracts already conceived in the mind that receives it. But because we could not give language to ourselves, we receive this means of knowledge also from the Creator. The human mind, constrained by the limitation mentioned above (FIRST PART), was unable to move unless it first received movement from the perception of subsistent beings or of their signs.

CHAPTER 20

Continuation. The divine origin of a part of language

100. Without signs we could not even conceive abstracts. Abstract ideas are simply qualities of entia that our mind contemplates in their ideality and by themselves; they are purely mental conceptions. And the only place where the objects of abstract ideas are found is solely in our mind.

101. The abstract idea of whiteness will serve as an example. I see a great number of white things outside me but I do not find whiteness by itself in any of them. The abstract idea of whiteness gives me a pure whiteness, unmixed and without gradation; if I add anything to it, it is no longer abstract — the idea needs to be totally pure and totally separate from every other concept. Separated in this way from every concrete thing, from every substance, I cannot possess it outside myself; outside myself I do not perceive it except as united to things whose weight, odour, form and other qualities I perceive with it. Hence, whiteness, as divided and abstracted from any other conception, from any thing or property of a thing, from any gradation, exists in this very simple, naked state solely in thought; it is purely a being of the mind. Outside, it certainly has its foundation while still united to other things, but in this case it does not retain its state, is not on its own, does not have its isolated existence. But it is impossible to confuse this abstract of whiteness, present by itself in the mind, with the mind, because the mind perceives it as something distinct from itself, in precisely the same way that all the other objects known by the mind and existing outside it are distinct. If we consider the matter more carefully, we will see how this way of conceiving something becomes possible.

102. It is done through an external sign of the abstract whiteness, a sign that gives the whiteness an existence, as it were, outside the mind and takes the place of the whiteness. The external sign is a sensible sign of the insensible idea of whiteness; in short, it is a word that isolates the whiteness from all the other objects that surround it in the things where it exists in

reality and is perceived in them. When the whiteness is thus isolated, the sign fixes it, reveals it and makes it subsistent before the mind; it arouses the mind to think of this pure idea suspended, as it were, in the word that expresses it. The word expresses solely the idea by itself, totally free from every other accidental or substantial being.

This explains why man needed external signs so that the mind could unite and bind abstractions to them. We could not invent these signs by ourselves: to invent them we would need the abstractions themselves. which, as I said, we cannot have without words. So God gave man a language. As supreme Master he taught him the use of some sounds in which the abstractions contemplated together with the sounds might appear as almost subsisting externally. These sounds were able to attract the attention of the human mind, and force it to fix itself on the qualities separate from the objects. This was due to the stable law to which the mind is subject, namely, that it must first be called into its act by the external objects that strike it.

[102]

CHAPTER 21

Continuation. Together with language, we also receive from God some principal truths preserved in the tradition of the human race

103. In the case of the first of the three objects discussed above, St. Paul gives us to understand how everything we learn from our investigation of the universe must be seen as the teaching of God.

104. In the quotation I discussed above, we saw that he condemns the intellectuals of paganism as those who, 'having known God, did not glorify him as God or give thanks: but became vain in their thoughts', as if they themselves, without any other help, had discovered such truths. He adds: 'They knew what is knowable about God,[32] solely because God had manifested it to them. God had inserted the light of his power and divinity in all created things so that if these were known, his invisible attributes would also be seen.'[33]

105. But how did the human mind, from the very beginning, rise by these means to the Creator? How was it first drawn to make this transition? Can our mind really move itself with a totally spontaneous motion? Does it have an activity, an agility totally independent of every external impulse, of every association of ideas? Or, as I said, is it first drawn by external objects to thought, and only later, through the association that objects have with one another, acquires mastery of itself as well as mobility and power to pass spontaneously from one to the other? What do the divine Scriptures say about this? In short, the question is: how was man, just created by God, first moved; how did he rise from sensations to the abstract concepts of his understanding and hence could form judgments about things? If he did not do this, things would be useless to him, almost unintelligible; they would vainly contain traces of

[32] *Quod notum est Dei* [what is known about God]. Note also here the absolute phrase 'what is known', meaning what is known to us, what is knowable by us.

[33] Rom 1: [19–21] [R].

the divinity which he could not separate and hence not use as stages by which to ascend to the Creator.

106. From the sacred Books we learn that God was the first to name the principal parts of creation, giving a name to it as soon as he had created it so that it was totally knowable by man. In creating it he had made it perceptible, but by naming it in the way he did he made it knowable by human understanding as a kind of type of species.

107. Thus, God gave language, when it was first instituted, a double purpose, and established it as a kind of mediator between the two great orders of visible and invisible things. Its first purpose was to make the sensible universe fully intelligible; the second, to make it a means by which we might pass beyond the confines of the sensible universe and rise to the knowledge of greater things. These things did not come under our senses but were supremely important for us as things that concerned the whole of our future destination and in which our total happiness was later to consist.

108. Consequently, in the gift that the supreme Master made to us of speech, there had to be more than simply speech as a purpose of divine teaching. The gift had to be bestowed in so wise a manner that language was taught us indirectly, as vesture of and access to the great truths that clarified the purpose of our existence and of the care that divine Wisdom had for us. For this reason, I believe, eternal truths were incorporated into speech and taught with it. Certainly, God did not teach language to us in the way a teacher of grammar would teach his pupils, but in the way that parents normally teach their children: they teach language with the very act by which they teach them the things contained in language.

109. Hence, every divine word must have been a great instrument for the first human beings who had not yet begun to speak. Nor is it surprising that they understood at once and, by imitating, spoke, because they were in fact endowed with a supreme power of understanding. Understanding had not yet become weak and uncertain, as we now receive it when we come into the world; we are not born adults, as our first fathers were created, nor are we born with all our powers intact and perfect.

110. This explains why divine Scripture assigns the gift of

speech to the Holy Spirit. The book of Wisdom says: 'The Spirit of the Lord has filled the whole earth. And this spirit, which contains all things in itself, has knowledge of speech.'[34] According to sacred Scripture, the knowledge of speech pertains solely to the spirit of God. In order to indicate to us the intimate connection between speech and the most sublime truths (which was the purpose of speech from the beginning), Scripture is not satisfied with saying that the Spirit of the Lord has knowledge of speech; it also adds that this spirit fills the whole earth with itself and contains all things in itself. We see that it unites the knowledge of speech with the knowledge of all things, or rather, that it unites this full knowledge with the knowledge of speech; it makes full knowledge precede speech. Because such knowledge is attributed to the divine Spirit, Scripture considers it necessary to say first that he fills the earth and all things with itself. Hence, the inspired Author apparently wants us to understand by these words how the invention of speech could not be proportionate to the limited strength of human beings because the task required universal wisdom in the inventor. Using language after it has been learnt is totally different from inventing it without having been taught it. Anyone who had to invent human speech could perhaps have no difficulty naming sensible, subsistent things, but, as I said, he would not be able to name abstracts because he did not perceive abstractions nor feel them either in themselves or in any sign that might show them. In the absence of this perception, it is impossible to imagine how man could have seen the qualities of things distinguished and separated from the things themselves or what could make him fix his mind on them alone, separate from their subjects. Without abstracts, he could not rise to the most sublime concepts that are either present in great abstractions or known solely through abstractions.

111. Moreover, if lesser abstractions are contained in greater, who could indicate the path that man must follow in order to pass from one class to the other, to descend from the more general to the less general, which is the first and indistinct path of the human mind? From the beginning, the highest truths and

[34] [Wis] 1: [7] [R].

most general abstractions had to be expressed in words. It is from these that the human mind always begins its path, which for the most part it does not know and is hidden from it. The words that God used from the beginning to signify the parts of the universe, which were taken as signs of fundamental abstractions, were precisely of this kind, as I might perhaps have the opportunity to demonstrate elsewhere. In order to give language such a solid foundation of wisdom therefore, the plan of the universe had certainly to be known: all things, their relationships and total ordering had to be known — in short, wisdom was required which, as Leibniz acutely says, 'according to the common notion of human beings, means simply the knowledge of happiness.'[35]

112. In many places of Scripture we find stated repeatedly that there is no wisdom if only a part of the knowable is known; wisdom must result from the knowledge of all things. Hence, we cannot find it by ourselves but only receive it from him who knows all things.[36] What we are saying about wisdom seems to me equally valid for the foundations of human language, because these two things have such a close affinity; they were given us united together, in the same way, we can say, that accidents were created united with matter.

113. The author of the book of Wisdom apparently uses this teaching to argue against those who dare to complain about the dispositions of divine Providence, and includes among the complainers people who in their inward thoughts detract from Providence. A paraphrase of the passage would be more or less this:

> O man, what kind of temerity is this? You misuse speech to abuse divine Providence, but it was the spirit of the Lord who gave you this speech that allows your mind to operate and you use it ungratefully to attack the Lord. Look to yourself. He will demand an account of the use you make of his gifts. He has knowledge of what is said and, filling the world with himself, knows all things. He sees thoughts, scrutinises hearts and hears all that is said.

[35] *Pref. cod. jur. gent. diplom.*

[36] Cf. *Saggio sull'unità dell'Educazione*, where the passages from Scripture are found.

Only he who has invented speech can know how to use it and use it wisely. If in the beginning eternal truths were bound with speech, it is only by loving these truths and meditating on them that you can talk with wisdom. Those who use speech to detract from these truths contradict themselves and become entangled in the words themselves, which nevertheless have a meaning independent of such people, a meaning that attests and confirms the truths they deny. Thus, those who speak evil things reveal themselves by their own actions, and condemn themselves before him who understands the meaning of all words and sees all contradictions. The wicked, in their very thoughts, will hear God questioning them about their contradictions. Nothing is to be gained by complaining. Do not use speech to detract, because your obscure declarations will have their effect: your lying lips will destroy your soul. Do not seek death in your wrong living nor use the work of your hands to cause your loss. It was not God who made death, and he does not rejoice over the loss of anyone. His plan is beyond your thinking, but it is a benign plan that he will bring to fulfilment by paths you cannot attain or imagine.'[37] Thus, in the way that knowledge is communicated from father to son, so the sacred author says wisdom 'is transferred into holy souls down through the generations and constitutes friends of God and prophets'.[38]

114. In antiquity, fathers were strongly urged to teach their children about the divine law and hand on to them the divine revelations and stories that united the human race to the Creator. These traditions showed traces of the first truths scattered throughout all the centuries and all nations, even if they were altered and falsified. But the negligence and infidelity of ancient people in telling their children the whole truth they had received from God was compensated mostly by the nature of language. Although language at the same time as the truths had changed and corrupted in its passage from father to son through many generations, it could not be totally extinguished. As long as it was preserved in the human race, it could not be separated from those elements which form not only the

[37] [Wis] 1.

[38] [Wis] 7: [27].

root of all human knowledge but the subject, and as it were substratum, of the first fundamental words. Consequently the fathers, by handing on language to their descendants, caused the greatest truths to be handed down throughout the centuries, even without being aware of doing so. These truths were safeguarded in a strong safe, so to speak, and handed on in the material form of language. Although languages, as I said, have been imitated, changed and multiplied, they all evidently retain the same root; and the traces of the same principal truths can still be found by anyone who critically investigates the fund of all languages.

115. In all these things we see that everything we know, we know because God communicates it to us through the objects he submits to our knowledge. These objects can be the subsistent things that compose the universe, or signs of abstract things, that is, words that he gave as sounds to our ears, or they can be truths of an order higher than the order of physical nature — truths which he revealed through, and closely united with, words.

CHAPTER 22

Natural reason alone cannot give us knowledge of happiness; this knowledge is learnt from God

116. Job drew comfort from this fact in the depth of his afflictions. As his thought ranged through the wonderful parts of the universe, he found everywhere difficulties that human thought was incapable of solving. But he also understood that even if he had known all these mysteries of nature, it would not have been sufficient to make people believe they have wisdom. Wisdom is not confined within the limits of creation but rests in the depth of divine eternity. The holy man asked:

'But where is wisdom to be found, and where is the place of understanding?' And he answered himself: 'Man knows not the price thereof, neither is it found in the land of them that live in delights' (it does not consist in created goods). 'The depth says: It is not in me: and the sea says: It is not with me' (wisdom cannot be extracted from all those goods that we naturally experience and from which we normally extract the notions we have of things). 'The finest gold shall not purchase it, neither shall silver be weighed in exchange for it. It shall not be compared with the dyed colours of India, or with the most precious stone sardonyx, or the sapphire. Gold or crystal cannot equal it, neither shall any vessels of gold be changed for it.' He then adds that this sought-for wisdom is drawn only from secret places hidden from human eyes. But again he asks what are these places, and answers: 'It is hid from the eyes of all the living, and the fowls of the air know it not' (it cannot be sought in corporeal extension). 'Destruction and death have said: With our ears we have heard the fame thereof. God understands the way of it, and he knows the place thereof. For' (here is the true reason) 'he beholds the ends of the world: and looks on all things that are under heaven. Who made a weight for the winds, and weighed the waters by measure. When he gave a law for the rain, and a way for the sounding storms. Then he saw it, and declared, and prepared, and searched it. And he said to man: Behold the fear of the

Lord, that is wisdom: and to depart from evil, is understanding.'[39]

117. In this sublime passage Job teaches how wisdom cannot dwell in any part of creation, that is, not in heaven, not on earth, not in the sea and not in the deep abyss, but only in the mind, which ranges through the different parts of creation comparing and uniting them. And this mind which possesses wisdom cannot be human because the human mind is neither simultaneously nor even successively present to the whole of creation. Wisdom, as we saw, is knowledge of happiness. But natural human knowledge is, Job says, only sensible and what we experience. This experience gives us knowledge only of external goods, of wealth and the pleasures of life, but happiness is not found in any of these, nor therefore is wisdom. Indeed 'the highest and most valuable things of the universe cannot be compared with it, and wisdom is drawn from hidden places'. But is it not possible that abandoned to ourselves, we will find wisdom after death? After death and deprived of divine companionship, we will have only a negative knowledge of wisdom, that is, we will know that in this life we had lost our way. As a result, our idea of wisdom will be the idea we usually form of anything far away, of anything we know by hearsay.

118. Even if we supposed that happiness might be found in some visible things, and that we could obtain this object that contains happiness, we could still not be independent of God, nor would our own knowledge and power be sufficient. We would have no certainty that our precious thing will not be taken from us and that we can enjoy it in all tranquillity. Do we really know the power of the creatures around us? Caught up as we are in the mutual action of creative forces totally independent of us, can we be certain that we will not be squashed in the continual, unrelenting course of nature, and I mean squashed, just like the insects that perish in their thousands on our streets under the feet of pedestrians. We are weak and ignorant people; even if we possessed all the knowledge we are capable of, or took pride in a power that oppressed thousands and thousands of people, we would be still be nothing. Do we really think we know the origin of things and are able to

[39] [Job] 28: [12–18, 21–28]†.

change their course, while at the same time censuring and complaining about God's arrangement of them? We are like a baby gurgling in its cradle, knowing nothing about itself, its destiny, the objects around it, and without the strength to satisfy its own needs, not to mention defend itself against external attacks, unless a provident care, a maternal love provides for all its needs? A brute animal can live tranquilly even in the midst of dangers because it cannot think, but we look for peace in the knowledge of things. Although we are reasoning creatures, we do not find peace. Yet the only way we can find it is through reason. What kind of knowledge will assure us and give us peace in this limitless universe around us? We are no more than a pin-point in the midst of a thousand forces and a thousand powerful, indifferent beings in movement all around us whose unbreakable laws we do not know, like the countless stars of heaven and the deep abysses of the earth, the great surgings of the oceans which seem at every minute to menace the continents, powerful hurricanes that flatten entire forests, fires that raze cities to the ground, electrical power, unseen and powerful, that seems capable of making the entire planet teeter on its foundations, and a thousand other invisible, insurmountable and inescapable forces. What kind of knowledge or human power therefore can live secure and free from apprehension in the midst of the relentless action of these inexorable forces? What are we in the midst of these terrible beings that are so much greater than we, greater even than we can imagine, we who can be laid low by a mere needle prick, an insect bite, a tiny sip of poison, a drink of water, a breath of air — little things such as these can even cost us our life?

But he who knows all the laws of nature and is their master can guide us among all these many powers that exceed our puny strength so that we do not fatally collide with them. Better still, only this great Being who knows everything and governs the universe can give us the knowledge to rise finally above these fearful powers and find happiness. How can any human being reliably know what is useful in the totality of events if God does not reveal it? If in our study of all that helps us we must base ourselves on what we foresee of the future, our knowledge will still be purely conjectural and limited: we simply cannot know all the events that can suddenly occur, all

[118]

totally outside our control, and yet in an instant can destroy all our fortune and defences. Only God, who knows and directs all the events of creation, can teach with certainty what will be most useful for us in the final outcome of all things: 'The way to find wisdom,' Job tells us, 'is known to God and he knows where it dwells because his gaze reaches to the ends of the world and he sees all things under heaven', and he adds: 'God sees this wisdom to be taught human beings. He will tell us about it, prepare it and investigate every point where he has fixed the strength of the winds, given the waters their measure, the rains their law, and the thunderstorms their path', that is, at the beginning, when he created and ordered the universe and at the same time disposed all things to serve the good of his faithful. God therefore was able to teach us the great secret of this wisdom when he tells us, 'Know that the fear of the Lord is wisdom, and to withdraw from evil is understanding'[40] — this is the road that will lead us to happiness because to this end he has disposed all the things of creation. To senseless human beings these things seem to act blindly and move purely by chance, but from all eternity, God has directed them in keeping with their immutable laws to serve unfailingly the salvation and perfection of the righteous.

119. Once again therefore we clearly see the need for faith and revelation. Even if we had the power to avoid everything we knew to be harmful, the experience of things alone would still not be sufficient for us to know everything that might harm us, to know all the dangers. Our experience does not stretch to everything and to all possible events, nor can we understand the whole course of the universe. Furthermore, experiential knowledge is acquired only with time, but we feel the need to follow the path of happiness and of a peaceful, secure life from the very beginning, without first getting lost on the path of error and misery. For this reason conjectural knowledge of our happiness is not enough for us.

120. Nevertheless conjectural knowledge can help us after we have been encouraged and made wiser by the assurances of divine revelation, which he who moves all things promises us as protection. In fact, experiential knowledge, which we

40 Cf. Job 28: [23–24, 26–28].

acquire through experience and continues to grow as the human race ages, always brings with it a new submission to revelation and a new comfort to faith. The more perfect this knowledge is, the more it accords with divine revelation, which simply, certainly and ceaselessly teaches wisdom to us all.

121. From all this we must conclude that reason alone with its particular arguments cannot solve all the difficulties raised about divine Providence. It alone cannot give peace to human thought, because reason lacks knowledge of the bond that unites everything. Thus, if we said to our reason, 'Even though you command me to cultivate virtue, I will not do so unless you can guarantee I will possess beatitude as a reward', how can reason confirm this? All it can say is: 'Experience tells me that the most virtuous people are generally the most happy.' But what if we were not satisfied with this and added: 'Can you assure me that as the reward of my virtuous life nothing harmful will happen to me today? that tomorrow I will not die, that my house will not be burnt down? Can you guarantee that my children will have a long life?' On such matters, both reason and experience, which do not exceed the sphere of sensible things and do not extend to everything, are silent. Reason can only send us back to the paternal voice of him who governs the present and future worlds. In sacred Scripture, he is referred to as the guide of wisdom 'because' (this explains the title of this chapter) 'all speech, all wisdom, all knowledge of facts, our learning and we ourselves are all in his hands.'[41] Only he, from the sublimity of his throne, can say to us with total confidence: 'Be virtuous, and I guarantee that one day you will find satisfaction. Nothing in the universe happens by chance. I have disposed all things for the good of the virtuous. Whatever misfortune befalls you, do not let it stop you from doing the good you intend. Everything happens for your good, including what seems contrary to your good; it all happens for a good that you will receive when all things come to an end, and this good will last for ever.'

[41] Cf. Wis 7: [15–16] [R].

CHAPTER 23

Knowledge of happiness is the result of all that can be known. Human reason does not attain this knowledge: God alone communicates it to us. Therefore faith is again necessary

122. Those who had faith in God when he said to man, 'Behold the fear of the Lord, that is wisdom: and to depart from evil, is understanding', needed solely this faith to be acquainted with the path that led to their happiness.

This great truth was simply a corollary of all God knew about the universe's system that he had mentally conceived and brought into reality, and did not reveal. Nor could he reveal the system to us in all its parts, nor was this necessary. It was enough to tell us what the end was of everything. We certainly do not need any great theoretical knowledge; we need no more than this practical corollary, which can truly be said to be the result of all that is knowable. It opens for us all equally the path to salvation, no matter how great or little our intelligence, provided we believe in the word of the Lord. God may not have given us all equal knowledge of unnecessary things, but he did grant us all equally the fruitful consequence of his universal knowledge which indicated the certain path to happiness. We cannot all be people of learning but we can all be wise and have faith in our most wise Master. People consider that true wisdom lies in the final propositions of knowledge. The hard-won knowledge of the learned is in the end directed solely to the discovery of simple truths, and in itself has no value; all the labour involved is for the result it can yield. From the moment therefore when the great Teacher and Lord of the human race communicated his law to us and promised us life if we kept it but death if we violated it, he gave us wisdom. God reasonably required us to believe his words, and because we could not learn the path to happiness through experience but solely through the authoritative assertion of our Creator, it was more necessary that we believed in his words. The limitation of our nature required us to be led by the only guide who knew the path.

123. Thus, we were given the happy necessity of paying a very noble tribute to our Creator: a *blind* faith in his words. I say a blind faith because we had not *experienced* anything that would explain the divine words, and it was most reasonable to believe in his words and submit our intelligence to such a great authority, that is, to admit our own insufficiency for such a task. Nothing is more reasonable than to trust someone who knows the route a difficult and unknown journey is to be undertaken. Proud people or independent thinkers may perhaps be contemptuous at the mere mention of blind faith, but when they have to take an unknown mountain track, they would not be so proud and independent as not to engage a local man as guide, a man who knows the mountains well. They now forget their great knowledge, and the uneducated peasant becomes their master and guide. The philosopher trusts himself blindly to such a master, and believes and fully obeys the instructions of the man of the mountains, as he follows him on very difficult tracks and over dangerous crags. He does not first ask for mathematical proofs or any other proofs, which in any case the guide could not give. He follows this course of action because public opinion says that the guide knows the way, while his own reason tells him he does not. Nothing therefore is more reasonable, more necessary, more ordinary than to submits one's reason to the authority of another; reason alone is truly never sufficient for any of us. So, *a fortiori*, nothing is more in agreement with reason than to trust ourselves to the truth of the Creator, acknowledging his power on the one hand and our own impotence on the other. It agrees even more with reason to fear him, because if we fail to fulfil his most wise and excellent will, he has at his command the whole of nature ready to vindicate him, and a thousand other means of punishing us. Consequently, to fear God and avoid causing him displeasure is with total reason held to be a teaching of wisdom.

124. But God's requirement that we have faith in his most truthful words was not in itself sufficient: he had to hide many unnecessary truths. In doing this however, he gave us a wider field for exercising fidelity to him, and at the same time left us with a great deal more material for meditating on his greatness and our littleness. Thus, even the little knowledge we can acquire agrees with, confirms and glorifies faith.

CHAPTER 24

Continuation. — Knowledge of times and places is beyond the power of human reason

125. In the orders of nature and of grace, God generally keeps hidden those particular things that depend on the complex of events, and we cannot deduce them through reasoning because we do not know the complex. Among such things, as Scripture tells us, is the determination of times and places, a determination that is indeed very relevant to the ordained movement of the universe. In Ecclesiastes we read, 'God has assigned to all things their proper time, and everything takes place under heaven, contained in their fixed place.'[42]

126. The distribution of these times and the allocation of these places certainly depend on the law of fittingness to the whole. Only one thought could establish this distribution, a thought that could include everything at once, because the great whole is only gradually attaining its completion through its places and times.

127. It is precisely in connection with the wise distribution of these places and times, in which God's plan is realised that Ecclesiastes warns us that we cannot know the great plan. Pointing out that even afflictions coming from God must have a wise purpose, the book adds, 'Certainly God has made all things good within their established time and given the world to human debate so that man can never resolve the great work that God has done and continues to do from the beginning to the end.'[43]

128. Thus, when the Apostles asked the risen Jesus Christ whether he would restore the kingdom of Israel at that time, he replied, 'It is not for you to know the times or periods that the Father has set by his own authority. But you will receive power when the Holy Spirit has come upon you; and you will be my witnesses in Jerusalem, in all Judea and Samaria, and to the ends

42 Eccles 3: [1] [R].

43 Ibid., [3: 11] [R].

of the earth.'[44] It is as if he were saying they should not be thinking about the particular dispositions which the heavenly Father makes regarding human things, but be satisfied with knowing simply that it is he who makes them; the Apostles should think of carrying out his will without considering how successful they might be, certain that the outcome would be no other than good, no matter how contrary things appeared.

129. Appearances at that time, and afterwards, were indeed very contrary to the restoration of the great kingdom of Israel, for which Christ's disciples had great hope and desire. Their faith however was not weakened by all these disturbing appearances. Like Abraham, they were certain that God would raise them up glorious even from their ashes, and if his word had first to be ineffective, they would risk and give their life with infinite joy. The innocent blood shed in three centuries by the most cruel masters of the world was simply a comfort for that living faith which is continually repeated in union with Job: 'Though he kill me, yet I will trust in him.'[45] Such greatness, such long suffering in human beings could not be produced by what their reason foresees or by their experience, but only by the most certain promises of the Creator accepted with a faith that fixes its loving gaze on an immense light far beyond all the limits of creation. Thus, in St. Mark, Jesus teaches: 'About that day or hour' (the end of the world) 'no one knows, … nor the Son, but only the Father;'[46] the universe depends on the Father's creating will, a will common to the divine Trinity, of which the Father is the source-principle.

130. We have seen in the book of Job that 'wisdom' does not mean the wisdom proper to God but wisdom as communicated to us. Similarly, elsewhere in divine Scripture we are often told that God comes to know (or some similar expression), meaning the knowledge he wishes to communicate to us. Hence, Scripture nearly always speaks of God according to the particular manner in which he united himself to the universe and made himself knowable to us. All reasonings that follow this form are intelligible and true for us. Thus we find verified that 'neither

[44] Acts 1: [7–8].

[45] Job 13: [15].

[46] Mk 13: [32].

the angels in heaven nor the Son know that day and hour, but only the Father'.[47] The Father knows the day through himself; the Son knows it in so far as in the Father and generated by him. But although the Son, as man, can know it if he wishes to read it in the divine essence, he does not know it in a human way nor in a way communicable to human beings and angels. Any knowledge therefore not communicated to a human being is quite correctly not called *human knowledge*. All that we call *human* knowledge must by its nature be made manifest to at least someone among mankind, and must pertain to that person in so far as a human person. But the last day, and generally the knowledge of the times and the moments in which the Most High moves and distributes events and leads all things to their unfailing end, is God's secret. And we can say that in this secret the eternal is pleased to place his formidable power, a power that does not upset nature but, in the twinkling of an eye as it were, strikes down wicked people scattering them to the ends of the earth and leaving the good triumphant. Job places this action among the works that indicate the greatness of the divinity.

131. Once again therefore the divine Master inculcates continual vigilance: 'Beware, keep alert and pray, for you do not know when the time will come.'[48] This alone is a convincing reason for vigilance. He describes the heavenly Father as the master who prior to leaving the house divides out among his servants the duties concerning the administration of his goods but keeps secret the hour of his return. And the divine Master, who wishes to keep that hour concealed from all equally, concludes: 'What I say to you I say to all: Keep awake.'[49]

132. The knowledge of times that the Eternal reserves to himself makes the works of the Lord wonderful and great in our sight, although we sometimes see events end abruptly in a way totally different from the way our own human providence was intently directing them.

Indeed, at every moment we are taken by surprise, as it were, by the Almighty. We never know or can ever know the future

[47] Mk 13: [32].

[48] Mk 13: [33].

[49] Mk 13: [37].

with certainty, nor foresee the results of our own actions, or discern how to deal with new circumstances that arise; we search totally in vain for ways to avoid them and protect ourselves against them. But circumstances are continually changing and we are caught in situations and complex predicaments that are always new and for which we have no skill. Only when things come to their pre-established and inevitable end do we become aware of the true situation, and remove the blindfold from our eyes. With the pressure gone, we can now think calmly about everything that has happened and even see it as most natural, we can reproach ourselves for not foreseeing such natural things, and because we consider our lack of vision as purely accidental, we can intend and hope to be more vigilant next time. In this way we can go on deluding and deceiving ourselves from one event to another as a punishment for not paying attention to the divine words and not knowing that we lack the key to events, that is, the knowledge of times.

We are never spectators at one and the same moment of a whole series of events, as the Eternal is, to whom both past and future times are present. To us, who are as changeable as time itself, individual events present themselves as separate from each another; they appear briefly on the stage of the present moment and then are gone. Their wonderful connection is seen only when they have for all intents and purposes passed and cannot be recalled; they are no longer under our control and are consigned uselessly to our memory. While each event was present, we were totally occupied with it as if no other event would follow; its action upon our sense-nature, the sounds that sometimes accompanied it, the complexity of its parts, the speed at which it passed, the thousand hopes it raised and the passions it set in motion, all these things conspired to prevent us thinking about the uncertain future; on the contrary, they made us presumptuous, bold and over-confident, as if we had been dreaming of kingdoms and treasure but were suddenly woken by the light of the sun that dissipated all our illusions. If only we could undeceive ourselves for once! Our task is to learn from experience and contemplate how, throughout all the centuries of the world's existence, God has sublimely guided countless series of facts, which have always confounded the futile hopes of the wicked, even when appearances seemed to support them in

[132]

their boasts. This should lead us to glorify God's supreme wisdom, and humbly proclaim: 'O the depth of the riches and wisdom and knowledge of God! How unsearchable are his judgments and how inscrutable his ways! For who has known the mind of the Lord? Or who has been his counsellor? Or who has given a gift to him, to receive a gift in return? For from him and through him and to him are all things. To him be the glory forever. Amen.'[50]

50 Rom 11: [33–36].

CHAPTER 25

The limitations of reason that we have discussed do not make reason contrary to faith but bind faith and reason together with mutual functions

133. The study of all these limitations, which arise from the nature of our mind, shows very clearly our need of faith to obtain happiness and the peace of spirit we desire. Nevertheless, reflection on the confines within which human understanding is restricted by its nature and condition has always been dangerous. If the confines are broadened too much, there is the risk of making the human mind presumptuous and confident with an illusory knowledge. If however, through fear of this, they are too restricted, there is the great danger of scepticism. The philosophers who have come to grief on one of these two hazards when treating this matter in some depth, are perhaps very few, but if I am not mistaken, the limitations I have discussed guard against *scepticism* on the one hand and the excessive *dogmatism* of reason on the other.

The limitations demonstrate that if God's word does not give us trust and comfort in the government of his Providence, then reason alone, abandoned to itself and taught only by the experience of sensible things, is not sufficient to give us complete peace concerning that government. Nevertheless the limitations persuade us that there is a conformity and bond between reason and faith: reason calls faith to its aid, while faith teaches and enlightens reason. But to prevent any doubt remaining about the bond between these two noble guides, I must consider any possible enmity and opposition between them, and show that reason maintains nothing contrary and hostile to faith.

The relationship between the two could differ in three ways.

First, a relationship of simple *diversity*. This is a negative relationship on the part of reason, that is, nothing known by reason need contradict in any way what faith suggests; reason simply lacks the knowledge of the things faith proposes. This kind of diversity does not remove reason's authority in the things it knows, nor does it affect the truth of all that faith proposes to be believed. We cannot use our ignorance to argue that what we do not know is false, although it is affirmed by a solemn, infallible authority. None of us knows everything. The part of knowledge we lack does not falsify the part we have, nor does the knowledge we have reject or condemn as false the part we do not have. This is the difference between reason and faith, and it comes from the natural limitations I have deal with. These limitations simply determine some objects that are hidden or veiled from us, but there is no opposition or enmity in this diversity of object, rather this is the reason for their close agreement. On the other hand, it is precisely because reason is ignorant of some part of truth that faith kindly comes to its aid by giving it what it lacks.

[133]

CHAPTER 26

The fallibility of reason gives rise to some apparent contradictions between it and faith. But reason can solve these contradictions by acknowledging its error

134. The second relationship is a relationship of *opposition* between reason and faith. The opposition is *apparent* if it refers to the way in which results are deduced, but *true* when the principles of reason oppose the principles of faith.

135. The first kind of contradiction is possible because reason is mistaken in its deductions, and sometimes it can lack sufficient facts on which to base an honest and complete argument. But because all these contradictions are apparent, they do not constitute a true opposition and enmity. When reason acknowledges that it does not know many things due to the limits restricting it, it necessarily feels obliged to acknowledge its ignorance in the presence of faith and bow to its teaching. Hence, when it is aware of deducing *consequences* contrary to faith, it must acknowledge its own imperfection and correct these consequences with the help of the light of revelation. The cause of these mistaken deductions can be easily detected: if we acknowledge our ignorance and the undoubted fallibility of reason, deductions of this kind must be expected, must be foreseen, and acknowledging our ignorance is the same as acknowledging our errors. Reason however cannot but be aware of its own ignorance: the limitations I have explained are deduced by the light of reason, meditating upon itself. If it is reasonable to submit to faith due to the *limitation* of our knowledge, it is still more reasonable to submit to it due to the *fallibility* of our reasoning. Human reason has no right to rebel against faith on the excuse that some of its deductions are contrary to the teachings of faith, especially because it has already implicitly submitted to faith by acknowledging its own natural limitation and fallibility.

However, this would not be the case if the very *principles* of reason (where error does not enter) were found to be in contradiction to faith. This kind of opposition would contain a true and evident enmity, a real contradiction. As a result, reason could no longer submit to faith because it is impossible for it to forsake the first principles, from which it receives movement and which direct all its steps. If reason could forsake the first principles, it would destroy itself because they constitute it — and no being can destroy itself. There is therefore no opposition whatsoever between reason and faith. No opposition has ever been found, and it does not come from the limitations I have posited.

CHAPTER 27

Sensism limits reason unduly and leads to scepticism

136. Thirdly: could reason doubt its principles?

It may think it can: if it considered the principles truthful and found that faith conflicted with them, it would condemn and destroy faith. But if it doubted the principles, it would simultaneously destroy both itself and faith.

137. This is *scepticism*, and it will help if I show how far my teaching about the limits of reason differs from this most pernicious system.

In doing this the opinions of some recent authors about this important question will become apparent, which will allow the reader to see whether I have contributed to a solution of the question. I could discuss at length the opinions of ecclesiastical authors who have always substantially possessed the truth, but I will concentrate only on those thinkers who have had a greater impact on the world that has acclaimed them as discoverers of great truths.

First, Locke brought back the Scholastic principle which people considered had been overturned by Descartes, namely, that there was nothing in the intellect which was not first in feeling. However Locke's explanation and application of the principle was much poorer and more materialistic than that of the ancient Scholastics: he deduced everything from sensation and reflection. Condillac hoped to simplify the system still further: he took pride in his success of explaining everything with only one principle: sensation. He persuaded himself that even the supreme rules of judgment that the ancient Scholastics had regarded as natural to man and as visible by a kind of instinct, can be composed of sensations. Unfortunately, both authors never saw any of the great difficulties that have always presented themselves to deep thinkers who wanted to explain the origin of human knowledge. They openly propounded, not without a certain air of contempt for all who went before them, everything that occurred to their presumptuous and rather limited minds. Anyone who argued against their school and proposed a profound idea was considered ridiculous; the tranquillity of their happy philosophy was not to be disturbed by any bold thought or solid reflection. Sensists derisively reject all the systems that go beyond their own superficiality, as if they are saying 'such things cannot be known. Abstruse things have no place in the discussion, nor do metaphysical obscurities, which fortunately have been banished from the enlightened, pagan world' — under their reign, all serious knowledge and higher thought is annulled.

138. When therefore these philosophers come to discuss the limitations of the mind, they have not the slightest difficulty in deducing everything from sensations and thus find no limits to human reason. They make reason immensely proud and arrogant, vainly flattering it that it knows everything that it needs through sensible experience alone, on which they base inexhaustible hopes.

Nevertheless, because many things, like the substances of bodies, are clearly not apprehended by corporeal sensitivity, they found themselves forced to posit in fact a limit to what is humanly knowable. But this did not frighten them and they did not doubt their system. Instead of solving the difficulty and seeing themselves as returning authority to knowledge, they dismissed the problem by gratuitously asserting that man can never know the essences and substances of things. This purely gratuitous limit to knowledge reduced philosophy and the knowable to very little or indeed to nothing but did not harm human reason. Reason had put all its treasures into the experience of the senses; on these imaginary treasures, contradicting itself, it had placed no limit. Thus, philosophy was reduced to the knowledge of accidents, inducing people to find satisfaction in these alone. It indirectly helped the material arts but retarded and annihilated moral knowledge. It produced a century that was in every respect extremely superficial and at the same time fiercely proud in its superficiality.

Next, Hume considered as beyond doubt Locke's principle that the only source of knowledge was sensations, produced in us by the action of the bodies around us.[51] But Hume's mind

51 The only true method to be followed in philosophy is undoubtedly that which begins from facts. The merit of the modern school is that it has

was much more penetrative and of greater consequence then Locke's, and we can suppose that this principle was received by him in the way that the prejudices of the time were received, that is, as authoritative propositions considered as true. Nobody thinks of examining them because they accept that the propositions have already been investigated and acknowledged. No one is prepared to check what is thought to have already been fully checked; no one wishes to find himself at the beginning again. But although Hume deduced the origin of human knowledge from Locke's thesis, which he accepted without examination, he did not do so with Locke's simplicity, because he saw that the principles of reason, as commonly accepted, cannot be deduced from experience. According to him, these principles present themselves as universal, whereas experience, even though repeated and multiplied, gives only particular results. Nevertheless the principle 'that everything we know we extract from the experience of the senses' remained in his mind and he did not doubt its truth. Consequently, Hume was drawn by the very process of ideas to doubt the value of the principles of reason: for him, they did not originate from experience, which he considered the sole source of knowledge, nor could their universality or necessity be drawn from experience. Therefore these principles were a product of the human imagination, an effect of blind habit. People see the principles realised so often in experience through the association of ideas and the tendency to turn to analogies that they suppose that the principles must always be realised as well. He thus reduces to general principles what are truly not general principles. In this way, Locke, by giving too much prominence to sensible experience and making human reason proud and bold in its declarations,

proclaimed this method and made it universal. On the other hand the omission of some facts and starting with incomplete observations is the ever-present defect. The gifts of the philosopher are the ability to observe all the facts, understand the most elusive (like the fact of feeling and of spiritual consciousness), and be indifferent to the results. To do this, we have to be very alert and pay continuous attention to ourselves. A philosophy that is capable of noting only what is external, what our corporeal senses experience from the stimulations of matter, is the crudest and basest of all. This is not mature philosophy but philosophy in its infancy, and such is the philosophy of Locke, Condillac, Destut-Tracy, etc.

opened the way quite unawares to Hume's abyss of scepticism and to the debasement of reason itself, whose dignity he sought to assert.

139. It is a constant effect of human error that extreme error immediately begets other errors that are defective in the opposite extreme, because error inevitably puts us at the mercy of the agitation and struggle of the most contrary opinions. Hume was struck above all by the principle of *causality*. Unable to see any way of deducing it generally from experience, he doubted it, or rather, we can say, he discarded it. Once this principle is discarded, the mind cannot pass from sensible things to insensible things. Hence, everything that did not come under the senses must be, at least for the sensist, very doubtful and uncertain. Thus, with reason dethroned, the right to testify to the truth was left solely to the bodily senses. These of course could do this only in the case of physical things, whose testimony reason was now no longer able to receive in any way whatsoever. But more or less at the same time Berkeley attacked the testimony of the senses, which now suffered their own dethronement. He condemned them as agents deluding the mind that was seduced by their appearances into believing in the external existence of bodies, which in reality did not exist.

CHAPTER 28

Transcendental idealism greatly limits reason, rendering it powerless to attain the truth, and results in scepticism

140. What I have dealt with above was the state of philosophy when Kant arrived on the scene. A man of great intellect, and more incisive than previous philosophers, he could not guard himself against the spirit of sophistry, which was a characteristic of the whole century.

It would be true to say that he opposed all his predecessors and brought together their contrasting teachings and errors, which he clothed in a new language and developed.

141. He felt the force of Hume's argument, namely, that truly necessary and universal principles could not be deduced from experience, no matter how often the uniform facts were repeated. On the other hand, in contrast to Hume, he saw that it was impossible to doubt the principles of reason; the whole human race has accepted and agreed on them throughout all time. But because Locke had acted too simply in deducing the general principles from experience and had thus given reason far too much confidence in itself, as something that took pride in its ability to attain all truth by experience, Hume had acted rightly when he demoted this arrogant reason that was so sure of itself. But in this Hume had done nothing more than *censure* reason: he had simply put a limit on the results of experience, and acknowledged that reason's vision had to be restricted by a certain horizon beyond which it could not go. He had neglected to make a *critique*, a judgment, of reason. Restricting reason's vision to an horizon was not sufficient; the nature of this horizon had to be established and clearly affirmed; in short, the limits of human understanding had to be determined.

142. Kant tackled this difficult question and laid down that the general principles of reason cannot, as Locke said, be drawn from experience (hence Kant acknowledged a *pure reason*, that is, devoid of experience). He also accepted Hume's opinion that these principles are true, universal and necessary. So, he

imagined an *hypothesis* that would reconcile everything — his system is in the last analysis only an hypothesis — he imagined that the principles were produced by human reason itself, or better, were a property of reason and, as it were, spontaneous acts of human nature; without these principles, reason could not judge what was presented to it. Granted that by means of this natural disposition, reason clothes the sensations received from experience with a certain universality and necessity, then according to Kant these concepts and the principles of reason make the experience of the senses possible, that is, they make us perceive intellectually and judge sensible objects. These concepts and innate dispositions are therefore the limits that Kant imposed on human reason; it *had* to use them in all its operations. Consequently, it had no power to judge them; if it judged them, it could do so only by using them and therefore was forced to have blind faith in them.

143. Kant claimed therefore that he had refuted Hume's *scepticism*, which had put these general principles in doubt. In truth however he refuted Hume's scepticism only by another *scepticism* taken a step further forward. If Hume wounded truth externally, Kant struck the mortal blow internally. Hume had doubted the existence of the general principles, whereas Kant, who supposed them to be connatural with human reason, accepted their existence, indeed their necessity. But by making them a product, an effect, of the subjective forms of reason, he rendered them incapable of testifying to the truth (which is essentially objective) and hence also to the real existence of entia outside us. In Kant's system the necessity and universality of these principles are purely formal laws of intelligence, which uses them to see things in a determined, constant way. Hence, according to him, everything that the human understanding sees is purely an appearance in the understanding, as in a *camera obscura*: the mind cannot see anything outside itself or must see it as its limited laws prescribe. In maintaining that the mind sees nothing real outside itself, Kant is acting like someone who lights a lamp to see only the lamp. This is what he calls *transcendental idealism* in opposition to the *empirical idealism* of Berkeley, whom he considers mistaken for having said that only bodies are appearances, whereas he should have said that all the principles of reason are also appearances. He refuted Hume's

scepticism therefore by pretending to deny the limitation applied by Hume who rejected the validity of the principle of cause. In fact however Kant increased Hume's limitation by subjectivising and invalidating all the principles of reason. He refuted Berkeley's *idealism* by transporting it from a part to the whole of human knowledge. He refuted *relative scepticism* and *idealism* by establishing an *absolute scepticism* and *idealism*. Moreover, in addition to finding clear contradictions in both experience and reason, he authoritatively declared that 'it is totally impossible to pacify pure reason in contradiction with itself' and he used this phrase as the title of a chapter in his Philosophy.[52] In this way Kant taught the *critique* of reason in a most *dogmatic* manner, declaring as supremely true a system that tended to remove all truth.[53]

I need to make a comparison between the limits I believe had to be assigned to human reason and the limits Kant assigns. But before doing so, it will be helpful to have a look at the origin of *transcendental idealism*.

144. Who would believe that such a system originated from *sensism* and even *materialism*?

Yet, as I have said, opposite errors attract one another and incongruously unite. In Locke's view, sensible matter had been the source of all human knowledge. Hume, following this principle with greater consequences than with Locke, had destroyed reason, depriving it of all power to know the truth and leaving the senses (in so far as they could be) as possessors

[52] *Critique of Pure Reason*. Cf. particularly part 2, *Transcendental Logic*, bk. 1, c. 2, sect. 2, and *Transcendental Dialectic*, bk. 2, c. 2, sect. 6, and *Appendix* to *Trans. Dial.*

[53] It seems impossible how Kant, after depriving theoretical reason of the capacity to pronounce on the absolute truth of things, did not see that he was bringing about the ruin of all previous philosophical systems, including the very system he himself was constructing. Criticism pronounced its own death sentence; it has nothing to offer except an apparent and subjective truth. Nor is it valid to say that it is a *negative* system that destroys and does not build up. Whether the propositions composing it are negative or positive, it is always true that the propositions have only a subjective, that is, an apparent truth. Whatever intellectual efforts the system makes, it will never escape the force of this argument. If it consists essentially in doubt, why is it put forward? And if doubt is put forward as a certain system, what right does it have to propose with certainty a system that removes all certainty?

of the power. Berkeley finished off the work already begun: he stripped the senses of this claimed possession. Kant on the other hand formed a totally material idea of the human mind and made feeling, intellect and reason into one single state. He was brought to this by the material idea he formed of the spirit, in the following way.

145. He noted that it was a property of matter to have only one limited form at a time, and to be incapable of possessing all the other forms. He *gratuitously* supposed that this must also be true of human reason: reason, enclosed within certain determined forms, is constrained to see things in accordance with those forms and with truth. He did not see that TRUTH ITSELF WAS THE FORM OF REASON and that this one form alone was precisely the form (as the word itself indicates) that did not give any of its own limitations to objects and therefore did not manufacture them but affirmed them according to *truth itself*.

146. Kant also explained his sophism with the material likeness of a mirror that produces the image of things according to its form: the image is misshapen, lengthened, shortened, twisted, divided and re-assembled according to the design of the surface of the mirror. Such, he says (and always *gratuitously*), is human intelligence, which perceives things only by adding its own form to them. In this way it informs them with itself and therefore can never be certain of their truth nor, he added, even of their existence, because the mind perceives only the representation of things, not the things themselves. Furthermore, it cannot pass from the representation to the things, as these are totally outside the mind, just as one body is always outside another — as he usually does, he was arguing with the analogy of bodies. Guided by these material ideas, Kant came to *transcendental idealism*, a system that denies all knowledge in human beings, that is, any knowledge that is more than apparent and subjective [*App*., no. 2]. How he punishes our wonderful mind! Although it often tries to rise above its natural limits, it finds itself ignominiously and unknowingly cast down by its own effort. With *transcendental idealism* Kant inflated reason, considering it a light unto itself and making it creator of the universe, which it brought with it and which continuously emanated from the laws of its activity. How wretched for human reason was so much honour! Alas, the whole universe is changed

into a dream; the divine is no more than a desire; the human spirit is indeed a great Lord, but only of chimera; truth no longer exists; thus the sun is extinguished in order to light a fatuous fire.

If we look at the tortuous route of such a system, we see it began with *materialism* and in the end acknowledged only the human spirit as the principle and end of everything. The human spirit was deified but unfortunately the system finished up back in *materialism*. It maintains that the only seat of what we call *matter* is the nature of the soul. Everything must therefore be reduced to one substance alone, which we are free to call *matter* or *spirit,* depending on the different properties we think it has. But this must surely finish up in *pantheism*? Only one substance is posited by *materialists*, in their consideration of matter; only one substance posited by *Spinozists*, in their consideration of God, and only one substance is posited by *transcendental idealists*, in their consideration exclusively of the human spirit. But is this not one system that starts from three different points and arrives at one and the same point? Whether these three entities are apparent or real, all these thinkers equally accept them and their properties, make them all into one being only and attribute their properties to this one being. Isn't this one being always the same, in that it is always the same body composed of three elements? It does not matter which of the elements is posited first, provided that after the addition of the other two, they are all so intermingled and confused that one cannot be discerned from the other: they are one whole thing. Hence, if the *materialists* arrive at their system with the first step, the *transcendental idealists* and the *pantheists* enter the same system with the second step. With the first step, one group stops at the human spirit, and the others at God. We should not be surprised therefore if Kant, after the first step, judiciously stops, calls his disciples around him and says: 'You see, I am certainly not a materialist; on the contrary I am the defender and champion of the human spirit.' Too many people all too simply believed these words, to which however it was sufficient to reply: 'Maybe, but finish the journey you have begun and when you have reached the end, we will judge the path you have taken.' This is the most dangerous snare of this author. Capable of all errors (we can say), he reaches the end after a very long

[146]

journey during which, while making frequent stops, he defends himself from the accusations of error with the excuse that he has not yet reached the end.

147. But materialism is not restricted solely to the beginning or middle of this system; it lies deep within it. The sole reason why Kant denies that the existence of objects is knowable must be because they are outside the mind. Thus, unawares, he adds the idea of space to spiritual beings. Moreover, he cannot conceive a spirit which, lacking matter, can have an influence on our mind. When the universe is judged to be apparent and the idea of God is solely that of a being who occupies a place outside us in the same universe, doubt about his existence must inevitably follow. This is why sacred Scripture truthfully notes that a material spirit removes the wings from intelligence; only a pure, spiritual soul succeeds in perceiving insensible objects. Hence, Scripture attributes to wisdom the characteristic of motion and penetration: 'For wisdom is more mobile than any motion' (that is, it reaches even where corporeal nature cannot reach) 'because of her pureness she pervades and penetrates all things. For she is a breath of the power of God, and a pure emanation of the glory of the Almighty; therefore nothing defiled gains entrance into her. For she is a reflection of eternal light, a spotless mirror of the working of God, and an image of his goodness.'[54]

[54] [Wis] 7: [24–26].

CHAPTER 29

The limitations I have assigned to human intelligence do not in any way lead to scepticism

148. Thus, from Locke to Kant philosophy continued to go astray and become complicated in its progress despite so many efforts, until it became wearisome. Frustrated, people were left prey to the vain authority of ever changing masters. Today,[55] rather than teach any philosophy, the schools prefer to relate its vicissitudes as a kind of popular history of long journeys and diverse errors of the human spirit. If philosophy is to be loved and believed once again, it must, in my opinion, on the one hand be reconciled with the opinions of the ancient thinkers and on the other express those opinions according to the method of modern thinkers. It must be presented in an attractive style, with a wide and practical application to human life, and finally, it must unify all opinions into one complete whole. The Scholastics, who have been greatly demoted, are the link between ancient and modern philosophies, and this link needs to be diligently studied. Scholasticism has certainly been degraded, and in recent times made to look childish and ridiculous. But this image is not found in its great authors, among whom it is sufficient to mention the greatest Italian philosopher, St. Thomas Aquinas, whose cherished footsteps I seek and will always seek in the difficult and dangerous paths of thought.

149. Our limitations certainly humble the human mind but do not plunge it into horrible *scepticism*, declaring the mind incapable of truth and certainty.

In the first limitation I established that we cannot form a positive concept of the supreme, necessary Ens because this concept would mean that we *necessarily* see how being, essence and operation are one thing in God.

But this is not due to the inability of our intelligence to know what is true, nor because the truth is restricted and constrained by some particular form, as Kant's philosophy supposes. It is due to the way the human intelligence must rise to the concept

[55] 1826.

of this most simple Being, The instrument we have for such a great task however is necessarily imperfect. It consists of our body and some very imperfect materials and symbols, like the substances that form the universe or our own spiritual but finite consciousness. We do not positively understand the nature of this Being because it is not shown to us in this life; we do not perceive it. Nor do we perceive or are shown any other ens that has a nature in common with that Being, because God has nothing in common with creatures. Faith comes to our aid and promises us that we will see him when he relieves us of the tent of this life. Then, according to the Apostle, 'We will know him as we are known by him', and according to St. John, 'We will see him as he is.'

150. We are not therefore, as Kant maintains, the unfaithful mirror that distorts the image. According to the Apostle, this mirror is the created things we observe. The mind is simply the eye that fixes itself on this mirror and sees what is there but does not see God, because he is not there. Hence, in conformity with this teaching, St. John tells us that at present not only do we not know much about God, we cannot even know what we ourselves will be like in the other life. This state is not yet given us to see; only by looking at present things can we guess what it might be. He says, 'Beloved, we are God's children now; what we will be has not yet been revealed. What we do know is this: when he is revealed, we will be like him, for we will see him as he is.'[56] Consequently, the first limitation I established concerns solely those invisible things that have no perfect likeness with visible things. But Kant, who applied the limitation to the faculty itself of knowledge, not to the manner and conditions of knowledge, corrupted the source, and spread obscurity and uncertainty about all knowledge.

151. In my opinion, pure human understanding is not restricted or limited. For me, there is only one form in us, which I call the FORM OF TRUTH.[57] In no way does it limit our

[56] 1 Jn 3: [2].

[57] Apparently, Kant understood the word 'form' in a material sense: he drew the concept from the form of bodies. But by 'form' I understand a perfecting principle, as the ancient philosophers understood it. Moreover, in my case, it is the *ideal object* that informs the soul. Consequently, those who said I had taken one of Kant's forms as the foundation of my system, did not

understanding because it is not a particular form; on the contrary it is a universal, categorical form, it includes all possible forms, specific and generic, and measures what is limited. With this measure alone I explain everything that in the operations of the human spirit transcends the senses and experience. This is not the place however to present a philosophical system; my intention is to show that although the limitations I have assigned to the mind may humble us, they do keep us safe from the depressing *scepticism* of our times. I will therefore continue with the demonstration of the other limitations.

152. In the second limitation I established that human understanding cannot comprehend the absolute infinite.

This also does not come from the limitation and constraint of the *form of the understanding*, but from the fact that real, infinite Being can never be fully represented before the gaze of our intelligence, that is, he cannot be totally perceived by a finite reality, such as we.

153. Through the form *of truth*, with which our mind is endowed, our mind can truly perceive and know all real entia of whatever kind that present themselves to it. But how do these entia present themselves to the gaze of our intelligence? Where do they place themselves, as it were, so that we can see them? And, if I may speak metaphorically, on what retina are they imaged? As far as I know, no one has carefully observed such things, but they are of the highest importance and not impossible to observe. In short, nearly everyone knew and admitted that entia cannot present themselves to the mind except in the human soul, of which the mind is a faculty. What was not well known, I believe, was the distinction between the part of the soul that receives real entia into itself and presents them to the understanding, and the part that understands them. This part, this pure understanding, is not limited, whereas the first part is, and it is this first part where real entia enter, as it were, with their reality, and where we must principally posit the substance of the soul. This part therefore — feeling — or rather, this substance, is put in communication with real entia and receives their action;

understand that the *form* I am speaking about differs essentially from all of Kant's forms, just as the *object* differs from the *subject* and from the *extrasubject*.

in a word, the essentially feeling human soul is necessarily limited. The reality of other beings cannot communicate themselves to the reality of the soul except in conformity with the measure of the soul. For this reason the soul can never comprehend God. Like a tumbler, it can certainly be filled to the full with divine nature, but never contain the totality of this nature. Hence, divine nature can never be totally presented to or perceived by the understanding. Therefore, if our intelligence can never perfectly know the divinity, this is not because it lacks an unlimited form but because this form resides in a limited nature that cannot contain the infinite. Hence, the infinite cannot be totally offered to this limited nature to be contemplated.

154. Equally, the third and fourth limitations cannot cause any doubt about the truth of the things that the mind sees, granted that it sees them in the way mentioned above.

These limitations simply note the mind's difficulty in seeing things. That things are placed in a position visible to the mind is not the effect of its will. The place where the mind can look at the things it would like to see and could see is not always visible to it. Sometimes it is difficult, and sometimes impossible, for the mind's eye to have things within its range. This difficulty and impossibility do not depend on the mind: if what it wants to see is not given to it to perceive, or does not at least have something in common with the things it does perceives, or has no bond with the truths it knows, then it is impossible for it to see. Sometimes the thing has a connection with these truths, in which case it acquires knowledge of them with varying difficulty and varying perfection. When we investigate nature to discover some law hidden from us, all our ability consists in succeeding to place the truth we seek in a location suitable and visible to our mind. The object takes up a location where our mind's eye can grasp it either by reason, through which the object is added to other truths we already know, or by some help distinct from us which, without our effort, places the object directly before our mind's gaze. The difficulty we experience when we have to reason to discover some hidden truth and try to equate it with other truths that we already know forms the matter of the third limitation. The argument of the fourth limitation is the free will of a being outside us, on whom we depend for the direct presentation of some entia to our mind.

155. None of the four established limitations therefore leads us to the disturbing doubt of the *sceptics*. None deprives our mind of its supreme and most valuable gift: knowledge of the truth. All four however express the conditions and measure according to which we can know the truth. These conditions show the true littleness of our mind in its true greatness; all of them, by which alone our mind learns, do not depend on our mind but on a being different from it, on that great Being on whom the subsistence of all things depends.

CHAPTER 30

Modern philosophy destroys theodicy

156. We have examined the difference between the teaching about the limits of the mind and the teaching of the most famous schools. But what results from the human spirit's difficulties concerning divine Providence?

First, we must set aside the school of Locke. It is not guided by any law in its deduction of metaphysical truths from experience; it simply follows its imagination and free will to deduce whatever it likes.

157. In regard to Hume, it is easy to see what his opinion had to be, granted the principles he embraced. He showed this in *Philosophical Essays concerning Human Understanding* under the title *Of a Particular Providence and a Future State*. He had resolved to follow rigorously Locke's principle that everything known by us is extracted from the experience of the senses and that we possess no innate principle or rule of any kind. He therefore had to deny or at least firmly doubt that those principles which the human race considered to be general are not and cannot be general because they arise from experience; tThey could simply be mistaken prejudices introduced into us by habit and by the association of ideas. Consequently, he had to doubt all *causes*, which as such are always invisible, and most particularly the final cause of the universe. This cause depends on the existence of a wisdom that is invisible in its relationship of cause and also invisible to corporeal sense because it is a subsistent spiritual being. With philosophical violence, as it were, he closed his mind to everything except the mechanical course of nature as the object of the senses; according to him, the understanding had no right to admit any other cause than natural causes, or better facts that succeed one another in nature. Moreover, after observing natural effects individually and finding them all finite, he denied that even granted the principle of causality, it was possible to deduce an infinite cause from them. With this conclusion he failed to note that, even if an infinite cause were unnecessary to explain the change of things

that already are, such a need would nevertheless seem obvious in order to explain how things began to be, how they continued to subsist, why certain ones subsisted and others did not, how they linked with each other, and how all of them, whether they liked it or not, tended towards a great unity — none of them whatsoever contained within itself the reason or cause for all this.

158. Kant also was caught up in Hume's sophism, but he was not subject solely to this sophism. The destruction of the consoling teachings on Providence had to come from the very centre of his imagined philosophy: he misguidedly applied his *transcendental philosophy* to divine Providence. We also find the same application in his *On the Failure of All Philosophical Attempts at Theodicy*, in his *Towards Perpetual Peace*, and here and there in many places of his other writings.

159. He claimed to demonstrate that it was beyond the power of the human mind to know whether a being existed outside the mind, because the mind cannot go outside itself and hence can have only phenomena and appearances of things delineated within it (he explained knowledge with these material analogies); much less could the mind conclude to an Ens about whom experience told the mind nothing. Consequently, from all this he had to deduce that it was impossible to demonstrate theoretically any governing Providence of the universe: any author of the universe would simply be a gratuitous affirmation by arrogant reason.

Unlike Hume however, he had not rejected the principle of causality. He had retained its semblance and, by doing so, had made it subjective and stripped of all the productivity of its consequences. As a result, he could no longer prove the existence of any cause which was not subjective and a mere appearance. Therefore, according to Kant's transcendental principles, the aspect presented by visible things leads only to a *cause of the world*. Whether this cause operates freely or through a necessity of nature is left undecided. Similarly no decision is made about whether this cause is connected to and fused with visible things, or else is distinct from them, or finally whether its existence is apparent or true. Because, for this philosopher of appearances, that which is material or mechanical is apparent, but not what is moral and free, he denies that the mind can argue from the mechanical course of nature to its moral ends that suppose a governing mind. He therefore distinguishes *natural theology* from *transcendental theology* (everywhere, as we see, he chooses words to make honest what in reality is not true). He says the former borrows the concept of a supreme intelligence from the nature of our soul, and supposes this intelligence to exist and calls it God. But this is purely a postulate or a supposition of reason, not an absolute demonstration. On the other hand *transcendental theology* admits the first *cause* but only in name, because it rejects the fact; this first cause that it admits is only an object of reason, a mere concept of the primal ens, the ens of entia. But this pure concept does not require the ens to exist in itself, outside our mind. Because our reason is held behind the unbreakable doors of its own concepts and ideas, it cannot in any way exit from these, but would exit if it were possible to argue from them to an ens truly outside them. Therefore, in a part of his *Theory of Pure Reason*, he makes a critique, as he says, of any natural theology, or better, demonstrates its impossibility, as something totally beyond the limits of human understanding. He calls those who follow these teachings *deists*, to distinguish them from *theists*, that is, from those who admit a natural theology. But this eliminates every proof of the divine existence that theoretical reason can provide. Hence, such a system could more appropriately be called *atheist* rather than *deist*. He says: 'In the concept of God' (this is an effort to avoid the title 'atheist') 'we do not usually understand an eternal and blindly active nature as the ultimate root of things but a supreme being whose intelligence and freedom must constitute the author of all things, and this concept alone interests us. Consequently, anyone wishing to be strict could refuse the *deist*' (the transcendental philosopher) 'all faith in God, leaving him solely with the assertion of a primal being and a first cause. However, because it is unjust to accuse someone by attacking what in fact they do not maintain, it will be more equitable and moderate to say that the *deist* believes in a God but the *theist* believes in a living God, a supreme intelligence.'

160. Thanks to this living God, we see that the founder of critical philosophy, although forced by the principles of his system to deny conviction to any theoretical demonstration of the divine existence, shows he feels how shameful it is to be an

n *atheist*. He diligently defends himself against this title and regards the reproach of not admitting the divine existence as a serious accusation of true guilt. In fact, quite a few who dismiss religion with vain arguments show that they feel a reaction in themselves. This is nature protesting in them, a nature that, even though depraved, is still the work of God, and by means of a hidden feeling ceaselessly informs man about the errors of his wayward reason and leads him back to its cause, the source of truth and good. Such people would like to be what they cannot be and abhor the very name of what they strive to be: is this perhaps because they are reminded of what they are? In fact the desire of the transcendental theologian to be called a *deist* rather than an *atheist* would seem pathetically puerile: on the one hand he denies there is any proof that a living God, a supreme, free intelligence, exists; on the other, in his search for something that he could name 'God', he is forced to use an abstraction and thinks up a kind of ultimate root of things which, although certainly active, is no different from things themselves. As a result he remains uncertain as to whether it is active in an intelligent way or is mechanical and resembles matter.

Surely, this is just an unending game and a deceptive use of words woven together for the less clever? The less clever have a feeling for admitting a God and hence are easily satisfied without further enquiry, but if they examined the meaning of the word 'God', they would see that the transcendental philosopher cunningly turns it about to mean anything other than what the human race understands by it. They do not see such a subtle snare; they accept words in their current meaning and, without suspecting anything, drink the hidden poison. However we have to admit that Kant himself sensed the frivolity of this subterfuge, of this miserable shield of a word. So, to avoid the blot of *atheist* he tried to add another explanation, although it also was just as puerile: he says that a transcendental philosopher does not deny the divinity but merely declares human reason incapable of demonstrating its existence. Surely he knew that the first teaching of any logic is that no one must accept the existence of anything that is not proved because this would mean a gratuitous, and therefore foolish, admission of the existence? He also defends himself in the same frivolous manner in his work on *Theodicy*: he says he is not impugning Providence by positive arguments but simply maintaining that human reason is incapable of defending it. But what does the word 'atheist' mean if not the absence of God? Hence, whether God is rejected because he cannot be shown to exist or because to admit him is considered absurd, I do not see how the system of transcendental philosophy can truly avoid a shameful stain and title.

161. It is true that if *theoretical reason* is denied the power to demonstrate the divine existence, one turns to *practical reason* to admit it. But isn't this simply another subterfuge? The name 'practical reason' is itself completely inaccurate. We do not have two reasons, only one, and the only thing that is different are the objects submitted to it.[58]

Kant showed he had sensed this when he denied every power of demonstration to practical reason. He granted it only the power *to make suppositions* or (to use his expression) *to admit postulates*. He determines this difference very clearly when he defines *theoretical knowledge* as that by which we know that something is; *practical knowledge* is that by which we represent to ourselves how appropriate it would be for something to be. Hence practical knowledge does not tell us that God truly is, but only that it would be appropriate for God to be, but this is a truth of appropriateness, a desire of nature, not a truth of the mind. Thus, when he gives the title of practical reason to our feeling that teaches and commands us to be virtuous and happy, he is simply enhancing and giving more beauty to the dignity of feeling under the specious title of reason. After having perhaps deceived himself with this false, or at least incorrect, title, he deceives his readers, making them believe that in his system God is admitted by a judgment of reason; in reality however, God is admitted simply through a pure desire of nature, through the desire which makes everybody require virtue to be joined with happiness. This forms the whole complex of everything Kant calls practical reason. It is true that among the postulates he distinguishes those that are merely supposed

[58] I have been accused of admitting two intelligences in the human being. How little people have understood me! For me, *practical reason* is simply the faculty of reflection as moved by the acting will, thus making it a principle of action.

and freely chosen (he calls these 'hypotheses') from those that are necessary as a *condition* of something *conditional* already known to us through theoretical reason (he calls these 'theses'). It is also true that he declares the existence of God a postulate accepted as a thesis. But that still amounts to nothing — the thesis has not been demonstrated. It seems to me that here again all he has tried to do is remove the wrong impression that could make people think he posited God only as some kind of postulate, adding all the authority he could to the word 'postulate'.

162. Moreover, if the teachings of theoretical reason are considered in their connection with practical reason, Kant's proof of the existence of God becomes even more deficient. He admits that according to theoretical reason the human spirit could perhaps be the centre of the universe: the universe could be nothing but appearances issuing from our nature.[59] Coherent with himself, with practical reason he saw man as the ultimate purpose of man. In theoretical reason there is no proof for showing that our spirit is not the Creator of nature; in practical reason our spirit is absolutely the legislator and promulgator of morality. In the production of the appearances of the things that we know, and also in the intimation of the precepts, our spirit follows only the laws of its nature. These laws make it do this, just as a mirror must reflect colours according to its form. Consequently, we cannot prove whether this kind of legislation that irrefutably commands us to do virtue is wise. The necessity of such legislation, a subjective necessity, is proved only by a kind of appearance. The legislation has exactly the same authority as the nature of our spirit, nothing more, and we are subject to it for only one reason: we do not have the power to escape its dominion. This is how Kant demonstrates that we are obliged to admit a God, but he has no proof whatsoever. In other words, the laws of our spirit oblige us to be foolish because it is foolish to admit what we cannot prove. Such laws, says Kant, in addition to requiring us to be virtuous, direct us to be happy. But because these two tendencies of virtue and happiness do not always accord in this life, that is, what is virtuous is not also

[59] Fichte came afterwards, removed Kant's 'could be', and made everything issue no longer *critically* but *dogmatically* from the Ego.

what is happy, we have to suppose another life, and in that life a just compensator, in order to make the two accord with each other. Such is his argument for the existence of God, and it comes down to this simple affirmation: admitting a God helps the human race because in the life-to-come this God will on the one hand reward the virtuous who have satisfied the most noble commands of their nature and at the same time resisted the less noble inclination of apparent happiness, and on the other punish the wicked because they have done the opposite.

163. This argument would have been valid if he had not previously robbed it of all its force, that is, if his system had contained a way of proving that the two tendencies of human nature must truly be in accord with each other. This is the major of his syllogism but he has not proved it. But how will he prove it? Because he has not previously admitted that the nature of man has been constituted by wisdom, he can indeed say that the lack of perfect harmony between the feeling of virtue and that of happiness seems to us repugnant. But he is forced by his fatal theory to grant that the accord is in the end purely apparent, and it is totally impossible to prove that it must be a reality. Indeed, to be able to affirm that everything that appears to be in agreement must some time be the case, we would need (according to Kant) to transcend the limits of human understanding. Thus, the inductions of practical reason and its postulates have a connection with theoretical reason such that practical reason pronounces them to be gratuitous.

From this depressing philosophy we can at least take something good: the valuable admission that the existence of God fills the vacuum of human nature, that our nature feels it as something necessary for itself, and ceaselessly and certainly longs for it. This admission of God's existence gives the greatest praise to those philosophies that teach that his existence can be demonstrated, and strongly condemns and criticises critical philosophy. No human being can embrace a system that declares the impossibility of demonstrating what is absolutely necessary for his nature to admit. If, according to Kant, human nature inevitably shrinks from denying God, if this repugnance forces us to admit God, then the same invincible repugnance will force us to reject Kantism, a system that denies any true argument for the existence of God. What value does philosophy have if it deprives me of every good? And if such a philosophy could be true, would not falsehood be better? So, the moral proof Kant would like to use to demonstrate the divine existence either proves nothing or, if it proves anything, proves not only the divine existence but the falsehood and impossibility of the Kantian system.

[163]

Chapter 31

Dispositions of spirit necessary for helping the mind to overcome the difficulties presented by the government of Providence

164. On the other hand, the teaching I have presented, which agrees with the divine Scriptures, opens up a broad and pleasant path that will calm our reason and satisfy our heart concerning the supreme dispositions of Providence.

165. I have distinguished two kinds of arguments, and both equally satisfy the difficulties presented by our weak reason. The first concerns *general arguments*. These are clear and easy to understand, and everybody can be helped by them. The second are *particular arguments*. These will not always help everyone because they often require a higher understanding.

General arguments concern many difficulties and use one reply to solve them; particular arguments reply to individual difficulties.

Among the first kind, some are more general and some less general. The most general of all is that the very existence of an unsurpassable, most wise and most powerful God instantly solves all the difficulties that confront human reason. Revelation is simply a means by which this greater knowledge is obtained, and faith is simply the firm belief we have in the words of this God who speaks to us from beyond a veil, from beyond a mysterious curtain draped between him and us, which will be removed when the material substance that envelops us is removed. Revelation therefore is not contrary to reason because any means that enlightens and instructs reason in the most sublime truths cannot be opposed to reason, just as the presence of bodies by which reason acquires knowledge of them is not contrary to it, nor are the words of the law-giver by which it learns what is taught. Nothing is more absurd than to consider as contrary to reason the means that help, perfect and instruct it. Without these, human reason, left in total darkness and much debased, would be almost annihilated.

166. Nevertheless, not even with reason, stimulated and enlightened by revelation, can we know or see in this life the essence of the divine nature. We have therefore the happy necessity of reasonably humbling our reason and believing that the God we know exists in the most fitting, though unknown, manner. To bear patiently this ignorance until it is taken from us, to acknowledge, profess and suffer it in this life without resentment, is to give the most reasonable submission to the Creator, a submission that pleases him greatly. Such submission is just, but irritating for unthinking, frivolous people or for those who are vain about their knowledge gained through the senses. The merit of faith lies precisely in this justice and in this humiliation of tiresome human pride; it prevents us from weakening our solid conviction of the existence of the supreme Being, despite the fact that we do not conceive the manner of that existence. Hence, those who are slaves to such pride, which is always unjust, are the only people who follow the path of unbelief. They find it hard to accept both the ignorance of their present state and the knowledge that revelation offers them. In fact they are afraid of revelation and avert their frightened gaze; they do not wish to see themselves. Rather than admit that they do not understand the mode of the supreme Being's existence, they deny his existence and strive to find fault in the arguments that demonstrate it, or they go to the opposite extreme and claim that they intuit God naturally.

Humility however, is a generous virtue, a reasonable submission of our total selves, particularly of our reasoning, to the one and only Wisdom. Acknowledging and confessing the definite limits of human reason, it prepares the path to faith and leads reason straight to the truth. Pride on the other hand darkens minds and generates errors; it confounds us and encloses us within our senseless thoughts because we have great illusions about our own excellence, which conceals all our weaknesses and imperfections. To attain this state, it denies, or as the Apostle St. Jude says, 'blasphemes what it does not know'.[60] To rid

[60] 'But these men blaspheme whatever things they know not' (spiritual things) 'and what things soever they naturally know, like dumb beasts,' (sensible things) 'in these they are corrupted (*in his corrumpuntur*)' [Jude 1: 10†]. Divine Scripture, speaking in the name of God, invites us to follow the path of faith but it also continuously accompanies us on the path of reason. It

ourselves of this object that we do not know, and ashamed of admitting our ignorance, we pretend humility and thus greatly restrict the power of reason itself. We know however that it is a useless species of virtue, which lacks all substance precisely because it lacks truth. Hence, no one, even those of little discernment, can be drawn into error by the false philosophical modesty that affects to downgrade divine incomprehensibility, or uses subtle fallacies to prevent us using our reason to know the real existence of entia outside us.

167. To sum up the whole argument. All human beings have the way open to them to dispel their anxieties about the dispositions of divine Providence. Intelligible reasons, some more general or less general than others, are available to all who can and must completely calm any concerns about the outcome of events. More general reasons are better adapted to a greater number of people; more particular reasons require more intelligence and study because of their difficulty and quantity. Precisely because they are particular, the problems unavoidably multiply. However, both general and particular reasons are equally valid and fitting.

Nevertheless general reasons, although clearer, require more virtue and *strength of spirit* if they are to help us stand firm in all the difficult problems that arise (cf. 29–30). On the other hand, particular reasons, when understood, help our human weakness because they are closer to the events and therefore are more easily applied. They help our unease either with sensible proofs or with explanations adapted to our thinking.

One general reason is *divine authority*. This by itself immediately removes all difficulties. I have called it the PATH OF FAITH by which the faithful do not hesitate, whatever new, painful and incomprehensible event happens. On the other hand, I have called the PATH OF INTELLIGENCE the investigation of reasons that are less *general* than this first reason, even down to the most particular. Not everyone is able to follow this path, in the way they can follow the first, which is open to all people of faith. Faith rests on a first reason, that is, the way of faith is not undertaken without intelligence, just as the way of intelligence must

offers us the most splendid and direct arguments for understanding the sublime ways of the Lord in his government of the universe.

not be followed and cannot be freely followed without faith. The path of intelligence thus aided by faith must be followed by all who free from all anxiety and disquiet love to keep their gaze fixed calmly on the shining path of wisdom. Because the first most general reason fully assures them that their meditation must reach a happy conclusion, they follow this path not so much to justify Providence, as to acknowledge and admire more greatly its sublime wonders.

168. Those whose spirit is more open to virtue forge ahead along this noble road. The enemies of truth however would have us believe that the divine Scriptures persuade us to be lazy and ignorant in our understanding. But this is not so: Scripture ceaselessly urges us to stay awake and be very attentive in our quest for knowledge. However, in doing so, it is not persuading us to reject the excellent means of enlightening ourselves, that is, revelation; we are not to limit ourselves solely to nature, which is the less valid means. The revelation contained in Scripture, together with the faith it urges on us, is given as the most solid base of knowledge and the beginning of all wisdom. Moses says to the Israelites: 'See, just as the Lord my God has charged me, I now teach you statutes and ordinances for you to observe in the land that you are about to enter and occupy. You must observe them diligently, for this will show your wisdom and discernment to the peoples who, when they hear all these statutes, will say, "Surely this great nation is a wise and discerning people!" For what other great nation has a god so near to it as the Lord our God is whenever we call to him?'[61]

But if there are some who in their arrogance wish to argue with God as if with their equal, and maliciously seek to find defect in his dispositions, we should not be surprised if the Lord abandons them to the illusions of their temerity and allows them to become entangled and small-minded in their thoughts. Hence, the book of Wisdom, which is a treatise on the sublime, provident dispositions of the Lord, begins with the precepts that will enable us to penetrate those sublime designs with the light of our mind. It tells us 'that for this end we must principally love justice' and then 'that we must have a good and kind heart, inclined to sense good and principally to sense good of

[61] Deut 4: [5–7].

God, as of him whose concept alone brings every love with it'. It desires 'that we look for the Lord in the simplicity of our heart, that is, not diverted by a particular interest, or by some passion that stimulates and blinds us. Instead, we are to silence all the voices of self-love and walk directly and openly towards the truth. If we think about divine things with a mind full of wrong affections, we are tempting God. God is found only by those who do not tempt him, and appears to those who have faith in him. Perverse thoughts bring division from God but tried virtue corrects the beginners, that is, sets on the road of virtue even those who might not have great intelligence to follow it. Wisdom cannot enter into an evil soul, into anyone who cunningly seeks to harm others. Nor can it dwell in a body subject to sin where the mind is continually agitated and menaced by the winds of passion. Moreover, the Holy Spirit desires frankness and avoids the pretence of a contrived and equivocal teaching, and withdraws from thoughts that lack understanding. And if a soul that he has entered does not act righteously, he makes it feel remorse.'[62] These are the admirable dispositions of heart that prepare the mind to penetrate divine secrets. The mind goes forward, moved by the will and guided by the will's affections. David therefore truthfully proclaimed: 'Lord, those who love your law enjoy a great peace and never take scandal or offence at all that happens to them, or that they see happen in the universe.'[63]

62 [Cf. Wis]: 1.

63 [Cf.] Ps 119: [165].

BOOK TWO

φυσικός [natural]

THE LAWS GOVERNING THE DISTRIBUTION OF TEMPORAL GOODS AND EVILS

CHAPTER 1

The purpose of this book is to present the particular reasons that justify Providence in the permission and distribution of temporal evils

169. Human understanding and everything it knows has limits. These limits were the subject of my investigation in the previous book, for the purpose I required. Any attempt to exceed these limits is an absurd temerity, an impossible task, but the legitimate requirements of our mind and heart can be satisfied without the need to go beyond them. Reason and faith can solve all the difficulties and doubts that may arise about the origin of evil and about the wisdom and goodness of Providence that not only permits this evil but, according to certain laws, allows it to be mixed with all the goods that Providence distributes abundantly among human creatures.

Indeed, all difficulties and doubts (for example, about the certain existence of a supreme being) collapse and totally cease before certain very effective and general reasons. I indicated these reasons in the previous book.

In this book I must descend to details and solve the doubts with reasons that are more particular, and deal with each doubt individually. This strengthens the human mind and nourishes the upright, compassionate heart.

170. However it is not my intention to treat all the questions that can be asked about evil. They can be reduced to two.

Whenever we consider evil, which continually afflicts the human race, we are faced with two well-known and immediately evident questions; they have been discussed throughout the ages by the sharpest minds:

1. How can human freedom, the source of moral evil, be reconciled with the inescapable truth of events, that is, with God's prevision, predestination and action in creatures? Leibniz saw this problem as one of the two labyrinths of human understanding.[64]

[64] The other labyrinth of the human mind, according to Leibniz, is the problem of mathematical infinity. Cf. *Théod.*, *Préf.*

2. How can temporal evil and its distribution among human beings as we see it, be reconciled with the divine attributes, that is, with the holiness, justice, goodness, wisdom and power of God?

171. I will limit myself to answering only the second of these two very important questions. For this purpose I will presuppose the first as already settled and take as postulates the following three propositions:

1. Man is free.
2. God disposes all things from eternity.
3. These two propositions involve no contradiction because there is a way to reconcile them.

I am fully convinced that the two questions can be separated because the connection between them is not so necessary that both must be treated together; the second can be treated, as many others have done, on its own.

172. Despite my limiting myself to the second question, the discussion offers inexhaustible material. Among the many authors, especially the first authors, who have dealt with the question, are St. Augustine, Leibniz, King and De Maistre. In fact, the great difficulty for any author who, like me, wants to justify Providence, lies more in the abundance of material than in its scarcity. My intention therefore is *to explain briefly the wise and excellent laws according to which God distributes temporal evils and goods among human beings*.

173. Even if I could add nothing further to all that has already been said, I would not think I had wasted my time; the subject is so worthwhile.[65] It seems to me to be a duty of compassion towards those who suffer from the hard demands of this life if I simply refresh their memory and repeat such noble, deep and true reasons by which religious wisdom can bring undying joy to the most distressful afflictions we suffer.

174. The problem of reconciling temporal evil with the divine attributes is not so simple as it seems. It has two parts, which

[65] The Abate Vrindts recently published in France, on the occasion of the jubilee, a work on the same argument (*Du Mal*, Paris, Méquignon-Havard, 1826). It seems therefore that in these days a need is felt for similar treatises. Even old arguments arouse new interest because the human race is itself always new, and always has the same nature and the same questions to ask itself.

must be distinguished for the sake of clarity. The first concerns the *origin of temporal evil*; the second, the *distribution of evil*. Because they are mutually related, I will deal with them both. However, they are different, and therefore I will deal with them in their order.

CHAPTER 2

The origin of evil — its nature — the usefulness of these two investigations

175. When we see good people suffering, we must consider whether they are suffering because they are good or because they are human beings. We see them suffering but can we be sure that the cause of their sufferings is their virtue? If we have no reason to believe that their virtue is the cause of their sufferings, we cannot say that virtue causes pain and affliction. On the contrary, we must say that it is humanity that suffers; no one suffers because they are virtuous but as a human being.

But why does humanity suffer? As creatures of an excellent God, should we not be free from all suffering of any kind?

This brings us up against the problem of the *origin and nature of evil*.

176. Seeking the origin of evil in humanity on the one hand and knowing its nature on the other are two distinct questions. But they are linked and sometimes fuse together. It will be helpful therefore to deal with them together because knowledge of the *nature* of a thing necessarily entails knowledge of its *origin*.

177. For the believer in God, faith alone in the most perfect Being must, as I have said, dispel every doubt that the origin of evil can harm the divine perfections. The believer, confronted with the difficulties that exceed his understanding, adores a wisdom higher than his because all the objections, even apparently unanswerable ones, lose all their force in the face of a direct demonstration, such as that given to anyone who believes in the concept of God.

Only a atheists can be scandalised by the existence of evil on earth, and thus use their ignorance as a new argument for denying God. My intention however is not to reason with atheists, who are beings of uncertain existence, but with people who admit an infinite Ens endowed with all perfections, and more particularly with Christians — I have already said that in this book I do not wish to avail myself of a very general principle to solve the difficulties against divine Providence. A person of weak understanding asks for other support. People in general find it too demanding if they have to accept that all the most sophistic objections have been answered solely by direct argument; direct argument must have a strong logical coherence if they are to accept all the light of a direct demonstration and feel its force so convincingly that all the contrary arguments no longer disturb their conviction.

178. Nevertheless, if atheists consider the particular answers I will give — and many other answers — which justify the Providence that permitted evil to enter the world, they will not be wasting their time. They can come to know that in the dispensation of goods and evils blindness does not reign; on the contrary such a vast, sublime and beneficent light shines so splendidly that our meditating on it can provide an unanswerable argument for a supreme Providence and a supreme Provider. I would like atheists to posit as an hypothesis all that the Christian religion teaches about the matter. I think they would find it difficult not to see that this hypothesis was superior in beauty, grandeur and perfection to all hypotheses, and was therefore something more than a vain hypothesis, that it was the truth.

CHAPTER 3

The existence of evil does not detract from divine perfection because evil is in finite natures, not in God, and its nature is not positive

179. In the search for the origin of evil, the objections that are raised against the divine attributes and present themselves to our understanding can be reduced to three:

1. Those that take to task divine *perfection and holiness.*
2. Those that target divine *justice.*
3. Those directed against divine *goodness.*

180. A defence of divine goodness will also serve as a full defence of the attributes of wisdom and power. If we can demonstrate that the evils of the universe do not in any way harm the unlimited goodness of God, the evils prove nothing against infinite wisdom and omnipotence; to conceive an infinite goodness is to conceive an unlimited wisdom and power. Wisdom and power are the two great arms of goodness that it uses to diffuse its immeasurable benefits: wisdom shows goodness what the best will is in all things; power makes this will operative, making sure that the love is applied to what is best.

I will begin therefore with the objections brought against divine holiness and perfection.

181. The first objection asks how evil can be possible under a most holy and perfect being. The objection indicates an ABSENCE OF KNOWLEDGE, that is, it is not known how to reconcile God's goodness with the evil in God's creatures. The idea of a being endowed with infinite perfection seems at first sight to exclude even the possibility of every evil: if the perfection of this Being is infinite, it must surely fill all things with itself? And because the infinite perfection of this Being fills and pervades all things as well as all times and all the space of the universe, evil ought to be eliminated from nature and, as it were, find no place or object where it can reside. This is how the narrow human mind reasons.

182. We note first of all: the objection is not directed against the existence of this or that particular evil but excludes the very

possibility of evil. Reduced to its ultimate terms it can be stated as follows: evil is impossible because a most perfect Ens is necessary.

183. There was a time when it was very difficult indeed to answer this objection; it seemed insoluble to anyone who confronted it directly. This was before St. Augustine. He had found and fully revealed the nature of evil in his refutation of the Manicheans, who had fallen into the error of the two principles,.

184. It is true that even before St. Augustine the philosopher Epictetus had known that evil is not a nature and had given this very fine opinion: 'Just as a target is not the cause of error, so the nature of evil does not exist in the world.'*[66] Here he acutely notes that evil consists in the failure of an action to attain its appropriate term, precisely in the same way that an archer fails when he misses his target. To hit the target, skill and expertise are necessary as a kind of actualisation of the power of archery, but to miss the target no skill and expertise are required.

Later on, St. Athanasius had written in a sermon against idols: 'Neither from God nor in God, nor from the beginning does evil exist. There is no substance of evil. But human beings, imagining and thinking the *privation of good*, began to construct for themselves what evil is and freely pretended that the things that were not, were.'[67] Thus, St. Athanasius noted that the mind had the faculty to conceive the negation of things under a positive form, and he admirably deduced from this faculty the origin of the *concept* of evil.

After him, St. Basil also demonstrated that he knew that evil is a privation and nothing more. Comparing it to death and darkness, he concludes: 'We must not look outside ourselves and go in search of evil, nor imagine some natural principle of evil, but we must all acknowledge ourselves as authors of our own wickedness.'[68]

Among the Latin authors, St. Jerome said the same in his *Commentaries* on the Lamentations of Jeremiah: 'Evils, which

[66] *Manual*, 27.

[67] *Orat. in idola.*

[68] *Hexam.*, Hom. 2, from which St. Ambrose drew a similar opinion, *Hexam.* bk. 2, c. 8.

by their nature do not in any way subsist, are not created by God.'*[69]

185. Despite this, the teaching was not sufficiently clarified and discussed before St. Augustine. He developed it fully with his very sharp mind and thus annihilated for ever the system of the two principles.

He irrefutably demonstrated that evil is not a real positive entity; God with his infinite perfection and holiness fills everything with himself without any need to enter evil, as it were, because evil is not one of the things that subsist. Hence St. Augustine demonstrated that in order to explain how evil arose we do not need to admit a first positive principle to produce it.[70]

St. Prosper next expressed this teaching of his master in verse:

> Through the Word almighty, one God created all things
> By whom nature is in no way created evil.
> And what the wisdom of the Word did not make rich
> Had no place in the state of things.
> Vice has no substance, no life
> That feeds the body and its matter.
> But when freedom departs from right order
> And good things do not retain their standard,
> In vice and fault, movement is wandering into contrary things,
> And evil is made to desert the true way.*[71]

After St. Augustine had added so much light to this teaching, every wise person embraced it and drew from it the most useful consequences.

186. Nowadays, the objection cannot be given any great weight because the truth that *evil is solely privation of good* is commonly accepted and no longer controversial [*App*., no. 3]. Evil has no positive cause but originates either from a defective form by which an ens does not have its full nature, or from a nature's weakness and slowness of operation. Clearly, this weakness and slowness of operation never happens in the most

[69] Chap. 3.

[70] The principal places where St. Augustine deals with the nature of evil are: *Confessions*, 2: 20; *Enchir*. 9–13; *De lib. arbitr*., 3: v. 8–15; *De Cod*., 9: 9; *In Jo. Trac*., 1, and in all his works against the Manicheans.

[71] *Epigr*., 95.

perfect Being; his operation is as perfect as his nature so that one enters into the other, and this perfect Being and its act are one most simple thing. It follows from this that the creature of finite substance is the cause of all evils. Because the act of being is not essential to the creature, it can receive this act imperfectly. Similarly, because potency and second act are different from being, they can be defective and deficient.

187. Evil therefore is not in the essence of things but in their naturation or in their operation and passion. These three things can be contained under the name 'act', or even 'operation' in a general sense. Thus, when the operation of contingent entia departs from its right path and directs itself to a term different from that established for it and required by their essence, there is evil in the operation. Here, we must pay particular attention to discerning what the thing called evil is, present in this act or operation by which the operating thing departs from the fixed term to which it is directly ordered. The whole act is not evil, because in its being it is always a positive thing. Hence, its being is not evil if, as I said, evil is negative, not positive, that is, privation of good. Thus, in every act that fails to attain the end assigned to it, there is something *positive* and good and also something *negative*, which forms what is called evil. The *positive* element, always present in an act, is, as I said, the being itself of the act, and being is good. The *negative* element that forms evil is the *term* that the act should have naturally attained, but did not; instead it terminated in something else and therefore failed. The *term* or the *object* to which the act tended was necessary for the act and required by its perfect essence and nature, but because the act has now failed, this term, which was needed for the perfection of the act, is totally lacking. The *lack of* the act's *natural term*, of its purpose, is precisely what forms the evil of the act. The act is futile, not having the good its nature needed, and therefore defective; it has *in se* a privation of good which harms it. The privation of what should have been its good has made it an act that is lost, irreparably lost, to the Ens that performed it; the loss is irreversible. The act itself therefore is not evil, but is evil because it has evil in it, and it has this evil because it misses the target, it does not attain its term; it is like seed that fails to germinate, like fruit that withers.

CHAPTER 4

Granted that nature is finite, the possibility of evil is necessary. Hence, even God could not prevent the existence of evil, because God cannot do the absurd

Every creature is enclosed within the fixed limits of its nature*

St. Ambrose, *De S. S.*, 1: 7

188. I am fully aware of the objections that will be brought against what I have said, and above all, of the following objection: If God is all-powerful and is supreme goodness and wisdom, why did he not make creatures so perfect that they would necessarily never fail in their operation?

189. A reply to this difficulty requires us to examine the nature of created things, in which evil is found as in its proper subject. We need to understand that if God, in creating the universe, could not make a repeat of himself, the universe and everything in it had to be limited: LIMITATION IS IN THE NATURE OF ALL THINGS OUTSIDE GOD. This is a fundamental law of creation and the key to divine Providence.

190. A consequence of the principle that all creatures, as creatures, must have a limited existence is that they must also have a limited operation, and because such an operation is accidental, it must be liable to failure. Let us look briefly at how the limitation of nature brings with it the limitation of operation that can always fail. This law is found in all three genera of things: material things, things that have feeling, and intellective things.

191. Material natures cannot extend their action beyond the place they occupy. One material thing cannot enter the place of another, so that when one collides with another in order to dislodge it, they break up and are reduced in size. I will stop to consider any further this failure of operation in bodily natures. It would involve me in a very difficult and long discussion. I would have to investigate first of all whether these natures have some subjective perfection of their own or whether all their

perfection consists in their being object of the intelligent nature that perceives them.

192. Natures that have feeling have the natural limitation of being very passive, and necessarily so. If this passivity were removed from feeling, the idea of feeling would disappear. The nature of feeling is such that not even God himself with his attributes could have prevented it from being *per se* subject to a pleasant and unpleasant perception. If it did not have this possibility, it would be another nature and no longer a feeling nature. God therefore could not remove the *possibility* that this feeling nature might suffer pain and sadness; in other words, he could not prevent its operation from being liable to failure.

193. But God wished to form a nature much more excellent than feeling nature: he formed the nature of the free, intelligent human being, which could choose good and evil as it wished. While God gave purely feeling nature an invariable instinct that made it pursue pleasant sensations and avoid painful sensations, intelligent, free nature could not act through blind necessity. This fact, we must note, pertains to its excellence, because the gift of having dominion over one's actions, of being able to choose this or that action according to preference, is an excellent gift. The nature that receives this gift has a very noble quality that allows it to perfect itself and also be a partner, as it were, of the Creator in the task of perfecting itself. But in order to have this noble quality, it had to have the limitation that enabled it to do the opposite, that is, to fail in the work of its own perfection. Even if God had wanted, he could not have created this excellent nature without its being subject to defect.

We see therefore that *the possibility of physical and moral evils is joined to the nature of everything that is not God himself.* The very nature of all created things and of everything that can be created requires some limitation proper to each, and this limitation opens the door to the possibility of evils. Thus, if the nature is not moral, it opens the door to physical evils, but if it is moral, it opens the door to moral evils.[72]

[72] This shows the link by which *privation*, which strictly speaking *evil is*, is connected to the natural *limitation* of creatures. Hence, limitation (incorrectly called by some 'metaphysical evil') differs from *privation* (called evil in a general sense), just as negation differs from both of them. *Negation*, *limitation*, *privation* have an affinity of meaning but are different. It will help

194. What I have said about natures considered singly must be applied to natures considered all together, that is, mixed with each other.

Because natures are endowed with some forces (in these I include every faculty of action and passion), they can, as a result of their intermingling, collide, unite and separate. Each nature necessarily profits or suffers from these actions and reactions: in the case of feeling natures they can both harm and help each other, while intellective natures, because endowed with greater activity, can do greater harm or give greater aid. This possibility of aiding and harming one another follows from their being arranged, as it were, in the same place, and endowed with the faculty of moving away from or approaching each other, that is, of being ordered in the universe. Because this mutual repulsion and attraction, this aiding and harming one another, is a result of their nature, and granted the positions and conditions suitable for this, God could not have united them to form a totality of the sovereign beauty that the universe presents to our gaze without at the same time allowing them to improve or harm each other through their reciprocal actions.

195. Summarising therefore, we can say that evil is solely and purely a lack; it is not a substance or a positive quality of a substance. Hence, it is not produced by any positive cause, nor is an essentially evil principle needed to explain its existence. The fact that God fills all things with his goodness does not render evil impossible. This lack that is called evil is simply the action of

if we determine the meaning of each. 1. *Negation* has a wider meaning than the other two, and is used to mean the lack or non-existence of anything. 2. *Limitation* has a wider meaning than *privation*: it indicates the *negation* of some entity considered as part of another entity. If this negated entity is not necessary to the thing, if it is excluded by the very nature of the thing, it is called *natural limitation*. 3. *Privation* indicates a *limitation contrary to nature*, that is, the lack of an entity necessary to the nature of a thing, for example, the purpose of an act required by the nature of the act. If I think of a man who does not exist but could exist, I am thinking a *negation*. If I think of what an existing man lacks, even when he has all that is necessary to him, that is, if I think he lacks a certain degree of energy that human nature can have, I am thinking a *natural limitation*. Finally, if I think of a hand that someone has lost, or of any other thing the person could or ought to have according to that person's nature, I am thinking of a *privation* and therefore of an *evil* for humanity.

some limited nature in so far as it fails in its term. The subject of evil is limited creatures. This limitation, which is the same as the liability to fail, thing, is so co-natural to all creatures that it would be absurd to think that they could exist without it — if they did, they would be infinite like the Creator; like him they would be eternal and independent. In short, they would exist through themselves, that is, they would have to be creatures without having been created, which is a contradiction. Consequently, the *possibility of evils* to which creatures are subject is metaphysically necessary, so that not even God's omnipotence can make it not be, granted that he wishes creatures to be.

Therefore, neither the *nature of evil* nor *its possibility*, or (and this is the same thing) the limitation of natures opposes or contradicts divine holiness and perfection: the nature of evil does not, because evil is a mere *privation*; the possibility of evil does not, because this is *necessary and connatural* to all created and creatable things.

CHAPTER 5

The *existence* of evil does not contradict the perfection and holiness of God

196. If the *limitation of the creature*, which necessarily makes evil possible, is itself not evil, how does *limitation* become *privation*, that is, become evil? The fact that the creature is limited does not mean that it is damaged; it can be limited, yet in its genus perfect, internally free of the evil to which it *can* be subject. Hence, if the *limitation* of creatures does not bring with it the existence of evil, to what principle must we attribute the creature's transition from a purely *limited* state to a state that is also *evil*?

197. To solve this difficulty, we must note that the *natural limitation* of creatures differs in character and quality according to the differences of creatures themselves.

Some creatures are totally *passive* or are such that they do not have within them any principle by which they move and act of themselves. On the other hand, other creatures are mostly *active* or contain an internal principle proper to them from which their operations proceed.

198. Because the first kind are moved to operation by a force outside them, their own efforts cannot make them pass from the state of simple *limitation* to that of *corruption*, they cannot become *evil* from being *limited* without the action or impulse of an external force. For example, the movement of bodies is always produced from outside. They receive this movement either from the contact or attraction (if attraction is considered a force) of other bodies; they do not initiate it by their own activity within them.

199. The second kind however, which, granted certain conditions, are active through their own effort, have a limitation that consists not only in receiving an impulse to evil but also in directly producing evil, if we can speak in this way. They have an *active liability* to failure, a liability that depends on them. As creatures they operate, and as creatures they do evil. If by their own action they fail in their operation, they place themselves in

a state of privation, passing spontaneously from being simply *limited* in operation to having an operation that does not attain its term — this is precisely where the corruption or evil of natures lies.

200. The principle therefore by which natures pass from *limitation* to *privation*, that is, to having evil in them, applies only to physical and moral natures. In physical natures the principle must be sought outside them; in moral natures it must be sought within them.[73] Indeed their limitation lies mainly in the principle; in other words the *limitation of moral natures lies in the active principle or internal energy that is able to move them to good and to evil*, is able to perform spontaneously an operation. This operation either attains or does not attain its natural end. If it attains its end, it attains perfection; if not, it is *deprived* of the perfection that it ought to have, and this precisely is evil.

We should keep in mind that the constitutive element of human nature is its freedom for good and evil. This freedom is an excellent endowment because it is the principle of *merit*. But the limitation of this excellent endowment is such that it can be directed to evil because merit cannot be conceived except on condition that demerit can also exist. If we consider human nature *per se*, it can, by its own movement, pass from a state of limitation to a state of evil. But we also know from the traditions of the human race that moral evil preceded physical evil and that it was intelligent man who abused his free choice and consequently incurred guilt before God. Man thus passed from being *limited* to being *wicked*, although the Creator had structured him for the perfection of virtue. Here then we have the source of all evils.

201. Once *moral evil* had been introduced in this way on earth, it is easy to explain how physical evil subsequently found the way open before it, because there is a strict, necessary relationship between the moral and physical orders, between moral and physical evil.

Indeed, due to this relationship, physical evil is understood as

[73] I said earlier that these natures *are partly active*. They are not *totally* active because they have a degree of passivity. Therefore, besides producing evil in themselves, they can receive it from outside, as happens in the transmission of original sin.

necessary and desired by divine perfection and holiness, which cannot allow moral evil to go unpunished.

Only physical evil, which punishes the sinful creature with sensible sufferings, can vindicate the divine holiness that the creature had attempted to insult and (unsuccessfully) to destroy and annihilate. Only chastisement re-establishes the order of justice infringed by sin. In this way, guilty and punished human beings give glory to divine greatness because, when they were just and rewarded for their justice, they had not wished to give it.

202. We see therefore that the evil found on earth cannot in the least harm or contradict divine holiness and perfection, whether the evil is considered *in its nature* or considered in *its possibility* or is the result of its passage from possibility to *existence*.

CHAPTER 6

Defence of divine justice against the objection concerning the evils suffered by the descendants of the first parent as a result of his fault

203. Here the following objection readily presents itself: after the father of the human race had failed in the way he acted, why should the evils that punished his crime fall also on his descendants? Doesn't this seem contrary to divine justice?

204. I must first point out how people generally confuse *justice* with *goodness* and bring against the former accusations which of their nature could harm only the latter in every case. We humans very easily attribute to ourselves rights we do not have. We easily complain that harm has been done to us in the case of things to which we have no claim whatsoever; the only relationship we have with them is purely their suitability for being owned by us. Self-love always makes distorted claims. Every day we consider as offences not only the evils we have received unreasonably from others but the good things not received. The slightest diminution of a person's great goodness or liberality (which the greed and cupidity of another would not like) immediately becomes *injustice* for the blinkered vision of the covetous and the cowardly, of which there are many. This supposed injustice offers them the occasion for a thousand complaints so that due to some light accident the benefactor, for whom no gratitude had previously been felt, now becomes an object of detestation and hatred.

205. If this is the way we often treat human beings, we treat God in the same way much more often.

But there is a vast difference between human justice and divine justice. People can withhold from us what in all justice is due to us and to which we have acquired a positive right. There can be situations where we complain about others because a right of ours has been violated. But can a similar situation exist in our human relationship with God? Can there ever be a case where we have a strict, solid right that makes us creditors of the Being from whom we have received everything and continuously receive all we have, and can God ever be a debtor to us?

These questions require an answer; if no title of true right can be shown that makes us creditors to God and makes God a debtor to us, we cannot conceive any possible objection to divine justice. Any such objection would be absurd by its very nature when we have a clear notion of God and man, that is, of a being who receives nothing but gives everything, and of a being who gives nothing but receives everything. Can beings like this understand justice in the same way? Can we say to God from whom we have received all we possess but to whom we have given nothing and cannot give anything: You have been unjust to me?

206. Someone may object: 'If we cannot naturally have a right relative to God, we can have a right if God has made us a promise.' This is true. If the promise God makes us is an act of goodness, and granted that it has been made, it gives us a right to expect its fulfilment. But relative to the temporal goods we are talking about, the promise is precisely what is lacking. Has God promised to reward in this life the merits of those who are faithful to him, and at the same time keep them safe from temporal calamities? Has he not rather prepared them to suffer calamities nobly and taught them to see such sufferings as the means he uses to purify and increase their virtue? Has he not shown them in his own self that humiliation is the path to glory, and sacrifice the path to happiness?

207. It might still be objected that even so, it is unacceptable that the Creator afflict his innocent creatures — under a true God only the guilty must be wretched.

I grant this, but a distinction must be made. Do we complain because God afflicts us positively by depriving us of what is ours, or negatively by denying us what is his. If we consider what we call *injustice* among ourselves, we do not complain of injustice when someone refuses to give us what is theirs and does not take what is ours, nor do we complain about people who may not do any good but at the same time do not do any harm or attack or kill; they may not be very beneficent in our estimation, but they are not unjust. If therefore we are arguing solely about justice and nothing else, let us apply to God the concept of justice that we apply in our relationships with others, and it will be easy to justify him.

208. The evils that have come down to us from the first father of the human race have not been positively inflicted by God. He did not deprive us of something belonging to our nature. It is true that he took from the first man-sinner the supernatural gifts he had given him but these gifts do not in any way belong to human nature; in fact it would be far truer to say that we ourselves wickedly rejected the gift of grace rather than that God had taken it back. It was after all we who made ourselves culpable and thus placed ourselves in a state in which the generous union of God with us became intrinsically impossible, precisely because essential holiness cannot exist where there is sin.

209. Even the damage left in human nature was not an effect of some *positive operation* by God, but of natural causes and of the sinful way we operate. Sin causes the human will to deteriorate and weaken. Consequently, the will of the first father, after his culpable transgression, was twice as weak as it was previously: it had lost *supernatural strength* because sin truly stripped man of the supernatural gifts. He also lost much of his *natural strength* because fault is also something contrary to nature and thus wounds nature. Hence, Adam's will was weakened not only in comparison with what it was previously but also in comparison with its natural perfection, because human nature, free of all sin, certainly has much greater moral strength than sinful human nature. We must keep in mind that we, fallen and reduced to the state of sin, can no longer raise ourselves, can no longer justify ourselves by ourselves alone. Moreover, no law of justice obliges God to restore us. Such restoration would be an act of infinite greatness and, if we consider the matter carefully, would seem to be an act greater than creation itself. In fact, according to the law of simple justice, the Creator had to inflict on the rebellious creature a punishment proportionate to the fault, in addition to abandoning the creature to itself.

210. But even if we suppose that God through his infinite, gratuitous mercy is moved to justify the sinful human being, this justification does not of itself mean that our will re-acquires all its previous moral forces. All it needs to recover is its rectitude, although the lower part of our will remains weak and inclined to evil. This is precisely what faith tells us happened when Jesus Christ accomplished the justification of the human race.

211. The objector may retort: such an argument may be sufficient to explain the state of the first parents, but what about their descendants? Surely, it is not just that these who have committed no fault should share the evils that the first father incurred?

Once again, the objection would be solid if God had stripped us of *what was ours*, or had chastised us. But what did we have before we were born? Nothing. Therefore nothing could be taken from us. Moreover, the evils we experience in the world after we are born do not come to us through a positive act of God but are the result of natural causes, of the laws of generation.

212. It has been demonstrated that both the moral and physical state of parents have an influence on the state of their children. Generation is not accomplished by the body alone but much more through the power and energy of the soul.[74] Consequently, if man, after sinning, was left with a very weak will, incapable of ruling his animal inclinations, it was in keeping that the children inherited the same defect, even if through the mercy of God the father and mother had themselves been fully justified. The justification would be gratuitous and, as personal, would be executed in the manner and within the limits God chose, and not passed on by generation. This meant that the offspring descending from the parents had to be defective in will and deprived of all justification, even if, as I said, we suppose that the parents had already been justified by God. Hence, there is absolute no need to believe that God positively inflicts evils on the descendants, as if these evils were punishments merited from Adam; it was sufficient for the offspring to be born according to natural causes and to the laws of human generation by which human nature is transmitted. St. Thomas says, 'Sin' (damage to the will) 'does not pass into the descendants from the first father *by the way of demerit*, as if he had *merited* death

[74] *RI*, 1358–1368. — All the ancient physicians have always taught that the mental and moral state of the parents influences the physical, mental and moral state of the children they have begotten. The teaching has been confirmed by the observations of modern doctors and naturalists, as can be seen in the recent work, *Thoughts on mental functions, being an attempt to treat metaphysics as a branch of the physiology of the nervous system*, pt. 1, Edinburgh, 1843, p. 178.

and the infection of sin for everyone. It passed *by way of transduction*, a consequence of the transduction of nature, because the act of a person' (human person) 'cannot *merit* or *demerit* for the whole of nature.'[75] The transduction of original sin therefore is simply a necessary consequence of the limitation of human nature, which either had not to be created or, if created, could not be made in any other way.

213. However someone may still maintain that while God lives and is sovereign in the universe, there is something contradictory in the concept of a being who, without having committed any fault, is in a wretched state. But I repeat: we are dealing with a question of justice, and there is no injustice if penal evil accompanies moral evil, that is, the damage done to the personal will, that constitutes sin (although without the concept of fault). Later, I will solve the other difficulty that can be caused by the concept of an infinite, divine goodness. Such goodness seems, at first sight, irreconcilable with allowing sin to enter human beings when they have committed no fault, even if this happens through natural and second causes and not through any direct or positive operation by the Creator.

214. For the moment, let us consider that human nature, which longs for happiness, was directed by the goodness of the most perfect maker to a goal so noble that he wished to draw human nature out of its nothingness. It is certainly *fitting* to this first goodness that, because it is infinite, it should be complete in every way, and therefore no human being should be tormented and afflicted without fault. But this title is not a title of strict right, nor is it a title that bestows the right to be exempt from suffering. It is simply human nature's need, human nature's own indigence. But indigence does not bestow a right; a thing is not mine simply because I need it; I cannot take

[75] 'Sin does not pass into the descendants from the first father *by the way of demerit*, as if he had *merited* death and the infection of sin for everyone. It passes *by way of transduction*, *a consequence of the transduction of nature*, because the act of a person cannot *merit* or *demerit* for the whole of nature, unless the act transcends the limits of human nature, as happens in Christ, who is both God and man. Hence, by Christ we are born children of grace, not through the transduction of the flesh but through the merits of an action. But from Adam we are born children of wrath *through propagation*, *not through demerit*,'* *In II, d. 20, q. 2, art. 3, ad 3.*

something, wherever it is, because I like it. Need does not come from God, but, as I said, from a limitation of our nature; it is purely an effect of the sequence of causes of the nature we ourselves have disordered. Let us look at the difference between this title of right and the titles that are the foundation of what we truly call 'right', of what people call right when speaking of their fellow human beings. The title of right is always something positive, not the mere necessity of something; it is some fact, the occupation of some land, for example, that was previously unoccupied. The only thing we can show God as a title is our indigence, just as the poor man shows his open sore to the passer-by and shouts out his dire need of food and of something to cover his bare flesh. There is nothing we have which is not God's; everything we possess is not acquired but received and remains the inalienable property of the one who first granted it. It is not the case therefore that we can find a true title of right which makes us creditors of happiness with God, and God a debtor to keep evils away from us and leave to us all that he initially gave us and of which we freely stripped ourselves. What we can find in this relationship between God and ourselves is that divine *goodness*, because complete and entire in every respect, cannot let its work be imperfect in us; it cannot allow us to have, without our fault, a nature that suffers irremediably; it cannot, without reason, allow a creature that is made for happiness to be subject to wretchedness.

But because this harmony between the happy, innocent creature and the infinite goodness of the Creator does not pertain to what is properly called justice but solely to the fullness of goodness, divine justice remains *per se* justified.

215. Indeed, the mere idea of Creator and creature makes impossible and absurd every complaint a created being might dare to bring against the justice of its Maker. If a complaint is apparently possible, it can be directed only against infinite goodness: whatever God takes from us of the good things he has given us, he is simply doing what he likes with what is his. A debtor can certainly complain about the cruelty of his creditor if the latter strips him of everything he needs for ending the pain of his wretchedness, but he cannot in any way complain about the creditor's injustice. It may also be unjust if someone reduces another to an extreme state by taking back what is due to him,

because no human being can have an unrestricted right to the goods of the earth, but no matter what God disposes for his creature it will never be unjust because God has a full, absolute, inalienable and necessary right over his creature. Consequently, there is no case against divine justice, not even a possible case. In fact, everything said to be contrary to God's divine justice is not in fact contrary to his justice but concerns divine goodness, which I will defend later.

216. But let us suppose that the objection that the evils of the first parent are applied to his posterity can be a question of justice. Does the objection have in fact any force?

We have already seen an answer to this, but I will present it again in different words. According to the condition laid on the first human being by God as supreme lord, he would obtain happiness if he kept himself innocent, but be condemned to death if he broke the precept laid on him. This is simple justice, and no one can object. After Adam committed the sin, death was postponed, but the seeds of death entered his body with the forbidden food and entered the whole of nature, of which Adam, the sinner, was part. Here there is simply mercy, because a judge acts mercifully in postponing the death that the guilty has merited. Some believe that in the fruit eaten by Adam there was probably a hidden poison, which was the punishment to be paid for the sin, and its power changed and weakened human nature. This opinion is found in Hebrew tradition. However, whatever way it may have happened, Adam's soul and body, after the fault, were very different from what they were before, and man found in himself concupiscence and mortality. I have said that by the law of generation the *child is born similar to the parent*. This law is not arbitrary but a consequence of our whole animal structure. According to the law, the child of a weak, mortal genitor will also be born weak and mortal. Hence, just as God had nothing to do with the origin of the first evil, which was totally the effect of the limitation of created natures, so he had nothing to do with the propagation of the parent's evil to the child; it is purely the imperfection of the generating parent that produces the imperfection of the generated child. If, as we saw, we have no reason to attribute Adam's defect to the first cause, then we have no reason to attribute the natural consequences of that defect to God. The limited creature erred and, through a natural law, the error produced other evils, and these evils produced others. Whatever the length of this chain of evils, one link emerges from another due the limited nature of things, and this limitation that opens the way to evil is necessary and hence impossible to alter. It would therefore be a contradiction to want non-limited natures created; indeed, that which *receives* being but does not *have* being *per se*, is by that fact limited. Hence, propagation of physical evil from parent to offspring is not difficult to explain, and in the case of the propagation of moral evil, this comes of itself because it consists in the prevalence of diseased animality over the weakened personal will.

217. No truly thinking person can assert with greater insistence that if human nature had to be imperfect, then it was fitting for God to create another better nature. This also is not valid for two reasons. First, the better nature would also be subject to its evils through the same law of limitation, and indeed subject to greater evils because *created nature's subjection to evil is as great as the good it is capable of*. Second, such an objection, even when well understood, would be impossible. In fact, when people make it, they do not truly know what they are saying: *no one can desire a nature other than the one they have*. We cannot nurture the desire to be an angel or an archangel or any excellent thing because such a desire would also include the other desire to destroy and annihilate our own nature, that is, to destroy the very thing from which every nature essentially and invincibly recoils — and this absurdity demonstrates the absurdity and impossibility of such an imaginary desire.[76]

[76] This teaching, that no human being nor any other being can desire another nature higher than their own, is taught by St. Thomas Aquinas: 'Nothing at a lower level of nature can desire the level of a higher nature,… because if it were transferred to a level of higher nature, it would no longer be. But our imagination is deceived: we want to be at a higher level relative to accidental things, which are able to increase without the corruption of the subject. We think we can desire a higher level of nature, which we cannot attain without ceasing to be'* (*S.T.*, I, q. 63, art. 3).

CHAPTER 7

Divine goodness is defended if we show that any objection against it would be rash precisely because we cannot know enough about it

218. We still need to see whether some element of divine goodness is perhaps harmed by God's permitting the first parent's sin. After the offence had been committed, punishment was necessary; and the effect of the punishment, which is moral and physical evil, had to pass into the descendants through the natural link between parent and offspring. Hence, if anything is to be brought against divine goodness, it can be found only in this permission.

219. In dealing with this question of permission we cannot use what I said about the possibility of evil, namely, that God's omnipotence could not prevent it because permitting evil is not as contradictory as preventing its *possibility*. If God had wanted Adam's sin not to happen, he could certainly have prevented it without harm to Adam's freedom. He could certainly have helped the free, intelligent creature not to offend. God has the extraordinary power to move freedom for a certain purpose without destroying it. Revelation tells us as much, and reason itself convinces us. Anyone who did not grant this, would have an imperfect concept of infinite omnipotence. We may indeed find it very mysterious in what way human freedom is joined to God's omnipotence, but both must be granted, and I posited these two great truths at the beginning as postulates.

220. So if God could have prevented man's first offence and removed this stain from him and from all his family, and could have also removed all the evils sadly caused by the stain, why did he not do so? Surely this was fitting to his supreme goodness?

This is precisely what I affirm. At first sight, a thing can seem an act of goodness but is a cruel fact. On the other hand, there are actions which at first make us want to protest loudly against their cruelty and barbarism, but when examined more deeply, contain a rare piety and exquisite affection. Only wisdom can guide goodness to its ultimate effect and true fulfilment. A goodness that lacks wisdom and is short-sighted and of little consequence cannot provide for what is remote and is not seen. But a wise goodness that grasps many and distant things, sometimes seems harsh and neglectful of partial goods. In fact however, it is not neglecting these goods; it is simply and gently by-passing them for the time being so that it can absorb them later on, because they have now increased a thousandfold, into the great whole that goodness always contemplates.

221. This explains why it is difficult to know what best suits a wise goodness that controls a wide range of enterprises, and this difficulty increases in proportion to the greatness and wisdom of the goodness. Thus, if we want to calculate the goodness of the Sage's works we need a wisdom equal to his.

This is all the more true if the Sage of whom we want to measure the goodness of dispositions is, as I said, head of a huge and very complex multitude.

222. A ruler's goodness equals the sum of the virtue and happiness he procures for the republic minus the sum of misery and vices. To know therefore how to judge correctly whether permission of Adam's sin pertained to the prudence of the best of rulers, we would need to know all the consequences of the sin and the new order of things that divine omnipotence had drawn from the sin. We would need to make a comparison between the new order established after the first offence and the order of things that would have followed if Adam had remained innocent. We would also need perfect knowledge of the primal order destroyed at its birth by the man-sinner, and our mind would have to be so powerful and penetrative that it could understand the present system of the human race (calculating all its parts and knowing all its rich endowments) which is bound up with the system of the universe. If anyone thinks he possesses all this knowledge, grasps the whole mass of things and can say whether the Eternal had done well or badly in establishing the present order and letting the ancient collapse, such a person could make the above objection with some force. But if he does not presume so much, then why does the presumptuous mortal not adore, in silence, the greatness of the divine wisdom that is beyond him?

CHAPTER 8

Divine goodness shines out in the permission of sin because God used the opportunity offered by sin to open for us, through the grace of the Redeemer, a fount of spiritual joys that were greater than the temporal punishments resulting from sin

223. Nevertheless, God has not left us entirely in the dark about these sublime reasons that come from a maximum intelligence; he has not denied us the light we could receive. When his word, always full of reasonableness and goodness, implants faith in us, it makes us sharers in the plan of the divine mercies because by meditating on the plan we are touched by it. His word clearly tells us that God, using the opportunity offered by Adam's sin, established another more sublime, more magnificent order on the ruins of the old order, and that where fault abounded, grace has superabounded. In their connection, his word has opened up sublime mysteries, although they are such that our difficulty in understanding them increases in proportion to our rash attempts to be unjust to God.

224. In the midst of temporal evils that have justly descended upon sinful man, the redemption that took away our sin and gave us grace has introduced into our spirit a new fount of contentment, flowing richly from a generous love of punitive justice and from the hope of a better, unending and most blessed life.

225. Many people who err by thinking that all goods and evils are in this present life, wrongly believe that bodily pain is the worst misery, and bodily pleasure the greatest satisfaction. They have great difficulty in understanding how happiness could increase in those who experience less and less pleasure, particularly if they are subjected to bodily afflictions. The truth is however that only the intelligent spirit is capable of supreme good and is the seat of happiness.

The pleasures and pains of the spirit are so infinitely superior to those of the body that people will often bear the greatest bodily sufferings to satisfy their spirit. Sometimes they will sacrifice their greatest pleasures for a mere illusion of their imagination (which itself shows the strength of the spirit), or for a desire for revenge, for a great ambition, for an ecstasy of glory, for some miserable vanity, but much more for the immense attractions of virtue — they will even sacrifice their life and have no fear of prison or of the stake. It is the strength of the spirit that bears all these things, not only with firmness but readily and joyfully; it treats light-heartedly every serious and long illness, and celebrates in being ready to die. We need only observe ourselves a little to find that we have in us a spirit capable of such greatness and such sublime happiness that an increase of virtue will compensate for any torment our body undergoes. We should carefully examine this sublime property that the spirit has to overcome bodily afflictions with an interior joy. People who do not feel they have this elevated moral energy can see it in a great many of their fellows and, if they note it with good faith, must be convinced that the human spirit can truly rise to the height of excellence, can obtain this strength so that it is not in the least disturbed when it sees its body crushed and oppressed, as its whole nature breaks up. Those who have not experienced such bodily sufferings cannot attain this peak of virtue and experience this great joy that is totally spiritual; it is a triumph over pain and hence over the pleasures of the body. Clearly then, the evils of this life can be of such great help that they can raise us to a virtue and joy of a higher order, not known before.

226. To object that God could have given this virtue and joy without our having to attain them through suffering would indicate a failure to understand the value and efficacy of the reason I have given. If virtue and the joyous triumph arising from virtue are formed by victory over suffering, the suffering is necessary to the act of virtue and to the exquisite pleasure; not even God could make suffering be overcome without suffering. We see therefore the sublimity of divine goodness, and if through sin God has allowed evils to enter the body of his creatures, he has simultaneously made them much richer in goods of the spirit, which are worth more than the evils because they result precisely from a triumph over the evils. Permitting the evils was necessary so that we could have these great goods in abundance, just as war is necessary if there is to be victory. All this is a result

of the natural limitation of things, which God could not change. We see therefore that our present state, when strengthened by faith in the Restorer and his promises and by the energy of the spirit that this faith gives to the spirit, must be preferred to the state of the innocent human being who is incapable of experiencing the pleasure of sacrifice and acquiring the honour of victory over suffering. And we must prefer it in the measure that the pleasure of the spirit surpasses it in the battle with bodily pain, that is, infinitely, because the order of spiritual things is more noble in species, not in degree, than the order of bodily things, and because the strength of the intelligent spirit can be limitlessly increased over the instincts of animal nature.

227. I am concerned solely with the state of man relative to the goods and evils to which he is subject in this life, and my argument goes no further than this. It is the most unfavourable standpoint for considering the new order of things caused by the offence of the first parent. It would be much easier to justify the divine counsel that permitted this first offence if we considered other parts of the new system and showed how superior this system was to the old system. We could, for example, demonstrate that an eternity of the most excellent goods has been prepared for man, and that he should strive to obtain just as the striving for greater virtue is put before him. We could demonstrate the great wealth of holiness and happiness of just one human being, the man in whom all things have been restored, Jesus Christ, a holiness and happiness that in its greatness is worth far more than the whole human race, just as the body has more worth than clothing. We recall how far the excellence of the new grace exceeds the old, and how the light of divine glory shines infinitely more brightly through the wisdom and goodness that are capable of drawing such great good from the creature's evil. We could keep before us the victory of the Lord's power over both rebellious sense-nature and diabolical spiritual nature defeated by its own weapons. We could acknowledge the joy of numerous angelic intelligences that give praise as they contemplate the immensity of the divine concept. And finally, we could set before us the justice that is glorified in the punishment of the wicked. God permitted their sin so that (as in the case of the sin of the first father) the virtue and happiness of so many just people might be built up and increased, and that the

universal order might become, granted the first conditions, not only the greatest and most beautiful but the *best* among *possible* orders; in other words, it would contain a *maximum pure happiness*, freed from all the unhappiness that had been necessary to obtain it. I say 'necessary' because of the limitation of created things — this limitation meant that there could be no definite kind of virtue or happiness without some opposing vice and unhappiness.

In the plan of created things, the eternal geometrician had assigned to himself certain conditions for solving a great problem of maxima and minima, that is, he found the way whereby the universe of predestined creatures contained the maximum happiness after the unhappiness had been subtracted — this is a just optimism. Can we really find an error in his calculation, and show that he has not chosen well? — But I will return to this great problem in book three, where I will present the data and investigate, as it were at a distance, the path to its solution.

[227]

CHAPTER 9

Recapitulation. Statement of the question concerning the distribution of temporal evils

228. To sum up. I have shown that:

1. Temporal evils entered the world through an act of *justice*, as a punishment for the sin of the first parent.

2. The *efficient cause* (if we can call it that) of the first evil that existed on earth, *moral evil*, was the human being, who is naturally free; *physical evil* now became necessary as a punishment for moral evil.

3. God was the *permissive cause* of Adam's offence and decreed his penalty as an act of justice. The propagation of moral and physical evil from parent to offspring takes place through natural laws, through the constitution of the natures that compose the universe, and among these in particular is human nature, to which generation pertains.

4. Even in permitting the sin of the first parent, God performed an act of both *infinite wisdom* and *infinite goodness*. The infernal spirit, the enemy of the Creator, had wanted to use the offence to harm God's work, but God drew from the offence an order of things immensely more vast than the first order; it was a new and better order that gave him greater glory, and human beings greater happiness, an order that he established in fact by the redemption.

229. I come now to the question concerning the distribution of temporal evils and goods among human beings, which is the second of the questions I proposed. The question receives some light from what has already been said. The difficulty is the following.

According to what I said, it is not absurd that temporal evils are present on this earth, and their presence must not cause us the least doubt about those sublime attributes that are fitting to the Creator and conserver of everything. But because in the life destined for us here below evils became necessarily mixed up with goods, we can ask whether these evils happen by chance without the Lord having any control and direction over them.

And if God does govern the goods and evils that are mixed together and follow one upon another in this world, will he not arrange that evils accompany vice, and goods accompany virtue, and in this way make life happy for the virtuous person, who is faithful to him and imitates him as much as he can in beneficence? Why do the guilty delight and triumph so often in their empty fortune, while the innocent suffer and are trodden under foot by the guilty?

230. Reflection on these complaints would be endless, because the complaints are more a weakness of the human senses than of human understanding. Among so many, I will choose the principal complaints, and these will open the way to an explanation of the excellent and most wise laws with which the Eternal moderates and dispenses all evils and goods for an end worthy of himself.

I will show therefore how in the final analysis evils are always reserved for vice, and goods for virtue, and we shall see that the completion of this sublime plan is wonderfully brought about through the short-lived irregularities that distress the weak and scandalise people who, with little faith in revelation, lack strength to believe in reason.

CHAPTER 10

Because no one is totally just, no one can say that they have been ill-treated by the distribution of temporal evils and goods

231. This is precisely what happens in the case under discussion. No one can prove to others and to themselves that they have been ill-treated by the way goods and evils have been distributed on this earth. This is true even if we supposed that virtue should be rewarded with temporal goods, and vice punished with temporal evils; it would be true if we supposed that the Creator did not have at his disposal other greater and more valuable goods with which he could amply compensate the just for their sufferings, and simultaneously humble and punish the wicked so that they could no longer enjoy the good things they had unjustly enjoyed. Nevertheless this is the fact, as I said.

232. Even granted all this, only the perfectly just can claim with any certainty that they are being unjustly afflicted by temporal calamities. In fact only the just can at the most complain that they are suffering. The unjust, even those who are only a little unjust, must confess to be most justly humbled and punished. If they do not, they are by that very fact most unjust; their complaint itself justifies Providence, and deserves punishment because the complaint is rash, irresponsible and culpable.

233. I maintain that temporal suffering is also justly inflicted on those who are in the smallest way unjust because there is no proportion between *moral evil* and *temporal evil*. Moral evil has a kind of infinite nature because 1. the authority whose law has been violated is infinite, 2. the moral order which has been assailed is necessary, and 3. God's dignity, which is offended, is infinite. Consequently, temporal penalties are not enough to punish even the least of formal injustices.

234. If therefore we cannot first prove ourselves totally just, any complaint against the Creator about the evils of this life is false and offensive. Can we truly prove ourselves just? Can we affirm this fearlessly and without telling a lie? If we are ready to listen to divine Scripture, even our upright deeds are tainted in

the sight of God;[77] we are told that 'everyone is a liar'[78] and 'if we say that we have no sin, we deceive ourselves, and the truth is not in us.'[79] We must carefully examine our conscience and find an answer to our inconsiderate complaints against Providence. All upright people always have a part of their conscience that witnesses against them. Even the pagans acknowledged this: they said that to err is human, as if, for them, erring and human nature are two indivisible things: error must be present wherever there is human nature. Conscience either shows us or does not show us to be the sinners that we are. If it shows us, why do we complain about evils? If it does not show us and we declare ourselves just, this blindness, this lie of our proud heart, makes us truly deserving of every evil and the most severe chastisement.

235. It is true that we can declare ourselves just if we do not limit our consideration solely to what we possess through nature but include what we, when united to Christ, have received through grace. But even the just Christian falls into light sin, for which the evils of life are not an excessive punishment. Moreover, those who are incorporated into Christ are just with the justice communicated to them by Christ. Christians therefore have first of all a thousand reasons to persuade themselves never to complain about the evils they suffer. They do not have to tear themselves apart to justify for themselves the Providence that they ceaselessly bless and adore in everything. Moreover, those who are just with the justice of Christ do not in fact know their just state with total certainty; they need a special revelation for this. They say, and indeed can only say, what the Apostle Paul says: 'I am not aware of anything against myself, but I am not thereby acquitted.'[80] Christians believe in Scripture, and Scripture says: 'Man does not know whether he is worthy of love, or hatred: but all things are kept uncertain for the time to come.'[81] Hence, on earth only true Christians can

77 'All our righteous deeds are like a filthy cloth' (Is 64: 6).

78 Ps 116: 11; Rom 3: 9–23.

79 1 Jn 1: 8.

80 1 Cor 4: 4.

81 Eccles 9: 1–2†.

merit the title 'just'; they clearly profess and declare themselves to be ignorant of their own justice, which they consider totally hidden in the hand of God.[82]

236. Even if their justice were expressly revealed to them, they would still not consider that they merit exemption from earthly evils because they know well enough that they cannot attribute this justice to themselves but that it comes to them from Christ. Despite the royal mantle that clothes and adorns them with Christian justice, they would still see themselves as sinners, for whom suffering is appropriate; indeed evil could come only from themselves. If good comes, it does not come to them from themselves alone but from themselves incorporated into their suffering Redeemer, while the root of evil remains in them as long as they live on earth.

82 'There are just people and wise people, and *their works are in the hand of God*' (Eccles 9: 1†).

CHAPTER 11

Under the best government of the universe, whose task is to obtain the greatest good, natural virtue enjoys no right to be immune from all evils. All it can claim is that the best ruler choose the series of causes and effects that is the most favourable to it among all possible series

237. I will retrace my steps a little. If just Christians do not have and cannot have any complaint against the evils they suffer, then the whole discussion concerns only those people who are just through *natural virtue*. But if our concern is purely with natural virtue, even perfect natural virtue (which is not found in any human being and, even if it were found, could not be recognised with certainty), we definitely cannot accept as true what we have conceded for the purpose of giving greater strength to the argument; in other words, we cannot accept that temporal goods and evils must be distributed according to the precise degree of natural virtue and vice, neither more nor less. If we consider only the natural order, which is governed by supreme wisdom and goodness, the only thing required from it is that it ultimately produces the greatest possible net good (cf. 222–230). But good cannot be totally free from evil, and even if this were possible, it would prove an obstacle to the greatest net good, which is the goal of an infinitely wise and best rule: some evils are absolutely necessary for obtaining incomparably greater and excellent goods. Hence, if we want to know what kind and how many goods the virtuous person can claim according to nature, we must look at the total great order formed by the things of the whole universe, that is, the whole human race and its duration.

238. In fact, if we look at this order as a whole, we see it governed by general laws, both natural, like those issuing from the very *nature* of the beings that compose the order, and supernatural, that is, the laws of *grace*, because grace also follows certain general laws laid down by divine wisdom. Among these laws there are some rare exceptions or miracles, both in *nature* and in *grace*, but these exceptions are also pre-ordained by God, and

have their own laws or reasons. Consequently, the opinion that every condition in which the world finds itself contains the reason for the next state is entirely true, provided it is correctly understood. Furthermore, the few exceptions do not impede the general sequence of things, it would not be difficult to demonstrate that these exceptions are also linked to the unity of the great plan. Hence, the whole sequence of this great order of things and the very last events are joined to the first events, as effects to their causes or consequences to their principles.

Therefore, the great work of divine Wisdom had to consist of 1. the position it freely chose for the first beings, 2. the motion of free natures and 3. the first events it permitted or commanded. And it did all this in accord with that prevision which was present at the beginning of all things and, with one discerning gaze, ranges over the whole immense series of future events up to the very last.

239. Temporal evils and goods are also part of these events, bound and intermingled with all the others. They came about through the same natural causes and according to the same natural laws that govern the universe. Hence, the good or evil distribution of these goods depends on the position of the first data. Hence, if we want to judge whether the distribution of temporal goods and evils is wise or foolish, just or unjust, we have to go back to this starting point; we have to transport ourselves to the moment when God, in creating things, gave a definite distribution to them all, and with his permission and his action controlled free natures in their first movement. We need to determine what God would have had to do, particularly at that first moment, in order that in the universe at the end of time, the amount of virtue and happiness would be seen to be maximum, compared with what might have been possible in any other combination of events. In short, knowing all the laws and all the relationships involved, we must calculate every small, great, past, present and future fact of the world. This is what judging the distribution of goods and evils means, and what the problem involves. The most mediocre of human beings discuss it, weak Christians grumble at it, and the impious blaspheme.

240. This reflection is itself sufficient to answer and settle all the mindless and rash objections brought against divine

Providence concerning the distribution of goods and evils. If a good man who has been mortally wounded in battle or struck by lightning or crushed under the ruins of his house, wants to complain reasonably to God, he must first calculate the whole series of causes that preceded and prepared that event. Going back mentally over such a long chain of effects and causes, he would not get back to the beginning, which is the first, true cause of his misfortune, without having come to the first moment when things came into existence and moved. He cannot with reason ask, 'Why did the arrow wound me; I was innocent, and I saved my comrade next to me, and he was a robber and blasphemer. Or why did God strike me with lightning, or cause the house to fall on me'. But he can ask: 'Why did God permit the whole immense series of events that produced my death? Why did he dispose things like this at the beginning, or why did he not save me with a miracle?' These last questions are different from the first. To reply sensibly to them he would have to know whether, if God had chosen to save him by another series of events from among those possible, the series contained, in place of his death, the deaths of many just people, or of people more just than himself. If God had saved him with a prodigy, we would still need to know what the consequence of this would be for the rest of the universe: would virtue have to suffer more due to the change in the chain of things, of which his death was a link? He would also have to know whether the miracles were part of and linked to the fixed laws of grace that give order to an invisible universe. All this clearly shows how every complaint against Providence, every moan, proceeds from a narrow mind, incapable of sufficiently understanding what it is complaining and moaning about.

241. To require an alteration in the pre-established order of things, whether a natural or miraculous alteration, requires from God a new universe, a new combination and interaction of facts among the infinite combinations or positions that can result from countless terms, that is, from the beings and the possible movements of beings that are in the universe, their places changing in all sorts of ways. Any average calculator understands that these combinations and contacts must be completely immeasurable. We can form some vague idea about them if we try combining in every possible way a large, determined

number of things, like the ninety balls of the lottery. If just people ask God to protect them from the death that results from a particular series of events, they are asking for nothing less that a new arrangement of accidents, that is, for a new universe. There would be as many universes required simultaneously from God as there are just people who are subjects of some temporal misfortune; indeed, the undetermined number of these universes would rarely, or rather never, mean that the same universe was asked for. Moreover, once the series of things had been altered, many just people would perish in the newly chosen series, who themselves would have a just reason for making the same request of God. Do we really know what we are asking? Could God really agree to our imprudent and contradictory wishes? The world would be an unfortunate place indeed if its destiny and government depended on human minds. It would be divided and torn apart by an incessant battle of desires and feeble opinions. All order would disappear, and in a short time everything would become confusion and chaos.

242. If the just suffer while the guilty enjoy a passing triumph, we should not complain. Such a situation is required by the order of the universe [*App*., no. 4]. The just must not grumble at their lot, and the guilty cannot glory in theirs. The situation of both groups is permitted by wisdom that postpones retribution for the sole purpose of accomplishing perfect justice at the end of the course of things. Natural virtue therefore cannot claim that the best organiser of nature should keep it always immune from evils and endowed with temporal goods. Natural virtue can rely on nothing more than that the organiser of the world has chosen the combination of cases most favourable to it among all possible cases.

CHAPTER 12

Human nature remains damaged even after justification. Temporal evils fall on the damaged nature, not on the justified person. They do not come from God, who simply permits them, but from the damage that nature has suffered

243. But the natural human being has never existed, and revelation and experience tell us that human nature is still not perfect today. Both these sources demonstrate that immorality is congenital in us. Our depraved tendencies so often obstruct the decrees of our will. Where then do we find the person whose nature is just if nature itself is corrupt?

Revelation tells us still more. It assures us that through the merits of Jesus Christ we, from being unjust, are made just. But it also teaches that alongside Christian justice which sanctifies our person, we retain in our nature a part of the primal weakness that makes us subject to little faults and moral defects, and only death destroys this weakness. This explains why we are deprived of every right to claim freedom from temporal evils; indeed, besides being just penalties, they are salutary medicines.

244. This is all the more true if we consider that these evils are the effect of the corruption of the nature common to all human beings. They come from the very laws of nature, not from God, who simply permits them.

This reason I gave to explain and justify the existence of evil is equally valid for justifying its distribution. The distribution is determined by natural causes, and affects only damaged *nature*, not the *person*, which with its spiritual excellence and virtue rises above sensible sufferings.

245. But let us look at the same truths from another point of view.

Human nature is so excellent that it understands truth and justice when these are manifested to it, and can love them. But this natural light that lightens up the beautiful face of truth and justice for human nature to see, helps human nature only in so far as it can dispose all its actions in an ordered way and direct them to its own natural perfection. This knowledge of truth is an abstract knowledge, a rule of life, delightful to the intellect, of which it is as it were the principal part. But it is not a real being, whose possession gives the total and full happiness we are capable of. God's goodness did not want to limit us to the perpetual contemplation of an abstract idea of the truth or a negative idea of the divinity: he had destined us to the possession of himself, who is subsistent truth, infinite being, that can be possessed and enjoyed. He spoke to us at our creation, and presented himself as our author and God. He imposed on us a commandment which we did not find present in our reason. In this way, he showed us that because reason applied to natural beings, it was not the source of a complete legislation; above nature there was a higher will from which we received new commandments. We were thus constituted in a positive relationship with the author of our life, a relationship that did not necessarily result from the conditions of our nature.

245a. Destined therefore to a supernatural end, we had to have a good that was infinite and different from ourselves. As soon as grace gave us practical knowledge of this infinite good, we began to savour it, saw the possibility of total enjoyment and the duty to obtain it for ourselves. But although we had received a sample of it, which made us want to unite ourselves with it, we could not do so by our own power. Like every creature infinitely inferior to God, we cannot receive any more of himself than what he graciously grants us. We need to understand very clearly that it is impossible for intelligent creatures, with their limited powers, to accomplish the conquest of infinite good and that this impossibility comes from their necessary limitation. Nor could God create an intelligence that could rise to the vision of God with its natural powers; God himself, enlightening the intellect, must present himself to it with his presence.[83] How else could the intellect find the divine essence that it neither has within itself nor finds in any created ens? Holy Scripture therefore, using a sublime expression, calls God a *hidden God*, and thus distinguishes him from the false gods dreamt up by human beings. This necessary limitation of the

[83] This is made clear also through the fourth limitation I explained in the previous book, chapters 17-18, that is, our mind needs some external energy to present the objects of its thoughts to it so that it can think of the objects.

intelligent creature means that we need divine grace and goodness in order to attain the supernatural end to which we were ordered from the beginning; we do not find our completion and satisfaction within ourselves.

245b. Revelation also teaches that God, after giving being to intelligent human nature, also endowed human nature, through his pure goodness, with his own friendship. Scripture describes the supreme God as conversing with the first human being as a loving father. Thus, God helped him by his grace to obtain the great end that would raise him to a great height and for which his nature was not, nor could be *per se* suitable. We should note that this friendship and supernatural help was pure grace, and that the first human being, after receiving it, rejected it with his sin. So God withdrew from nature, which he was protecting and perfecting with his presence. According to the expression used Scripture, it seemed as if he were saying: 'I will withdraw because they do not want me. I will hide my face from them so that they see it no more and, hidden in this way, I will stand by to see where the wretches, now abandoned to themselves, will end up.'[84] We were therefore deprived of necessary help; we had nothing but our nature, a nature wounded by its own self through the free commission of sin. As a result the descendants of Adam were bound to find themselves deprived of supernatural help, just as their father was. God did not deprive them of what was theirs; he simply withdrew what was his. Thus, they received the whole of human nature, but as their father had made it, the nature he was able to give it. Nature, now fallible and fallen, deprived of the supernatural help that prepared it fittingly for the possession of God, was inevitably left with a perpetual thirst for a happy state, and this thirst was the thirst for supernatural water whose sweetness it had savoured. Sadly, the thirst was such that no drink could quench it because damaged man found no order or moral peace within himself. But he

[84] God made this threat, which is as terrible as it is mild, against the Hebrews through Moses: 'I will hide my face from them, I will see what their end will be'* (Deut 32: [20]). Our human powerlessness and extreme need of God could not be better expressed. God has no need to strike us to lay our pride low. It is sufficient that he abandons us to ourselves, that he leaves us alone and free so that we can experience doing everything we want to do and are able to do.

could not get rid of the desire to quench his thirst for happiness. He had to wander about, continually experimenting and looking for it in created things or in himself.

246. Pride and sensuality now rear their head. Man, fallen back upon himself, no longer looked to the divine help he did not have. Instead, the feeling of his own power became stronger and bolder; he was confident he could still obtain his full satisfaction with that power alone. This was pride. When at times he felt that this confidence was failing him, he turned to creatures, threw himself greedily on every delightful object, sought happiness everywhere, followed every false light that vainly allured him wherever it seemed to shine out. United no longer to God, he united his soul to material things. This was sensuality. Human nature was no longer sufficient for itself. The divine Judge had done nothing to it nor harmed it, but simply left it to itself, as it had in fact made itself. The only thing that was taken from it and belonged to it was the free gift. This happened through its own limitation and not because it had been imperfectly constituted by the supreme craftsman who had formed it. Human nature thus contained within itself a seed of the most wretched corruption and disorder, a seed that had been fully fertilised by the sinful act. Man's confidence therefore of finding peace in himself or in various creatures (even if no fault could be imputed to the descendant of Adam because the fault was necessarily inherited), would always be a true disorder and produce a continuous torment, because he would always be seeking happiness and finding only unhappiness.

247. Let us consider the wisdom and justice with which God has permitted temporal evils to spread from the first parent to the descendants. I have no doubt whatsoever that the just withdrawal of supernatural help from the spirit of the first human being was alone sufficient to drain his strength already disordered by sin and deprive him naturally of dominion over his body, which had been kept alive by the power of the companion-soul close to the source of life. From the description in Genesis, I consider God as inserted in the universe as if part of it, close to his creatures, delighting in them as it were, and clothed in some natural, visible form, in which he presides over the government of creation. But I do not doubt that when he withdrew from nature, after the bonds uniting him to it and

forming part of the general plan had been severed, he left that nature sterile and wretched as if deprived of its soul, and prey to all the evils expressed in the divine curses. However, whatever the case may be, it is sufficient we understand how human nature, separated from its author by sin, and even granting that it kept all that pertained to it, carries within itself a source of necessary disorder and woe, which affects and damages its moral part. The final effect of the development of so sad a seed therefore can be only unhappiness and desperation, so that man, never finding what he seeks, finds ultimately total wretchedness. If the disorder and the ruinous wound to the will that constitutes original sin in the descendants do not have the concept of fault (because not free), similarly my argument does not require us to say that evils and sufferings must be seen as personal penalties. Just as original sin can be taken as a fact pertaining to the moral order but arising from the limitation and the liability to failure of human nature, so evils and sufferings can be taken as a consequence of original sin, founded on the connection of the spiritual moral order to the corporal order.

[247]

CHAPTER 13

The permission of temporal evils that fall on the just and unjust is an act of justice and goodness because the evils act as a medicine for the moral infirmities common to all human beings

248. It is not only just and necessary but a decree of goodness that happiness is not found by those who seek it where it does not exist. Let us suppose that we can find some satisfaction in ourselves or in the things outside us, or at least suppose (and this would have required a miracle) that God had greatly reduced the sufferings we experience as we follow uncertain and wearisome paths in our search for happiness. Would this have helped us any better? The more weariness and pain we find in ourselves and in creatures, the less we trust such things and have any affection for them. On the other hand, the more pleasure we experience in creatures, the more does disorder enter our life, the more does the foolish hope increase of finding total satisfaction without God. We thus grow ever further and further away from him. Hence, if God left human nature to itself, the seed of disorder present in human nature would become much more harmful; in fact it would ultimately bring upon itself greater troubles because justice is obliged to straighten out all wayward things and return all disordered things to order by making them a burden to themselves. All this would happen in proportion to the extent that human nature found its delight in uniting itself inordinately to created things against its God. Hence, the burden of the sufferings and misfortunes we experience in temporal life is not only a penalty for the first sin and the result of our nature constrained by limitation, which begets disorder of which pain is a just offspring, but also a reparation and, I would add, a defence against the assault of this angry nature that is not sufficient to itself and perpetually turns to itself.

249. But if we look at the grace brought us by JESUS Christ, we see a new supernatural help, more excellent than the first, given to the human spirit. It joins us again to God who of his

own free will has come once again to the aid of human nature. Human nature had been exhausted by sad experience, but this taught it that the rest it so arduously seeks lies neither in itself nor in anything created. It therefore turns from its troubles and gives itself into the care of a loving God, and draws from him a new and infinite strength. Thus, its burdens and temporal sufferings not only help it by checking the force of its disorders but become a call to return to its true rest. It now sees the greatness of divine goodness shining more clearly in what it suffers.

250. Any complaint which a mortal being might make against temporal afflictions is therefore totally unreasonable. We come into this world turned from God and limited in our nature, which brings with it disorder in our will, and this disorder subjects us to suffering. Hence, the law which imposes suffering is both natural and just because common to all defective human beings. It is also good because it opposes the natural disorder and corrects it as much as it can and also because the obstacle of the evils with which our disordered nature has to contend helps us through JESUS Christ to turn back, and admonishes us to return quickly to the God who himself comes to meet us.

251. It is true that JESUS Christ, as Redeemer and Saviour of humanity, wanted to restore humanity in regard above all to the *person*. This meant that until the general resurrection our *nature* was left weak and subject to the death that destroys it, but at the general resurrection he himself would regenerate it in all its fullness. God was led by sublime reasons to follow this economy in justifying and restoring humanity, and many of these reasons can be known. I have just presented one.

252. But even when none of these reasons is known, human arrogance cannot impose a law on God and on his liberality. It cannot claim that the divine goodness which comes spontaneously to the aid of human miseries (although we do not have the least right to this aid) must bow to our understanding of the situation and act in one particular way rather than another. God is certainly acting fully legally when he restores the disorder of human nature to the level he likes, whether totally or partially. He may indeed have left us prey to the temporal infirmity to which we are subject, but he has saved us from the

eternal evils of the spirit. This alone should make us totally grateful to him, should make us bless our liberator in a fitting manner. But humanity is truly ungrateful: the very God who fills us to overflowing with benefits is himself called before the tribunal of fallen man!

253. As I said, misfortunes and temporal sufferings have been purposefully left so that we might be healed. The universal disease from which we suffer is a rash sense we have of our nature separated from God through sin, a sense that is identical with pride, and multiplies concupiscence. The only way this disease can be cured is by misfortunes. These, together with the light of grace, were able to open our eyes to ourselves and to other creatures, and see and sense our nothingness and the nothingness of other creatures in regard to our satisfaction. After repeated maulings and the daily experience of deep afflictions we were able to conclude finally: 'Peace is not found in any creature, so I turn to you, my God; in you alone is our souls' rest.' Even if we had not suffered such a bitter experience, we might indeed have found our peace in God, but we would not have had so certain a feeling, or at least such a vivid feeling, like the feeling we have from our painful experiences. In these we felt that peace is not only in God but in God alone, and that all other natures are nothing, because they cannot give rest to intelligent nature, for which all other natures are made.

254. Human understanding reasons about the things provided by the senses. It therefore had to use experience to remind human feeling, as it were, that human nature continually needs its Creator. This resulted in our having a greater knowledge of divine perfection on the one hand and of our own imperfection on the other: the glory of the supreme Creator shone with all its light in our minds. His victory over all creatures shone brilliantly before the eye of our intelligence and before the senses of a humanity humbled under his sublime and powerful hand. But the splendour of this glory of God, seen by human nature, is precisely human nature's great salvation. Here is its contact and union with the Lord, because the grace of intelligent nature abounds in proportion to the extent to which the divine glory or power penetrates that nature, as it were. If human knowledge begins from sense, and sense needs experience, God could not lead us to such perfect knowledge

unless he allowed us to experience our own weakness and the evils we brought upon ourselves. There is no other way God could bring human beings to such a high degree of conviction of their own nothingness and of divine greatness, or indeed to such a sublime indication of their salvation and grace. Did God have to abandon his own laws in order to train human nature and could he in fact do that; a stone cannot be moved by a force that is less than the inertia of the stone, nor can the feeling of an animal be moved by something it cannot feel; no action can be produced in a being unless the action acts on the being's forces or faculties. Should God therefore have used miracles to prevent those very evils that alone could teach the composite being we call man? Divine wisdom and goodness are indeed sublime! These two attributes have left us with temporal evils (which were all our work) in order to lead us to the highest perfection and greatest salvation. The Christian needs to understand what Plato himself understood when he made use of the remnants of the first traditions: 'The Lord God of gods,' he said, 'having seen that the beings who were subject to generation had lost the most precious and most beautiful of things, decreed to subject them to a treatment that could both punish and regenerate them.' This would be more than sufficient to dispel the difficulties levelled against the distribution of evils. It was the state of our defective nature that made us subject to all evils. But these evils themselves are a remedy (confirmed by the grace of the Redeemer) for the ugly disease with which nature has infected itself through its own fault. Those people therefore who encounter few evils in life can naturally rejoice in having, as it were, accidental good fortune, while those who are burdened by many temporal evils can see in them a supernatural divine mercy.

[254]

CHAPTER 14

The efficacy of prayer is a means given by Christ that removes every irregularity in the distribution of temporal evils

255. But not all people keep before them this original imperfection of their nature, and even if they do, they do not keep it *constantly* before them. We do not all give thought to the sin we carry with us, the continuous tendency to delude ourselves about our power and about corporeal things. The acute, habitual sense of our strength, when isolated from the sense of the Creator, can be defined as an instinctive pride. We complain that temporal evils and goods are not divided justly according to the merits of vices and virtues; I mean the vices and virtues we call actual, that is, those we ourselves cultivate and do not inherit. But I certainly do not wish to force such people to become aware of their inattention; I do not want to claim that the one argument, based on the disorder common to us all, answers every complaint about the evils we all experience. I have already pointed out that the continual use and application of the same general principle is too difficult for many people. If I can therefore, I will help this lack of understanding with arguments that are less general but closer to their thinking.

256. Earlier I indicated the connection that exists between the events of the universe. We saw how the course of all things (and therefore the distribution of evils and goods) depends totally on the primal position of beings and their first movements, both of which are pre-chosen by divine wisdom. I also observed that it is beyond all our intellectual capabilities to form a direct judgment about the wisdom that in the beginning established this position of things in the universe and their movement through it. I then considered that the best position for things could not be that which kept all just people safe from temporal misfortunes, but on the contrary was that which did the least possible harm to the just and allowed only the smallest possible number of evildoers to escape punishment. When I say 'the just', it is clear that I prescind from the innate disorder

of nature, from its actual effects and from the defects to which those who share in the grace of Christ are generally subject through their weakness; in fact these realities strengthen my argument.

We would of course require proof if we were to affirm that the combination of things willed by God at the beginning was not the best possible for favouring virtue and harassing evil; indeed the concept of God leaves no room to doubt that it was the best. The teaching of Christianity however, which is used to answering the most difficult questions, provides us with a greater light that confirms all that reason reveals. The divine Master assures us that God guards his just with special protection, and dispenses blessings to them with great largesse. Among other things, he teaches this most consoling truth: *prayer made in the name of the Mediator obtains all it asks.* Very rarely do those who pray very rarely ask for miracles, but many temporal goods can, according to Christian philosophy, be obtained by prayer without the need for miracles. This truth presupposes another truth, that when at the beginning God had chosen the order of events that follow one another, he had foreseen, from that very moment, all the prayers and the desires of the just (in fact the just usually ask their God for what they desire; they keep their gaze fixed on him every day, and even their desire itself is sometimes valid as a prayer), with the result that he had predisposed things in such a wonderful way in the universe that those prayers were answered in the natural succession of events by granting the requested good or some greater good. In this way God disposed that this or that thing was in harmony with the universal good. We know this disposition because we know that he hears every one of our prayers.

Christian teaching also tells us that the only innocent life in the state of reparation is that which comes through new grace, which prays. We are taught that prayer is not only an effect of grace buts also its means. As an effect and means of grace, prayer becomes a measure of grace and hence a measure of virtue. Consequently, the amount of virtue is equal to the amount of prayer. And because the extent to which prayer is heard corresponds to the prayer itself, then according to this system of Christ's religion, 'all goods are distributed according to virtues, precisely because they are distributed according to prayers'.

[256]

CHAPTER 15

Using only the rational law and prescinding from the positive promises of God, we cannot prove that temporal evils must be distributed according to virtue and vice

257. It will be helpful if we examine more closely the merits of the virtue that complains that it is rewarded so little for its merit. First of all, let us look at this shameful complaint and see whether we are in fact dealing with virtue — we are often deluded and take pride in even the vainest appearances of virtue. After we have distinguished true virtue from false virtue, we can see which of the two has more claim: true, solid virtue or the pretence of virtue, and which has more merit: modest virtue that holds its peace or proud virtue that boasts openly.

258. I shall first distinguish between virtue in the natural order and virtue in the supernatural order.

259. Natural virtue differs greatly from supernatural virtue. The latter, considered solely in its external characteristics, differs from the former in the quality of the law it follows and in the promises that sanction its law. Its law is positive, that is, communicated under God's authority. The promises made to those who observe it are also positive, clear and solemn. In contrast, the guiding law of natural virtue is manifested through the sole light of natural reason, and does not display or preserve any deposit of positive promises.

I will not delay to examine whether our presumptuous human reason can boast of the smallest truth that it has discovered totally by itself and therefore can actually so little called a promulgator of any legislation, or whether in fact all the enlightenment it is so proud of is not, when taken back to its origin, due to the positive instructions received by man from his Creator at the beginning, with legend added afterwards. These instructions moved the minds of the first fathers to the free use of their reason and placed in them the seeds of all human wisdom. These seeds were then handed down by the fathers to their descendants who knew so little. I truly believe this to be the case. I side with the opinion of those who deplore the blind pride of the human spirit that attributes to itself and sacrilegiously takes to itself the glory due solely to the Master and Wise Being.[85] But leaving aside the investigation of how our reason originally attained its lights that now beautify it and make it resplendent, I take these lights as they are, and readily acknowledge in reason's arguments (from whatever source they derive their principle) the solid bases of a moral legislation. Because these bases are consequences of principles of reason, all of which shine with an eternal truth and not purely as the pleasure of a sovereign will, I call them *natural legislation*, and from observation of this natural legislation I draw the concept of natural virtue.

260. I admit therefore a natural virtue, but this virtue is as uncertain in its commands as it is hesitant and tremulous in its voice in difficult matters. It is its own law, inspired more by feeling than by deep reflection. This noble, moral feeling which never leaves us is certainly not void of light, and certainly shows itself as a companion to a function of reason, which is to perceive entia; it also suggests to us great respect for all that is intelligence and freedom, and persuades us gently to love our fellow human beings, to share with them every good in which we abound, and sometimes to forget ourselves for them, without hoping for any other reward than the joy of making some unfortunate person happy, of benefiting another — it is a feeling that is certainly good, upright and a happy harbinger of some good event. Nevertheless, despite the sublime abstraction of virtue that the contemplating mind draws from it, this feeling fails to give to our weakened reason, which easily accepts flattery, such a strong and continuous demonstration of itself that reason is bound to acknowledge it or will not test it, or doubt its legitimate authority. But if the legislator himself comes to someone who doubts and says: 'I assure you: listen trustingly to the voice within in you. That voice comes from

85 The first book explains what I mean by the light of reason (cf. 148–155). I have distinguished three kinds of things given by God to human knowledge: 1. natural objects; 2. God himself and all that concerns the supernatural end of man; 3. language and with it the principles of reasoning. When the third, which is the means of reasoning, is united or applied to the first, it can be called *natural reasoning*, and when applied to the second, *supernatural reasoning*.

me', the doubter, in the face of such testimony, can no longer withhold trust from the law that he feels written in his heart; if he does, he is totally inexcusable. The authority of the hidden law becomes open and fully authenticated; it is no longer a voice from an unknown source or that can be doubted. This legislator, who earlier was veiled and hidden, is now seen and either honoured in the fulfilment of the law or manifestly injured in its violation.

261. The law of justice therefore, when applied to God who has revealed himself to us, acquires an obviousness and an infinite, unassailable authority. This explains why, as I said, God never left the world without those traditions that could help it raise itself mentally to him. Hence, those people among the pagans who applied themselves to the study of wisdom had no excuse. As St. Paul says: they held the truth of God in injustice, although the existence and attributes of God were clear to them. God had manifested these things to them; he had given them a mind which, enlightened and made productive by the words communicated to it, could rise above visible things to form a concept of invisible things, a concept of the virtue and divinity of this supreme Lord and legislator.[86] But those who abandoned this light of tradition and shut themselves within their own limited knowledge laid only a weak foundation for virtue; indeed they could not have laid any foundation if they had completely abandoned the knowledge received from human contact. To this uncertainty and hence to this weakness of nature's law, and also to the certain and powerful impression of feelable things, whose persistent voice sows false doctrines in us and rejects unseen virtue as an illusion of our imagination, we must attribute the universal and unfortunate fact that while moral philosophy abounds in many books and is ostentatiously discussed by prudent human beings, it is almost absent in the lives and behaviour of the same people. Acting in an impressive manner, which is more demonstrative than virtuous, they claim they are upright but cover up their crimes for years or certainly their daily infringements of this strict law, against which a single deed removes the right to the title of innocence — and innocence is only the first level of virtue.

[86] Rom 1: [18–20].

Consequently, if there are people we can call totally virtuous, let them come forward and appeal against the sufferings of this life so wrongly distributed. But, I repeat, let them first of all prove their innocence (if they can), at least to themselves, in those few, fleeting moments when in solitude and silence their heart ventures to calm their artificial, benumbed state and tell them the truth.

262. But to whom will these unique people, outstanding among all others, direct their reproaches and complaints? They do not know who their legislator is and he has not revealed himself, nor do they know the sanction of the law, a law which, we supposed, they generously observed despite all their terrible ordeals. Their legislator was of course their reason that gave them the law they observed so carefully. But after their reason has stated the law, it immediately confesses how powerless it is to reward and punish. It declares that its office is neither to distribute rewards nor to inflict punishments, but simply to demonstrate with complete clarity what is upright and just, and to present these qualities as so absolute and necessary that their obligatory force does not depend either on expected rewards or feared punishments. In fact, independently of these things, the law is promulgated by the light of natural reason, which proclaims authoritatively to all: 'Obey'.

We certainly see that the consequences of our obedience to the law of reason is peace, while remorse is a result of disobedience. But this peace and remorse are, in the last analysis, simply the voice of reason intimating the law. The law applies a different measure in response to our behaviour: it approves if we obey the authoritative directive, but rebukes if we disobey. Its sole concern is our obedience; it is not interested in what is a good or an evil for us; these things are unknown to it, as if they did not exist. Hence, for as long as the law is not clearly proclaimed by God but is proposed by reason alone, it certainly has full authority and is self-evidently and by moral necessity unbreakable. At the same time however it is not joined to any reward or sensible punishment, which differ naturally and totally from the moral law. The moral law is received by pure intelligence and proposed in all its simplicity to the free will; it is not involved or mixed with anything in a lower sphere, that is, the sphere of the senses, because there is no communication between what is essentially sensible and what is intelligible and moral. It is true that they are mysteriously joined in the unity of the human being, but they are not confused or become one. This is why what is essentially moral neither promises nor desires nor bestows anything sensible, just as what is essentially sensible cannot aspire to any of the pleasures of what if essentially intelligible — these pleasures do not in fact even exist for what is essentially moral. Hence human beings, each of whom is, in an extraordinary way, a double being, wrongly complain when they confuse the rights of the two essences that compose them, and claim that their sensitive nature must receive pleasures through the merits of their intelligent nature, or they are scandalised because one nature suffers while the other seems worthy of reward, that is, worthy of the reward found in the good testimony of conscience, and this testimony does not fail because it is the natural and necessary consequence of the practice of virtue. It is therefore unreasonable to require that those who obey the law of their nature be rewarded with sensible pleasure and those who break the law be punished with feelable suffering. This would be like wishing that another human being should be rewarded or punished for the merits or demerits gained by a particular human being, or that even another nature should be rewarded or punished, a horse for example that is rewarded or punished for the bravery or cowardice of its rider.

Prescinding from God therefore, the testimony of conscience is the sole sufficient reason why human nature must receive a secure reward.

263. If the generous legislator has made no special promises, we will never have a reason authorising us to imagine we possess a right to sensible rewards that differ from the reward of peace of conscience. The natural law, which is known solely through the light of reason, can make no other promise — in fact not even peace of conscience is promised; it is simply a necessary, natural consequence. Only when the moral law is positively promulgated by an external legislator, may the legislator add rich promises to it. This addition is worthy of him, and it is made from his liberality, from his perfect goodness. On the other hand, if he adds other positive precepts to the natural law both through intimation and through the things intimated, it

would seem that a certain equity requires promises to be added.[87]

264. Hence, when human beings want to join together without God and limit themselves solely to the natural law, they lose (I repeat) all positive promises; they distance their minds from nature, just as they distance the light from reason. For them, reason and nature are now simply facts; they can demand nothing from them. As human beings, they are constituted to be listeners to what reason says and spectators of whatever happens in nature. They hear reason and feel its authority without knowing the result; they do not ask of reason what real support it has for its authority, but this does not stop it from being more absolute and inexorable in its command. They see the spectacle of nature and feel that they are actors in it and even a spectacle themselves and perhaps a cruel spectacle, but it is a necessary cruelty, a fact against which they cannot appeal nor even cry for mercy or pity. This is what reason is, this is what nature is, considered in itself, deprived of God. Reason simply commands, nature simply operates. The command of reason lacks indulgence as well as hope; the operation of nature is blind, and order cannot be demanded of it as something fitting to it; order can only be looked for, as a fact noted in nature.

265. Nevertheless, this fact observed in nature can lead us, by use of reason alone, to knowledge of the existence of a supreme mind. But who is going to acknowledge such an existence if the order is not seen, if all that is apparent is a system of many irregularities in which the good and the wicked are jumbled together and tossed about, with the good perhaps oppressed and the wicked enjoying life? The person who is generous and

[87] This feeling, that observance of the law must be accompanied by positive rewards, is universal and deeply rooted in the human race. It is proof that the human race received the moral law from an external legislator who once spoke with it, or at least is proof that the law was deduced from the concept of a supreme legislator. If the human race had deduced the moral law solely from reason, without the intervention of the thought of a being who is lord of all, it would never have had in its spirit such a great expectation and exigency of an external reward. This is so true that only with difficulty are we persuaded that it is not a natural suggestion of our reason. The same applies to many other truths which, according to the expression of a learned man, were not *naturally* in us but *naturalised* in us.

has a noble conscience will reply: 'It cannot be like that. I can never admit that there is a contradiction and opposition between the order of reason and the order of nature. On the contrary, I believe that after this life both will definitely be reconciled, and I cannot renounce a belief that is good and consoling. For me, what is good will be the argument for what is true.' This kind of courageous earnestness leads the human spirit not to look for an order between virtue and happiness on earth but to wait for it after death. Again therefore it is unreasonable and groundless for people to complain because they suffer on earth, even though they are faithful disciples of natural virtue.

266. All this is nevertheless true. Even those who reject the positive lights of the Christian religion and, with an unbiased mind, observe themselves and the universe around them, must accept that they and the universe are a fact. They cannot require that these two things must harmonise according to a rule that they themselves consider good or wise. They can only observe and, with this observation, extract the law to which the universe is subject. And let us also observe with them, and see, by noting events, if we can discover the *law* according to which goods and evils are divided on earth, whether they fall indifferently on the good and the wicked, and whether there is a constant difference between them so that the good are perhaps more favoured, or the wicked are more prosperous.

CHAPTER 16

Observation demonstrates that temporal goods continually tend to be united to virtue, while evils generally speaking follow vice

267. If we find even on earth some order of goodness and justice in the sequence of events, we can certainly argue for the existence of the Creator, whom we have pretended for a short time to forget.

268. We see at once (or think we see) that the order is not perfect, that is, not free from irregularities. Many cruel actions are certainly not punished immediately, nor is every act of virtue rewarded. To be convinced of this, it is sufficient to look at the sun that shines every day on so many crimes and disasters that are arrogantly and boastfully inflicted on others. But this does not necessarily prove that there is no order of justice and that the order that must exist and is the only order that can exist is lacking.

269. As we have seen, no one can reasonably affirm that things should combine and events follow one another in such a way that all the just are spared temporal sufferings, and no unjust person escapes them. It is therefore equally unreasonable for us to conclude from our observations that there is a perfect order and harmony between merits and goods, between demerits and evils. But if we find that in general the wicked are temporally punished and the virtuous temporally rewarded, it will be a consoling relief, and sufficient for us to dismiss our doubts and set us on the way to belief in the existence of an excellent mind that regulates the universe.

270. Indeed we have seen that death and the other common evils to which the whole human race is subject originate from the limitation of the nature that suffers them and at the same time is separated from its author. It would therefore be unreasonable to search nature and natural virtue for some defence against these evils. We cannot expect to find accord between moral good and moral evil and between eudaimonological good and eudaimonological evil in the case of evils that are

common and necessary to nature, but only in the case of evils that are eventual or accidental.

The first, accidental good is internal peace of spirit, and we saw that this natural reward is never absent from the virtue that respects the abstract dictate of justice, whenever we are obliged to apply the dictate. It is a kind of cult of God who is present (I would even say hidden) in the virtue and unknown to us.

271. Many other excellent consequences can be added, because the beings we encounter in the universe and to whom the dictate can be applied are our fellow human beings and ourselves.

We have in fact no difficulty in seeing that those who are just to their fellow humans and to themselves avoid evils (granted all other things are equal). Temporal goods follow more easily for such people than for those who are unjust towards themselves and their neighbour.

272. Virtue relative to one's fellow human beings consists in such a well-balanced spirit that it has a great love for the good of everybody and seeks this love through action, just as vice consists in ignoring the regard due to others and thinking only of oneself. By a law of nature, everyone prefers to vote for those who are known to love all people rather than vote for those who are known as the enemies of everyone; the former therefore receive the majority vote. As a result, those who love their fellow humans have the greater probability of acquiring all goods. Although the interests of individuals will be against them, individuals, relative to their own personal interest, stand alone and are overridden by the power of all. It is true that others who simulate the same virtue can compete with them, but the pretence of virtue cannot be as frequent, constant and certain as genuine virtue. In some cases, those who have a greater love for the common good are sometimes overcome by other people's individual passions that have been unified by accidental causes, but this must be less frequent because less probable.

273. We must also note that irregular cases, although most rare, make a greater impression than cases that follow from the very nature and reason of a thing. The opinion therefore that irregularity occurs very often is typically the opinion of the uninformed; it is not founded on a serious calculation, but arises from the resentment at seeing the wicked so successful.

The fact itself of the resentment proves that the case is contrary to nature, and hence less frequent than its opposite; the number of times it is contrary to nature is very low; the number of times it is favourable is never-ending. This is another proof that human beings act justly when passing judgment on others, and are only unjust when judging their own case. Hence, in the world the greatest number of judgments about the external merit of people is correctly made because the votes given in judging others exceed those given in judging oneself, and are almost as many as the number of judges multiplied by itself.

274. My proposition that the good enjoy a greater probability and expectation of obtaining human goods can be doubted if insufficient importance is given to the condition I laid down when positing it, all other things being equal. It is true that more powerful enemies will certainly oppress the virtuous, weaker person. But I am asked what is the more probable distribution of goods among human beings, and among these goods this power, whose abuse we deplore. The question supposes that the goods are not yet distributed, and the desire is to know the law that continuously governs their distribution. This law therefore, according to which goods and evils are distributed among us, is in my opinion the following:

NATURAL GOODS HAVE A CONTINUOUS TENDENCY TO UNITE THEMSELVES TO NATURAL VIRTUE; EVILS, TO VICE

275. Whatever the state of the world and no matter how irregular the distribution of these goods, this tendency never ceases to function; it is *always* true that goods continuously have, as it were, a kind of inclination to unite with truth. Thus, even when a body is at rest, it is still drawn towards the earth. Consequently, if human goods are continuously drawn towards virtue, they must, as time passes, approach a regular distribution, and this balance must become more and more perfect, or must certainly drive events incessantly towards this perfection in the moral order, whatever the accidental disturbances the perfection may encounter.

276. We will see this better explained if we consider for a moment the *law of probability*, a sovereign law that presides over the execution of all the other laws of the universe. All these are directed by it, and its sublimity will be seen when I

publish *Cosmology*, if such studies can hopefully find favour and encouragement in Italy.[88] The law, stated briefly, is the following.

277. If ninety balls, one sixth of them yellow, one third red, and half of them black, are put into a bag and then emptied out, there is no certainty which colour will come out first. There is a half probability that a black ball will come first, a third probability for a red, and a sixth probability for a yellow. Whatever colour emerges first, it is always an irregularity because that colour has, so to speak, no full right to emerge first; it has only a half, third or sixth part of a right, as it were. But if the ball is replaced in the bag, and the balls are taken out a great number of times (the colours being noted), their number for each colour will approach the proportion of the colours, that is, a half of them will be black, a third red, and a sixth yellow. The more times the balls are taken out, the more the irregularity diminishes, and the regular pattern appears. Any accidental disturbance of this regular pattern does not prevent the continual fulfilment of the law that tends to make the colours of the extracted balls regularise themselves. And if the balls were drawn out *ad infinitum*, the law clearly indicates that every irregular assortment would disappear.

In the case of the universe therefore, those people who consider only particular cases cannot see its beauty; on the contrary they must see deformity because they meet inevitable irregularities. But those who consider a long series of events will discern a marvellously regular and symmetrical order. For example, if we looked at a piece of very beautiful embroidery and examined each stitch or thread individually, we would see only one colour at a time without noticing the attractiveness of the whole; to appreciate the work we would have to hold it at a distance, and with our view encompassing the whole work enjoy all the colours that the intelligent embroiderer has put in their proper place. Therefore:

> *In applying the laws of the universe the great craftsman has arranged an irregularity in the detail but regularity in the whole, making the irregularities subject to his wonderful, eternal plan.*

[88] The author was writing in 1825.

278. We can see this in the division of temporal goods and evils. If we see a virtuous person suffering, we see it as only one incident, but if we looked at the whole of his life, we might find many more goods than evils. If it is still not sufficient to see regularity when we consider someone's whole life instead of just one event or part, we can consider whole tribes. In doing this, we will see that the more prosperous tribes are those that have a greater total of virtues. The irregularities we see in an individual tribe will noticeably diminish if we consider many tribes instead of one; the irregularities will diminish even more if we consider whole nations. The history of nations constantly demonstrates that they have perished through excessive vice, and flourished through predominant virtue. If we look at the entire history of virtue and vice in the whole human race, we will see even less irregularities, and see them as decreasing still further in proportion that we examine ever longer and longer periods of the history.

279. I said I would keep the explanation brief. I will therefore use only one example to illustrate the matter. We must first note that what sometimes seems irregular contributes excellently in fact to a general regularity. It is a common and very true observation, made throughout the ages, that certain vicious and virtuous inclinations of the spirit pass from father to son. This explains in great part why diverse clans are seen to have diverse temperaments, have their own way of thinking and their own habits and customs. This observation enables us to see how hereditary diseases that seem irregularities can fulfil a wise purpose of Providence. The sins of the fathers who have been punished by illnesses are also punished in the offspring because the inclination to the same vices passes into them. If to this we add the education and examples by which the father leaves his impression on the offspring, the result is the greater probability of the same faults, and generally of the multiplication of those faults. It was necessary that lineages, morally vitiated in this way, were also afflicted by greater corporal ills so that they might be extinguished sooner than incorrupt lineages, and thus virtue might always survive in the world.[89]

[89] Laplace uses this argument in his *Saggio filosofico della probabilità*: 'It is certainly interesting to see that if the only thing we consider in the eternal

CHAPTER 17

The punishment due to those who do evil is sometimes deferred, and this can favour virtue. We should not therefore be scandalised by this

280. Here I must make the subtle but true observation that Plutarch makes in his work entitled: 'Why divine justice sometimes defers the punishment of evil doers?'

According to Plutarch, God does not punish immediately, because he considers the totality of things, not things individually. He considers not so much what each of our actions would require, but rather what helps so that a perfect order of justice and goodness might shine out throughout the whole of our life.

When wicked people change their behaviour and are morally renewed, says Plutarch, they often advance in the path of virtue perhaps even further than they previously advanced in the way of vice. If God had removed such people, inflicting on them a prompt punishment at the moment of their first sin, there would certainly not have been the particular irregularity that the crime went unpunished for some time, but the great order that resulted from the crime would also have been lost. Indeed, in this case the claims of justice were strengthened in the totality of the life of each one and to the great advantage of each by the mercy shown by the legislator and by the earth's acquiring a greater sum of virtue.

281. Plutarch drives his observation home:

> Great characters do not produce anything mediocre. Because their energy cannot remain inactive, they are in continual agitation like ships battered by waves and storms until they have formed very solid habits. Those who are not experts in agriculture are not interested in land which

principles of reason, justice and humanity are the happy chances that constantly accompany these principles, there is a great advantage in following the principles, and serious difficulties in rejecting them. Their chances, like favourable chances in a lottery, always prevail in the end in the midst of the uncertainties of chance. I would invite philosophers to consider the reflections expressed in this essay and direct their attention to a matter that is truly worthy of the time they give it.'*

> is nothing but scrub, wild plants and stagnant water; on the other hand an expert sees the excellence of the soil precisely because of these things. In the same way, great characters are initially subject to the danger of producing bad and perverse fruit. We however have no time for such produce and wilderness, and consider that the best thing is to cut it all down. But the expert who knows more than we about the art of husbandry sees the great good and generosity in such people, and patiently waits for the time of reason and virtue when their strong temperaments produce fruit worthy of them.

282. According to this concept, Plutarch very appropriately likens the norm followed by divine Providence in this particular situation to the law of the Egyptians which ordained 'that if a woman with child is condemned to death, the punishment must be deferred until she is delivered of her child'. He says there are many guilty people like this woman; they deserve death and are perhaps already sentenced by God. But they have, hidden within them, some beautiful action, some magnanimous deed. Hence, the wisdom and goodness of the legislator requires postponement for a time of their punishment until they have produced the good fruit of virtue that is maturing in them unseen.

283. Even if this fruit were not the result of true virtue, we could still suppose there are people who, when they have returned to an upright life, are able to compensate spontaneously and liberally for what their prior evil behaviour had denied to justice. The same reasoning would also apply if the fruit produced helped others: the wisest and most excellent Judge would surely have to preserve evil doers if he had destined them to bring some good to their fellow human beings, even perhaps without their wanting and knowing this?

> If the tyrant Dionysius had been punished at the time of his usurpation, no Greek would have survived in the whole of Sicily, because if the Carthaginians had seized the island, they would have forced all the Greeks out. The same would have happened to the cities of Apollonia and Anattorio, indeed even probably to the whole island of Leucadia, if Periander's punishment had been delayed long after his usurpation of power. And I have no doubts

that Cassandra's punishment was deferred for the sole purpose that it might help in the rebuilding and repopulating of Thebes.

284. Plutarch is speaking about the use God makes of tyrants to punish people's crimes. He gives the examples of Phalarides for the people of Agrigento and of Marius for the Romans, but points out that with good and benign reason, God reserved to the end the punishment of the tyrants themselves. This is a truth that is evident and confirmed in all ages by manifest experience. It could be supported by more recent and equally impressive examples that could be substituted for Plutarch's ancient examples, but this is not really called for because cases are all too common. Indeed it seems that the ears of the whole world are still itching for them.

285. It should be noted how well Plutarch's observation agrees with the principles I have laid down. We are asking why punishment should be deferred for the guilty, because according to the law of justice this is an irregularity. This may be so, but the irregularity is a partial irregularity that gives order to the totality; it is a transient irregularity that is corrected in the course of time, when it generates a more beautiful regularity. We may ask whether this total, more beautiful regularity could not be obtained with the simple passage of time and thus avoid the need for the disorder and fleeting irregularity. But this cannot so because the seeds of virtue and moral greatness in those who have at first been wayward but later, through extraordinary virtue, have become a light to humanity, would not have developed if at their first sin they had received the punishment they deserved. Hence divine Providence could not have used them as instruments (even unwilling instruments) to save thousands of innocent people from a catastrophe, or punish thousands of guilty ones. Thus, their wickedness, which for some time remains unpunished and as such presents an apparent irregularity, becomes precisely a minister of justice and serves to strengthen the moral order much more extensively. This procedure is necessary because all creatures are limited, they cannot simultaneously unite all goods to themselves and escape all evils: while avoiding some, they fall into others, and while trying to obtain certain goods, they are naturally subject to the

loss of others. Consequently, the great skill, as it were, that divine wisdom uses to correct and govern the things of this world is precisely to dispose them in such a way that greater goods come from the permission of evils.

CHAPTER 18

Those who complain about Providence often have a false concept of virtue. However virtue, even as they understand it, does not lack temporal advantages

286. People who complain about divine Providence often use the word 'virtue' inappropriately. They use it for all those actions that are directly beneficial; this is natural virtue. But it can be truthfully said that according to the strict sense of the word there is no true *natural virtue*, that is, that terminates in created nature. The moral law, in which every virtuous action must terminate, is eternal, although its presence in created intelligence had a beginning. Moreover, when we are separated from God, we turn our affections and thoughts solely to useful temporal things, whether we want to obtain them for ourselves or, if we have a good nature, enjoy giving them to others. We always work for a limited interest or at least a limited end that can always be overruled by a greater interest or end. Furthermore, the cold judgment of our mind can restrict us to a pure egoism, and we help others only for our own advantage. On the other hand the instinct of our heart, which is never totally extinguished in the human being, inclines us to benevolence. Although an instinct is not a virtue, we nevertheless want our internal, mysterious enjoyment to be a virtue, we want to take pride in it and applaud it. We also see that to oppose this instinct is to oppose truth, and that to oppose truth is objectively evil. How then do we persuade ourselves that this objective evil is also the greatest evil for ourselves as subject, and carries no possibility of reward? The most we can do is make an effort to interpret in the pure, noble voice of nature the will of a hidden legislator and magnificent remunerator whom we have lost sight of; it is with an act of faith that virtue becomes efficacious and begins to reign in us. This great and wonderful word 'virtue' therefore is heard by people who have lost sight of God and do not understand its meaning. The title 'virtue' is fitting only for those actions that are performed for love of a law, which then becomes more lovable and powerful when we

discover in it a most loving and all-powerful legislator. Virtue, rooted in an infinite good, becomes immovable in us, just as the law on which it depends is immovable; it becomes queen of all human passions and feelings, exceeds the value of every interest and of everything useful in this life.

For the moment however I will postpone discussion about true virtue, and discuss those people who complain about Providence and understand 'virtue' as the study of only those things that have temporal usefulness.

287. These utilitarians who complain that their virtue brings no success, certainly contradict their definition of virtue. If we keep to their definition, then those people are perhaps more virtuous who are more capable of searching for and finding temporal advantages? Are they not also the most prosperous?

288. I will deal first with the relationship we all have with others and then with the relationship with ourselves.

We all defend ourselves against our aggressors. Society also defends itself. In all societies there is an order of justice that outlaws crimes against peaceful and secure ownership. Civil society itself arose from the need of human beings (each of whom is made stronger by what all contribute) to defend their peaceful ownership against the wicked, and from the need for a fixed order that might more securely give the virtuous the distinctions and rewards of their honest life. Hence, in society generally considered, punishment of the guilty continuously exists alongside the safety and honour of the good. In the world, in all nations and at all times, an external and temporal public justice exists, considered sacred, like a sword of God. Those who escape this justice can be only an exception to this, a particular irregularity.

289. But while everything done for the good of society pertains to virtue, and all that harms it pertains to vice, virtue is also acknowledged in the good rule we follow for our own sake or, more straightforwardly, for the advantages we seek for ourselves. A prudent, temperate person is praised, and rightly so, but doesn't this kind of virtue bring its own reward? It cannot claim any more than the temporal good it bestows, and is called virtue precisely because it obtains good. The vices contrary to this kind of virtue could be punished by diseases and by other misfortunes that accompany disease. A prodigal man soon

finds himself destitute; avaricious people, in addition to the wretchedness that consumes them, are hated and abhorred by everybody. Intemperate people bring many illnesses upon themselves. If, from the world, we banished the throat and intemperance, the majority of illnesses would disappear. The longevity of hermits and priests is clear proof of the advantage which the virtue of temperance bestows in the present life.

290. We must also consider the following. We hear very often these days that the greatest criminals, in the midst of their vices, possess something of what the world calls virtue. The world admires and praises the cleverness and foresight that result from this virtue; it is impressed by the criminal's plan, by the way the plan is boldly executed, the resolution of the criminal in the face of dangers, the dexterity in escape and the vigilance for the unexpected. In fact these things have their own special worth and their own natural goodness. Again, it is surely fitting that people who are careful, industrious and provident should acquire goods greater than those obtained by lazy, neglectful and foolish people, who think only of the present moment. The acquirement of human goods in the world is, as it were, a kind of castle or territory to be conquered: we fight for the goods, and they go to the bravest. Sometimes of course the opposite happens due to unforeseen accidents, but it is still a fact that when the conditions are the same, the bravest fighter always has superiority. This superiority, which produces a greater probability of victory, always gives the advantage to those who possess the courage I am talking about.

291. However, we need to consider very carefully the reason why a person's gifts and merits, which are admired and extolled, sometimes fail to obtain their temporal reward. We can easily understand this if we remember what I said earlier: gifts and merits are qualities of human nature, hence they can fail in their operation because human nature can fail.

Great people who have temporal goods as their objective show prudence. The practice of justice, equity and beneficence make other people benevolent. Temperance and austerity strengthen the body for performing demanding work. Some face and bear dangers with firm resolution, while others display a kind of magnanimity when they put fame before life. These virtues and all similar virtues are simply an effort by human nature to grow, to make itself noble and happy. But to obtain these perfections, nature needs some external help from someone who possesses the perfections themselves and can therefore communicate them to it. Consequently, it is not only fitting but necessary that human nature be frustrated in all its efforts. In this way it gives glory to God from whom it is separated. However, although those who have the above-mentioned virtues obtain temporal goods without much difficulty, sometimes they do not obtain them because the *possibility of failure* is proper to such virtues. Even those who obtain temporal goods lose them after a short time through death, which demonstrates how empty their human powers are. Human powers are granted only one thing: THE ABILITY TO TAKE POSSESSION OF HUMAN GOODS, BUT ONLY WITH UNCERTAINTY AND FOR A SHORT TIME, SUCH THAT ALL THE POWERS ARE CONFOUNDED.

292. Even here, whatever good there is the goodness of the author of nature, because all the noble gifts mentioned above are given to us together with nature. We do not even own truth; it belongs to God. In the goodness proper to human beings, we find only a love of self, which uses personal gifts and faculties with varying degree of energy and wisdom, and without colliding with the interests of others; this produces a reputation for justice. But the love of ideal justice fails when all interests seem opposed to it. We find good and noble instincts in the soul, but these move the will more than they are moved by the will, and they do not always help reason in a suitable way. Nevertheless, divine power and wisdom dispose that natural justice and prudence have the ability to remove many evils and procure many goods for us. Although this law attaches good to righteousness and wisdom, and evil to wickedness and foolishness, and also sometimes fails (as was fitting), nevertheless, people did not find reasons in it for honouring supreme Providence, but only arrogance and pride. Consequently, they thought up a presumptuous doctrine, which sometimes promises constant natural happiness to the imperfect virtue of nature, sometimes defines virtue as purely the study of what is useful, and virtuous people as those who are able to enrich themselves with human goods. Ultimately therefore the utilitarians, with their system, acknowledge and justify, without intending to do so, the Creator's Providence.

[292]

CHAPTER 19

Why temporal goods tend to be aligned with natural virtue, and evils with vice

293. But why is it that the distribution of natural goods and evils follows the law I have noted; in other words, why do temporal goods have a continuous tendency to unite with natural virtue, and natural evils generally result from the absence of natural virtue?

This fact is not only the effect of God's wise disposition at the beginning of beings and of the choice of their free movements but also of the perfection the Creator gave his creatures when he created them. This perfection pleased God when he saw that all things were good. Although this goodness comes to creatures from the likeness to their Creator, it does not, as I have indicated, exclude the limitation by which the intelligent creature, the most excellent of all creatures, needs the ever-present help of its author, the most perfect being.

HENCE, TWO ELEMENTS ARE DISTINGUISHED IN CREATURES; ONE, A NEGATIVE ELEMENT, IS LIMITATION; THE OTHER, A POSITIVE ELEMENT, IS PARTICIPATION IN EXISTENCE. Limitation makes creatures capable of all evils if they are not freely helped by God; participation in existence renders them capable of order and all goods. They received this participation at creation from their Lord, but the limitation, or rather deficiency, came from themselves, that is, they retained it from the nothingness from which they came.

294. Ancient philosophers had already seen and stated these things, although in a somewhat confused way. They might have received some light from very ancient traditions, whose importance we cannot at the present assess. Alternatively, some extraordinarily brilliant minds might have broken through the darkness in which humankind had immersed itself, and glimpsed some light of the highest truths; alternatively (and this seems probable), both of these possibilities were involved. Whatever the case may be however, we certainly find in the writings of scholarly men that have come down to us traces of a great wisdom, superior to what we could expect of those

disadvantaged times. As an example I will take a passage in Plato where he presents the teaching of Timaeus, a philosopher of Locris, and where he comes close to the theory of the two elements that are in the nature of all created things and from which all the laws constituting the universe derive. However, later on, Plato could not defend himself against some erroneous consequences of Timaeus' concept, probably because he had not sufficiently clarified his own concept. He says: 'Timaeus of Locris said that there are two causes of all things', that is, everything we observe in the universe can be explained by two principles: 'First, *mind*, cause of all the things that have some reason behind their origin'; these are the divine ideas that are causes and exemplars of all natures, of the positive element of nature; 'and *necessity*, which is the cause of the things that exist through a certain energy according to the powers and faculties of bodies'; this is the limitation that, as we saw, results in necessity, and is demonstrated far more in corporeal, material things than in all other things.

295. The mind can be charmed when considering how all the laws of the constitution of the universe originate from only two elements.

Indeed, THE LIMITATION OF CREATURES (the first element) PRODUCES THE COSMIC LAW THAT ALL NATURES, WHEN ABANDONED TO THEMSELVES, ARE SUBJECT TO EVILS. This is a most universal law that appears in all its light through the fault of the intelligent creature; hence that sublime, mysterious saying of the Gospel: ALL WHO EXALT THEMSELVES WILL BE HUMBLED, AND ALL WHO HUMBLE THEMSELVES WILL BE EXALTED.

296. THE GOODNESS CO-CREATED IN BEINGS AND NOT DIFFERENT FROM THE BEINGS THEMSELVES (the second element) IS THE SOURCE OF THE OTHER COSMIC, CONSTITUENT LAWS. THESE LAWS ARE SIMPLY THE STABLE RELATIONSHIPS BETWEEN FINITE BEINGS, CONSIDERED IN THE LEGISLATING MIND.

297. The primal position of these beings, determined by divine wisdom, could not alter the laws that govern the universe; it simply regulates the verification of the laws. This primal position established the cases to which the laws of the universe would be applied, that is, the number of times, the place and the length of time when entia would affect each other in the way dictated by the law. If we imagine two clouds in the

sky charged with the two poles of electricity, and a conductor between them, we have the combination of three objects that is necessary for the law of electrical equilibrium to be visible. If there were no combination, the law would not have been true, and yet it would have been true even if it had never made itself visible.

298. Cosmic law therefore, in its application has conditions imposed on it by the combination of things.

From this we can see how little the sophists understand when they object to the efficacy of prayer. God does not alter the laws of the universe because of our prayers. To hear our prayers, he certainly does not need to change the laws but simply arrange their fulfilment in one way rather than in another. It is enough to have pre-arranged with wise foresight the combinations of things and hence the instances where the laws are applied and manifested. It is not a case of removing the law of equilibrium from electricity but of foreseeing the combination of the two clouds and the conductor, which reveals the law. The combination of the poles is prevented at the time of the primordial arrangement of things.

CHAPTER 20

Temporal miseries serve to dispose us for virtue and hence for supernatural happiness

299. But let us now consider the human excellence to which the noble title 'virtue' pertains in all its fullness. All the prominent and splendid external actions we see of virtue are its body not its spirit. The spirit, which is the form of virtue, lies in the sublime, totally pure end for which those actions are done. This end is located in the hidden depths of the human will where virtue has its seat. As I have said, virtue strives upwards from the earth to heaven, uniting the limited with the infinite. Indeed, in its present state, it is simply knowledge of the limitation proper to human nature, and the uniting of this nature with God. Christianity says that this uniting of the human being with God is pure grace that God gives to consenting human nature; nature itself does not go to God by its own movement but God comes to it. Because God loves nature first, it receives from him the power and duty to return that love. Such then is the nature of this virtue. God had loved human nature from the beginning, and human nature, inebriated with the perfection it had received, miscalculated the reasons for its need of God's love, because a need that is fully satisfied is not felt. But when human nature was deprived of God, it felt a strong need for him, or rather felt its own insufficiency among all the evils that originated with its insufficiency. And although God loved it again with a free, spontaneous movement, man could not now think what the loving help of his Creator was: sin is such a deadly evil that it opens a great wound deep in our nature, and in doing so also removes our very sense of the wound because it wounds and corrupts in us the precious instrument, so to speak, by which we know moral evils and our moral necessities. Hence the benign decree of human reparation was 1. all human beings had to experience physical evils so that they might have a continuous feeling of their insufficiency, and 2. a particular human being who was without fault and, as it were, absorbed by the divinity into a divine person, would

voluntarily subject himself to these evils and thus acquire an immense credit with divine justice. With this credit, guaranteed, as it were, by the endorsement of a divine bank, this particular human being could pay our debts and communicate back to us that union with God which he, as God-Man, possessed through nature. Once the debt of the human race had thus been satisfied, we could be rejoined to God, with a union like the first but much closer and more excellent. Perfect human nature placed no obstacle to its supernatural union with God, whereas sinful nature did. In the first state therefore, God could supply a less effective grace than in the second. Thus the greater our imperfection in the state of decadence, the more abundant the grace that comes to our aid.

300. How wonderful that the glory of divine grace shines forth so strongly in the infirmity of nature! Human virtue becomes more sublime, because through grace we have the power to be supernaturally virtuous.

The further we are from God therefore, the more virtue and effort we need to go to God. But as I have said, the experience of temporal miseries disposes us to such a step because we are not a pure intelligence; we are also endowed with organs. Consequently, it is solely by what our feeling experiences that we are fully persuaded of the extreme need we have of God.

301. This explains why virtuous people, when victims of temporal miseries, never complain about divine Providence. Their continual wish is to advance in self-knowledge and union with their God. This makes them unite their will with eternal wisdom that reveals its secrets to them and blesses their sufferings as something that, with the aid of feeling, helps to raise their minds to the efficacious acknowledgement of their own natural imperfection and hence of their need for their abandoned master. With humble joy, they see in their own imperfection the place where divine grace happily resides and its glory shines forth. They rejoice that God does much in them and that little is left for arrogant nature to do. Therefore they are happy to suffer and from their suffering draw an extraordinary sweetness that has no earthly quality. In their voluntary humiliation they are aware that they have received a new and unexpected greatness. They can joyfully tell themselves that they have conquered and, having become one with Christ, have

become lords of nature; if the whole universe were to collapse on them, it could only complete the triumph of their sacrifice. Here is something truly wonderful! The just groan under their sufferings but do not complain; on the contrary they rejoice greatly in a life hidden in their sufferings, and their joy increases in proportion to their justness. Those who complain about Providence are falsely just, and the more they complain that they are the victims of injustice, the less just they are. Nevertheless, this earthly justice generally has a prompt reward, as I said earlier, and obtains this reward for itself — if it does not obtain it, it is defective. But it is still not content: it grumbles about its very gifts, a crime for which alone temporal misfortunes do not sufficiently atone.

[301]

CHAPTER 21

The complaint brought against Providence by those who are not truly just justifies Providence. This shows that they are unhappy even when they are rich in earthly goods

302. The above-mentioned complaint is itself another justification of Providence.

If it is made by unjust people and if they quarrel with and complain about divine dispositions in proportion to their distance from perfect goodness, they clearly reveal a ceaseless disquiet of spirit and demonstrate that human goods, abandoned to prevailing desires, do not satisfy them.

303. Possession of human goods certainly differs from our enjoyment of them. We are much deceived if we think that human happiness should be dispensed according the distribution of external goods. What is the use of possessing a great quantity of goods if we cannot use them? What good does it do if goods, rather than giving us pleasure, disturb us by stimulating desires that cause many troubles and anxieties? If we wish to judge wisely, the simplest of meals enjoyed in peace and innocence, seasoned as it were with a good name and human kindness, is better than all the well-stocked tables of the rich who are torn by enmities, quarrels, suspicions, the curses of God and man, and comfortless remorse.

304. We must not therefore be concerned about goods themselves but about their use and effect. If we are concerned about the degree of satisfaction they bring us, all apparent irregularities will disappear because the level of satisfaction is always proportionate to true virtue.

CHAPTER 22

The truly just are content with temporal evils. This contentment does not reduce but rather increases their right to a heavenly reward

305. Nothing I have said so far weakens the argument which philosophers of a future life have put forward based on injustices carried out in this world. Hence they sometimes have sympathy for good people who are oppressed, and abominate wicked people who are exalted.

If the just find in their conscience such a sweet peace that they are not disturbed by temporal calamities, they owe this peace only to God and themselves. As a result, all their credit is continually available to the unjust who have rashly afflicted them. The latter therefore, to balance the account and because a most just God rules over all, must humble themselves before the just and make satisfaction for injury.

306. Moreover, the contentment that the just can draw interiorly from their sensible evils, is itself a merit demanding a reward. We see here the marvellous goodness and wisdom of the Most High: although he leaves us subject to temporal misfortunes, he teaches and strengthens us to be content with them, and to be so with a contentment that exceeds the evils and at the same time gives us further pleasure as compensation. God does in fact generously reward the pleasure, even the very intense pleasure, that comes from faith and hope in the promised compensation.

CHAPTER 23

Positive and natural penalties of evildoers. — God's goodness towards them

307. But we will leave the argument about internal joy, in which alone consists real happiness, a happiness that is not purely nominal or apparent. Instead, I will deal with the external distribution of evils. We have seen how vices that are harmful to society, are generally punished by society, and that vices against oneself are punished by illnesses. Only crimes against God seem less vindicated in this life because these are punished only when they harm us; in other words, vice has to be done. Among such offences against the Creator we must include certain faults that do not harm society except when frequently repeated. However, every time they are committed, they offend God's law and reverence for him. The following are the temporal punishments attached to these offences.

308. When they harm society, as I noted, the offended society seeks to vindicate itself. Here, we must note that people who infringe divine precepts already have a guilty and evilly-ordered spirit. Hence, they often suffer misfortunes. The faults that they commit against human beings incur the penalties that divine patience was postponing for them.

309. Secondly, we cannot fully calculate how much the human soul is debased and brutalised by fault and the knowledge of fault.

No matter what effort the soul that feels guilty may make to hold itself erect, no matter how often it struggles with its pride and its insane temerity, it is always prostrated by the blow it has received: wherever it goes, it carries with it a dark stain that humiliates it and stamps with its baseness and inexplicable weakness all its actions, all the enterprises it attempts and all its efforts to be important, which are more desperate than bold. This dark stain of guilty souls becomes darker as their faults increase in number. Vileness grows, and the spirit's energy diminishes; its very efforts exhaust it so that finally it suffers a total collapse and depression. The fault descends to its penalty through these stages of abjection. I believe that certain races, debased by the crimes of their ancestors, are thus insensibly reduced to a state of poverty from which it is very difficult to rise. Some souls, deprived of vitality and of all foresight and light, feel no stimulus whatsoever and are closed to all persuasion — perhaps savages originated in this way. Fear is the first offspring of crime, and also the pitiful dread that trembles at the slightest movement. The final state of such fear is a very disturbed spirit, the most shameful carnal behaviour, provocative theories, desperation and suicide.[90]

310. The extent to which society punishes offences against God depends on the depth of this degradation of soul and how important religion is acknowledged for the social good. We see in diverse times therefore the extent to which religious misdeeds are punished and virtues rewarded.

311. Clearly then, there are two parties offended by our vices, God and other human beings. The latter vindicate themselves in this life, but among all those who are offended, God is the best and most patient. He frequently gives temporal life space for repentance and emendation, even though in this life nothing we suffer would be sufficient to make amends for such offences. This gives greater validity to the argument for future life, drawn from the insufficiency of present justice.

[90] *Saggio sulla Speranza*, 1: 1.

CHAPTER 24

The question of the distribution of temporal goods and evils is completely solved when the supernatural order is taken into account

312. When God arranged beings and their movements, he established the distribution of evils and goods not so much in keeping with the sublime virtue that aspires to eternity, but more in accord with two other laws dictated to him by his supreme wisdom and goodness towards human beings.

These are precisely the laws with which the whole of this present work is principally concerned. They bring total peace to Christians; indeed they fill Christians with the tender acknowledgement and devout admiration of their Lord's greatness.

313. In the last analysis, only Christians are given knowledge of the whole great plan of Providence and contemplate it in its entirety, with no part hidden from them. Only they know where they stand in the universe and all the links that bind human beings to the created things around them and to the eternal Creator who fills all things with himself. On the other hand, non-believers, who lack the highest truths about their nature, do not know where they are, do not know the relationships that bind them to beings different from themselves. Like mindless animals, they vegetate without reason in the midst of a splendid universe, which solely for them is dark and inexplicable, just as they themselves remain inexplicable.

314. The philosophers who resemble unbelievers are those who are keen to draw knowledge from themselves and begin by cutting themselves off from even the possibility of thinking, when they impose on themselves the foolish law that God and revealed teachings must be excluded from all arguments. In this way they render themselves incapable of applying their minds to divine decisions, and instead make a pact with their own pride to exclude wisdom. Anyone who reasons with them is forced to use a dry, disconnected kind of discourse because with their mole-like eyes that narrow in the presence of light, they cannot explain the totally visible magnitude of the most

provident order of the world. They worship their own reason as much as they hate the truth, and precisely due to this they place senseless limits on reason itself. They bind it with arbitrary bonds so that it cannot range over a rich, spacious territory that is not theirs but belongs to a liberal master, and rather than depend on him they choose to perish in their destitution. Alternatively, they totally discredit and curse anyone who does not accept their argument, which generates nothing but darkness. Hence, in so far as their strength permits, they enter the fearful road of nothingness which has no welcome for all that God's word has created.

Up to this point my discussion of Providence relative to the distribution of goods and evils has done no more than sample, as it were, the subject. I was restricted to this lighter treatment because I needed to speak about natural virtue, that is, argue more according to the few, basic concepts of human philosophy than according to the fullness of Christian wisdom. Now, however, I can go more deeply into the subject and discuss supernatural virtue, in that I am talking to Christians, to people who are not children relative to the truth but have become adults and are strengthened by the hidden things concerning divine and human nature as revealed by revelation.

Indeed, in the present state of sinful humanity what is needed and is important is solely what relates to supernatural virtue. Born as we are in sin, there can be no salvation without faith in the Redeemer, and this faith, this sole principle of salvation, is simply a supernatural relationship we enjoy. Everything in our present state therefore that leads us back to moral perfection and happiness is supernatural; all that is truly important for us, all that contains salutary instruction and not hypothetical speculation begins and ends in this supernatural relationship.

[314]

CHAPTER 25

The first law of the distribution of temporal goods and evils: they all serve the perfection of the Church of Jesus Christ

315. Returning therefore to the laws by which divine Providence governs temporal goods and evils relative to supernatural virtue, the first law is:

God, in his plan, permitted our downfall so that he could draw from it a virtue and happiness that we could enjoy and was greater than the first. This virtue is the virtue of Christ, which is a love that binds the sinful creature with the God who has been provoked.

316. This virtue and consequent happiness had to be brought down to earth and, on earth, had to triumph over everything. This could not happen unless supreme Providence gave perpetual existence to the society of human beings who possessed this virtue. But the society of human beings needs external goods in order to live on earth. Therefore external goods had to be assured for it. Furthermore, it had to triumph and increase, cultivating this particular virtue. Finally, it had to call to itself every human being; all temporal goods had to serve it and draw all things to it. This is precisely the history of the Church of JESUS Christ and is the first law. According to this law God distributed and ordered all temporal goods at the beginning. In his sublime mind, he did not assign them to particular individuals who were just, but to the whole society of his just. Nor did he assign all goods in an instant but through the course of ages, and not as a reward for his just but as a means of their subsistence, multiplication and triumph over human greed.

The first law therefore according to which God distributed goods and evils is:

> EVERYTHING SHALL SERVE THE PRESERVATION, INCREASE AND SANCTIFICATION OF THE CHURCH.

317. The prevalence of virtue over vice was not sufficient for

this end. I mean the prevalence by which virtue and justice have a majority of favourable votes in the world.

This is true if we are talking about human virtue, where human interests and cupidity are involved; and whenever a certain equity is exercised towards general cupidity, particular cupidity is helped. Christian virtue however is something quite different. It consists in not basing one's hopes on nature alone but solely on God. It strikes deep into carnal hearts, confounding their arrogance, which it shows up as false and nothing. It clearly reveals the shameful insufficiency of all the affections, passions, plans and provisions of those who have separated themselves from their God and presume they are capable of giving themselves greatness and happiness. The anger therefore of all this human nature is aroused against such great and unexpected light, and when this light with all its strength forces nature to look at itself, the anger rages against the light. The result is the incitement and instigation of all the wrongs done to Christian virtue, of all the hatred and torment of so many pious people, of the continual persecutions of the Church.

Nature by itself knows nothing about greatness, beauty and the sublime; it knows only what is in itself. And those who follow this one norm must inevitably despise all those they see who set little value on bare gifts of nature. They must despise Christians who take little account of such gifts, because Christians know goods that are incredibly greater, and they are also totally helped by God and are full of God. Equipped with this great gift, they clearly understand the little value and short duration of all natural good. As a result, they have no interest whatsoever nor desire to deceive themselves in calculating this little value.

CHAPTER 26

Three divine decrees concerning the execution of the first law of the distribution of goods and evils relative to natural virtue

318. This struggle between Christian piety and all that is famous in the world is a truth of observation apparent at all times and in all places.

According to the world's values, there is nothing more ignoble, weak and stupid than such piety. But God has decreed that this supposed ignobility, weakness and stupidity should triumph in the struggle, and that the invisible grace that is in the human being should triumph over all visible nature, and triumph finally with great splendour and, as it were, in all magnificence.

319. To do this God expressed this fundamental law at the very beginning in three sublime decrees. The first was:

> ALL THOSE WHO OPPOSE GOD'S JUST PEOPLE CAN START PROSPEROUSLY BUT NOT END PROSPEROUSLY.

A look at history shows that all earthly kingdoms rise, flourish and collapse. In their midst, we see God's Church in its humility always the same, outliving all mortal kingships. From its very first appearance in the most despised and contemptible nation, and guided by a few poor fishermen, who were disciples of a condemned man, it declared that it must fill the earth. But nobody ridiculed its great promises; everyone took them seriously. Princes mobilised, and those who ruled the whole earth applied their great power to annihilate the Church. The struggle (or more accurately, the butchery) lasted three centuries, and in every region innocent blood was spilt. But when the struggle ended, we see who the victors were. The emperors, finally exhausted by the massacre of just people who offered no defence but allowed themselves to be torn apart like lambs by wolves, were punished one by one, the majority of them struck down by God's anger. The Church won a victory in its mission every time it was laid low. Bearing these trophies, she continued to make progress, even to reaching the royal palace where she received the Emperor of the universe as a son; in her mercy, she embraced the descendant of tyrants. They were able to begin but not finish. The harsh tests however did not cease, because they must never cease, yet the outcome of all her diverse battles is the same as the first. It does not matter whether she is attacked by cruel power or by the sophisms and cunning of a dominant philosophy, or by the pernicious evil of heretics, or the barbarisms of the times, or by the immoral behaviour of her own children, or the hypocrisy of her intractable ministers, or indeed by all these things put together. She is certainly afflicted and distressed, and concerned more for her children than for herself. All her enemies always proclaim triumph in the face of her groanings, and boast their victory throughout the world. Nevertheless, the suffering Church still lives, still resists with her faith, meekness, unconquered patience and prayers; she still offers her blood. But this beautiful spouse of Christ need not weep: a calm look around shows that her enemies no longer exist, they have passed like shadows of the night, they are under the earth; their memory has gone or is abhorred. But the Church exists and lives, and the universe applauds her triumph.

320. This observation of history supposes that from the beginning God had so disposed human goods that his Church did not lack anything it needed. If we examine the events with their causes we find that they are for the most part natural, for the reason I explained earlier, that is, God willed all things to be connected together as cause and effect. But the fact that these events follow one after the other, from the first disposition of beings until the final events, is no less willed and ordered by God; indeed, the events demonstrate far better his supreme wisdom displayed in that first distribution ordained to favour the good.

It is therefore reasonable that in the permutations of human things we continually admire and adore the great wisdom, the ineffable goodness and actual divine will. We also know that there is nothing more foolish than to oppose the natural chain of events in order to avoid adoring God's will in all things, because the whole concatenation of events is his will.

321. The second decree that God enunciated to execute the first law is:

THE VIRTUE OF THE JUST SHALL CONQUER MORE COMPLETELY THROUGH THEIR TEMPORAL OPPRESSION.

322. I have said that human beings, left to themselves, dispute and compete among themselves for possession of human goods, which are divided according to the strength and valour of the combatants. This is *natural law* corresponding to natural virtue, and goods are divided according to it.

But a new kind of virtue, supernatural virtue, was brought into the world by Jesus Christ. This virtue was directed to our acquisition of an eternal, not a temporal good, provided we did not entrust and abandon ourselves to nature's force but solely to the power of grace. A new law therefore entered the world to direct the division of temporal goods and evils. It stated that contempt for temporal goods, or better, total lack of trust in them, resulted in possession of these very goods.

323. We should not be surprised therefore if Christian nations always stand out, even in human greatness, among the other nations of the world simply because they have greater contempt for human goods.

The Church, totally humble and poor in its spirit, will be continually enriched. The priesthood will become richer in the measure that its ministers sincerely love poverty and are outstanding with their generosity in the holy use of their riches. This is the amazing but inevitable course followed by things: poverty was chosen as an educator and teacher of Christians. It is, I would say, their first virtue; they are strongly enjoined not to be solicitous about anything. Only God thinks of them; indeed, God had thought of them from the beginning of all things. Their superior wisdom enthusiastically embraces God's plans, to which their wisdom tranquilly abandons itself, expecting everything from God, because it desires his, not human, triumph. It is this complete and humble poverty of spirit that must prepare and grant to Christians those goods for which they have no affection whatsoever. But the society of Christians, after teaching the world detachment from these goods by the example of its faithful people leading a poor and hard life, is also charged with teaching the world how to use the goods well. It must therefore practise and demonstrate successively in itself all the virtues involved in the administration of human things.

While directing all things externally, it must keep its spirit at a distance from them, as it did when it first received them. The Christian society, made rich and powerful by God, not by human beings, and putting its trust in him alone, must in the course of the centuries witness to what its divine author said: *OMNIA TRAHAM AD ME IPSUM*, I will draw all things to myself, I will draw them to the nakedness of the cross.

324. Finally, the execution of the first law could not be complete without the following decree, again made by God:

> THE JUST SHALL HAVE, IN COMMON WITH CHRIST, VICTORY AND DOMINION OVER ALL THINGS.

Because Christian virtue is distinguished by detachment from natural things, produces victory over them and guides our external possession of them, Christians continually rejoice in their hearts over external sufferings; through these sufferings they intimately feel their immense superiority over all the forces of nature, and hence regard suffering as a happy event, not simply for their salvation, but also for the salvation of their fellow humans. If some of them, justified in Christ, suffer more than their faults require, they are compensated by God; they have a kind of excess credit with God and, after being redeemed, this excess makes them redeemers of others. They also participate in everything possessed by the author of grace, even in the work of redemption. Hence there must be great joy in the awareness of this sublime participation, a joy that at every instant returns upon itself, as it were, and in this continual return, incessantly renews and multiplies itself. It is true that it is hidden from the world, but it is all the more precious for that. The profane should keep their distance: it is the ineffable secret of the saints!

CHAPTER 27

The second law of the distribution of temporal goods and evils: the distribution tends to prepare people for the Gospel

325. But society, as the custodian on earth of perfect virtue, could not subsist in an uninterrupted succession until the end, unless God, at the beginning of things when he determined the distribution of goods, took into account the weakness and infirmity of the nature in which he was resolved to insert his grace. He did not need to destroy the elements of that nature, but simply perfect it. This had to be done sweetly, through those laws of his grace I discussed above. These laws manifest in the redemption of souls the same wisdom as in the creation of the material universe, which proceeds harmoniously and is preserved through uniform and regular operations.

Hence, the second fundamental law followed by divine Providence in the distribution of goods and evils is:

> TEMPORAL GOODS AND EVILS SHALL BE SO DISPENSED ON EARTH THAT THEY EDUCATE GOD'S PEOPLE TO SUBLIME VIRTUE.

Divine grace, in its distribution, definitely follows certain laws enacted by God, laws that for the most part are hidden from us. Man had to be directed to that total supernatural virtue that lies in the victory of the spirit over the whole of rebellious nature. This could happen only by degrees, in keeping with the development of human nature into which grace is inserted, a development brought about mostly through the action of temporal goods and evils on us.

CHAPTER 28

Three divine decrees concerning the execution of the second law of the distribution of temporal goods and evils relative to natural virtue

326. For the execution of this second law God made another three admirable decrees, the first of which is:

> TRUE BELIEVERS SHALL ENJOY PROSPERITY OF FAMILY OR NATION WHEN, THROUGH LACK OF INTELLECTUAL DEVELOPMENT, THEY CANNOT SUFFICIENTLY CONCEIVE A HAPPINESS TOTALLY SEPARATE FROM SENSIBLE THINGS AND, IF NECESSARY, WILL BE HELPED BY MIRACLES, SO THAT THEY MAY BE ASSURED THAT THERE IS A GOD WHO REWARDS VIRTUE.

327. This decree fulfils two purposes: 1. the preservation and uninterrupted continuity throughout time of the society of the just, and 2. the help given to the weakness and imperfection of any just individuals.

328. In the case of the society of the just, this decree was in force up to the time of Jesus Christ, who purified this society with his blood and made it totally spiritual. After Jesus Christ, it is applied only in keeping with the good pleasure of divine mercy, for the sake of just individuals who need it.

329. Why this comfort was much more necessary to people of good will before Christ than at the present time can be explained briefly. The key that unlocks everything wicked in the history of the development of human nature, of its needs and of its errors, is the law governing the development of the faculty of abstraction. Man who in the beginning was, as it were, one whole thing to himself, was, with the passage time, divided into many things. At the beginning he could not, with his judgments, divide anything into parts; the further back we go, human judgments become more and more simple and one. Even a little observation shows that *the source of ancient errors is lack of distinctions, and the source of modern errors is the excess of distinctions*. Hence, at the start, man could not abstract from sensible things, or think solely of spiritual things. The individual, it seems, was bound to the family, and when nations

began, we see a particular unity in them, very similar to family unity.

330. This unity and, as it were, compaction of thoughts and feelings that man had at that first time must be carefully understood. We need to be aware of this indivisibility with which primal man perceived both himself and the world, and also this incapacity for considering things in only one individual respect. Indeed he had to consider things in their totality, just as they were and presented themselves to him; he did not detach and separately consider special qualities or relationships. It is important that all this be noted because the fact alone allows us to form a true, adequate concept of that first state of human beings, from which the human race has become ever more distant and pursues its course of development. We must value this concept because without it we would never know man. This human being cannot be known by considering him solely as he presents himself to us in some individual, or in a small society or even in civil society and in the whole human race. Humanity is very varied and multiple in its aspects, aptitudes and forms, which through the course of centuries are successively manifested and unfolded. Nevertheless, it always has within it new and deeply hidden seeds that cannot be observed and recognised until they have germinated and presented themselves in their time to our observation and analysis.

Just as a seed is not seen if it does not put out a root or shoot, so vice versa, when we examine a tiny branch of the wonderful plant that humanity is, we forget to go backwards to its first root, to its seed and thus we fail to conceive the state from which it first began its development. As I said, we truly need to know this state if we want full information about all the conditions and modifications that this varied, multiple and reasoning animal takes on.

The origin of so many futile and totally inapplicable theories about the education and government of humanity must surely be a partial and inadequate knowledge of humanity? If we study the human race solely in the individual, the individual provides us with only a few observable facts. We note what human beings are like at the present time, and we believe that they have always been and will always be like this. But if we look back we see them in many states so diverse from our present state that we do not even suspect their existence, nor have any idea of them, nor even conceive their possibility. Similarly, because they are subject to continual movement, they will take on other new states as they progress; they will seem to be almost another nature different from our present nature. I grant that if we wanted to conceive useful institutions, it would be enough to know the present state of the human race, but how can we know this state fully if we do not continually compare it with past states? Only comparison lets us see the properties of things and we take note of only the differences.

331. Moreover, what is the origin of so many false judgments about antiquity? Where do we get this incredible audacity to condemn everything, to judge everything our ancestors did as shameful and culpable? Why do we desire to see in them extreme ignorance and foolishness so that we can see in ourselves supreme wisdom, to see in them the model of improbity so that we can show off our own virtue and uprightness, all of which in turn will not be readily believed by posterity? What truly is the origin of this disordered pleasure in finding that a short time ago the human race lacked even the most elementary good sense, that it was a mindless race linked to the race of monkeys? The answer must be a proud presumption which neglects to study the human race that it judges so partially, and forgets to study the diverse states and modifications of this race, while it excludes goodness or the depravity of morals and institutions which are also relative to the state of the human race. I am firmly convinced that man cannot be known if the study is based on present society alone and not on complete facts. The most varied, extensive and original facts must be gathered; opinion must be founded on a faithful and unbiased investigation of the very varied conditions of humanity at different times, particularly the primal condition from which its first development began, and the laws of its first steps. Such a broad base of observations is necessary for the study of human nature; only with the union of these facts will we know what is more fitting to it. In this sense the whole of the human race, not the individual, is the witness of truth, as a learned man recently said.

332. In fact the various states of the human race provide the *materials* for our most important judgments, and no one can be more aware of these than the human race itself, which is subject

to them. The only thing anyone can testify to is what is seen. To use the wise words of the learned man I have referred to, we must not confuse the power to produce something with the faculty to perceive something.[91] We ourselves certainly do not create truth; we do not generate it in our mind, form it of our own substance and then give birth to it. We can only receive it, not produce it; we are limited to the presence of the objects of our thought (cf. 85–87). These are presented to us by some invisible force; we see them and pronounce them, we divide and unite them. Our reason can do no more than this; our strength goes no further. It is foolish to try to cross this limit and produce something true for ourselves; it is like the attempt to claim that by chemical action we can increase the elementary particles of matter created by God. The reason is that we know only what we experience with our senses or learn from others through speech. How then could man at the beginning separate what pertained to the spirit from what pertained to the body, what pertained to the individual from what pertained to the family, what pertained to the family from what pertained to the nation, and what pertained to the nation from what pertained to the whole of the human race? He could not do this through his own arbitrary movement but only through diverse occasions that were presented to him and enabled him to make these distinctions and separations. It is true that God, after giving him some words (cf. 99–115), had guided his mind to apply a sign to the first abstractions. But these few, principal abstractions were

[91] 'We do not stray because we glory in our reason but because we misunderstand our nature by attributing to ourselves what is not ours. *In our pride, we confuse the capacity for knowledge with the power to produce*. We forget that our intelligence, which in the beginning is purely passive, is born and develops by the help of truths given to us; we possess only what we have received. Endowed with the power to combine primal truths and draw consequences from them, a power that is limited like all the actions of a finite being, we search in ourselves for the certitude or ultimate reason of things and because we do not find it there, we begin to doubt. The truths withdraw, darkness comes. In the midst of this darkness, we cease to recognise ourselves. Alone and proud of our solitude, we try to create; we awaken obscure memories and believe we are peopling our empty understanding with real beings, because we evoke ghosts. But we are soon disillusioned and, exhausted by this vain labour, we close our eyes and sleep in eternal darkness'* (De Lamennais, *Essai sur l'Indifférence*, etc., c. 19).

[332]

insufficient because the faculty of abstraction had to be applied to the whole of life and to the judgments that needed to be made daily about things. From the beginning man knew that an immortal spirit existed in his mortal flesh, but he could not apply this first abstraction to all his judgments about the meaning of things nor draw from his judgments all their consequences. To do this, he needed the experience of goods and evils to lead him to the conception of a good that existed solely in the spirit, and of a happiness that contained nothing materially sensible. This separated him from everything bound to him most intimately by ties of nature, love and habit; it concentrated him on himself, a state he had not yet experienced or begun to experience. In short, he could conceive only a happiness of his total self as he was, endowed with body and spirit, but not a purely spiritual happiness.

332a. We must say the same about virtue. Virtue shows itself in actions, but man had to pursue a long series of reflections and experiences before he formed a very clear idea of the intimate essence of virtue, that is, of a totally spiritual virtue that consisted solely in the entirely free act of an intelligent will acting in conformity with the universal order of being. He certainly knew what virtue and vice were, but contemplated these within actions, without actually distinguishing the external and material part, as it were, of the actions from what was the pure form of virtue and vice. Before he reached this high level of reflection, he needed to see the actions of virtue separate from internal virtue, to see human beings simulating virtue, or alternatively find some actions similar to virtuous actions, produced by simple instinct, as in animals, which he saw he could not praise as virtue or condemn as vice. He also had to experience the situation where a person with the purest and most sublime intentions was prevented from externally realising them. There were many similar cases where actions that were nevertheless virtuous came under his observation but lacked what gives them the title of virtuous; there was also the opportunity to note many virtuous intentions that lacked their external effect. All these observations led his mind to distinguish them and abstract the purely moral element.

333. But man not only had a spirit, the seat of virtue and happiness, and a body that shared in these two qualities, he also

lived in a family, with a spouse and children, whose love made one sole thing with him, which, we could almost say, was more complete than the union that nature could achieve between his own flesh and spirit. Once again he had to learn to mentally separate the happiness and virtue of his totally naked and sole spirit from the happiness and virtue that extended into those that were his cherished parts, into that quasi extension of himself. To do this he needed a new experience, new occasions for abstraction, new situations where the things he was accustomed to seeing as united were presented to his mind as separate. He had to see other human beings who, although endowed with all the goods of family-society, were nevertheless anxious and troubled, but he also had to see others who despite the misfortunes of their house, like Job, found within themselves such an invincible strength of spirit that they were able to bear all the weight of their misfortunes. Only then did man have the occasion to see family goods separate from happiness of spirit; he could now divide the latter from the former and thus finally know that external goods are simply something extra and that family is not essential to happiness but something into which essential happiness spreads and diffuses itself.

However an increase of family means an increase of relationships, and at the same time of human ties. Man acquires a more extensive existence, a national existence. New abstraction now becomes necessary. Just as he first had to distinguish the spirit (the seat of virtue and happiness) from the body that shares in it, and then subsequently distinguish it from the family through which virtue and happiness spread, so he had finally to distinguish essential and total happiness and virtue of spirit from national happiness and virtue, which is purely an application and extension of the former. With the nation man acquires around himself a much wider sphere of activity. Because it is his understanding that unites this whole sphere of things to himself and makes it a quasi-part of himself, he must also know that this new extension is not necessary for his complete happiness and that, although he certainly diffuses all he possesses of morality and happiness into this extension, he does so like the sun, as it were, that fills all the surrounding sphere with its light but this illuminated sphere does not become the sun. But he cannot understand this without new abstractions, which in turn he

[333]

cannot make without new experiences. He must therefore see national prosperity possessed by unhappy people, and happy people who have no prosperity. Having seen this, he comes to understand clearly how these things differ, and that what belongs to the nation differs from what belongs to pure truth, pure virtue and pure happiness, just as the modifications of human nature differ from what is the common and general foundation of that nature.

334. Clearly then, no one can arrive instantaneously at all these abstractions. We are forced make them one after the other and with repeated attempts: in fact, one abstraction presupposes the one before it, so that we must proceed step by step according to an immutable law of human understanding. On the other hand, if we bypassed and omitted just one of these abstractions, we would have no verification whatsoever of any virtue and happiness within us; our idea of virtue and happiness would still be somewhat muddled and, as it were, confused with sensible goods and evils, mixed up with things foreign to their essence. As a result we would not have obtained the perfect knowledge and spiritual love of virtue alone nor know the best direction our spirit should take for immutable happiness.

335. But many centuries had to pass before we could have the necessary time for pursuing step by step a series of abstractions, and have the occasions to see these things actually separated and divided from each other so that we could make the necessary comparisons between them and note their differences. Centuries had to pass before we could finally become familiar with these separations and apply the abstractions to each and every case. The same amount of time was also required for our spirit to prepare itself for such tests and trials. It is certain that not only the development of our understanding but the preparation of our spirit requires a long time. Our spirit had to grow gradually stronger in virtue and, as a result of the abstractions carried out by our intellect and continually purified, had to ennoble its love, making it intense and in control of external sensations.

336. The human spirit follows the path of reason, and love follows upon knowledge. As long as humanity did not have pure knowledge of virtue, it could not have a love whose object was purely virtue. But even when the intellect has come to

know the lovable thing, time is often needed for love to be aroused and become intense.

Love also requires a decree, and even when the will has decreed love for the thing known by the intellect, love has not yet arrived at its perfection. Again it needs time to grow in intensity; its warmth grows gradually, and when it is as it were internally enkindled, it blazes up and burns brightly. In the same way, the love whose object is virtue and happiness that have been stripped and purified of all the foreign trappings surrounding them, begins only when the purest knowledge of virtue and happiness has begun in the understanding. This knowledge also requires much time for its formation. After this, love does not begin again unless it is preceded by the will, but the power of the will is not exempt from the law of time: it must make repeated and long acts to give that most pure love sufficient strength to rise above the allurements of all sensible things. This at least is the ordinary course followed by love in humanity if not in each individual. Clearly therefore, a great deal of time was required for love to follow such a long course and finally reach perfection. But that is not all. We must ask: can we human beings with our extremely weak and infirm moral nature attain such a great height of most perfect virtue and such a love for it that perfect virtue is more valuable to us than the attraction of all sensible things?

337. This could never be accomplished with our sluggish nature. Virtue, as a pure abstraction, is too feeble and vague when obtained by the mind's natural energy. Also, our heart would never be satisfied by being permanently united to such a weak phantasm; it would find more satisfaction in the things we see and touch. Only the grace of the Saviour was capable of adding solidity and reality to the abstract idea of virtue, revealing God himself; only the grace of the God-man was able to reinforce the power of the will and enkindle an immeasurable love in the ice-cold human heart.

But because this operation of grace accompanied and seconded the operation of nature, it followed the law of time by which nature operates. Its course is the following.

338. Grace first helped us to remove all sensible things from the idea of virtue. Human intelligence had to make this purification by means of the successive observations and experiences I

have described, and for these a good period of time was necessary. Because we had this purified idea, grace could make it effective, could divinise it (the second step). In fact, the human heart began to feel the force of virtue when it began to see the beauty of the divine reality that was joined to virtue, and began intensely to enjoy its pleasure. The third step was the human heart's capability of a sublime love: grace could move our heart to fix itself on this, and the will, moved and maintained by grace in its constant act, could produce the infinite, most pure and invincible love I am speaking about.

339. All this explains God's infinite goodness. Knowing fully the human nature he had created, he did not force us from the beginning to carry out the most difficult operation of abstracting perfectly from human goods, particularly from fatherhood and nationality. Indeed, a sudden movement like this was contrary to the laws of our mixed nature. God acted like the wise farmer,

> And while the vine in its first age
> Matures with fresh leaves,
> Tender shoots must be spared.
> And as the vine-branch reaches joyfully out
> To the gentle breeze,
> And, freed from its bonds,
> Directs itself towards the heavens,
> No sharp pruning-hook must be applied.*[92]

340. But in acting like this, God certainly did not deprive us of the exercise of virtue; he did not deprive us of religion, happiness and union with himself. On the contrary, his divine wisdom found a way to unite human goods with the sublime cult of sacrifice, and to make all these goods wonderfully serve this cult alone.

341. It is also true that he could not have done this without a great many prodigies. If at that time we had seen our virtue rewarded by solely natural means, we could not have raised ourselves high enough to determine continually for ourselves the mind of a God who ordered things from the beginning, because we no longer had any means of mentally separating the

[92] Georg. 2: 362–365.

forces of nature from the one who directed and sustained them. It was therefore necessary that also here our faculty of abstraction was helped by external objects in which we saw things divided. In this way we could learn to distinguish them whenever they presented themselves in an intermingled and confused state. On the one hand we needed to see nature's operation, and on the other to see God's operation in the prodigies that suspended nature's laws. Without this, we could not fully distinguish nature from God, and later, not distinguish what nature did through its own forces and what the mind carried out in nature; in short, we could not distinguish the *physical forces* nor *how they were directed* by a wise distribution of all entia from the very beginning of the universe. Virtue and vice were therefore accompanied by sensible and often miraculous gifts and punishments in life, so that sensible goods and evils might be used like signs and words to teach our human sensitivity the value of virtue and contempt for vice, and at the same time, we might not attribute anything to ourselves, or to some unknown cause in nature, but only to the God who surrounded us with portents.

342. Thus the Lord very early on identified the cult of himself with the vicissitudes of a family, thus making the cult *familial*. This form of religion was maintained in the house of the Patriarchs until the descendants of that house were mature.

God next made his cult *national*, that is, he identified it admirably with all the interests and vicissitudes of the chosen nation.

But when human beings were eventually able to separate not only the interests of the family from the interests of the nation, but the interests of the nation from those of humanity and religion, the human race was perfect. It was now the fullness of time. JESUS Christ appeared on earth and proclaimed a religion separated and abstracted from all earthly interests, both small and great, and from everything to do with corporeal nature. This religion therefore rules over itself; it is thus pure from flesh and blood, just as God is pure.

343. As a result, all people had to be educated by Providence to this religion. To accomplish this end, Providence used caresses and shocks, that is, corporal goods and evils distributed

according to his wisdom. In this distribution we note a second decree:

> THE SENSIBLE GOODS GIVEN TO THE HUMAN RACE IN ITS INSUFFICIENTLY DEVELOPED STATE AS A REWARD FOR ITS FAITH AND OBEDIENCE SHALL BE DIRECTED TO STRENGTHENING HUMAN BEINGS IN THEIR SUBMISSION OF SPIRIT TO ALL THAT GOD MAKES KNOWN TO THEM AND THAT THEY ARE UNABLE TO KNOW. THEY ARE THEREFORE DISPOSED TO EMBRACE IMPLICITLY THE PURE VIRTUE OF THE REDEEMER, AND BY MEANS OF THIS DISPOSITION ALL SENSIBLE GOODS SHALL BE DIRECTED TO THEIR SALVATION.

344. As in the case of the Hebrew people, God truly regulates temporal goods and evils according to our human weakness and according to our greater or lesser materiality. However he always directs the goods and evils to teaching us spiritually and leading us to that sublime virtue which is destined to conquer all things. Because we cannot reach the peak of such great virtue all at once, grace is given us by degrees, in the way that nature develops in us by degrees. God does not want us to think that our nature is sufficient; on the contrary he wants us to acknowledge our need of supreme help. This approach to God comes from the faith that raises us up to him; indeed, if God had not spoken to us we would have had no means of attaining him. Hence, *grace* is given according to the degree of faith, and the degree of faith depends on the degree of *revealed truth*, that is, grace depends on revelation. The old grace therefore was basically the wait for the Messiah and the acceptance of everything he would teach, while the new grace opens up into an explicit faith in all he taught, and embraces the wait for the fulfilment of his infallible promises. The ancients were disposed, through a certain implicit faith, to receive the sublime spirituality that the Messiah would later proclaim and we understand, but they, with the exception of a very few holy people, did not yet understand.

345. Such then is the ingenuity of divine goodness. It condescends, so to speak, to help all levels of human nature and all the different states of this nature. Two conditions were necessary for accomplishing man's salvation after the sin of the first father. First: salvation had to be obtained by means of such a pure virtue of man that this virtue consisted in a total sacrifice of his

corrupt substance, and that all earthly goods were offered by him as satisfaction for offended justice. Second: it was necessary that this most pure justice, totally independent of anything on earth, totally spiritual and totally alone, formed the sole end of man's acts and that he was in fact able to make this justice the aim of his actions, the ultimate term of his desires. But how could he take as aim something he could not even know? This certainly did not mean that the human race born during the time that its intellectual powers were not yet sufficiently developed to attain to such sublime abstractions would perish. God found a way to save everyone in whatever state they might be and at all times, and always by humbling all human nature; in other words, he found a way to satisfy the above-mentioned conditions of human salvation. When humanity was finally able to abstract pure virtue, God saved it by teaching it to sacrifice its nature to him, as in fact the disciples of the Crucified do. But at the time when humanity was still incapable of using its intelligence to raise itself to such heights, God saved it by giving it a docile spirit ready to do all that he might say and command. Hence, without fully understanding the matter, humanity was now disposed to the mystic sacrifice, horrendous to nature, which the divine exemplar had to consummate on the cross in the sight of all. This was the state of those ancient, just people who languished in the expectation and desire of the Redeemer.

346. Finally, divine wisdom made a third decree for the execution of the second law:

> MAN, IN HIS INSUFFICIENTLY DEVELOPED STATE, SHALL BE MENTALLY HELPED TO SEPARATE NATURAL GOODS FROM SUPERNATURAL GOODS BY MEANS OF TRIBULATIONS APPORTIONED IN KEEPING WITH HIS CAPACITY AND WITH GRACE.

According to the words of Scripture, God uses afflictions to test, prove and purify his saints. They see and bless God's just intervention in the world and also see their virtue accompanied by temporal calamities. Hence, applying their ever-present faith, they conclude that beyond this world there must be a far more excellent happiness in the divine treasures with which the Almighty rewards virtue, and the Almighty fully guarantees this with his word. Consequently, the idea of true happiness is purified ever more in their minds. While they experience the fragility of human, natural things, God gives them a taste of the spiritual consolations with which their hearts are filled and which makes them aware of their happiness, of their strength and of the heavenly balm that the consoler-spirit diffuses in their souls. They therefore dedicate themselves sincerely to detaching themselves from all mortal things, gradually caring nothing for them and finally despising them. In this way they embrace their Saviour's naked cross as a unique and priceless treasure.

347. All this clearly demonstrates how the distribution of temporal goods and evils on the earth is not the same for everyone, nor does it follow the same law. To those who are perfect, God applies the first law. For the imperfect (and many nations are still in this state, nations that are being prepared for the call to faith), he uses the second law. But in the case of those who trust in their own nature he leaves them to the laws of nature, and in the case of all who war against his kingdom he fights and defeats them.

BOOK THREE

ὑπὲρ-φυσικὸς [supernatural]

THE LAW OF THE LEAST MEANS APPLIED TO THE GOVERNMENT OF DIVINE PROVIDENCE

> I, *wisdom*... was present, when he prepared the heavens, I was present: when with a certain law, and compass, he enclosed the depths: when he established the sky above, and poised the fountains of waters: when he compassed the sea with its bounds, and set a law to the waters that they should not pass their limits: when he balanced the foundations of the earth; *I was with him forming all things*: and was delighted every day, playing before him at all times; playing in the world: *and my delights were to be with the children of men*†*
>
> Prov 8: 12, 27–31

CHAPTER 1

Recapitulation of the two previous books

348. Because many years have passed since I wrote the two previous books, I must briefly summarise the argument I have followed so far.

In books one and two, I justified divine Providence in two different ways. In the first, I used *negative arguments* to show that every censure human beings presume to make against the sublime Providence of the Creator and ruler of the world is totally vain because presumptuous; no matter how incisive the human mind may be, it is inferior to the tremendous task of passing judgment on the government of the world and on the supreme Lord's apportioning of good things and bad things. In the second, I presented *positive arguments* to prove that the existence of evil on earth does not detract from the divine attributes, and that the distribution of evil things and good things (as we see it in reality) does not contradict the holiness, justice and goodness of the Creator. On the contrary, whenever the natural light of reason aids and strengthens the teaching of divine revelation, the divine attributes shine forth with new and brilliant light.

349. In regard to divine *holiness* and *justice*, it seems to me that after what has been said we can have no reasonable doubt about these two attributes, nor should anyone who has understood them have any hesitation about them. God's holiness is immune from defect if we understand that there is no evil in divine nature, that is, not the evil that is ultimately a defective operation in created ens. Evil is a defect that is so much part of finite nature that we cannot conceive this nature as not subject to evil, whereas infinite ens cannot be conceived subject to any defect. Hence, Almighty God, who is infinite, excludes all evil from himself and is therefore essentially holy and perfect. And because it is absurd that an infinite thing be created, and also absurd that any created, finite thing be exempt from the possibility of evil, which follows necessarily from the thing's limitation, God could not draw from nothingness an ens that was not subject to evil; he cannot do the absurd.

Similarly, we see that *divine justice* is free from reproach relative to the permission and distribution of evils. We need only consider that created natures are themselves the cause of evils, and that good and evil is done principally by free natures. Just as justice requires us to let each person have what is theirs, so injustice consists in depriving them of what is theirs. Hence, when we allow finite entia to act according to their nature, and even more according to their free will, we are not depriving them of what is due to them; on the contrary we let them have what is theirs. Because finite natures are, as a result of their limitation, causes of evils, they are causes of the distribution of evils; indeed, the way that evils are produced determines the way they are naturally distributed.

350. In the case of divine goodness however I used more extensive arguments to corroborate it. But more than that: it is such a beautiful and rich cause to justify that I cannot be satisfied with what has been said; its fruitful and splendid nature has motivated me to add this third book so that it may fully triumph in minds and spirits. Nevertheless I still believe that the argument already put forward would by itself be sufficient to convince minds that everything done in the universe is a sign and proof of the Creator's supreme goodness.

However, the human spirit's conviction could waver when the intellect ceases to contemplate the truths I have explained. Although these truths are sublime and totally spiritual, they gradually lose their force and become weak by the continuous impressions on our senses that hold our attention. It will not be a waste of time therefore if I present new arguments that can strengthen the mind and demonstrate the emptiness of the remaining objections that can be brought against this matter, so that these salutary truths can be engraved more deeply and solidly in the human spirit.

351. This is all the more necessary because the noble idea we conceive of God and of his goodness often makes us claim and expect from him unreasonable things that may indeed seem appropriate to an omnipotent, excellent being, but in truth are neither good nor even things; on the contrary, they are nothing, because *in se* they are contradictory. We think like this because our concept of divine goodness is vague and confused. The argument we put forward is basically this: 'God's

goodness is as infinite as his power. So, why doesn't he free us from all evils and accumulate all goods for us? He is able do this, and if he did it, surely his action would be a greater goodness than leaving us subject to so much suffering? Therefore we do not see him acting like an infinitely good being — his action could be better.'

I do not accept this very common objection, which seems to be so true that good people usually settle it by applying a faith that adores rather than a reason that understands. It is certainly most reasonable that anyone who believes in God should also believe that God can never fail to act with infinite goodness even when, according to human understanding, the opposite seems to be the case. But I am convinced that human reason itself, if it thinks about and examines the matter honestly and perseveringly, can discover (at least, when strengthened by revelation) a way to overcome the objection and acknowledge that its origin lies in the ignorance and superficiality of the person making it. In the previous book, this conviction led me to present some reasons that directly refute the objection. I will summarise and present them again in another way.

352. The objection claims that God should not allow the natures he has created to act always according to their forces and laws but, whenever their action is about to fail, he should intervene in such a way that he prevents the failure by suspending the action. Directing natures to a perfect action in this way, he prevents the production of every evil. This requires God to intervene in reality in creation, that is, to intervene with a supernatural force, where 'supernatural' means a direct agent superior to the whole of nature, that is, God himself. This explains why I have called this present book ὑπὲρ-φυσικὸς [supernatural]: I wanted to continue the solution to this difficulty and deal with the action of God that modifies the actions of natural things — in the previous book I only touched upon it.

353. I noted that all finite things, not merely this or that created thing, are subject to evil through their natural disposition. This cuts the ground from under those who object that God should have made the universe with better substances rather than with the present substances. Leaving aside the fact that we cannot wish that other entia be created instead of ourselves or

that we should be a better ens than we are, none of the substances of which we are made could be exempt from the *possibility of failure* proper to everything limited, which is the origin of all evil. I also demonstrated a necessary consequence of this principle: no matter what distribution and connection of created entia was determined at the beginning when the world was created, evil could not have been avoided. Hence, in the distribution and concatenation of the various natures composing the world, God would have acted with infinite goodness and wisdom only on condition that the choice, distribution and concatenation had produced the greatest possible net good, once the evil (that could not have been entirely avoided) had been subtracted.

354. But this is not the objection commonly made. Generally, people do not think of making God intervene at the very beginning when he creates and disposes all the different natures; they want him to intervene in the universe after it has already been created. As I said, they claim that God should help the finite beings already created, and should always protect them and keep them from falling into evil. This is the common objection that must be answered.

355. In the previous book I did two things to answer this objection. I first limited my argument to human good and evil, because the goods and evils of material natures and sensitive natures (all these natures lack intelligence) are strictly speaking goods and evils solely in relationship to us; the complaint we bring against Providence concerns our own personal evils, and simply expresses our pain. I then observed that in order to know whether we would be better off if divine intervention freed us from evils, we had to know what human nature is, and what its limitations are. After investigating these limitations, I found that we as human beings are in fact so limited that if certain evils are suppressed, we are deprived of certain goods, because these goods would not exist if we were not subject to evil. I therefore understood that permanent relief from an evil is not, as it seems at first sight, the work of supreme goodness. Supreme goodness will not suppress an evil if the suppression means the loss of goods, or of goods that are more desirable than the cessation of the evil. When we are in this situation and are asked what do we desire more, and granted we can calculate

both the evil and the goods attached to it, we will doubtlessly prefer the evil to remain together with the great goods that accompany it rather than be deprived of both. All goods and evils, pleasures and pains are weighed in a scale that tells us which of them satisfies our spirit more. Weighed thus against each other and granted they are not equal, they leave in our spirit either a happy or a sad effect, depending which is heavier.[93] If this were not the case, how is it that people are often happy with a paltry gain that cost them much effort and fatigue? A merchantman will entrust his life and goods to the sea, but when he is safe in port with a ship full of goods, he considers as nothing the hardships, dangers and illnesses suffered on the long voyage: he is fully content with his increased wealth. Love of a little glory can give such great value to a good that is more imaginary than real, that it is desired at all costs, even at the cost of death. A soldier, when showing the scars of his wounds and speaking about the terrible battles he has endured, experiences a kind and degree of pleasure which he could not have experienced if he had not really borne the acute pain of the wounds and courageously overcome his fear of death. Similarly, anything won by hard, strenuous work, by long deprivations and small savings, has a particular pleasure that is totally lacking when greater wealth is obtained simply through a gift or by inheritance. The conclusion must be that for the human spirit there are certain joys that are the fruit and consequence of certain pains, and that the joys are so naturally joined to the pains that it is impossible to separate them; not even God could separate them because he does nothing absurd. How could he let us experience the joy we can derive from knowing that we are authors of our own goods, if we are not in fact the authors? How could he make a rich person take delight in the thought of the abundant wealth gained by great effort and hardship if acquisition of the wealth had cost nothing at

[93] Cf. *SP*, 581–585 where it is demonstrated how pleasures and pains which seem so different that we do not know how to measure them against each other, are nevertheless balanced and measured against each other in the totally simple unity of the human spirit, with the result that the spirit is satisfied or not satisfied. The good or evil state, the happy or sad state of the human being must be deduced from this effect of *satisfaction*, not from the individual pleasures or pains.

all? How could he make brave people enjoy in their old age the thought of their courage and bravery and of the harsh trials overcome if instead of facing opposition or suffering they had always lived in easy comfort? Did he do these things by impressing on human imagination hardships and dangers that in fact never existed; in other words, did he use empty illusions? If we thought like this, we would be changing the One who is truth itself into a vain magician, which is another absurdity because contradictory to divine nature. If such a thing happened, God's goodness would not be true because he would no longer be a truthful God. I must repeat therefore that there are some human goods that are the result of certain evils, and that human nature is content to have these goods, even at the cost of some inevitable evils. But if human nature is content with the goods, indeed is happy to have those evils on such a condition, we surely cannot complain? Human nature does not complain; only individuals complain. They are not faithful interpreters of human nature, they do not accept its preferences; instead, they are guided by their own abstract and false speculations.

356. Nor must we forget that our need to experience some evils in order to have certain, much desired goods is precisely one of the limitations of finite nature. Our concept of limitation would be too narrow and incomplete if we restricted it to the kind of limitations proper to bodies. Every finite nature has its own limits, and the quality and form of these limits cannot be known except by observation of individual natures, what kind they are, their endowments, the laws to which they are subject. Hence, just as bodies are limited in their extension, so the animate being is limited in the laws of feeling which form it. The human being, composed of matter, feeling and intelligence, shares in the limits of these three elements and also has the limits resulting from the relationships of the three elements and from the physical and dynamic connection that unites them. We can see therefore that if infinite Being enjoys essential good without any limitation whatsoever, every finite being enjoys only good with certain limitations and limited by certain conditions. Thus, each finite being has its own good, but not every manner and form of good can be appropriate to it. Consequently, whenever we want to know in what way infinitely good being (that is, God) must treat human beings or any of his

other creatures and still truly act with infinite goodness, it would be wrong to investigate whether he deprives them of some goods or leaves them subject to some evils, because this would be contrary to the concept of infinite goodness. Instead, we must investigate whether he gives to the finite being the good proper to it, the good that fits its nature, and therefore whether this kind of good, proportionate solely to that particular finite being, is as great as it can be. We must also establish whether such a good, in order to be the greatest possible, can be free from all evil or must have some evil intermingled with it. I agree that from someone who is supremely good we can and must expect a supreme good, but not a supreme good contained in an abstract concept; it has to be a supreme good proper and fitting to the finite ens to whom it is given — any good that is not proper to the ens is not good, nor does the ens desire or will it. The question therefore must be reduced to investigating which good is proper to the finite being in question, and how and when this type and form of good can be called supreme in its kind. This principle, applied to ourselves, gives precisely the consequence that the good proper to the human being can be conceived as having attained its highest degree only when it is preceded or accompanied by some evils, which help to form and complete the good. The existence of evils therefore in no way detracts from supreme goodness; on the contrary, their existence proves it.

357. This principle, valid for an individual human being, is also valid for the whole of humanity. When we examine the nature of individuals, we see that they could not enjoy the goods they supremely value unless they accepted some evils whose negative value, measured against the individuals' feeling, is far below the positive value of the goods. But the same is true of the human race: it could not fully develop all its faculties or acquire deep knowledge of itself or reach the apex of civilisation, virtue and prosperity except by the experience of misfortunes, the impetus arising from necessities and evils, a ceaseless struggle and, above all, the sublime battle (which is so pleasing in the sight of the most wise and excellent being) that is sustained and won only by naked virtue against material force, against the power of the wicked, and the greatest disasters. Elsewhere I tried to show that, once all the goods have been

totalled and the evils subtracted, a government is only supremely good when it strives to give humanity the maximum of net good, no matter how this good is distributed or whether it had to be accumulated only in a few individuals, or whether some individuals had to be left in a wretched state.[94] In the case of government by Providence, the whole of humanity is its object, and a supreme, governing goodness aims solely at procuring humanity's greatest good. If this greatest good cannot be obtained without the loss of some individuals, a loss included in the overall calculation, this is a defect not of the controlling goodness but of the limitation inherent in humanity, whom the intention is to benefit to the greatest degree.

358. The foregoing is the substance of the principles from which I draw the arguments I presented in the second book to defend the supreme goodness of Providence. The arguments show that, although God's goodness is unlimited and ready to bestow every good and remove every evil, humanity is not unlimited, nor capable of receiving every kind of good free from every kind of evil. This means that finite ens (the object of divine goodness) limits, I would say, this goodness and prevents the full effect that divine goodness would like to produce.

The principles became much clearer and more effective in settling doubts against divine goodness by means of some particular applications I made of them to man. I will give a brief summary of them here.

359. The applications begin from the general principle that 'the perfection of an ens requires it to be author of its own good'.

This principle is not deduced solely from the nature of the human being but is completely universal; it applies to every ens, follows from the intrinsic order of ens, and hence pertains to those principles I call 'ontological'. It calls for our attentive consideration as a principle that places yet another condition on the operation of divine goodness. In fact, it shows that divine goodness cannot be supreme if it limits itself simply to bestowing goods on us; it must also act in such a way that we ourselves become authors of our own goods; otherwise, we

94 This most important rule, most apt for measuring the level of a government's goodness, deserves full attention. Cf. *SP*, 594–629.

would lack the highest perfection of being authors and cause of our own good.

360. All human goods are reduced to two supreme classes: *moral goods* and *eudaimonological goods*. With God's help, we can in some way be authors of both for ourselves, and this is something we value and cherish more than anything else. If therefore divine goodness was to be supreme in its relationship to us and correspond to the aspiration of our nature, it had to bestow on us what we could not procure for ourselves, and also help us obtain all we could.

361. But the order proper to these two supreme classes of goods is that eudaimonological good follows moral good as its appendix. This order is an eternal law of justice, and also an ontological principle because contained in the universal order of ens: there can never be a well-ordered, happy ens in which there is only eudaimonological good and not moral good as well, or in which the latter is expected to be at the service of the former. A disorder like this would mean that moral good has immediately disappeared because its essence requires it to be superior to every other good. Hence, a person without virtue cannot be well ordered or happy. Thus, for divine goodness to be supreme it must preserve this moral order at the same time as it bestows benefits on humanity. It had to first direct its attention to making humanity virtuous by moral good and then making it happy by the addition of eudaimonological good.

362. Furthermore, divine goodness could not show itself truly supreme if it did not first make us authors of a supreme moral good that benefited us. Hence, if we want to know what the goodness of the supreme Being should fittingly do in order to show itself greatest in its beneficence to humanity, we need to investigate what divine goodness had to do 1. to make us authors to the highest degree of our own moral good, and 2. to make the moral good whose authors we had become, *the greatest*, that is, the greatest possible.

363. In regard to the first, we are authors of our moral good by virtue of our free will. If divine goodness had not left us free for good and evil, the goodness could not have been the greatest; indeed, it had to permit us the greatest possible amount of freedom of indifference because the amount of *merit* is proportionate to the amount of our freedom (granted that the other

conditions of merit are not absent). Generally speaking therefore, it was not fitting that God, in moving us to good, should reduce our freedom by removing or diminishing its indifference, at least in those cases where the diminution in an individual was not compensated in the whole of humanity or by the greatest sum of moral good.

364. In the second case, the amount of moral goodness that we might procure for ourselves is as great as the two elements that compose the amount, that is, 1. the effort to obtain moral good, and 2. the divine object, which is the only good communicated to the human mind and heart.

365. The first of these two elements demonstrates the need for a eudaimonological evil. The effort to be virtuous is as great as the opposition to be overcome, whether this opposition is moral or physical; and the greater the effort, the more valuable the good. I call 'moral' the opposition that we come up against in practising virtue and that arises from the inclination to evil we carry with us. Associated with this inclination is the allurement of sensible pleasures, which must also be conquered. I call 'physical' opposition that which comes from corporeal and temporal evils; sometimes we have to bear these in order to practise virtue. This double opposition allows us to increase our own moral good in two ways:

1. The amount of effort we make to rise above pleasure and pain is an act of great love for what is upright and just; it means we value uprightness and justice in practice above the other goods that we despise for their sake; we render them honour that is founded in God as the one who is subsistent justice and uprightness. Thus, the degree of effort we make to obtain virtue is also the degree of intimate union between ourselves and the eternal principle of virtue. We can acquire moral good by means of greater *intension* and greater *extension*. The effort to acquire it increases the intension of the good but not its extension; the effort inserts us more deeply into good, although it does not make us dilate in it; it unites moral good and ourselves ever closer together without changing the kind of good.

2. The more we give, so to speak, of what is ours in order to obtain moral good, and the more we sacrifice eudaimonological good, the more credit we acquire with eternal justice. The law of eternal justice requires that those who suffer for

justice must be compensated; in fact, in order to purchase this justice, they reject everything delightful. This compensatory and remunerative law reduces to the ontological principle that 'being, under the moral form, when placed in opposition to being, under the real form, must triumph and draw from the latter infinite glory'. It follows logically that we can reject a real good for love of moral good, and can suffer because we attach immense value to moral good and desire to possess it at all costs, but in doing so we must ultimately gain from our loss. If this did not happen, moral being would not fully triumph over real being, and hence the lover of moral being would have suffered the loss of real being, or have lost it without any gain. This explains why eternal justice arranges a most abundant retribution for the virtuous who suffer patiently, so that in the end they see they have not lost the real, eudaimonological good they renounced in order to acquire virtue; on the contrary they have changed it into a greater good. More important still, they recover all they generously gave (which itself was God's gift), not as a gift but as a reward, not as a fortuitous acquisition but as a credit of justice. Thus, the eudaimonological good they had previously possessed in isolation and separate from moral good was later acquired back as an appendix to the moral good. This time however it is enhanced with a new, supreme dignity and splendour. Such then is the happiest thing that can happen to us, to see ourselves rich with supreme eudaimonological goods that are due to us and that we ourselves have obtained. They are, in a true sense, our own, given to us by an unambiguous, immutable justice. This fact is the foundation of the argument for a future life that I discussed earlier, and the pure hope of it gives Christian people a certain happiness in this life.

366. Because all these things are certain, it follows that if supreme goodness was to guide human beings to the greatest good possible, it had to place them, or allow them to place themselves, in a state in which the acquisition of virtue required the GREATEST EFFORT and the GREATEST SACRIFICE accommodated however to human strength — an exception would be the other conditions for the greatest good that might require or entail some reduction of that effort and sacrifice. The difference between *effort* and *sacrifice* must be noted: the intensity of effort leads us to the moral state that consists in the *intensity* of

the very act by which we seek and seize good, whilst sacrifice, that is, our loss of eudaimonological good, although involving no effort, is of great advantage as it gives us credit with divine justice for the eudaimonological good that we have voluntarily lost and for which we must be abundantly compensated.

367. Moreover, the noble kind of moral perfection we attain by effort and sacrifice brings with it many other goods. We could not obtain these if we did not bear the evil present in the very fatigue of making the effort and in the privation and the suffering.

In the great struggle we have for the sake of virtue and in renouncing other goods for the sole purpose of procuring virtue, we have an experiential and most effective knowledge of its sweetness and beauty. And because God is the object of supreme virtue, we also have an intimate knowledge of God himself; we learn by experience how much more God is worth than all other things, which are now nothing for us and no longer attract us. On the other hand, people who have not had this experience can have only a kind of cold, negative knowledge of the supreme good, like the knowledge obtained through hearsay or repute.

Consequently, in the great plan by which God undertook to educate the human race to virtue, he applied the medicine of temporal evils to counter the unhealthy attraction of goods that was so dangerous to human weakness, and the medicine of temporal goods to counter the opposite danger that great evils could be for human weakness. He did this in the first age of the world when man had not yet mentally attained high abstractions nor come to understand and experience the intangible goods of the spirit.

368. Another good, resulting from the virtue acquired by our struggles and sacrifices, is the sweet awareness we experience of our victory. This awareness of being vanquisher of all things makes us feel greater than all things, and like God, because of the divine virtue God has communicated to us and with which we conquered. This gives us a supreme, ineffable joy which spreads through our soul, and also a powerful security which, while we live here on earth, raises us as it were to heaven, from where we look down on and spurn the sensible world as something too little for us.

369. I come now come to the second element from which we derive the greatest amount of the moral good that we must procure for ourselves. I said this is God himself in so far as we share in him. Granted the condition mentioned earlier that 'the moral perfection of human beings is never the greatest if they themselves are not its author', it necessarily follows that God would not be acting in harmony with an infinite goodness if he did not offer and, as it were, administer himself to us according to two laws: first, he must not place any limits to the communication of himself; second, we must be permitted and committed to attain and draw to ourselves divine good and divine nature as much as we wish, aided by God and given the ability by him. Thus, in keeping with the first law, God's communication of good was entirely unlimited and infinite; in keeping with the second law, we became authors of divine good for ourselves and were able to obtain it in proportion to the extent of our faculties, nature, effort and the greatness of our desire for it. In fact, God himself exhorted and stimulated us to obtain precisely as much as we could and desired with the great precept: 'You shall love the Lord your God with all your heart and with all your soul and with all your mind.'[95] The fact that divine goodness followed these two laws becomes clear in the Incarnation, in which the divine Word was united personally to human nature. Thus, the Word was given to man and to every human being as the great and inexhaustible fount where unlimited divine good could be obtained. Furthermore, in sacrifice, in the sacraments, in prayer and in supernatural works we were given other means of wonderful efficacy which can of themselves produce every moral good and perfection and are limited solely by our human will and work. The amount we draw to ourselves of that good increases in proportion to the extent we use those means and dispose our will.

370. Such, substantially, were the reasons with which in the previous book I justified the divine goodness in permitting physical and eudaimonological evil. They demonstrate that this evil was necessary if on the one hand we were to attain maximum moral perfection (from which every eudaimonological

[95] Mt 22: [37].

good inevitably comes) and on the other the universe were to obtain its sublime, most excellent purpose.

We cannot retort that God has no need of physical evil to obtain the supreme moral good — in God moral good is supreme and not preceded or accompanied by any evil whatsoever. But, as I said above, the reply must be that moral good in God does not exist under the same conditions as in us. Moral good must not be considered solely in the abstract, but as it is in God and as it can be in us. The different natures in which it is, change its state: in God, the divine nature itself is moral good, God himself, eternal and most actual; in us, moral good is a pure accident: it does not exist but is formed; it cannot be a good proper to us unless we ourselves (with divine help) form and produce it. We can operate only with our faculties and forces, purely according to the laws of our nature. Hence, if moral good in us is something produced, we need to study how it is produced and brought into being. We have seen that it is produced and set in being by acts of the will whose efficacy and perfection is proportionate to the ardour of the effort and sacrifice manifested in the acts. This therefore is a condition of human virtue, not of divine virtue.

371. But why did God permit moral evil? I answered: because moral evil is a condition for a much greater moral good. The work of redemption, an abyss of divine goodness, is due to the fall of the human race. Even if there had been no sin, God could certainly have incarnated himself, and thus communicated himself in a supreme mode to his creatures — this would have been fully compatible with the essence of supreme goodness.[96]

96 St. Thomas proves the *fittingness* of the Incarnation in a general way from the fact that God is the *essence of goodness*. His fine thesis is: 'Because God is the very essence of goodness, it was fitting that he communicate himself to his creatures *in a supreme mode*. Faith tells us that this was fulfilled in the work of the Incarnation'* (*S.T.*, III, q. 3, art. 1). As proof of this he says: 'Whatever is fitting to each thing is fitting according to the concept of the thing's nature. For example, reasoning is fitting to man because it pertains to him in so far as he is rational according to his nature. God's nature is the essence of his goodness, as is clear from what Dionysius says (*De div. nom.*, c. 1 [lect. 3]). Therefore, all that is part of the concept of good is fitting to God. But part of the concept of good is the communication of oneself to others, which again is clear in Dionysius (ibid., c. 4 [lect. 1]). Consequently, it pertains to the concept of supreme good to communicate itself *in a supreme mode*.

But our discussion concerns the work of *redemption*, not of the *incarnation*. The redemption is the complete triumph of moral being over real, intellectual being in so far as this being is divided from moral being in the world of contingencies. By means of the redemption moral being overcomes and subjugates real, intellectual being which wanted to separate from it; it leads real, intellectual being captive like a trophy proclaiming its victory, and having thus saved it, makes it sublime and perfects it. This moral being that triumphs over real being that has rebelled against it is the holiness of God, the supreme good communicated to human beings despite the opposition of their sin. God's communication of himself to sinful human beings and his destruction of sin is an act of goodness infinitely greater than the communication of himself to the just; the supreme Being permitted sin, precisely because it pleased him to come to this extreme expression of his goodness. He was not content simply to display the infinite magnificence of his goodness; he wanted us to cooperate with him in such a divine prodigality of beneficence; he wanted us to become with him authors of our own redemption, and to this end he disposed things in accord with the great principle I gave: that the greatest benefit possible for us is not to give us good but to let us be our own authors of this good. Therefore, the Word was made flesh and dwelt in us; a human being immune from all sin, assumed in a divine person, became redeemer of all other sinner-humans, and died to redeem them. This act of beneficence on the part of the God-Man was so great that the evil of all the sins of the world weighed nothing in comparison with it. Hence, it was fitting that infinite goodness permit human sin so that the God-Man could practise divine virtue as great as the virtue shining forth

This happens in a most particular way whenever this good unites created nature to itself so that one single person is composed of three things, the Word, flesh and blood, as St. Augustine says (*De Trinit.*, 13: 17). Clearly therefore, it was fitting for God to incarnate himself.' This intrinsic reason for the fittingness of the Incarnation retains its force whether we suppose man had sinned or not sinned. Hence, we do not need to know with certainty what God could have done if man had not sinned because, as St. Thomas says a little further on (ibid., a.3): 'Those things that arise solely from God's will, over and above what is owed to the creature, are made known to us only by holy Scripture that reveals the divine will to us.'*

[371]

in the work of redemption. Indeed, in divine wisdom's just weighing scales the moral good present in even the lightest of Christ's sufferings had to outweigh the moral evil of all the sin human beings committed or could commit. Consequently, by means of the occasion of the sin permitted by God, humanity was given so great a mass of moral good in Christ that nothing can compare with it. Even if all other human beings perished eternally, Christ's humanity, saved and glorified, would not only compensate for such a great loss but would immeasurably outstrip the loss.

372. But this was not the only advantage that divine wisdom had before it in permitting sin. We have to add the effect that followed from the moral good that Christ had actuated and accumulated in himself and merited through the giving of his life for the salvation of the world. This effect was indeed the salvation of the world: through faith in the divinity and power of the Saviour and through the waters of baptism, sins are cancelled and we are incorporated into Christ and made sharers in all his infinite goods. In fact, the application of his merits made through baptism is so certain that not even sins committed after baptism can totally abolish it. Those who sin after baptism do not lose the impression of the priestly character imprinted on them by baptism, which makes them capable of receiving the forgiveness of their actual faults through the power and the sacrament of Penance.

373. They can also obtain from Christ, principally through prayer, the grace of an efficacious compunction, by which they become in a certain way redeemers of themselves. If Christ's power did not reform sinner-humans, they could not be converted, could not raise themselves to God. Sinners, on their own, cannot satisfy divine justice nor rise from the depth of their sin, because they cannot perform an act that has the power to please God, find him once more and possess him as their good. To make sinners capable of the supernatural act, which they need for recovering divine goodness, divine power had to come to their aid. This power was given them by the God-Man in baptism. Here we see the immeasurable splendour of the divine goodness and the supreme charity of the God-Man towards human beings, with the result that they have a reason for infinite gratitude because they have received a gift so

gratuitous that they could not hope to acquire it by themselves. And once again, this infinite gratitude is their occasion for a moral good great beyond every kind. They could not have had this good without having first been redeemed; the good is precisely the feeling of their voluntary gratitude by which they glorify the Saviour. Again therefore, the wretchedness of sinners becomes their source of greater good. In the case of baptised adults, they must also have supernatural faith in Christ who has been announced to them, and it was in baptism that they received the power of this faith. Thus, although they did not, with voluntary faith, cooperate in the impressing of the priestly character on themselves, which is impressed solely by the power of Christ, they do cooperate in receiving the fruit of the character, that is, their full justification. But human beings baptised through the mercy of Christ are in another way made quasi-authors of their justification when, as I said, they repent of their actual sins committed after baptism. Hence, those who sin after baptism still have open to them both the way of prayer, by which they beg God for effective compunction, and the sacrament of Penance. The forgiveness of sin belongs to God alone, but the responsibility of sinners is to approach the sacrament and have the dispositions necessary for receiving absolution. In doing so, they cooperate by their own action with their justification by disposing themselves for it with divine help.

374. When the sacrament of Penance is well received, it necessarily and properly supplies what we cannot do, and also gives us power to do what we ourselves could not do, that is: 1. it forgives serious guilt by the infusion of sanctifying grace, 2. it forgives eternal punishment, and 3. it strengthens us against relapses. When we are not in the state of serious guilt and have in fact received grace, we have re-acquired the power to merit supernaturally, and are therefore suitably disposed for the virtue of expiatory and meritorious penance. The exercises of penance, through the grace of God that accompanies them, can now produce two effects: 1. they can cancel the residue of sins [*App*., no. 5], and 2. they can satisfy the temporal punishment accompanying the residue [*App*., no. 6]. Thus, the tears, the contrition of heart, the penal works with which we daily purify ourselves, receive from divine grace and from the merits of

Christ so much power that the Fathers call such acts a 'baptism by strenuous effort'.[97] These acts with which we satisfy God, emend us and, as it were, redeem us from the consequences of sin. They are moral goods of infinite value, of which humanity would have been deprived if sin had not been permitted. No one can perform such an excellent act, no one can have within himself such a great and lively feeling of God's goodness, no one can glorify and extol God more than the sinner who is converted. We have seen that moral virtue consists in a movement that raises us to the supreme good, because we do not have virtue in our essence but must procure it with accidental acts. Consequently, sinners redeemed and aided by God are the most suitable subject for a great virtue, because the movement by which they raise themselves from the depth of iniquity to the summit of divine sanctity is the most prolonged and greatest of all, requiring greater effort and sacrifice. Indeed, sinners who turn from their evil living die and are reborn another being.

Here, it seems to me, we find the clear explanation of what Christ said, that the Angels in heaven rejoice more over one sinner who has turned from evil living than over ninety-nine just. This rejoicing is also felt on earth by all souls zealous for the divine honour; they have no greater joy than that which they experience in the conversion of a single soul. But if we question sinners whose heart is converted, it is almost impossible to describe the great sorrow they experience. All their austerities and penances are infused with a sweet, soothing balm. And if they sometimes seem to someone who does not know the disposition of their heart to be merciless and cruel towards themselves, it is because the sufferings, mortifications and satisfactions that they give to God have lost all asperity for them and have become their dear treasure, their daily food, of which they never have enough. Light shines in their souls, and this new light gives them such a knowledge of God that its depth is as great as the magnitude of their offence; they would prefer to annihilate themselves, as it were, in order to restore the honour and love they took away from God. They are saddened and reproach themselves because they cannot do all they would

[97] John Damasc., 4: 1.

[374]

like; all their affection and efforts to love him do not compensate worthily for the love they have denied him, because such things always fall short of what he deserves. As a result, the vivid, deep and experiential knowledge that true penitents acquire of God and of themselves, the immense gratitude that opens in their heart, the burning, insatiable ardour with which they study how to restore outraged justice and make compensation to their offended God are all acts which perfect the human being. If infinite wisdom had not permitted humanity to sin, these moral goods of the highest degree could not have been obtained. Thus, with all reason the Church exclaims: 'O happy fault that merited to have so great a Redeemer'.

375. Someone however may retort: the infinite goods communicated by the Redeemer to humanity bear fruit only for those who are saved, so why was the Gospel not announced to every human being? And why does God allow many of those to whom the Gospel has been announced, who have been baptised and have believed, fall into sin and are even lost?

We should not think that those who without their fault have not received the grace of baptism and faith, or have not had Christ announced to them, or babies who die without baptism, are totally deprived of every benefit of the Redeemer. If Christ does not communicate to them the grace that raises them to the supernatural order (a grace that is bound with baptism), we can be certain that he restores their body at the future resurrection, which pertains to the order of natural life. In this he uses, on behalf of all, the power and authority he has over all flesh, as I have demonstrated elsewhere.[98]

376. Moreover, the reason why God does not communicate the supernatural grace of the Redeemer to every human being, and why he permits the actual sins they commit with their free will, causing many to perish, must be found in the principle mentioned earlier that the supreme goodness of a government must tend to produce the maximum, comprehensive good of the governed (it is the same whether the good is distributed or accumulated) provided justice is preserved. Hence, whenever this maximum good cannot be obtained without evils being

[98] [Rosmini is referring to an Appendix that he added to the edition of 1845–1846 and strictly speaking is outside the argument of this work.]

permitted, it is a supreme goodness to permit them. We have then both the total of goods which at the end of things will be present in those who are saved, and the total of natural goods that will be in those who are not saved. These two totals added together, minus all the evils to which every human being has been or will be subject, must in fact be the comprehensive maximum of goods among all possible goods that the supreme, divine governor of humanity can obtain, with due regard for the divine attributes. Therefore we must also accept that the faults and perdition of the wicked are the indispensable conditions of such a great a good. In the final part of the previous book I explained how this could be: I demonstrated that divine Providence guides all events for the perfection and triumph of the Church of the Redeemer, which is the great means used by God to attain the purpose of the universe, that is, the maximum moral good in humanity, followed necessarily by the maximum eudaimonological good.

[376]

CHAPTER 2

The final, more subtle objections against the above reasons given to justify Providence

377. Some objections however remain that seem to weaken the light of the reasons that I have recapitulated here and that I have explained more at length to justify divine goodness and make it prevail. These last objections seem indeed to be ingenious and subtle, but precisely because of this they only give further proof of the narrowness of human understanding, which sees them as learned and subtle. Moreover, arguments that do not present the truth, indeed hide the truth from the intellect, are difficult. My intention in this book therefore is to present these objections in all their apparent force and solve them.

378. In order to make the supreme goodness of divine government shine forth, I established the principle that 'divine government is supreme when the good it produces in humanity is the greatest possible'. I wanted to demonstrate that no argument exists capable of proving that this maximum good is not obtained in humanity. Hence there can be no valid argument against any of the divine attributes. Consequently, the apparent irregularities in Providence's government of the world in no way support any conclusion against God's existence or justify the complaints against God by those who suffer evils. I established this by showing that of all the qualities of goods, moral good is the most excellent, and that eudaimonological good acquires the concept of complete good only when it comes after moral good as a natural appendix.

I next investigated the elements we can use to calculate the amount of goods (mainly moral good) and said that this amount must not be taken from and measured solely against the amount of good considered abstractly; we must also acquire this amount by using our own strength so that we become authors of it for ourselves. The supreme, moral and simultaneously eudaimonological good is God, infinite good, but because the only way we can unite ourselves to this good is by our own strength (which God creates in us), we cannot have total possession of it, precisely because our strength and powers are finite. Hence, taking into account all humanity's strength and limitations, humanity has reached the ultimate level of its good when it can do no more. But, as I said, no one can prove that God has not procured this maximum fruit from the human race. In fact, if we examine closely an argument that would seem to prove the opposite, we see that on the contrary the argument itself contains the clear characteristic of one of the conditions I have given for procuring the greatest good. The argument is:

378a. 1. It seems at first sight, and I grant this, that our moral state would have been happier if all freedom had been taken from us and we could do only good. However, closer consideration of the matter shows that without freedom we cannot be the authors of our own good.

2. It also seems that it would be better if good cost us no effort at all. But further reflection will show that effort and struggle are an indispensable condition for the amount of merit we can obtain.

3. It seems that it would have been more desirable for us to obtain good without any sacrifice. But a deeper examination of the truth reveals that the total credit we acquire relative to eternal justice and the abundant reward we expect are conditioned by sacrifice. A life deprived of physical evils may indeed seem preferable, yet physical evils are the powerful stimuli for activating the best human faculties; they are the means by which we become wise and acquire experiential knowledge of ourselves and of other things. They are also the necessary occasion for the sacrifice which allows the human will to rise above all the material, external world on the one hand, and on the other allows moral being to triumph over physical being.

4. It seems that the affairs of humanity would have fared better if sensible goods had not seduced us to neglect the law of justice. But again, reflection shows that this seduction is itself a necessary condition for a greater victory of virtue that rises above it; a whole field of heroism is opened up for the virtuous person, where we learn to know ourselves even more and our relationships with other things.

5. It seems above all most desirable that all moral evil should

have been excluded. But this also is a necessary condition for the maximum good of humanity. It offers the occasion for penance and the conversion of heart, which is a miracle of moral virtue and divine goodness. It becomes a stimulus for the most exquisite feelings of love and gratitude towards God, and for feelings of great sweetness. Finally, the wickedness of some individuals increases the virtue of the good who suffer greatly, and therefore increases the total of overall good.

In regard to the eternal loss of souls, this cannot be avoided, granted moral evil and the safeguarding of the attributes of divine justice and sanctity. This inevitability is particularly true if we consider that the moment when life is taken from us is an accident linked into the whole series of events. If this series is regulated by supreme goodness, it cannot and must not have regard for this or that individual but must concern itself with the maximum, overall good of the whole human species that can be obtained from the series.

Nevertheless, against all the above arguments the following very subtle objections, as I said, can still be made:

379. 1. It is certain that God can move human freedom to good without either destroying or diminishing freedom. It would therefore seem conformable to the *essence of goodness* that God, who is essentially good, direct the freedom of all human beings to supreme good, and they would still be the free authors of their own actions.

2. It is true that effort, sacrifice and therefore victory over corporeal evils and over the seduction of goods are conditions that increase the moral value of actions. But the quantity of moral good does not depend solely on these elements but more on the quantitative mode of the supreme, divine object, which is the purpose of morality. Therefore, the moral good we lose when our effort and sacrifice might cease, could be compensated abundantly by a spontaneous and very abundant communication that God could make of himself to us. In short, God can communicate himself to us in the measure that seems good to him, and could thus give us a sanctity of any degree whatsoever without the need for any effort or sacrifice on our part. It would therefore seem in conformity with an infinite goodness that we are relieved of the need of our efforts and suffering which are our present means for our acquiring virtue.

And all that is said here about moral good can equally be said about eudaimonological good: God could compensate the knowledge and joy we draw from our struggles and sacrifices and from our own repentance by the direct infusion of a knowledge and joy of another kind but of greater intensity.

3. Therefore God could save all people and also make them attain any degree of sanctity either by moving their freedom or by giving them sanctity without any need for their free cooperation, or finally by giving sinners on the point of death an instantaneous grace capable of changing them from wicked people to very great saints.

I will now give my solutions to these three objections, hoping I can do so in the most complete way.

[379]

CHAPTER 3

The solution to the objections will be general, that is, one for all of them

380. The objections could be solved in several ways. For example, in the case of the second, we could correctly say that the objector's system would exclude the increase of the moral good that humanity could obtain through its own effort and sacrifice, and we would therefore have to conclude that humanity could not attain the maximum of its perfection. But God can communicate to humanity that quantity of himself, no matter how great, that he wishes to communicate, and still leave humanity the glorious opportunity to acquire this quantity with its own efforts. Hence, the communication that God makes of himself in any quantitative mode does not exclude effort and sacrifice. The effort and sacrifice simply increase our moral good, or rather they enrich us with a good whose quality and nature is so different and proper to us that no other kind can compensate for it or equal it, especially because the human spirit has a natural, greater love for the good it has acquired by its own effort and sacrifice than for any good donated to it.

381. But in this book I do not intend to solve the objections individually, with particular reasons. Rather I want to give to all three a single reply that is most convincing for anyone who understands it, and I will draw it from the laws according to which wisdom operates, laws that can be found in the very essence of wisdom.

To this end, I will first examine what the objections claim God should do for us if he is to be seen as operating with supreme goodness.

Chapter 4

The objections are based on uncertain and erroneous principles

382. The authors of the three objections claim that God cannot be acknowledged as exercising supreme goodness in the government of the universe because 1. he does not use his almighty power to move the freedom of all individual human beings to choose the best, 2. he does not infuse into them that amount of virtue and grace which would amply compensate for the moral excellence that comes from effort, struggle and sacrifice, and finally 3. he does not save everyone with his omnipotence, at least at the moment of death.

But are these judges and censors of divine goodness in fact certain about what they say? Is it really certain that they do not false rules to distinguish when goodness is supreme or less than supreme? Is it so easy (as seems to them) to measure the *maximum of goodness*? Surely, it is more difficult to measure the depth of divine goodness than to measure the distance of the fixed stars or the length of their light beams? If this is so, and if moreover the wise people who authoritatively pronounce that the government of the universe is not as good as it could be are not really certain and secure about the efficacy of the rules with which they measure the highest summit of goodness, then they should be silent and rely on the judgment of him who holds the reins of the world. As long as these rules of their judgment are uncertain, their objections will also be uncertain, and hence they cannot conclude anything. Divine Providence therefore remains unharmed and fully justified if we can simply demonstrate that the goodness God uses towards us *can* be supreme, even if we cannot measure it or have sufficient norms to define the conditions necessary for it to be maximum (cf. 12). Truly, ignorance cannot be the foundation of an objection. The fact that an ignorant person does not understand someone else's wisdom does not prove that the other is not wise.

383. To determine accurately the measure of the Creator's goodness we must also simultaneously measure his wisdom,

which guides his goodness. Only the wisest person can act with supreme goodness. Foolish goodness is not goodness because foolishness itself is an evil. If foolish people can perform some good, they do not do so as good people, but because they are partly wise and not completely foolish; if they were completely foolish, they could not be the author of any good whatsoever. Hence, vice versa, a being cannot be all goodness in its operations unless it is all wisdom; to produce maximum good, it must use maximum wisdom. The essence of goodness therefore must lie in the essence of wisdom — such is the intimacy of the bond binding the divine attributes. Consequently, if the censors of Providence wish to show that the rules they claim to impose on supreme goodness are totally certain and doubtless, they must also show that the rules are simultaneously laws of supreme wisdom. But this is precisely what they cannot do. Anyone who asserts something must prove their assertion according to the axiom of logic: *asserenti incumbit probatio* [proof lies with the assertor], and as long as they offer no proof, a single gratuitous negative destroys the gratuitous assertion. Nevertheless I will undertake the task of showing that what they assert cannot in fact be proved. I will also demonstrate that the laws which the adversaries impose on divine goodness are not laws proper to wisdom but contrary to wisdom. For this purpose I must now examine at greater depth the very concept of wisdom and determine the intimate, essential laws according to which it must operate.

CHAPTER 5

Three laws of the activity of being

384. Ontology shows us that being has a triple act, that is, it is in three modes.

In the first mode it is called *real*, in the second *ideal*, in the third *moral*.

385. Ideal being exists only in the real. Real being that contains ideal being is called *intellectual being*.

Moral being exists only in intellectual being.

Therefore the human mind conceives three kinds of real being: *purely real* being, *intellectual-real* being and *moral-intellectual* being.

386. Each of these three real beings has an intrinsic order and consequently an *order in its operation*; therefore three laws, to which the three kinds of real beings are subject in their operation.

387. The law obeyed by the operation of *real being considered as such* is the law of *causality*. It states: 'If something begins, there must have been an entity that made it begin to be (a cause).'

388. The law obeyed by the operation of *real being as intellectual* is the law of *sufficient reason*. It states: 'Intellectual being does not operate without an end proportionate to its operation (a reason).'

389. The law obeyed by the operation of *real being as moral* is the law of *moral freedom*. It can be stated as: 'Moral being tends to unite itself to the whole of known entity without being prevented by any partial entity' [*App*., no. 7].

390. These three laws, governing the operations of triple being, are necessary and immutable. Let us see how they are *necessary*.

391. *Real being* cannot act without the law of causality. Here, 'act' does not mean its first act, with which it is, but its second act with which it makes an entity begin and exist that previously was not. This necessity is absolute because if real being were not, it could not produce anything new; and if it is, it is precisely a producing cause.

392. *Intellectual being* operates necessarily as the result of a sufficient reason because if it did not do so, the operation would not be intellectual. This manner of operation consists in following a reason which, like a light, precedes the operation. Nevertheless, because intellectual ens is, as I said, not only intellectual but also real, the being that is called intellectual sometimes operates blindly, without reason or without sufficient reason; in this case it is strictly speaking pure reality that acts, not intelligence. It seems therefore that intellectual being is not necessitated to operate according to a sufficient reason. This is true for an intellectual ens composed of both reality and intelligence, but not true if the reality is removed from the ens by abstraction and the ens is considered purely as intellectual; as such, it can operate only on condition it follows a sufficient reason, and if it does not, it does not operate.

393. *Moral being* is necessitated to operate with moral freedom, that is, it is not determined by an external cause. Moral being is an internal principle with the tendency to unite itself to the whole of known entity, and in this union finds pure pleasure, enjoyment, good.

But here I must make an observation similar to the one I made concerning the necessity proper to intellectual ens. The ens called moral is not purely moral but is also simultaneously real and intellectual. Hence, it does not always operate as moral: sometimes it operates as intellectual, sometimes as purely real. Consequently it seems that it does not always operate according to its law of moral freedom; in fact this is the case whenever it does not operate as moral being but as purely real or intellectual being, and in these instances it follows the laws I have attributed to it. Indeed, if we maintained that a moral entity in its operation did not tend with spontaneous movement to unite itself to all being, it would be a contradiction in terms because the operating entity would lack precisely what gives it its name and the quality of moral.

394. We see therefore that a purely real individual always maintains its law when operating because it stands alone and is not contained in any other mode of being. On the other hand, an intellectual individual and a moral individual sometimes wander from their laws, not because their laws do not have the same absolute obligation for these individuals but because

being is in them under other forms, which makes the individual follow other laws. *Real being* individuates *ideal being*, which is within real being, and individuates *moral being*, which arises from the active relationship between real being and ideal being that is within real being. As a result, every moral and every intellectual individual without exception is first of all real.[99] The intellectual individual therefore operates in two modes: according to the law of real being and according to the law of ideal being, because it results from these two beings. The moral individual operates in three modes: according to the law of real being, to the law of ideal being and to the law of moral being, because it is composed of these three elements, as they could be called.

[99] In *AMS* 782–788 I explained how *real being* can be the *principle of individuation*.

CHAPTER 6

The law of virtue and the law of wisdom

Recta ratio ipsa est virtus [Right reason is virtue]

St. Aug., *De util. cred.*, 2: 27

395. The law of virtue is the law of moral being, which I have defined.

396. But the *moral individual* does not always follow the law of virtue and avoid vice because, as I said, the moral individual is not only moral but also intellectual and real. He has a triple activity: the activity proper to real being, to intellectual being, and to moral being. Thus, when operating as real being or intellectual being, his operation can be in opposition to the law of moral being.

397. But how can being under one form be in opposition to being under another form? Does one form combat the other? Is there a continuous and essential battle going on within being [*App.*, no. 8]?

This is definitely not possible. On the contrary, being under its three forms is wonderfully in agreement with itself, and the triple law of its operation produces that most perfect, primal harmony which is the origin of all other harmonies.

But I repeat: why does the moral individual, when operating according to the law of reality or the law of intelligence, sometimes contradict and oppose the law of morality?

The answer is: the moral individual does not possess either real being or consequently intellectual being in all their fullness; in other words the moral individual is *limited*, and *limitation* is, as we saw earlier (cf. 293–295), the reason for all evil. If we consider the fullness of real being, its operations accord entirely with the law that governs the operation of intellectual and moral being. If, for example, we imagine a most perfect, intellectual being, its operation will never infringe the law of moral being; on the contrary, its operation will accord with it naturally. But a real being, and therefore also a limited, intellectual being, can easily place itself in contradiction with the law of moral being, not because its operations proceed from a real or intellectual being as such but from a *limited* real or intellectual being. This being, precisely because limited, does not operate entirely according to the law of reality and of intelligence, and therefore operates contrary to the moral law that always directs itself to the *totality of being*.

398. Applying all this to ourselves, we are each a moral-intellectual-real individual. Even if these three activities operate in total isolation without any relationship between them, we cannot say that they are in conflict with each other: for example, animal acts carried out independently of the will, like the circulation of the blood, digestion, etc., pertain to real being. Although this operates by itself *independently*, this does not put it in *opposition* to the laws of intelligence and morality.[100]

However the three activities do not always operate in isolation but often with an active and passive relationship between them. This relationship is one of either accord or discord, and is produced by the *will* which brings together and unifies in itself the three principles of operation. I have called these principles *instincts*, and classed them as *animal*, *rational* and *moral*.[101] These three activities are therefore rooted and unified in the *individual*. The activity of the individual is precisely the will, and this, with its unity, posits the three principles or operative instincts in close connection and relationship with each other, making them either accord or discord with one other. As I said, the individual is always formed by reality, which is the root of the other two modes of being. This means that the *will* also pertains to real being that has within itself ideal being and moral

[100] If we think of someone as naturally perfect, would actions of this kind have to depend on their free will? I believe that their free will would have to possess the power both to *suspend* and to *stimulate* all animal activities. But if the will had abstained from intervening with its action, whether preventive or stimulative, the animal operations would have continued because their proximate cause is animality. Even in our present state, the will can have a greater or lesser influence on these functions, but they do not *necessarily* depend on the will. They *can* therefore take place in us without the intervention of the will. Cf. *CS*, 69.

[101] *CS*, 66.

being, which individuate in real being. The will, as an activity that follows upon knowledge, is a power that arises in *real being* by means of the intelligence that is in real being. But because knowledge can extend to all things, therefore the animal, rational and moral instincts can be equally objects of knowledge. Consequently, the will can determine us to operate according to the good presented to it by either the animal or rational or moral instinct. Thus by means of the will the human individual chooses which of the three instincts he will follow in his operation. This choice posits the three instincts in a relationship of either peace or conflict with each other.[102] It is not an isolated instinct that operates but the individual who chooses between the various instincts.

399. After explaining how the three instincts are placed in relationship and accord through the unity of the individual or of his power, that is, the will, I must now explain how these instincts can contradict each other and how the preference of one can damage and harm another.

As I said, if the being in each of the three modes were full and complete, there would be no struggle between the modes, and hence being's three instincts would be in perfect harmony. But because the real being that constitutes the human individual is in no way the *whole of reality* but only a very small part of it, the instinct arising from it is not the instinct proper to the totality of real being. Therefore the instinct of human reality does not tend to give actuality and perfection to the whole of real being but only to that tiny particle of reality that is in us. As a result, we oppose the demand of moral being that tends always to totality, seeks the completion of being and requires every part of being to be proportionately an object of acknowledgement and love.

400. But a description of how the law of moral being is

[102] Therefore St. John Damascene says that *choice* has its origin in the mind: 'The choice of these (things) is with our *mind* because it (the mind) is the source and origin of the action' (*De ortodoxa fide*, bk. 2, c. 24). These words authoritatively confirm *practical knowledge*, which is the principle of operation I distinguished from ineffective, purely *speculative knowledge*. If, according to Damascene (and to St. Thomas who follows him), the mind itself is the principle and source of operation, then we must necessarily find in knowledge the first strands, so to speak, of human activity.

constituted will shed more light on the origin of the struggle in question. If we consider the pure reality in us, we seem so restricted; if we consider ourselves in so far as intellectual being, we expand on the one hand to the infinite and on the other remain, as before, limited. Our form is ideal being, which is infinite, but this alone does not put us in communication with real being; it does not make us perceive reality (cf. 153) — as we saw, it is given to us in a very limited mode in our feeling. If we consider ourselves in that part that intuits ideal being, our mind has something of the infinite because ideal being is the essence of being and gives formal knowledge of the whole of being. But because the reality and subsistence of being is communicated to us solely in the smallest part, we can perceive only very little of reality, which is everything that occurs in our feeling. It is true that in addition to the realities that occur in our feeling we can argue to the existence of other realities. Information about the existence of other realities can also be communicated to us through what we hear from other beings who communicate with us. But the realities we come to know in this way are not all the realities that subsist. Furthermore, if these realities, whose existence we *believe* in by trusting others or have accepted through reasoning, are not like the realities we ourselves have perceived, our knowledge is empty; we obtain no knowledge of *what* these real entia *are like*; we know only their mere existence and the relationships they can have with perceived entia. I call this empty knowledge *negative-ideal.*

We have therefore three kinds of knowledge: 1. *ideal knowledge* or knowledge of intuition, with which we know the essence of being, and although this knowledge is universal, its degree of determination can vary; 2. *perceptive knowledge* or perception, with which we know the subsistence of being; this knowledge is particular and very restricted; 3. *negative-ideal knowledge* or reasoning; all the information that comes from the authority of others reduces to this, and by it we know the existence of certain subsistences but not the *mode* of their being. We also know some relationships they have with other perceived or intuited entia, and these relationships determine them but none of this puts us in communication with the reality itself. These three kinds of knowledge can be reduced to two: we can have either information about *the essence of entia* or information about *their subsistence*, and this second kind can be subdivided into positive and negative-ideal information. Granted all this, how is the law of the operation of moral ens constituted?

401. I said that it originates from the law of the operation of intellectual ens, which is the law of *sufficient reason*. I will explain how.

First of all, the *law of sufficient reason considered as an operative principle* pertaining to practical reason[103] must not be confused with the principle of causality. If we operate, our operation always has an efficient cause because there is no effect without a cause, which is the law of every operation in so far as it is real. But this efficient cause is not always *in se* a sufficient reason. On the contrary we sometimes operate against reason, in which case we do not make the principle of sufficient reason practical, and because this principle does not determine us to operate, we do not operate according to the law of intellective being.

402. Nevertheless, this law requires us to operate for a *reason*. Reason is equivalent to knowledge, independently of the mode of knowledge. The fact that our knowledge may be either ideal or perceptive or negative-ideal does not make it any the less knowledge and also a reason for operating. All the things we know, relative to our intellective activity, constitute as many reasons for operating; the mode of knowledge does not make them more or fewer reasons for operating than what they are in themselves. For example, we know human beings by the perceptive mode, whereas the supreme Being knows them only by the negative-ideal mode. The perceptive mode has a particular

[103] The reader must bear in mind the nature of *practical reason*. I defined it in *Principles of Ethics* (*PE*, 186–187). There are two modes of *knowledge*, *speculative* and *practical*, which means that the principles of reason have two values, one *speculative*, the other *practical*. They have a practical value when taken as efficient principles of our operation, in the following way. In the speculative order the principle of sufficient reason is the *cause* conceived by the mind as a reason that explains the existence of the effect. But *in the practical order* the same principle of *sufficient reason* is totally different; it is that which makes the operator reasonable. When we have a good reason for doing an action, and this reason determines us to do the action, the *reason* has become the primal cause of our action; the *principle of sufficient reason* has become effective, operative, practical. This is the law proper to the operation of intelligence.

efficacy for initiating human activity, but the negative-ideal mode is much less efficacious. However this does not give human beings greater value, and God less value. The things we know constitute a reason for operating in proportion to their value and to what they are, not in proportion to the mode of knowledge that is more or less efficacious in moving and determining us to action.

403. But how is the *perceptive mode* of knowledge more efficacious than the *ideal mode* or the *negative-ideal mode*? The answer as follows. In perception real being is communicated to us. Hence, the efficacy of perception to move us proceeds from the activity proper to reality, which acts as an *efficient cause*, but ideal or negative-ideal knowledge give us nothing more than the *sufficient reason*, without effectiveness.

Because *reality* is purely the matter of knowledge and not the *form*, the operation proper to intellective being proceeds from the *form* of knowledge, which is present in all the modes of knowledge. Therefore, the law of sufficient reason in the practical order consists in our operating *according to formally known objects* and not *according to materially perceived objects.*

404. Thus, if an ens were solely intellective, and hence knew entia only formally, such an ens would operate always according to the law of intelligence, that is, according to the entity or value of the entia, and thus according to a sufficient reason.

Similarly, if an ens knew all entia only in one of the three modes mentioned above, whichever it might be, this mode of knowledge would have no influence in determining operations that were contrary to the concept of the entia. Hence, its operation would always be guided by a sufficient reason because it would be proportionate to the values of the known entities and not to the different modes by which they are known.

405. These teachings enable us to explain how the law of the operation of moral being has its origin in the operation of intellective being, and how we sometimes fail in one or other of these operations.

The principle of moral being is a tendency to unite itself to the whole of being, taking pleasure in and enjoying this being. This can be called natural, universal love. Strictly speaking, it is not *affectivity* that constitutes moral essence but the *universality* of the affective tendency. Moral essence lies in that quality of an ens through which every other ens, as ens, is a good for it, and the more this other ens is ens, the more it is a good for the ens. I am speaking about an ontological fact purely and simply observed. The proposition, 'Every ens is a good', is founded on the fact that 'complete ens loves itself', that is, '*in rerum natura* [in the nature of things] there is an ens we call complete, that is, moral, because it has an affection for entity itself'. The existence of this affection is the ontological fact I assert: its characteristic is that the proper object of the affection is *entity itself*, and therefore it descends in degree exactly in keeping with the degrees of entity. But when we speak of affection or love, we must understand something rational. This means that the object is given by knowledge prior to the principle of love. We have seen that the only formal knowledge we can have as human beings is that which extends equally to the whole of entity without determination, and with determination to all known entia; in other words, of all the objects we know, we know their ideal part, but not their material part. Hence, human activity cannot be moral, that is, it cannot extend virtually to the whole of being and actually to the whole of known entity, unless it follows formal knowledge; in other words, it must love being in so far as it knows it, without any regard for the mode by which it knows it. We therefore operate according to the law of moral being, only when we distribute our affection in proportion to the degrees of entity contained in the entia we know in whatever mode we know them.

406. But I said the same about the kind of operation proper to intellective being. I said this being acts according to the law of sufficient reason, and that the sufficient reason is the known ens, prescinding of course from the mode by which it is known. Consequently, the law of *intellective operation* would be exactly the same as the law I called the law of *moral operation* in that intelligence could never operate without having some primal affection by which it moved its operation. In order that this affection be proper to intelligence, it must originate from a known ens, it must be an esteem of this ens. The known ens however cannot be esteemed unless it is a good for the ens that knows it, because 'good' expresses a concept relative to an

affection; *good* cannot in fact exist without *affection*, the one involves the other through the law of *synthesism* that I dealt with elsewhere.[104] Good and affection are the distinct terms of the ontological fact I indicated above. Hence, intellective being would either have no activity at all or necessarily have embedded in it a principle of universal love, which is precisely what is appropriately called 'moral'. For this reason I always distinguish between a speculative and an operative knowledge. *Speculative knowledge* has no action outside itself, it stays with the ideas it contemplates. *Operative knowledge* is esteem and affection with which ens tends to enjoy known ens. This practical act of the intellective act is precisely what constitutes moral being.

407. I have distinguished two laws, the law of *sufficient reason* and the law of *moral freedom*. The law of sufficient reason presides over both speculative and operative knowledge. In the order of speculation, intelligent being seeks the sufficient reason for what it knows, and finds the reason in principles and causes. Once the principles and causes are found, speculative intelligence is satisfied and rests. There is still no morality here. But in the order of operation and of that affection through which intelligent being tends to unite to and enjoy the whole of entity (which makes all entity a good), the principle of operation is this affection itself. The affection applies and distributes itself to the entia in the degree that accords with their entity (their entity determines their capacity to be loved), and in doing this, it makes the sufficient reason operative, thereby turning it into a practical reason. Known entity therefore becomes a sufficient reason for operating, purely because it is naturally loved, that is (and this is the same thing), because it is naturally a good. Hence, the sufficient reason that explains to intelligence its cognitions is not the same as the sufficient reason for intelligence's operations. The first of these two functions of sufficient reason serves as light to the mind; the second serves to move the operations. This second function identifies with the law of morality. As soon as an affection is added to intelligence and the known ens shows itself to be lovable, intelligent being becomes active with an

[104] *PE*, 21–42.

operation determined by the grades of known entity. These grades become the sufficient reason for operating, and operating morally. Moral being now exists in intelligence. Hence, *sufficient reason* changes into *moral freedom* as soon as it becomes operative.

408. This law of moral being has therefore a double name: it is called *moral freedom* when considered as an active principle independent of the mode of knowledge and independent of the instincts of reality; it is called *practical sufficient reason*, when considered in the universality of the moral affection distributed according to the known entities, which are also reasons.

409. Here, I must point out again that we, although moral beings, can deviate from the law of morality and contradict it with our actions. This deviation is explained by exactly the same explanation I gave for the deviation of intelligent being from the law of intelligence. The deviation is one single deviation with two different relationships: a relationship with knowledge, and another with pleasure in known being, so that *sin* is *practical error*. We have seen that if intelligent being were solely intelligent, it would never deviate from its law. In the same way therefore, if moral being were solely moral, it could operate only morally. But we human beings are not only intelligent and moral, we are also real, and reality provides us with the matter of our knowledge. Consequently, our knowledge is partly materiated or perceptive, partly without matter and purely formal. Pure, formal knowledge constitutes the sufficient reason for intellective and moral operation because it alone makes entia known for what they are in themselves. But materiated and perceptive knowledge disturbs the order of the entia presented by formal knowledge, and impels us to operate not according to the order but according to the stimulus of reality, which has an influence on materiated knowledge. A struggle now takes place within us: the noble instinct of our morality draws us on the one hand to operate according to the value of formally known beings, and on the other to operate violently in an opposite way by the instinct of the real being we have perceived in a limited, narrow way.

410. In the midst of this great struggle the will presides as

arbiter. As I said, the will is the power of the one human subject.[105] This power differs from the three instincts mentioned above in the same way that the one subject differs from the three entities: it differs mentally from real entity, intellectual entity and moral entity. But strictly speaking it does not constitute a fourth entity; it is the union of the three entities. These, in the act of issuing from the unity of *real being* as from their root, become three and then re-unify in *moral being* as in their perfection. Thus the will is the power of being in so far as being is embedded in moral intelligence. In the struggle therefore it is the task of the individual, of his will, to determine himself either in favour of the intellectual and moral law, which tends to operate according to *formally known* entia, or in favour of the law of real entity, which initiates operation according to *materially known* entia, that is, according to feelings and their instincts. When the will determines itself in favour of the moral instinct, it becomes one thing with it and adds strength to it. When it determines itself in favour of real being, it becomes mixed up with it, and thus sin arises. The will is a power of the subject which each of the two contrary instincts tries to commandeer and keep for itself. But often neither succeeds, in which case we remain in a state of bilateral freedom or of indifference. But if one of the instincts attracts and commandeers the whole will, as happens in those in heaven and in the damned, the will necessarily and spontaneously wills and operates moral good and moral evil, and hence draws no merit or demerit upon itself. We are now in a position to determine the true concept of the *law of virtue* and the *law of wisdom*.

411. The *law of virtue* is: 'Ens shall always operate in conformity with the law of moral being.'

412. The *law of wisdom* states: 'Ens shall always operate in conformity with the law of intellective being.'

413. The law of virtue is therefore the law of moral freedom,

[105] This can explain the passage of St. Hilary where he writes: 'In the human being we find only three things: *body*, *soul* and *will*. Just as the soul is given to the body, so power is granted to each of these to use itself as it wishes'* (*In Matth*., 10: 23). His distinction of the *will* from the body and the soul shows that he considers the will as an arbitrating power that can use equally the animal instinct, which comes from corporeal reality, and the intellectual and moral instinct, with which the soul is endowed.

by which we do not allow ourselves to be dominated either by the instinct of limited real being or by the instinct of intellectual being that has been limited by materiated knowledge as opposed to formal knowledge.

The law of wisdom is the law of *sufficient reason*, by which we do not allow ourselves to be moved by an *efficient cause* without a reason.

414. Thus, the *law of moral being* becomes the *law of virtue* when it refers to the possibility present in an ens to operate in opposition to the law, and allow itself to be determined to its operations by the active principle proper to real being, either alone or united to materiated knowledge. This can happen because the operative ens is simultaneously real, intellectual and moral.

The *law of intellectual being* becomes the *law of wisdom* when it refers to the possibility of an operative ens breaking the law by again allowing itself to be moved by materiated knowledge and influenced by its own real principle in opposition to the reason clearly visible in formally known entia.

415. We see then how the laws of virtue and wisdom unite and merge into one law, which explains why the whole of antiquity gave the name 'wisdom' to *virtuous knowledge*, the basis of virtue, totally complete virtue.

416. Returning to my purpose in discussing these matters, I wanted to justify divine Providence and goodness against the three last objections. I have shown that

1. the law of moral goodness and the law of wisdom are one and the same law,
2. the law of wisdom is the law of *sufficient reason*, and
3. it is also the law of moral goodness.

Consequently anyone operating without sufficient reason would be neither wise nor virtuous.

If I can now show that those who raise the objections are not judging divine goodness according to a true and safe rule, I will have shown that the objections clearly have no validity. And the rule cannot be other than the law of wisdom that I have discussed, because it is impossible to demonstrate that there is a sufficient reason that obliges God 1. to move the freedom of all human beings in such a way that they all obtain the supreme good, or 2. to communicate himself to them to such an extent that they are dispensed from every effort and sacrifice yet retain all their moral good, or at least 3. to use his all-powerful action to convert all obstinate human beings at the moment of their death and thus save them from hell. In fact, to show that God is failing in wisdom or virtue or goodness, it would be necessary to demonstrate that because he does not do these things, he operates contrary to the law of sufficient reason. The objections therefore have no weight, and what I shall now add will make it fully clear that because this sufficient reason cannot be found, the objections are vain and void of all force.

CHAPTER 7

How the law of sufficient reason changes into the law of the least means

> *Sapiens operator perficit opus suum breviori via qua potest* [The wise operator brings his work to completion by the shortest possible route]
>
> St. Thomas, *S.T.*, q. 3, arts. 4, 5

417. The law of *sufficient reason*, considered as a law of *practical reason*, is the law according to which wisdom operates. I must now reduce this sovereign law to an equivalent formula by showing that it is the same as the law of the least means; in other words, the *law of the least means* is the same *law of sufficient reason* which wisdom necessarily follows to determine the quantity of action and expedients it must apply in its operations. The following reflections will help to give a clear understanding of the identity of the two formulae.

418. When wise people are about to operate, they ask themselves three questions.

1. Do I or don't I go ahead?
2. What effect do I want from my operation?
3. In what way shall I operate, that is, how shall I produce the effect I want?

Their answers cannot be affirmative if they do not find a sufficient reason for their affirmation.

419. Hence, the sufficient reason governing the operations of wise people is threefold; they must, in all their operations, follow three sufficient reasons:

A first sufficient reason must determine them to operate rather than not operate.

A second sufficient reason must determine them to want their operation to produce one effect rather than another.

A third sufficient reason must determine them to produce the effect in one way rather than another, with one particular action rather than with another.

420. In the order of facts these reasons, which abstractly

understood are three, constitute one single comprehensive reason because, if only one were lacking, wise people would not have that truly sufficient reason that makes them operate.

421. In the previous chapter I said that generally speaking formally known entia are the sufficient reason according to which wisdom operates. In fact, the following arguments, carefully considered, show that it is precisely entia themselves that can provide wise people with all the three reasons necessary for their operation.

I. What kind of *sufficient reason* can determine the wise to operate rather than not operate?

Clearly, it must consist in an *end* they propose to themselves. But no end can be found outside an intelligent, moral being, whether this being is wise or not. In other words, every operation of a wise person must have as its end the esteem, love, respect and perfection or production of a moral-intellective being. We must look at this in detail and classify all the operations that an intelligent being can perform.

422. The operations of an intelligent ens are of three kinds:

1. To know, esteem and love entia, and determine its other actions according to this esteem and love.
2. To add perfections to known subsistent entia.
3. To make subsist entia that do not subsist.

423. If the entia which must always be the object of these three kinds of operations of wise people were not moral-intelligent, they would never provide a sufficient reason to determine the wise person to operate, because purely real entia have only the reason of means.[106] Consequently, there would never be a sufficient reason to love or help or produce an ens, if the ens were not moral-intellective, or was not ordered to the good of a moral-intellective ens. Every non intellective-moral entity lacks *selfness*. Therefore it cannot refer anything, either good or evil, to ITSELF because this ITSELF to which it might refer something, does not exist; we supply it by means of language and imagination. The non moral-intellective entity certainly has an existence but a relative existence and solely the existence of means. As such, it is

[106] *PE*, 101–105.

incapable of good because again this PERSONAL ITSELF does not exist. Hence, it cannot be an object of another's love and benevolence because it lacks the object necessary for benevolence. It can of course be esteemed when ordered to something which might exist *per se* and has enjoyment *per se*; we can even imagine that it has an enjoyment of its own. But in these cases the object, the end that the imagination has supposed for the action, is still an ens that has *selfness*, and therefore is intellective and moral.

424. If the three kinds of actions had as object a purely real good and nothing more, they would not be wise. On the contrary it is a contradiction to think that intelligent ens might ever produce them on this condition. Even when it seemed to love or help or produce as an end an ens lacking intelligence, careful analysis would show that in doing this it would have *itself* as its end or, as I said, would, in its imagination, bestow an intelligence, that is, a *selfness*, on that particular ens that does not have it. As a result, its operation would always finish up with a being considered intelligent, or wrongly supposed to be such. In this last case the operation would be *foolish* because it lacked truth, although it would still be an *intelligent* operation.

None of these three kinds of actions therefore could be posited by an intellective ens if the object of its actions were not a moral-intellective ens. Only this kind of ens can constitute a sufficient reason that determines the wise person to operate rather than not operate.

425. Before continuing, I must point out that the same condition (that the object has to be moral-intellective) is also necessary if the actions in question are to be moral. The reason is again that wisdom and morality of operation conform and identify with each other.

We have in fact seen elsewhere that no operation can pertain to the order of morality if the action's end does not involve an intellective being.

What kind of esteem or affection can an intellective ens give to an ens that lacks intelligence?

Either it will give no esteem or love.

Or it will esteem and love it for the benefit of the thing itself.

Or it will esteem and love it relative to another intellective ens, as a means for its own advantage and pleasure or for the advantage and pleasure of another.

In this third case its esteem and affection become moral because they finish in an intellective ens.

In the second case its esteem and affection pertain to the order of morality in the opposite sense, that is, the esteem and affection are immoral because they harm an intellective ens by falsely giving intelligence to what does not have it. Here again, it is the relationship to an intellective ens that makes the act pertain to the order of morality in the opposite sense, that is, the act is contrary to this order.

Finally, in the first case, there is no act and therefore no moral act of any kind.

426. The same can be said about the perfection of an ens. If the ens that is making itself perfect is intellective or moral, the act it does is also moral. But if a non-intellective, non-moral ens is perfecting itself, no good is done, unless the perfection is produced to the advantage of another moral, intellective ens.

427. Again, the same can be said in regard to the operation that produces a previously non-existent ens. If the newly produced ens is neither intellective nor moral, nor produced for the sake of and to the advantage of an intellective, moral ens, the production has no moral quality. It will be the effect of a real being operating blindly, and never the work of a moral being.[107]

In conclusion, no work, no act has any moral value if its object or final end is not a moral, intellective ens. As I said, moral ens is simply that which tends to the *whole of being*, to the *completeness of being*, and not to only one form of being. It does not stop at reality, but adds intelligence and love to reality. In this way being is completed, and the act becomes moral.

[107] Production as such is generally neither a good nor an evil. No moral law determines that there must be production rather than no production, as long as the discussion concerns production without the manner or object being determined. But moral good and evil pertain to the *manner* of production and lie in the perfection of the product in such a way that if the producer does not stop at making his work solely real, but instead makes it also intelligent and moral, bestowing on it corresponding endowments and perfections, then what is produced is truly a moral good. This operation is also wise because the work has an end, a sufficient reason.

428. II. What is the *sufficient reason* that determines the wise person to produce one effect rather than another?

Again, it is intellective being, object of the operation. This being can provide either a morally necessary and absolute sufficient reason or an unnecessary and relative sufficient reason.

429. In the first kind of actions (esteem, love and the resulting operations), the intellective ens that is their object provides a sufficient reason which is in part necessary and absolute, that is, it imposes a moral obligation. The obligation comes from the degree of entity measured according to our formal knowledge of the being. This degree determines precisely the correct measure or quantity of esteem and love to be given to it, and determines the resulting operation. Thus, if we give to a moral-intellective ens an esteem greater than that determined by the quantity of entity present in it, we operate neither wisely nor morally because the excess of the esteem and love is arbitrary and blind; it does not have its sufficient reason in the entity when correctly esteemed and loved. If we do not give the esteem that the entity merits, our operation lacks a sufficient reason; it is therefore defective.

430. Note: this first kind of obligatory moral actions is not limited to esteem and love, but extends to the operation that follows. When this operation expresses internal affections, it is *cult*; when it does good to others, it is *beneficence*.

Thus, exterior actions, which is where our affections naturally show themselves, must not be repressed if no other motive intervenes. This also provides proof of the obligation of an external cult of divinity. Similarly, a father is obliged to feed and educate his son as a result of the esteem he must have for his son and for himself, and for the paternal love that is a natural part of himself.[108]

[108] It must be borne in mind that although the esteem for a moral ens that is suffering must induce anyone to help who is able to help, nevertheless not every suffering nor every misery endured by an intellective ens is a sufficient reason for determining an esteem and an affection that might move a moral ens to give help. If the need was the willed effect of the fault of the one in need who has acted wickedly, then the degree of esteem and affection necessary for stimulating a person to help ceases. Love of justice is now involved, which requires the sinner to be punished and afflicted. Only an infinite, omnipotent and totally gratuitous goodness, like that in the supreme Being, can take away

431. The second and third kinds of moral actions [cf. 422] do not have a sufficient reason that obliges morally. Hence, they contain actions of pure, gratuitous goodness.

The *sufficient reason* for actions of this kind is certainly not the right of an ens whose perfection we want to increase or of an ens we want to reproduce. Nobody has the right to another's gratuitous beneficence, and much less can someone who does not exist claim rights.

Nor is the *sufficient reason* the moral obligation I have excluded. On the contrary it is the pure *goodness of the benefactor* who operates according to his nature, expressed in the adage: *bonum est diffusivum sui* [good diffuses itself].

432. However the effects of this goodness have limits. These limits determine a good ens to produce certain effects rather than others, and are the result of:

1. the limited power and knowledge of the benefactor;
2. the limitation of his goodness;
3. the limited capacity of the being whose perfection or production is sought.

Hence, the sufficient reason that determines the *quantity of beneficial effect* we are talking about must lie in the *instinct of the goodness* of the benefactor-ens who is determined 1. by his own limitation, 2. by the limitation of the means applicable for the benefit, and 3. by the limitation of the nature of the ens that is the object of the benefit.

433. III. But this determination of the *quantity of beneficial effect* whose production is desired does not mean that the *manner of action* is determined, that is, the mode and means intended to be used to produce it. The same effect can be obtained by diverse modes and by diverse actions and means.

The sufficient reason therefore that determines the means of action for producing a determined effect is the quantity of the desired effect.

If several means present themselves to the mind of a wise person, and all can be used to obtain the proposed effect, obviously he will choose the simplest and easiest, the least of all, provided

sin and at the same time satisfy justice, as was the case in the redemption. But this work pertains to the second kind of moral actions I have listed, not to the first.

it truly gives the desired effect with equal perfection. If the effect he desires determines him to operate and he desires only the effect, the only means he will want to use will be precisely that which is sufficient for obtaining the desired effect. To produce it therefore, he will choose the least cause, the least possible quantity of action, the least means. This is what I call the law *of the least means*. It is the law of *sufficient reason* applied to determine wisely the *manner of operation* for obtaining a determined effect.

CHAPTER 8

The sense in which the law of the least means can be said to dominate in the real world

434. This law, on which I must base my argument, is so important that I cannot continue without indicating its domination even in the order of real things.

I stated the law as: 'Intelligent being, when wanting to produce a determined effect, will choose the least cause to produce it.' This formula contains the words 'effect' and 'cause', which are part of the law that governs the operation of real being: the law of causality.

435. An intellectual ens is, as we have seen, a real ens that contains ideal being. Hence, although it directs its operation according to sufficient reason, every operation it carries out with a sufficient reason must be subject to the law of causality because the operation is real. Intellective ens is aware of this law and understands its necessity. Reason therefore determines intellective ens to a given operation and also determines it to follow the law which obtains the effect, that is, the law of cause. This law can be expressed as: 'The cause corresponds to the effect'; in other words the quantity of the effect determines exactly the quantity of the cause. If we compared a given effect with a cause and found that the cause exceeded the quantity of the effect, then clearly all the excess quantity is lost relative to the effect; indeed, the excess is not a cause of the effect. Consequently, in the order of real being, there can be no doubt that every effect is always *maximum* relative to the cause or, vice versa (and this is the same expressed in other words), every effect is produced by the *least* of all the causes that can produce it. If the cause were not the least, it would exceed the need, and in so doing, it would not be cause.

436. Nevertheless, the concept of a *maximum effect*, or respectively of a *minimum cause*, is not strictly speaking drawn from the consideration solely of *real nature*. In real nature there is nothing more than cause and effect; the relationships of maximum and minimum are added by intellective being, which

considers the *effect* as an *end* it proposes, or as an effect determined by a mind that wanted the effect. I will explain.

437. Real nature produces only real effects. These always have exactly the same quantity as their causes; they neither exceed nor fall short of their causes. But our understanding conceives a possibility that the effects may be greater or less, although this possibility does not exist what is real. Consequently, in relationship to the imagined possibility, our mind finds that the effects are always maximum and respectively the causes minimum.[109] For example, light that passes through a less dense medium to a denser medium refracts towards the perpendicular. If we supposed that the light were endowed with intelligence, it would have proposed to itself to reach its destination by means of the shortest path and least speed, that is, it wanted to save as much as it could in distance; in which case, the only path it could follow would be the path it follows in reality.[110] In fact

[109] In fact a close look at the way mathematicians solve the problems of maximum and minimum shows that they always suppose a series of possible terms and among these they propose to find the minimum or maximum term. The terms are not things in nature but purely abstract possibilities conceived by the understanding. Thus, when the theory is applied to natural effects, the natural, necessary effect is found to correspond solely to the maximum or minimum term they are looking for and not to the other terms. This is precisely why this term alone is real; the other terms, which I said were assumed hypothetically, are ignored so that they can succeed in finding only the important term.

[110] Pietro Martino was the first to demonstrate that the minimum for light passing through various densities is the result of the speed and the distance travelled. Thus, if the speeds maintained by light in two media is indicated by a and b, and the distance it travels, by x and y, the minimum is given by the expression $ax + by$. If the mass of the bodies is added to the distance and speed and, generalising the principle, we say that in all the movements taking place in the universe, *MDV* is always verified as minimum, that is, the mass multiplied by the distance and the speed, we have what Maupertuis called, 'law of minimum action'. This law, as conceived by Maupertuis, would require a long argument to demonstrate its accurate and inaccurate parts, and I cannot do that in a footnote. But it is not necessary for the present argument: it is enough if we note that the law of minimum action, as Maupertuis conceives it, must be combined with and corrected by the law of the 'conservation of living forces' that we owe to Huygens, because Maupertuis' formula does not take living forces into account. But even this would still not be sufficient. Later on however I will discuss the *quantity* of the minimum action generally considered, and not limit myself to the *minimum action* of bodies but apply it

however it does not have many paths from which it can choose: there is only one possible path for it, the path determined by the forces that move it. But the human mind, with its intellective imagination, imagines many others as postulates. Thus, it considers as possible something that in reality is impossible, and comparing the real path with the supposed possible paths, it finds that the path followed by the light is, of all the paths, the path of the least action.

We also observe that nature often gives an hexagonal shape to what it produces, like the shells of the grain of certain plants (according to the observations of Mairan), the scales of some animals, and sometimes snowflakes, etc. This shape is the natural result of soft, flexible bodies next to each other; assembled in this way, they cannot produce another shape. But human intelligence, considering the properties of this shape, finds that of all shapes it saves the most space, and would therefore have been chosen by a geometrician who had wanted to create those natural entia according to the law of the least means. This happens because intelligence compares that shape with other shapes imagined as possible, even though in the cases where nature produces the shape, it is the only one possible.

We still need to see how, why and for what need human understanding usually turns a purely human way of mentally conceiving things into a law of nature. The general reason is that when intellective being mentally conceives *reality* it always adds something of its own, which it then finds appropriate to separate by reflection, because it wishes to purify its concept. It thus makes the operation of real nature appear as its own intelligent, voluntary operation. But an ens that operates according to intelligence and will is not tied to only one mode of operation; it proposes an end for itself, it proposes to produce a given effect determined by its free will, and this conceived effect is independent of the order of *pure reality*. Reality does not choose the ends of its operation; indeed strictly speaking, it does not have *ends*, it has only *effects*, determined exactly by the blind forces or activities that directly produce the effects. Hence, if reality cannot choose the effects of its operation, it cannot in any way

to all beings, which will change it into an *ontological* law. Also, what I will say about determining this quantity will be sufficient for my intention.

choose the means and paths for obtaining them. It has always only one path of operation, only one mode of producing the effects; other paths and modes are impossible. Therefore the effects it produces cannot strictly be called maximum, nor can the causes be called minimum, because there are no other possible effects or causes with which to make comparison. On the other hand, intelligent being proposes for itself the ends it wants; it sees the diverse paths from which it can choose in order to obtain these ends, and chooses the simplest, the easiest; in short, it chooses the path that will bring it to the desired effect with the least means. Anything extra, because superfluous, would be a waste of action and devoid of sufficient reason.

438. This is true of intellective being even when the effect proposed for the determined end can be obtained only with the action of real forces, for example, the forces of corporeal nature. If the physical effect desired by an intellective ens equalled the total complex of effects of the quantity of real, material ens at its disposal, all it would need do is wait for the overall effect that the real ens produced by itself, and this would be the effect sought.

But because intellective ens has some special requirements of its own, different from those of brute ens, it does not desire the total complex of effects that corporeal-real ens produces or can produce. It directs its will to only one among the many effects that the material-real ens naturally produces or can produce, whether an individual effect or a complex effect, and this effect must serve as means towards the intellective ens' moral and intellectual ends. It is therefore forced to search for this particular effect in nature but finds it mixed with other effects to which it is indifferent, effects it does not seek. Hence it must free the effect from all that is superfluous in the effect's nature, that is, it must simplify the effect in order to have it alone. In this way the effect becomes a *minimum* relative to the complex of all the effects with which it was naturally mixed. Hence, the direct cause chosen to produce this one effect must itself, in this sense, also be minimum. Moreover, the intellective being must not desire to use any of the forces or causes that produce other unwanted effects.

439. Let us suppose that an intelligent being wants to make a spherical body roll down from a higher to a lower point, and the

only thing it expects from the forces of nature is that the sphere descend. What will wisdom or intelligence suggest? There are numerous paths the body can follow in its descent: straight paths, curved paths or a mixture of these. Nature has all these paths, and the brute body descends by whatever path it is set on at the beginning. But the intelligent being, whose sole end is descent, will certainly choose the path where nothing superfluous occurs. Clearly, the path to be accepted among so many possible descents will be that which offers the least resistance to the body, because any resistance is contrary to the desired descent, contrary to the easiest and quickest descent for the body. Pure wisdom will find this path immediately, but the human being, who possesses only a snippet of wisdom, must search for it with long and demanding study, comparing all possible paths in order to find the path that will satisfy the conditions. He will compare the straight, the curved and the mixed paths, and after reflection will be persuaded that the desired path is a curve and not a straight or mixed path. But because the curves by which the body could descend are themselves infinite, he will look for and finally find among the possible infinite curves the path that makes the descent easier. Mathematicians have called this curve 'cycloid', that is, the curve described by the point of a wheel that touches a plane, when the wheel completes a perfect revolution on the plane. A wisdom therefore that wishes to make a sphere roll from a higher to a lower plane will trace only a cycloid curve for the descent. With this path it obtains the proposed end free from all other possible effects, whereas with other curves or inclined planes there will be superfluous effects as well as much opposition and resistance, all of which is contrary to what is intended.

440. When it became known that the cycloid was the line of the fastest descent, the following conclusion was drawn: all the points of a circumference that rolls along a plane, as the wheel of a wagon does, always move through the line of the quickest descent, as if brute nature follows this law and thus shows wisdom present in nature. But in this movement of the wheel the points of the circumference follow this path for the simple reason that the motor force applied to the circular form of the wheel turns the points through the path without any choice being made. Therefore, because it is the only possible path

followed by the points, we cannot say whether it is the easier or more difficult path. Nevertheless, relative to our human intention, it is the easiest when we want to make a body descend from a higher to a lower plane by a path that is not vertical. Intelligent being therefore attributes the laws of its own operation to material-real ens, and thus it seems to it that this ens follows the law of the least action or means in producing its effects. However I will add a few other examples of a truth that deserves much consideration. It will be a good foundation for the argument I wish to build on it.

441. Let us suppose that intelligent being wants to find in nature an isochronous movement, that is, a movement that always takes the same amount of time whenever it is repeated. Nature can certainly produce this effect but it does not distinguish this particular effect desired by intelligent being from all the other effects; it equally carries out the effects that it is capable of carrying out, according to the factual positions and circumstances in which it finds itself at every moment. When intelligent being wants to obtain the particular effect of continual, isochronous movements for any period of time it wishes, it is obliged to place certain bodies in the positions where in obedience to their own law (the law of causality), they satisfy the intelligent being's desire. Consequently, the intelligent being will apply the cycloid to the pendulum and thus obtain a constant proportion between the circular movement and the translation movement. These two movements compose the cycloidal movement, and the invariable constancy of proportion makes the durations of the movement precisely equal, which is what is desired. Once again, intelligence chooses the cycloidal curve from among all curves. It thus removes every irregularity and superfluity from the production of the effect.

442. The same argument can be applied to the invention of machines. All machines are systems of bodies devised by human intelligence to obtain a determined effect. Their perfection lies solely in simplicity, which always means action is saved. Their construction conforms best to the principle of intelligence when their action for obtaining the desired effect is least. Thus, a machine made by an infinite intelligence, by a perfect wisdom, must use the least action for its effect.

443. Nothing like this however exists in material nature. It

cannot desire this special effect because it is determined equally to all the movements its forces produce in reality. And when I say that material nature does not follow this law of the least action, I mean it produces its effects solely with its forces. This does not in any way exclude whatever might come to it from an intelligence presiding over it. I must explain this.

A material-real ens can be considered either in its individuality and in its relationships with space or with many other material individuals. The material individual (extrasubjective) is the atom, that is, the first indivisible particle, as it is thought, of matter. The forces conceived as pertaining to these atoms do not determine the place the atoms must occupy in space; wherever they are located in space they preserve their identity, and hence the identity of their forces. These forces, from which each atom results and which do not move the atom (because the material atom never passes from rest to motion by its own effort, or vice versa), do not make it seek one place rather than another; they are not the cause that makes the atom to be here or there; in other words, the cause of their location in space does not reside in themselves. This absence of cause determining their position, this negation by human imagination, was often converted into something positive and real, and this reality, created and invented by human understanding, was called 'hazard' or 'chance', such that hazard or chance were said to be the *cause* of the location of atoms in space. How did human understanding fall into such an enormous error as to transform nothing (the absence of cause) into a cause? Intellective instinct played no small part in this.

444. A property of the intellective instinct is the inclination that human understanding has to use its own principles to judge the being of things. The principles of reasoning give rise to a corresponding number of instincts in the faculties of judgment. One of these principles is the principle of cause. Our understanding is so much inclined to see effects united to their causes that whenever it does not find the causes, it readily creates and invents them with a hasty judgment. False human judgment therefore, finding no cause that locates atoms in one place rather than another, calls the absence of cause hazard and chance, and with these words gives reality to the absence of all reality. I have already noted on other occasions that words bind the understanding to

themselves; the understanding takes words as signs of things and always supposes that some thing underlies the word even when it does not underlie it. Thus, by virtue of the word 'nothing', we conceive nothing as something positive; here the word 'nothing' takes the place of the absent thing, it is a representation without the represented thing. But we find this absence of the represented thing irksome, and instead of examining the word's proper task, we blindly accept it as a true representation, although that particular word truly resembles an impostor whom no one has authorised to carry out the task he presents.

445. In the case of atoms therefore, the cause of their location in space is not in them, nor in their nature nor in their forces; hence it must be sought outside of them, whatever it is. Moreover, this cause must have determined the place in space for all atoms at the beginning of the universe. From these first positions, by means of reciprocal action and the mutations that followed successively afterwards (according to constant laws), the present location of atoms, that is, the present state of the material universe, came about after that first period. It is clear that such a cause, which is outside matter, must be intelligent.

But if it is intelligent, it must have had present to it some ends that required it to locate the atoms in one way rather than another because, as we saw, *ends* constitute the sufficient reason according to which intelligence operates.

These ends in fact can be only the good of pure, intellective and moral entia.

If we suppose this intelligent cause to be infinite, it must have observed exactly the law of the least action, that is, of the least means, in locating the atoms. Hence, it would have located them in such a way as to obtain the maximum desired effect with a respectively minimum action.

Consequently, whenever the relationships between the position of many atoms are considered in connection with effects that are helpful to intellective-moral beings, then the law of the least means, of which there can be no trace in the real atom, must become evident in the complex of atoms, that is, in the world, if the world is to be truly the work of wisdom. Because these relationships cannot have material reality as their cause, they have to be attributed to intelligence. Therefore:

1. if the observation of nature leads us to discover that material nature spontaneously produces a quantity of effects helpful to intellective beings, and

2. if these effects follow the law of the least action,

then clearly, a cause endowed with intelligence has intervened, and a wisdom presides over the material world.

Because this fact is observed in so many effects produced by atoms and material causes that are associated in a given way in nature, the law of the least action, or of the least means, is usually considered as governing material, real being. Strictly speaking however it is simply a law of the intelligent author, who remains hidden as he presents his work (nature) to our senses.

446. From all this we can conclude that the law of the least means is present in brute nature in two ways:

1. in purely material effects, and

2. in effects seen as ordered to the good of intellective-moral beings.

In the first way we give no thought to the usefulness these effects offer intellective-moral beings. An example would be the least action with which light passes through media of different density, or in the shortest path taken by electricity to reach a given term by means of conductors of equal substance and different length, etc.

In these effects it is human intelligence that gives the law of the least action to nature. It does not compare the way that natural effects are produced with other ways that are physically possible (these ways in fact do not exist, because material nature has only one path, only one way of action). Instead, it compares the production of natural effects with ways that intelligence supposes to be possible: intelligence reasons about material nature as if this nature were an agent free to choose between diverse ways of its operation. Here, the law of the least means is clearly not a law of purely real being but is added by us who subject real being to the law of our intelligence.

In the second way, the effects depend on the harmonious union of many material entia, a union not determined by any power or force found in entia but by an intelligent cause that must have disposed and brought the entia together in this way. We see yet again that the law of the least means pertains not to material and brute being but to intelligent being. Nevertheless, it is applied to material and brute being because the law is seen as followed in material and brute being due to the intelligence that presides over and governs blind reality.

447. So far I have considered the real being that is present to us in the universe in one respect only, as purely *material* or corporeal, that is, sensiferous or felt by us.[111] But we must also consider it in its other respect, that is, as *that which feels*. The purely feeling soul of brute animals is indeed real but not intelligent. Does this soul therefore, in its operation, follow the law of the least action or means?

In the brute animal, we must note, sensitivity is not purely and simply sensitivity but is organised and individuated. Hence, to know whether it follows the law of the least action, we must consider it as it is in itself, prescinding from what it owes to organisation, which is precisely what I did when I discussed matter. I examined matter first of all according to what it contains, in its visible forces, and afterwards according to what it receives from its location in space. The latter adds to it certain active and passive relationships between its parts, which gives rise to this sensible universe.

448. Sensitivity, considered purely as such, that is, in its pure concept, is simply a uniform feeling diffused in space, which becomes its term; it is not greater in one place than in another. It has no fixed principle on which it depends, but the same principle of feeling is found equally and with the same activity in every point of felt space. Such is the pure concept of sensitivity, stripped of everything that can come to it from elsewhere.

When understood in this way, sensitivity, or more accurately feeling, does not operate according to the law of the least action and means but according to the law of cause.

But what in fact is the activity of corporeal feeling as such, what kind of activity does its concept present?

449. The activity of feeling must be sought in the sentient act. The property of this act is to actuate a *maximum feeling* among possible feelings, in the way that happens with every act of real being does, and with every cause that achieves all the effect it is capable of. We have already seen that in the order of material real ens the effect is always equal to the quantity of the cause,

[111] *AMS*, 230–246.

and that human intelligence considers this effect a *maximum*, because it compares the effect to other minor effects seen in the idea but not physically possible. In the same way, the act of feeling produces a maximum feeling, because with our understanding we can imagine lesser feelings, inadequate for the act, and in comparing these lesser feelings with the effective feeling, we see the latter as maximum. But granted the act of feeling, and its determinations, and the conditions that come to it from elsewhere, feeling is still neither greater nor less; it is what it must be. Consequently, it cannot be called maximum: it is simply proportionate to the act that produces it. Hence, the maximum found in feeling does not pertain to reality but to the way the intelligent human being conceives it.

450. Nevertheless, the circumstances and conditions that determine the act of feeling can vary infinitely. What then is the sufficient reason which makes a given feeling have particular conditions and not all the others, and is determined in one way rather than another? Is this sufficient reason found in sensitivity?

This reason will certainly not be found in sensitivity. As we saw, the position of atoms in space is not determined by their forces; the cause must be sought outside them. Similarly, the conditions that determine whether the intensity of the act of feeling is greater or less, whether it has this or that characteristic, etc., are not found in the act of sensitivity itself. Sensitivity is indifferent to whatever its act may be; it simply posits the act to which it is determined by the conditions imposed on it. Therefore, the cause of its determinations does not exist in itself but must be sought outside it.

451. What then is this cause that is external to corporeal sensitivity and determines it to one act rather than another?

It is the location of the corporeal material molecules that are the term of feeling or, to use a more common word, the organisation. In fact corporeal sensitivity is an activity that consists in the *adherence of feeling* to a body. It is therefore so dependent on a body that if it were possible to withdraw the body from it, corporeal sensitivity would no longer exist.[112] Consequently, the

[112] Cf. *AMS*, 262–349, 367–494, where I explain how I consider *sensitivity*, determined by organisation, as the principle of all the instinctive operations of

location of the corporeal particles destined to be a term of feeling, and the passions to which the resulting body is subject, are the conditions that determine the act of feeling and hence determine the feeling itself that is brought into being. If the felt body is more extensive, the feeling is also more extensive. If the felt body changes place, the feeling accompanies it. If intestine movements take place within the felt body, and they do not make the body withdraw from the feeling, the feeling feels these movements, receives stimuli and sensations. If the body loses its continuity, the feeling is multiplied in accord with the multiplication of the continua, and if many bodies unite, many feelings unite and blend into one sole feeling. In all this, sensitivity operates with its own activity, which is 'adherence of feeling to bodies'. In short, whenever a body, in certain given positions and conditions, is given to sensitivity, sensitivity infuses its proportionate energy of 'adherence of feeling to it', effecting the maximum possible feeling in the way explained above. Because every activity, every act, is a force that posits itself, the felt body, subject to sensitivity, comes under an influence of sensitivity that restrains it or maintains its intestine movements, or increases or reduces them, according to the nature of the force or sensitive activity.

452. An obvious consequence can be drawn from this. The determination of corporeal feeling does not lie within corporeal feeling itself but in the location of the atoms and molecules that constitute its term. And as we saw, the cause or explanation of this location cannot be attributed to corporeal forces, but must be outside bodies. Hence:

if 1. observation tells us that the atoms and molecules are distributed in such a way as to produce an organisation, a unity of feeling, so that effects useful to intelligent beings are obtained, and

if 2. a complex, permanent feeling is also obtained, which

an animal. This opinion, which I discussed at greater length in *Psychology*, is not new, but perhaps has not received the great development it is capable of. Bonnet expressly admits the same principle: when discussing the marvellous works of bees, he says: 'I do not say that bees, and all animals, are pure machines, clocks, looms, etc. A soul probably adheres to the machine; it feels its movements and takes pleasure in these movements. Through the machine it receives pleasant or unpleasant impressions. This *sensibility* is the great and *sole movement* of the animal'* (*Contemplation de la Nature*, p. 11, c. 27).

in its operation produces effects according to the law of the least action,

then clearly the foreign cause that has determined this harmony of corporeal parts for such an excellent end and with great wisdom, is an intelligent cause. Therefore, if we acknowledge that animal operations obey the law of the least action or of the least means, we cannot conclude that this law pertains to purely real being, but on the contrary, to an intelligent being that rules over real being and makes real being obey it.

453. Consequently, I do not deny that in the composition of the animal and in its operation we note an end and a mode grounded in intelligence; indeed this is established.

If for example we consider the composition of the most perfect animal, the human being, we find that the composition has an order directed to the service of intelligence; indeed, it has an order directed to the production of intellective being, such as we precisely are. The composition of the human body therefore, which cannot be explained by corporeal forces or sensitivity, must be attributed to an intelligent author.

454. In regard to the other animals, we make use of them in numerous ways, and new uses are discovered as science progresses; we even discover new advantages that unknowingly they bring us.

Consequently, they also are ordered to the good of intelligent being.

455. We can of course find certain traces of the law of the least means in the composition of animal bodies. Philosophers have given little thought to the composition of bodies, but the little they have so far given is sufficient to demonstrate this fact in the many effects produced by animal bodies. Moreover more and more traces of the great law of intelligence will be discovered as a result of observations, findings, and reflections on animal operations. If we were to go into this subject more deeply, we would never finish; it is sufficient for me to touch upon it.

456. First, we must note that the animal results from organisation, from a given distribution of the atoms that together constitute the living machine. There is no argument to prove that the sensitivity of the atoms ceases when the organisation breaks up, but there are many arguments to induce belief that feeling

always continues to adhere to the atoms, whether the feeling is multiplied in keeping with the number of divided and organised parts, or in keeping with the number of atoms themselves. This explains the gradation of animals from the most complex to the most simple, terminating with living molecules or living atoms. But when only individual atoms remained, certainly no movement could be revealed in them because they are indivisible and unchangeable; there would also cease the combination of many feelings into one as well as their stimulation and the harmony of movements and feelings that gives unity to the multiplicity and preserves and reproduces this unity, which strictly speaking constitutes the *animal*.

457. This concept of the animal shows us that the law of the least action regulates both the composition of the animal and its operations. Everything that is the animal and is operated by it for its life, preservation and reproduction, arises from one sole, most simple cause, the cause of *sentient activity*. An infinite wisdom gave this activity diverse occasions to operate in ways as wonderful as those we see in each animal. In the beginning this wisdom united corporeal atoms in such a way that they became fertile seeds. Granted these first aggregations of atoms that we call seeds, perhaps in all possible varieties and posited in relationship with other external, suitably disposed atoms, *sensitive activity* is sufficient to do all the rest: to constitute the animal, to nourish, develop and reproduce it; to constitute all the countless forms of animals that, as I said, I believe must be as many as the possible aggregations capable of constituting a living machine. This gives us the gradation, not of beings, but of animals. In fact, observation, which every day becomes richer and more complete, supports what Leibniz called the *law of continuity* in nature, granted that this law is restricted to the sphere of animate entia and is correctly understood [*App*., no. 9].

No design could be more simple: the animal is produced with all its countless species distinguished into one continuous gradation by means of a most simple *sensitive activity* and of a varied disposition of atoms, which give the animal the opportunity to operate in various ways. This process must not be seen as something arbitrary but as issuing from the intrinsic order of being.

458. Constituted in this way, the animal is endowed with organs, whose action is so harmonious that the animal's

preservation and the development and propagation through which it perpetuates itself are not an effect produced by the action of one organ alone but by the conspiring actions of all its various organs. If we take nutrition as an example, we see how the digestive and assimilative apparatus maintains a constant harmony with the apparatus that takes and prepares the food for the stomach. For example, the intestines of animals that live off vegetables are longer than those of carnivorous animals. Because a vegetable is a less nutritive food, it had to remain longer in the body so that the nourishing substance could be extracted. The mouth, teeth and oesophagus of this species of animal has a form that best serves the taking, breaking and preparation of plant food; on the other hand, they have no apparatus suitable for obtaining animal food. If we examine the beaks of birds, it is truly amazing to see how they have a form proportionate to the food appropriate to each genus. Birds of prey that feed on living flesh have a strong, hooked beak for seizing and tearing the prey. Seed-eating birds have a short, thick beak necessary for breaking and, I would say, for grinding seeds. Those that live off spiders, moths, mosquitoes and other delicately-formed insects have a sharp, gentle beak for gathering only the smallest and softest insects without, at the first bite, breaking them into pieces. The snipe, feeding off vermin found below the surface of swamps and mud, could not feed itself without its very long, delicate beak, used for searching in that kind of terrain; the same beak would be an impediment for all other creatures. In short, the organs of every animal species are the most suitable and adapted instruments imaginable for the needs of their species. The greatest suitability and adaptation of these instruments is a saving of action because an appropriate instrument expends less action in obtaining the effect than an inappropriate and badly designed instrument.

459. It may be objected that the organisation develops by itself under the influence of the primal instinct that operates as a formative or shaping force. This may be so, but the simplicity of the means that nature uses to assemble the animal and make all its parts harmonise and serve each other, shows that the law of the least action is applied to these complex beings by an incomparable wisdom. Moreover, why does the instinct's power, unique in its concept, vary its operations to develop so many

and so varied species of animals instead of one species only? And why do the tiny bodies of the simplest animals have the above-mentioned internal order and correspondence between their parts?

460. Corporeal sensitivity, I said, is purely one in its concept; instinct is simply the activity exercised by sensitivity on the sensiferous, felt body. But the operation of sensitivity and instinct changes and follows another direction and mode of operation only when the combination of the sensiferous, felt atoms changes. To explain the animal therefore, we must suppose, as I have said, a primal organisation whose cause is not in sensitivity, we must suppose a seed organised in a given way in which the sensitivity acts through its own instinct. We must also suppose a variety of seeds, which explains the tremendous variety of the different generations of animals produced by the formative force of instinct.

Therefore, we have to turn to an intelligence which, instead of dispersing the atoms into infinite space, assembled them so that they were ordered into various groups. These groups were various animal seeds but each seed was perfect, that is, composed and devised by such wisdom that the action of the sensitive instinct had the opportunity to develop a perfect animal body, a tiny totality with ordered parts, where life, stimulus, and individuality of feeling were maintained and reproduced in a perpetual cycle. All these parts, developed with the greatest accord between them, had a role to play in this process and were capable of producing the one sole effect that results from a complex of harmonious effects, the one sole feeling in which countless feelings that constitute the animal are fused together.

461. If we also consider that every animal, in order to preserve itself, must be in relationship with the external and sensiferous world and must act on this world in order to produce diverse effects necessary for its maintenance and reproduction, we will find everywhere traces of the law of the least action, and the progress of this study will be proportionate to the multiplicity and manifestation of such traces.

462. We can in fact say in all truth that all the movements an animal makes are directed by the law of the least action. The animal does not perform all the movements it could but always chooses only those that bring it the greatest enjoyment with the

least effort. This explains why, for example, an animal that could walk on two legs walks on four, and why an animal walking on two chooses this position as the most comfortable. Every animal lies down, arranges its limbs, carries its body in the most comfortable way, although it has the strength to place itself in another position, but the principle that determines it is always the principle of doing the least possible to obtain the same end, that is, an equal enjoyment, free from all discomfort. This principle determines the use of the animal's forces so that it regulates the speed of its step and its walking; it produces the stops, the dashes forward, the leaps, the quick turns, every variety of its movement.

463. The sounds made by diverse generations of animal are determined by the same principle. Each has the faculty to produce sounds and always maintains the same tone and measure of call, whistle and song, according to the choice it makes which depends on what costs the animal least and has equal or more enjoyment for it. The principle also explains the multiplicity of languages and dialects among human beings: the organs of speech, modified in different ways, produce diverse sounds, not because they could not make all the sounds the same but because the law of the least action determines the faculty they have of forming words to produce those particular words that are the most spontaneous.

464. The discussion would be endless if we considered the habitats and nests that diverse animals construct for themselves, where the law of the least action sometimes manifests itself geometrically. I will limit myself to the familiar example of bees.

As is known, all their cells have an hexagonal form, and among all possible polygons only this form occupies precisely the least space. But more than that: the hexagonal cells terminate in a pyramidal base by uniting three similar, equal rhombi. The angles that the rhombi could have made when joined in a pyramidal form are infinite — the pyramid could be more or less acute, more or less obtuse. But among all these possible angles, which does the bee constantly choose in its task? They were very accurately measured by Maraldi who found that the greatest angles are generally 109 degrees 28 minutes, and the least, 70 degrees 32 minutes. Koenig, an outstanding mathematician, sought a solution. He asked: 'What should be the angles of an hexagonal cell with a pyramidal base, such that the cell requires the least material possible for its construction?' He found the answer in calculus, which indicated that the greatest angles of the rhombi had to be 109 degrees 26 minutes, and the least angles 70 degrees 34 minutes. He also demonstrated that by preferring a pyramidal base to a flat base, the bees economically use all the wax necessary for constructing a flat base and simultaneously acquire more space and more comfort.

The construction of the hive according to these splendid geometrical rules is certainly the necessary effect of instinct. But where does the instinct originate? Certainly not in the concept of sensitive activity, which is totally indifferent to the way it operates. This activity is, as I said, determined by the organisation, the union of the atoms to which the sensitivity together with its instinctive force adheres as to its term, and by which it lets itself be directed and actuated in various ways. This aggregate of atoms is the origin of the seed of the bee, which in turn becomes the little body constructed and animated in such a way that it determines the formative instinct of the hive. But what is the cause of this aggregate? It is not in the nature of atoms nor in the nature of sensitivity; it is therefore an external, higher intelligence governing the universe.

Thus the law of the least action is uniquely a law of intelligence and is seen faithfully maintained in real being that composes the universe. Therefore the universe is ruled and directed by an intelligence.

465. This great truth is precisely the source from which flow, as from their principle, the logical rules that the most famous and scholarly investigators of nature have laid down for all those who are open to understanding and interpreting nature and discovering its secrets.

Newton's two laws are of this kind:

1. 'The causes of natural things must not be admitted to be more than those that are true, and suffice to explain the phenomena of things.'*

2. 'In so far as possible the same causes must be assigned to natural effects of the same kind, like the fall of a stone in Europe and in America, like the reflection of light on the earth and on the planets.'*

These two rules are true solely because, as Galileo said prior to Newton, ' nature, through common consent, does not use many things to do what can be done with few.' This is precisely the principle of the least action and means, universally acknowledged by naturalists under diverse names, including sometimes the name 'law of parsimony'.[113]

[113] Giovanni Bernoulli also proclaims the same principle: 'We can never fail to wonder that the effects of nature always concord with the most general metaphysical rule that "nature does nothing useless; it always follows the shortest path, and what it can accomplish with few things it never accomplishes with many"'* (*Op.*, vol. 4, p. 271).

[465]

CHAPTER 9

What has been said can solve the objections put forward

466. The law of the least means is therefore the law of sufficient reason in so far as it determines the *mode of operation of wisdom*. Nature is seen as following this law, and also both sensitive and insensitive *real being*. But it does not have its cause in nature. Therefore it is proof that intelligence presides over the real being that composes the universe.

The law of the least means also becomes the law of virtue when it is considered in relationship with moral freedom, that is, with the affection present in intelligent being and with the will.

Therefore God would be failing in the attributes of both wisdom and goodness if the *mode* of his operation towards human beings were not regulated by the law of the least means. This is the important corollary that was established by the argument used up till now for the law. It is in fact the corollary on which I will base my solution to the proposed difficulties.

467. Three reasons can be given in support of the claim that God does not treat human beings with *supreme goodness*:

1. God could move the will of all human beings equally to good. He could do this with guaranteed effect and without destroying freedom.
2. When God communicates moral good to human beings, he obliges them to sacrifice something. But God himself could communicate in abundance all the good obtained by the merit of their sacrifice.
3. God could move the will of all people with irresistible effect, even at the moment of death, and determine them all directly to good. Although it is true that this action will destroy their *meritorious freedom*, the good arising from this freedom could be compensated by a great outpouring of good without their loss of freedom.

These assertions suppose that if divine goodness is to be supreme, it must do these three things; and if it does not do them, it is not supreme. But the objectors must prove that this kind of action is required by supreme goodness. As I pointed out, if they do not prove it, they have proved nothing; their objections are simply ignorance and rashness. They should first consider what they must do to demonstrate effectively their proposition that 'if divine goodness is to be good, it must carry out the three things they impose on it'. They must demonstrate that if God fails to act in this way, he is not following the law of the least means. This law determines the operations of wisdom and goodness in such a way that if either wisdom or goodness stray from it, they cease to be wisdom and goodness. Hence, if the objectors do not demonstrate this, they have proved nothing: their objections are empty words, not objections.

They should consider whether it is easy or difficult for them to prove, with some probability at least, that 'the law of the least means must determine the most wise and excellent God to operate in the manner they claim'. To help them find an answer and realise the difficulty of the assumption in which they enmesh themselves (or rather the hazard on which they unfortunately founder), I will state the question more precisely which they claim to have so neatly settled.

468. It is clear that if God is to move everyone to supreme good with guaranteed effect, his action in them must be greater than it is at present; he must move some with guaranteed effect, while to others he gives only the faculty, if they wish, of being successful in their actions, allowing them not to be successful through their own defect. To have God act therefore in the way the adversaries want and prescribe, he clearly would have to apply and produce in us a greater quantity of action than he in fact does.

Similarly, it is clear that if God wished to dispense all human beings from all sacrifice and bestow on them moral good without any sacrifice on their part, he would again have to do much more than he does at present if they are to be compensated for the moral good they would have lost. Therefore in this case also he would have to apply a greater quantity of action.

Moreover it is evident that if God wished to move the human will by such a great efficacy that he determined it to supreme good and the forces of freedom could not oppose this movement, he would again have to do far more in us than he does at present. Therefore once again he would have to increase the quantity of action he uses and produces in us for our good.

In short, the proposed objections claim that if God were supremely good, he would have to increase the *quantity of action* that he presently uses towards his human creatures.

469. Let us suppose therefore as a kind of postulate that God does deliberate about using a *quantity of action* greater than he actually uses, in favour of his creatures. Does this mean that this greater quantity of action which he decides, as it were, to expend, must be directed to obtaining the three goods that the objectors lay down?

Whatever quantity of action God disposes to use in his creatures, he must use it according to the law of wisdom which, as I showed, is the law of the least quantity of action or of the least means. Hence, in order to demonstrate that any *increase of action* by God in his creatures must, strictly speaking, produce the three goods required by the objectors and not other goods, the three goods must be shown to be the *maximum effect*, that is, the maximum good that God's increased action can obtain. As we have seen, a given quantity of action is said to be minimum when used in such a way that it has its maximum possible effect. Consequently, if the objections are to have any meaning, the following proposition must first be demonstrated:

> The quantity of action necessary to obtain the three indicated goods, or to obtain two or just one of them (for example, that all human beings be saved), cannot be applied to obtain any other *greater good* than this: the eternal salvation of all.

This is what the adversaries must prove if they understand sufficiently the meaning of their argument and if it is to have any force.

470. But they have never proved nor ever undertaken to prove this. Hence, their objections were never more than the gratuitous assertions used by ignorant and rash people who claim to lay down the law of the Creator's operation. They say to God: 'You must operate in this or that way if your operation is to be most wise and excellent.' They then consider themselves absolved from explaining 'why God should operate in the way they prescribe'.

471. There is much more. Not only do they fail to understand what they need to prove if their reasoning is to be reasoning and

not arbitrary judgment, not only do they never suspect the need to investigate such a difficult assumption, the assumption itself, whenever made, can be shown to be totally beyond the intellective forces of humanity. Only infinite intelligence is sufficient to solve the great problem, as the following demonstration shows.

472. A government that has many intelligent beings under it is not the best if it does not procure for them the greatest good possible. This greatest good results from the sum of all the goods attained, minus the sum of evils, if there are any. I think that this proposition can be taken as certain; anyone wanting proofs can find them where I have given them.[114]

To reduce the proposition to the formula appropriate to the present question, I will change it (as mathematicians do with equations) into the following, which still means the same as the first: 'A government is best only when it exercises its providence in such a way that the quantity of its governing action procures the maximum good purified of the evils that its action is capable of doing, because in this way the effect is obtained with a minimum action.' Hence, the overall good minus the evils can be maximum when the good is distributed among more rather than fewer people (except of course what pertains to them by right); all that is required is that the good be maximum.[115] The good obtained by the government does not have to be without evils, provided that when these are subtracted, the good remains maximum. For example, let us suppose that the quantity of governing action available to the government can be used in two ways for two overall effects, each maximum in its kind. One of the effects is the greatest possible sum of goods not accompanied by any evil. The other effect is the greatest possible sum of goods accompanied by evils but in such a way that when the evils are subtracted, the sum of goods remains the greatest possible. Clearly, governing wisdom must measure the two relatively maximum sums: the sum of good that brings no evils with it and the sum of good left over when purified of the evil it brings with it. Governing wisdom must see which of these two is greater, because wisdom will always choose the

[114] *SP*, 581–628.

[115] Ibid.

greater: only by choosing this, will it obtain an absolutely maximum good, and hence operate according to its law of the least quantity of action.

This reasoning supposes that the goods and evils are measured in the human spirit which acts as their weighing scales, and that they cancel each other out, just as weights do on a balance, so that an evil compensated by a good that outweighs the evil ceases to be an evil; in fact we desire it for love of the greater good that comes with it.[116] We must add that in the case of an excellent governor this balancing and cancelling out of goods and evils takes place in his own spirit because all the goods he produces are a good for him, and all the evils mixed with the goods that he has produced are evil. Hence, if he is excellent and the evils are removed from the goods, he will want to obtain the maximum total of goods that remains.

On the other hand, if his wisdom showed him that the sum of goods resulting from the greatest goods possible not mixed with evils exceeded the sum of goods mixed with evils but from which the evils had been removed, he would certainly be acting in conformity with his perfect goodness if he produced only pure goods without permitting any evil.

473. If we now apply these basic calculations to God's government of his intelligent creatures, we will clearly understand the difficulty our adversaries must have in proving their thesis, if their objections are to have any force. They maintain that God ought to save all human beings and prevent all evils. But, as is clear from what has been said, this pertains to the supreme goodness of his government only in the case that the salvation of all human beings, or the removal of all evils, is an absolute maximum of good relative to the *quantity of action or means applied*, that is, the quantity of overall good must be greater than the good that could be obtained by allowing some people to be lost or suffer some evils. The objectors must prove that such in fact is the case, namely, that the *quantity of action* they want God to exercise to obtain the effect they demand cannot be better applied than by making it produce that effect; in other words, they must prove that the quantity of action used to prevent the evils would produce a good absolutely greater than it

[116] I also demonstrated this in the place indicated.

would if God had used it to produce other goods mixed with evils. Indeed, if we want to make God apply a greater quantity of action than he actually applies in favour of his intelligent creatures, we must still ask:

'Are we certain that this increase of action or means that we claim from God, according to the law of wisdom, must properly be directed to produce the required effect, that is, make all human beings attain salvation? Could the case not be that when God has determined to produce the *greater quantity of action* or means that we desire, he could draw another good greater than the salvation of those who are lost, or greater than freedom from the afflictions we suffer? Could he not perhaps multiply the number of intelligent natures with the same quantity of action and thus draw a good that cannot be calculated? No one can say or prove with certainty that, by means of another combination of circumstances, the increase of action we have claimed could produce a far greater good than the evil we want prevented, even if the good produced were mixed with evils. No human being, no angel, can calculate this; it exceeds all the power of finite intelligence. To solve the problem, we would have to know every single procedure God could follow and every way he could use the quantity of action. It is therefore great ignorance and crass rashness to claim of God that in the government of his creatures, 1. he applies a quantity of action greater than he does, and 2. in applying this action, he applies it as *we* want it, not as his wisdom directs.'

Certainly, when evils affect us so much that we want them all banished from the world, we operate blindly; we are calculating only one thing and do not consider that the quantity of action sufficient to end those evils could perhaps be applied differently and produce goods infinitely greater than the evils. I say greater, even if the goods are mixed with evils, even if the sum total is calculated after the removal of the evils that might accompany them. It is therefore purely an illusion of our own making when we affirm that God cannot be supremely good if he does not make all evils cease; it is a totally unproven prejudice, a gratuitous proposition, incapable of being proved by anyone. In fact, to prove it we would have to prove precisely that the quantity of action used to make evils cease could succeed better if God guided it in another way. Our adversaries do not even think of this; moved by the sight of evils, they make confident declarations without comparing the evils with the much greater goods that would certainly be lost if the evils were removed, indeed without comparing them with the much greater goods that a most wise God could produce with the very quantity of action used to abolish the evils.

It is true that the law of the least action does not include the condition that 'the quantity of action of a wise person must produce only goods free from every evil'; the law simply determines that 'the quantity of action of a wise person must produce such an effect that, after the evils have been compensated by goods, the effect is maximum'. Nevertheless the law of the least action is the only law that determines the mode of operation of wisdom and goodness. The condition therefore that some may wish to add to the law does not pertain to the law of wisdom and goodness. It is false to claim that God must follow this condition if he is to be seen as most wise and excellent in his operation. Consequently, the condition imposed by the adversaries on divine operation is arbitrary. Whenever we see that it is not observed in the works of the Creator, we cannot conclude that he is less wise and less good. The objections of the adversaries therefore collapse of themselves, they are totally without meaning.

474. Indeed, by imposing on divine wisdom a condition that in no way pertains to it, the adversaries certainly destroy divine wisdom. Any wisdom that operates with laws that are not contained in the law of wisdom is not wisdom. The adversaries restrict wisdom and divine goodness; in a word, they are really complaining because God is not as foolish as they are. Such then is the outcome of objections which at first sight seem so serious and so effective to human short-sightedness.

475. No problem can be correctly and truthfully solved if it is not free from all the conditions that do not pertain to its nature. The problem of wisdom is this: 'What is the maximum good that can be obtained with a given quantity of action?' The adversaries want to add to this problem a condition that does not pertain to it; they say that 'the maximum good must not have any evil joined to it'. With a single arbitrary condition they prevent a solution to the problem of wisdom; they denature the problem, they change it into another more limited problem. If

God is directed by wisdom in his operation, he will, through the very essence of his nature, let his censors protest as long as they like, while he continues on in the way that befits him.

476. This mode of divine operation shows us in fact that the great problem of wisdom, to which only the infinite mind can apply itself, is solved by God in this way: 'A sum of pure good obtained from a given quantity of action, while allowing some evils to accompany the goods, is greater than the sum of the goods that have no evil mixed with them.' This serves as a commentary on the famous words of St. Augustine: 'God has obtained more goods from evils than he would have if he had allowed no evils'* [*App.*, no. 10].

CHAPTER 10

Response to the objection that it costs God nothing to do more or do less

477. From all this we see that the adversaries' propositions are nothing more than commonplace objections which, when thoroughly examined, disappear.

But the objections are the kind made by uneducated people against Providence. Instead of examining more deeply the intrinsic reasons of good government, they are guided solely by their desires and subjective affections. I must therefore answer another very simplistic objection, similar to the previous objections.

The objection can be presented as follows:

— It costs God nothing to employ a greater or smaller quantity of action in favour of his creatures; he has no need to save his action.

Even if he could obtain a greater good by using the same quantity of action in another way, this greater good would not necessarily be lost, because he could easily obtain it by adding another quantity of action sufficient to obtain it.

— But surely, this second quantity of action could itself be used to obtain a greater good?

— Certainly, but the greater good could be obtained by a third increase of action.

— And what about the greater good that could be produced by using this increase of action in another way?

The objector still replies: it could be obtained by yet another increase of the quantity of action. Thus, the argument can go on to infinity, because God's action is infinite and not determined by any quantity.

478. Carefully considered, this reasoning is similar to the suggestion given by a courtier to the Duke of Urbino. The foundations of his magnificent palace were being dug. Castiglione relates that there was no place to put the excavated material, and that a courtier advised the Duke to have a large hole dug in which it could be buried. When the Duke asked him where the excavated material from that hole would be put, the courtier

replied that he should have the hole made bigger to take that material. When the Duke repeated that making the hole bigger would mean digging out a greater quantity of material, the courtier insisted that the hole be made bigger to take this increase of material. The Duke could never make him understand that the same problem kept recurring because the courtier thought that the problem was solved by making the hole always bigger until it was sufficient to hold all the material of the foundations and the hole.

479. But to reply directly to the objection: in my opinion it contains two errors, indeed two absurdities.

The first is that if the law of the least action is essential to wisdom, as I have shown, then to claim that God should abandon it and follow a different law is to claim that God should act foolishly. The only people who can think that God should abandon the law of the least quantity of action when he operates are those who have not really understood the law, who have not understood that in the mind and soul of an excellent governor evils are cancelled out whenever they produce greater goods, just as a thermometer's degrees of cold would be cancelled out if of themselves they produced a greater heat.

480. The second error and absurdity contained in the proposed difficulty is the supposition that God can produce outside himself an infinite quantity of action. I say 'outside himself' because the quantity of action we are discussing is produced in the world, which can be considered as an aggregate of means and ends. The ends are the goods produced, that is, the overall, final sum of moral-eudaimonological good. The means are all the entities and actions directed to producing that sum of good. The law of the least quantity of action is upheld when the *sum of the means* is least relative to the sum of the ends or, vice versa, when the sum of the ends is greatest relative to the sum of the means. But neither of these two sums can ever be infinite, although God who produces them is infinite.

481. The objector may now say: But if God's goodness is infinite, as it must be, will it not naturally want to diffuse itself infinitely? And if it wanted to diffuse itself infinitely, why not produce infinite entia, where it would find no limit at all? Surely, to deny God this power would be a limitation of his omnipotence?

I reply: Not at all. When we say that God cannot do absurd things, we do not limit his divine omnipotence; absurd things are not included in the vast ocean of being.

To claim that the *number* of finite entia that God had to create should be infinite is to claim an obvious absurdity. An infinite number is a contradictory, repugnant concept; no number exists that is not determined and cannot have another number added to it to make it greater. Moreover, each of these entia would itself be finite and limited to a certain finite quantity of good. Even the means necessary for guiding each ens to the good it is capable of would also have a finite quantity.

482. Again, if we think that every created ens should have had an *infinite nature* so that God could manifest an infinite goodness in each, we fall into another, no less obvious absurdity. The plurality of entia contradicts the concept of the infinite because only one infinite is possible, and this infinite is God. Hence, his goodness is infinitely diffused and spread within himself by those hidden operations with which he subsists in three persons. But if God's goodness extends infinitely within himself, no one can prevent it from diffusing itself in the creation of finite entia and communicating to them the good they are capable of. Forbidding him to so would mean limiting his goodness on the plea that his goodness is unlimited. This is true even granted that the action of his goodness supposes an infinite object and, we might say, an infinite production, which is the case, as I said, in the generation of the Word and in the procession of the Holy Spirit. Nevertheless, because finite entia are *in se* possible and are capable in a limited way of good, it is absurd to forbid God to create them; they are not evil; on the contrary they are good, even if limited.

483. On the other hand, no limited being (and hence our adversaries) can ever propose such an objection if they really understand its force. Every created ens endowed with intellect loves its own existence and also the goods it is capable of; it considers both as a supreme beneficence of divine goodness.

484. There is nothing contradictory therefore — indeed it is fitting to the concept of divine goodness — that in addition to diffusing itself infinitely within infinite being, it also diffuses itself in finite beings, creating them and enriching them with the endowments they are capable of. This clearly closes the door to

every other objection that can be made about the dimensions of these beings. No human reasoning whatsoever can prescribe their dimensions in such a way that God must act exactly according to the measure imposed by that reasoning. Moreover, even if our reasoning had the foolish temerity to prescribe this measure, reasoning always remains finite and at an infinite distance from the infinite. Hence, the quantity of real entity of creatures cannot be determined by the simple concept of divine goodness. We must in fact leave the determination to *divine free will*, or at least find another way to determine it.[117]

485. In creation therefore, no matter how much it extends endlessly beyond human imagination, only a finite quantity of real entity can exist, that is, entia limited in nature, dimensions and number. As a result, the *ends* and *means* are *limited.*

Divine goodness of course has *in se* no limits, but when it is made the principle of contingent being, it receives a kind of limitation, not proper to itself but proper essentially to the effect it produces, because the capacity of finite ens for good is finite.[118]

486. Thus, divine goodness cannot extend itself any further than the capacity of created ens allows, and here again it is following the law of wisdom. We must see therefore how far the capacity of created intellective and moral ens extends, whose good alone can be the purpose of creation.

487. The nature of moral-intellective being — for example, human beings — is such that on the one hand, as we saw, it participates in the infinite in that it intuits ideal being, on the other it possesses reality in a finite mode, and therefore as real it is finite. Its extension to the infinite in the sphere of ideality allows it to have an infinite *extrinsic end*. Therefore, God's goodness, which has no limits, ordered his intelligent creatures

[117] In saying this I do not deny that we could still ask one of the most sublime questions: 'Because God's goodness is infinite, it certainly tends to produce the maximum good. Therefore, when considered in its relationship with possible finite entia, does it contain a principle of appropriateness which in some way determines the dimensions and number of created entia?' Here however I need not deal with this great question; my argument is complete and fully effective without it. But I will deal with the question in Cosmology.

[118] The capacity of finite ens is finite because whatever is given to it is given only in a finite mode.

to the enjoyment of himself. In this respect those in heaven who are said to have obtained their great end, see the whole of God, but because every created real being is finite, the whole of God's reality cannot be communicated to it. Hence, those in heaven are correctly said to see the *whole* of God, but not *totally*. They are also said not *to comprehend* him. God himself is said to be incomprehensible and to dwell in inaccessible light.

488. Someone may answer that when God communicates himself in reality to intellective being, he is not fused with, nor becomes the same as, this being but always remains external. But this is not sufficient: finite, real being has not only finite faculties and forces, but in addition objects must also make themselves in some way finite in so far as they make themselves proportionate to the act of the faculties. It is absurd and contradictory to imagine an act of a finite being that can perceive God totally. To use a simile, although a very inadequate simile, we can say that if a body, a hand for example, touches a much larger body, for example, the earth, the area the first body touches of the large body is only as extensive as the area of the first body itself which, in our example, is the hand. And if the globe of the earth could have such great unity and simplicity that no division could be conceived in it, we would correctly say that the hand that touches it would be touching the whole earth but not totally.

489. Consequently, when God wishes to benefit an intelligent creature, he acts in conformity with infinite goodness when he gives the creature infinite good as an extrinsic end, that is, gives himself, because the creature is capable of so great a benefit. However, when we ask in what measure he can communicate his reality, we must reply: in a limited measure.

490. If we also want to know how great that measure is, I leave it to the reader to choose the reply considered best, either the reply that seems to determine in some way the extent of the measure, or St. Thomas' reply that the measure can always be indefinitely increased provided it remains always finite. I myself accept both replies because both come to the same conclusion that the real good which God can give to a finite ens must always have a finite *quantity*.

491. It is true that if the measure can be always and

indefinitely greater,[119] there is no sufficient reason to determines its quantity. In this case God could choose equally this measure or another greater measure. The choice would depend purely on his freedom, and this act of his freedom would constitute the only sufficient reason for the choice. All this results from what has been said, but the matter will be better understood if we argue as follows. Let us accept that God fixes a measure of good to be shared among his creatures. We certainly could not say that he should have chosen a greater measure, for example twice the amount. If the amount were twice the first, it itself could be doubled, and then doubled again, and so on indefinitely. Only one of the following choices can be accepted: either the measure of good that God must destine for his creatures is infinite, or it stops at a finite quantity. The first is absurd; hence it must stop at a finite quantity. But every finite measure, when increased, never approaches the infinite, which is always at an infinite distance. Hence, we cannot prescribe one measure rather than another for God's goodness. If we had a valid reason for requesting an increase, we would have an equal reason for asking for a second increase and a third — we would never come to a halt and therefore never determine a measure, which in any case must be determined.

Clearly then, in every system there is either a sufficient reason that determines a fitting measure of good that God must share among his creatures, or this determination depends on an act of his free will, without any other reason. It is always equally certain that the good destined for his creatures must have a definite quantity, a limited measure.

492. In the end therefore the quantity of action God uses to produce the good cannot be infinite but limited.[120]

119 'Indefinite quantity' means a quantity that can always be increased, but never be actually infinite.

120 In many places St. Thomas deals with the question whether God does the *better thing*. He distinguishes a *material better* and a *formal better*. He excludes the first but admits the second. In one place he presents this objection: 'Nature does what is better, and God much more. It would therefore be better if there were two worlds rather than one, because many goods have more value than one.' He replies: 'No operator makes material plurality his end because material multiplicity does not have a material term but tends of itself to the infinite. The indefinite however contradicts the

493. The law of wisdom however requires this quantity of action, whatever it is, to be minimum relative to its effect, that is, its effect must be respectively maximum. Granted that the divine mind is presented with all possible effects to be obtained by the quantity of action applied in various ways, and granted that the effect of maximum overall good does not consist of pure goods alone but of goods mixed with evils (and often occasioned by evils), then God, in order to act in conformity with his infinite wisdom, must prefer the composite of goods mixed with evils. He cannot prefer the composite of pure goods, because the composite of goods mixed with evils, after the evils have been subtracted, returns a net sum of greater goods, which is the end of divine goodness.

494. If in the concept of the world, which served as type for his creative power, God saw that the sins and the loss of those who damn themselves were necessary evils for obtaining the greatest good from the least action, he had to permit them. Not to permit them would mean he was departing from the law of wisdom and goodness, from which of course he could not depart in his works because he himself is wisdom and goodness.

495. Everything I have argued demonstrates that the case could have been precisely as explained, and no human intellect could demonstrate its impossibility. Hence, the adversaries have not proved that sins and damnation contradict the concept of divine goodness and wisdom, even though they could be prevented by divine power. Their objections cannot prove anything, but are prejudices of an ignorant rashness.

concept of end. When we say that many worlds are better than one, we are speaking about material multiplicity, and this better does not pertain to the intention of God in his operation. If he had made two worlds, it would have been better to have made three, and so on indefinitely' (*S.T.*, I, q. 47, art. 3, ad.2). Here, the Saint admits that the *formal better* pertains to the end God proposes.

CHAPTER 11

After answering the objections, we can now turn to the moral and eudaimonological evils that happen in the universe, and demonstrate by positive arguments that they do not in any way harm divine wisdom and goodness; on the contrary, they prove them. — Preliminary notions about how the quantity of action is measured to determine whether the action is minimum

496. We have seen that no one can assert that the sins and eternal damnation to which mankind is subject prove a defect in the goodness of God, who could prevent them but does not do so. It is impossible to prove that the removal of these evils from the world would not violate the law of wisdom, which is the law of the least quantity of action. This fact is sufficient to justify divine Providence.

But if adversaries cannot prove that the universe can be formed and governed by the least quantity of action without these evils, I believe that the opposite can be proved, that is, that the evils are necessary if the law of the least action (which is the inescapable condition of infinite goodness and wisdom) is to be maintained in the universe. Even if the available proofs had only the force of probable conjectures, the work involved in assembling them would still be consoling and useful: although not necessary for justifying infinite goodness, they help us to raise our mind to such goodness, and strengthen faith and trust in the creator and preserver of everything.

I will present these extra, almost superfluous proofs. For those who have understood them, they will ultimately be not only far more than conjectural but rigorously demonstrative. I will present only a few because this field of investigation is rich with an inexhaustible harvest. Even if I presented many, I am certain there would still be many more for others to investigate.

497. The investigation to demonstrate that the evils of this life and of the future life give us a reason for praising rather than impugning God's wisdom and infinite goodness concerns first of all how the quantity of action can be measured and therefore

how it can be shown that this quantity, in order to be minimum, must permit evils.

498. The investigation will be helped if we proceed with the greatest clarity of ideas. The subject is so intricate that our reasoning can go astray if the terms used are not clearly understood. I begin therefore with considering how the quantity of action is measured in general, and then determine which quantity of action is the object of our problem.

499. I. The quantity of action we are talking about is relative to the *effect*, that is, the action is not in itself called *minimum* but is minimum relative to the desired effect.

500. II. Because the desired effects can be multiple, the measure used to determine the quantity of action relative to one effect cannot be used to measure the quantity of action relative to another effect. For example:

a) If the desired effect is solely that a body reach a given place, then granted the speed, the straight path will be that of the least action; in a system of straight paths, the paths that take the body by the shortest route will be the system of the least action. This is the principle of Ptolemy, the shortest path in optics and catoptrics. The space travelled is the *means* used to obtain the end, and also the means that must be saved if there is to be less quantity of action in the production of an effect. This is called a minimum quantity of action, based solely on the distance saved. The shortest route is therefore called the least action relative to the *saving of distance*.

b) On the other hand, if time were considered as the *means* for obtaining an effect, clearly the least quantity of action would be the least time spent in producing the quantity. We must therefore look for the maximum *saving of time*. Applying this principle to the movement of bodies, we obtain the least action by calculating the speed of the movement and the shortest distance: the faster a body moves, the quicker it reaches its term.

c) If we consider *force* as the means and we want to *save force*, we need to establish that the quantity of action is less when the same force is used to move a body at a greater speed. Hence in this case also the quantity of action is in indirect proportion to the speed. Moreover, if the force and the mass of the body are fixed, the resultant speed is in indirect proportion to the number of obstacles the body encounters, as happens when bodies follow the cycloidal path in their descent — here we have Leibniz's principle of *the easiest path*.

d) We can conclude that under these two aspects a greater speed does not constitute a greater quantity of action (which was generally maintained by Maupertuis), except on one condition: the saving of speed must be considered an *effect* to be obtained, that is, speed is considered as the *means* for obtaining another effect. In this case, if a reduced speed gives the same effect in the same time by the same movements, the quantity of action will be less, precisely because *speed is saved*. Euler[121] applied this principle together with the principle of saving space to the trajectories traced by central forces. He demonstrated that the velocity multiplied by the element of the curve is always a minimum. Lagrange extended this principle to every system of bodies that are subject to the laws of attraction that they exercise on each other in any way whatsoever.

e) If the desired effect is simply *uniformity of motion*, the more uniform the motion becomes, the greater the effect, and this is maximum when perfect uniformity is obtained. In this case, the quantity of least action will consist in the least means used to transform an irregular continuous movement into a uniform movement. This is the problem of the clock, where the accelerated movement of a weight or of an expanding spring has to be converted into the uniform motion of the clock's hands. Here, neither the maximum speed nor the maximum space traversed, etc., are desired. The *simplicity of the means devised to obtain uniform motion* constitute therefore the perfection of the clock.

f) But if the desired effect is to make a utensil or instrument out of some material, so that the *material* is considered as means, then the saving will concern the material. We can say therefore that there will be the least action if the instrument is assembled in such a way that *minimum material* is used. This again is the principle of Koenig, who, as I said, demonstrated that bees, when constructing their cells, use the least wax possible.

501. III. We must also bear in mind the consequence that if

[121] Cf. *Mémoires de l'Académie de Berlin*, vol. 7, yrs. 1750, 1751, and also his work on the problem *De Maximis et Minimis*.

the desired effect is not simple but compound (many effects are desired), the *saving of means* cannot always be obtained by one effect. In this case the maximum effect results from the compound of the desired effects, and the least action results from the least quantity of one means or of various means understood as one. The mechanics of muscles can serve as an example. Nature has devised the machine of the human body in such a way that movements were large and endowed with great speed, and at the same time used the least energy. Here therefore, there was no concern to save space or speed; rather the desire was for a movement that would cover a greater space. Space and speed did not have the concept of a *means* but rather of *effect*, which had to be maximum for both. Thus, the *means* that had to be rendered minimum was *force*. The muscles and bones mostly constitute levers of the third kind.[122] In this kind of lever the force acts without loss, and therefore with maximum effect when applied to the lever in the normal direction. But when applied obliquely, the force divides and the part that is not normal is lost. In the case of muscle applied to bones, it acts on them in an almost normal direction because muscles that contract are attached to the underneath of the enlargement found at the extremity of bones. Here *force is saved*. On the other hand, if we note that the part of the lever where the resistance is much longer than the part where the power is exerted, we see that a greater force is needed to obtain the desired motion than if the resistance part were shorter. This is because the wisdom of the Creator wanted to obtain simultaneously a faster and greater movement, and could not do so without applying greater force. Thus, if we stretch out our arm and, let us say, the part where the muscle is attached moves five centimetres a second, the extremity of the arm moves at a speed of about sixty centimetres per second, precisely because the resistance part is twelve times longer than that of the power part. Hence, if the desired effect had been solely to move the lever, and no other effect (the speed and extent of the movements) had been simultaneously sought, it was impossible to save all the force that could have been

[122] In the science of mechanics a 'lever of the third kind' has the fulcrum at one end of the lever, the resistance at the other end and, in the middle, the force applied to move it.

saved. Consequently, because the desired effect is compound, a little more force was necessary to make the quantity of the total desired effect greater.

502. IV. Finally, it can happen that the desired effect is one simple effect but the means used to obtain it can be only many, and they must operate together in such a way that all the profit that one means could give cannot be obtained without impeding the action of another. Here again it is necessary to sacrifice a part of the action of each of the means if the total effect is to be maximum. I will take an example from political economy. The purpose of a tax imposed when a given product is introduced is to bring a maximum income to the State. Two means are available: increase the tax and increase the introduction and consumption of the product. But if the tax is increased, the introduction and consumption will clearly decrease. On the other hand, if the tax is greatly reduced, it brings little return because it is so small. Neither of these two means can be used without diminishing the efficacy of the other. The maximum will be obtained by reducing the tax to such a term that the resulting increase in the introduction or consumption of the product will compensate advantageously for the loss resulting from the reduction. — The position of the light of a street lamp is a case in point: the higher it is placed the more area it illuminates but less powerfully; the lower it is placed, the less area it illuminates, but more powerfully. Hence, to obtain the maximum effect, a height must be determined where the strength of light compensates most advantageously for the area lost at a greater height. This opposition of efficacy of means is present in the majority of the problems of maximum and minimum, and its cause is the *limitation* that I said is inherent in all finite things.

503. All these examples allow us to reduce the principle of the least quantity of action to another more general formula, which is so precise that in every case of the general problem it precludes all possible questions about the measure to be used in determining the minimum *quantity of action*. The formula will be: 'Use the *least means* to obtain the effect desired.' This effect, relative to the means, is maximum. Thus the principle of the least quantity of action becomes the *principle of the least means*, and this is the formula I will now follow in my argument.

Chapter 12

The problem that had to be solved by essential wisdom for marking out the path for essential goodness[123]

504. That the formula 'the principle of the least means' is more accurate than the formula 'the least quantity of action' is seen from the following. 'Means', which corresponds to 'end', indicates that the minimum aimed at is a relative minimum. On the other hand, 'the least quantity of action' seems to indicate an absolute minimum. Hence we find in the universe that the least means is always used to obtain the desired end, but we do not always find the least quantity of action, except by changing the meaning of the phrase, that is, by using different measures to measure the quantity of action. In fact, anyone who claims to measure the quantity of action by always using Maupertuis' formula 'distance multiplied by speed', would often find the principle inapplicable. But if we see that distance and speed are saved in many movements of the universe, then nature seems to achieve, as its end, that the movement is smooth and free from violence. We also often see that nature, far from saving distance and speed, prefers to increase them, as in the case of muscular movements, where it saves energy. On other occasions, nature apparently wants to obtain the greatest possible quantity of motion and save time, energy and obstacles. In short it is always the *means* it saves in order to obtain the *end* that is put before it and varies according to need.

505. This variation of the *end* contains no contradiction in nature if we bear in mind everything I said above. I noted that in the case of matter and sensitivity, that is, in the case of what constitutes *real being separate from intelligence*, no true end and therefore no principle of the least means can be found. Instead,

[123] It is not necessary to point out that in the case of the operations of the divine mind, we use a language that is human and insufficient, because we do not have a better. The reader knows that divine intelligence knows everything with one single act, without a sequence of thoughts. Divine intelligence does not reason, does not need to solve problems to find a conclusion, which we, considering the limit of our faculties, must do.

we see only forces and activities that produce what they must exactly produce; in these cases, there is neither a possible maximum nor a possible minimum. But in the case of an intelligence that desires to obtain an effect from nature, it can make this effect an end and find the least means for obtaining it. If it is a case of particular ends, intelligence can propose many of them, and often one excludes another: for example, relative to a material nature, the end proposed by intelligence varies: it can be to position a body in a given place, or to obtain speed, a quantity of motion, smoothness or uniformity of movements, or a given shape, etc. Intelligence finds the least means to obtain each of these ends, seeking the means (and often finding it) in the forces of nature or in the way these forces have been distributed and combined. But whereas real nature does not itself change its ends, intelligence considers the operation of nature partially, under diverse relationships, sometimes for an effect changed into an end, sometimes for another effect contrary to the first and also changed into an end. Human intelligence is moved to do this because it needs these particular, even contrary, ends to obtain a higher end, which is to enjoy satisfaction. But if the same intelligence finds the forces of material nature distributed in the universe in such a way that they can be easily adapted to the many and contrary effects it wants to obtain in the easiest and simplest manner, that is, by the use of the least means, then clearly the diverse forces and parts of nature have been given a wonderful distribution and combination by a supreme intelligence.

506. But we must now take the discussion to a higher level because it concerns the end Providence had in view; we must investigate whether this end is obtained by the least means, that is, by the inviolable law of wisdom and goodness.

The end desired by Providence is the final end. Providence seeks the *greatest moral perfection of intelligent creatures*, followed by the *greatest eudaimonological good*, that is, the greatest happiness. As we have seen, the only end that moral-intelligent being can have is moral-intelligent being itself and the good of this being; there can be no other *sufficient reason* for its operation. This good of the intelligent being is an absolute, universal end; all other goods are relative and partial ends; hence, relative to the final end, they are only means.

We must therefore establish how much moral perfection and happiness God had to communicate to his creatures so that his supreme goodness might be praised.

We have seen that it was not possible for this quantity of eudaimonological moral good to be infinite because the creature could not be infinite. But as long as the quantity was finite, and no other conditions were added to the problem, it could increase indefinitely according to God's free will.

However, we need to discover whether another condition or another application of the principle of the least means has added a fixed limit to this finite quantity, without which it would remain indefinite or indefinitely augmentable?

In fact it is inconceivable that divine goodness, which by nature is infinite, can be restricted to a certain measure of benefits, unless wisdom places a limit on it, and if it does, the limit does not diminish God's goodness; on the contrary it perfects and completes it. Nevertheless, the absolute quantity of the external effect diminishes in order to give the effect a greater relative quantity, that is, make it maximum relative to the means.

Therefore we now see what the nature of the problem was that divine wisdom had to solve in order to lay out the path for essential goodness to follow in its operation. The problem was 'to determine the quantity of eudaimonological-moral good that the Creator had to distribute to his creatures so that this quantity was maximum relative to the means used.' Indeed, if the good produced in the universe were ever maximum, and the quantity of means minimum, the universe would be perfect, nor could an infinite goodness have given it better order.

507. Consequently, if in such a universe, conceived by the divine mind with so perfect an order, there were sins and also the damnation of those who sin or damn themselves, it would be patently clear that both the sins and the damnation, far from prejudicing the supreme goodness of the Creator, would confirm it.

As I said, nothing demonstrates that this is impossible, and this was sufficient for me to reply to the objections against Providence. If in fact the thing is possible, we must suppose that the supreme Being operated in this way; otherwise we would have to demonstrate either that God does not exist or, if he does, that in his operation he does not follow a way in conformity with his divine attributes — both of these things are equally absurd. In order to doubt divine existence (although it is confirmed by many other proofs), we would need a *rigorous demonstration* that eudaimonological and moral evils cannot be part of a universe which, among all possible universes, is precisely most wise and excellent because totally governed by the law of the least means. Hence, if no such demonstration exists, and no finite mind could conceive such a demonstration, then God exists (as other proofs show), and he permits the evils as links in a most ordered universe.

But the task I had set myself goes further. I have defended the *possibility* that such evils are part of the universe as a result of wisdom ordering the universe in conformity with the law of the least means, and I have also supposed this to be the case. Now however I want to demonstrate *positively* that these evils are in fact present in our universe for the reason I have given, namely, that the law of the least means had ordered the universe in this way so that it might be perfect and totally worthy of God.

[507]

CHAPTER 13

The principle to be used for solving the problem concerning wisdom in its relationship to the creation and government of the world

508. The demonstration I have just mentioned requires us to find a principle that can guide us in applying the law of the least means to the universe. It must be the same principle that divine wisdom had to use to solve the great problem and thus mark out the right path for divine goodness to follow.

The principle, which results from what has been said and is clearly indicated in the Gospel, can be expressed as follows: 'The principle of the least means will be maintained when created entia are so governed that the greatest possible good can be drawn from their activities.' The principle of the least action clearly requires that all created entia and all their activities are used in such a way that their use and, so to speak, their mutual trading, give the greatest return.

509. JESUS Christ seems to have indicated that the providence of the heavenly Father harmonised with this principle when he said that the Father's glory consisted in drawing the maximum fruit from his disciples: 'My Father is the vinedresser. Every branch of mine that bears no fruit he takes away, and every branch that does bear fruit he prunes that it may bear more fruit,' and he gives the reason: 'By this my Father is glorified that you bear MAXIMUM fruit.'[124] These words expressly say that God's providence tends to produce a *maximum* good, that is, the maximum fruit possible that can be drawn from his vine.

510. This great principle can be translated into another formula, equivalent in meaning to the first, but more adapted to my need to apply it in certain ways. The formula is: 'The principle of the least means will be maintained when created entia are so governed that not one of them and nothing of their activity are left unused, that is, are lost or do not bear the fruit they could if used in another way.' This also seems to be expressed in divine Scripture in Job's words: 'Nothing upon earth is done

[124] Jn 15: 1, 2, 8 [R].

without a cause,'[125] that is, without an end intended by Providence, as the context seems to indicate. Christ himself also taught that no sparrow falls to the earth independently of the heavenly Father's will,[126] meaning that no event, no matter how small in the world, is wasted but is directed by God's wisdom to obtaining some good.

Such then is the inviolable law of wisdom and divine goodness, that there is no entity or activity in the universe, nor anything done, without all the fruit it can give being gathered from it — all such things are considered an organic part, so to speak, of the universal system.

[125] Job 5: 6†.

[126] Mt 10: 29.

[510]

CHAPTER 14

First consequence: when God can obtain a given quantity of good by using created entities and activities, it is not fitting that he obtain it by an extraordinary and direct intervention of his power

511. The undeniable and evident principle I am discussing enables us to apply the law of the least means to the government of the world, and to draw as corollaries some propositions which demonstrate that the eudaimonological, moral evils permitted by God are part of the plan of an infinite goodness and wisdom.

We begin to see this from a proposition that originates directly from the principle of application: 'God would not be acting wisely if, instead of drawing a certain quantity of good from created entities and activities, he were to obtain it by a direct and extraordinary intervention of his power.' The reason is obvious: in such a case the entities and activities that he left unproductive would remain unprofitable, unused and lost because he disposed that the fruit they could produce be obtained by the use of another means, by a different use of his own activity, not by the activity of his creatures. Hence, one cause would be used as two causes to obtain an effect as one effect, whereas the extra cause and action that would be used in this way and granted the wish to use them, could obtain another fruit different from that obtainable from the created activity.

512. For example, let us say that divine wisdom, by using creatures and exploiting their activities to produce good, could obtain a quantity of eudaimonological and moral good equal to a hundred, after all the evils mixed with the good had been subtracted. Instead however of doing this, let us suppose that divine wisdom wanted to obtain the same amount of good by miracles and by any other extraordinary intervention of its power. God's infinite goodness would still not be satisfied because, in the second case, a complex of means was employed which, used in a different way, could have produced an amount of goods equal to two hundred and more. Therefore, a loss of a

good equal to one hundred and more has taken place. Hence it is not valid to say, as I showed earlier, that the good obtained by the action of natural entia is mixed with evils that could have been avoided by a direct, extraordinary intervention of God. In fact we saw that in the weighing scales of the universal Governor of the world, evils and goods must neutralise each other, as they do in human affections, and that the total of goods is obtained by first subtracting the evils, so that only a total of pure good is left. Granted therefore that in the case of created entities and activities, the greatest amount of good cannot be obtained without the admixture of evils (which is a limitation proper to all contingent beings), it does not follow that divine power must intervene to remove and prevent the evils. Such an intervention would entail a loss of so much good that we would have the absurdity of a great means being used to obtain a little end.

513. If it is in fact certain that 1. the extraction of all the good possible from created activities cannot be done without simultaneously permitting evils, 2. these evils cannot be removed without the extraordinary intervention of divine power, and 3. this extraordinary intervention is contrary to the law of wisdom, which is the law of the least means, then the eudaimonological-moral evils to which creatures are subject, the sins, and the damnation of some, do not destroy but rather establish the wisdom and goodness of God.

CHAPTER 15

Continuation: the necessity of second causes

514. The principle we have discussed gives rise to another corollary: the necessity of second causes.

The purpose of divine wisdom and goodness is to obtain a maximum fruit from creatures, but creatures could not produce any fruit if they were not causes.

515. We should carefully note this truth: if creatures were not causes, creation would lack a purpose worthy of God. When God created, he could have no other purpose than to make his creatures good, just as he is good. If creatures were solely passive, they would not be good with a goodness of their own because they would receive everything: to receive is not goodness, much less moral goodness. Only those natures that desire, love and do moral good are capable of their own goodness and of moral goodness. Hence, with their own acts they make themselves causes of good.

Not only divine wisdom, but divine power shines more powerfully when it produces cause-beings rather than beings lacking action. A power that is not complete and perfect cannot produce other causes that are perfectible by their own acts; an ens that is totally inert and impotent to do anything does not attain the order of perfection. Producing only one cause is much more powerful than directly producing many effects.[127]

Therefore not only divine goodness, not only wisdom, but the very display of power required that God create beings that were second causes.

516. Although this was certainly necessitated by the divine attributes, it seems that it was also required by a metaphysical necessity arising from the nature of being. We cannot in fact

[127] St. Thomas says so well: 'This' (the existence of second causes) 'does not result from the insufficiency of divine power but from the immensity of his goodness through which he willed to communicate his likeness to things, not only in so far as what they might be, but in so far as they might be causes of others. In these two ways, all creatures receive divine likeness in common, as we showed above (c. 21). This made the comeliness of order visible in created things'* (*C. G.*, bk. 3, c. 50). Cf. also *S.T.*, III, q. 72, art. 2).

conceive an ens that is totally devoid of action, and if it has some action, it already has the more or less perfect nature of cause — here, entity, actuality and cause become synonyms. Hence, the concept of entia that are not in any way causes seems to involve a contradiction. Moreover, the more a thing is ens, the more it is cause. Accordingly, if God could not be satisfied with creating the lowest level of entity, he could not be satisfied with the lowest level of causes.

517. These arguments that prove the necessity of second causes considered both in their nature and individually are not the only arguments; another can be added, drawn from the order and harmony of many causes. This order and harmony, which makes a whole out of many individuals, increases created good a hundredfold, indeed a thousandfold. But I will discuss this later and demonstrate the necessity that entia created by God must be placed in connection with each other.

518. If the universe had to be composed of causes, God had to make these causes fruitful, that is, produce in their overall complex all the good they could. This is the principle of application of the law of the least means, which I wanted to establish.

519. Once again therefore, it was necessary that the natural order and the subordination of second causes be maintained as much as possible without interruption throughout the course of the world.

520. Moreover, because entia are constant natures, they are also constant causes, and because they are bound harmoniously with each other, they have a permanent order. The result is another very beautiful corollary: 'It conforms to divine wisdom that the universe be ruled by universal, permanent laws and not through individual, arbitrary actions.'

521. This corollary, which has its origin in the principle that the universe is a complex of cause-entia, a complex of substances that have their own operation, can also be proved directly by applying the law of the least means. When created natures are left to operate with their laws and capacities, God acts far less than if he were to intervene at every turn to achieve what can be simply obtained through these laws and capacities.

CHAPTER 16

Second consequence: granted all the good that God's government can draw from all the activities of the creature, it is appropriate to his goodness 1. that he adds his direct action to produce in them and obtain from them the good they could not accomplish by themselves, no matter how they were governed, and 2. that in the use of this supernatural action he still upholds the principle of the least means

522. The second corollary resulting from the principle of application is: 'The direct, supernatural intervention of divine power in creatures is certainly not impossible, but it cannot take place except to obtain those goods that the creatures could not produce by themselves, no matter how they are governed, but can produce when helped by God.'

523. This intervention takes place in fact when *grace* is communicated to the creature, which raises the creature to a supernatural order. No human being, no moral-intellective creature could ever have attained the *perception of God* with the forces of its nature alone, nor communicate directly with God, if God had not communicated himself to it; in a word, it could never have performed one single act pertaining to the supernatural order and, much less, enter habitually into this order.

524. The communication of divine grace is like a new creation: through it a new entity, a new ability is created in us.

God gratuitously endows his creature with this gift that is outside nature, and it is a gift very fitting to his goodness because his goodness, which is infinite, tends to produce every possible good. In this gift God upholds the law of wisdom, which is the law of the least means, that is, he gives his grace in such quantity and in such a distribution that, joined to the activities proper to human nature, it can produce the greatest fruit.

525. Consequently:

I. No quantity of grace is lost, none is given fruitlessly by God; it produces the good that he intended when he gave it.

We find that God himself says this in Isaiah: 'His word will not return to him empty'.[128]

526. II. In bestowing grace, God calculates the dispositions of his creatures and foresees the use they will make of it. He also foresees all the consequences that will come from it not only to the individual to whom it is given but to all other individuals as well, to the whole human race and to all intelligent creatures. He bestows grace at the time and to the extent he foresees that that particular quantity, united to the natural and supernatural activities of the creature, will produce fruit greater than could have been obtained by any other distribution.

527. For example, let us suppose that the quantity of grace to be distributed is equal to ten[129] and that there are two unfaithful nations. One of the nations has sufficient natural probity to produce with its own forces a natural-moral good equal to a hundred,[130] while the other nation is corrupt, and the moral good it produces is equal to ten. But in his infinite wisdom, God sees that if he communicates the ten degrees of grace to the first nation, it would produce only ten degrees of supernatural, moral good, perhaps as a result of the pride that makes it believe it is virtuous because it is not corrupt; on the other hand, if he

128 'For as the rain and the snow come down from heaven, and return not thither but water the earth, making it bring forth and sprout, giving seed to the sower and bread to the eater, so shall my word be that goes forth from my mouth; it shall not return to me empty, but it shall accomplish that which I purpose, and prosper in the thing for which I sent it' (Is 55: 10–11). When he says that his word comes from his mouth, he means that grace comes directly from him and not from any creature, it does those things he wills in sending it: 'It shall accomplish that which I purpose, and prosper in the thing for which I sent it'.* Even if grace does not sanctify or convert the person who resists it, it obtains other ends, other goods which were God's intention in bestowing it.

129 The reader should bear in mind what I have already demonstrated, that the quantity of grace God distributes, whatever it is, never increases infinitely; it is always a finite quantity.

130 There is no need here to enter into the question whether fallen man can with his natural forces alone produce a moral good entirely free from evil, even from every element of *philautia* [self-love]. My argument will be sufficiently compelling if human beings can do some moral good solely with their own forces, which all Catholics grant. Moreover, I do not see why, when moved by respect for the moral law, we cannot perform *some act* with our natural forces — this is not beyond human nature.

bestows the ten on the second nation, which is humiliated by the sense of its own disorders, it will be welcomed with gratitude,[131] and thus bear a supernatural-moral good equal to a hundred. Clearly, divine goodness that wishes to draw the greatest fruit from its gift will give the ten degrees of grace to the corrupt nation.[132] Thus, the first nation continues to produce a hundred degrees of natural good, the second however a hundred degrees of supernatural good. However, if the ten were given to the first, the supernatural good produced would be equal only to ten, resulting perhaps in a diminution, not an increase of their natural good due to the greater perversion that arises from opposition to grace, and due to the very little natural good of the other nation so advanced in moral corruption.

528. This throws light on why God has certainly wise reasons for deferring the grace of faith for particular nations and anticipating it for others, also for deferring for a very long time the coming of the Saviour into the world, which had fallen into the greatest darkness of sin by the time the star of justice rose.[133]

[131] Can the acceptance of grace with a feeling of gratitude be a purely natural act? I think it could be if grace is not considered as grace, that is, relative to its supernatural effects, but as a means to strengthen us against natural corruption. The reason is that the object of the act (the reduction of natural corruption) is substantially natural. But if we mean gratitude for the supernatural effect of grace, the gratitude is supernatural and can result only from grace. We must distinguish therefore the two effects of grace (although in reality they cannot be distinguished): one strengthens nature, rendering it capable of natural virtue, the other gives us the power of supernatural virtue. The first effect, granted it is produced in us by any cause, can be known with natural light; the second can be known positively only with the light of grace. Hence it is possible to be grateful for the first with natural will, but for the second only with supernatural will produced by grace itself. I am speaking about the first feeling of gratitude which, although natural, presupposes the grace without which the gratitude cannot be.

[132] This shows that God does not give grace according to merits and that natural virtue neither merits grace, whether *fitting* or *congruous grace*, as the theologians call it, nor is an occasion for God to give his grace, although it sometimes can be.

[133] One of the reasons that facilitated the promulgation of the Gospel was certainly the awareness people had of their own corruption and the urgent need they felt for some reform in order to safeguard human things, which were collapsing under the mass of vices. St. Augustine observed that we cannot conceive what state of degradation the human race would have come

But we must not think that the above case of the two nations allows us to conclude that God always distributes his grace in proportion to greater natural corruption. I used the case purely as an example. In other cases God will bestow his grace on naturally upright people but not on the corrupt. Nevertheless it will always be true that in bestowing his grace, he does so according to the law of his wisdom, that is, he distributes grace in such a way that he obtains from it (all things considered) the greatest fruit it could ever give, whatever the distribution.

529. I say 'all things considered' because the calculation must not be restricted solely to the immediate effect that grace produces in those to whom it is given and offered. Although they can reject it, it can be fruitful in others to whom it was offered at the same time, or for whom the others' refusal serves as an example and a profitable teaching; it can also help in other hidden ways. Thus, the divine Master tells us that his preaching and miracles were not well received at Chorazin and Bethsaida, to which towns grace was offered in addition to his preaching and miracles. The same grace however was not offered to Tyre and Sidon, but if these two towns had heard Christ's preaching and seen his miracles, they would have been converted.[134] But Christ's preaching and miracles were not solely for the Galilean towns where he performed them; they were for the whole world. They did in fact bring about the conversion of some Galileans, among whom Christ chose the Apostles and his disciples, who carried the light of the Gospel to all the nations of the world. Therefore, if we suppose that such a rapid spread of the Gospel would not have followed the conversion of Tyre and

to if it had not been given the unexpected aid of Christian law: 'I thank the Lord God who sent us extraordinary help against these evils. Where would this flood of humanity's terrible wickedness not take us? Who would escape, and into what depths would it not plunge us if the cross of Christ were not grounded more eminently and firmly in such a great rock of authority? With trust in its strength, we would be so stable that although we are caught up in the vast whirlpool of this world, no evil persuasion or force for evil could conquer us. Heavenly authority had to come and help us in this dregs of depraved customs and our loss of past discipline'* (*Ep*. 138). Cf. *SP*, 451–493. What he says immediately afterwards is also excellent.

[134] 'Woe to you, Chorazin! Woe to you, Bethsaida! for if the mighty works done in you had been done in Tyre and Sidon, they would have repented long ago in sackcloth and ashes' (Mt 11: 21; Lk 10: 13).

Sidon at a time when the world was not yet disposed to receive the Gospel and, to use Christ's words, 'the regions were not yet white for the harvest',[135] we can understand how wisdom and divine goodness could prefer to give the grace of the Gospel message to Chorazin and Bethsaida, which did not accept it, rather than to Tyre and Sidon which would have accepted it [*App*., no. 11].

530. Nevertheless the preaching given to those who through their pride were badly disposed would not have been given if there had not been others who through their humility were well disposed and would profit from the preaching. The Gospel message was ultimately proclaimed in favour of people who were downtrodden and humiliated and were the only ones to welcome it as good news with abundant fruit. Hence, the Saviour said that he had been sent to 'evangelise the poor',[136] applying to himself the prophecy of Isaiah, who described the mission of the future Messiah precisely in such a way: 'The Spirit of the Lord is upon me, because the Lord has anointed me to bring good tidings to the afflicted; he has sent me to bind up the broken-hearted, to proclaim liberty to the captives, and the opening of the prison to those who are bound.'[137] In whatever way and for whatever cause people are humiliated, they nevertheless, in their desolate, dejected state, welcome with immense gratitude the comfort of anyone who helps them, or a ray of hope brings light to their eyes. In such a low state, in which their formerly hardened and vicious heart has softened, they are cast down by misfortunes and the corruption that produces the misfortunes. No better way could be found for humiliating and prostrating people who, because they know that they are made for truth and justice, experience internal remorse and sorrow through the awareness of their darkness and injustice. Hence the first Christians, as the Apostle noted,[138] were mostly poor,

[135] These words demonstrate the possibility of a certain natural disposition to which God was pleased to add his grace.

[136] Lk 4: [18].

[137] Is 61: [1].

[138] 'For consider your call, brethren; not many of you were wise according to worldly standards, not many were powerful, not many were of noble birth; but God chose what is foolish in the world to shame the wise, God chose what

simple-minded, desolate people who found in the proclamation of the Gospel the comfort and refreshment they so much needed and hopelessly longed for but had not experienced. Christ says that, among the signs indicating that he was the promised Messiah, *PAUPERES EVENGELIZANTUR* [the poor are evangelised].[139] This verified the prophecies which had assigned this characteristic to the preaching of the Redeemer. Also, only God has the power to come to the aid of all humiliated and desolate people, and finally only divine wisdom could find in the most despised human beings a disposition for his gift, in the way that only divine power and goodness could communicate so great a gift, and could use human infirmity as a kind of support for attaching a new deiform structure to defective human nature. This fact is far greater than the restoration of sight to the blind and the raising of the dead to life, among which Christ places the sign of the evangelisation of the poor and the meek.

531. III. It also follows that when God gives a person a particular quantity of grace in order to draw the greatest fruit from it, he makes the grace help not only the individual to whom it is initially given, but also others who, having been brought to a correct disposition by the individual, receive the grace through the individual.

532. This shows how God had good reason for wishing to obtain the sanctification of *many* by means of a *few* of his saints, the chosen ministers of his mercies. St. Thomas uses the same reason to show how fitting it was for the Word to assume only one suppositum of human nature, not all supposita: 'The short path,' he says, 'followed by wise people in their operation means they do not use many means to obtain what one means will obtain. Hence, it was most fitting that through one man only all other human beings should be saved.'[140]

533. Why then, we may ask, does God sometimes use an overpowering grace to calm and tame the most rebellious and obstinate of wills? This is certainly a great intervention by God

is weak in the world to shame the strong, God chose what is low and despised in the world, even things that are not, to bring to nothing things that are, so that *no human being might boast* in the presence of God' (1 Cor 1: 26–29).

[139] Mt 11: 5; Lk 7: 22.

[140] *S.T.*, III, q. 4, art.5, ad 3.

in his creature, an immense dispensing of his action. But if he bestows his gift so generously, we cannot doubt that he operates according to the law of wisdom, which is the law of the least means. Hence we can reasonably believe that in the sudden conversion of the hardened sinner God prepares a means for innumerable, great goods arising from that good. That particular quantity of grace is mostly wisely applied because of the great abundance of fruit it produces. Consequently, the purpose of these great conversions would seem to be not only the salvation of the soul that is gained through them (although nobody can calculate the treasure of good that that soul alone is worth to God), but the salvation of many others. Examples are Saul, who became the apostle of the Gentiles, St. Augustine, who became the doctor of grace, Dismas, Mary Magdalen and other sinners whose story is in the Gospel. They became not only outstanding examples to all the world but evidence of divine pity for all time. This explains why the common sense of Christians expects great things from such sudden and impressive changes of heart, and when they occur, is accustomed to saying that God who brings them about must have a great purpose for the Church.

To sum up. In the bestowal and distribution of his grace, God follows the same law of wisdom that he follows in the bestowal and distribution of the gifts of nature, in his creation, preservation and government of entia. Anything still needed to be said will help me indicate, in so far as I can, the paths that wisdom marks out for the supreme Being and are faithfully followed by this Being in his operation in nature and in every direct intervention of his power, whether the intervention is ordinary or extraordinary.

CHAPTER 17

Third consequence: the law of excluded superfluity

534. A third consequence of the same principle of application is: Because God draws the greatest possible good from everything he does in the universe, 'the law of excluded superfluity' must apply in what he does.

535. From this law Aquinas astutely deduces the necessity of contingent fallible causes that make the universe a perfect work. He indicates the law of excluded superfluity with these words: 'In things that are properly ruled by providence, nothing must be left useless.'* After positing the law, he argues: if all the causes in the universe were to operate out of necessity, their effects, even though superfluous, could not be prevented. If many effects that were not necessary for the production of the greatest good could not be prevented, there would be a superfluity. In this case, the governing wisdom of the world would fail in its great principle that excludes anything superfluous.[141]

536. This principle presides over both the natural and supernatural orders. The divine Saviour taught this when he said to the Apostles: 'My Father is the vinedresser. Every branch of mine that bears no fruit, he takes away, and every branch that does bear fruit he prunes, that it may bear more fruit.'[142]

537. It was fitting therefore that divine wisdom prevent all these effects of natural, prolific causes; they could be overabundant and left unused relative to the sum of total good. For this reason, when created entia are posited together in a most wise way, they limit each other in their propagation and action. The

[141] Although others understand the words of St. Thomas differently, I think this is the true argument he wishes to make. The passage reads: 'In things that are properly ruled by providence, nothing must be useless. But some causes are clearly contingent because they can be prevented from producing their effects. Consequently, it would be contrary to the concept of providence that everything must necessarily happen' (*C. G.*, III, q. 72, art. 8). I explain this text as: 'There must be nothing useless in the universe. Consequently, causes must be contingent so that their effects can be prevented and, when superfluous, removed.'

[142] Jn 15: 1–2.

excessive luxuriance of plants is tempered by different levels of soil sterility and by other causes limiting vegetation. The excessive multiplication of an individual species is moderated by the proximity of plants to one another and their struggle for nutritious soil. Their exuberant fecundity is further limited by animals, for which they serve as food. Animals themselves are exposed to the action of a great number of natural agents that impede the propagation of each species beyond a certain limit. A very notable cause among those limiting the number of individual animals is the ceaseless battle between them, in which the weakest and most prolific become food for the strongest and least prolific. This kind of struggle, seen in all nature, is a means used by the most provident Author of the universe to remove the excessive effects and superfluous actions of created causes that would prejudice the total good. He places, and considers, entia and their actions in admirable proportion and wonderful harmony, of which none in particular has its own cause within it and, to use the expression of a recent author, he 'uses death itself to profit life'.[143] He makes corruption serve generation, and with the destruction of previous forms renews and continuously reinvigorates the world.

538. Even human death is regulated by supreme goodness according to this law, and serves the great end of removing what is superfluous or unused from the universe. The same truth was taught by JESUS Christ: he used a parable to show that the good are called to a reward only when their fruit is complete, and have been left on earth to produce that fruit. 'The kingdom of God is as if a man should scatter seed upon the ground, and should sleep and rise night and day, and the seed should sprout and grow, he knows not how. The earth produces of itself, first the blade, then the ear, then the full grain in the ear. But when the grain is ripe, at once he puts in the sickle, because the harvest has come.'[144] Here we should note the words 'at once' (*STATIM MITTIT FALCEM* [at once he puts in the sickle]). They express exactly how God never leaves the elect on earth for one instant

[143] Roselly de Lorgues, *De la mort avant l'homme*, c. 2. This chapter deserves to be read. It correctly demonstrates that for brute animals neither pain nor death have the concept of evil.

[144] Mk 4: 26–29.

longer than the time necessary for the abundant fruit they must give. The same law determines the hour of death of the reprobate, that is, of all those who God foresees will no longer bear the fruit they should, either directly by their emendation or indirectly by occasioning sanctity in others and, more generally, by occasioning a greater amount of total good. 'Every tree,' Christ says, 'that does not bear fruit is cut down.'[145] Hence, when St. John saw the great crowd of Pharisees and Sadducees coming to his baptism, he said that they were simply fleeing the anger that was coming upon them; he exhorted them to bear fruit worthy of repentance so that God would not wipe them out: 'You brood of vipers! Who warned you to flee from the wrath to come? Bear fruits that befit repentance, and do not begin to say to yourselves, "We have Abraham as our father"; for I tell you, God is able from these stones to raise up children to Abraham. Even now the axe is laid to the root of the trees; every tree therefore that does not bear good fruit is cut down and thrown into the fire.'[146] Note in these words how the Precursor says that the axe is laid to the root of the trees, because the Messiah has already come into the world and is ready to begin preaching the Gospel. The ingratitude and unteachability with which people might confront the incarnate Word was a fault that made them unworthy of every other grace. Therefore, with their hearts hardened, they would have made themselves for ever barren and deserved to be cut down.

538a. This very sober truth that the abuse of graces and the unwillingness to bear fruit for JESUS Christ, who cared for them all, can distance the soul from heavenly gifts as a most just punishment, and in the soul's barren state merit its removal from his garden, is appropriately signified in that most mysterious fact when Christ, in his hunger, looked for fruit on the lush fig tree, and not finding it (because outside the season) spoke one sentence over it, and immediately it shrivelled up.[147] From this we

[145] Mt 7: 19.

[146] Lk 3: 7–9; Mt 3: 7–10.

[147] Mk 11: 13–14. — This is why Simeon, and before him Isaiah (Is 8: 14), said of Christ: 'He is set for the fall and for the resurrection of many in Israel' (Lk 2: 34). Just as acceptance of his grace was the same as rising from sin, so its non-acceptance was a fall into the depths. Hence Christ himself says: 'If I had

also learn that we cannot preserve our life unless we do two things: bear fruit and bear it at the time Christ looks for it, which is the time when our fruit can be of help to the good of the universe, the final sum of good. Hence, we can rightly conclude that even if by continuing to live we could bear some fruit, we would nevertheless be removed before producing it whenever our delay in producing it is longer than the universal order requires. This late fruit, which does not increase the sum of the final good, is not calculated as fruit because the master has no need of it at that moment and refuses it. He therefore passes the awesome sentence on the lush tree that is proud of the abundance of its foliage: 'May no one ever eat fruit from you again.'*[148] In another case however, the landlord has been coming to visit his fig tree for three years without finding fruit on it. But at the request of the honest gardener who has promised to dig around it and manure it, he is prepared to wait another year before having it cut down. This demonstrates the efficacy of the prayer of pastors for the sinful souls committed to their care. These prayers are a new accident that causes a change in the universal calculation. The fruit, because it was late, would not be suitable for the good and harmony of the universe and hence not worth waiting for. However through prayers it becomes suitable and harmonious again, and the most wise Master waits for it.

539. It will help if I use an impressive example to explain the nature of the time when the most wise Lord looks for fruit from his plants and if he finds none, consigns them to the fire. The example is the Flood, and the plant that had to bear fruit was the human race — the allegory is equally valid for an individual, for society and for the whole of humanity.

The human race had become depraved by disordered pleasures of sense. Because God is essential goodness, he wanted to restore it, but because he is also essential wisdom, he wanted to use the least means to restore it. He had two possibilities open to him: correct the depraved human race by threats, warnings, exhortations and other means of his providence, or destroy it

not come and spoken to them, they would not have sin; but now they have no excuse for their sin' (Jn 15: 22).

[148] Mk 11: [14].

while saving some incorrupt root from which it would retake, regrow and become a new plant. Wisdom found this second means much simpler and more readily applicable than the first. It therefore chose it for its purpose: it submerged all flesh in the waters, saving one good family as the stock for all the new generations. Even today, with our weak understanding, we can comprehend how God had to calculate that this arrangement would allow the world to be repopulated in a few centuries with a new, incorrupt people, as at the beginning. If he had not taken this measure, a great number of centuries would have had to pass before the generations born and raised from the corrupt stock were cured of the universal disorder and made good: the depravity and scandals would have passed down from father to son, from age to age, with the possibility of increasing rather than diminishing. Even if we granted that a time would have come when the world could have reformed its behaviour, ridding itself of the perverse habits in its families, who knows which and how many means would have been necessary for this? And granted that the far distant time of this reform of the human race had to dawn (which is uncertain), the time for it would have been the season for the fruit of the fig tree. But God was not looking for the fruit at such a remote season: he wanted it before that time, and wanted it to be more abundant and better. The fig tree therefore became barren, leaving only one little shoot, and thus produced a new humanity in a very short time. Once the contagion of the previous perversity had been removed, this new humanity was capable of a greater abundance of fruits which, if the whole of humanity had been totally preserved, it would not have borne because it retained the propensity to evil; indeed, the propensity to evil would probably have taken hold of the only stock that remained incorrupt, with the result that the sum of evils would have been appallingly multiplied.

540. The same calculation by Wisdom destroyed the Pentapolis, and it declared the nations living in Palestine to be anathema; according to the same calculation, many other peoples had to perish, and the lives of families and individuals were terminated.

541. However there seem to be exceptions to this law. Many wicked people are allowed to live for a long time; many peoples

are preserved who seem to produce nothing but thorns and poison. — But the exception is only apparent because there are no exceptions to the principles of divine wisdom. To understand this, I make only two observations.

1. The reason why it is better for an individual, a people, a nation to be eliminated from the earth is not the scarcity of the particular fruit it produces for its own advantage but the scarcity of the fruit it produces when the consequences of its action in the whole of the human race and throughout all time are considered. The calculation therefore must concern the virtue of the good that is exercised and perfected through the iniquity of the wicked; the virtue is an exquisite fruit which the wicked do not, in all truth, bear for themselves but for other people, for the master of the vineyard, whose infinite goodness considers the overall good of all his creatures as his own good, as his own glory. Hence the calculation must include all those countless goods that Providence draws from the wicked. No one has written more copiously about this than St. Augustine, and I will quote a part of his admirable thoughts on the matter. After he has pointed out how the wretched impel the good to take refuge in God, to place their hope in him alone, to turn to him with fervent prayers (with the result that the good soul is enhanced and enriched with moral perfection), he adds that God uses the wicked to correct the good and bring them to that great act of most perfect charity which is to love one's enemies and do good to them:

> He certainly tests and afflicts us by this means of evils, and does so for the sake of the kingdom of heaven. Is there a father who does not discipline his son? God, in doing the same, instructs us for the eternal inheritance. This is the good he often draws in our favour from evil people, in whom he tests and perfects our love, and it is his wish that this love extends even to our enemies. Indeed, the Christian's love is not perfect until it fulfils Christ's commandment: 'Love your enemies, and do good to those who hate you, and pray for those who persecute you.' In this way the devil himself is conquered, the crown of victory is procured... The weapons on the left of the just are the malice of the wicked, as the Apostle says: Through the weapons of justice *on the right and on the left*, that is, through glory

> and disgrace. He next lists the other things: the weapons on the right are the glory of God, a good name, the truth by which the just were known, life, not being dejected but joyful, enriching many, possessing everything; the weapons on the left are when people are seen as ignoble and of evil name, as seducers, unknown, killed, constrained, wretched, in need and possessing nothing.[149]

542. 2. When God wishes to eliminate an individual, a family, a unproductive nation, from the earth, he does not do so with a miracle — this would be contrary to the law of the least means. Instead, he arranges the series of second causes in such a way that they produce the willed effect. To obtain this effect therefore he needed to give a particular order to the chain of second causes, all of which he saw with a totally simple act of his mind and which cannot be changed without alteration to the total, very complex fabric of creation. Hence, eternal wisdom had also to calculate whether the order given to the second causes harmonised appropriately with the intention of obtaining the maximum good. Creation, which is precisely the complex of second causes, is so limited that sometimes a partial good effect cannot be obtained without the loss of a greater effect, or an evil eliminated without opening the way to a greater evil. Therefore, the tree, which itself is barren for its master, is not however totally barren if cutting it down and throwing into the fire would harm the field or vineyard. In such a case, tolerating it saves other greater produce of the property. Thus Christ tells us that he leaves the darnel, which is harmful, together with the wheat, because by pulling out the darnel, the wheat would be uprooted with it.

543. Clearly then, the law of divine wisdom is one single law without exceptions of any kind. Its applications however vary greatly, according to the many circumstances that one infinite mind can simultaneously embrace. Not a single circumstance, not even the least, escapes this mind, which can completely and most exactly explain the reasons for them all.

[149] *Enarr. In Ps.*, 93: 28.

CHAPTER 18

Fourth consequence: the law of the permission of evil

544. The same law gives us the reason why and according to which God permits evil.

545. The reader should recall what evil is. I have called it a privation of good (cf. 183–187). Because good is the entity of things, the more entity there is, the more good there is; and there is more *entity* where there is more *action*.

It follows that the permission of evil comes directly from the law of the least means. This law requires God not to intervene in nature as creator, preserver and sanctifier except only with that quantity of action that produces the greatest possible good in whatever way the quantity is used. On many occasions God will not intervene; on many occasions he will cease to act or produce second causes or their capabilities or perfections because, if he did act, the activity used or produced would not bring forth the greatest fruit, which alone satisfies his infinite goodness.

546. This abstention of God from operating is the permission of evil. God is the *first cause*, and all effects, including those of *second causes*, go back to this first cause. Hence, if the first cause ceases in some measure to co-operate, many effects of the second causes also cease. This absence of effects or of their fullness and perfection is not therefore operated by God. Whenever God operates, he produce a good, but whenever he abstains from operating, the absence of effects comes of itself. The first cause is certainly the universal cause of all things, but just as it does not remove the free will of intellective creatures when they do good, so the absence of its action does not remove their free will when they fail in their operation and thus do evil. This second fact is no more difficult to understand than the first: if there is mystery in the first, it is not surprising to find mystery in the second, but if it can be shown that this is in fact the case, then it is the case, even if we cannot explain how. We know that God, as first cause, is universal cause of all finite activities; if he were not, we would have an absurdity because there would be entities, or

acts of entities, *independent* of God, and if something existed independently of God, God would not be God. Consequently, any activity that escaped his creative act would exist through itself, and *that which exists through itself* would be divided into many. The absolute infinite would therefore cease because the concept of the absolute infinite is of an ens that embraces in itself with a totally simple unity all that is through itself.

547. On the other hand, if we have formed a clear concept of creation, we will easily understand that creation produces things together with their order ('creation' is understood here as every action of God *ad extra* because God in fact operates always in a creative mode in so far as he produces at every moment that which without him would not be). Creation therefore produces accidents as subsisting in substance and as issuing from substance; it produces the acts of second causes as acts of second causes and issuing from these causes according to the mode of the causes' operation, whether this mode is free or necessary. Hence the intervention of God never removes free operation; on the contrary it produces it, makes it free, as indeed it is. He acts in such a way that the free act is the act of free choice of an intelligent cause, to whom the act is rightly imputed, and to impute something means simply to refer the thing to the free cause that produced it.

548. Consequently:

1. If a created, free cause does evil, it is imputable to that cause. The imputation is the relationship of the action solely with the free, direct cause that produced it, not with the first cause.

2. The sinful, created, free cause could have avoided the evil, could have chosen good; otherwise it would not be free.

3. The first cause produced this free cause that chose evil, and produced it such that it could have equally chosen good or evil. If this were not so, the first cause would not have produced it free.

4. This free cause, in choosing evil, fell short of the fullness and perfection of its act, but it could have avoided falling short.

5. The first cause continued to produce the free cause in the very act in which the free cause fell short of the fullness and perfection of its act, even though it could have avoided falling

short, that is, the first cause made the free cause able not to fail, but did not produce the failure of its act. This failure, as something privative, cannot be produced by a cause that is total activity, that never fails and has an infallible operation.[150] There was thus no privative act in the first cause, only a mere negation of act, a limited negation that did not remove from the second cause the power to do the complete act. The first cause simply allowed the act of that power to lack its perfection, a perfection that the second cause could have given but did not.

548a. 6. The *permission* that God gives for moral evil is not itself the cause of evil. The cause of evil is a *deficient cause*, but in God there is no deficiency; his every act is perfect. This perfect act of God however, precisely because perfect, having maximum good as its object, does not extend to producing all the perfect acts that second causes can do. As a result, deficient causes can posit some imperfect, deficient acts, not because they could not have done otherwise but have done so through their free choice. This free and actual deficiency is *demeritorious moral evil*, from which follows afterwards *a necessary moral evil*, as in the damned and in sinners. The *first cause* therefore does not produce any evil; the *second cause* does, which alone is deficient.

7. God's permission of evil does not deprive the free cause of its ability to avoid evil; it simply does not prevent the free cause from committing evil. The object of the permission is not *antecedent* in time to the evil committed, as if the evil were necessary because of a powerful impulse to evil, or because the ability to avoid it has been taken away. The object is *contemporaneous* with the evil, it is the actual evil itself. Hence, the evil is not *caused* by either *positive* or *negative* permission but is *simply permitted*.

8. *Non-free*, *moral evil* is a consequence of *free*, *moral evil*. It sometimes comes about through the withdrawal of moral forces, willed by divine justice. Hence, necessary moral

[150] St. Augustine, with his powerful mind, has perhaps investigated this matter more deeply than anyone else. He expresses the truth we are discussing as: 'The product of God, that is, angel and man, has indeed sinned but they sinned by their own operation, not by God's operation. They themselves are the good product of God but their sin is their own evil product, not God's product'* (*Operis imperf. contra Iul.* 5: 64).

evil is penal evil, that is, a just penalty for previous free, moral evil. It is willed as punishment by eternal justice in that God concurs in it negatively, that is, by not giving moral strength or by subtracting it through just judgment, which is precisely the case of the damned. As St. Augustine says: 'The necessity of sinning because freedom to abstain is lacking is a PENALTY for the sin from which there was freedom to abstain, at a time when there was no pressure of necessity.'*[151]

9. Finally, God concurs negatively in penal evil by denying or withdrawing eudaimonological goods from those creatures who by sin have made themselves unworthy of them.

549. God is not therefore the cause of the evil of fault. If Scripture sometimes says he is cause of this evil, he is called cause in a sense different from when he is called cause of penal evil. God is neither *positive cause* nor *deficient cause* of either the evil of fault or of penal evil. He is certainly not the cause of the evil of fault, not even negative cause, because this evil is free; he does not withdraw power from the free will of the creature; on the contrary he bestows it and maintains the power with which the creature can freely avoid this evil. God simply abstains from obliging the creature to choose good, allowing him to choose evil. It is true that when the creature chooses an act that has all moral perfection (this constitutes good), God concurs positively with the fullness of the act. And when the creature chooses an act that lacks due moral perfection, God does not concur in this deficiency. However, as I said, this non-concurrence does not precede the existence of the deficient act, nor determine it, nor make the opposite impossible: God simply does not produce the perfection of the act simultaneously with the human being's choice of the imperfection of the act (*simply permissive cause*). Neither of these two things is prior to the other nor influences the other.

550. But in penal evil, in physical evil and in all necessary acts of nature, God is *negative cause* in so far as such acts do not happen precisely because he does not give the productive activity; if he did create that activity, they would undoubtedly take place because they are necessary acts, not free acts. Hence physical, penal evils (these strictly speaking would not be evils if they

[151] St. Augustine, *Op. imperf. contra Iul.*, 1: 105 [*App.*, no. 12].

were not penal, that is, if they did not punish intelligent nature) are acts of God's justice and as such are fair matter for praising God. Nevertheless they are not something God inflicts positively on his creatures, to whom he gives only good. They are penalties that nature suffers for its own imperfection, to which God justly leaves it. St. Augustine says: 'When God punishes as judge, he punishes those who have transgressed the law. HE HIMSELF DOES NOT INFLICT EVIL ON THEM; he rejects them because of what they chose, in order to complete the total of miseries.'*[152]

551. Here, it will be helpful to clarify further the nature of this *negative cause* of penal evil. God is negative cause of penal evil in two ways: either by not giving the activity that would produce the complete effect, as in the case of purely physical evils (*non-giving cause*), or by ceasing from action, as in the case of necessary-moral evils, which are also penal, as in the damned, from whom he withdraws his grace (*ceasing cause*).

552. Relative to defective, physical acts (the Scholastics called these *peccata naturae* [sins of nature]), God is not their negative cause by withdrawing nature's forces; on the contrary he maintains these forces, and this preservation of natural things preserves uninterrupted the series of second causes from the beginning of the world to its end. But God foresaw from the beginning the immense series of causes and defects that would be more suitable to his plan[153] and, in the same series, all the failed and defective effects that were necessary also to his plan and were fitting punishments for crime. Therefore, from the beginning he created and gave natural things capacities that were so limited, and placed them in such relationships with each other, that they necessarily collided in certain ways. This resulted in those real and just defects that were the source of punishments of guilty being. In other words, he *did not give* to nature those entities, capacities, order, nor add those aids by his own hand that would prevent every defective act in nature being a penalty for man. In fact, at the beginning he so arranged things that during the time of human innocence no one suffered

[152] *In Ps.*, 5, n. 10.

[153] St. Thomas says precisely: 'Natural effects are provided by God in such a way that natural causes are ordered to these natural effects, and without the causes the effects would not happen'* (*Summa*, I, q. 23, art. 8).

from the forces of nature. Thus, during that time none of the penal evil I am talking about existed on earth. However, because God knew how long that first period of innocence would last and knew that a time of sin would follow, he arranged that nature, in keeping with the series of causes and effects, should develop penal effects through a pre-established harmony between the physical and moral evils in which man would co-operate with his will.

553. Thus all the primal forces proper to nature remained as they were. God did not diminish them; he simply left them to the natural development pre-established by his wisdom. However, when he withdrew himself from nature, it is certainly true that he also removed the beneficial influence he had given nature through his special presence. But I will discuss this cessation of the Creator's beneficial action on nature later when speaking about the *ceasing-negative cause*.

554. It is a fact of course that at the beginning God did not create and order the second causes in an unlimited quantity, but determined them *in pondere, numero et mensura* ['in measure, number and weight'].[154] This however does not contradict what I said previously that the creative act extended to all the acts of individual, created substances. This act does not remove the efficacy of the second causes; on the contrary it produces them. Hence, the disposition God gave to creatures at the first moment of their being simply means that the law determining their successive acts was included in that disposition; the whole creative act embraces and produces those acts exactly in the way they are determined: in short, the order of creatures is the order of the creative act. This act is so constituted that all the successive states exist already potentially and virtually in the first state of creatures, together with the actions by which one state changes to its following state.

555. At the beginning therefore God's sublime wisdom inserted this order in all natural things so that he could use all their defective acts as punishment for sin. All this was a consequence of the *least means*, which requires God to obtain all he can from nature through the forces and capacities inserted and arranged in nature. Hence Scripture often calls us to

[154] Wis 11: 20.

contemplate that first order so that we can understand the sublimity of creative wisdom. For example, we read in Sirach: 'From the beginning the works of God were carried out with right judgment and, from the moment of their institutions he distinguished their parts. Their beginnings' (the stars, and their rulers the angels) 'are in his hands for all generations. He elaborated their movements for ever. They suffered no impoverishment; they neither tired nor ceased in their operations. For all eternity they never crowd one another, and they are always faithful to his word. Then the Lord looked upon the earth, and filled it with his good things. He covered its surface with every living soul, and into it every soul will return.'[155] This clearly indicates the primal formation and distribution of natural causes and the whole series, pre-established by wisdom, of their effects. The same book also demonstrates how God gave an order to things in their first institution that benefited the good and punished the wretched; we read: 'From the beginning good things were created for good people, and for the wicked good things and evil things,' and further on: 'Fire and hail and famine and pestilence, all these have been created for vengeance; the teeth of wild beasts and scorpions and vipers, and the sword that punishes the ungodly with destruction. They will rejoice in his commands, and be made ready on earth for their service; and when their times come they not transgress his word.'[156] We must also note how often Scripture tells us that God foresees all times and has assigned things and events to their appropriate times, and that they are all good at the times assigned to them: 'From everlasting to everlasting he beholds them.'[157] Hence: 'No one can say, "This is worse than that," for all things will prove good in their season.'[158]

556. But because at the moment of creation all natural beings were so arranged that at certain times they had to fail in their operations and thus result in punishment for the wicked, the limitation of all creation meant that the good also were sometimes involved in disasters together with the wicked; the good

[155] Sir 16: 26–31 [R]. See also the Greek.

[156] Ibid., 39: 25 [R], 29–31.

[157] Ibid., 39: 20.

[158] Ibid., 39: 34.

were, as it were, accidently present when the collision of punitive causes produced penal evil. This required eternal wisdom to make another calculation to solve another problem. This suffering of the good, which they did not deserve, had to be taken into account by wisdom. Prior to regulating the things of the universe, wisdom had to answer this question: 'Is the activity required to avoid this suffering of the good such a good that it is sufficient to make the activity most wise?', or put another way: 'The quantity of activity would have to be sufficient to bring to an end the accidental sufferings of the good that happen as it were *praeter intentionem* [outside the intention] of the author of nature. When this quantity has been calculated, including the punishment of the wicked that would end, would the activity be exercised in the best way, would it return the greatest fruit?' In certain cases Wisdom answered 'No', in others 'Yes'. The affirmative applies to those cases where the wicked, for the sake of the good, escape the punishment (or part of it) deserved in this life, but pay the debt in the next life. The negative answer applies to the cases where the good undergo sufferings they do not deserve or are greater than they deserve. This was the case of JESUS Christ, the Virgin Mary and many Saints, whose undeserved evils were richly rewarded by God in eternity.

557. The limitations of entia therefore require us to distinguish the rule from the apparent exception that arises when the rule is applied. According to the rule natural things must be arranged so that their effects favour the good and punish the wicked. The exception is the opposite. Hence, the rule divides into two:

1. Natural effects should be so ordered that they aid the good, not harm them.

Exception: the wicked enjoy the advantages of the good, as much as is necessary, so that the order and series of natural causes is not interrupted.[159] Because of this God makes the sun

[159] Job said: 'God willed that my sins whereby I have deserved wrath and the calamity that I suffer, were weighed in a balance. As the sand of the sea, this would appear heavier' (Job 6: [2–3†, with Rosmini's variation]). But Baldad, one of his friends said, among other things, that Job's evils could not be avoided without interrupting the course of natural things. It was not right to claim that God should prevent them because nobody could calculate how many greater evils would have followed from such action and how many

to rise on the good and the wicked, and sends his rains on the lands of both.[160]

2. Natural effects are to be arranged in such a way that they bring suffering to the wicked.

Exception: the good are subjected to natural evils destined for the wicked, also as much as is necessary, so that the order and series of causes is not interrupted. An example is the blindness of the man cured by Christ, although he himself and his parents had not sinned.[161] Another is the death of the Galileans whose blood Pilate had mixed with their sacrifices; also the eighteen on whom the tower of Siloe fell, who were by no means the greatest sinners there were, as Christ himself testified.[162]

558. Both these laws are proclaimed by Scripture. Relative to the first, St. Paul says that God has donated to human beings all things together with Christ.[163] Jesus Christ does not want his followers worried about temporal things: 'Seek first the kingdom of God and all these things will be added to you,' because the Father has already disposed that they finish up where there is true virtue.

Relative to the second, the temporal sufferings threatened for the wicked are innumerable because 'fire, hail, famine and death: all these were created for vengeance.'[164]

559. The punishments that follow as natural effects are produced negatively by God, that is, he does not act. At the beginning he arranged created natures in such a way that they should not produce relative goods but fail in their act, not always a physical act but often one of order and harmony, because in things and in the complex of things, order and harmony is an extra act, an extra entity.

560. Sometimes however God is a *negative cause* of necessary evils, not simply by omitting to act but by withdrawing his

goods prevented: 'Shall the earth be forsaken for thee? and shall the rock be removed out of his place?'* (18: [4]).

[160] Mt 5: 45.

[161] Jn 9: 3.

[162] Lk 13: [1-5].

[163] St. Paul, letter to Eph. 1: 10.

[164] Sir 39: [35†].

beneficial action. St. Augustine explains the expression ‘hardening hearts’ used by Scripture as: ‘God does not harden by bestowing malice but by not bestowing mercy.’*[165] But if we examine the matter more closely, we see that God does not withdraw his grace with a positive act from one who sins, in the way, for example, that a person takes back from another an article he has lent. Although the effect of the light and sanctification of grace in the sinner ceases, and hence in this sense divine action ceases, grace does not cease through a special action of God himself in that he positively takes it back for himself; it ceases more like the light of the sun when we close our eyes, although the sun continues to shine. Thus, Bellarmine teaches that we are born without grace not because God was not ready to give it to us but because grace encounters the impediment of original sin in the new-born. This impediment is like blindness preventing the enjoyment of light, but the blindness and obstacle in the new-born is not in the material eye; it is in the will, and the will constitutes the human person, the subject of sin, who is cured solely by the healing grace of Jesus Christ. The obstacle itself consists not only in a contradiction between the sinful will and illuminating grace, but also in a contradiction that a holy God should come to dwell in the soul of a sinful being, which is something that clashes totally with the divine attributes.

561. The reason why Adam was deprived of the enlightening grace he possessed was his transgression. For the same reason God’s beneficent influence in nature, which was at the service of man in grace, also had to cease. As long as man was united to God, and hoped in God and not in nature, he was protected by God, who subjected and ordered nature to him.

[165] *Ep*. 194: 14.

Chapter 19

Recapitulation, and its connection with what follows

562. To sum up. God is *first cause* of all that happens in the universe, but sometimes he is *positive cause*, sometimes *negative cause*.

563. The first cause, as positive, can always be called *creative*, because God does not directly intervene in what a second cause can produce. Hence, when he intervenes, or in so far as he intervenes, he does something new, that is, there is no sufficient reason for it in nature.

564. I have subdistinguished the negative cause into *deficient* and *non-deficient*. I showed that God is never deficient cause — deficient cause is proper to second causes.

565. The non-deficient negative cause is twofold: *permissive* or *inactive*.

566. The *purely permissive cause* removes neither second causes nor their forces that are capable of producing the full effect; it simply permits them to fail in producing this effect. Thus, God is cause, or more accurately, is not cause of the moral evil of fault. This is the moral evil that the creature produces by its free will against the eternal law. God, far from withdrawing this free will from the creature, in fact creates and preserves it in the creature.

567. The *inactive negative cause* does not produce entia or their forces or their effects. Thus, God is not cause of superfluities but cause of their absence and that there is *penal evil*.

God is not the cause of superfluities, that is, he does not produce them, he excludes them from the universe.

Penal evil also comes from God in that he does not produce the contrary good.

568. Penal evil is *physical*, *intellectual* and *moral*.

Physical evil is lack of the goods necessary for life, bodily pain, bodily imperfections and death.

Intellectual evil is ignorance, slowness of understanding, etc.

Moral penal evil is original sin, necessary sins, unavoidable moral defects.

569. These evils are necessary and hence arise from necessary causes which lack something for their perfect operation. This missing element can be called very generally an activity or an entity that is not given them. The strength of a power and the disharmony between many powers are a lack of some actuality, and if the absence is not always in individual entia or individual powers, it is at least in their complex whole.

570. God is *inactive cause*, sometimes by *not carrying out* an action, sometimes by *ceasing to carry out* an action.

Thus, at the beginning God abstained from making entia or, more generally, second causes that were superfluous to his end. He did not give to created powers the order by which, as they developed, they would produce superfluous goods or avoid the evils that were helpful and necessary for the great end.

With regard to *ceasing to carry out* an action, strictly speaking God never brings to an end what he has begun to carry out, granted that the second cause does not reject his gift and make itself incapable by its own action, which was precisely what the first father of the human race did when he removed himself from God and his grace. As a result, grace ceased to operate in him, not because grace was absent but because man abandoned it.

571. All these distinctions explain how God can intervene in the production of the good and evil of the universe. They also help us understand those places of Scripture where God is called first cause, even of evil.[166]

572. We see therefore that whether God operates as *positive cause* or intervenes as *negative cause*, it is always the law of wisdom that directs him, always the law of the least means that determines his operation. He carries out nothing except that from which he can draw the greatest fruit, and abstains from producing anything that does not give him this fruit. For the same reason he does not impede but permits the evil of fault, or allows penal evil by not producing the activities and their order that would prevent penal evil; if he produced those activities or their order, his action would be badly applied because it would not bear the greatest fruit, and he does not act if his actions do

[166] Gen 45: 5, 8; Ex 7: 3; Deut 2: 30; 2 Sam 16: 10; 1 Kings 12: 15; Job 12: 10, 17, 24–25; Is 10: 6; Jer 10: 23; Ezek 3: 20; Amos 3: 6; Jn 6 44; Acts 2: 23; 4: 27–28; Rom 9: 16, 18–20; I Cor 4: 7; 13: 6; Eph 2: 10; Phil 2: 13.

not bear the greatest fruit. He always weighs out not only the goods that his action would give but those that it would impede and those that it would bring with it.

573. All these teachings are important for continuing the discussion. Knowledge of the nature of God's positive and negative operations allows us to investigate in greater detail his wisdom and goodness in the universe. We can investigate 1. when he operates as positive cause, or 2. has the concept of negative cause (when he is not operating), or finally 3. when he is operating simultaneously in both ways. This last kind of operation gives rise to the mixed effects of entity and limitation, and of evil and good. We can also meditate on his infinite wisdom as regulator of all the above three kinds of operation, which contain the events we see in creation, and we can investigate what his wisdom suggests that his infinite goodness should do in every circumstance. I will begin with wisdom as regulator of the actions and *positive dispositions* of God, and then examine wisdom as regulator of the *negative* and *mixed effects*. This will reveal the great order of everything.

Relative to the positive dispositions and operations, let us see how God had to order and choose the entia of the universe and the end to which he had to direct them. We can then consider the wonderful means he had to use for this great end. Finally, relative to the means, we can look at his negative and mixed dispositions.

CHAPTER 20

Fifth consequence: it was fitting that God should establish a connection between the entia he wished to create, and make them one harmonious whole

574. Many particular reasons can demonstrate that when God wished to create many entia, it was fitting that he put them in relationship and communication with each other, so that linked in various ways they should form one whole. But all these reasons can be reduced to the law of the least means, or at least this great law certainly requires the connection and unity of created things.

575. To begin with, we see how one thing needs another in order to subsist and develop. Human beings need food provided by brute animals and vegetables; we need air to breathe, light to see, and we need those like ourselves in order to multiply and form societies, etc. All the other animals also need entia different from themselves to maintain their existence and perpetuate their species. Vegetables themselves need minerals, earth, water and various juices on which to feed, various fluids in which they live, etc. If vegetables did not release oxygen into the air and take in hydrogen, after a short time the air would become unsuitable for breathing. Thus the animals, exhaling hydrogen, supply the substance plants take in and live on. Fish need water and suitable food. Electricity, fire and other weightless things are strictly necessary for the preservation of animal life. If there were no sun, everything would perish. The earth turning on itself, and its annual encircling of the sun have a particular relationship with certain periods of life, with pregnancy, etc. In summary, we can say that no living thing can stand on its own, and the whole universe concurs in making it exist, endure and act for its ends. It is true of course that if God had wished to separate one ens from another, he could have preserved it by miracles of his omnipotence, but if he had done this, the capacities that entia have to help and sustain each other would have been left unused; there would have been an immense and useless expenditure of activity. But according to the law of the least

means no entity or activity must remain fruitless; rather each must produce all the good it can. Hence the intelligence outside the world disposes and locates it in the place, time and manner most appropriate to the end. God therefore would not have observed the law of wisdom (which is the law of least the means) if instead of placing various entia in a fitting relationship with one another, he had isolated and disassociated them, and in so doing had removed from them the possibility of helping and completing each other.

576. Moreover, two kinds of effects result from the wisely ordered connection of the variety of entia: effects that can contribute to the production of the final end (*goods that are means*), and effects that are ends themselves (*final goods*). If God had not joined entia by his wisdom, both these goods would not have been produced.

577. Goods used as means pertain to the order of both real things and intellectual things; goods used as end pertain to the eudaimonological-moral order. It is not difficult to see that in the real order the conjunction of entia results in infinite effects, and without this conjunction there could be no effects. Indeed, we can say that all physical effects knowable to us originate from the connection and composition of entia — in fact, in the universe we see nothing that is simple, totally on its own and separate. All these effects that God orders as means to the final good would certainly be lost if created entia were not put in communication with each other. The immense number of physical effects resulting from the various interactions of atoms and other entia exceeds all calculation. Moreover, each effect, through its varying quantity, gives a new effect that otherwise could not have been. If we unite the forces of some given nature, their union as one will give what they could never have given when separate. If, for example, I have a hundred units of force to move a certain mass, and I apply each unit individually one after the other, I will not move the mass and will uselessly lose all the forces I applied a little at a time. But if I apply all one hundred units at the same time and at the same point on the mass and in the same direction, I will have the effect of movement. Again, a room can be easily heated with a hundred kilos of wood, but not with one piece at a time. If one piece at a time is burnt, the hundred kilos will not obtain the effect gained by

burning the whole quantity at the same time. From the union of entia therefore, new, innumerable effects that vary in nature and quantity are obtained, and each, when well ordered by infinite wisdom, will produce a good.

578. The same is true of the intellectual order.

Human beings are an ens endowed with the means of knowing, but initially we lack all knowledge about the *real ens* outside us. The fundamental feeling, the modifications of this feeling, the real entia that produce these modifications, constitute the first matter of the knowledge we later acquire when, once our attention has been aroused, we apply to these realities the means of knowledge, which is *undetermined ideal being*. Human knowledge therefore could not develop and grow if bodily realities did not act on us, did not stimulate us, did not produce our instincts and needs. We had to be surrounded by the universe from which we glean the matter of our knowledge, that is, the matter about which we begin the reasonings that raise us to the Creator, where we contemplate his wisdom, goodness and perfection. The whole complex of the information we obtain in this way results from many occasions and means that enable us to develop our affections and thus to operate morally, practise virtue, and also gain merit. Clearly, we had to have a connection with the universe, experience its action and be continuously modified by it. But let us grant for a moment that the omnipotent God could have communicated all this knowledge directly to us without our having to be subject to the action of the material universe, and that we did not have to act on other entia. If this were the case however:

1. human nature's capacity to receive knowledge of created entia, and its capacity to operate on the universe and learn through its experiences and practise virtue, would be lost and ultimately unused and fruitless, and

2. the capacity that the various entia composing the universe naturally have to modify us, provide us with great knowledge and give us the opportunity to perfect ourselves by practising moral virtue, would also be lost, left unused and not bear the fruit it could have.

Because all this is contrary to the law of the least action, it was appropriate that we and other beings were connected in such a way that the activities we possess could bear fruit.

579. But let us consider briefly the goods that have the nature of end and are drawn from the connection and mutual action of entia.

580. The only way we know that the cause of the universe is wise is by contemplating the traces of wisdom present in the universe. These traces are visible in the harmonious connection of many entia helping one other and forming one whole, ordered to one end. This truth was known and proclaimed by philosophers prior to Christ, particularly by Italian philosophers, who named the complex of all things κόσμος and *mundus*, as if they meant something ornate, beauty *par excellence*,[167] and considered this order and beauty of the universe as a very clear proof of the existence of God, and considered the unity of the order as a proof of the unity of God, its author. Hence, St. Thomas says: 'The world is one, because all things want to be ordered with only one order for only one end. Hence, in the 12th Book of Metaphysics, Aristotle concludes from the unity of the existing order in things to the unity of God who governs them.'[168] Hence, the universe is as it were the book in which we apprehend the knowledge that makes us capable of virtue. The characters with which this book is written are the entia that compose it together with their mutual actions and passions, tendencies and aversions; all these things constitute a most wonderful order and a stupendous harmony. We can of course imagine that God could have created man in an isolated state, and then by showing him the order and harmony within himself, could have instructed him without having to make use of the wise connection of creatures. But such a divine procedure (even if we think it possible) would have been contrary to the law of the least means because, by means of it, the capacity of creatures to provide us with the traces of wisdom, and our own capacity to extract teaching and instruction from these traces, would have been left unused, like lost wealth; God would not have drawn from the creature the good it could give by itself.

581. Moreover, if we had no connection with other creatures

[167] Thus Pliny says: 'What the Greeks called κόσμον, ornament, we call *mundum*, perfect and absolute elegance' (Bk. 2: 4). Varro says the same, *De L.*, bk. 9: 19.

[168] *S.T.*, I, q. 47, art. 3, ad 1.

and there was no continuous exchange of action and passion between them and us, we could not make ourselves virtuous by using the least means. Just as the knowledge we have comes from this universe in which we are, so we are given the occasion for practising virtue and, by our own efforts, acquiring moral perfection to which all the good we are capable of reduces. Eudaimonological good acquires the concept of true human good only if it is an extension of and a very appropriate sequel to moral good. If several individuals had not dwelt together, the human species would not have multiplied, and there would have been no social virtues, which are strictly speaking human virtues. The use of the entia of the universe and of the goods and evils they produce is the material in which are embodied, as it were, all those moral virtues that philosophers describe: justice, fortitude, prudence, temperance. If we had no companions, all useful enterprises, all heroic actions would become impossible. Hence God said that 'it is not good for man to be alone.'[169]

Moreover, all human affections, which is where the great part of our happiness lies, and all the countless pleasures put before us by the wonderful variety of many creatures adapted to satisfy our natural tendencies, would also be impossible. One of the greatest pleasures of human understanding is the contemplation of the harmonious Whole which, through creative wisdom, is the result of the interweaving of so many various and contrary things. Equally, one of the greatest delights of the heart is the delight that comes to individuals from the society of their fellows, living in each other through the action of love. Furthermore, through the effect of supernatural charity one person lives and takes pleasure in all those who share in the same charity. Thus, in each one, life is ceaselessly multiplied, increased and accumulated.

582. Again let us suppose for a moment, or better, let us pretend in our imagination that God could have compensated human beings in another way, by giving them the opportunity to practise virtue generously, to develop the affections of their heart and enjoy the pleasures of intellect and spirit they are capable of. He could do this however only in two ways: either through creatures or by revealing himself directly, in which case

[169] Gen 2: 18†.

everyone would see essential wisdom and goodness, and love him. If we choose the first (through other creatures), we are back to human beings in relationship with creation, and my thesis is confirmed. If we choose the second (God reveals himself), we come to grief on many hazards, particularly those indicated, and the law of least means is thrown to the winds, for the following reasons: 1. all the forces, tendencies, faculties and appetites that are natural to us and for which creatures are proportionate objects, would be unused and, having no reason for their existence, would be lost; 2. if God revealed himself directly and openly to us, we would be constituted in a final state, and therefore could not merit, because we would be deprived of freedom. Hence, all the merit of the virtue we are capable of would be wealth we had lost.[170]

583. If it was appropriate for finite entia to be put in communication with one another for the reasons given and that they exercised mutual actions and passions, it follows that evils as well as goods must result. As we have seen, every finite ens is necessarily susceptible to evil through the limitation of its nature. In the case of physical or eudaimonological evil, this must arise from the action and mutual reaction of forces: the force that produces pleasure also produces pain, where each different effect depends on the different way the force acts and the degree to which it acts. Nevertheless, it is sufficient that these evils are less in number than the goods and therefore allow the greatest possible quantity of net good to be attained. This is the

[170] Someone may object that God could have infused ideas into us without having to give us the vision of himself or putting us in relationship with other creatures. But the objection is not valid for the following reasons: 1. the law of the least means would always be violated because our ability to obtain ideas for ourselves by use of our senses would be useless; 2. *ideas* are not sufficient for the full practice of moral virtue because ideas give us knowledge only of possible things, whereas virtue is mainly practised towards intelligent real beings who can be known only through *perceptions*; 3. ideas alone are not sufficient for *happiness* because happiness is found solely in the union with real beings and not with purely possible things. We must not think that even angelic knowledge, prior to the angels being admitted to the vision of God, consisted in mere ideas. It consisted in true affirmations of both themselves and created beings, where they saw traces of the supreme Being. Hence according to St. Augustine the angels' knowledge continued to increase as God formed and beautified the universe. Cf. *Super Genes.*, bk. 3.

fruit that Providence proposes to draw from the complexity of creatures and their capacities; the capacities resemble the capital that the divine master uses to trade with and, without this trading, they would have remained unused and, as it were, buried in the ground. No on will ever be able to demonstrate that the physical goods in the universe (to limit ourselves to these) are less than the evils, while on the other hand it will be very easy to demonstrate that the goods are far greater in number, where good is seen as ordinary and continuous, and evil as the exception. Thus, life is a good because life is an agreeable feeling, whereas death, which concerns only one point of time, is an evil; health is a good, illness an evil. In illness we are never deprived of all goods, of all pleasures, and never of the feeling of existence which, if it were not good, we would never love so much as to judge its loss a very great evil. Generally speaking, every act is pleasurable, so that pain is simply an impediment that sensitive nature encounters in carrying out its complete act. Thus reason fully supports us when we say that all that is, is good in both the metaphysical and the physical senses, in so far as every pain or trouble consists in some privation or failure of an act to attain its completion and reach the term to which it tends and in which it rests. Hence, the universe is simply a complex of goods which suffer some limitations and reductions as a result of their co-existence and mutual action.

584. Moreover, anyone wishing to determine exactly the sum of goods and compare them with the sum of evils, ought first of all to distinguish between *individual pleasures* and *satisfaction*.[171]

Some individual pleasures, we should note, could never be obtained if they were not preceded and accompanied by certain evils. The pleasure we experience in recovering our health, for example, which is a very intense pleasure, could not be enjoyed if it were not preceded by illness. The pleasure of food and drink is made very intense and gratifying by hunger and thirst. Rest and sleep are among the greatest enjoyments only when we are exhausted and tired or have kept long vigil. We can say that generally speaking people of very comfortable, soft life enjoy the world less, and that the simple and uneducated find more taste

[171] Cf. *SP*, 509–639.

and savour in eating their gruel and drinking their spring water than anyone who dines daily at a table laden with every kind of rare and choice foods and fine wines. This is a truth of common experience so well known that our two gifted philosophers, Ortes and Verri, claimed to deduce from it (falsely however) a general principle, maintaining that 'every pleasure is nothing more than a cessation of pain.'[172] Plato touched upon this where he tells us that when Socrates had had the chain taken off his foot on the day he died, he rubbed the mark left by the chain and said to his friends: 'How wonderful this thing seems that we call *pleasure*. It has a natural and wonderful relationship to *pain*, of which it seems to be the opposite, like something that refuses to exist in us alongside pain! But if find one of them (pain or pleasure), we are, as it were, forced to accept the other, as if they were joined at the same apex.' And then he adds this beautiful thought: 'Indeed, I believe that if Aesop had observed such a thing, he would have written a fable about it; that is, when God wished to reconcile things that conflicted with each other but could not do it, he joined their apices, so that when we experience one of them, we soon experiences the other.'[173] It could not have been said more elegantly. This Socratic or Platonic thought (that God wanted to reconcile contrary things), calls for a deeper investigation, which I will undertake elsewhere. For the present, it is sufficient to note that pleasure, in the act that we receive it, is a movement or transition from a state less agreeable to nature to a more agreeable, perfect state. Therefore, pleasure must come from pain, and its intensity is proportionate to the intensity of the painful condition. Nature begins to move away from this painful condition, making the act more agreeable, because the act is greater in proportion to the length of its path, that is, in proportion to the distance apart of the two extremes between which it moves. A pleasure must also be more intense, the more rapidly the transition is accomplished. From this we can draw several very useful consequences.

[172] Before Verri published his book *Sul piacere*, Ortes had defended a similar paradox in *Calcolo sopra il valore delle opinioni, e sopra i piaceri e i dolori della vita umana*, which was inserted into volume 24 of *Economisti Italiani, Parte moderna*.

[173] *Phaedo* [60 b-c].

585. First of all, we can deduce that, just as every act presupposes a potency, so actual pleasure (the kind proper to human nature) presupposes a lower state from which our nature passes to a better state. This lower state prior to the act of pleasure, although not always *painful*, is always at least a *limitation* that is proper to sensitive nature. This shows us the error of Ortes and Verri who would have found the truth if they had made the act of pleasure arise not from *pain* but from the *limitation* and failure of nature.

586. Second, we deduce that the limitation of human nature is such that it enjoys the most intense pleasures on condition that it is subjected to pain. Consequently, supreme Providence which, granted the law of the least means, has to draw from natures all the good that their forces and faculties can attain, had to permit us to be subject to pain, if Providence wished human nature to enjoy all the pleasures of which it was susceptible.

587. Third, we see why many pleasures result in exhaustion, vexation, stupefaction and harm to health. This is a new reason why Providence had to moderate pleasures and mix them with their opposite.

588. But let us consider pains not in relationship to the act of pleasure but to the satisfaction and contentment of spirit, where true human good lies Here, we have the ability that the Creator has given us as a gift to rise above pain with constancy of spirit and strength of will, even preferring it to pleasure, and in this way changing it from evil to good. And if we denied this ability, we would have to reject the noble nature of our human intelligence. Leibniz, after dealing with the teaching of the Stoics, adopted Descartes' opinion that 'even in the midst of the most wretched misfortunes and the most severe pains, we can always be content provided we can use reason.'[174] Bayle retorted mockingly that 'this is a remedy which almost no one knows how to prepare';[175] he rejected the great riches of human nature, and blamed the Author of nature rather than the ignorance of those who do not use the gifts they have in their spirit. Leibniz answers that the matter is more possible than it seems:

[174] Vol. 1, letter 9.

[175] *Rép. Au prov.*, vol. 3, ch. 157.

Leaving aside true martyrs and those who receive extraordinary assistance from above, there were false martyrs who imitated them. The Spanish slave who killed the governor of Cartagena to avenge his master and took great enjoyment in the cruellest torments he suffered can truly shame the philosophers. Surely it is possible to attain what he attained? Whatever we can say about a fortune, we can also say about a misfortune:

*What is possible for anyone can happen to anyone.**

But still today entire nations like the Huron, the Iroquois, the Galibi and other peoples of America give us beautiful lessons in this matter. We are amazed at the fearlessness and almost insensitivity with which they faced their enemies whom, we read, slowly roasted them and ate them piece by piece. If such people could preserve the advantages of body and heart, adding them to our knowledge, they would be better than us in every way,

*He stands out in the midst of hovels like a tower rising to the sun.**

Among us human beings they would be as a giant to a dwarf, a mountain beside a hill:

*Father Apennine, like Eryx, like Athos, revels in the snowy heights bearing himself upward to the heavens.**

Although this extraordinary strength of body and spirit in these uncivilised people, unyielding in a point of honour, is most amazing, we could acquire it by education, by mortifications carefully adapted to the purpose, by an overriding joy founded on reason, and by a diligent effort to preserve a certain presence of spirit in the midst of distractions and experiences that can so easily disturb the spirit. We read something similar about the ancient Assassins, subjects and pupils of the old man, or better, lord (*Senior*) of the mountain… The gymnosophists of the ancient Indians had perhaps something similar. Galanus, who presented Alexander with the spectacle of having himself burnt alive, had certainly taken courage from the great examples of his masters and of tests of great sufferings sustained in order not to be afraid of pain. The wives of the Indians, who ask to be burnt with the bodies of their husbands, still seem to retain something of the courage of the ancient philosophers of the country.[176]

[176] *Théod.*, 3: 255–257.

589. God therefore placed deep in us a strength that makes us superior to pain and sometimes enables us to choose pain as something preferable to pleasure and capable of satisfying our desire. Consequently, Providence could not leave this internal capacity unused which raises us to such great heights, and we ourselves desire to activate it with wonderful ardour of mind. Hence, in order to draw from it the sublime act to which it is ordered, Providence had to arrange that there was no lack of opportunities for its display, that is, no lack of great (even extreme) sufferings. We can therefore again conclude that if the Creator had prevented physical evils, he would not have operated with wisdom, because he would not have fulfilled the law of the least means which requires that everything useful in nature be extracted so that none of its potencies, none of its possible acts, is lost, but rather each produces that quantity of good it is capable of.

590. This reasoning has much more force if we consider the *moral good* that human beings can draw from painful feelings. I have already touched upon this; here it is sufficient to recall that moral good, which alone has the concept of end, has a value far beyond every other kind of good, which must be regarded as means.

591. Moreover, physical evils are not only an occasion for those who suffer them to obtain great good, if they wish to; these evils can also become for all who know about them a source of knowledge concerning human nature and an occasion for doing good.

592. It is true that if the human race had remained innocent, as God had created it, there would have been no physical evil on earth. It would have been contrary to divine holiness that a nature totally devoid of fault and sanctified by God could be afflicted in the smallest way. But this absence of every evil was not the simple effect of human nature and material forces, because even if distributed with supreme wisdom, these forces would still have clashed, collided and damaged one another due to their limitation. The absence of all evil was the effect of a special providence which, with the help of creatures superior to us, like the angels, kept death and other bodily afflictions of us mortal beings at a distance. In this state of things therefore, the law of the least means could not be fulfilled, nor was it possible

to draw from all human faculties and all possible human acts as well as from the corresponding actions and passions of the rest of the world, all the good that these things could have bestowed. Consequently, supreme wisdom followed its own counsel and permitted the human race to be tempted, and to succumb to the seducer's temptation. This opened the field to all the possible development of human nature and the path to all the tremendously greater fruit that infinite goodness had decreed.

593. In this new order of providence therefore, all the evils are present together with all the goods, both physical and moral, that could be obtained from the evils by means of reparation. But in the beginning the distribution of natural causes was so arranged that they produced the physical evils at the times and in the manner, number and degree that, when everything had been calculated, would finally produce the greatest moral good of humanity and, consequently, the greatest eudaimonological good. I presented some laws of this distribution of causes in book two.

CHAPTER 21

Sixth consequence: it was fitting that the universe should be ordered according to the law of continuity or gradation

> It pertains to divine Providence that all possible levels of entia are filled*
>
> St. T., *C. G.*, III, q. 72, art. 2

594. Another law can be drawn from the principle of application of the law of the least means. It is the well-known *law of continuity* of entia that Leibniz explained. It is demonstrated from what has been said, in the following way.

595. When God wished to create contingent beings, he could create only a finite quantity, not because he lacked the power, but because

if he did otherwise, he would contradict the limitation inherent in these entia and in the nature of numbers. It is therefore absurd to argue with God and demand to know why he had created this particular quantity rather than another, these particular entia rather than others. The fact is that the quantity of entia created by God has to be accepted as a primal datum. All we can reasonably demand is that 'God, as most wise, draw from the quantity of entity that he willed to create all the good it could give by distributing it in the way most suitable for this'.

596. What kind and quantity of entity therefore did God propose to create, and in fact created?

It results from many kinds of things. We shall concern ourselves with the primal, elementary kinds.

Those known to us are three: 1. *material elements*; 2. *sensitive principles*; 3. *intellective principles*.

597. We saw that the law of the least means requires God to draw from these three kinds all the good they can give. But for this to happen God must not allow the loss of any of the forces, capacities, passions and modifications that can give some good. Therefore, in the previous chapter, I concluded that it was fitting for God not to leave entia isolated and separate from each other but to unite them into one whole, putting them in contact

with each other so that through their mutual interaction and modification they would exercise all their capacities and faculties, and none would be left unused. The result would be that they each could contribute something to the sum of good.

Using a similar argument here, we can arrive at another conclusion, equally evident: it was fitting that God use these three elementary kinds to form all the entia that could be formed from them, uniting them in all possible ways, precisely because each of their different combinations is a new entity from which supreme wisdom could draw some good. But this would not be true if a particular combination within the universal order could not increase the sum of good. In this case the loss of the combination would be justified.

598. Thus, if we suppose that the three kinds of elements had to be composed and intermingled in all possible ways so that no capacity and aptitude was lost, the result must clearly be the law of continuity between them, that is, the universe had to embrace a *continuous gradation* of entia from the simplest to the most complex, from the lowest to the highest, according to the quantity that infinite wisdom could form from the three elements.

599. This law does not prevent the three elements having a nature that remains inconfusably distinct. Their nature is immutable, as each element corresponds to a different idea, which is the foundation of a different species. If the atom, which is matter, could change into a sensitive principle, it would cease to be. Similarly, if the sensitive principle, in so far as sensitive, changed into an intellective principle, it would no longer be a sensitive principle. Using Aristotle's simile, often repeated by the Scholastics, we can say that the three elements differ in the way numbers differ.

600. On the other hand, the three principles can be joined together in various ways according to their reciprocal affinities. It is my belief that the material element (atoms) is always informed by feeling (I will present proofs elsewhere), and when the appropriate organisation is attained, the animated atoms form the animal. The animal principle however can be joined to intelligence, and the two principles can acquire a common root, as in the case of the human being.

601. But because this conjunction is not necessary, intelligence can also have a subsistence separate from animality, as in

the case of human souls deprived of the body, although they preserve the root of the animal principle. The same applies to the angels. Hence the opinion of Leibniz, Bonnet and other modern thinkers, and also ancient thinkers [*App.*, no. 13], that every intelligent being must be clothed with some kind of body, even the most tenuous, is gratuitous because, among their various reasons, they could not conceive purely spiritual substance. These philosophers did not note that the body, whether tenuous or solid, is always a body, because the tenuousness or solidity of bodies is relative to our senses; bodies, whether tenuous or solid, do not lose their corporeity or come closer to spirituality; they always differ from spirits not only by degree but by nature.

602. In his demonstration of how fitting it is that creation does not lack pure spirits, Aquinas uses a reason that is close to the reason I give for the law of continuity. According to him the series of levels cannot lack the highest level, which concerns more the purpose of the universe:

> What is accidental to a nature is not always present in the nature, just as having wings does not suit every animal, because it does not pertain to the concept of the animal. Thus, because understanding is not an act of the body nor of any corporeal capacity, the possession of a body does not pertain to the concept of intellective substance as such. The body comes to this substance as an accident for some other reason, that is, it is fitting that the human soul be united to a body because in the genus of intellective substances the human soul is imperfect; having a state of potency, it lacks in its nature the fullness of knowledge which it must draw from sensible things through the corporeal senses… But if the imperfect is present in a genus of things, the perfect must pre-exist in the same genus. Therefore, in intellectual nature there must be some perfect intellective substances that do not need to obtain knowledge of sensible things.[177]

This explanation is valid only if we presuppose the wisdom and goodness of God that gives order to the universe and requires the law of continuity. Without this presupposition we could not

[177] *S.T.*, I, q. 51, art. 1.

prove the principle that what is accidental to a being must vary and sometimes be present, sometimes absent, because only possibility, not necessity, is seen to be present. Nor would the consequence that Aquinas draws from the principle be valid: he concludes that pure spirit must exist because it is what is perfect in the genus of intelligent beings. But we could have replied that the perfect in the genus of intellective things is God. Hence, Saint Thomas turns to God's wisdom and goodness where he argues:

> The object of the divine intention in created things is good, and this consists in assimilation to God. The perfect assimilation of an effect to a cause is accomplished when the effect imitates the cause according to that through which the cause produces the effect, as heat produces heat. God produces the creature through intellect and will... Hence some intellective creatures are necessary FOR THE PERFECTION OF THE UNIVERSE. But understanding cannot be an act of a body nor of a corporeal power because all bodies are determined to the here and now. Therefore we have to assume that an incorporeal nature exists that makes THE UNIVERSE PERFECT.[178]

Note here that in his arguments St. Thomas frequently supposes the *universe to be perfect*, otherwise the product would not correspond to the infinite wisdom, goodness and power of the Craftsman who formed it. It is surprising therefore that there are authors who take great trouble to attack such an obvious truth and do not acknowledge that here we have a most reasonable optimism.

603. The law of gradation or continuity therefore results from the principle that it is fitting that God should draw from the three component elements of creation all the good they could give with their various unions, modifications, faculties and acts. This law, visible in the universe, has two parts: 1. the *greatest number of species of entia* that intermingle without confusion; 2. within the same species, the *greatest number of grades*, according to the level of participation of individuals in the species.

604. The first part of this law explains why creation is

[178] *S.T.*, I, q. 50, art. 1.

composed of 1. atoms that give no sign of sensitive life, 2. brute animals, 3. intelligent animals, 4. pure spirits. The first two can, in my judgment, be reduced to the same species, the only difference being in their organisation. The intelligent animal is the middle ens that links the extremes: the brute and the angel.

605. The second part of the law explains why each of the three or four species of things covers an almost infinite gradation. Minerals are composed and recomposed in all sorts of ways, revealing diverse forms, properties and capacities. There are also some constant things that cannot be changed by the forces of nature that are known to us at present and, because these things are immutable, they are understood as so many scientific species,[179] which are the fifty or fifty-nine elements so far listed by chemistry. Then there are the animals: these have such a gradation that the scale of fixed kinds, understood by naturalists as species, begins where the traces of life are almost insensible and doubtful, and ends with the human being. Evidently in this gradation no intermediary links are missing.

606. Finally the angels. Faith tells us that they are divided into choirs and countless legions. The sequential gradation of their nature is unknown to us but is certainly one of quality and of an inconceivable and unattainable number. Moreover we can accept that this gradation is immeasurably more extensive than the gradation we see in the sensible universe, and that one angel is more sublime and distant from another angel than a star is from the furthest star.

607. This teaching resolves a difficulty that might arise: 'How did God unite an entity as limited as corporeal nature to an intelligent being that extends *ad infinitum* and is by nature immortal?' Composed being, that is, the human being, is necessary by virtue of the law of the least action, which is the law of wisdom. Such a being is necessary as a link in the chain of entia. Through this link God draws all the possible good from the elementary entities: *matter*, *feeling* and *intelligence*, and not only

[179] I call *scientific species* or *species by opinion* those seen as different species because they demonstrate in themselves something stable that separates one from the other. But this is not enough to constitute a truly different species. Species is constituted solely by an essentially different act of being, as I demonstrated in *New Essay* [646–659].

from each but from their conjunction and various admixtures. We must remember that matter and animal feeling are raised to a higher level through their union with intelligence, of which they become instruments, participants in moral perfection, in happiness. The path followed by contingent being is its transition from nothingness to existence, from imperfect to perfect, from matter to feeling, from feeling to understanding. It is indicated by the Aristotelian definition: 'Man is an intelligent animal', which is true if explained as 'an animal raised to the state of intelligent being'. If in this elevation of merely animal being to the state of intelligent being, animality does not match the greatness of intelligence, this is an inevitable consequence of the limitations inherent in finite nature. Not even infinite power can make these limitations not exist, because they are contained in the *essences* of entia, and these essences cannot be changed even by God because this would mean changing his own essence. Hence St. Thomas says: 'Matter has a double state. The first state is chosen because it is a fitting state for the form; the second follows necessarily from the first. Thus to make a saw, the craftsman chooses iron as the matter, capable of cutting hard things. But the fact that the saw can rust or become blunt results necessarily from the nature of the matter. It is precisely fitting therefore that the intellective soul be given a body that has a uniform constitution. But it also follows that the matter makes the body necessarily corruptible. If someone objects that God could have avoided this necessity, I reply that in the constitution of natural things we must not seek what God could have done but WHAT IS FITTING TO THE NATURE OF THINGS, as St. Augustine says.'[180] In other words, God does not operate according to the measure of his power but according to the norms of his wisdom. We can also say: to make an organic body that by its nature is incorruptible is absurd, although God could have preserved it from natural corruption, which in fact is what he did in the primal institution of humanity.

[180] *S.T.*, I, q.

Chapter 22

Seventh consequence: it was fitting that the universe be ordered in keeping with the law of variety in the actuations and modifications of entia

608. Divine wisdom, which cannot by its very nature decree any deviation from the law of the least means, must draw the greatest profit from creation. From this principle I deduced the necessity of the *law of continuity* of the entia that make up the universe. The same effective reasoning can be used to deduce the necessity of the *law of variety in the actuations and modifications of entia*.

609. This law is: the entia that make up the universe and are mixed and grouped together in all possible ways must undergo all the modifications they are capable of and perform all the diverse acts for which they have the faculties, in so far as divine wisdom can draw from each a good that increases the overall total good. Thus, if there were only one possible modification of a created ens, only one capacity, only one act that could produce for divine wisdom the fruit of a very small good to be added to the sum total, and if God neglected to squeeze out, as it were, that drop of net good from his creature, he would be deviating from the path prescribed by his infinite wisdom, because the modification, activity or act would remain unused and would be lost.

610. From all the variety of modifications and acts therefore, divine wisdom can draw some good that increases the total good. Consequently all possible varieties in created entia must be present, unless there are some that cannot be harmonised with the order of the universe and with the maximum good desired of them. I cannot in fact demonstrate this to be impossible, but I think it probable that there are no such varieties.

Every *essence* therefore of created things must be realised and represented in the universe, clothed with all the possible varieties of accidents from which some good can be obtained. A created ens must be found in all possible states from the lowest state to the highest, in all acts from the most imperfect to the most perfect, in all its relationships with other entia that differ specifically from it.[181]

611. Consequently, every created nature, because of the *limitation* necessarily inherent in it, is susceptive of a certain number of imperfect states, of a certain number of acts that lack their term (evil consists in this lack). But if divine wisdom can draw some good from these states and evil acts, they also must have a place in the universe. Moreover, it is certain that there is not a single evil in the universe from which an infinite wisdom does not draw some goods, as was repeated so often after St. Augustine who gave us the fine sentence: *Deus utitur et malis bene* [God also uses evils well].[182]

612. Indeed, numerous physical evils give us the occasion to exercise virtue, even heroic virtue, as I have said. The moral evils of some people also certainly offer a great and continuous occasion to others to exercise patience, charity, zeal for the glory of God and the salvation of the wicked. In fact, human nature is made in such a way that a contrary produces a contrary. Those who are well disposed would not know the beauty of virtue if they were not starkly confronted with the deformity of vice, to the point of finding it abhorrent, or see vice attack virtue and even divinity itself in the attempt to overthrow it. People of good will, faced with this shameful spectacle and aware of the danger, take courage and robustly defend themselves and humanity and even, in a sense, God himself, that is, his external glory. And if vice becomes deeply engrained, they will even avenge eternal justice, as Scripture says: 'The whole world shall fight with him against the unwise.'[183] Hence, if the wicked were eliminated from the earth, an immense quantity of virtuous

[181] Observation of the entia that make up the universe confirms the truth that the mind has *a priori* knowledge, if we argue from the *law of wisdom*. The ancients had also noted this variety in nature. In a letter Seneca writes: 'Among other things that reflect the wonderful *ingenuity of the divine craftsman*, there is the fact, it seems to me, that total sameness is never present in a great abundance of things. Even things that seem to be similar are diverse, when we compare them: there are so many kinds of leaves, but each is marked with its own characteristics; so many animals, but none is like another'* [*Letters to Lucillus*, bk. 19, letter 4].

[182] *De C. D.*, bk. 18, c. 2; bk. 16, c. 2.

[183] Wis 5: 21†.

works would also be eliminated at the same time; even the number of the just would diminish, due to the lack of an effective stimulation to the practice of a more sublime virtue, as Christ taught in the parable of the darnel and wheat: the weeds sown by the enemy could not be gathered without harm to the wheat; both would be pulled out.[184] The divine Master added that in order to form the greatest sum of good, to which the divine goodness tends, God had to permit scandals (*NECESSE EST ut veniant scandala* [Mt 18: 7]). This passage tells us that the Gospel uses the word *necessity* not solely in the sense of *absolute necessity* and of metaphysical necessity, as it is called, but also in the sense of *hypothetical necessity*, based on the supposition that the intention is to draw from created things the overall maximum of good they can give. We see this in the Saviour's words that follow: *vae autem homini illi per quem scandalum venit* [woe to that man by whom the scandal comes], which show that in our nature there is no necessity, whether metaphysical or physical, to sin; on the contrary, every moral evil has its first cause in free will. Certainly, the amount of good for humanity that God drew from heretics, from the impious and the wicked, is incredible. St. Augustine has admirably explained this fact.[185]

613. Furthermore, many wicked people are converted and saved. I said that the moral act of the human spirit that moves towards virtue becomes greater, the more it moves from a greater depth of sin. Hence, in this respect there is no greater

[184] Mt 13: 29.

[185] One of the many passages relative to the matter, found in the works of the holy Doctor, is the following: 'It has been said in all truth: 'many heresies must arise so that those who are of good character may be revealed among you' (1 Cor 11: 18). Let us all take advantage of this beneficence of Providence. The people who become heretics are those who, even if they were in the Church, would go astray. But outside the Church they are of great help, not because they teach the truth, which they do not know, but by stimulating sensual Catholics to seek the truth, and spiritual Catholics to open it up to others. In the holy Church of God there are innumerable acceptable people, but they do not reveal themselves to us as long as we choose to sleep. We are satisfied with the darkness of our ignorance rather than fix our gaze on the light of truth. Hence, heretics awaken many to see and enjoy the light of God. So let us make use of them, not to approve their errors but to uphold Catholic discipline against them and become more vigilant and cautious, even if we do not succeed in recalling them to salvation' (*De Vera Relig*., c. 8).

good than the conversion of a sinner, over which 'the angels' rightly 'rejoice more than over ninety-nine just,'[186] because angelic wisdom can measure the moral greatness of the act.

614. Even though others are pardoned, they are still necessary for the perfection of the universe, for the great end God has proposed, which is to draw from human nature all the good it can give. We cannot deny that God can draw good even from the damned; he can draw a great abundance, using means of which we are totally ignorant. Nevertheless he permits us to know a great part of the good he can draw from them. The terror of eternal punishment, in addition to stimulating us to good, can produce many other useful thoughts in the good, both those who are still pilgrims in this life and those dwelling in eternal beatitude. St. Augustine gives us some of those thoughts:

> Let us thank the Saviour because we see that in the damnation of our fellows we have not received what we certainly know is due to us. If every human being were saved, then what is owed to sin through justice would certainly remain hidden; if no one were saved, then what grace generously bestows would remain hidden. It is preferable to use the words of the Apostle in this very difficult question: 'What if God, desiring *to show* his wrath and *to make known* his power, has endured with much patience the vessels of wrath made for destruction, in order *to make known* the riches of his glory for the vessels of mercy.'[187] This mass of people, deservedly condemned, pays the shameful debt *with justice*, and *with grace* gives honour that is not due, not earned by the privilege of merit, nor by necessity of fate, nor by the TEMERITY OF FORTUNE but by the sublimity of the richness of the wisdom and knowledge of God, which the Apostle contemplates not displayed but veiled, exclaiming in wonder: 'Oh, the depth of the WISDOM AND KNOWLEDGE of God'![188]

In this extract we should note that in the divine Scriptures the *penal consequences* following naturally upon sin, that is,

[186] Lk 15: 7.

[187] Rom 9: 22–23.

[188] Rom 11: 33. — St. Augustine, 194, c. 2.

through the intrinsic order of ens, are called the *anger of God*.[189] The good which the Apostle wishes to reveal (and also St. Augustine who presents the authority for it), comes from the punishments of the reprobate. This fact is precisely what I said: their punishments serve as a natural teaching for us; without them we *would not understand* how wicked sin is, how inviolable justice is, how great God's power is to vindicate justice, how great mercy is and how gratuitous the grace of salvation. God could of course infuse these salutary concepts into us with a direct act of his infinite power, but in this case the creature would not render the good resulting from these concepts, even though the creature could give it. Such action by God would violate the law of wisdom because the creature would not produce of itself all the good it could produce. It is true that the total calculation of God's wisdom is not open to us, so that what applies here applies in the other things of faith, part of which we understand and part we do not know. Hence the Apostle's exclamation: 'O the depth of the riches of the wisdom and knowledge of God! How unsearchable are his judgments and how inscrutable his ways'! Nevertheless, we understand enough of it to conclude that whatever God disposes, he does not do so by chance or, as St. Augustine says, with the temerity of fortune. On the contrary, in everything he follows the law of wisdom, which is the law of the least means. We see therefore that the Apostle does not call God's judgments incomprehensible and his ways unsearchable because they set aside the law of wisdom and follow a blind free choice, but because they fulfil this law so faithfully and with such admirable constancy that no mortal mind can penetrate it or embrace its unlimited extension.

615. Our conviction in this matter can be further strengthened if we consider the good that the comprehensors in heaven receive from the just punishment of the reprobate. They see with total clarity that the lowest parts of the universe are joined to the highest in a most harmonious bond. They also see that wicked beings contribute to the holiness of the virtuous; they see that the equilibrium of violated justice is restored through the punishments, and see this justice triumph over all the power that the creature who battles against it with its own forces is

[189] Cf. *CS*, 108.

capable of. They see that every good comes from God alone, but every evil from the creature trusting in itself. They see themselves reigning with supreme authority in the kingdom of God's justice who dwells in their essences; they reign over all those who hoped and hope in injustice. Finally they see an order of great justice and unity, an order produced by a providence that desires good alone and hence maximum good, on which the necessary limitation of created being lays the necessary and indeclinable condition of the existence of evil. These things are contemplated and experienced by the souls who have realised in themselves the end of the universe, which the whole universe served and serves. It is impossible to say what kind and what amount of happiness this contemplation produces for them and how great the opportunity it gives them to praise the Creator on whose face they gaze.

616. Once again therefore I conclude with the two great authorities of Aquinas and St. Augustine. The first, agreeing with the second, says: 'If all evils were prevented, many goods would be missing from the universe. The lion would not have life if there were no killing of animals, nor would there be the patience of the martyrs, if there were no persecution by tyrants. Hence, St. Augustine says in the *Enchiridion*[190] that Almighty God would not permit the existence of any evil in his works if he were not so omnipotent and good that he can make good even out of evil.'[191]

190 Chap. 11.

191 St. Thomas, I, q. 22, art. 2, ad 2. — Cf. also *C. G.*, q. 3, art. 71, for the same argument.

CHAPTER 23

Continuation. — The end of the law of wisdom is the complete realisation of the species, not a multitude of individuals. — The law of *excluded equality*

> Individual things exist for the sake of a universal nature. A sign of this is that in those things in which a universal nature can be preserved through one individual, there are not many individuals of one species*
>
> St. Th., C. G., III, q. 75: 10

617. To clarify the two previous *laws of continuity* and *variety*, and to remove every possible difficulty concerning the teachings I have so far given, I must, before proceeding further, say something about another cosmic law that I call the law of *excluded equality*.

618. This law lays down that in the whole of creation there cannot be two intellective individuals of the same species who in their *final state* are perfectly equal in all their accidents and relationships. My law of *excluded equality* approximates to the more general principle Leibniz called the law *of indiscernibles*, but it is not truly the same.

619. To make sure therefore that what I say does not involve ambiguities, I will deal with the different related questions that can be raised about the equality of individuals of the same species.

First Question. Can there be two or more individuals of the same species totally equal in *substance* and *accidents*, and even in *reality*? — Reply: the multiplicity of equal individuals of this kind is excluded through metaphysical necessity, because it removes the element that is the principle of individuality and multiplicity: the element is a different *reality*.[192]

620. *Second Question*. Can there be two or more co-existent

[192] I have said that in my opinion *reality* is the *principle of individuation*. Cf. *AMS*, 782–788.

individuals of the same species who differ only in their reality and individuality but are equal in everything else, in *substance*, *accidents* and in *active and passive* relationships with other beings? — *Reply*: this cannot be proved to be metaphysically impossible: many individuals could exist equal in this way. They would be indiscernible to other intelligent beings to whom they had equal relationships. They could however be discerned by God, whose action, in creating them, would have had two terms instead of one only, because the creating action would have had two realities for its terms. Similarly, in the case of intellective entia: each intellective ens, perceiving its equals, could distinguish the others from itself by means of the awareness of its own reality. But if an individual intellective ens knows others equal to itself, each of these must know the others and in an equal way, otherwise they would not have the equality required by the hypothesis. However if this level of equality of intellective entia is conceived as possible, the equality would last only an instant, but we cannot in any way understand how such entia could be kept equal during their development and in their relationships with other entia, which are also subject to development and to change. Such equality would require not only that the equal entia performed perfectly equal actions but that all the other entia surrounding them maintained an equal active and passive relationship with each of them. This is truly impossible, granted the connection of entia — unless of course we posit the hypothesis of diverse equal worlds where the same accidental combinations are perfectly repeated. But such a hypothesis (prescinding even from the diversity of place) contradicts the above-mentioned principle of the unity of the world, and also, as we shall see, the principle of excluded equality.

621. *Third Question*. Can there be two equal and real possible things, of which God creates only one? — *Reply*. I think that the human mind can conceive this. For example, instead of Adam, I can conceive that God could have created another human being totally like Adam, except in individuality. I will explain. The *idea* we have of something is the same for all equal individuals.[193] But the *subsistent-reality* itself is not included in

[193] Cf. *New Essay*, 3: 1176–1193. King had said the same in his work on evil.

the idea,[194] and much less is it the idea itself, as Hegel wrongly claims. So, where in God does the reality of the thing exist? Certainly not in the idea of things but in the act of his most powerful will,[195] with which he creates them and makes them *subsist*. But the reality he creates never exhausts his creative power, which is always able to create new realities. Consequently, infinite, equal individuals can correspond to the same idea (whenever the nature of the ens, which is the term of the creative act, does not have special conditions that exclude the plurality of individuals). Hence, the reality of another human being totally like Adam could not be absent from God if he had wanted to create that reality, that is, make it subsist: this reality that he could have created is called *possible-reality*. Leibniz tries to prove that it is impossible for God to choose between two equal possible individuals, the kind that the human mind can conceive.[196] He objects that the creator would not have sufficient reason to choose one rather than the other. But the objection arises from the false Leibnizian supposition that intelligence always operates not only according to a *sufficient reason* but also according to one *reason prevailing among different reasons*, so that there is no sufficient reason unless one reason naturally prevails over another. Therefore Leibniz does not accept that the human will is free to choose *between volitions*.[197]

194 Ibid., 402–405.

195 God's will as the cause of contingent things is demonstrated by St. Thomas, *S.T.*, I, q. 19, art. 4.

196 The human mind can conceive the *possibility* of many individuals not because their possibility as uniquely distinct beings is understood in their specific idea but because the existence of a real individual is already known by us, and we relate this individual to our idea and thus know that the individual does not exhaust or realise everything understood in the idea. Therefore we understand that the idea contains the possibility of an infinite number of equal individuals. I have shown in many places that the possibility is not the idea, as many falsely attribute to me, but is a relationship which the mind adds to the idea of the ens. Cf. *NE*, 2: 540–557.

197 In Leibniz' *Riflessioni* dealing with the controversy between Hobbes and Bramhall, whose acts were published in London in 1656 in the book *Questions touchant la liberté, la necessité et le hazard, éclaircies et débattues entre le docteur Bramhall, évêque de Derry, et Thomas Hobbes de Malmesbury*, in quarto, the German philosopher says: 'Human beings choose objects with their will, but do not choose their actual volitions. These come

[621]

I reject this teaching, which would destroy the bilateral freedom necessary for producing *merit* strictly understood. Instead, I demonstrate that this faculty of bilateral freedom exists, and that its nature consists in 1. choosing between volitions, and 2. increasing by *practical force* the prevalence of one reason over another so that the reason that prevails and determines the choice is not always prevalent *per se* but is made so by freedom. I agree with Leibniz that intelligence always requires a reason according to which it operates, but I maintain against him that if there are two reasons struggling equally in favour of two volitions, free will can choose one of the volitions rather than the other by adding some weight to one of the two and thus determine its indecision. This is a truth which I first draw from the observation of what happens within us, and then confirm with arguments taken from the absurdities that would result if the opposite were the case. I will deal only with three of these absurdities:

621a. 1. Without bilateral freedom we cannot explain a true moral merit in mankind.

2. It is not impossible to conceive two equal reasons for two volitions. Thus, in the case I considered above, we can conceive that at the beginning of the world God could have created another perfectly equal human being in place of the human being he did create. This would mean that the activity of an intelligent being is fettered in its operation. We know that intellective activity, by its nature, always chooses the best, as long as the best exists, but granted that in the nature of things this best does not exist (this follows from the hypothesis of two perfectly equal reasons), the activity is no longer bound to the law of the *per se* sufficient reason, because there is no sufficient reason. Someone will object that in this case the activity is not intellective. But it is simply a question of the meaning of words: if intellective operation means to operate on the condition that there is a reason, the operation is intellective. However, an operation that chooses arbitrarily

from reasons and dispositions' — Leibniz repeats this opinion in many places. But I demonstrated the opposite: *meritorious freedom*, strictly speaking, can consist solely in *the choice between volitions*. This is precisely where freedom is distinguished from will, the freedom I have called bilateral. Cf. AMS, 636–643.

between reasons does not have to be called intellective. There is no absurdity in this: not every activity can in fact be reduced to intellective activity because, as I have shown, real being has an activity of its own.

Moreover, I also said that strictly speaking every activity without exception pertains to real being, and this being is always in operation and uses the various reasons of the understanding solely for its direction. Hence an activity is not *formed* by the knowledge of what is possible but is *directed* by this knowledge. An activity is not therefore destroyed when it finds no direction in the knowledge of what is possible; its reality continues, left free to do what it likes, licensed by the understanding to operate by itself in whichever of the modes presented to it by the understanding; the understanding does not direct it in one way more than the other, or rather it shows it both ways equally. Consequently, the answer to the question 'whether in such a case the activity is intellective or not' is that it is partly intellective (in the principal) because it operates with reason, but not totally intellective (in the accessory) because there is something (the direction of the movement) that is arbitrarily chosen through its own energy.

3. God's divine power would be limited if, in place of the intellective ens that he creates, he were denied the power to create another totally equal ens. Leibniz did not venture to deny this metaphysical possibility, and Baldinotti, accepting Leibniz' concession, could refute him with the same reason I use against him concerning the choice of possible, totally equal individuals, the kind that the human mind can think.[198]

622. I say 'the kind that the human mind can think' because divine understanding and operation differ greatly from ours. God has no need to choose; with one single act he wills all he wills, and the object of this one perfect act is placed before him

[198] 'But if two perfectly equal things are *in se* possible, which Leibniz has not denied because he could not see that there was anything contradictory in this, surely God can chose one of them as the term of his action?'* (*Metaph. Generalis*, 73). However, it does not follow that God could have made subsist at the same time any two equal entia whatsoever, without distinction. This would contradict the connection between the entia of the universe, that is, the unity of the world, as I have said. Thus, Clarke's and Baldinotti's explanations are, relative to this passage of Leibniz, deficient.

by his wisdom and by his essentially good will; no act of choice precedes this. Hence the *possible equal human beings* that we supposed do not exist for God with a distinct existence. Although individuals acquire existence and distinction by God's decree that creates them, they do not have these things prior to this decree and cannot therefore be objects of a true choice. The human mind however forms for itself their possibilities and distinct images, and thus begins to conceive and form the idea of a choice, which it then tranfers to God. In God mere possibles are virtually indistinct, because such is their true being. It would not therefore be far from the truth to say that in God there is the possibility of possibles, as I have explained elsewhere,[199] and there is also the relationship between the creature and God's inexhaustible power. We would therefore be uselessly straining ourselves to conceive a true choice between Adam's reality and other equal realities; Adam's reality is distinguished from other things, just as the distinct is distinguished from the indistinct, and what is first from what is second, that is, as a first creative act is distinguished from another creative act which might succeed it and can therefore now create an ens totally equal to the first, including its relationships. Only in the system of emanantism could a choice of individuals be introduced, because in such a system, in which creatures are composed of divine substance, their substance or reality is made to pre-exist in God. But this is not the case in the Catholic system of creation, where the reality of creatures is not prior to the creative decree and cannot therefore be an object of choice. Consequently, the third question I proposed has both its origin and solution in the imperfection of human understanding. When applied to God however, it disappears into nothingness, as something that is not possible.

623. I return now to the second question, which is related to the purpose of this chapter, and I will demonstrate what I proposed, namely: 'It is not appropriate to the law of wisdom to make many intellective individuals exist that are totally equal in their final state'.

The proposition is restricted solely to intellective individuals

[199] *Il Rinnovamento*, etc, bk. 3, cc. 52 and 53.

because only these have the concept of end for operative intelligence and morality.

624. In the case of *non-intellective beings*, which have only the concept of means, it would be difficult to prove the same thesis. Leibniz extended his principle of indiscernibles also to these, with the result that the principle presented a weak flank to the attacks of Clarke. He objected that if God could find it necessary to create many equal individuals for some purpose, why could he not do so?[200] Here we see Clarke arguing from the *concept of means*, which created entia can have, and not from the concept of end, as I do.

625. Furthermore, we must carefully consider what is necessary if two or more individuals can be said to be equal in everything except their individuality. Such perfect equality requires them to have equality in all that constitutes them or makes them what they are, that is, substance and all their accidents. In my explanation of the second question, I added *relationships with other entia* in addition to substance and accidents. Certain relationships have a role in making entia be what they are, as in the case of intellective ens; here, knowledge can be considered as a relationship with other entia, constituting and determining intellective ens. But not all entia or all relationships are of this nature. Thus, for bodies, the external relationships of space and time, that is, a place and a period, constitute neither their substance nor accidents, nor do they pertain to the body. Hence, if we said that the material universe is composed of perfectly hard elements of the same nature, having the same size and shape, like Anaxagoras' ὁμοιομερεῖς, then certainly these elements would be totally equal entia, except for their reality, even though they are located in different parts of space and considered in different periods of time. If on the other hand different efforts towards movement or different movements change something in the corporeal elements, the question is not easily solved because it now depends on knowing whether effort towards movement and movement itself pertain to or are alien to corporeal nature. I believe that neither movement nor effort towards movement is part of the *idea of matter* because matter has the *concept of term*. However, the faculty of receiving and

[200] *Cinquième réplique de M. Clarke.*

transmitting movement together with effort towards movement is certainly part of the idea, whatever the faculty may be.[201]

626. According to this opinion the elements we are talking about would not be equal in everything if they were not all at rest or did not possess the same effort to movement and the same velocity of movement produced by the same part of the element. The different directions of the movement must also be indifferent precisely because the different parts of space in which a body is, do not change anything in the body.

It is not therefore my intention to maintain or deny that perfectly equal corporeal elements can and do exist. The question has no importance for my present purpose.

627. In the case of *non-intellective animate entia*, they are certainly modified by sensations which they receive from outside and from the action they themselves exercise on other bodies. These relationships would have to be equal for equal animal entia, otherwise they would vary, but as I said, I think this is impossible except solely in the inadmissible hypothesis of two or more equal worlds, or at least in the hypothesis that there is equality between the little worlds (so to speak) in which the action and reaction of the animate entia are enclosed, that is, the group of foreign entia in contact with or influencing them. This does not involve absolute impossibility when the thing is reduced to a single moment. But in the case of enduring equality it seems inconceivable due to the interconnection of all the parts of the universe and of their continuous, reciprocal actions and consequent mutations. Again however, this is outside my argument that concerns only intellective beings, which have the concept of end.

[201] Francesco Orioli, a professor at the University of Corfù, in the periodical that he publishes in that city under the title *Spieghe e Paglie* put forward the hypothesis that when the movement of the body is terminated by the impact of a contrary movement, virtual movement or the tendency to continue the movement remains in the body. Consequently, continual tendencies remain but are made ineffective through what opposes them: 'Hence, every material substance would preserve in itself, at least virtually, all the tendencies to motion impressed on it in all past time and would maintain these tendencies in the order they were impressed' (*Quaderno VI*, no. 1, year 1844). I mention this hypothesis as a new consideration, but I do not see the least proof for it nor even the simple possibility of its truth.

628. Turning therefore to intellective entia, I deny that there can be many that are perfectly the same in their final state. In this denial, I am not following Leibniz' opinion. He held that there can be no reasonable operation if the reason for the operation is not *per se* sufficient. But his opinion fails on two accounts: 1. he starts from an erroneous concept of meritorious freedom because he fails to recognise the freedom that has the capability of changing the efficacy of the reasons present to the spirit, a freedom which makes possible the choice between two *per se* equals — the freedom itself makes them unequal; 2. he does not see that two equals could exist, not because God might have chosen one of them to exist but because God could make them both subsist without preferring one to the other, which is one of the reasons Clarke used against Leibniz.

629. I am also not content with the explanation that I gave above concerning the connection of entia which gives rise to the unity of the universe and concerning their perpetual, reciprocal mutations. The explanation, although effective, excludes instantaneous equality.

630. The explanation that I need to establish here concerns solely the final equality of many intellective individuals. It rests on the intimate nature of intelligence and wisdom, which never sees individuals as an end but as realising in themselves a *species* of eudaimonological-moral good.

631. We must remember that the form of intelligence is an *idea*, and an idea is always the foundation of a *species* (class). Even generic ideas reduce to specific ideas, of which they are abstractions.[202] We must also remember that the will, which is the principle of intellective action, always terminates with its action in a known object proposed to it by the intelligence. The will therefore wills objects in exactly the same way that they are known by the understanding.[203] Hence the question reduces to determining how we know real entia, into which the will's inclination is borne.

202 Here, the reader must be keep in mind the teaching I gave about *species* and *genera* in *NE*, 646–659.

203 Note: we are talking here about the *way* we will, not the *degree* with which we will objects. The *way* depends in part on the will, and it is here that we find the efficacy proper to bilateral freedom.

Real entia perceived in feeling are recognised by the spirit when it refers them to the *idea* in which it intuits their essence. Hence knowledge of a real being is purely the awareness that a given essence (which is a part of the universal essence) is realised, that is, it has passed from potency to act.[204] Thus, the entity present in a real individual is simply the entity in its essence knowable in the idea. This entity constitutes the good that the real individual has, and the more entity it has, the greater is its good, because *ens et bonum convertitur* [ens and good are interchangeable].[205]

Moreover, because good is the object of the will, the object inclines the will to itself in proportion to its goodness. If we suppose that we are dealing with entia that have different and opposite substances and accidents, one individual alone cannot receive into itself all the entity to which its essence extends because it does not simultaneously admit all the accidents of which its essence is receptive. Also, an individual in its final, permanent state, which is the state we are discussing here, cannot realise all the good that the intellect contemplates in the essence. Consequently, the will, which has as its object the good it sees in the essence, is inclined, after producing an individual, to produce others in which the portion of ens and good is made real that could not be made real in the first individual because the first individual was incapable of taking the portion into itself. However, for the same reason, the producing will has nothing else to make real when it has posited in being as many individuals as it needs in order that all the modes and accidents to which the essence extends are made real. It therefore ceases producing other individuals: the good it tended to make real is already fully realised; it finds no further object that it can will. But if the producing cause, after producing all the different individuals in their modes and accidents, repeated the production by positing in being individuals equal to the first individuals, it would produce neither good nor ens that was new to the understanding and will, that is, that was not already produced. It is true that an ens produced equal to another would be a good for itself but it would be as nothing to the understanding and will of

[204] Cf. *NE*, 3: 1176–1193.

[205] Cf. *PE*, 20–45.

its author; it would be a superfluity to the realisation of the ideal world because it would not add any good to this world which it might not already have. Hence, the being that operates essentially through intelligence and will (like divine being) will never produce such an ens, not because the being does not have the power to produce it, by willing it, but because it does not will it. Producing it contradicts the law that guides wisdom in its *end*, which is 'to realise all the good that is in intelligible essence'. It also contradicts the law that guides wisdom in the *mode* of its operation, which is 'to use the least means for the end', a law that excludes all superfluities.

632. St. Thomas adds something more to this demonstration, which makes the demonstration still more complete. He observes that creatures participate in divine goodness through *form*, not through *matter*; the form has its origin in God because it is in the divine exemplar and consequently in the Word. God makes things only in so far as they can participate in his goodness. St. Thomas says: 'In substances however the matter exists for the sake of the form, BECAUSE THROUGH THE FORM THE MATTER PARTICIPATES IN DIVINE GOODNESS, FOR WHICH ALL THINGS WERE MADE.'*[206] From this he deduces the exclusion of individual things as superfluous to the realisation of the form: 'Clearly then, individual things exist FOR THE SAKE OF A UNIVERSAL NATURE IN ALL ITS EXTENSION. A sign of this is the fact that in those things in which a universal nature can be preserved through one individual, there are not many individuals of one species.'*[207]

633. Consequently, two intellective entia, totally equal in their final, permanent state, cannot be the object of an infinite wisdom. The same applies to the law of morality, which coincides with and resides in the law of intelligence, or certainly is guided by intelligence. I will explain.

The principle of morality is 'the practical acknowledgement of the good that is in a known real ens'.[208] If therefore the moral act has for its object the *good* that is in a known real ens, the esteem and moral affection does not stop at the reality of the

206 *C. G.*, III, q. 75: 10.

207 Ibid.

208 Cf. *Storia comparativa e critica de' sistemi interno al principio della morale*, c. 1. [Cf. also *PE*, 167].

individual but passes on to its eternal essence contemplated in the idea. The mind measures the individual precisely with the idea in which the mind intuits the essence of the individual, and it esteems the individual in proportion to how much of the essence it finds realised in the individual. Whether the *reality* that constitutes the individual as an individual is this or that reality entirely indifferent to morality, so that if there could be two perfectly equal, intellective individuals, the esteem and moral affection whose object they would be, would be morally identical, not different, although their reality and individuality would be different. I say 'identical' to indicate that a moral affection whose object was two perfectly equal, intellective entia would not differ either in quality or quantity, granted that the deficiency of the lover is excluded. If we consider affection as it is in human beings it seems that it must be greater towards two equal entia than towards only one, but this is because human affection is mostly weak and deficient. Affection in God, however, where the total notion of affection is made real, is complete affection; here, one single ens is clearly sufficient to exhaust all the possible affection required by the essence it expresses and makes real. And I have explained why: the object of rational, moral affection is an ens in so far as the ens realises its own essence. Granted therefore that in a perfect lover, such as God, and also (in due proportion) in those in heaven, there is an affection for only one real ens, where the essence is seen subsistent, every possible affection for other entia that are equal to the first and are realised dissolves into that affection. To love one is to love all, because it means to love their species and nature, the object of the intellect and of intellective love. Moreover, neither the intensity nor the morality of this love can grow with the multiplication of the entia, nor can their multiplication give the lover an opportunity to make himself more virtuous or happy in his love for them. As I said, love in us who are viators is deficient, whether the love is potential or habitual. Because of this fact, our love grows with the repetition of acts, but it does not become a more noble species if the species of the object does not change. However, the acts can be repeated in favour of a single ens without many equal entia necessarily existing.

It is not therefore *individuality* and *reality* as such that constitute the proper object of morality, but the realised *essence*. Thus, if instead of Adam God had created a human being equal to Adam, differing solely in reality (which is possible to conceive), the moral act for which this being would have been the occasion in other intellective beings that might have known him, would have been exactly the same: morality would have neither gained nor lost anything. Hence, if we suppose an infinite goodness, it will want to produce all good, but wanting to produce all good means wanting the complete realisation of the essences of entia. When this creative goodness has obtained this end, it will cease its activity; it will no longer have any reason to create new individuals who would add nothing to the perfect realisation of their essences and give no occasion for any new act of moral goodness. The love for individuals which completely realises all the essence of the specific ens to which they belong, is the act which fully esteems and loves that essence; in this way all the moral good possible for them can be expended. Therefore supreme, creative goodness will never produce two individuals that are perfectly equal and endure in their final *state*. This would be superfluity, because the moral end sought by supreme goodness can be obtained with one single individual.

634. But if the principle of the *realisation of species* produces the law of *excluded equality*, it also confirms the law of *variety*.

We must bear in mind that an *abstract species* is an imperfect species, which cannot be a proper object of perfect understanding, such as God's understanding. The norms or types of operation for divine understanding are *full species* that are distinguished by his creative act. But for each ens there are as many full species as there are modifications and varieties in good and evil, and these modifications and varieties can be given to the ens and mutually exclude each other.

It is true that the other species seem to be virtually contained in the archetype or complete-full-species, but:

1. It is not proved that each ens has only one archetype. Perhaps for some entia the contrary can be demonstrated (I myself consider this fully probable in the case of entia that are composed of several elements).

2. Even granted that the archetype is one only, it does not follow that it contains in itself every possible endowment of the ens, because certain endowments are excluded due to the limitation of the ens. For example, if we suppose that white is

the archetype of the colours, it in no way follows that white has within itself the capacity to produce the pleasant sensation produced by green or red or any other colour. We can perhaps say that a particular colour, for example green, at its greatest intensity virtually contains all the weaker sensations that that species of colour is capable of stimulating, but we cannot maintain that the maximum intensity of green gives to the spirit and eye all those delightful sensations that the colour's graded tints usually stimulate, each of which excludes the other and imparts it own enjoyment.

3. Even if all the endowments of which an ens can receive could be contained in the archetype, they would be so intermingled and confused that this fact alone would make a thing different from what the endowments are when separate and distinct. This is something very similar to the way that two colours mixed together produce a third which is neither one nor the other.

4. Again, even if all the very distinct, possible endowments could be comprised in the archetype, as in the case of the archetypes of composite things, some would necessarily limit others because they would have to keep an order among themselves and produce a harmony. In this case, none of them could be brought to the greatest degree of intensity without damaging the harmony of the whole. Thus in a very fine painting it is impossible for all the colours to excel and be very intense; this would destroy the total effect of the picture.

5. The archetype does not contain the deficient part of the ens. This part is the absence of endowments and the presence of disorders or evils, which are also found in all the other incomplete full species. The absence and evils are nevertheless necessary in order that the essence be fully realised and manifested to created intelligences, because it is precisely the absence and evils that make known the limitation and deficiency of the essence.

635. For all these reasons eternal wisdom, tending to realise essences completely, had to make them exist in all their possible varieties. But two more reasons can also be added:

1. Without these varieties many goods would be lost in the universe. Every variety, every endowment of an ens, all the different combinations of endowments, every defect, every

disorder (granted that all these are wisely related to other entia and other varieties) will produce or give the occasion to producing both particular and universal goods as a result of the harmony of things. Thus in the case of a well-disposed spirit, corporeal pain occasions the virtue of fortitude and, when related to all the vicissitudes of human life, produces most pleasant memories, as the poet says:

> You have experienced the Cyclopean rocks;
> Recall your courage and banish sad fear.
> Perhaps even this distress will some day
> be a joy to recall.*[209]

Misfortune forms lasting friendships, stimulates feelings of compassion, opens the way to such a great amount of charitable works that without it the love binding people together would be far rarer, and all human activity would be diminished and almost brought to an end.

636. 2. Without all the possible varieties, we could not *know* or fully esteem entia in their essences because one essence alone, whether abstract or archetypal, does not manifest all the endowments and varieties that an ens can receive. The finite intellect of the creature cannot simultaneously contemplate many entities with the same intensity of thought with which it contemplates them separately and one at a time. Hence, accidental entities had to be separated from each other so that we could know created things in the best way and, through them, know God. As this is a very important matter, I will return to it later.

637. For the present, this teaching, which shows that divine operation has as its purpose the full realisation of the eternal essences of entia, has many and very relevant consequences. I will mention some here.

First consequence. This has its origin in the teaching, and concerns the question discussed by theologians and philosophers as to how God can love creatures and create them through an act of goodness, when he has no need of them; they cannot add any good to him, and his love can have no worthier object than himself. William King, in his well-known work *De origine Mali*,

[209] Virg., *Aeneid*., 201–203.

maintains that God determined himself to create with a freedom of such perfect indifference that for him creation and non-creation were the same. King conceded that creatures cannot be the object of a divine desire, like creatures who are not good by their nature but by the will of God; God makes them good simply by willing them with the result that, prescinding from the relationship with the divine will, neither evil nor good could be found in entia. To this Leibniz rightly retorted:

> It is difficult to conceive how authors of merit could espouse such a strange opinion… It seems to be proved by the fact that all creatures have all their being from God, and they can neither work on it nor determine it. But this clearly changes the question. When we say that an intelligent substance is moved by the goodness of its object, we do not claim that this object is necessarily some being existing outside the substance, and if it is conceivable, that is sufficient. It is its representation that works in the substance, or rather the substance acts on itself in so far as affected and disposed by the representation. With God however, his understanding clearly contains the IDEAS of all possible things, and as a result of this, everything is eminently contained in it. God therefore determines himself by himself: his will is active in virtue of goodness, but it is specified and directed in its action by the intellect full of wisdom… Now, if IDEAS are independent of the will, the perfection and imperfection that are represented in them will also be independent. Indeed, is it due to God's will or rather to the nature of numbers
>
> that, for example, certain numbers are more capable than others of admitting many exact divisions, or are more appropriate than others for forming squares, composing polygons or other regular shapes,
>
> that the number 6 has the prerogative of being the least among all the numbers we call perfect,
>
> that in a plane, six equal circles can touch a seventh,
>
> that of all equal solids, the sphere has the least surface,
>
> that certain lines are immeasurable and consequently little suited to harmony?
>
> Do we not see that all these advantages and disadvantages come from the idea of the thing and that the contrary implies contradiction? Can we claim that God is indifferent to the pain and difficulties of sensitive creatures, and

> particularly the happiness and unhappiness of intelligent substances? And what about justice? Is this also something arbitrary; would God have acted wisely and justly if he had resolved to damn the innocent?... In God therefore a reason existed prior to the resolution and, as I have often said, God did not create this world by chance, or without purpose, or even through necessity; his *inclination* led him to this, and his inclination always guides him to the best... Therefore, to create or not to create is not absolutely indifferent to God; nevertheless creation is a free act. Nor is it more indifferent to him to create this or that world, to create either a perpetual chaos or a system full of order. Thus the qualities of objects, included in the IDEAS of the objects, were the reason for his choice.[210]

637a. In this excellent passage many things are true and well stated. The definite distinction between *real being* and *ideal being*, a distinction that is the foundation of philosophy, greatly clarifies the argument. — The *principle of operation* is always in real being, while the idea simply directs the operation. But the difference between human and divine operation is this: in God the principle of operation is so perfectly contained in divine, real being that God cannot receive any stimulation from any other real being outside himself, whereas in us the principle of operation is imperfectly contained in our human real being such that this being can receive stimulation and motion from other real beings different from it. Consequently, we are moved to operate by the action of a created reality foreign to us. Because, as we have seen, reality is the principle of individuals, we as real individuals receive the action of other real individuals. This action sometimes produces in us an enjoyment, which gives rise to the operative inclination or pleasant instinct that tends to unite individual with individual, reality with reality. Nothing of this happens in God: the only reality, as reality, to which God has an inclination is his own; he takes pleasure only in himself.

The enjoyment and instinct that arises in one contingent reality towards another is not something *per se* intellectual and moral. It is certainly true that our understanding perceives the enjoyment and we make it precisely the end of our operation,

210 *Adnotationes in librum De origine mali, haud ita pridem in Anglia evulgatum*, n. 21.

and at the same time we also second the instinct arising from it. As a result, created intellective being does not always operate for the good it sees in the *idea* but sometimes operates by means of the individual impulse of the reality that is conceived by the intellective activity and allowed to operate by the will, or also seconded by the will. But if an operation resulting from the impulse of the contingent reality thus becomes an intellective operation, it still does not acquire any morality because morality never considers the individual as individual and reality but as the realisation of an eternal essence, in which all esteem and moral affection always terminate. Consequently, God, whose operation is always intellective and moral, can never have as the purpose of creation the individual as individual, that is, the individual's pure reality that does not exist before he has created it. Instead, he has as his purpose solely the *individual's eternal essence*, which merits esteem and moral love and is in the divine idea. This fact is the origin of the inclination of God's goodness to produce the created reality as an actuation and realisation of the eternal essence lying in the depth of his being. Hence, St. Thomas says with his usual acuity and truth: 'It is not appropriate to the first agent that is pure agent' (and not patient) 'to operate to acquire some end' (as in the case of passive agents that tend to acquire). 'His end is solely to COMMUNICATE HIS PERFECTION, WHICH IS HIS GOODNESS.'[211] This communication, which he enjoys, consists precisely in his making the essences of contingent things become subsistent from possible, because creation consists in making their reality pass from non-being to being.

638. Once again this explains why the Fathers and Doctors say that God's knowledge (I would say 'practical knowledge') is the cause of things. St. Thomas says: 'The *intelligible form*' (the essence of the thing intuited by intelligent being) 'does not indicate a principle of action in so far as solely in the intelligent being, if we do not add an inclination to the effect, which arises from the will. Because the intelligible form has a disposition to opposites (the knowledge of opposites is one and the same knowledge), it would not produce a determined effect if it were not determined to one by the appetite...[212] It is clear however

[211] *S.T.*, I, q. 44, art. 4.

[212] Arist., *Metaph.*, 9, text 10.

that God causes things through his intellect because his being is his understanding. Hence his knowledge must be the cause of things in so far as it is joined to the will,'[213] which is precisely what makes it practical. The *operation* therefore responds to the *cause*, and because the latter, in God, is practical knowledge, he creates the quantity that is sufficient, and suffices for realising the essences of the things he wishes to create; it is these essences that constitute the knowledge. From this we conclude that God loves contingent things for himself because he loves them for the eternal essences that lie indistinct in his nature and which he distinguishes by producing them in time with the creative act.

639. *Second consequence.* Although the evils that contingent being can receive develop in contingent being, this being is not less loved by God. The evils are in fact already indicated in the eternal essence of the creature. Moreover, because the love that God bears for real creatures is directed to their essences shining in the divine ideal, and not to the realities as such, and because the evils to which he permits creatures to be really subject are necessary for completing the divine ideal, the evils do not diminish the love he bears for the totality of his creature. As I said, the measure of this love is the measure of entity and hence of good that is in the eternal exemplar.

Just as the object of divine love therefore is not *individual good* as such, that is, prescinding from the relationship this real good has with its eternal type, so contrariwise the object of divine hatred is solely *individual evil*, as individual and real, prescinding from the relationship the evil has with the eternal type, in which the evil is contained and which limits the good without destroying it; on the contrary it plays its part in completing the good. Again therefore, just as God does not produce an ens that is not necessary for realising its type, so he does not permit any evil that is not necessary for realising the accident of evil contained implicitly in the archetype. Although this increase of evil, if God permitted it, harmed only individuals and not God, it would nevertheless prevent the sum of good from being maximum and would also be a superfluity. For these two reasons it would contradict divine wisdom. But as the lovability of creatures relative to God remains totally in the divine

[213] *S.T.*, I, q. 14, art. 8.

archetype which the creatures express, so it is not real evil that limits this lovability, but possible evil, which is necessary. We see therefore that if the possibility of evil, which is necessary, does not detract from divine holiness, nor can the existence and realisation of evil detract from it in any way.

640. *Third consequence*. In heaven, among the multitude of saints, no saint can be equal in everything to another; on the contrary each will be unique and supreme in his or her form, which will increase the glory of each. We can therefore say of every saint what the Church sings equally of every pope: 'There has not been found another like to him who kept the law of the most high', and we will see verified the words of St. John, when he was in ecstasy: 'To everyone who conquers I will give some of the hidden manna, and I will give a white stone, and on the white stone is written a new name that no one knows except the one who receives it.'[214] This name unknown to those who do not have it written on them must surely be the characteristic or type of the holiness proper to each saint, a type of holiness that no one else will experience and which will give to those who manifest it in themselves an incommunicable delight symbolised in the hidden manna. Furthermore, if something similar is verified even on earth in the spouse of Christ, how much more must it be verified in the final state, in the spouse who has entered her marriage in heaven 'clothed in many-coloured robes', as the Psalmist says?[215] Hence, we should not hesitate to believe that there are as many types of holiness as there are places in the heavenly mansion, and only one individual attains one of these places. We can thus better understand the apostolic simile: 'Do you not know that in a race the runners all compete, but only one receives the prize? Run in such a way that you may win it.'[216] Many run in this life to obtain a place in heaven, but only one receives that place, although anyone who fails in one place can perhaps gain another, which only that individual occupies.

641. Finally, the *fourth consequence*. The whole of this teaching explains why the knowledge of individual things as

[214] Rev 2: 17.

[215] Ps 45: 14.

[216] 1 Cor 9: 24.

individual things gives neither knowledge nor perfection to the understanding, and why we say that all knowledge lies in universals. Therefore, the knowledge of individual things as such adds nothing to the speculative understanding; it simply helps the practical understanding to operate.[217] But practical understanding does not operate with wisdom and moral goodness if it does not turn to some speculative information and gives due esteem and affection to the *essence of entia* in proportion to the share this essence has in the infinite and *universal essence*.

[217] 'Knowledge of individual things does not pertain to the perfection of the intellective soul according to speculative knowledge. However it pertains to its perfection according to practical knowledge, which is imperfect without the knowledge of individual things in which operations exist, as stated in the sixth book of Ethics (c. 7)'* (St. Thomas, *S.T.*, III, q. 11, art. 1, ad 3.

[641]

CHAPTER 24

Eighth consequence: the law of unity in divine operation

> Although she is but one, she can do all things, and while remaining in herself, she renews all things*
>
> Wis 7: 27

642. It is not enough to be aware that the end of divine operation, in creating the reality of things, is grounded in *ideality*. In God this ideality is not divided into parts but is totally simple and united, hence the unity and complexity of divine operation.

643. This unity of divine operation that calculates the whole and not simply a part is a new consequence of the law of the least means. But because this law makes the will tend to the maximum good, it obliges the will to calculate all the particular goods and evils in order to find that ultimate result of good which, as maximum, becomes the sole and excellent object of the operation of an excellent will.

However, in order that everything in these teachings is seen to be harmonious, I want to show in this chapter that the unity of divine operation originates more from the essence of God than from the law of least means.

644. God is *absolute being*. This being has three forms that I call (using a human, inadequate language) reality, ideality and morality. These three forms of being harmonise into a totally simple unity. The mode of operation of absolute being must be the same as itself, that is, one and trine. Operative action pertains to reality but is always directed by ideality. Hence, in the previous chapter we saw that God is inclined to create contingent natures not because he loves their reality as a kind of end, but because in their reality he loves the *ideal essence* that shines in his intellect. Consequently, the Creator's divine affection ultimately terminates in himself, as Scripture says: 'The Lord has made all things for himself: the wicked also for the evil day'[218] — even the

[218] Prov 16: 4†.

wicked find their eternal types in the ideal of the divine intelligence and contribute to the realisation of these types.[219]

645. It is clear that God finds the purpose of his operations in the essences that are in him, which is a law of all intellective operation and of all moral operation. As we saw, morality is not a tendency that is satisfied with what is finite and temporary but extends to the infinite and the perennial, which is where morality begins. This explains my opinion that an ens that lacks intelligence cannot be the object of moral virtue: if intelligence is lacking, the divine element is lacking.

Moreover, God operates not only as intelligent but as infinitely and essentially intelligent, which gives us another law of his operation: the law of *unity* that we are discussing.

646. If we consider only his power, he must do everything he does with one totally simple act and from eternity because the concept of power at its absolute greatest necessitates this manner of operating. But the same truth applies if we consider what the operation of an infinite intelligence must be. Infinite understanding must know everything with one entirely simple act and know it from eternity. Hence a single, most simple act of God's intelligence embraces from eternity the exemplar of all he wishes to operate, and is the act itself with which he operates.

647. We have seen that God would not have been able to extract from the universe the greatest good that it could give if everything was not interconnected and all its parts were not bound together. Therefore I deduced the unity of the universe from the law of the least means.

But here I add that this most totally one universe, as it had to be, could not give the greatest good possible (and in this sense be a work appropriate to the supreme craftsman), unless it was first represented in his essence by the most simple act of divine understanding, and carried out by that very act.

This act of the divine understanding is practical, that is, operative; it is the powerful, creative act of the world. As an intellective act it had to be initiated by the will. However, we must not think that the divine will, gazing into the *idea* where the whole of being sheds its light, had delayed for a moment to

[219] Note carefully: the *idea* of evil is not an evil thing, nor is the *type* of the wicked person tarnished by any wickedness.

see the *perfect world* it wished to create, or that it passed from willing potentially to determining the desired world, as if the divine will had first taken a moment to deliberate and determine the kind of the world that was necessary for the world to be perfect. We humans will potentially: when we begin to will, our knowledge of what we will is only general and imperfect. But in God it is nothing like this: a choice between possible worlds is not totally excluded for the divine will. Such a choice supposes a kind of comparison between these worlds, and if this were the case, we would be attributing to God our own imperfect human operation. We have to say therefore that no investigation and choice of any kind whatsoever had to be made by the most excellent and perfect divine will: by means of a totally perfect and totally divine instinct, the divine will went immediately and directly to its object, that is, to the *perfect world* which it wished to realise. Thus it instinctively moved the divine understanding to that totally simple act by which the perfect world was drawn from nothingness without any other determination than the natural perfection of the divine volitive power. This explains how the world which *per se* was indistinct in the divine knowledge of *simple intelligence* was distinct in the *knowledge of vision* or *approbation*, as St. Thomas calls it,[220] which is the equivalent of my 'practical knowledge'.

The divine will therefore had been determined from eternity by its own totally free goodness and excellence to create the perfect world. It had neither to compose it nor investigate it nor choose it from infinite possible worlds.[221]

648. This simplicity and unity of the intellective act with which God willed and created the world results in a few corollaries that are helpful to our purpose.

1. The practical, intellective act with which God willed and created the world did not have as its object one part of the world separate from another, one ens divided from another. Its object was *the whole*, the complex of things, bonded most wisely together in unity. *Good* therefore, which is the ultimate

[220] *S.T.*, I, q. 14, art. 8, resp.

[221] I have shown how 'possibles' in God do not have *per se* a real distinction but are distinguished by the creating will. Cf. *Rinnovamento* etc., bk. 3, cc. 52–53 [1836 edition].

purpose of the divine will, is the good of total result, is all good, the good that is the result of all the entia composing the world and invisibly united in the divine understanding.

649. 2. The individual parts and entia of the world are willed by the *creating will* solely within the *whole*, as part of the whole, as fitting to the whole, in other words as necessary for producing that *total of ultimate* and most simple *good* of the divine act that is the divine reason for the divine act.

650. 3. Anything that is not the final eudaimonological-moral good, nor part of it, is willed only for its role as a *means* towards the final good understood in its totality. In this way God wills permissively physical and moral evils, he wills real contingent being and intellectual contingent being (if we mentally separate both these from moral being), and finally he wills the same moral being considered in potency and not yet in act, although in the potency of moral good there is a primal act, which has the concept of end and therefore forms part of the sum of final good.

651. 4. God's supreme wisdom and goodness determine him to permit particular evils, both physical and moral, whenever he finds that, due to the limitations of created things, evils cannot be excluded from the universe without diminishing the final sum of goods into which his most excellent will is essentially borne — he would be acting contrary to his will if he sacrificed the whole for the part and the end for the means. We are unable therefore to investigate why God wishes this or that particular evil, but we can investigate why he wills this whole, this world which includes that evil, because no particular thing cut off from the whole can an object of the creative, provident will. The reply therefore to the question why God willed to create such a world and not another is that a world of such a kind was suited to supreme goodness as the world that produced the greatest good with the least means, and hence was the only one possible.

652. 5. Whenever we see divine intellections and volitions as directed to only one part and not the whole of the universe (and we do so because we suppose that in God there is a plurality of acts of understanding and willing), we are simply attributing to God the impersonal manner of our own understanding and willing. Everything we will is not willed with one single act because everything we understand is not understood with one

single act; we understand bit by bit and therefore with very many acts. It certainly can be helpful to conceive divine operation in this human way, but we must correct it afterwards by reflection: we must note that the multiple intellections and volitions we have presumed in God are not separate in reality, not even mentally separate. It is we who divide them through the limitation of our understanding, which depends on the analytical process. This human conception caused Leibniz to say the following about divine understanding:

> God's wisdom is not satisfied with considering all the possibles, investigating and comparing them, weighing them against one another to evaluate the degrees of their perfection or imperfection, looking to see which is stronger, which weaker, the good and the evil. His wisdom goes beyond finite combinations, carries out an infinite number of infinite combinations, that is, an infinite number of possible series of universes, and each possible series contains an infinite number of creatures. Thus, divine wisdom distributes all the possibles it had already seen individually in many universal systems which it also compares. The result of all these comparisons and reflections is the choice of the best among all the possible systems that divine wisdom composes in order to give total satisfaction to goodness. Such is the plan of the subsistent universe.[222]

All these multiple acts of comparison, reflection and choice do not take place in the mind of God: they are presumed by Leibniz, like so many postulates. He then adds: 'Although all these operations of the divine understanding have an order and a priority of nature, they are all carried out together, without the involvement of any priority of time.'[223] But even this is not sufficient to correct what is inaccurate in the multiple acts, because he still allows for the subsistence of the plurality of acts of the divine intellect, even though they are all done together. Indeed, divine understanding is one most simple act which, when conceived by us, changes into a great many and very diverse acts as in human speech. We should rest satisfied with this division of the operation of the divine intellect; it can give us some

[222] *Theod.*, n. 225.

[223] Ibid.

understanding of how far-reaching divine intellect is. But if, instead of limiting ourselves to this, we want to base arguments on the division and draw consequences from it, as if the division existed in God, we would immediately lose our way and finish with a false conclusion.

Limiting the discussion therefore to the practical, creative understanding, this understanding excludes also every prior comparison and choice, as I have said. The will, because supreme by nature and using a totally divine instinct, moves the creative intellect to what is perfect and most excellent. It does not need to search for what is most excellent and perfect; it already has, from eternity, an inclination to love, from which issues the entirely free decree of creation.

653. Leibniz also speaks in a human way about God's will when he says:

> God has, by virtue of supreme goodness, a firm inclination to produce or to will and bring about the production of, every good and every praiseworthy action, and the inclination to prevent or not to will and bring about, the obstruction of every evil and every evil action. But through his goodness, joined to an infinite wisdom, and through the concourse of all his antecedent and particular inclinations towards each good and the prevention of each evil, he is determined to produce the best plan possible for things. This constitutes his final, decretive will.[224]

But the truth is that the divine will has only one act whose object, relative to creatures, is the perfect universe which, as the natural object of the creative act, has become possible. Only this universe can exist, and the only inclination of the divine will that can exist in reality is the inclination whose object is God himself and the subsistent universe. The ideal essence of this universe is in God and is determined by the same will that eternally creates.

654. Nevertheless, the limitation of our human mind necessitates us to place in God many hypothetical wills to explain divine operations. For example, when we consider that God is essential goodness, we at once deduce that he loves every

[224] *Réflexion sur l'ouvrage que M. Hobbes a publié en anglais, De la liberté, de la nécessité et du hazard*, n. 11.

particular good and hates every particular evil; he therefore wills every good and does not will every evil. That God loves every particular good and hates every particular evil is indeed true, but it is only hypothetically true that he wills that every possible particular good we conceive should subsist to the exclusion of every evil; in other words, it is true only in the hypothesis that the particular good and the particular evil, separated out, were able to be the object of the essentially synthetical divine will. These volitions relative to parts and, in the case of a decree, hypothetical volitions reduce to what theologians call the *antecedent will*, to which something true in God corresponds; it is the inclination to or love for all good, and hatred for all evil.

But many goods exclude each other, due to their limitations, and also many goods are limited by many evils which condition them. In addition, a will is not the best will when it wills the subsistence of a lesser good rather than a greater good or, to avoid willing a small evil, wills and decrees the loss of a greater amount of good. Therefore, God prevalently loves with his will the greatest sum of good in comparison to the means used to obtain it. Theologians call this will *consequent*, and it is the only will that directs divine operation because it concerns the whole of the divine work. The divine work is the one and only object of the one and only volition with which from all eternity God makes everything he makes.[225]

[225] God loves and wills the essence of good. From this truth the human mind correctly deduces that God loves all the particular goods conceivable by the human mind, some of which he produces, others he does not. Relative to these ultimate goods, the Scholastics called the divine mind, conceived in this way, *antecedent*. The *antecedent will* is simply the divine will that loves and wills the essence of good and hence loves and wills all the things in which the human mind conceives to some extent the essence of good. When I say that in God there is only one act of will, I mean a complete, distinct act. Moreover, the antecedent will is, to use Leibniz' words, 'totally firm and pure and must not be confused with the *velleity* of the person who would will if he were able, and would will to be able, something that does not happen in God, not even with the *conditional will*, which we are not discussing. — Clearly, antecedent wills are not unproductive but effective, although the effect obtained is never full and entire but restricted by the concourse of other antecedent wills. The *decretive* will, resulting from all the *inclinatory* wills, always attains its full effect' (*La cause de Dieu plaidée par sa justice, conciliée avec ses autres perfections et toutes ses*

655. This doctrine explains better the efficacy of prayer. It is certain that if prayer asks for the increase of the overall and final good, it cannot fail to be heard because God himself wills that good, and obtains it precisely by hearing prayers according to the full, overflowing measure that he saw and decreed from eternity. Moreover, if we ask perseveringly and appropriately for our own eternal salvation, we must obtain it, even though what we ask is a particular good. The reason is that granted the infinite goodness of God, the overall and final good requires that a prayer which has been properly made be heard, although not always in the same way. The special request for salvation however has only one way of being heard, and that is the granting of the salvation asked for. In fact, what would be the value for us if the salvation of the whole world were granted and we lost our own soul? Such a prayer would not be heard. On the other hand, the prayer we might make for the salvation of someone else can be heard in many ways: either the particular grace requested (the salvation of the other) is granted or a greater grace. The greater grace must be implicitly contained in our request, for example, the salvation of many other persons, or our own salvation, and finally goods and events that can increase the final sum of good to which the universe is ordered and to which all good wills must tend with their desires and prayers. In fact, anyone who loved another's eternal salvation so much that it was preferred to a grace which would increase the final sum of good would certainly not pray well. This final result of maximum good is the object of God's will, therefore anyone who excluded it from their prayer would not be conforming to the divine will. This would be all the more true if anyone asks for a particular good as a means, like the ending of some corporal suffering. When we pray, we should, in order to pray properly, add the condition, 'if granting the good is for the

actions [nn. 25–27]). The antecedent will, as conceived by the Scholastics and terminating as it does in the essence of good, is true, firm and pure. But it lacks *decree* because the essence of good cannot be realised where we think and believe it can be; it must be considered as a true and efficacious love because it has an influence in producing the consequent will, which is volition by decree. Were it not considered in this way, we would have to give up conceiving it humanly as a will. If discussion about God begins in a human way, it must continue in a human way; not to do so is to incur the danger of falling into error.

greater glory of God, that is, it contributes to the increase of the final sum of good that God intends to draw from creation'. Any prayer made in this way that does not always obtain the requested good, obtains a greater good.

656. This enables us to understand Christ's prayer in the garden. When he was tormented by the representation of the imminent passion, divine wisdom moved him to pray to the eternal Father in these words: 'My Father, if it is possible, let this cup pass from me; yet not what I want but what you want.' And again: 'My Father, if this cannot pass unless I drink it, your will be done.'[226] Why did he say 'if it is possible', 'if this chalice *cannot* pass unless I drink it' — everything was certainly possible for his Father, if we consider the Father's power in itself, separate from his wisdom and goodness. However, because God never operates solely with his power but directs the works of his power according to the norm of wisdom and goodness, it was not possible to obtain that grace, and indeed it was not obtained, as the event demonstrated. Granted that the passion of Christ was necessary for drawing the greatest good from creation, it could not in any way be avoided; God could not operate without the law of essential wisdom and goodness. The Father did of course take into calculation the desire, human will and prayer of the Christ, and included the suffering of his incarnate Son in the calculation. Nevertheless, taking all that into account, he had to conclude that after contrasting all the great evil with the good that must come from the divine passion, the abundance of good that finally remained was so great that he had to judge that the sublime sufferings, the atrocious death of the God-Man, the refusal to hear the prayer of the just, the extreme mortification and abnegation of his human will, were most reasonably applied as a means for the most excellent end. Even if Christ, praying as a human being, doubted whether it was possible or not for the chalice to pass from him and not be drunk, nobody can think that he, as God, was ignorant of the impossibility of the request. Christ wished to demonstrate in this way that the calculation of the ultimate good must be left entirely to the Father, a calculation surpassing all human thought and determined deep in the divine intellect, where

[226] Mt 26: 39, 42.

infinite things are weighed, in this case the sufferings of the Word made flesh and the overwhelming, eternal mass of glory that would result from these sufferings in the humanity of Christ and in his faithful followers. As a result, the reasoned solution of the great problem was hidden from Christ as a human being, even though a most perfect human being. He therefore submitted the human will, whose sole determined object is what is contained in human knowledge, to the divine will, whose determined object is the maximum good contained in divine knowledge. This teaches us all to subordinate the object of our own will to the object of the divine will, precisely because we are blindly and totally ignorant of this object which is the complete good that only God knows. We, with our human mind, cannot attain such an object but can certainly know that the object of the divine will, although unknown to us, is a greater good than every object of our human will known to us. Thus the divine will, which is total light and essentially supreme, determines the *operative divine intellect*, and there are no other distinct possibles than those to which the divine will guides the practical, divine intellect.

657. But why does the risen JESUS Christ say to the Apostles: 'All authority in heaven and on earth has been given to me. Go therefore and make disciples of all nations, baptizing them in the name of the Father and of the Son and of the Holy Spirit'?[227] Why does he send them to all nations and not to all individuals, when he has been given all authority in heaven and on earth? He most certainly loved the salvation of every single individual, and loved each one infinitely, because his love was divine. His purpose however is the overall good of the whole of humanity. Also, his desires whose object was the salvation of each individual, the desires for the particular goods collided with and mutually excluded each other. As a result, prevalence had to be given to the desires for greater goods, to the maximum desire whose purpose was the maximum sum of final good. And in order to have this sum he also had to permit the loss of some individuals, as a necessary condition. Nevertheless, we could still apparently conclude from Christ's words that if some individuals necessarily perish for the greater good, this necessity is not verified for

[227] Mt 28: 18–19.

nations, to each of which incarnate wisdom, which never commissions anyone fruitlessly, sent its missionaries. Consequently, Christ's words harmonise wonderfully with the words that the same wisdom declared many centuries earlier: 'I have stood in all the earth, and in every people, and in every nation I have had the chief rule.'[228] It does not say 'in every individual'; the words fulfil the ancient promise made by God to Abraham: 'And in your seed shall all the nations of the earth be blessed,'[229] not 'all the individuals'. We have therefore the prophetic canticle, repeated so frequently in the ancient covenant: 'Praise the Lord, all you nations! Extol him, all you peoples!'[230] These passages and many others do not speak of individuals, but with the comprehensive vision proper to wisdom they confirm the salvation of all the races grown into nations.

658. The principle that the Most Wise one has only one object of his operation, the sum of good, and obtains it with a totally simple act, also throws great light on the whole economy of the divine government of the human race, and particularly on the mystery of the censure of the Hebrews and the vocation of the Gentiles. St. Paul says of the Hebrews 'the salvation of the Gentiles came from their offence', 'their offence is the riches of the world, and their diminution is the riches of the Gentiles', and 'the loss of them is reconciliation of the world'.[231] By these words he simply means that God, in his eternal wisdom, saw that the greatest good could not be obtained by the least means unless he permitted the necessary evil of many Hebrews refusing faith in his Christ. He therefore permitted this refusal, sacrificing some Hebrews to the salvation of all the nations of the universe. To explain how this was necessary would take time and I will return to it, but the Apostle clearly tells us what God's purpose was in abandoning for a short time a part of the Hebrews to their willed incredulity: 'God has concluded all in unbelief that HE MAY HAVE MERCY ON ALL;'*[232] the purpose of divine

[228] Sir 24: 9–10†.

[229] Gen 22: 28; 12: 3†.

[230] Ps 117: [1].

[231] Rom 11: 11–15†.

[232] Rom 11: 32†.

operation is always good, always the maximum possible good, subject of course to the law of the least means. Indeed, if this law prescribes that the whole of good must spring from and be made fruitful by the intelligent creature without any extraordinary, superfluous intervention, then the Most Wise one, who had to fulfil this law, must draw from the very weakness of the creature, from its incredulity and malice, every good that could directly or indirectly be obtained from it. This waywardness of the peoples, permitted by God for many centuries, was therefore a factual proof to humanity of the insufficiency of their reason and of the powerlessness of their freedom to procure final, eudaimonological-moral good. In the case of the Hebrews, their waywardness was a factual proof of the insufficiency of the positive law, although it was revealed for their salvation. Clearly then, humanity needed the God-Man to redeem it from its perdition. It had experiential proof that only a totally gratuitous gift, the grace of Redemption, given by God, could obtain its end. Humanity could not acquire this valuable knowledge except by experience; without experience it could never know itself, nor could this good of self-knowledge come to it except through the law of the least action, which forbids divine intervention to give humanity what it can draw from itself. Although this experiential knowledge, informed by grace, humbles us, it raises us to God on whom we see that our whole self and our eternal happiness depend. This acknowledgement of the need for God and his merciful grace, open to all who acknowledge that need and value its excellence, was for us *holiness*, the sole maximum good. To obtain this maximum good, it was wisely permitted that many would be lost. As a result, this permission, in the judgment of an excellent and most wise God, was equally just and good because we were left with what is ours and everything was included in the calculation; it was in fact an act of supreme goodness, a totally wise goodness, because a necessary means to what is most excellent.

659. Finally, if we consider that in the whole, in the maximum good that creation can give, we must not see simply a union of entia but an order and extraordinary harmony, we will have a new argument for the necessity of evil, because we will see that evil contributes to the beauty and moral perfection of the whole. St. Thomas explained the argument:

> The good of the whole takes priority over the good of the part. A prudent governor will allow a part to lack some good in order to obtain an increase of good in the whole. The builder hides the foundation under the earth so that the whole house has stability. If evil were removed from some parts of the universe, a large part of the perfection in the universe would perish. The beauty of the universe has its origin in the appointed combination of goods and evils because evils come from goods that fail. Nevertheless, from these evils certain goods follow through the providence of the governor, just as the use of a pause makes a song pleasant.[233]

We must note here that the beauty of order is not a quality foreign to the good of intelligent beings because they contemplate the beauty and receive light and pleasure from it. Also for this reason, to put order in the world is to produce good for intelligent natures.

[233] St. Thomas, *C.G.*, III, 71: 7.

[659]

CHAPTER 25

Ninth consequence: God has to operate in the world according to the above laws of wisdom in order to draw divine glory from the world, which is the purpose of the universe

> *Hominem fecit, cui* innotesceret [He made man, to whom *he was to be known*]
>
> St. Theoph., *ad Autolyc.*, 2: 10

660. From what has been said we can form a clear concept of *divine glory*, the purpose of the universe.

For intelligent, moral natures 'glory' means the manifestation of power, wisdom and goodness in the unity of divine operation.

661. If God, setting aside his wisdom and goodness, had made everything with his power alone and not used his wisdom and goodness, he would have drawn no glory from it. To be powerful and use power blindly, not ordered to a good end, is not glorious.

Glory is simply the applause that intelligences give to an intelligence. But intelligences do not applaud (nor can they) pure power; they applaud the operation where power is applied with wisdom and goodness. Hence maximum glory is due to God who, when operating, must always and through his essence follow the laws of wisdom and goodness, which incline him to economise his power.

662. Hence the Fathers of the Church note that God never wishes to combat the wicked with his power alone, with which he could annihilate them with one blow, but conquers them principally with the use of his wisdom and goodness, a courtesy he uses even with the devil. This is why St. Justin, a martyr of the second century, said that God had arranged for Christ to be born of a woman who had a husband, in order to hide the birth from the devil. St. Bernard argues according to the same concept:

> It was necessary that the sacrament of the divine counsel

> be hidden for a certain time from the prince of the world, not because God feared any obstruction from the devil if he performed the work openly, but because everything he wanted to do he did both powerfully and wisely. Just as in all his works he maintained a certain fittingness of things and times for the sake of the beauty of order, so in this magnificent work of our restoration, he was pleased to demonstrate both his power and his wisdom.[234]

663. In these words we see shining forth the truth I am teaching: how the law of the least means obliges God to economise as much as possible with his power (in which alone his glory does not consist) and make the greatest use of his other attributes of wisdom and goodness that draw just praise from intellects. To this end (obtaining just and worthy praise), the great Pope St. Leo also attributes God's will that the human nature assumed by the Word in one person should overcome the devil. Thus, God concealed under weak and mortal elements the omnipotence with which he could have subjected the devil at his pleasure but without receiving any glory:

> This struggle undertaken for us (by Christ) was fought according to a great and wonderful concept of equity, when the almighty Lord came against such a cruel enemy not with his majesty but with our lowliness. He opposed this enemy with the same form and nature as ours, sharing in our mortality and immune from all sin. In the fullness of the time determined by the sublimity of the inscrutable divine counsel, the Son of God assumed the nature of the human race in order to reconcile this nature to its Author so that the devil, the inventor of death, would be conquered by the same nature that he had conquered.[235]

We see here clearly that God preferred to use human nature to defeat the devil rather than directly use his omnipotence: he made human nature itself bear such great fruit, but it could not do this by itself. Therefore the Word added himself to it, verifying that this extra cost, as it were, that God assumed, was applied so well and wisely that human nature produced the maximum, exquisite fruit.

[234] Hom. 2 super *Missus est*.

[235] *Serm. 1, De Nativ. Dom.*

664. In many places the book of Wisdom praises God for this economy and reduction of his power, motivated by his most wise goodness. Thus, in the plagues with which he afflicted Egypt, the inspired author admires how God punished the Egyptians by sending them a multitude of tiny insects:

> For your all-powerful hand, which created the world out of formless matter, did not lack the means to send upon them a multitude of bears, or bold lions, or newly-created unknown beasts full of rage, or such as breathe out fiery breath, or belch forth a thick pall of smoke, or flash terrible sparks from their eyes; not only could the harm they did destroy people, but the mere sight of them could kill by fright. Even apart from these, people could fall at a single breath when pursued by justice and scattered by the breath of your power. But you have arranged all things by measure and number and weight.[236]

In the chapter that follows we see how divine wisdom and goodness restrained divine power by not allowing it to expel from Palestine the corrupt peoples living there:

> Yet even those you spared as men, and did send wasps forerunners of your host, to destroy them by little and little. Not that you were unable to bring the wicked under the just by war, or by cruel beasts, or with one rough word to destroy them at once: But executing your judgments by degrees, you gave them place of repentance, not being ignorant that they were a wicked generation, and their malice natural, and that their thought could never be changed. For it was a cursed seed from the beginning: neither did you for fear of any one give pardon to their sins. For who shall say to you: What have you done? or who shall withstand your judgment? or who shall come before you to be a revenger of wicked men? or who shall accuse you, if the nations perish, which you have made? For there is no other God but you, who has care of all, that you should show that you do not give judgment unjustly. Neither shall king, nor tyrant, in your sight inquire about them whom you have destroyed. For so much then, as you are just, you order all things justly: thinking it not agreeable to the power, to condemn him who deserves not to be

[236] Wis 11: 17–20.

> punished. For your power is the beginning of justice: and because you are Lord of all, you make yourself gracious to all. For you show your power, when men will not believe you to be absolute in power, and you convince the boldness of them that know you not. But you being master of power, judge with tranquillity, and with great favour dispose of us: for your power is at hand when you will. But you have taught your people by such works, that they must be just and humane, and have made your children to be of a good hope: because in judging, you give place for repentance for sins.[237]

The noble title given to God of 'master of power' shows how the attributes of wisdom and goodness direct and moderate his power. The words, 'your power is the beginning of justice' demonstrate that the power is, as it were, informed with justice, such that it does not move unless justice, its form, moves it. Here, 'justice' is to be understood according to the customary wider meaning used by the divine Scriptures, that is, all moral good, and therefore also mercy. Mercy uses the power to perform the marvels of mercy; it changes hearts, and restrains the power by mitigating and delaying punishment.

665. The divine glory that penetrates and shines throughout the universe is of two kinds: substantial, which is the glory God gives to himself, and accidental which intelligent beings created by God give to their creator.

Because glory is the applause that an intelligent being gives to an intelligent being when the latter operates with wisdom and goodness, the glory that God gives to himself is the approval he gives to his own works. This is expressed in Genesis by the words: 'God saw everything that he had made, and indeed, it was very good.'[238] This does not mean that in God there is a distinction of time between the operation itself and his seeing in the operation the traces of his wisdom and goodness, in which he takes pleasure. On the contrary, from eternity he was inclined, as we saw, to realise contingent being, loving it as the realisation of the eternal ideas, indeed as the realisation of that ideal which is the sole type of the universe and in which his

[237] Ibid., 12: 8–19†.

[238] Gen 1: 31.

essentially excellent will found what could be manifested as wise and good in the contingent. Hence this approval that God gave to what he saw from all eternity as wise and good in the exemplar of the world and inclined him to create and govern the world, constitutes also the eternal glory he gives himself for having created it. For God there never was a time when the world was only possible; he certainly created it in time but with an act as eternal as the possible is.

665a. The exemplar in which from all eternity God saw the world created in time and in which he commended his work, and most justly and holily took pleasure in it and glorified himself, is the divine Word. Hence, when the Redeemer prayed: 'So now, Father, glorify me in your own presence with the glory that I had in your presence before the world existed,'[239] he recalled the glory he had and still had as divine Word. The Father, approving from all eternity the world presented in the exemplar, saw this world in the divine Word and, seeing it, created it. The Word therefore, with that sublime prayer, was asking that the glory that the Father was already giving him from all eternity should, as the Father gazed upon the exemplar of the world in him, be realised in time (which is what the Father himself willed from eternity) and should be communicated to the humanity of the Word. Although in fact the divine Word contained the type of the world and never lacked that glory or paternal approval, the glory had still to be realised and communicated in time to the Word as man, because the humanity of the Christ was the humanity of the divine person. Consequently, the Redeemer did not ask for the glory proper to the Word as image of the Father who dwells in an inaccessible light, but for the glory proper to the Word as having in himself the typical world. The Father, in his loving act, saw in this typical world the human being assumed by the divine person, and also saw all the things, all the glory of the Word that had been communicated to this human being, who received personhood from the Word.

If the glory of the Word communicated to humanity was seen in the eternal type, it had to be realised in time, and this is what the Christ asked. He asked for the realisation because it had to be effected in time by virtue of his prayers in the form of a

[239] Jn 17: 5.

request, and these prayers are seen in the eternal type. The realisation also had to be effected through merit, preaching, heroic virtues and the magnanimous offering of his life that the Christ made — and all this was indicated in the same eternal type by God's decree. Thus, the realisation of the glory that the Christ had to receive as a risen human being was conditioned by the operation of the Christ himself. Hence he tells the Father that he has accomplished all that had been enjoined on him; in other words, before receiving the glory, he had already realised that part of the exemplar that was his task to realise. With all justice now fulfilled by a most holy life, it was the Father's turn to fulfil and realise the other part, for whose implementation he was responsible: 'I glorified you on earth by finishing the work that you gave me to do. So now, Father, glorify me in your own presence with the glory that I had in your presence before the world existed.'[240] The Christ said he had carried out the work (although he had not yet suffered) through the fullest and most perfect offering already made of himself, as well as through the unbloody sacrifice celebrated at the supper, which was equivalent to the reality of death, to the *consummatum est* [it is consummated] that he pronounced on the cross.

666. When the Christ, as a human being, asked the Father that the glory destined for him from eternity be realised, he was asking only that God's one sole inclination and will to produce the world should receive its full effect in time. And because the exemplar of the world, although only one, resulted from many successive states, all these were unfolded and successively realised in time, including the last and final state. This final state had to last eternally as the accomplished, excellent state of created things; relative to it the previous states have the nature of means and way. However, the world contemplated in this ultimate, permanent state, which is like the *archetype* of the previous states, has an order in its parts, even though it is a totally perfect unity and harmony. Some of these parts concern the purpose of the world, others do not strictly speaking concern the purpose but are indispensable conditions for the final parts. The parts that constitute the purpose are the elect in the state they will enjoy after the resurrection; and Christ is their head. Hence St

[240] Jn 17: 4–5.

Paul writes:

> Each (will be vivified) in his own order: Christ the first fruits, then at his coming those who belong to Christ. Then comes the end, when he hands over the kingdom to God the Father, after he has destroyed every ruler and every authority and power. For he must reign until he has put all his enemies under his feet. The last enemy to be destroyed is death. For 'God has put all things in subjection under his feet.'[241] But when it says, 'All things are put in subjection', this obviously does not include the one who put all things in subjection under him. When all things have been subjected to him, the Son himself will also be subjected to the one who put all things in subjection under him, *UT SIT DEUS OMNIA IN OMNIBUS* [SO THAT GOD MAY BE ALL IN ALL].[242]

This is the outstanding part of the divine exemplar of the world; all other parts are ordered to it, and its realisation is, as St. Paul says, the end of all things. Therefore the creative, ordering wisdom takes pleasure in and rests in this final state of his elect, as wisdom itself says in an inspired book: 'I alone have compassed the circuit of heaven, and have penetrated into the bottom of the deep, and have walked in the waves of the sea, And have stood in all the earth: and in every people, And in every nation I have had the chief rule: And by my power I have trodden under my feet the hearts of all the high and low: and in all these I sought REST, and I shall abide in the INHERITANCE OF THE LORD.[243] These are precisely the elect. The divine Master therefore gave us the prayer to the Father: 'Your kingdom come'. This petition hastens on the complete realisation of the eternal exemplar, the *final state* of things when, as the Apostle said, Christ hands back to the Father the kingdom won by his valour.

667. St. Paul also calls this 'a sabbath rest of the people of God'. It is the final state which wisdom, after finishing its work, enjoys and glories in eternally, and is represented at the beginning of things by the seventh day: the book of creation says, 'On the seventh day God finished the work that he had done,

[241] Ps 8: 8.

[242] 1 Cor 15: 23–28.

[243] Sir 24: 8–11†.

and he RESTED on the seventh day from all the work that he had done.'[244] This purpose of all things, this great PURPOSE, for which human beings were specially created and to which they must direct all their affections, studies and operations, had to be deeply impressed for ever on the whole human species. To do this, I believe that the sabbath was instituted as a solemn day from the beginning of the world, a day of rest from all material fatigue, and was later inculcated very strictly by many laws, and sanctified by many rites.

668. God therefore, from all eternity, takes pleasure in his work, the world, and glories in it. He does this not through blind reality (reality is an effect of his power), but because traces of his infinite wisdom and eternal goodness are expressed and shine forth in the world's reality. He glories because infinite power, moved by wisdom, is displayed there, and it is goodness that moves wisdom to display and diffuse itself. We also, as intelligent and moral beings (the same can be said of every intellective creature), see the traces of wisdom and goodness in the world in varying degree. From these traces we learn to know the wisdom and goodness of the infinite craftsman; we approve them, and we applaud him and give him unending glory. We must note that we attain this deep knowledge of the wise and excellent Creator by various degrees because we do not have in us the whole exemplar of the world, as God has; we extract it from the perceptions we receive from creation and from our reflections upon them. Aided by the light of revelation and grace, and proceeding gradually from the sign to the thing signed (because the world is only a sign), we trace and determine in our minds the exemplar of the world. The paper on which we draw this exemplar is ideal, undetermined being that we naturally intuit and includes indistinctly the whole of entity, just as a block of stone contains all the statues the artist intends to sculpture from it, or a surface contains all the shapes that can be drawn on it.

Although the perceptions we obtain from creation are few in comparison with the immensity of things, they are sufficient for us to acknowledge the bright light of divine wisdom and goodness that leads us to guess at the huge sun, so to speak, from

[244] Gen 2: 2.

which the light comes. Consequently, seeing the creative wisdom and goodness reflected in so small a mirror, as it were, we have cause for exercising our *faith* and for adoring the depths of divine wisdom and knowledge that we cannot completely penetrate. But the more our understanding draws on this wisdom, the more we understand created things, and penetrate them in a religious spirit with our thought. Everything we draw from them is a spark that enkindles in our hearts the affection we owe the Creator. But not only is our contemplation of the traces of supreme wisdom and goodness limited by our inability to grasp with our understanding the vastness of creation in which, no matter how much we penetrate it, we never come to understand more than the tiniest bit; we are also limited by the fact that the real world unfolds itself before us through a succession of facts, presenting one state at a time of the many that it must pass through and are contained in the eternal exemplar. Here we have a fresh reason why intelligence must lead us to faith: whenever our mind sees one link of the immense chain, it tells us that there are other links hidden in the future. But before the world finishes its journey, we each finish our own journey, and granted we have consented to the light received and to grace, we come to see the face of God, as Scripture says: 'For the wisdom of doctrine is according to her name, and she is not manifest unto many, but with them to whom she is known, she continues even to the sight of God.'[245] Here then we find our purpose and, contemplating the eternal exemplar, we wait at rest for the final state of the universe. The grandeur of the knowledge of creative wisdom and goodness becomes the material of a new canticle, with which the comprehensor gives to God a more explicit and final glory, and which will also receive abundant material from the inaccessible light that even at that time overcomes the power of the creature.

God will therefore be praised and glorified mainly because of this final state pre-ordained long ago as completion and apex of the universe. The events that have previously taken place and will take place have a very close relationship of means with this final state, and make a tremendous unity with it. Because this is the final perfection of every intelligent creature, the whole order of creation had to be ordered and disposed in such a way

[245] Sir 6: 23.

[668]

that moral-intelligent beings could know through that order and see in it the wisdom and goodness of God. They would do this first through its parts and then in its overall composition; by admiring and loving God's wisdom and goodness, they would give him tremendous and unending praise. This praise is like a natural outlet for intellective substance and a final word with which it declares and consents to what is right, and in which it finds satisfaction and beatitude. This assent, this applause that the creature voluntarily gives to the known, loved and admired Creator as most wise and excellent is itself a part, and indeed the final part, of the eternal exemplar. The very encomium itself that the creature pays the wisdom and goodness that it contemplates in creation now becomes the most sublime witness of this wisdom and goodness of creation. Hence the very praise of God, through which the creature perfects itself, gives the creature new and better material for praising the Creator. Once again we see reproduced here that marvellous, eternal circle that we have admired elsewhere in the order of moral things,[246] and through which moral good is made a perpetual object of a new and more sublime moral good.

669. Before continuing, I will summarise this teaching which is rich in important corollaries. It can be reduced to the following propositions:

1. The *praise* that I have described constitutes the final moral perfection that the intelligent creature can attain, and is given by the intelligent creature to the wisdom and goodness of the Author of the world, which is the complex of contingent entia and of all their successive states.

By 'praise' I mean the final act of approval which intellective substance is inclined to carry out and voluntarily carries out when it perceives and acknowledges God's wisdom and goodness in the real signs and traces communicated to it. We, as mixed beings, have a body whose movements aid the senses of the soul; the body also has a vocal organ inclined to produce as many sounds as the words said internally by the spirit. We find in these spontaneous sounds indications of the things we have pronounced internally, and these indications strengthen the

[246] Cf. *Storia comparativa e critica de' sistemi intorno al principio della morale*, c. 8, art. 3, §7.

passing pronouncements in our minds, make them consistent for us, and their repetition easier. Therefore we take pleasure in these sounds and use them to satisfy the need we have to make our internal judgments vivid for ourselves, and to multiply and produce them; without such help our judgments easily disappear. This is the cause of poetry and canticles, especially of those canticles that God's Church on earth has used from the beginning of the world in order to celebrate the Creator. But spoken words and all sounds are not truly the essence of the praise that the intelligent being directs to God; they are simply the effect and spontaneous expression produced in our animal part by the internal, intellectual praise — as I said, we use such sounds to help us conceive the praise mentally, to store it in our memory, reproduce it and take pleasure in it. But if the essence of the praise given by an intellective being is solely the *approval* that this being pronounces interiorly, then clearly, if the object is supreme being, such praise must be the final act of the moral perfection of the creature. In fact, knowledge of the Creator is so definitely the perfection of the intellective creature that the Christ said: 'This is eternal life, that they may KNOW you, the only true God, and JESUS Christ whom you have sent.'[247] He says that this knowledge is *life* because positive and practical knowledge of God must be accompanied by a feeling of joy. He also says it is *eternal* because the joy *per se* never fails, nor ever loses its vitality. The final part of this knowledge, which actuates and completes the knowledge, is the internal judgment that exults in a full and totally voluntary approval, and by means of this approval the person of the human being consents to and takes great delight in the light it sees.

670. 2. The *moral perfection* of the intellective creature is the purpose of the universe, the only purpose worthy of God. In exactly the same way, the praise or *glory of the Creator* is also the purpose of the universe.

671. 3. Again, this praise, this final act of the moral perfection of the intelligent creature, this purpose of the universe, is the most sublime part of the divine exemplar of the world; everything else is ordered to its realisation. Therefore God, who loves the world in the exemplar, of which the world is the

[247] Jn 17: 3.

realisation, loves above all this praise that creatures give him and takes pleasure in it from eternity. He applauds himself for having realised such a great good and having thus generously diffused his goodness in creatures. In God also, the approval he gives to himself is conceived as the apex of moral good, which he is for himself. Creatures who give him this praise find the principal cause for praising him in the praise itself to which they are ordered, and they approve of their approval as the greatest good that God communicates to them of himself. Thus, by redoubling the praise and glory they give to God, they also redouble for themselves the joy in which they exult, making their joy the matter and cause of joy. This makes them sharers in the moral goodness of God, because the thing that is the object of God's goodness becomes the object of their goodness; they are thus adapted to God and are consummated in one term only.

672. 4. Therefore the object of the moral perfection and intellectual enjoyment of the viators on earth and the comprehensors in heaven is God, author of the world — 'world' here means the complex of all created things and of all the diverse states through which they pass until the very last state of the vision of God. Because intelligences perceive in this vision the divine act that realises the world, and intuit its exemplar, they see in the act the beatific vision itself, which is the culmination of the act and destined for them as the reward of their merits and at the same time a gratuitous gift. Hence in the beatific vision the work of the world will be that which will make intelligent creatures know and praise God. They will see, as it were, the great canvas of the world displayed in him and also in the vast, resplendent complex of infinite wisdom and goodness, because the divine work, in the exemplar and in the eternal decree that designs it while creating it,[248] is God himself, the divine face. It is

243 The essences of things created in the divine Word have no real distinction because the Word is totally simple. Their distinction arises from the decree of the creator, and hence must be considered a *relationship* between the creator-decree, that is, the terms of this decree, and the Word. Consequently, distinct creatures in God cannot be seen unless God as creating is seen and also the Word to whom the terms of the decree refer. This indicates the weakness of Malebranche's system: when he posited that corporeal things are seen in God, he necessarily posited that God himself is seen. Gerdil's defence of this is also insufficient. He tried to prove that things can be seen in God without

true that in addition to what they see and comprehend of God, they will also understand that God is inaccessible light, that they cannot attain. This is a reason for eternal adoration by every creature who abases and consumes itself in the incomprehensible infinite. This loss of the creature in the abyss of divine essence is also part of the purpose of the universe, and is present and seen as such in the Word creating and acting as exemplar. Thus, although God is, without the intervention of any means, the object of the beatific vision and form of the intellect of the blessed, he is such in so far as author of works *ad extra*. These are in him in an ineffable manner, as the Scriptures tell us and in so far as they were created in him: he is at the head of all and 'he sustains all things by the power of his word,'[249] and again 'in him we live and move and have our being,'[250] also: 'He is the image of the invisible God, the firstborn of all creation; for in him all things in heaven and on earth were created, things visible and invisible, whether thrones or dominions or rulers or powers — all things have been created through him and for him.'[251] It should be noted here that the word 'first-begotten' is appropriate to the divine Word as exemplar of the world and creator,[252] and as such he is the wisdom about which it is written: 'I came out of the mouth of the most High, the firstborn before all creatures: I made that in the heavens there should rise light that never fails, and as a cloud I covered all the earth;'[253] this is followed by a description of the works of creation. He is also God the beatifier of souls; hence it is said of Christ: 'on whom the angels desire to look.'[254] The meaning here is that the angels do not look on the part of the Word which is incomprehensible to every creature but on the part he reveals. Hence the angels

God being seen. If things were seen in God without God being seen, the things in God would have to be distinct from God and really distinct from each other. This would deny God his supreme simplicity; the only distinction in God is that of the persons.

249 Heb 1: 3.

250 Acts 17: 28.

251 Col 1: 15–17.

252 *Rinnovamento*, etc., c. 52, at the end.

253 Sir 24: 5–6†.

254 1 Pet 1: 12†.

contemplate him as author and redeemer of the world, and thus desire to look on 'the face of the Christ' or the incarnate Word. This explains the teaching of the Apostle that God poured so much wisdom and goodness into the world system precisely in order that this wisdom and goodness might become the object of the knowledge and admiration of the angels and be the matter for their praises, in which they are blessed: 'so that through the church THE WISDOM OF GOD IN ITS RICH VARIETY MIGHT NOW BE MADE KNOWN TO THE RULERS AND AUTHORITIES in the heavenly places'[255] and generally, when speaking about all created intelligences: 'so that in the ages to come HE MIGHT SHOW THE IMMEASURABLE RICHES OF HIS GRACE.'*[256]

673. 5. The difference therefore between our contemplating divine wisdom and goodness in creatures and contemplating it in the heavenly mansion is the following. Here on earth we toil hard to find traces of divine wisdom and goodness in real creatures. Creatures act like mirrors in which these attributes are reflected, and like enigmas that contain the attributes in an attenuated form. With the passage of time we come to see them and imperfectly compose for ourselves some little part of the eternal exemplar. In heaven on the other hand we shall see the whole of creation in God, and what we shall see will be God. Consequently, at present all creatures are, relative to us, simply *signs* of eternal truths and unchangeable essences;[257] they are like a language that God uses to make himself understood by his

[255] Eph 3: 10.

[256] Eph 2: 7.

[257] This observation explains the metaphysical element and sublimity of some phrases of the divine Scriptures in which great and glorious human beings are called symbols and seals, that is, signs of divine power and wisdom. Job 38: 14 is interpreted in this way, and in the Vulgate is rendered as *Restituetur ut lutum signaculum, et stabit sicut vestimentum*, which Martini translates as: 'The seal will come back as mud, and subsist as a garment,' where 'seal' expresses the greatness and power of human beings, a sign of God's power, in the way that Ezekiel 28: 12 calls the king of Tyre 'seal of resemblance', that is, a seal that has a resemblance of God: 'You were the seal of resemblance, full of wisdom and perfect in beauty'†*, and also in Aggeus [Haggai] 2: 24 God promises Zorobabel to make him as his seal: 'In that day, says the Lord of hosts, I will take you, O Zorobabel the son of Salathiel, my servant, says the Lord, and will make you as a signet, for I have chosen you, says the Lord of hosts.'†*

creatures endowed with intellect. But creatures themselves are not truth, they have nothing final in them; they are, as I said, expressions and indications of what is final and divine. Once again we see the wonderful circle that pertains to the *synthesism* of being. If contingent natures are only some signs, signs that manifest being and what is eternally true to created intelligences, what then are these intelligences? They are entia to which the *signs* are given to raise the intelligences to eternal ens, and at the same time the intelligences are themselves *signs*. As *intelligent subjects* they read everlasting truths in the book of the universe. But in so far as they make themselves *objects* to themselves, they are some of the letters with which the whole of the book of the universe is written, and whenever these letters are read, they signify and show divine ideas. Consequently, intellective creatures can be fittingly defined as living letters that present and give their own meaning.

674. 6. The comprehensors however no longer need to read the true and eternal entity in this book of created reality, because this entity is given them to contemplate and perceive directly. Nevertheless the traces of the wisdom and goodness of creation, far from becoming useless to them, are in fact necessary. All the traces are in the eternal exemplar and are precisely the part of the exemplar that is accessible to them. The traces therefore justify the praises that those in heaven eternally give to God, so that not a single fragment of creation is lost in the eternal centuries, not one little event is lost to memory; they are all engraved in divine being. No accident that has occurred in the flow of time is useless or superfluous to the beatitude of those who enjoy the beatific vision. These see the wonderful interconnection of things in God, the unity of the whole in the incalculable multiplicity of the parts, the appropriateness of the smallest part to the whole and its necessity for the most simple and sublime end of creation. They perceive all this in the act of the most holy divine will which sees in the intelligible essence the contingent in all its excellence, and seeing it, loves it, and loving it wills it, and willing it creates it, a volition of mighty power. In seeing all this, I say, they spend all their energy in giving glory to the Creator, and in this they are blessed, while still feeling their inability to give him all the glory they ought.

675. 7. It follows also from this that God could not have

obtained the end of the universe, that is, this manifestation of himself, of his wisdom and goodness to intelligent creatures, if he had not ordered the world, as he in fact did, in complete accord with divine art, where the essential norms of wisdom were constantly followed and, principally among them, the law of the least means that we are discussing.

676. If all these things have been understood, no one will dare claim any more that God should use his power to make exceptions to the laws of his wisdom, as those people do who complain about Providence and say: 'If God is omnipotent, what do miracles cost him? Can't he banish all the evils of the world? Could he not prevent sin, save the wicked, prevent the damnation of many?' He certainly *could* but this world was neither produced nor formed solely by his power; if it had been, the purpose of the world was lost because the purpose was that the world should be a complex of *signs* of his wisdom and goodness. Finite intelligences were to use these *signs* to raise themselves to the acknowledgement of the most wise and excellent Being, and thus give him unceasing glory; in this offering of glory to God they were to find the final term possible of their moral perfection, and thus also attain their everlasting beatitude.

677. At this stage, another difficulty may present itself to the mind. The argument could be: 'If God has made everything for the purpose of the universe, and if this purpose consists in the beatific vision, could he not admit created intelligences directly to this vision, and omit all the rest?' The objection has no value if the theory I have given about the vision is borne in mind, and the principle 'of the limited state of all created things' is never lost sight of. This limitation even puts a kind of limitation on the power of God itself, I mean on the effects produced by his power. As a result of the limitation, no creature, even though admitted to the vision, can fully comprehend the divine essence; there is a part where God always remains hidden and inaccessible for finite beings. If God could not communicate himself totally to finite beings, not even by the light of glory, an investigation into how he could reveal and communicate to them his essence reveals that he could certainly communicate himself in a way that conforms to the nature of created intelligences, and this is precisely by the relationship he has with them as their creator, provider, redeemer, and sanctifier. It must be carefully

noted that God himself is the creating act; God is also the provident act, he is the act of the incarnation and of the sanctification of the world, because every act of God is God.[258] For as long as we are viators, we see and experience the effects and the *term* of these divine acts, but when we become blessed, we see these same acts in their *principle* and their essence. The acts are actually only one act, which is the act of the divine essence. Thus, we see all the divine essence that can be communicated to created minds flowing into them as it were, and it could not be otherwise. Hence God had to create the universe and execute in it everything his wisdom and goodness could do in order that the divine vision might be possible for the creature, that is, the vision of the divine essence in so far as it does everything that concerns the creature.

678. I repeat therefore: none of the traces of wisdom and goodness that are diffused throughout the universe, or rather are the universe, is lost in regard to the purpose of the universe, which is the beatific vision. This vision is nothing other than seeing these traces, that is, the universe at its source, and the universe at its source is the divine essence communicable to the creature. Hence nothing that happens in the universe perishes: the evils permitted by God in order to draw goods from them, the lower levels of created entia, the imperfections that unfold at each level with all the possible varieties, are all things ordained to result in a totality arranged by infinite wisdom and goodness. The blessed see this infinite wisdom and goodness in God, and in God these attributes are God. They constitute the manner in which the blessed see God and in which alone they can see the original power, wisdom and goodness, which are God. The God they see is not detached from the universe but united most closely to it as its principle, from which the universe continuously receives the being it has and keeps for ever.[259]

679. Although the laws of divine operation so far presented

[258] Hence St. Thomas acutely says: 'Creation understood as an action means a divine action which is his essence that has a relationship to the creature. In God however a relationship to the creature is not real, but only seen by the mind'* (*S.T.*, I, q. 45, art. 3, ad 1).

[259] I say 'for ever' because nothing God has created is annihilated, although it changes form.

(the laws of gradation, variety and excluded equality) demonstrate, as we have seen, God's infinite wisdom and goodness in the universe that has not yet arrived at its final state, we can and must transport all these things to the final state and consider them as necessary for obtaining this most excellent and sublime state, a state in which the series of entia and events no longer has succession but is very much present and gathered completely into the full unity of divine harmony and of every kind of good.

680. Indeed, if we consider the contribution made by the law *of excluded equality* to the maximum good of the blessed, we see that it bestows on them a good that they could not have obtained in any other way. In fact, the law makes each of the blessed unique in the full species that each has,[260] and to be unique in possessing a given excellence increases the joy drawn from its possession. Nor must we think that this detracts in any way from charity, as it may seem at first sight and as happens whenever individual passions are involved in the appetite for unique excellence, which is the case on earth, due to human weakness. But this is not the case in heaven: the uniqueness of personal excellence is loved by the one who has it, precisely because the possessor sees himself or herself chosen to realise sufficiently the full-specific essence, and for this great purpose there is no need for anybody else to share in it. Hence there is also delight that everyone else is unique in their own essence. But because this delight refers to the eternal essence of things, it refers to God, in whom these essences are grounded. Consequently, we see that this extraordinary delight that the real intellective being draws from seeing itself unique with a specific excellence, is not the kind that comes from the limitation of entia but from the nature and order of being; it is an ontological, not a cosmological law. God himself therefore enjoys his unicity in so far as he sees in himself the whole of realised being.

681. If we also take into account the laws *of gradation* and *variety* as contributing to the increase of the eternal happiness

[260] The *abstract species* includes a great number of *full species* (among which at least one *complete species*) that are also modes of the same species. Cf. *NE*, 2: 646–659. Thus the *abstract* human species is one only, but the *full species* are as many as the ideal varieties of human beings.

of the just, we can draw two important considerations from them.

1. No ideal essence could be fully known by intelligent creatures if the ideal essence were not realised in all possible modes; as long as it is not realised, the modes in it are indistinct or rather, as modes, they do not exist. Therefore the creature cannot see the fecundity of an essence if distinctions do not exist. Also, in the simplest essence of a thing the mind distinguishes modes by limiting the essence. But the mind cannot limit an essence with its thought if it does not find the limits which, like signs or boundary lines, it uses to mark out particular modes in the essence. These lines which the mind draws in the essence to mark out modes that are the possibilities of real entia are found only in realised entia so that none of the realised entia equals or exhausts the total essence. Some of these limitations are arbitrary, that is, the reason for them is not in the idea of the ens under consideration. An example are limitations of quantity: for the most part the reason for these is not in the idea, and as such they are not necessary for knowing the fecundity of an ideal essence. Other limitations however are necessary, like all those that concern qualities and accidents that exclude each another. The existence of many real entia is therefore necessary in order that all the modes in which an essence can be realised may be distinctly understood. Thus, if wisdom and goodness wished to communicate themselves to created intelligences, they had to give these intelligences the mode for seeing all the fecundity of the essences of entia; only in this way could the understanding and affection of creatures rise from perceived real beings to the full comprehension of ideal beings, where, as we saw, the act of knowledge and moral will terminate. Solely through the gradation and variety of the real entia that compose the universe could man who is in the state of viator raise himself to the perfect contemplation and moral esteem of the essences of things. Therefore this gradation and variety were necessary for our intellective and moral perfection, and similarly for all other created intelligences.

681a. Let us apply this reasoning to the beatific vision as I have described it. In this vision there is in fact gradation and variety, and we contemplate these throughout their total range. But we certainly cannot do this here on earth where we perceive only a few links of the chain, a few varieties. Moreover, in heaven we contemplate them at source, God, because God himself is the gradation and variety present in the divine creating act and in the divine Word, with whom they have a relationship. Hence, the wisdom and the goodness of the gradation and the variety are a part of God's essential wisdom and goodness because the act that produces them and in which they are seen is the divine essence. If this act is the divine essence visible to the blessed, and if it is determined by its terms, which the real gradation and variety are, then this real gradation and variety of entia are a condition of the beatific vision and determine, so to speak, its quantity and mode. We see here then how strong the connection is between created things and the Creator, how close indeed the connection between all the successive states of the universe and the final state of the comprehensors in heaven, and finally we see how necessary these states are for their happiness and the glory they give to God in heaven.

682. 2. The second consideration resembles what I said about the law *of excluded equality*. I noted that this law had to dominate in creation because without it one of most exquisite goods that those in heaven can enjoy would have been lost: the joy of seeing themselves endowed with a totally unique excellence. We must also note here that without the law *of the gradation* of entia and *of their variety* humanity would have lost a good it supremely desired, the good of *superiority*. This observation, although not new, is beautiful and important. Aquinas used it to defend Providence when he said: 'There would be no perfect goodness in created things if they had no order of goodness in such a way that some were better than others. Otherwise, all the possible degrees of goodness would not be realised (NON ENIM IMPLERENTUR OMNES GRADUS POSSIBILES BONITATIS),' (this is the law of gradation seen many centuries prior to modern philosophers) 'nor would there be any creature that was like God in so far as eminently above all the others.'[261]

[261] We should also note the words St. Thomas next uses to demonstrate that the inequality among entia and evils is necessary if all *possible goods* are to be drawn from a given essence of things: 'If there were total equality in things, there would be only one created good. But the degree of good is higher so that there may be something good that cannot fail in goodness. There is also the lower degree because something can fail in goodness. The *perfection* of the universe therefore requires both degrees of good. It pertains to the providence

683. It is certain that we are naturally pleased to see ourselves more superior than other beings. But two questions can be asked about the nature of this *appetite for superiority*: 1. Is it simply an effect of the damage in human nature and would not be found in a perfect human nature? 2. Is it at least a consequence of the necessary limitation of contingent being, and therefore does not pertain to the order of being, that is, it is not an ontological but a cosmological property?

684. In reply to the first question I say that the appetite for superiority, considered in itself (without the abuse and the evil application that corrupt nature makes of it), does not stem from damaged humanity but from humanity itself. Our reason for doubting that it stems from humanity is the same as our mistaken suspicion that the appetite for unique excellence has an evil origin: we doubt and suspect because both these appetites are frequently abused by fallen humanity. In the state of decadence fallen humanity, which wants to satisfy its natural appetites independently of the laws of justice and goodness, makes its appetites causes of blind, exclusive and irresistible instincts. But if we consider appetites in themselves and strip them of their evil qualities, they are good. To understand how they can be good, we need to investigate whether the *uniqueness of excellence* and the *superiority* of an ens over others can be just, and is even required by justice and goodness. If there is only one such case where these two things considered as goods do not offend justice or goodness, we can ask if they have in themselves the nature of a good. The uniqueness of excellence does have this nature, as we have already seen, but I also say the same for superiority, because superiority can be just and good if distributed by God according to merit. Is therefore the superiority of

of a governor to preserve, not reduce, perfection in the things governed. Consequently, it does not pertain to divine providence to exclude entirely from things the potential to lack good. Evil comes from this potential, because that which can fail, sometimes fails' (through the *law of probability*, as I explained elsewhere); 'and this lack of good is evil. — It does not therefore pertain to divine providence to prohibit evil in governed things'* (*C.G.*, III, 71: 3). St. Thomas, it should be noted, constantly begins from the principle that *the universe must be perfect* and we cannot think of anything better happening in it than what actually happens. If we thought otherwise, the work would not correspond to the infinite skill of the Craftsman.

one being over others a natural object of appetite for human beings who are incorrupt, granted that the superiority is free from all moral evil.

684a. I say 'yes' because I demonstrate it with the principle I used earlier, that 'the excellence of a prerogative intuited in an abstract essence can be understood only if the excellence is perceived or seen distinct at all the levels at which it can be realised. By itself, an abstract essence shining before our understanding is not sufficient to show our understanding all the fecundity that the essence is capable of'. If a human being or any other intelligent being possesses a given excellence, it is just that they enjoy it and, moreover, draw from it all the enjoyment it can give. If infinite wisdom did not give them the occasion and means for fully knowing their own excellence, they would lack a part of the enjoyment which they could justly extract from that excellence, with the result that one of the goods obtainable from created nature would be lost. But a created being cannot fully understand its own excellence without regard to the lower levels in which the excellence can be realised. Lower beings must therefore exist in which higher beings see that the excellence they possess is divided into parts and they can come to know its full value; because of this they can enjoy their own superiority. This enjoyment at finding themselves having superiority over many others is simply the means for fully knowing their own excellence and hence for enjoying it as much as possible. The enjoyment is just and good; it does not originate, as it seems to, from a corruption of nature but is an appetite resulting from nature. Therefore we find a superiority bestowed on humanity when first created: 'And he said: Let us make man to our image and likeness: and let him have dominion over the fishes of the sea, and the fowls of the air, and the beasts, and the whole earth, and every creeping creature that moves upon the earth.' And to those he had created male and female he said: 'Increase and multiply, and fill the earth, and subdue it, and rule over the fishes of the sea, and the fowls of the air, and all living creatures that move upon the earth.'[262] Dominion is given to both male and female because the latter, having human nature, also had an appetite for

[262] Gen 1: 26–28†.

superiority. But God places in Adam a superiority relative also to his similar, that is, to Eve, and to the children that would be born from him. Hence God calls the woman *help* of the man and is made from the man. St. Paul, commenting on this, says that 'the man is head of the woman'.[263]

685. If *superiority* is a good that is appropriate to human nature and if God, through the law of his wisdom, is moved to draw all possible good from his creatures and to dispose things so that every good attains its summit and develops to the final fruit of which it is capable, it is fitting that the *good of superiority* proper to human beings must also increase to its maximum measure. But the first state of the human race did not favour this effect. The only dominion human beings could exercise over their similars was a limited dominion, because they differed little from each other in excellence, nor did they have great need of another's government. Here we have a fresh reason why it was more becoming to eternal wisdom to dispose that that first state changed into another, a state more favourable to the development of this great good, that is, the superiority proper to human nature. Without this disposition, human nature could never have realised every good whose seed it contained, and hence in its developments could never have exhausted all its essence, which was contemplated and willed by God. Hence *sin* was permitted, an accident that provided the occasion for maximum inequality among human beings. God immediately gave a very clear indication of this inequality that resulted from sin when he said to the woman: 'You shall be under your husband's power, and he shall have dominion over you.'[264] Moreover, sin makes human beings unequal in different ways. First of all, our consequent weakness, vacillating thoughts and inclination to evil require that our associating together be constituted in a stronger and more compact order, that the wicked be forcefully restrained, the ignorant taught by more knowledgeable people, and the inconstant governed by fixed laws, or certainly that an individual or a collective will must rule others, keeping them to a definite rule, from which they are continuously inclined to escape in disorder. This

[263] 1 Cor 11: 3–10†.

[264] Gen 3: 16; 1 Cor 14: 34†.

explains the origin of rulers, sovereigns, masters, legislators, etc., and under them weak people, subjects, disciples, citizens, etc. Second, granted that God still wished to give the unjust the means of justifying themselves, he reopened the path of justice to anyone ready to follow it. The outcome was an immense, completely internal inequality between the state of the wicked and that of the just, as we see in the first ages of the world. The wicked were *sons of men*; the just, *sons of God*;[265] these two groups formed as it were two cities, one of which has God as superior, the other the devil. The distance between the just and unjust is infinite, most fittingly symbolised by the firmament that divides the upper waters from the lower waters,[266] and from the *caos magnum* [great chaos] which, as we are told in the Gospel, for ever divides and separates by an impassable distance the unjust rich from the just poor.[267]

686. Because human nature, according to the law of the least means, had to render all possible good, all possible inequality had to be present in the human race. To achieve this, both the *extreme of iniquity* and the greatest possible *extreme of justice* were necessary so that the most just human being ruled over all the others in due gradation down to the most unjust. This was the only way to obtain in humanity the *maximum superiority* of all possible superiorities. According to this plan there had to be someone in the human race who descended to the level of ultimate possible evil — this will be the Antichrist — and someone who rose to the ultimate possible of holiness, who was Christ. The Antichrist's appearance is permitted by God; Christ's birth was a work of God. We see that the *superiority* of Christ over all the human race and over the demons is glorified throughout the whole of Scripture: he is seated at the right of the Father, above all the angelic choirs, while the sequence of events goes on unfolding in order to put everything under him, according to the sublimity of the words addressed by the Father to his Son, which begin: 'Sit at my right hand until I make your enemies your footstool.'[268]

[265] Gen 6: [2†].

[266] Gen 1: 7†.

[267] Lk 16: 26†.

[268] Ps 110: 1.

687. It is important also to note that all the diverse kinds of *superiority*, like all the classifications of things, can be reduced to three categories. In fact, just as there are three categorical excellences: *power*, *wisdom* and prevalent *moral goodness*, so there are three superiorities. Humanity had to attain the ultimate possible summit of these three superiorities, just as it had to attain the ultimate possible depth of the corresponding inferiorities.

688. Vengeance against one's enemies reduces to the superiority of power reduces. Two societies therefore had to separate out in humanity, one good, the other evil, and the former had to have supreme dominion over the latter. But both had to have a graduated hierarchy: in one, thrones of power rose higher and higher to the right of the divine Father; in the other, thrones descended ever lower and lower to the bottom of the abyss. In the hierarchy of the good the less good had to be below the better, but without losing any of their fullness of joy. The good do not love or desire every superiority for themselves but only the amount that is just, and because the superiority is just in those above them, they love that these have this superiority and they love their subjection to them. On the other hand, those above them enjoy being of higher rank because with full justice they can and must be such. In the hierarchy of the wicked however, all superiority is hated and insufferable, nor can those who have it draw enjoyment from it because they hate justice, and the hatred of justice is a torture.

689. In the second question we asked if the appetite for superiority was *ontological* or simply *cosmological*, that is, if it came from being as such, or from the limitation of contingent being. I reply that it is natural for God to give himself glory through his works *ad extra*; they reveal to finite intelligences the magnificence of his wisdom and goodness. He is infinitely pleased with the works that are in him; they are in him through the act with which he creates them, seeing them with a creative, willed vision. He must therefore delight also in the fact that he is superior to contingent being, whose infinite source he is. This relationship between contingent and necessary being is, in God, an argument for the glory he gives to himself, and pertains to his own excellence which he knows. We must say therefore that the enjoyment felt in superiority is, strictly speaking, intrinsic to

the order of being and, considered in itself, does not originate from the limitations of contingent things. However it does involves an eternal relationship with contingent things, just as the word 'supreme' involves a relationship with what falls short of what is supreme.

690. If we apply all this to the beatific vision of the comprehensors in heaven, their superiority lies in this vision. The gradation of everything that is or was below them demonstrates most clearly to them how great is the good contained in their excellence, just as the gradation of what is superior to them demonstrates the greater excellence of other entia. This gives them the occasion to love ever more in them the justice present in the just superiority of another. These graduated excellences are all seen in God, and seen as pertaining to him out of eminence. Whoever sees God, sees that all the ineffable excellence and goodness of creation reduces to and resides in God, as in its source. It is now totally simplified, eternal, essential, no longer the goodness of creation but of the God whose face they see. And this divine goodness creation gives a little intimation.

CHAPTER 26
Continuation

691. Everything said so far results from the principles I have posited. But the arguments will be followed more easily if I summarise the principles.

The law of operative wisdom is the law of *sufficient reason*. This determines the *end* and the *mode* of operation of a wise person.

When applied to the *mode* of operation it produces another law, that of *the least means*.

The law of the least means needs a principle of application. I found that the principle of its application to the government of contingent entia is: 'It must govern in such a way that all the good that these entia can give is in fact obtained.'

The fecundity of the principle became clear when I considered it as the generator of various other laws that presided over the government of the universe. These laws were: the law *of non-intervention by God* in nature without necessity, the laws *of necessary intervention*, *of excluded superfluity*, *of the unity and harmony of the universe*, *of the gradation of entia*, *of variety*, *of excluded equality*, *of the unity of divine operation*, *of divine manifestation in time*, *and of divine manifestation in eternity*, where all passing events become consistent and necessary, the means of divine glory, the ultimate purpose of creation.

Particular attention must be paid to the last two laws, which I developed in the previous chapter and are founded on the principle: 'Divine wisdom and goodness could not be manifested to the intellective creature except through the work of creation, either perceived *in se*, as is the case of man as viator, or contemplated in the divine essence creating the world, as in the case of the comprehensors.'

Because this very important truth deserves deep meditation, I will take a little more time and offer some fresh considerations.

692. No created being can understand the supreme goodness of another being if it does not understand the wisdom of the other. For goodness to be supreme, the will must be guided in

its operation by a supreme wisdom so that the operation will produce the greatest good possible. If we understand that divine wisdom could not have manifested itself to finite intelligences without creation, we will understand that creation was also necessary if divine goodness was to manifest itself to them. Let us see if divine wisdom could have made itself known to contingent intellective being without the work of creation.

693. First, without creation there would not have been contingent intellective being. Hence, nothing could have been manifested to it.

694. Let us suppose that God had suddenly communicated the vision of his essence to only one created intelligent being, without anything else of the universe. The communicative relationship between God and this being would be a supernatural complement to the creative act[269] because with only one operative, creative and beneficent act God would terminate and rest in this creature, who would consequently see God in so far as God acts in it as creator and perfecter. In this case, the object of the vision would always be the divine essence not as it is *in se* cut off from its operation, but in so far as it operates with wisdom and goodness in the creature. Hence all that the creature could understand of divine wisdom would be what is manifested to it in the creative, beatifying act. In this act, the divine essence would reveal itself to the creature as root, source, principle and foundation, and in any other more appropriate mode we might wish to name. The quantity, as it were, of divine wisdom knowable to creatures therefore is exactly that which shines forth in the divine essence in so far as this communicates its goodness to them and in so far as it produces creatures in the varyingly perfect state in which they are, that is, relative to the degree of wisdom and goodness it uses when operating in them. Thus, if creatures, if their overall composition, or in a word, the universe, is more or less perfect, and if the traces of wisdom in them vary in degree, there must be a corresponding degree of manifestable divine wisdom, because the wisdom manifested in the divine essence is proportionate or analogous to the created traces of wisdom. Thus, supreme wisdom had to have a teaching

[269] Therefore St. Thomas says: 'Charity is that which unites us to God, who is *the final end of the human mind*'* (*S.T.*, II-II, q. 184, art. 1).

authority that shone in creatures so that divine wisdom could be intuited in a supreme mode in the divine essence. It is true that those who see God know that in addition to the wisdom they see in him in a limited way, there is another abyss that remains hidden from them. This serves as matter for eternal adoration. But everything not understood in God, not seen by the creature, is a help to the creature only because the creature forms a kind of negative concept of it from what it positively understands and sees.

695. Someone might say that if the creature can see God, God can communicate to it as much of his essence as he likes, and hence can show the creature as much as he wills of his essential wisdom and goodness. He certainly can do this, but on one condition: he must first make the creature apt and able to receive the modal part[270] of his essence that he wishes to communicate, because this part must be received by the capacity of the perceiving creature. Consequently God could not manifest his essence to a stone or to a brute animal unless he first gave the stone intelligence (which is absurd) or raised a brute animal to a state of an intelligent being, which would then cease to be a brute animal. This is why the communication of the divine essence can be made only in a mode adapted and proportional to natural faculties — to claim the contrary involves contradiction. Although *natural faculties* can never attain the divine essence, they have the *capacity* to perceive that essence, that is, the capacity to receive from God the *faculty of that perception*. This new faculty is, as it were, grafted by God on to the natural faculties by the communication of the *light of glory* (as the theologians call it), which is the divine essence itself. Because God is intellectually seen, the intellect is the natural faculty to have the supernatural faculty of the vision grafted on to it. Therefore, although the object of the vision is infinite, the faculty to see it, which is subjective, is finite (because the subject is finite) and is proportionate to the natural-subjective faculty on to which it

[270] God's totally simple essence cannot be divided, not even in so far as it is conceived by us. But the *mode* of conceiving it can vary, and vary in perfection. We can say that finite being perceives the divine essence in a limited mode in the sense that the essence itself, in so far as corresponding to the limited mode in which it is perceived, is called a *modal part* of the essence.

(the supernatural faculty of the vision) is grafted.[271] So if we wanted to investigate the *necessary limit* of this faculty of vision that is given to the human being, we would have to investigate the nature of the human intellect and see to what it is proportionate, in the way that if we wanted to discover the necessary limit of the faculty of vision in another intellective being, we would have to consider the nature of that being's intellect.

695a. The quality of the human intellect is known from its form, which is universal, undetermined being. In this being, no species, no genus of things, no difference, no reality manifests itself by its own means. Hence, we are given *feeling* so that we can know reality and the differences of diverse realities. Feeling, in its general definition, is not limited solely to the external senses but is 'the faculty to perceive every reality that acts on and in the reality of the human being'. This definition should be carefully noted: it embraces the feeling both of the human being and of every perceptive being, because every perceptive being has a feeling, without which it would be dead. We therefore draw the consequence that 'because the reality of the perceiving subject is that which suffers the action of another reality (feeling follows from this action)', every faculty of feeling has a limit determined by the amount of reality which makes up the perceiving subject. The feeling therefore that the human subject is capable of is proportional to the amount of the subject's real entity. This amount can be ascertained by considering the subject's real, sensitive faculties. They are: 1. the faculty of animal feeling; 2. the faculty of spiritual feeling; and 3. the faculty of mixed feeling. Because the last is the effect of the first two, resulting from the unity of the human subject, it cannot help us to determine how far human feeling can be extended. I will therefore consider only the first two.

695b. Animal sensitivity produces feelings which determine some differences in the *universal being* intuited by us. Hence, there are specific ideas of these feelings, and from these specific ideas abstraction extracts generic ideas. These generic and specific ideas are so determined by feelings that without them the

271 St. Thomas says: 'The created intellect does not see the divine essence according to the mode of the essence but according to its own mode, which is finite'* (*S.T.*, III, q. 92, art. 3, ad 3).

ideas could not be.[272] Thus, whenever God might want to infuse feelings in someone who has never experienced them, all he could do is arouse in that person the feelings, or corresponding images or traces to which those species referred. The contrary would be absurd, because the species of a feeling is solely the connection between the feeling and the idea of being, and this connection cannot exist without terms.

In regard to pure spiritual sensitivity, the feeling we have of ourselves originates in us as a result of animal feelings. It can therefore be called mixed sensitivity. Indeed, as intelligent (that is, as people intuiting being), we each have a feeling of our own subject, and this can be called pure spiritual sensitivity. Note however, this pure feeling is not such that it can become an object of our thought without some particular feeling moving us to reflect on ourselves. Granted therefore that we reflect on our own intuiting subject, we form the specific idea of the human being as well as the affirmation of ourselves. But again, God could not infuse this idea or this perception into us if he did not simultaneously infuse the human feeling to which the idea and the perception refer, and this for the reason indicated above, namely that the idea is only ideal being limited by the feeling, and the perception is only the affirmation of the relationship between ideal being and feeling, a relationship that cannot exist without the terms from which it results.

695c. This allows us to understand what the sensitivity of the human intellect is and the feeling of the human subject intuiting being. It is a feeling produced by intuited being in the intuiting agent, by the object in the subject. The subject feels the presence of the object, and if this object is not the pure ideal essence of being but adds its own reality to this ideal essence, it increases the fundamental feeling of the subject, and hence the subject itself. From this we can deduce how human beings can perceive the reality of God. The reality of God corresponds to and conforms itself to ideal, universal being, which is the form of the human intellect.[273] God therefore must let himself be seen as real

[272] How we know entia solely by the way they act on us was shown in *NE*, 3: 1209–1212. It is indispensable that the reader has a good understanding of this teaching.

[273] Cf. *NE*, 3: 1158–1175.

form of the intellect; in ideal being we must see revealed, feel and apprehend the real. This communication of the realities of God must be made in such a way that, although it makes us sublime, it does not change us into another being. Our intellect must retain the same nature and must remain a human intellect, although made sublime. Ideal being, the form of the human intellect, is in fact so ordered that it bears the imprints of the diverse realities whose action we feel with our sensitive powers; it is ordered so as to receive precisely into itself all these diverse imprints that are all virtually contained in the fundamental feeling that constitutes each of us the subject we are. If God therefore, when manifesting himself, conforms himself to all the imprints and realities of which ideal being, proper to the human intellect, is capable, and adds nothing else (which would change the nature of the intellect), he must manifest himself as the principle and source of all the realities that are destined to produce the imprints; in short, he must manifest himself as the act by which he creates man and the universe, and in which alone the universe subsists. In this way the divine essence adapts itself to human limitation or subjectivity, and only in this way can it fulfil all our human potencies and give them delight with itself.[274]

[274] This does not mean that the blessed must see God in everything that God knows through the *knowledge of vision*. Perhaps not all created things are proportionate to us and our feeling. Perhaps, due to the special nature of our feeling, we are constituted in a limited system of things which is also proper to us. In fact St. Thomas says: 'It is not necessary that in knowing a cause, we know all its effects, unless we comprehend the cause, which the created intellect is not able to do. Hence the quantity of things seen in God's essence by those who see him in his essence is proportionate to the clarity of their vision of the divine essence. Consequently, a human being can instruct another about these things. Thus the knowledge of angels and of holy souls can increase until the day of judgment, and also knowledge of other things that pertain to the accidental reward, but goes no further because it will be the *final state of things*. In this state it is possible for everyone to know everything that God *knows with the knowledge of vision*'* (*S.T.*, Supplement, q. 92, art.3, resp.). Nevertheless, even when the final state of things has come when all the blessed will see all contingent things (or at least those things that pertain to their system), they will see in the divine essence only a part, not all of them, and Christ will teach them about the others. St Thomas again: 'Not everyone will see everything in the divine essence. However, *the soul of Christ* will clearly see everything there, just as his soul sees now. Other people will see more or fewer things according to the degree they know God. Thus Christ's

696. Note carefully: if God wanted to manifest himself to us only in so far as he corresponds to undetermined being that shines in the human mind and not as he corresponds to the imprints that undetermined being can receive, we would certainly feel an infinite, absolute ens, and consequently affirm it to ourselves. This alone would suffice to place us in a supernatural state, which constitutes the state of grace. If we reflect upon ourselves in this state, we are aware that there is an infinite reality, and the reality of this ens is identical to the intelligible ens we see in the idea. The feeling of the identity of this real and infinite ens intelligible to us gives rise to a complete joy infinite in nature, which we feel to be a new act of the same identical being in three modes. However we distinguish nothing further in this being, which is the whole of being, because there is no other contingent reality we can refer to it, nor see any other finite in it. God is thus communicated to us as TOTALITY, but we do not necessarily see the action proper to this totality, nor the internal action it exercises on us or on other things; in a word, we see only a real that conforms to the *undetermined ideal*, and which is the beginning of this ideal. This is certainly the state in which the holy people of the New Testament are constituted on this earth; it is the order of the gracious justice of the Saviour. There is perception of God, but the act with which he produces everything that he produces remains hidden in him; it resembles more the perception, rather than the act, of divine power that virtually comprehends everything. God's power however is God's essence. Consequently, there is a kind of vision, a vision however that is possessed through the light of faith but not sufficient to make visible before us the mystery of the universe, and give us total delight.

697. Here I must add another consideration. The wisdom that directs supreme goodness in the three categorical operations *ad*

soul will illumine all other souls about the things which, better than other souls, it sees in the Word. In Revelation 22: [23] we read that 'the glory of God will enlighten the city of Jerusalem and its light is the Lamb'. Similarly, higher things will enlighten lower things, not with a new light such that the knowledge of lower things is increased, but by a certain continuation of the light, just as we can understand that the setting sun lights up the air. Hence in Daniel 22: [3] we read that those who teach many about justice, shine out like stars in perpetual eternities'* (ibid, ad 12).

extra has a necessary relationship with these operations, and hence it can be manifested only through this relationship. In fact the wisdom and goodness by which we know and praise the Creator is that through which God *freely* operates good and disposes the means from which he can obtain the greatest possible sum of good. This free wisdom and goodness of God is not present in operations *ad intra*. These operations are posited by *necessity*, not by free choice, and with them divine nature is, as it were, constituted and posits itself identical in three modes, in three acts and, strictly speaking, in three persons. Even if we were granted to see these internal operations, we would not necessarily see the free goodness and wisdom that constitutes the reason for God's praises. Such a vision would, by itself, make us blessed but we would not know the divine wisdom and goodness of God's operation *ad extra*, if his relationship with creation and with himself remained hidden. The reason is the principle laid down by Aristotle and acknowledged as true by St. Thomas: 'Only act, not potency, is knowable through itself'; potency is known only through its act.[275]

It is true that when we mentally separate from the divine essence the act with which it produces the contingent things of the universe, there would still be wisdom and goodness towards these, but the wisdom and goodness would be only radically and potentially present, and hence could not be seen and acknowledged by the creature. The attributes of wisdom and goodness, if seen in act in the divine essence, would certainly be known, but such a vision cannot take place if the relationship between the essence and creation, or better, the creative act itself, is not seen as well, because the creative act cannot be seen without its term that determines and specifies it. An intellective being therefore would be blessed if we supposed that its vision of the divine essence was such that the creative and governing act of the world were hidden from it, but it could not know either free divine wisdom or free divine goodness. It would not therefore glorify God through these attributes but glorify him only as its own good. Nevertheless, in glorifying God as its

[275] 'A thing is intelligible in so far as it acts, not in so far as it has potency, as is clear in the ninth book of Metaphysics'* (*S.T.*, Supplement, q. 92, art. 1, ad 1).

good, an intellective being would glorify him through his relationship and communication of himself to it. Consequently, the object of the vision would still be solely the divine essence in the act in which it communicates itself to its creatures. Because the divine essence is not perceived without the reality of God, and because the reality of God is not perceived except in the reality of the perceiving creature, the divine essence is always and in every case perceived in the way it is communicated to the reality of the creature, and this is an act *ad extra*.

698. In all this we see confirmed what I said in the previous chapter:

1. The end of the universe is that intelligent creatures should know and exalt divine wisdom and goodness. This action constitutes the divine glory.
2. Creatures, due to their limitation, cannot know this divine wisdom and goodness except through the works of creation where the traces of these attributes, that is, the essential laws of wisdom and goodness, clearly shine out.
3. In the present life, we know divine wisdom and goodness by garnering their traces from the perception of creatures, and by reflecting on this perception.
4. In the future life, we will know divine wisdom and goodness from the perception of the divine essence in so far as this is an act which, with infinite wisdom, produces and communicates its goodness to creatures.
5. It was necessary therefore that God regulated the universe according to the above laws of wisdom and goodness so that the glory that is the end of creation might be made known to and obtained by creatures.
6. The universe and all that happens in it, and all its successive states, are permanent in the act of the divine essence, which is their first cause. They form a single, most wise and excellent whole, which is revealed at certain levels to blessed intelligences, and are the eternal reason for the praises that these intelligences raise to their Creator and are the completion of their happiness.

CHAPTER 27

Tenth consequence: in operating, God follows the law of heroism, that is, the law of extremes

699. The laws of wisdom and goodness that I have presented so far are necessary: God could not have ignored them in creating and governing the universe, not only because he is essential wisdom and goodness but without them he could not have obtained their end, which is his glory.

Because this new argument, taken from the purpose of the world, confirms the necessity of these very noble laws, we can continue developing them in their applications. These applications will make the laws more effective in solving the objections that human ignorance brings against the sublime government of Providence.

700. I will begin by drawing a new consequence from the laws of *continuity*, *variety* and *unity* in God's operation, as follows: 'God, operating in the universe, follows the law of heroism, that is, the law of extremes.' In fact, this is the difference between the operation of ordinary human beings and that of heroes: the former do not leave the beaten track and keep to mediocrity, heroes, according to their goodness or wickedness, take good and evil to their ultimate, attainable extreme. Stopping at nothing, they want every enterprise to which put their hand, to attain the completion it is capable of, and of which they have the type vividly before their mind. If therefore heroes are good, they are excellent, but if evil, they are very wicked. God always acts in this way, and he is certainly the greatest and most excellent of heroes.

701. Holy Scripture indicates this characteristic of divine operation. It says that wisdom 'reaches from end to end mightily, and orders all things sweetly.'[276] The *might* of divine operation is clearly visible in the infallible attainment of every effect proposed; the *sweetness* is demonstrated in what is done to obtain the desired effect. Second causes themselves are left free to run their course, even when they seem to operate in a

[276] Wis 8: 1†.

contrary way, although in the end despite appearances they all conspire in the Omniscient's plan.

The law of extremes therefore embraces the *end* and the *means*.

702. If we consider the law relative to the end, that is, to the effect God proposes for himself, it is a consequence of the unity of divine operation. Through this unity, all things are carried out with one eternal act, and the government of the universe is directed to only one preconceived purpose, that is, to obtaining the greatest good that can be drawn from created things. And precisely because this *final good* is the greatest that creatures, directed and helped by God, can give, it is the ultimate extreme attainable. Hence, the passage of Scripture quoted above, where it says that God reaches from end to end, is preceded by the reason for this divine practice which, as I said, is the unity of divine operation. The sacred text says: 'And being but ONE,' (wisdom) 'she can do ALL THINGS: and remaining in herself the same, she renews all things, and through nations conveys herself into holy souls, she makes the friends of God and prophets. For God loves none but him that dwells with wisdom. For she is more beautiful than the sun,' (which lights up all the world) 'and above all the order of the stars' (whose rays extend a tremendous distance): 'being compared with the light, she is found before it. For after this comes night, but no evil can overcome wisdom' (which shines equally at all times). She reaches, therefore' (this is the consequence), 'from end to end mightily, and orders all things sweetly.'[277]

703. If we now consider the *law of extremes* relative to *means*, the law originates from the laws of *continuity* and *variety*. All graduated beings, and all their varieties and acts, are means in the hands of divine wisdom; they are all ordered to its one intention, which is to make evils serve the final sum of good. The words quoted above refer precisely to this, that 'no evil can overcome wisdom'. Evil itself is a means for the excellent intention of wisdom, and no deficiency in the creature, no perverse will, can impede or diminish that end; it can only contribute to it, as a necessary means for accomplishing it.

704. Divine wisdom therefore orders and uses for its end all

[277] Wis 7: 29–30 — 8: 1†.

things, from the greatest to the least. Hence Scripture says: 'I fill heaven and earth.'[278] In the admirable Psalm, 138, God is exalted because he reaches everything with his wisdom and power; nothing escapes his gaze or his hand. In the psalm, a human being speaks to his Maker:

> O Lord, you have searched me and known me! You know when I sit down and when I rise up; you discern my thoughts from afar. You search out my path and my lying down, and are acquainted with all my ways. Even before a word is on my tongue, lo, O Lord, you know it altogether. You beset me behind and before, and lay your hand upon me. Such knowledge is too wonderful for me; it is high, I cannot attain it. Whither shall I go from your Spirit? Or whither shall I flee from your presence? If I ascend to heaven, you are there! If I make my bed in Sheol, you are there! If I take the wings of the morning and dwell in the uttermost parts of the sea, even there your hand shall lead me, and your right hand shall hold me. If I say, 'Let only darkness cover me, and the light about me be night,' even the darkness is not dark to you, the night is bright as the day; for darkness is as light with you. For you did form my inward parts, you did knit me together in my mother's womb. I praise you, for you are fearful and wonderful. Wonderful are your works! You know me right well; my frame was not hidden from you, when I was being made in secret, intricately wrought in the depths of the earth. Your eyes beheld my unformed substance; in your book were written, every one of them, the days that were formed for me, when as yet there was none of them.[279]

This is appropriate language for humanity; the sentiments are those of perfect humanity that knows God as he was in Christ.

705. God therefore, with his wisdom and his action, touches the extremes of both the natural and supernatural orders. This is a common argument in the canticles of praise in divine Scripture. David exclaims: 'From the rising of the sun to its setting

[278] Jer 23: 23–24. — In this place God says he is not far from all things but near them: 'Am I a God near by, says the Lord, and not a God far off? Who can hide in secret places so that I cannot see them? says the Lord. Do I not fill heaven and earth? says the Lord.'*

[279] Ps 138: 1–16.

the name of the LORD is to be praised! The Lord is high above all nations, and his glory above the heavens! Who is like the Lord our God, who is seated on high, who looks far down upon the heavens and the earth?',[280] touching the two extremes of height and depth. St. Paul, alluding to this, exhorts the Ephesians to obtain the knowledge of these extremes of divine greatness; he prays 'that you may have the power to comprehend, with all the saints, what is the breadth and length and height and depth.'[281]

706. With his power God touches the extremes in the *sphere of real being*, creating all the links in each species from one end of the chain to the other, and developing all their varieties.

God touches the extremes in the *sphere of intelligence*, establishing total harmony among all the graduated and varied entia (excluding the replicas of the same type), and making them all work towards one purpose.

God touches the extremes in the *sphere of moral being*, and in so doing turns this unique purpose of all entia into the *greatest* possible eudaimonological-moral *good* that they can give. Even though the whole mass of real being is blind, and the whole complex of intelligent beings is free, he makes them all serve *moral being* and contribute to producing it in the greatest possible abundance, to making it happy and paying it honour. Thus, the Psalmist says that he raises 'the poor from the dust, and lifts the needy from the ash heap, to make them sit with princes, with the princes of his people. He gives the barren woman a home, making her the joyous mother of children';[282] in other words, he guides to happiness and glory the just person who trusts in him against all appearances; he makes the just triumph when faced with all the power of real being and with the prudence of intellectual being which at times opposes the just.

707. God also makes all the *natural order* serve the *supernatural order*. For this end, he makes the Word come down from his infinite height to become the least of human beings.[283] Later, he makes this last of mortals follow the same path in the opposite direction, rising back up to the right side of the Father: 'He who

[280] Ps 112: 3–6.

[281] Eph 3: 18.

[282] Ps 113: 7–9.

[283] Is. 53: 3.

descended,' St. Paul says, 'is the same one who ascended far above all the heavens, so that he might fill all things, UT IMPLERET OMNIA.'[284] Even natural reason gets a glimpse of how fitting this is to God, as Plato's words can demonstrate: 'In keeping with the ancient opinion, God, who embraces the *beginning*, *end* and *means* of all things, follows a good path, moving in conformity with nature. He is always accompanied by judgment, and punishes those who deviate from the divine law.' Plato draws the consequence that 'those are made happy who, keeping to this judgment, follow it humbly and temperately'.[285]

708. The glory that comes to God from his touching both extremes with his wisdom and goodness, can be appreciated through the wonder experienced by created intelligences. Aware of the immensity of divine operation, they clearly understand the greatness and goodness of its purpose, which is to draw from all things that are, and from all their acts, the greatest universal good these things can give, the greatest increase of the final sum of good. They also understand the extent and difficulty of the calculation needed to obtain this sum. According to our way of thinking this calculation requires God to foresee and take into account all the possible combinations of all entia, all their relationships, mutual actions and influences, and to choose to give existence only to those that correspond to the purpose. He has to harmonise everything, even down to the atom that is beyond our senses. Hence, he will not choose to give existence either to a wisp of straw or the movement of a leaf or a thought of an intelligent being without first considering it relative to all the other tiniest entia and their tiniest actions, and finding it opportune. Thus, determining whether it is appropriate to

[284] Eph. 4: 10.

[285] *De Legibus*, bk. 4: [715e–716a]. — the following observations are necessary concerning this passage of Plato:

1. He does not give this opinion as his own but as received from ancient tradition ὥσπερ καὶ ὁ παλαιὸς λόγος.

2. From knowledge of the divine greatness, which disposes all things and which no one can resist, he draws the precept of *humility* by which we submit to divine Providence and let ourselves by ruled by it κεκοσμημένος ταπεινὸς. It is one of the rarest places in pagan authors where humility is named and commended. The Greek word ταπεινὸς corresponds to the Latin *humilis*, that is, low, despised.

create, or how to give motion at every single moment to a molecule of air or of light must be just as just difficult as determining the form of the entire universe. Finally, created intelligences understand that the realisation of such a great calculation requires total dominion over everything. Because, for created intelligence, such an immeasurable task surpasses all its thought, it admits defeat in the face of such a great light of wisdom, and the created will finds no affections that correspond to so great a goodness. This annihilation of the creature in the face of divine greatness increases in proportion to the creature's understanding of the Creator's work by inductive reasoning, and this understanding is completed in the vision of God.

[708]

CHAPTER 28

Continuation. — The law of antagonism

709. We need to examine in more detail how the *law of extremes*, which is the law of heroism, is verified in divine operation.

The heroism of God's operation stands out more brilliantly when it is opposed, and particularly when opposed in a terrible and incessant battle in which God, as protector of the just and contrary to all appearances, is always the victor. In this battle he uses only the least power necessary to draw the greatest possible good from created things and from the power he has used. This is the law I call the *law of antagonism*.

710. It is clear that if divine wisdom found it fitting to produce entia in a continuous gradation and have them develop in all their possible varieties, the most terrible struggle between them had to result because they could not but develop in the most contrary directions, even to the extremes of the oppositions they could arrive at. Therefore, the form of evil had to descend through its levels to the lowest degree possible; similarly the form of good had to ascend through its levels to the highest possible point. Moreover, because entia are simply a complex of activities, there had to be a supreme activity for evil and a supreme activity for good, each tending to prevail over the other and increase at the expense and ruin of the other.

711. This state of the problem made it more difficult to solve in the way intended by infinite goodness. Despite the fact that all possible opposition was permitted, and evil was allowed to apply all its possible forces without encountering any obstruction, despite all this — indeed in the presence of all this — infinite goodness wished to obtain the complete triumph of good by wisely directing things. The good had to consist in such a great quantity of final good that this final good would have been less if there had not been the opposition of great evil, or the evil had been prevented from applying all its possible strength. It is in this supreme difficulty of finding a happy solution to such a great problem that divine

wisdom and goodness stand out in their maximum light before all intelligences.

712. Hence, throughout the whole of Scripture we see God described as a champion, a hero who conquers enemies: 'The Lord is as a man of war, Almighty is his name.'[286] In the Psalms he is called 'Lord God of hosts',[287] 'The Lord, the Most High, is terrible, a great king over all the earth',[288] and he is continually invoked as such. 'Contend, O Lord, with those who contend with me; fight against those who fight against me! Take hold of shield and buckler, and rise for my help! Draw the spear and javelin against my pursuers! Say to my soul, "I am your deliverance!"'[289] To St. John, JESUS Christ appears as he will be at the end of events, as a horseman, a conqueror of all peoples, of all things, but only after he has endured a most bitter and bloody combat.

> Then I saw heaven opened, and behold, a white horse! He who sat upon it is called Faithful and True, and in righteousness he judges and makes war. His eyes are like a flame of fire, and on his head are many diadems; and he has a name inscribed which no one knows but himself. He is clad in a robe dipped in blood, and the name by which he is called is The Word of God. And the armies of heaven, arrayed in fine linen, white and pure, followed him on white horses. From his mouth issues a sharp sword with which to smite the nations, and he will rule them with a rod of iron; he will tread the wine press of the fury of the wrath of God the Almighty. On his robe and on his thigh he has a name inscribed, 'King of kings and Lord of lords'.[290]

713. This complete victory however is not obtained by a display of his power. If he wanted to display his power, all combats would be impossible; with his power he can annihilate his enemies how and when he wishes, even before fighting them — after all, it is he who gives them existence. Or he can make them

[286] Ex 15: 3†.

[287] Ps 80: 4, 7, 19; Ps 68: 12.

[288] Ps 47: 2.

[289] Ps 35: 1–3.

[290] Rev 19: 11–16.

incapable of carrying out any hostile act against him, because at every moment he himself gives them strength and life. Alternatively he can make them submit and humble themselves before him as one who is the first cause of their good acts, despite the fact that these are voluntary and free. But he does not fight with his power; he fights with his infinite wisdom, which is a faithful guide of his infinite goodness. His wisdom restrains his power and prevents it being wasted; in fact his wisdom imposes on the problem the great condition I have mentioned 'of having to draw from the creature, when brought to its full realisation, all the fruit that created nature can give. Beyond the level necessary for producing this full realisation, no other level will be used if such a level did not bear maximum fruit, that is, more than it would when used in another way'.

714. Consequently, due to the certain foreseen effect of his most wise dispositions, God said to the Hebrew people: 'I put into your hands such and such a king, or such and such a country, or I do not put them into your hands'. This did not mean that he had to use his extraordinary power or work miracles. As I said, he used his wisdom, which had already disposed natural things to result in the victory of his people or, if he had predicted otherwise, their defeat.[291] He alludes to this arrangement in which he used second causes to accomplish his plans where he says: 'This day will I begin to send the dread and fear of you upon the nations that dwell under the whole heaven: that when they hear your name they may fear and tremble, and be in pain like women in travail.'[292] Moses then relates

[291] When the time destined by God for the conquest of Palestine was near, he said to Moses: 'Today you are going to cross the boundary of Moab at Ar. When you approach the frontier of the Ammonites, do not harass them or engage them in battle, for I will not give the land of the Ammonites to you as a possession, because I have given it to the descendants of Lot.' Moses notes here that the land of the Ammonites was first inhabited by giants and 'the Lord destroyed them from before the Ammonites so that they could dispossess them and settle in their place. He did the same for the descendants of Esau, who live in Seir, by destroying the Horim before them so that they could dispossess them and settle in their place'. The Lord continues: 'Proceed on your journey and cross the Wadi Arnon. See, I have handed over to you King Sihon the Amorite of Heshbon, and his land. Begin to take possession by engaging him in battle.' Cf. Deut 2: 18–22, 24.

[292] Deut 2: 25†.

how the war against king Sihon had a title of equity and justice, that is, Sihon would not let the people of Israel pass through his lands despite the promise of no damage of any kind, a promise that was kept in the case of the sons of Esau and the Moabites who had permitted the transit. Moses says however: 'But Sihon the king of Heshbon would not let us pass by him; for the Lord your God hardened his spirit and made his heart obstinate, that he might give him into your hand, as at this day.'[293]

715. If God had wanted to use only his power to make these events happen, there was no need for the Hebrew's enemies to be seized by fear, which is an effect of nature, or for the king of Heshbon to obstinately deny the transit over his lands, which also can be a free, natural disposition. But God, who orders second causes with infinite wisdom, had so disposed these causes that the terror and the obstinacy took place at the due time and thus justly made Israel conquerors. The people who through their corruption no longer produced the universal good that God wishes to draw from the creature, were destroyed at the hands of Israel. Hence, when the old and new faithful gave and still give God the title 'Lord of hosts'[294] or when they said he 'fought for Israel'[295] they did not mean that he always worked miracles but rather that he assured victory for Israel through the second causes that are in his power from the beginning, and whose series he disposes so that they carry out his will with totally certain success. Hence, all the effects of the second causes were very correctly referred to God, as to the first cause, and he alone was glorified by them.

716. To clarify better the *law of antagonism*, we must examine the reason for the factual opposition and hostility manifested by the creature. It must be sought in the essence itself of contingent being.

Contingent being is real, but through intuition shares in ideal being. Real contingent being is finite, while ideal being is infinite. The antagonism is therefore the struggle between the finite

[293] Deut 2: 30–31.

[294] 1 Sam 1: 3.

[295] Deut 3: 22; Josh 10: 14, 42; 23: 10; Judg 9: 17; 2 Chron 20: 29; Jdt 5: 16; Wis 5: 20; Is 51: 22.

and the infinite. I have already given an indication of this very important truth, but must explain it better.

717. Real being has three acts, its own and two others that arise in it through ideal being that is added to it; they are the intellective act and the volitive act.

Real being is contingent being as presented to our perception. Considered solely in its own act, it has three modes: 1. extension or space, 2. corporeal matter, 3. feeling.

718. Extension or space presents itself as immutable and hence incapable of antagonism.

719. Corporeal matter seems indifferent to every state of union or separation because it contains no reason for its movement. Hence, if we conceive union as natural to matter and give it a continuous tendency to be totally united, this concept itself means we have added something to it that does not pertain to it. What we have added pertains, strictly speaking, to feeling, which is the manifest cause of movement in matter. Nor is it valid to say that this way of conceiving matter strips it of its forces and therefore annihilates it. It can in fact exist when helped by forces other than its own, which are precisely those of corporeal feeling. The only consequence (which is neither absurd nor improbable) that we can draw from this concept of matter is that, on its own, it is not a complete substance but, in order to subsist, needs to have some other principle joined to it. Therefore this concept of simple matter contains no antagonism.

720. Antagonism begins to show itself in the animal sensitive principle. This principle truly tends to individuate itself and form an organism, settling itself in the easiest and most pleasurable mode. Hence, there is a struggle between itself and matter, or better, between the diverse individualities to which feeling unites itself wherever it finds occasion, because each individuality tends to constitute itself in the most perfect mode, taking matter to itself and absorbing other feelings. This continuous activity on the part of feeling is the source of the movements of the world, the combination of forms, their disintegration and renewal, and a universal effort by all struggling nature to organise and disorganise.

721. It is here that a necessary struggle truly appears. And without the intervention of an outside force, that is, an intellective force, I do not know whether this struggle could

ever end, could ever establish a state of nature in which feeling, organised and united into perfect individuality, would form one great animal of all matter. But even if feeling could attain this state of peace, it is certainly not ordered to it because it is not on its own and does not have within it an end but must serve intelligences, which are many and multiple.

722. Hence, even the antagonism present in the order of animality does not finish in animality, nor is its reason founded in animality but in the intelligences to which it is ordered. The multitude of these intelligences, destined to use a corporeal feeling (as in the case of human intelligences), requires many individuations of feeling. As soon as feeling is obliged to be constituted in many animal individuals, it is already divided and finds itself in a necessary state of combat and struggle with itself. Thus, divine wisdom remains fully justified relative to the conflict between various individual sentient principles and relative to the conflict resulting from the material world. We are left therefore with only the conflict seen in the order of intelligences to be discussed, for which the conflict in animality becomes a condition and instrument.

723. This verifies what I said, that the antagonism from which God draws his great glory is a struggle between the finite and the infinite. I will explain this concept better.

We are each a finite real being that intuits the essence of being, and this essence has no confines. With this intuition we are equipped for knowing every being. But we can either will or not will, love or not love, known being. This faculty makes us moral because moral good consists 'in willing and loving the essence of being, and hence *all being*, without exclusion of any kind.' If the nature of moral good requires us to will and love all being, it also requires us to love every particular being in proportion to the essence of being that it shares in. This proportioned distribution of our esteem and love is the sum of moral duties. We are therefore perfect in proportion to the extent we maintain and love this distribution. But to maintain this just proportion sometimes costs us effort and suffering, which entails struggle and sacrifice. The greater our moral perfection and merit, the greater the cost to us in the effort and labour with which we will and love every ens in proportion to the essence of being. Clearly therefore, no supreme moral perfection can be conceived in the human being without conflict, indeed a terrible conflict, more terrible and ruthless than we can imagine.

724. Our esteem and affection for all entia therefore must be distributed in proportion to entia's participation in the essence of being. But why must this distribution cost us effort and suffering?

The reason is not morality as such but our LIMITATION.

We are finite but we have the infinite (the essence of being) as the object of morality. Consequently, we have to make an unceasing effort to extend our limitation, opening ourselves to the infinite. This effort by finite being to make itself equal to the infinite is very demanding indeed, because it entails a kind of disruption of itself, of breaking out in some way of the limits in which created ens is enclosed. These limits, because natural to finite being, are loved by finite being, which therefore naturally shrinks from exceeding them. If it exceeds them it sees itself as losing its individuality and, as it were, annihilating itself, allowing itself to fall into and be absorbed by the infinite. But we have here the great act of Christian HUMILITY, the continual and voluntary annihilation of self before the infinite. Eastern philosophy however abused this great truth; it changed voluntary, *moral annihilation* into *real annihilation*. According to it, supreme perfection and happiness consisted in the absorption of created entia into God together with the total loss of all their individuality.[296] Although such an error seems monstrous, it is a truth in disguise: it witnesses to the approval given involuntarily by wise but mistaken people to the Christian teaching about the humility of the creature towards the Creator.

725. This is even more obvious if we consider that we naturally operate with our practical understanding, that is, with our will, which assents and adheres to the entia that the intellect presents to it, and as I said, the will is good and perfect when it adheres to them according to the proportion of entity. Therefore, our operations cannot be good if they do not come from

[296] 'Thus, man who acknowledges in his soul the supreme soul that is present in all creatures, shows himself the same to all, and obtains the very happy outcome of being finally absorbed into Brahma' (*Manava-Dharma-Sastra*, 12: 125). The teaching about the *absorption* of reality is a consequence of the teaching of *emanation*.

the will and conform to it. But human understanding does not know all entia in the same way, although it knows the entitative essence of them all. It knows some as present and acting on its feeling; others have already been perceived by feeling, and it knows these remotely through imagination or simple memory; others, which it neither perceives in the present nor has perceived in the past, are either only intuited, as is the case with the essence of ens (ideal knowledge), or else induced through reasoning, that is, their existence is induced and determined solely by relationships and nothing more (negative-ideal-inductive knowledge). I said that if all the entia that we must will and love were known in the same way, it would be easy for us to make our affection and operation proportionate to the degree of entity they possess; we would thus be operating according to moral exigency. However the opposite happens: we are moved more by some entia than others, not because of their greater entity, which constitutes the *moral norm*, but because of the different way we know them. This explains the effort we have to make to use them according to the degree of their entity, and ignore the stronger movement they produce in us due to the way we know them. Hence there is struggle. I will give some examples.

Human essence is in itself equal, and is the same in every human being. We therefore owe to others a respect and love equal in kind to the love we have for ourselves. This is the norm for our operation. But we know ourselves through an intimate, essential feeling, and know others through an external perception and imagination. The way in which we know ourselves moves us to operate much more in our own favour than in the favour of others. Therefore we are often tempted to prefer unduly ourselves to others, which is contrary to the norm of morality: we love ourselves as end, and other people as means, which is a different kind of love. Hence, in order to be virtuous we have to struggle and conquer this temptation.

The moral law that imposes on us love for all entia, first tells us not to do them any evil because love knows nothing of evil. It next tells us to do good to them in proportion to the love we should have for them, giving this love in proportion to their essential entity. The whole moral law reduces to these two precepts, one negative, the other positive.

[725]

Beginning with the first (the duty of justice), let us see how on many occasions and due to our human limitation it cannot be fulfilled without a struggle.

It may happen that I suffer a pain, for example hunger, or suffer a danger, like death, but can avoid the pain by causing it directly in another (by stealing his food let us say) or can escape the danger of death by killing an innocent person, then I will not remain innocent unless I struggle with the hunger or submit to death. I am certainly not obliged to do an evil to myself, indeed I am obliged to do no evil to anyone no matter whom, whether myself or others. But precisely for this reason, when some evil happens to me and I cannot avoid it without doing an evil to another, I must calmly accept the evil because the moral law is universal and says: 'Do not make yourself the author of evil.' This struggle, which virtue must often undertake, is clearly the result of human LIMITATION: I perceive myself more vividly than I do other beings because I am a *limited reality*. But the law of morality requires me to direct my action to esteem and love *every ens according to its essence*, in whatever way I know it and provided I know it.

The positive precept says: do good. This becomes obligatory if doing good is understood as working to remove evil from intelligent beings (duty of charity).

I see my country in danger, and the only way I can defend it is by exposing myself to death. If I give my love to things in proportion to the quantity of entity they have, I must prefer my country to my life. But my reality seeks refuge from fulfilling such a demanding duty because my reality is LIMITED. If the reality of all my fellow citizens were my reality, I would have the overall instinct of such reality, and it would cost me nothing, indeed I could at least sacrifice a portion of it, that is, myself, for the preservation of the larger reality, the reality of my fellow citizens, to which the same instinct would certainly lead me. But because I am moved by the feeling and instinct of my individual reality alone, it makes me seek refuge from the exigency of the moral law. The moral law however takes no account of this limitation; it says absolutely, 'In your esteem, love and undertaking prefer the greater entity to the lesser; sacrifice yourself for your country.' This law is exacting, and once again requires struggle, sacrifice.

[725]

726. I said that this moral struggle is always a struggle between the finite and the infinite. This is true even when the larger entity, which I must prefer to my reality, is finite, as in the case where I must offer myself for my country. The law that says, 'Prefer the larger entity to the lesser', is only a consequence of the other preceding law that decrees: 'Acknowledge the essence of being', where the essence is infinite. The respect owed to this infinite essence is the ultimate reason for every moral law, for every moral obligation; it is the essence of morality, even though the infinite essence is respected in the real ens that participates in it in a finite mode.

727. But the moral struggle between the finite and the infinite stands out much more clearly if the object of moral duty is directly the essence itself of being, either the ideal or realised essence.

728. Fidelity to promises and truthfulness are duties whose direct object is the essence (of being) intuited in the idea. Sometimes these can be satisfied without the loss of one's life.

729. The fully realised essence of being is God. Duties to God therefore deal with subsistent being, which not even in its reality admits confines. Hence, the respect owed to this being tolerates no comparison with the respect we owe to our own reality, which is nothing compared to the divine reality. The result is the necessity to honour God and carry out the divine will always and at whatever cost, at the cost of all sufferings, of death itself. If we fail in such a clear duty, we lose our personal perfection and make ourselves morally perverse. Moreover, the LIMITATION of the reality that constitutes the human being is the necessary occasion of moral struggle, of that struggle which obliges the finite to break out of its own environment in order to extend into the infinite that is communicated to the intellect, and thus share in infinite good, which moral good always is by its very nature.

730. This perfection is manifestly greater in proportion to the act and effort we make to acquire it. Hence, without antagonism, supreme moral perfection for us could not have been posited in being. But God's goodness is infinite, and as such tends to draw from the creature ALL the moral good it can give. Thus it was fitting to divine wisdom and goodness to give such an order to created things that in them and through them MAXIMUM

ANTAGONISM had to develop as an indispensable means for THEIR MAXIMUM MORAL PERFECTION.

731. Everything therefore had to conspire against the virtue of the creature, and the creature's virtue had to triumph: the infinite in the creature had to conquer ALL THE FINITE. Such is the triumph of the Creator's wisdom and goodness; such THE GLORY OF GOD.

732. In order that the antagonism might act with maximum force, the opposition of the warring parts had to be maximum. But the opposition could not be maximum if it were individual. Consequently, there had to be an organised opposition, of many things, many persons working together against virtue.

733. On the other hand, virtue and moral good are individual. But because the creature had to have a force capable of repelling organised opposition, a defence of virtue had to be organised; many things and many persons had to unite in favour of virtue.

734. Therefore *two societies* on earth, one composed of those whom Scripture calls 'sons of God', the other, of those whom Scripture calls 'sons of men': two cities, the city of God and the city of the devil. As soon as human beings multiplied, these two cities appeared distinct and hostile, and they fight each other onto death until the end of time. They supplied a sublime argument for St. Augustine, who took the name of his immortal work from the name of the better city.

735. The divine Scriptures describe how all kings and nations conspire against the Christ of God. Thus in the psalms: 'Why do the nations conspire, and the peoples plot in vain? The kings of the earth set themselves, and the rulers take counsel together, against the Lord and his anointed, saying, "Let us burst their bonds asunder, and cast their cords from us."'[297]

They also describe all the kings and nations who favour the Christ of God: 'May all kings fall down before him, all nations give him service.'[298]

All kings and all nations therefore belong to the city of the devil, and all kings and nations belong to the city of God — what extraordinary antagonism! What a conflict! It seems we can say that God will probably allow powerful enemies of his

[297] Ps 2: 1–3.

[298] Ps 72: 11.

kingdom to arise from all royal lines, and that in all nations there will be periods of corruption and wickedness to the extent that everything is against good. But we can also say that faithful servants of the Lord will come from all the royal lines, and that periods of virtue and piety will be found in all the nations, so that everything may favour good.[299] Thus, good will finally triumph over evil with a tremendous and unexpected victory.

736. It is indeed written that God will mock his enemies and 'shall bring all the nations to nothing,'*[300] humbling their pride and wickedness when they seemed more certain of victory. Again, Scripture says, predicting the empire of Jesus Christ,:

> He who sits in the heavens laughs; the Lord has them in derision. Then he will speak to them in his wrath, and terrify them in his fury, saying, 'I have set my king on Zion, my holy hill.' I will tell of the decree of the Lord: He said to me, 'You are my son, today I have begotten you. Ask of me, and I will make the nations your heritage, and the ends of the earth your possession. You shall break them with a rod of iron, and dash them in pieces like a potter's vessel.' Now therefore, O kings, be wise; be warned, O rulers of the earth. Serve the Lord with fear, with trembling. Adore the Son, lest he be angry, and you perish in the way.'[301]

He says he will annihilate the nations in order to recreate them; he will rule them with a rod of iron, and break them in pieces like a potter's vessel. He does this however to make them vessels of honour, ornaments of his royal palace. Thus we see the most famous idolatrous kingdoms fallen, ancient nations destroyed, and the world continuously renewed by the Gospel, that fulfils the longings of the human heart. Hence, Christ is called 'the hope of all the ends of the earth and of the farthest seas.'[302]

737. Here again we can consider a new reason why this immense antagonism was necessary so that divine wisdom

[299] We see here a reason why Scripture speaks about both the part and the whole, according to St. Augustine's observation, *Ep*. 149: 20.

[300] 'But you, O Lord, shall laugh at them: *you shall bring all the nations to nothing*'* (Ps 58: 9†).

[301] Ps 2: 4–12†. ['Adore the Son' in Rosmini's quotation reads 'kiss his feet' in the RSV].

[302] Ps 64: 5.

could draw all possible good from its creatures. This victory of the principle of good (the infinite) over the principle of evil (limitation) has an effect in creatures who are the fortunate object of the victory, and in whom the principle of good conquers. The victory causes a feeling of infinite gratitude to, and exultation in, the sovereign Lord, to whose wisdom and goodness alone the victory is owed. In fact those who are seen to pass from evil-living to justice, from deserved punishment to promised reward, cherish an acknowledgement and an infinite joy. These very fortunate creatures enjoy not only the good they have but draw pleasure from comparing this good with the evil they had. The memory and sight of this evil brings intensely before them the grace they have received and gives them a full appreciation of the grace. Lacking righteousness, they received this grace without any merit on their part; they were given it by God, when he used his great wisdom and power in their favour, the same wisdom and power that he applies to the government of the world and was totally necessary for the salvation of each individual. This exultant gratitude becomes infinite matter for those canticles that divine Scripture puts in the mouth of the good, or are the faithful expression of their intimate feelings. They say to themselves: 'He does not deal with us according to our sins, nor requite us according to our iniquities. For as the heavens are high above the earth' (these are the extremes), 'so great is his steadfast love toward those who fear him; as far as the east is from the west, so far he removes our transgressions from us. As a father has compassion for his children, so the Lord has compassion for those who fear him.'[303] Other warm praises (of moral value for those who pronounce them) are proclaimed. Such praise would not have been in their souls if they had had no clear information and painful experience of the misery from which the kindness of the Creator raises man. Moreover, because this transition from evil to good with which the whole race is united brings with it such great knowledge of divine goodness and such great rejoicing, we read that Mount Sion, the city of the great king, is founded amid the exultation and joy of all the earth.[304]

[303] Ps 103: 10–13.

[304] Ps 48: 2.

[737]

738. A deeper investigation of the intimate nature of this tremendous conflict, this unbounded antagonism between the infinite and the finite, will make us more aware of the greatness of God's goodness.

We have, on the one hand, nature, which is contingent and a limited reality. This limited reality is a limited substantial feeling, which has limited instincts and limited principles of action. These all tend to the limited good which a limited reality is capable of.

On the other hand, there is the unlimited moral law, the essence of being that shines before minds and has no confines; there is an unlimited real being, God.

The fact that limited nature tends to its own limited good is not a disorder; on the contrary it is a law of nature. But that it should prefer to esteem and love its limited self as it is and not the unlimited being that is made known to it, this is disorder, injustice, an outrage against the infinite.

This kind of collision between the finite and the infinite was not in itself necessary, because we can easily conceive the possibility of harmony and peace between the finite (as created nature is) and the infinite (which is manifested to created nature).

But God wished to act in another way, a way more fitting to his infinite wisdom and goodness. He disposed things in such an order that moral virtue might conquer the greatest temptations, and that the infinite might thus conquer the whole of the finite, and the creator receive maximum glory from creation.

To obtain this end it was necessary to permit sin for the following reasons:

1. Without sin the creature could not develop through all its possible states, because the eternal idea contained virtually not only the creature's *limitation* and *deficiency*, but its *fall* with all the degrees of wretchedness through which it descends.

2. In the intelligent creature, sin left a state of malice and disorder, and hence of moral impotency. As a result the struggle of sinful nature with vice became very difficult, indeed disproportionate, to the point that it could no longer conquer with its own forces. Therefore the salvation of the creature required God to give extraordinary help. And his direct intervention found a sufficient reason for this because, without

his intervention, the creature could no longer give the maximum fruit for which God had drawn the creature out of nothing.

739. Nevertheless, at the same time as the creature, strengthened by such great help, produced all the fruit it could, all the glory was God's alone; only he, with his extraordinary intervention, drew this great good from the creature who had fallen and become powerless. Hence St. Bernard, agreeing with the whole of ecclesiastical tradition, writes:

> You ask where are our merits or where is our hope? I reply: 'He has saved us according to his mercy, not through the works of righteousness that we may have done.'[305] Did you perhaps think that you yourself created your merits, that you could save yourself with your righteousness, you who cannot say 'Lord JESUS' except in the Holy Spirit?[306] Are you forgetting who he is who said, 'Without me you can do nothing',[307] and 'It is not the one who runs nor the one who wills but God who has mercy'?[308]

St. Augustine glorifies the Redeemer's grace as superior to the grace given to Adam; according to him, the Redeemer's grace showed itself very powerful by drawing good from wicked man: 'Hence, these' (fallen human beings) 'need a more powerful grace, although now' (that is, in this life) 'not a happier grace.'*[309] When humanity had fallen, the Word of God had to put himself at the head of the battle that man had lost, and under this captain the victory was no longer in doubt. However we should note that if God actually intervened in the conflict, he did not intervene in a way that destroyed the forces of the adversaries which sin had so greatly increased. On the contrary, wishing to conquer these forces in regular conflict, he let them keep all their strength. As a result, the struggle was enormous, and the antagonism we are talking about was greatest. God certainly did not wish to conquer by annihilating the opposing

[305] Tit 3: 5.

[306] 1 Cor 12: 3.

[307] Jn 15: 5.

[308] *De gratia et libero arbitrio*, n. 1.

[309] *L. De Correptione et gratia*, n. 30.

forces, as he could well have done, but solely by adding a divine force to those people who would fight for justice, that is, he added his Word to conquered humanity, to whom he have grace of the Word.[310] For the rest he left the forces of opposition intact. These forces are: the devil and his principality in the world (hence he is banished only after a just victory), the stimulus of the flesh, the inclination to evil, disordered nature (no longer in harmony with virtue), death and all the other penal consequences of sin that test us to the extreme even when we are united to the Word or the grace of the Word. All this was necessary so that the invincible strength of divine grace might shine forth. St. Augustine says:[311]

> What grace is more powerful than that of the only begotten Son of God, equal and co-eternal to the Father, made man for them (sinners), without any sin whatsoever whether original or personal, and crucified by sinful human beings? Although he rose the third day, no more to die, he underwent death for mortal beings, he who gives life to the guilty so that after they had been redeemed by his blood and received such a wonderful pledge, they could say, 'If God is for us, who is against us? He who did not withhold his own Son, but gave him up for all of us, will he not with him also give us everything else?'[312]

740. We see therefore that although a great number of victories come only from God, God nevertheless fights with and in us; it is still we, in the hands of God, who produce much fruit. St. Augustine says: 'And (human beings) receive so much freedom through this grace (of the Saviour) that although they battle on earth against the concupiscences of sins, and fall into some sins, for which they say, "Forgive us our debts", they are no longer slaves to mortal sin.'[313] This new force of free will, this

[310] See *Dottrina del peccato originale*, quest. 5, concerning how the justification of human beings through Jesus Christ is not brought about by the destruction of something in them but by the addition of a new supernatural principle of operation, superior to the other principles of natural operation.

[311] Rom 8: 31–32.

[312] *L. De Correptione et gratia*, n. 12: 35.

[313] Ibid.

greater freedom acquired by redeemed sinners from Christ, is seen in the greater battle they have to win in order to obtain the greater victory — as St. Augustine says: 'A greater freedom is certainly necessary against such great and serious temptations, which were not in Eden, a freedom fortified and strengthened by the gift of perseverance, in order that this world with all its loves, terrors and errors may be conquered.'[314] Augustine continually glorifies the valour and merit of redeemed sinners, particularly of martyrs, over and above the valour of the innocent first human being:

> Finally he whom no one threatened but who used his free will to thwart the command of God who threatened him, did not maintain himself in such a happy state, in such great ease of not sinning. Redeemed sinners however remained faithful, although in this case the world was not content simply to threaten them but acted cruelly against their constancy. The first human being saw the present goods he had to abandon;, the redeemed did not see the future goods they were to receive. This was solely by the gift of him from whom they obtained the mercy to remain faithful; they had a spirit not of fear that could make them give in to the persecutors, but of courage, charity and continence, which could make them overcome all threats, all invitations, all torments. Although the one who was immune from all sin was given a free will with which he was created, he made it serve sin. But the will of the one who was already a slave of sin, was freed through him who said:[315] 'So if the Son makes you free, you will be free indeed.'[316]

741. At this point we need to consider again (and never enough) that the human race had fallen into sin and been raised from abject wretchedness to the eternal kingdom and that in this tremendous transition which it had to make from one extreme to the other (extremes separated by an immense chaos), it experiences sensibly its own nothingness and also the greatness and goodness of its Creator.

[314] Ibid., n. 35.

[315] Jn 8: 36.

[316] *L. De Correptione et gratia*, n. 35.

The moral perfection of the human race lies in an intensely vivid knowledge of this greatness and goodness of God because, as I said, perfection consists in the *practical acknowledgement of God*. Hence, I repeat: we are a potency,[317] and our perfection consists in act. The act is as great as its *extent*, that is, as the distance between its starting point and the point it attains and to which it leads. The most extended act of which we can be the subject therefore moves from the extreme of moral evil to the extreme of good, and the greater and more rapid this transition, the more we know and feel God who, as good and powerful, makes us, who are wicked and inept, undertake the transition.

742. Furthermore, the value of the moral act is proportionate to its *intensity*, and it is made intense through lively combat. At the time of the institution of the human race this combat could not have been great or difficult because God could not be the author of evil or create a nature opposed to virtue. On the contrary he had to dispose everything in favour of, and therefore for the easy acquisition of, virtue. As a result opposition could originate only from the free will with which the created ens could sin. Divine wisdom and goodness permitted sin therefore in order to allow the tremendous opposition to be the occasion of God's power in us for a great victory. The opposition originated from sin in the following way. Justice required crime to be punished. Granted therefore the crime of the creature, God had to permit the cessation of the harmony he had placed between real, intellectual and moral being; he had to allow being, under these three forms, to clash disastrously with itself and, by causing itself great pain and affliction, be punished for its free rebellion. Therefore, the penal consequences of sin, in accord with divine justice and ordered to good by a most wise Providence, generated the intimate struggle in nature. St. Paul most fittingly compares this nature to a woman in childbirth crying out in pain. This similitude is very apt because it shows correctly that the stress suffered by the whole of nature is not destined to a sad outcome, rather it is ordered by God to good, just as birth accompanied by such harsh pains is followed by the joy over the newborn child. St. Paul says:

[317] *SP*, 545–573.

> For the creation was subjected to futility, not of its own will but by the will of the one who subjected it, in hope that the creation itself will be set free from its bondage to decay and will obtain the freedom of the glory of the children of God. We know that the whole creation has been groaning in labour pains until now; and not only the creation, but we ourselves, who have the first fruits of the Spirit, groan inwardly while we wait for adoption, the redemption of our bodies.[318]

After describing the battle we see in the broken order of nature, the Apostle says that this struggle remains even in those redeemed and justified by Christ. The cause of this struggle is the corruption of the body and the natural will of the flesh, which are the consequences of sin. They desire what is contrary to the spirit, that is, contrary to the supernatural principle which is the apex of the human spirit, the saved personhood, the new man, the new creature, whose task is to fight and conquer the old man.

743. This supernatural will and activity, engendered in us by the grace and power of Christ, is what Christ placed as opposition to damaged, disordered nature. In fact, if Christ had not created this new active principle in us, the combat was already over, because human power had been overcome and spent — we were lost people, prisoners, dead for ever. Thus two terrible enemies were born who clashed in atrocious and ferocious battle: nature with its free perversion that God has permitted originated the power of evil; God produced the power of good, which is his incarnate Word together with the grace of his Word infused into the souls of human beings. Here it produces insuperable force capable of sustaining the combat with a sure outcome. A maximum antagonism was thus made possible, and the most glorious of victories assured.[319]

744. A consideration of this great plan of divine Providence shows that it was the only one corresponding to an infinite wisdom and goodness that wills to draw all possible moral good from the creature and spur it on to the greatest moral perfection

[318] Rom 8: 20–23.

[319] In *Society and its Purpose* I explained how Christian nations resist the greatest temptations without suffering corruption. Cf. *SP*, 715–741.

that can be obtained with the least means. Maximum moral perfection, to which maximum happiness is always joined, consists (to repeat again) only in the maximum practical knowledge of God as good, and the goodness of God is known only by its act, and the act is known by experience. In order that the greatest knowledge of God might be given to the intelligent creature, by which in loving God freely it could sanctify and perfect itself, it had to be made to feel the greatest act of divine goodness, and to place all hope and love in this goodness as in its only good. Consequently, it had to be given a way of comparing the good it could receive from God with the good it could have in itself or in the universe of contingent natures. To make this comparison profitably, we cannot conceive anything better than God's plan. We all feel the total deficiency and nothingness of our fruitless and helpless nature, and even rear up in rebellion against moral good and human perfection. At the same time we do not see in ourselves, or in any other part of creation, a single ray of hope for our moral salvation — on the contrary we experience ourselves as an enemy of ourselves; all entia are enemies of our virtue, enemies if they make us suffer, enemies even more if they praise us. But while lost and without comfort in this state, we again see God coming towards us and, as a loving Father, saying, 'See! I am your salvation.'

It is true that as long as we were laid low in evil we did not even know our state sufficiently; we were so numbed that we let our enemies seduce us; we were their slaves and even trusted in them. But as soon as we were raised from such an abyss and from death, our heart changed so that we knew our previous, desperate state and also our very fortunate, present state. Hence, people who are fortunate enough to make this great transition still have engraved on their souls their past woes but also their present goods in which they see themselves gratuitously blessed; they must therefore experience an ineffable admiration for divine goodness. And after they have removed every disordered affection they have for finite natures, to which they were subjected by an irreparable disaster, they rightly place all their affection in the Creator and Saviour to whom they are indebted for such a great liberation from evil and for such a great abundance of good. God is the one and only Saviour of the creature — this is the great concept that had to be revealed to intelligent

[744]

creatures through experience. It alone could furnish the matter for the greatest love, the greatest perfection and the most perfect hymn of glory to the supreme Being.

745. Thus, through the sin permitted by God, the finite being became the adversary of good, a power fighting for evil. The only power that was fighting evil in favour of good was the infinite being, God. Isaiah's words were now completely fulfilled: 'The Lord ALONE shall be exalted.'[320] But because this exaltation directed only to God was lost relative to the great salvation of the creature, God acted as a power of good in favour of the human race: he united himself to the human race in the incarnation. Thus the Christ became the hero destined to fight the great war. He could therefore say: 'I have trodden the winepress alone; and of the people there was none with me.'[321]

746. Consequently, the only contribution human nature made to its salvation (before it was redeemed and saved by God) was no more than its presenting itself to God as the object to be saved. St. Bernard's observation about free will is relevant here:

> You ask, 'What about free will?' I briefly reply: it is saved. If you remove free will, there is no longer anything to be saved, and if you remove grace, you no longer have the means to save. This task cannot be accomplished without two things: one by which the task is done, the other for whom or in whom it is done. God is the author of salvation; free will is only capable of being saved. Only God can give salvation; free will can only receive it. Hence, what comes from God alone and is given to free will alone cannot lack the consent of the one who receives, just as it cannot be without the grace of him who gives. Thus it is said that free will cooperates by consent with grace that operates, which is the same as saying by being saved, because to consent is to be saved.[322]

Here, free will is understood as the human will that is certainly free to do some natural good, but in itself is incapable of procuring eternal life. Hence, it is saved by God when made capable through Christ.

[320] Is 2: [11].

[321] Ibid., 63: 3.

[322] *De gratia et libero arbitrio*, n. 2.

747. But we need to consider the two great adversaries individually, the two powers that do battle on the stage of the world for as long as the world lasts: the power of evil and the power of good.

The power of evil, I said, is formed by the whole of finite being after its fall from the first order of things that the Creator had given it. The finite being susceptible of moral evil is the being that has intellect and will. We know two kinds: angels and human beings. God permitted both to sin so that the power hostile to good might be greatest.

748. The transgressing angels became demons, and we can believe (granted the law of variety) that as many fell as there are degrees of the evil that angelic nature is capable of. Similarly, just as many remained faithful as there are degrees of good their nature is capable of. The power of evil therefore began with the demons.

749. Later the devil seduced man, winning a first battle as it were, and thus damaged human nature. But whereas a part of angelic nature had kept itself incorrupt, the damage to human nature was such that it had to propagate itself to all the individuals of the race, except one, the predestined restorer.[323] From that moment human nature became the object of the most terrible war between God and the devil. Humanity, which the devil wished to draw to himself and thus strengthen the power of evil, would be saved by God and, after acting as the field of battle for the two adversaries, would become the trophy of divine victory. It was inferior to all other intelligent creatures; it was weak, mortal and obliged to extract the basic matter of its knowledge from bodies. Nevertheless, from eternity God had decreed to raise humanity by his omnipotent goodness and grace above all nobler creatures, including all the angelic intelligences, even to making it sit on the throne with himself and be adored by the whole of creation. According to this divine concept, all the most sublime creatures were to bow before it, even adore it.

But before this great plan was carried out, it seems that God showed it to the angelic intelligences, while keeping hidden

[323] The Mother of the Saviour was also *obnoxia peccato* [subject to sin], but preserved from the original stain by the grace of Christ.

from them the way he would carry it out, called in Scripture *mysterium absconditum a saeculis* [the mystery that has been hidden throughout the ages — Col 1: 26]. This was to be the expedient used by God's wisdom to raise the angels to maximum moral perfection and hence to their greatest happiness. By revealing to the angels the great mystery before its fulfilment, God offered them the opportunity to raise themselves to the highest knowledge of him and themselves, and to make the greatest act of esteem, love, confidence and faith in their Creator. Hence, by trusting firmly in the divine word, although inexplicable to them, and adhering with all their heart to God's sublime will, they were able to acknowledge the infinite as everything and the finite as nothing in comparison with the infinite; in other words, they were able to acknowledge that, as the finite depended on the infinite, so all the exaltation and happiness of the finite did not come to it by its own forces but depended solely on the free will and power of the infinite. As a result, the finite was obliged not to hope in itself but in its Creator, to whom its forces were no obstacle — he kept the forces intact but did as he pleased with the finite. After the angelic intelligences had been enlightened with the knowledge of such a great truth, and freely adhered to it, they would be able to actually give God all honour and glory; with blind, steadfast faith in the divine word, they could submit to his will and declare themselves ready to humble themselves (even though so sublime in nature) under that human being who in comparison was so small and yet destined from eternity to be made the consort of God himself and to sit on the right of the Father. The maximum glory of God and, simultaneously, the maximum moral perfection of the angelic creature consisted solely in this willing annihilation of the finite creature under the infinite Creator.

750. Some angels, following the instinct of their finite reality, refused to satisfy the moral exigency of infinite being that wanted this humble act. The act would have given them perfection and obtained protection and grace from the Almighty. Hence they fell. Other angels however willingly humbled their finite reality under the decree of the infinite and, annihilating themselves as it were before him, fulfilled their moral duty. Then the infinite, whom they had chosen, took them to himself and made them blessed. With their humble act, they acquired a

maximum practical knowledge of the greatness and goodness of God, who immediately gave himself to them to be perceived and eternally enjoyed.

751. God had thus used this man, this system of the world of humanity, as a kind of sign to reveal his divine attributes, his wisdom, goodness and power, to the angels [*App*., no. 14]. The man, the system, presented the angels with a free choice of either perdition or salvation, according as they acknowledged or did not acknowledge the divine greatness signified and indicated to them in the creation of the human world. That same humanity now became the reason for the great conflict between the rebellious angels and God; they wanted to ruin his plan, using their natural forces to prevent it, the forces in which they had so audaciously trusted when they sinned in the beginning.

752. In Scripture God is very often introduced as taking humanity under the wings of his protection; he saves it from the enemy, and is glorified and proclaimed by this salvation, obtained amid great dangers. Psalm 93 uses the same argument; like other psalms, its language is a very ancient form of speech proper to Scripture and is enigmatic. Instead of mankind, 'earth' is used; instead of the powers of the abyss, 'sea' and 'rivers' are used. This kind of allegory of sea and rivers is constant in Scripture: they rise up, billowing and foaming, against the earth in order to engulf it; God breaks their impetus, placing obligatory limits on the proud sea and defending the land against the onslaught of its waves. The words, although brief, are beautiful and sublime. I quote them here in a plain translation:

> The Lord has reigned, he is clothed in majesty, he is clothed and girded with strength. He has established the earth, and it will not be moved. Your throne, O God, was prepared from of old; you are eternal.
>
> The rivers have risen up, O Lord, the rivers have lifted up their voice. The rivers have lifted up their waves with the roar of many crashing waters.
>
> How wonderful the surging of the sea, how wonderful is the Lord on high! Your testimonies are faithful. O Lord, holiness is fitting to your house for unending days.

753. My interpretation of this psalm is not arbitrary, as can be

seen from the title at the beginning of the Hebrew text. It says that this canticle of praise is for the day preceding the Sabbath, that is, the sixth day of the week when man was formed. The earth, said to be established on that day, is precisely humanity, whose defence God undertakes against the enemies signified by the sea and raging waters,[324] because on the day man was created, the only enemies he had and was to fear were the rebellious angels of God. Hence, the throne that the psalm says was prepared for the Lord from of old is the throne destined for the God-Man by the eternal decree with which God made man. The divine testimonies, called faithful, are precisely this decree, which was to be totally fulfilled in the face of all the tremendous power of the demons. This interpretation receives confirmation and new light from the verse with which the whole psalm concludes. It speaks of the house of God; and its everlasting ornament must be holiness, the purpose of the world. The house of God is humanity, where God came to dwell by becoming incarnate and communicating himself through grace to believers. Thus his chosen society, the Church, is composed of human beings, and fittingly called temple or house of God. The characteristic of this temple is to be holy in order to fulfil the good that God planned when he created man and the world; Solomon's temple was simply a symbol of this house.[325]

754. But because God did not need to use his naked power to conquer the devil but simply oppose him with his wisdom, of which the constant law is the law of the least means, he permitted the devil to do all the evil necessary for drawing every kind of good possible from the forces of the creature, from its development in all senses, from its limitations and from its deficiencies. God permitted the devil to tempt the stock of human nature, to seduce and destroy it. But in the resulting sin and contamination of the whole human race, God reserved for

[324] Ernest Rosenmüller also admits as certain at least the fact that the sea and rivers mentioned in this psalm must not be understood as sea and rivers in a material sense, but as hostile powers: 'The power and terrible onslaught of the enemy is meant, and often huge armies; everything is compared to rivers under the image of flooding waters. Cf. Is 8: 7–8; 17: 12–13; Jer 45:7–8.'* And he notes: 'Virgil used similar imagery to describe the invading army of the Greeks, in the Aeneid, 2: 494ss.'* (Scholia in h. 1).

[325] The same argument is found in Psalm 24.

himself a daughter, guaranteeing and protecting her from all original contamination.[326] From her blood, without human intervention, a human being would be generated, who was also God. This God-Man was to restore humanity abundantly, and thus conquer and confound the devil. This was also necessary through the *law of variety*, which required this form of excellence in the human species.

The Son of the Virgin was therefore the one in whom humanity attained the apex of its greatness and magnificence, indissolubly united to God with the maximum bond of possibles, as the personal bond is. This single individual was superabundantly sufficient to redeem all his fellows, other human beings, from the hands of the enemy, raising them from the depths to any degree whatsoever of moral perfection. Consequently, it was necessary that he was in the human race both through the *law of the least means*[327] and by the law of *excluded equality*.

755. The result of all this was the great individual of the human species who was to be at the summit of all those in whom the species would be propagated, indeed he was to be the summit of creation. Linked to the Creator by a bond of personal union, he was the realisation of not only the *archetype of humanity* but of *deified humanity*. Thus, man, who is lower than all other intelligent beings, indeed flesh, which is the lower element in humanity, is elevated to such a great dignity as to be justly and necessarily adored by all angelic intelligences, *ET VERBUM CARO FACTUM EST* [AND THE WORD WAS MADE FLESH]. This followed the ancient divine decree which at the constitution of the world had been a scandal for the transgressing angels and an occasion of

[326] Because the distortion of the will, which constitutes original sin, arose from the harm done to generated flesh, God could have disposed the natural causes of generation in such a way that at a fixed time an individual might be born without the physical contamination that constitutes the proximate and efficient cause of moral contamination. He was able to raise this individual from the lowest level to any degree whatsoever of moral perfection. It was entirely a most singular grace, which means that this individual was also *peccato obnoxius* [subject to sin], as I said earlier.

[327] St. Thomas gives this reason: 'It pertains to the shortest path followed by the wise operator that he does not use many things to do what can be done by one. Hence, it was most fitting that all human beings were saved through one human being'* (*S.T.*, III, q. 4, art. 5, ad 3).

moral perfection of unending beatitude for the faithful angels. Thus the demons, who had not believed in the mystery so repugnant to their pride, saw the mystery unveiled and fulfilled, as God had told them. But they themselves had cooperated in bringing it about more fully and gloriously by the very means with which they thought they had thwarted and prevented it, that is, by the seduction of the first human being and the poisoning of the source of life, of the generative principle.

756. But humanity needed to develop in every respect, from the highest to the lowest and in all its varieties, as the law of wisdom required. After its head had been established and made master of the universe; after the CHRIST had been realised, who was a divine person, raised up to God whose nature he enjoyed as his own, it was necessary for every full species without exception, that is, all the types contained in humanity's essence, to be realised. This required on the one hand a tremendous series of human individuals who corresponded to the types of good, and on the other a tremendous series of human individuals corresponding to the types of evil, this latter in the service of and for the glory of the former.

757. The individuals destined to correspond to the types of good had to be taken from the corrupt mass in virtue of Christ and made vessels of election. The individuals destined to correspond to the types of evil had to be the work of the devil and of themselves. This was not willed by God but simply permitted, so that the devil and his own, although deceived, might contribute to the production of the maximum good that had to result from creation with the least intervention by God.

758. But how could Christ communicate a part of his holiness to other human beings whose sin had made them useless? The obstacle to his carrying out this act was justice, of which the eternal law is:, 'The total of moral evil must be balanced by eudaimonological evil.' Hence, any created will that preferred the good of its own finite reality to the moral demands of the infinite, must find in its own reality a suffering that equals the amount of satisfaction it sought in itself. Christ himself therefore took on the payment of the great debt of human nature and, having profitably paid it, was able to save all those human beings who were more fitting to receive his supreme goodness.

759. But in order to expedite this payment owed to eternal

justice, the power of evil was again used, that is, the power of the devil and of those human beings whom God permitted to be added to the devil's cause. This is another example of the good God draws from evil and from the necessity of antagonism in order to obtain the greatest good with the least intervention on his part, while allowing the creature to do as much as possible. He permitted the devil and the human beings allied to him to put the CHRIST to death. Christ could not be seduced, as Adam could be, but he could die if he willed it. Hence he said in the garden: 'Do you think that I cannot appeal to my Father, and he will at once send me more than twelve legions of angels?'[328] These words teach many truths. First, the Christ underwent his passion willingly and not through a strict command imposed on him by his Father. In fact, if he had absolutely asked his Father, the Father would have freed him from death, dispatching legions of angels to help him. But he did not want this except on condition that nothing be lost of the maximum good that could come from his death, because 'he savoured the things of God and not those of human beings,'[329] the things of the infinite, not those of the finite. He had already prayed that his chalice might pass him by, *if it were possible*, that is, if its avoidance would lose nothing of the maximum good that could be obtained from creation by using the least means. But the fact that this maximum good could not be obtained without the death of Christ (a calculation incomprehensible to the human mind) was contained in the eternal decree and already recorded in the ancient Scriptures. Thus, Christ added: 'But how then would the scriptures be fulfilled, which say it must happen in this way?',[330] meaning: 'I would ask my Father to send his angels to defend me if I did not know what is recorded in the divine books, that I must die. This clearly means that my death is necessary for the great purpose of infinite goodness that wishes to obtain the maximum good with the minimum means, and to this goodness I fully adhere. This greatest good is the will of my Father, therefore he himself offers me this bitter chalice.[331] This is also my

[328] Mt 26: 53.

[329] Mt 16: 23 [R].

[330] Mt 26: 54.

[331] Jn 18: 11.

[759]

will, because I, as God, will this maximum good that the Father wills, and as man I will this divine will blindly; I do not consider the profound reasons for it, as if I did not know them; it is enough for me to know that my Father's will can be only the best for his purpose, and is in itself adorable. Consequently, if I had made legions of angels intervene in my defence, which the Father would have done if I had requested them unconditionally, all this angelic power would have been wasted because relative to the desired end the least means would not have been used, and hence I would be doing something contrary to eternal wisdom and to my Father's will. I therefore submit myself and prefer the undeserved passion and death. I very willingly let the hostile powers operate against me with their natural forces, and let them win another battle over humanity, and then the Father will be able to convert this momentary defeat into an everlasting victory.'

760. It would indeed be an injustice that a just person should suffer the cruellest death if the person had not accepted it and voluntarily renounced their right. But as accepted by Christ such great suffering, undeservedly received and of infinite value, became credit. The justice of the Father had to pay this credit because a law of eternal justice requires that 'anyone who suffers undeserved suffering should be compensated with equivalent happiness'. And the compensation and joy Christ desired from his Father was the salvation of his brethren, of all human beings. Hence his love for them used its immense credit of justice as the price for cancelling the debt of sinful humanity. In this way the causes were equally balanced, to the great advantage of humanity: the equilibrium ordained by eternal justice between sin and punishment was re-established. With the obstacle removed, humanity could now be restored from all its moral evils through the communication of the grace of the incarnate Word, who was able to communicate himself to every single human being in the measure he wished. This measure was precisely that determined by infinite wisdom and goodness, the measure that fitted the law of the least means. God applied and continues to apply to every human being the quantity of grace which he knows will return him the greatest fruit.

761. Thus Christ could choose all the individuals of the human family that corresponded to the many mansions in his

Father's house;[332] not one would remain empty. These mansions are the types of humanity in which are all the various possible forms of good emanating from the essence of human nature. These forms were distinguished at the beginning in the creative act, in which Christ, even as man, sees them and which is the exemplar shown him according to which he builds up the temple of the Lord with living stones.

762. But below this hierarchy of the predestined, another series of realised human types begins where, at the end of things, there will probably be all the forms that can be assumed by human nature that has been deprived of grace and fallen into evil. These forms of evil may possibly develop with time but not all of them remain until the end of the world: only those will remain as final forms that according to divine calculation are necessary for the greater glory of the saints and, more generally, make the total good of humanity full and overflowing.

763. We must not forget that all these human individuals, who represent the moral evil of which human nature in all its forms and gradations is capable, are in their wretched state due to the action of the devil and of their own free will, not to the action of God. God does no more than permit different degrees of evil and prevent it with varying degrees of his grace, so that in the end there is the variety necessary for the supreme beauty of the world and there is also the greatest fruit the world must produce.

As I have already said, this greatest fruit would not have been obtained without a maximum antagonism. But there could not have been this greatest antagonism without a maximum hostile power, a power composed of the rebellious angelic powers and of humanity seduced and allied with them, or rather servant to them. The only member of this humanity who remained on God's side was a virgin whom the prophets called the rod of Jesse, which was to put forth a flower on which the spirit of the Lord would rest.[333] This rod in flower was all the power for good.

764. It seemed therefore that human nature was very unequally divided between good and evil, having placed itself

[332] Jn 14: 2.

[333] Is 11: 1–2.

totally on the side of evil. But there was one exception, an individual of the weaker sex, who was not of noble family and had no influence in the world. She was not preserved from evil by any natural power of her own but by a disposition of the Creator who wished to make her the starting point of his glory: the glory of the infinite over the finite. When the whole of human nature, with the exception of the poor Virgin of Nazareth, had become utterly useless for producing good, the infinite said: 'Behold I come':[334] I come to draw an infinite good from the finite which has become totally useless. Thus, the Word was made flesh, and the terrible war was engaged, not between the forces of nature but between the natural and the supernatural.

765. The flower that blossomed on Jesse's rod was in itself a product of infinite beauty and value, a human individual raised beyond all human greatness, a GOD-individual. If all the rest of the human species had subsequently been lost, human nature would still have produced most abundant fruit: this by itself was sufficient to guarantee victory over evil. But, as I said, the Christ did more: he saved innumerable human beings by paying their debt abundantly. He in fact saved those whom his Father had given him,[335] to which in the Scriptures the great mystery of predestination refers. Predestination involves calculation of the maximum good, and only the divine mind is capable of this calculation. The Father used it to make the eternal decree in which the Word, who made the same calculation, saw how many blessed and which blessed he would have to draw from the human race in order to reap the maximum from his vineyard, and in seeing these blessed he created them.

766. The God-Man therefore had to give his gifts to human beings in the order that would produce the maximum good. How did he accomplish this great purpose?

He first divided the restoration of human beings, his brethren, into two parts according to the two elements that composed them: 1. the restoration of the *personal element*, and 2. the restoration of the *natural element*.

He then arranged to carry out the double restoration in two periods, very distant from each other according to human

[334] Ps 39: 8†.

[335] Jn 17: 6–24.

reckoning: the restoration of the *human person* takes place as soon as people believe and are baptised, whereas the restoration of *human nature* is accomplished at the end of the world, by the resurrection of the body. In the Scriptures both restorations are called *regeneration*,[336] because in the first the person is regenerated; in the second, human nature, which is constituted by the union of the soul with the body. Clearly, the two restorations or regenerations have a great interval between them, and part of this interval is the present life we lead here on earth. In this life, in which we are regenerated relative to the spirit, we find ourselves united to a damaged, disordered, dead body, that is, a body deserving destruction and death. Hence, for each just person, the battle and antagonism seen as necessary for the perfection of virtue was able to continue; without this battle the moral value of the combatants is not visible, nor a resounding victory gained, nor the most glorious palm won.

767. If the soul had not been regenerated by Christ, and if the supernatural principle, which is the foundation of a new person, had not been created in it, there would have been neither battle nor victory. The champion needed to fight in favour of good and to conquer would have been missing, and the champion is the supernatural principle that struggles against all defective nature. If JESUS Christ had immediately restored both the body and the soul (he could easily have done this with his power), there would still have been no battle because there would have been no adversary. Without the regeneration of the soul, battle was impossible; only the power of evil would have existed. Without the regeneration of the body, battle was impossible because only the power of good would have existed. In both cases, the two adversaries necessary for the struggle would have been absent.

768. The present life is therefore the time of battle for the redeemed *individual*. It is written: 'The life of man upon earth is a warfare.'[337] The duration of the world is the time allotted for the battle for the complex whole of redeemed individuals, for the *city of God*. Hence, Christ likens the kingdom of heaven to the field of wheat in which the enemy sows weeds that war

[336] Mt 19: 28.

[337] Job 7: 1†.

against the wheat and stop it growing. But the owner is aware that the weeds cannot be rooted out without harming the wheat, and therefore commands his servants to wait and collect them at harvest time. Christ says: 'The harvest is the end of the age, and the reapers are angels. Just as the weeds are collected and burned up with fire, so will it be at the end of the age. The SON OF MAN' (the conqueror) 'will send his angels, and they will collect out of his kingdom all causes of sin and all evildoers, and they will throw them into the furnace of fire, where there will be weeping and gnashing of teeth. Then the righteous will shine like the sun in the kingdom of their Father.'[338] The sun is JESUS Christ, and his imitators will be like him.

769. We have discussed the time assigned to the cosmic struggle. Let us now look at the course it can follow.

The following should be borne in mind:

1. God's infinite goodness wanted to raise his creature to the highest degree of moral perfection.

2. This supreme degree lies in the most perfect knowledge of God's goodness, wisdom and power.

3. Such knowledge can be possessed by the creature only by comparing its own nothingness with the whole, which is the Creator, and comparing the whole of the Creator with its own nothingness.

4. God therefore had to give to the creature an opportunity of abasing itself to an infinite degree under him and acknowledging its own nothingness compared to his greatness.

5. He gave the angels this opportunity by revealing to them the mystery of divinised humanity.

6. Some angels, adoring this humanity and willingly abasing themselves, acknowledged the divine greatness, and thus attained that high knowledge in which the summit of moral perfection consists. Others however, trusting in their own nature and not in the power of grace which gave promise of making human nature so great, became unclean demons.

7. Man, seduced by the demons, also trusted in his created nature rather than in God and his word.

8. Finally, this same arrogance was propagated in man's children, except for the virgin MARY, in whom the divine Word

[338] Mt 13: 39–43.

found a pure and spotless dwelling for incarnating himself and thus infusing into humanity a principle of salvation.

We must also remember that the incarnate Word gave human beings 'the power to become children of God.'[339] But because these also had to be raised to that supreme moral perfection to which infinite goodness tends, God wanted them to cooperate in their own salvation. He therefore offered them again the alternatives: either they acknowledged the nothingness of nature in comparison with the Creator and instead of placing all their hope in the finite, placed it totally in the infinite, or they hoped in the finite and adhered to it. He gave them the supernatural power to adhere to the good alternative and instructed them how to do so, and he promised them the good, final outcome. Because this instruction was very necessary for them, he gave them lessons in a wisdom previously unheard of; he said: 'Blessed are the poor in spirit, for theirs is the kingdom of heaven. Blessed are those who mourn, for they will be comforted. Blessed are the meek, for they will inherit the earth. Blessed are those who hunger and thirst for righteousness, for they will be filled. Blessed are the merciful, for they will receive mercy. Blessed are the pure in heart, for they will see God. Blessed are the peacemakers, for they will be called children of God. Blessed are those who are persecuted for righteousness' sake, for theirs is the kingdom of heaven.'[340]

All this meant: 'Blessed are those who consider nature as nothing compared with what is above nature; blessed are those who do not trust in the finite, but in the infinite, who place God before creation so that they consider the creation as nothing relative to God; who know perfectly what God is, compared with what every other contingent being is.' But there is still more meaning.

770. If nature itself had not been damaged by sin, and if human nature, even after regeneration in the spirit, had not been disordered, JESUS Christ would never have said blessed are the poor, because wealth as such is not an evil, nor would he have said blessed are the meek who submit to violence, because the

[339] Jn 1: 12.

[340] Mt 5: 3–10.

use of power in just defence is not an evil, and he would not have said blessed are those who weep, because the smile of pleasure is also certainly not an evil. In the order of incorrupt nature natural goods were meant for human beings; wealth, power, natural pleasure would have been in harmony with their moral virtue, and would certainly not have caused their seduction. Now however, these goods are often an incentive to evil. Furthermore, they have become transient and perishable, just as human nature, abandoned now to death, has itself become transient and perishable. Finally, even if the goods were not seductive, deceptive, perishable, they could never give happiness to the regenerated human being, raised high above the natural order, born of the Holy Spirit and destined to such a great good that whatever the whole of nature can give in compensation is painful. Hence the beatitude of the redeemed sinner is infinitely superior to all created goods. Indeed it is independent of these, so that not even created goods can increase this beatitude, and created evils are the occasion and means for obtaining it in a most full and superabundant measure.

771. For this reason, human beings, thus restored and reborn, were also instructed to mistrust natural good as infected with a fatal poison, according to the words of St. John: 'For all that is in the world, [is] the lust of the flesh and the lust of the eyes and the pride of life… And the world passes away, and the lust of it; but he who does the will of God abides for ever.'[341] We were taught and exhorted to consider such goods to be deceptive pride, because nature is weak and mortal, whereas the supernatural principle gives what nature cannot give, immortality, and immortality means everything to us. 'Brothers and sisters, we are debtors, not to the flesh, to live according to the flesh — for if you live according to the flesh, you will die; but if by the Spirit you put to death the deeds of the body, you will live.'[342] This immortal life that God promises to those who trust only in him and not in nature is most blessed; relative to it any suffering caused by our present corrupt nature is no longer considered suffering: 'I consider that the sufferings of this present time are not worth comparing with the glory about to be revealed to us.

[341] 1 Jn 2: 16–17.

[342] Rom 8: 12–13.

For the creation waits with eager longing for the revealing of the children of God.'[343]

772. This is a truly just reason why God permitted nature to become disordered and lose that admirable harmony it had with moral virtue which at the beginning was served by it. Nature had provided every good necessary for moral virtue and inflicted no evil. But now, by its frequent opposition to virtue, like a rebellious servant, and oppressing virtue with evils rather than delighting it with goods, it makes more prominent than ever the sublime power of virtue, the new virtue grafted on to damaged nature by Christ. It gives more prominence to virtue's independence from the finite, over which the infinite (the source of this conquering virtue) had such a beautiful victory.

773. Such is the teaching given us by the Redeemer. Some have accepted it; others, not. The former, associating themselves with Christ, belonged to the power of good; the latter, associating themselves with the devil, increased the power of evil. Once again God allowed the defection of the latter because he saw this as necessary for producing the greatest good and ultimate triumph.

774. The moral good acquired by those who believed in Christ and followed him was so great that every moral good in the order of nature is annihilated before it. The moral evil of the others who, lacking belief, did not wish to follow Christ, was of immense gravity. Hence it is written that Christ came to put division between us all,[344] that he is set for the ruin and resurrection of many,[345] and that he is the corner stone, and 'the one who falls on this stone will be broken to pieces; and it will crush anyone on whom it falls.'[346] Indeed Christ said: 'If I had not come and spoken to them, they would not have sin; but now they have no excuse for their sin.'[347] They have no excuse because all those to whom the Gospel was preached were offered grace with the Gospel. Due to their evil disposition they refused it, and with

[343] Ibid. 18–19.

[344] Mt 10: 35.

[345] Lk 2: 34†.

[346] Mt 21: 42, 44.

[347] Jn 15: 22.

this refusal 'the thoughts of their hearts were revealed', according to Simeon.[348] Granted therefore their evil disposition, they were not planted by the Father, and 'Every plant,' said Christ, 'that my heavenly Father has not planted will be uprooted.'[349]

775. It is true that because only God must be glorified in every good, even those who believed did not believe through their own power but through a gratuitous gift, through a pure choice made of them from eternity. Isaiah says, 'I was ready to be sought out by those who did not ask, to be found by those who did not seek me.'[350] If God had not arranged the order of their salvation in this way, they could not have known the infinite and essential goodness of God, nor have had the feeling of ineffable gratitude for him that forms their ultimate perfection. Nevertheless those who believed the Gospel had to have some remote disposition for faith, which was perhaps a kind of disenchantment with creatures and a low esteem of their own virtue. The Hebrews lacked this low esteem of themselves, and the lack caused their infidelity: they did not accept the grace of faith in Christ because they trusted their own works, the exterior works of the Mosaic law and the natural goods promised to those who observed the law. Hence God could not draw from them his full glory in which the creature attributes everything to the Creator and nothing to itself. Such is the mystery of the rejection of the Hebrews and of the vocation of the Gentiles, explained by the Apostle:[351] 'The Gentiles who followed not after justice have attained to justice, even the justice that is of faith. But Israel, by following after the law of justice, has not come unto the law of justice. Why so? Because they sought it not by faith, but as it were of works. For they stumbled at the stumbling-stone. As it is written: "Behold I lay in Sion a stumbling-stone and a rock of scandal."[352] And "whosoever believes in him shall not be confounded."'[353]

[348] Lk 2: 35.

[349] Mt 15: 13.

[350] Is 65: 1.

[351] Rom 9: 30–33†.

[352] Is 8: 14.

[353] Is 28: 16.

776. The power of evil hates the power of good, but the more that evil hates good, the more it perfects the good against which it is directed. The summit of good was in Christ because his human nature was assumed into a divine person and was the source of every moral good for those who adhered to him. The good they derived from this union was supernatural and deiform; it was therefore the highest and most perfect good. Three necessary consequences followed: 1. the power of evil targeted the Christ as its special object of hatred; for this reason he was called 'a sign which shall be contradicted';[354] 2. the greatness of the good caused the hatred to become inevitably unbounded and enraged, and 3. the hatred had to include proportionately all those who shared in the holiness of the Redeemer. For this reason the divine Master warned his disciples:[355]

> If the world hates you, know that it hated me before it hated you. If you were of the world, the world would love its own, but because you are not of the world, but I chose you out of the world, therefore the world hates you. Remember the word that I said to you, 'A servant is not greater than his master.' If they persecuted me, they will persecute you; if they kept my word, they will keep yours also. But all this they will do to you on my account, because they do not know him who sent me. If I had not come and spoken to them, they would not have sin; but now they have no excuse for their sin. He who hates me hates my Father also. If I had not done among them the works that no one else did, they would not have sin. But now they have seen and hated both me and my Father. It is to fulfil the word that is written in their law, 'They hated me without a cause.'[356]

The world is the finite human reality that loves and exalts itself rather than the infinite, but Christ does not pray for this reality. Therefore he says, 'If you belonged to the world, the world would love you as its own'. He guards his disciples against the world so that they will not trust in finite reality but

[354] Lk 2: 34†.

[355] Jn 15: 18–25.

[356] Ps 35: 19.

in the infinite, and this is why the world hates them. Finite reality, centred on itself, cannot know in a practical manner the dignity and majestic beauty of infinite reality. Hence Christ says that the world does not know the Father practically and intimately but knows him well speculatively and externally, because Christ had shown it the Father's works, and this speculative, external knowledge, although enough for hatred of the Father, was not enough for love: 'Now they have seen and hated both me and my Father.'*[357] These two kinds of knowledge, the *speculative* (necessary knowledge) and the *practical* (willed acknowledgement), occur frequently in Scripture.[358] The world lacks the second kind because it chooses not to acknowledge God, but it has and must have the first, which makes it inexcusable.

777. The hatred proper to the power of evil was therefore enraged by the excellence of Christ's virtue which, far exceeding the whole of damaged and corrupt nature, supremely despises this nature and does not regret its demise — his virtue trusts in God alone, as the only source of good.

This explains the furious, persistent, frenzied and totally inexplicable persecutions, of which Christ and his Church were a fixed target throughout the past centuries, and will be in the future. It explains the tremendous clash, the battle to the last drop of blood, between the two universal and everlasting cities.

778. The victory to which each of these cities tends is ultimate happiness. And part of this happiness is domination of the universe, because intelligence aspires to domination, aspires to carry out all it wills, and to dispose everything with its will. The *city of the devil* hopes to find great independence of will and domination over everything in its own forces and those of the creature. The *city of God* has no trust in the finite but hopes to find everything in the infinite, in the virtue of the Christ, in God. Therefore the city of the devil can only be violent by habit. Lacking any interest in moral virtue, it moves and stimulates all the created forces it finds within its grasp to destroy the city of God as an obstacle to the domination and independence in which it seeks its contentment. The city of God moves

[357] Jn 15: 24.

[358] *ER*, 194–201.

essentially in a peaceful, calm manner because it distrusts finite forces and expects everything from God alone. It is interested only in moral virtue and is firmly convinced that God will bestow this virtue as a most just reward. Consequently, with meekness and as if abandoned to the fury of the wicked, it aspires to the perfection of virtue, according to the word of its divine Head, who said to those he had invited: 'I am sending you out like sheep into the midst of wolves,'[359] and he assured them of his infallible promise: 'Blessed are you when people revile you and persecute you and utter all kinds of evil against you falsely on my account. Rejoice and be glad, for your reward is great in heaven.'[360]

779. In this decisive battle God plays the role, we might say, of two characters: a champion who, after becoming human, fights, and an impartial judge who watches the battle in order to give the prize and crown to the most deserving.

As champion, he conceals the weapon of his power in a sheath, as it were and, fighting with his humanity, makes it give every proof of courage in moral perfection.

Nor does he make use of his power as judge but of his impartial justice and his equity, pronouncing most just judgment. He reserves his power till the end in service of this judgment, and solely for sanctioning the unbiased sentence he will hand down to the combatants and for rewarding those who have legitimately conquered.

780. Note: the power of evil and of good place their victory in opposite things.

The power of evil would believe it has already won the struggle by its success in two things: 1. its seduction of humanity by depriving it of all justice, and 2. its destruction of it with the death that follows from sin.

The power of good however places the victory it seeks in preserving the justice in human souls against temptations, and leaving the consequences to God.

781. Therefore, when the power of evil came into conflict with the God-Man, it made every effort to seduce him. The angel of lies, making false use of the inspired word, tempted him

[359] Mt 10: 16; Lk 10: 3.

[360] Mt 5: 11–12.

with intemperance, presumption and ambition.[361] When this bold affront failed, only death remained as the means of destroying his human nature, in which the power of good existed. The God-Man, concerned solely with maximum moral perfection while leaving the eudaimonological consequences to God, suffered death, but could have saved himself if he had wished. However he did not wish to save himself, because death offered him the opportunity to exercise the greatest, most heroic act of trust and charity towards the Father. Thus, for a moment, the power of evil thought it had destroyed the power of good and totally triumphed.

782. But it was a vain illusion. Although the human nature of Christ had been destroyed, the power of evil did not realise that the two elements of that nature remained: the body and the soul. These, which on their own could never have united, were joined to a supernatural principle immune from death, the person of the divine Word consubstantial with the Father. Thus, the conquering subject had not, as it seemed, been destroyed through death; he had been harmed in his lower part, in his humanity. Once again, it was the finite that perished, the finite that had tortured and destroyed itself — the infinite had sustained no wound or damage. As Scripture says, only his clothing had been stained with red while he trod down his enemies like the grapes in the wine-press;[362] in other words, God had subjected the humanity to punishment, although, with infinite condescension, he had taken this humanity as his dwelling.

783. The Father then stepped in as judge and decreed victory to the conquering person who was not dead but alive for ever. This person, in agreement with the Father, resurrected the humanity that had trusted God without limit, and had demonstrated and exercised a perfect moral perfection. This moral perfection consisted in such a great reverence and love for the Father that, although the resurrection and glory could be attributed to the most faithful, religious humanity as a fitting and due reward for its merits, nevertheless Christ as man preferred to have moral perfection through the grace of the Father. All

[361] Mt 4: 1–9.

[362] Is 63: 1–4.

Christ's glory therefore was founded solely on the Father's goodness, as if he had not merited such a great favour (his renouncement of the right to an extraordinary reward for this reason was also a supreme perfection): 'In the days of his flesh, Jesus offered up prayers and supplications, with loud cries and tears, to the one who was able to save him from death, and he was heard because of his reverent submission.'[363] Here his human nature, acknowledging its mortality, acknowledged that immortality was not due to it as its prerogative but through pure divine clemency. It also acknowledged at the same time that virtue and fidelity to God deserved to be maintained even without any claim of reward, and that it was fitting for the finite to be a holocaust to the infinite. Hence Christ's request to the Father that his life be preserved is based solely on the foreknown will of the Father, that is, on the eternal predestination in which the Father had decreed immortal life and glory for the humanity that was immolating itself for love, for confessing the Father and for his glory: 'I glorified you on earth by finishing the work that you gave me to do. So now, Father, glorify me in your own presence with the glory that I had in your presence before the world existed.'[364] Everything of the Christ that had to be realised in time (his passion and consequent glory) were present in the creative act from eternity. Christ, seeing them in this act, asked that they be accomplished in time because they were already with the Father.

784. When God, the most just judge, had therefore declared victory for the immortal, invincible conqueror, the latter (the person of the Word who had never left the soul and body of Christ), reunited the two things. Thus humanity, formerly destroyed by the power of evil, was reunited by the person-subject whose responsibility it was, and appeared glorious in the act of triumph. The power of evil certainly could not complain that God had shown little equity in this great deed, as if he had intervened with his omnipotence. The Christ whom the power of evil had killed rose by his own effort, without the intervention of any alien force. His personhood had not been killed; it was divine and, raising its own

[363] Heb 5: 7.

[364] Jn 17: 4–5.

humanity, which it could do in any case with full right, it had conformed itself to all that from eternity, had been declared both just and most fitting to the infinite goodness of God and decreed as such. His personhood had conformed to what the humanity of Christ, with a deep sense of humility, had requested as a free grace. Infinite goodness could not turn a deaf ear to a prayer of this kind.

785. Thus the power of evil, in conflict with the Christ, had lost the two battles rashly waged against him: the battle of *seduction* and the battle *of destruction*; the first in the order of virtue, the second in the order of force. The first, far from succeeding in seduction, gave the Christ the fitting opportunity to make his resplendent, perfect sanctity shine with infinite merit before intelligences. The second, although permitted to do all it could with its forces, was weaker than Christ; the most it could do was kill the one in whom all the power of good lay, but could not destroy his person. With the death of the human nature, the person was given the opportunity to reunite the separated humanity and embellish it with all the splendour of power and glory that the divine person was equipped to give, wanted to give, and could and had to give to it.

786. At this stage it seemed that all combat was ended. The risen Christ himself had said: 'All authority in heaven and on earth has been given to me.'[365] Even before his death, Christ, who in the creative act saw this power given eternally to him as risen, had said: 'Father, the hour has come; glorify your Son so that the Son may glorify you, since you have given him authority over all people, to give eternal life to all whom you have given him.'[366] Christ's most just victory had given him power over all things. From that moment he could do as he wished with all the world because, as Isaiah says, 'the will of the Lord shall prosper in his hand'.[367] If he wished, he could save the whole human race, free it from all temptation and illness, and strengthen it in good. But guided by the sublime counsel of his

[365] Mt 28: 18.

[366] Jn 17: 1–2.

[367] 'Yet it was the will of the Lord to bruise him; he has put him to grief; when he makes himself an offering for sin, he shall see his offspring, he shall prolong his days; the will of the Lord shall prosper in his hand' (Is 53: 10).

most wise goodness he did not wish this. Instead, he wanted to do more and even better for humanity; he wanted to draw from it, from the acts of each person, all the moral good that each could give. Operating not only as God but as man, he would do this according to the law of wisdom, which is the law of the least means. This law of the least means was the law according to which eternal predestination was ordered. Christ kept this order continuously before him and saw in it all he wanted to do, because he saw the most excellent and sublime object of the divine will, the exemplar from which to copy. The divine calculation, carried out at an infinite depth within eternal wisdom, obtained a greater abundance of good from the human race. This allowed all the redeemed to gauge their strength and combat the power of evil, just as the Redeemer had done. Courageously, they could win the victory and crown, even if some perished in the struggle, a loss that was richly compensated by the huge gain accumulated in those who conquered. Hence, Christ often speaks about those whom the Father had given him while he was alive on earth, the Apostles and his immediate disciples. He also prays for those who believe in their word; he does not pray for the world nor that all people believe. He does so not because he was not Lord of everybody but because he wishes to exercise his dominion for the overall, total and greatest good of all humanity, which could not be done without the loss of some when their will was tested. Consequently, according to his good pleasure and granted the greatest good, he wishes to save all who can be saved, and only these. As God, his will is identical to the Father's; as man, it agrees with the Father's. In the Father's will therefore he reads which human beings are to be saved so that there may be the greatest good willed necessarily by infinite goodness and wisdom. He says:

> I have made your name known to those whom you gave me from the world. They were yours, and you gave them to me, and they have kept your word… I pray for them; I am not praying for the world, but on behalf of those whom you gave me, because they are yours. All I have is yours, and all you have is mine; and I have been glorified in them… Holy Father, keep in your name those you have given me, so that they may be one, as we are one… I pray not only for them, but also for those who will believe in

[786]

> me through their word, so that they may all be one single thing, as you, Father, in me and I in you; so that they may be one single thing in us, and the world believe that you have sent me.[368]

He does not ask for his disciples to be taken from this world in which and against which they must fight, nor does he pray for the world, for those who base their joys and hopes on the finite reality of the creature. He prays for those who do not put their hope in the finite but believe in his words and the words of those he has sent, that is, of his Church, so that the world may believe in his mission and thus cease to be world, or if it remains world, is conquered by the shining light of eternal truth and its glory. He prays all this through the love of the Father because even in the salvation of the predestined he seeks and loves the will and glory of the Father 'because they are yours, and all I have is yours, and all you have is mine'.

787. The Book of Revelation, the revelation of Jesus Christ, is the manifestation of the supreme battle which the risen Christ, now in glory, still wages and will continue to wage with the power of evil until the end of the world. He is not obliged to this but does it with a spontaneous and generous will through the instrumentality of his faithful servants. The Fathers say that this mysterious book contains a kind of history of the experiences of Christ's Church, a history that in the final analysis is an account of many conflicts.

788. In the first chapter, Christ's apparition to John leaves us in no doubt about the full power with which he was clothed after his resurrection and his place at the right hand of the Father: 'I am the first and the last, and the living one. I was dead, and see, I am alive forever and ever; and I have the keys of Death and of Hades.'[369] If he does not use the fullness of his power and allows death and hell to war against humanity, it is not because he could not prevent their rage with full justification, but both his generosity towards the power of evil in order to throw it finally into greater confusion, and the greater good which in his wisdom he sees as the outcome of the great struggle, induce him

[368] Jn 17: 6–21 [R].

[369] Rev 1: 17–18.

to leave the hostile forces free to renew the conflict, which in turn must renew the victories of the saints.

789. Revelation has two principal parts, because John is commanded to write *quae sunt* [what is], that is, the state of the Church at that time (this is done in the second and third chapters), *et quae oportet fieri post haec* [and what is to take place after this],[370] that is, the states of the Church that were to follow the first state (after the death of the Apostles), which the remainder of the book relates.

790. In chapter five the book of eternal predestination appears, which contains the names of the elect.[371] These constitute the maximum final good which, as was decreed, had to be obtained from human nature; the opening of the book is the realisation of this excellent, eternal decree. This realisation is carried out by the work of CHRIST, conqueror and risen, and appeared to be a desperate task to fulfil. St. John says:

> And I wept much, because no man was found worthy to open the book, nor to see it. (Who among sinful human beings was able to see the decree of eternal predestination, never mind realise it?) And one of the ancients said to me: Weep not: behold the lion of the tribe of Juda, the root of David, has prevailed to open the book and to loose its seven seals. And I saw: and behold in the midst of the throne and of the four living creatures and in the midst of the ancients, a Lamb standing, as it were slain, having seven horns and seven eyes: which are the seven Spirits of God, sent forth into all the earth. And he came and took the book out of the right hand of him that sat on the throne. And when he had opened the book, the four living creatures and the four and twenty ancients fell down before the Lamb, having every one of them harps and golden vials full of odours, which are the prayers of saints. And they sang a new canticle, saying: You are worthy, O Lord, to take the book and to open its seals: because you were slain and have redeemed us to God, in your blood, out of every tribe and tongue and people and

370 Ibid., 19.

371 The fact that the closed book contained only the names of the elect is understood from 20: 12, where the book of life is distinguished from the books in which the works of other men are written.

nation: And have made us to our God a kingdom and priests, and we shall reign on the earth.[372]

This is the ancient Church of Israel that was in limbo. After the death and resurrection of Christ and after being admitted to see the creative act in God, this Church sees the glory of the Christ and how he will realise the predestination of the saints belonging to that ancient Church by gathering together the remnant of the Hebrews destined for salvation from all the nations among whom they have been dispersed. The twenty-four elders, corresponding to the heads of the twenty-four priestly families, represent the Israelitic priesthood. The four animals represent the prophets who prophesied about the four prerogatives of Christ: his divinity, humanity, kingdom and priesthood; and the whole Israelitic Church is represented by *priesthood* and *prophecy*. When this Church is admitted to the vision of the creative act, it gives glory to God with the following words which witness to the honour due to him for the wisdom and goodness of his providence: 'You are worthy, our Lord and God, to receive glory and honour and power, for you created all things, and by your will they existed' (in the creative act) 'and were created' (in themselves).[373] The lamb receives the book from the right hand of the Father because the Father committed to him the accomplishment of the predestination.[374] He committed this task to his humanity because the lamb saved the world by his immolated humanity. Moreover, with the perfect virtue of his humanity he sought only to execute the paternal will that he saw in the holy mission, and he accomplished the predestination with the all the wisdom of his humanity directed by his divinity as the principal and personal agent. Hence he had said about his disciples: 'They were yours, and you have given them to me.' But it says that 'the lamb was standing as if it had been slain' because Christ received the right and faculty to realise the predestination after he had consummated his sacrifice, before his resurrection; in the sepulchre he seemed

372 Rev 5: 4–10†.

373 Rev 4: 11.

374 Rev 5: 5.

finished, but only his humanity was prey to death. The person, because divine, lived, and united with the soul, appeared as liberator to the Fathers in limbo.

791. Why is it then that when the lamb opened the book, John's visions begin again, and the book's seals, as if the book were still closed, are broken open one after the other at different times and with various events?

CHRIST's conquest through his death had removed every difficulty that prevented the opening of the book of predestination. He had merited the fullest power to activate the eternal decree for saving the elect. After he had risen and led into heaven the ancient saints imprisoned in the underworld, the great book was opened to them, who had been made 'a kingdom and priests serving our God'.[375] But the predestination of other holy people, members of the new Church, also had to be accomplished. These however could not be united in the heavenly kingdom except after many centuries, as required by the law of wisdom that had dictated the book in which the conqueror read what was fitting for him to do. Thus it seems to me that the breaking of the seven seals indicates the seven great means to be used, the seven great operations by which JESUS Christ, now Lord and ruler of the world, accomplishes the mysterious paternal will. He alone can naturally read this will in the essence of God, and as man was the only one worthy of reading it because of his heroic virtue. In fact these great means and the great, divine operations are fittingly called seals because in the Scriptures this word, as I have said, expresses the marks of the divine greatness and as it were its imprint, which God's operation leaves in creation.

792. We have seen that the first opening of the book signifies the fulfilment of the predestination of the ancient house of Jacob, and is indicated to John by one of the twenty-four elders representing the ancient priesthood that is custodian of the Mosaic law. In the same way, the opening of the first four seals is indicated to John by the four animals representing the prophets who proclaimed the greatnesses of Christ to all humanity invited to the Gospel.

793. The risen CHRIST operates in the world as King, Priest,

[375] Rev 5: 10.

Man and God. Apparently, to these four prerogatives correspond the four ways of operating by which he leads humanity, his inheritance, to the final end to which humanity must come, that is, the maximum glory of God and its own maximum good. Because Christ must be glorified under all four of his magnificent gifts, I think that in the diverse ages of the Church he takes pleasure in making one age stand out more brightly than another and uses a manner of operation more analogous to one than another.

794. As King, he obtains all he wills with infallible effect through the fullness of his power. The royal manner of his operating shines out most especially in his resurrection, when he comes forth from the tomb as conqueror of death, and in the final triumph and judgment. This prerogative is particularly demonstrative at the beginning and end of the Church, and thus at the beginning and end of Revelation.

795. As Priest, Man and God, he disposes the means with which he infallibly obtains the above effect: he exalts the supernatural principle communicated to his servants and at the same time humbles nature that must appear as almost annihilated before the infinite.

796. He does this in the following way. As Priest, he immolates victims, and just as he immolates himself first, so he offers us as a holocaust to the Creator, with a different effect in the good and the wretched. In the good, who have had their nature humbled and destroyed, as happened with Christ, the supernatural, personal principle remains alive; they hope in it alone, and through it they receive back abundantly all they had lost.

797. But in the wretched, whose nature has failed, every foundation of their hope has disappeared for ever. Hence Christ said to his disciples: 'Do not think that I have come to bring peace to the earth; I have not come to bring peace, but a sword,'[376] and again: 'Whoever does not take up the cross and follow me is not worthy of me. Those who find their life will lose it, and those who lose their life for my sake will find it.'[377] But the wicked he will lay low and punish with violent death and with wars, ordained by creative providence, and these disasters in the wicked are atrocious and irreparable evils. In the first centuries of the

[376] Mt 10: 34.

[377] Ibid., 38–39.

Church, Christ's priestly mode of operating shines in the sacrifices of the martyrs and in the cruel deaths suffered by their persecutors.

798. As Man, he is the first to fast, and makes his followers fast, who thus greatly purify themselves in a spirit of penance. They also know that 'One does not live by bread alone, but by every word that comes from the mouth of God,'[378] and in the likeness of their Master have another food in addition to the earthly.[379] Finally Christ gives them a suprasubstantial food, his flesh and blood under the species of bread and wine, together with the sweet fragrance of his grace, a fragrance that can never be spoilt.[380] But he uses famines to scourge the world, to humble it and convince it that it does not have what is necessary for its subsistence. Christ's mode of operation in humanity shines out in the penitents and monks who followed the martyrs. This was the medieval period, a time when famines were very frequent and, in general, poverty and decadence of productive skills, and ignorance. All this, inflicted for many centuries, humbled the world.

799. As God, he comes to the death bed of the elect to take them to himself, like a royal spouse who comes to conduct the very beautiful spouse into the magnificent, festive palace.[381] He abandons the obstinate wicked to an evil death, casting them down into hell. Thus, he opposed the heresies of the 16th century and the unbelief in which they all ended with the rejection of many and with a great number of extraordinary saints who beautified his Church. To the former he ministered justice with his divine power, and to the latter, grace and mercy.

800. Here then are the first four opened seals:

The lion, symbol of royal dignity, shows John how at the opening of the first seal 'a white horse' came out, 'Its rider had a bow; a crown was given to him, and he came out conquering and to conquer.'[382] He was already a conqueror but nevertheless

[378] Ibid., 4: 4.

[379] Jn 4: 32–34.

[380] Rev 6: 6.

[381] Song 1: 4.

[382] Rev 1: 2.

came out to conquer. This is Christ risen as King of glory who is traversing the earth and doing what he wills, and nothing can resist his bow.

801. The calf, symbol of priestly dignity, shows John how, on the opening of the second seal, 'out came another horse, bright red; its rider was permitted to take peace from the earth, so that people would slaughter one another; and he was given a great sword.'[383] This is the time of persecutions. The horse and its rider marked with blood represent the power of Christ to scourge the world from region to region with violent, cruel death. This is perhaps the angel-minister of Christ, charged with this action, as representative of Christ.

802. The third animal with the face of a man, symbol of the human nature of Christ, shows John how, upon the opening of the third seal, 'a black horse' comes out, 'Its rider held a pair of scales in his hand', and a voice said, 'A quart of wheat for a denarius and three quarts of barley for a denarius.'[384] This is the middle ages: the horse and its dark rider represents the power of Christ to scourge the world from region to region with famine and hunger. Perhaps this is the angel, minister and representative of Christ, deputed for this task.

803. Finally, when the fourth seal is opened, the eagle, symbol of Christ's divine nature, shows John 'a pale green horse' coming out, 'Its rider's name was Death, and Hades followed with him; they were given authority over a fourth of the earth, to kill with sword, famine, and pestilence, and by the wild animals of the earth.'[385] This is the time, after the middle ages, when arrogant intelligence abuses knowledge to corrupt the world with errors and unbelief. The pale green horse, death and hell represent the divine power of Christ to punish reprobates with eternal damnation, leaving them to be brought down by death and sin. This again is perhaps an angel, minister and representative of Christ, that presides over the execution of the terrible just sentence.

804. When the last three seals are broken open, events take place in which Christ intervenes with the three prerogatives of priest, man and God, and the whole great drama is finally

383 Ibid., 4.

384 Ibid., 5–6.

385 Ibid., 8.

unravelled with the return of Christ as King. After judging the world and conquering his enemies, he enters into marriage with his royal spouse, the Church of his elect.

805. Thus, when the fifth seal is broken, the prayers of the martyrs are heard; they ask for vengeance against those on earth who have shed their innocent blood. They believe that the time for vengeance has come because Christ has now been glorified in all four modes, as King, Priest, Man and God. But he must be glorified again in these four modes, as is written: 'I have glorified it, and I will glorify it again.'[386] He has been glorified in *individuals*; he must now be glorified in *society*. The powers of evil and good on earth have not yet been fully organised: each must be organised in the most perfect way. Evil is permitted to become stronger and develop all its forces so that it can then be conquered with greater glory by good. Thus, the martyrs receive the reply that their number of victims is not yet complete: they must rest a little under the altar until the eternal Priest has consummated the great sacrifice in his servants. The vengeance that divine justice owes to the martyrs hastens the coming of God's kingdom. The martyrs' prayers, which cannot remain unheard, is a fifth means added to the first four, and together they continue to further the completion of the great plan of Providence. It indicates a time of new persecutions, those that are happening even today in Japan and China, and in other regions where the Gospel is being preached. The difference between these persecutions and those that will take place in the final age is that here it is a question of persecutions and martyrdoms undergone for the diffusion of the Gospel throughout the whole earth, whereas in more distant times it will be persecutions caused by apostate human beings within a world already Christian.

806. Good is organised on earth in the Church of Jesus Christ, which is the society of believers. The fifth age is destined to preach the Gospel to the faithless nations, and its preachers sprinkle it with their blood.

807. Hence, during the time that the number of those who give their life for Christ and voluntarily make themselves victims with him to spread the Gospel among the most distant

[386] Jn 12: 28.

peoples, the sixth seal is broken. Here the action of the humanity of our Lord JESUS Christ is the principal element. With the breaking of the seal, the planetary phenomena foretold by the prophets and by Christ himself begin. With these phenomena he shows his power as man over nature, just as he had shown it over humanity in the three previous seals. An earthquake first prostrates the whole world that has become very civilised and proud of itself, as described by Isaiah.[387] 'Then the kings of the earth and the magnates and the generals and the rich and the powerful, and everyone, slave and free, hid in the caves and among the rocks of the mountains, calling to the mountains and rocks, "Fall on us and hide us from the face of the one seated on the throne and from the wrath of the Lamb."'[388] Mankind, now terrified and its self-assurance completely shattered, acquires the fear suitable for divine pity. And the CHRIST, mindful of his Ancestors according to the flesh and of God's covenant with them, brings into the Church the remnant of Israel, a fixed number of the different tribes. The Church lives once again with a new fervour and welcomes among its faithful a countless multitude of all peoples. The conversion of the Hebrews was predicted by Moses and the ancient prophets.[389]

808. This is the time when baptism, which marks human beings with an indelible character, and the other sacraments instituted by Christ that operate through the power communicated to them by his most sacred and glorified humanity, are received very fervently by many people, who draw holiness from them. However, human pride still continues in others. Christ therefore must finally apply new means pertaining directly to his divinity. These are new interior lights given to the masters of his Church to defeat errors. They also include the new power of his interior grace, and of his charity communicated to the saints of his Church to conquer the coldness and

[387] Is 2.

[388] Rev 6: 15–16.

[389] 'When all these things have happened to you in time to come, you will return to the Lord your God and heed him. Because the Lord your God is a merciful God, he will neither abandon you nor destroy you; he will not forget the covenant with your ancestors that he swore to them'* (Deut 4: 30–31).

hatred of human beings. This is indicated by the breaking of the seventh seal, which now follows.

809. After the Church has enjoyed so much prosperity and peace, and piety is flourishing everywhere, God permits it to be shaken more than ever by systems of false teachings. This is a new release of human and diabolic wickedness. It produces great disorders in the world and must finally be suppressed and overcome by the wisdom and power of the Word of God. Therefore when the seventh seal is broken, seven angels appear. These apparently correspond to seven prelates and doctors in the Church (as indicated at the very beginning of the revelation in the angels of the seven Churches of Asia). Each has a trumpet which, I think, means the good or harmful teaching they spread about with great effect in the world. But before they blow their trumpets and convulse the world, another angel casts fire from the altar in heaven down onto the earth ready to receive it and produces sounds and lightning and great movements of land. This angel represents a great saint (perhaps a Roman Pontiff of sublime holiness), who with the fire of divine love performs prodigies in the world, to the terror and confusion of the wicked. Next, the first four angels sound their trumpets in succession. At their sound, four perverse teachings cause very serious evils. Then the fifth angel sounds his trumpet, and the infernal teaching indicated by this sound initiates a war that has the support of the secular powers. But the discord produced by the preaching of the sixth teaching is even greater: it causes wars that are still more murderous, in which, it is said, two hundred million horsemen will appear (perhaps in succession), armed with guns — the invention of these must doubtlessly be meant here.[390] These teachings and tumults, which Christ called the *initia dolorum* [beginnings of sorrows][391] will again corrupt the earth to the point where idolatry will reappear.

After the power of evil has been allowed to cause such a ferment, Christ will intervene with the works of his divinity for the salvation of the world in its perverted state. He will give such light to his servants that far from being scandalised by what has happened, they will clearly see wonderful motifs of divine

390 Rev 9: 16–18.

391 Mt 24: 8†.

wisdom. The mystery of divine predestination will shine out and be justified in all its brilliance such that they must give infinite glory to God. Christ who reveals the great mystery is called angel: 'And I saw,' says the sacred Text, 'another mighty angel coming down from heaven, wrapped in a cloud, with a rainbow over his head; his face was like the sun, and his legs like pillars of fire. He held a little scroll open in his hand. Setting his right foot on the sea and his left foot on the land, he gave a great shout, like a lion roaring.'[392] The open book is the hidden mystery of Providence revealed, and the sea and the earth mean both angelic and human nature ruled over by Jesus Christ. The communication of the lights that Christ makes here to his Church is indicated by sounds similar to the seven thunders that John is forbidden to write down; he is ordered only to indicate them, that is, note them in figures so that the great teaching of God's work remains hidden, preserved until the time set aside for the good of humanity for whom it will have become necessary.

This teaching that will be revealed and explain the unfolding of God's work, will announce what will happen when the trumpet of the seventh angel sounds; this is why the book of providence and predestination is given to John to eat,[393] as representative of the saints of the time to whom the light will be given. Eating the book indicates practical, not simply speculative knowledge — speculative knowledge is the reading of it. Hence John is told: 'You must prophesy again to many nations and peoples and tongues and kings.'[394] This revelation is indicated in summary form, not written down but indicated in the oath made by the Angel of the testament, Christ Jesus: 'Time shall be no longer. But in the days of the voice of the seventh angel, when he shall begin to sound the trumpet, the mystery of God shall be finished, as he has declared by his servants the prophets.'[395] The phrase 'in the days of the voice of the seventh angel' means a long period. 'When he shall begin to sound the trumpet, the mystery of God shall be finished' means its end will begin because the Christ's operation as King will begin and

392 Rev 10: 1–3.

393 Ibid., 8–10.

394 Ibid., 11†.

395 Ibid., 6–7†.

his kingdom be founded immovably on this earth. Thus, at the sound of the seventh trumpet, loud voices will be heard in heaven, saying: 'The kingdom of the world has become the kingdom of our Lord and of his Christ, and he shall reign for ever and ever.'[396] The facts assigned to the seventh trumpet are announced at the time of the sixth trumpet in order to enlighten and sustain the faithful servants. These are represented by John who measures God's temple, sees it as if already finalised, and knows the two prophet-witnesses who must preach, perform miracles, suffer martyrdom, rise after three and a half days and ascend to heaven in the presence of their enemies, who at that very moment will be hit by an earthquake that kills seven thousand of them, 'and the rest were terrified and gave glory to the God of heaven.'[397]

810. The kingdom of Christ on earth therefore is completed in the days of the seventh angel, the representative Christ, who comes to oppose the previous false prophets and remedy the evils that happened to mankind at the sound of the six trumpets. The twenty-four elders celebrate its completion with these words: 'We give you thanks, O Lord God Almighty, who are, and who were and who are to come; because you have taken to you your great power, and you have reigned.'[398] Also implied is the great, royal act of judging the reprobate and of rewarding the elect.[399]

811. The first judgment made at the sound of the seventh trumpet, is the judgment against the demons. The sentence is carried out by the good angels: 'And war broke out in heaven; Michael and his angels fought against the dragon. The dragon and his angels fought back, but they were defeated, and there was no longer any place for them in heaven.'[400]

812. The expulsion of the demons from heaven means they are thrown into total confusion by the wisdom of God, which wished to use its power against them only after it had removed

[396] Ibid., 11: 15.

[397] Ibid., 11: 1, 14.

[398] Ibid., 11: 17†.

[399] Ibid., 11: 18–19.

[400] Rev 12: 7–8.

all the cavils and exceptions that the prevaricating angel, with his very acute intellect, brought against the victory that Christ had won for humanity. God's wisdom seconded this angel in all the tests he asked to carry out against Christ's saints to prove their virtue, just as he had done with Job, but all of the tests failed. When they and all the temptations Christ had allowed the angel to present to his disciples were over, the devil, in confusion, could no longer return to the presence of God to dispute with him and ask to hear what was new. But even though he is silenced, he still does not submit to justice; on the contrary, he rejects the punishment that Michael and the other heavenly spirits powerfully inflict on him. Nevertheless, despite the fact that all the devil's reasoning has been confused and he has been expelled from heaven (the region of intelligence), he can still cause intense unrest, not by reasoning but by using against human beings his blind power that he himself knows is evil — this is the meaning of his having been cast down from heaven to earth. 'The great dragon was thrown down, that ancient serpent, who is called the Devil and Satan, the deceiver of the whole world — he was thrown down to the earth, and his angels were thrown down with him. Then I heard a loud voice in heaven, proclaiming, "Now have come the salvation and the power and the kingdom of our God and the authority of his Christ for the accuser of our brothers has been thrown down, who accuses them day and night before our God."'[401] The accusations are precisely the cavils used by the devil to sow doubt about the victory that Christ had won in his saints, and are the tests he asked of God in order to try the virtue of the saints, but are now all ended.

813. The devil had now been stripped of his power to continue arguing against the firmness and fullness of the strength and grace with which Christ had endowed his disciples. Enraged, he fought the battle with only the brute forces provided by his real being, which were not yet bound. Hence it is written: 'Woe to the earth and the sea, for the devil has come down to you with great wrath, because he knows that his time is short!'[402]

[401] Rev 12: 9–10.

[402] Rev 12: 12.

814. Thus Christ's equity, generosity and perfect wisdom and justice gradually subdue the devil and, expelling him from one place to another, reduce him to hell. The great struggle no longer took place in heaven but on earth, no longer a struggle of wisdom but of power. This power had to be totally conquered by Christ's power, and to conquer it, the strength of the dragon had not to be bound at the beginning; on the contrary, it had to be left entirely free to reveal all its cleverness in battle.

815. Consequently, diabolical wickedness and human wickedness, indicated by the two beasts, one rising out of the sea, the other out of the land,[403] will be organised and given supreme power. This will be the time of magic. Portents will be seen of such a kind that, if it were possible, even the elect would be deceived.[404] The beast is a great emperor who has under him many kings. One of the portents he will perform and that will shake the world will be the cure of a fatal wound of one of his kings, who seemed dead.[405] The emperor, who has been raised up by the dragon and given a magic power by the dragon, will overcome the saints and form a universal monarchy, and have worship paid him. Because there will be violent persecution, the prophecy concludes: 'Here is a call for the endurance and faith of the saints,'[406] that is, the extreme, maximum test of their faith and constancy. This potentate will reign for three and a half years, with the two prophets already announced appearing under him. These two prophets must, it seems, be Enoch and Elijah who combat the false prophets with true miracles and whose preaching will last the same length of time, that is, one thousand two hundred and sixty days.[407] Finally they are martyred: 'When they have finished their testimony, the beast that comes up from the bottomless pit' (which is the sea) 'will make war on them and conquer them and kill them.'[408] A very

[403] Rev 13: 1, 11.

[404] Mt 24: 24.

[405] Rev 13: 3.

[406] Rev 13: 10; 17: 9.

[407] Ibid., 11: 3–7.

[408] Ibid., 11: 7.

cunning man will becomes a minister of this potentate, this blasphemer of God and instrument of the devil, a warrior full of violence and cruelty. The minister is the second beast who has risen out of the land and represents human wickedness. He will pretend to be mild and will seduce people with clever hypocrisy and subtle sophistry. Hence he is said to have 'two horns like a lamb and it spoke like a dragon'.[409] He will give great scope for power to his master, who is the supreme politician for evil, the one in command, that is, the first beast. Thus we read: 'It exercises all the authority of the first beast on its behalf,'[410] and to indicate that the minister of the first beast is meant, it adds: 'And it makes the earth and its inhabitants worship the first beast, whose mortal wound had been healed.'[411] This shrewd man will use natural sciences, which will have reached their peak at that time, to simulate miracles, even to making fire come down from the skies (perhaps by means of large electrical apparatus), and give life and speech to the image of his Lord (perhaps because he had found the way to organise living principles). In this way he will seduce the world. And although he causes the death of those who do not worship the statue of his Lord, to whom apparently he has given life, he is more shrewd and violent: he publishes laws, one of which forbids buying and selling for all those who do not carry the mark of his Lord.[412] Thus human cunning is kept as a minister of diabolical fury because the former had not yet been fully conquered in all its complexities. Hence the description of this manner of persecution concludes: 'This calls for wisdom,'[413] that is, the wisdom of the saints, because they will need the greatest wisdom to oppose such a seducer and not be deceived by him.

816. It should be noted that at the time of this persecution, which will be greater than all the previous persecutions, the Church will have a certain number of saints of supreme, invulnerable virtue. But these, whom all the power of the two beasts

[409] Ibid., 13: 11.

[410] Rev 13: 12.

[411] Ibid.

[412] Ibid., 13: 15–17.

[413] Ibid., 13: 18.

will strive to overcome, will be humble, excluded from social power and living in solitude, where they will make religious life flourish more than ever before. Thus, what happened under Nero will return, that is, the opportunity for solitary, contemplative life, particularly through the fathers of the Egyptian desert. The prophecy contains evidence of this.

817. The ancient Church conceived and gave painful birth to its child, the Redeemer. The dragon's attempt to devour him was in vain because the Redeemer was taken up to heaven and to his throne. The dragon, now confounded in the arguments he had first used, fell down to the earth but did not find the Christ against whom he could hurl the forces of his real nature and rage. The Catholic Church therefore, which does not differ from the ancient Church (the Church that flourished before Christ and that which flourished afterwards are one and the same), withdrew with its more elect portion into the desert for the duration of the tremendous persecution carried out by the two beasts, as it had done at the beginning of Christianity: 'And the woman fled into the wilderness, where she has a place prepared by God, so that there she can be nourished for one thousand two hundred and sixty days,'[414] which are exactly the three and a half years that the appalling persecution of the two beasts will last. Although the serpent persecuted the woman even in the desert, he later lost all hope of being able to destroy her: 'The dragon was angry against the woman: and went to make war with the rest of her seed, who keep the commandments of God and have the testimony of JESUS Christ.'[415] Contemptuous of those in the desert, he stopped persecuting them and turned to the Christians in society, where he aroused or continued the persecution which, as I said, had already been revealed during the sounding of the sixth trumpet. The temple mentioned in the prophecy means the Church in the desert; the temple atrium is society where the Christians live — John was commanded: 'Come and measure the temple of God and the altar and those who worship there, but do not measure the court outside the temple; leave that out, for it is given over to the nations, and they will trample over the holy city for

[414] Rev 12: 6.

[415] Rev 12: 17†.

forty-two months,'[416] which is precisely the time the two beasts were given to vent their rage.

818. The greatest force of this terrible and cunning persecution ends with the resurrection of the two prophets and their assumption into Heaven, and with a fearful earthquake that kills seven thousand people and prostrates the others to the extent that they give glory to the God of heaven.[417] But the city of the devil, established on our planet, does not yet fall.

819. With the human race laid low by terror, the coming of JESUS Christ in his kingdom on earth draws near. But before that takes place, John is shown the glory of those living in the desert. During the persecution carried out by the two beasts they lived in perfect continence far from such a depraved world; of them it is said: 'These are they who were not defiled with women: for they are virgins. These follow the Lamb wherever he goes. These were purchased from among men, the first fruits to God and to the Lamb. And in their mouth there was found no lie: for they are without spot before the throne of God.'[418]

820. Next, the famous of the world are evangelised. They are indicated as those who 'sit upon the earth and over every nation and tribe and tongue and people'.[419] The evangelisation is done by an angel who, it seems, is a great pope. The Gospel, resplendent with so many victories, is proclaimed as eternal, and the future judgment that must complete the revealed work of Providence is intimated: 'Fear God and give him glory, for the hour of his judgment has come; and worship him who made heaven and earth, the sea and the springs of water.'[420]

821. This angel is followed by another angel, another holy preacher, who foretells the fall of Babylon. And then a third angel, who announces the punishments for those who have worshipped the beast or its image or have received his mark on their foreheads or hand.[421]

[416] Ibid., 11: 1–2.

[417] Ibid., 11: 11–13.

[418] Rev 14: 4–5†.

[419] Ibid., 14: 6†.

[420] Ibid., 7.

[421] Ibid., 14: 8, 11.

822. The earthquake and the preaching of these three angels restrains in some measure the wicked fury of Babylon but in general people do not listen to the preachers and do not repent; rather they continue to take their pleasure, as Christ describes them: he predicts how the charity of many will grow cold, and how, when he comes, he will hardly find faith on earth.[422]

The fall of Babylon is therefore reserved for the coming of Christ the King. He comes down on earth, on which the dragon has descended, in order to totally overthrow the latter. Then will take place what the two angels said to the Apostles as they watched JESUS Christ ascend: 'This JESUS, who has been taken up from you into heaven, will come in the same way as you saw him go into heaven,'[423] that is, received into a cloud. Thus at the time of the world we are dealing with, John tells us: 'Then I looked, and there was a white cloud, and seated on the cloud was one like the Son of Man, with a golden crown' (the symbol of the royal dignity) 'on his head, and a sharp sickle in his hand.'[424] This apparently must be a coming or appearance that is peaceful and visible only to holy people, as was his ascension into heaven from the Mount of Olives; it is not therefore his public, solemn and terrible coming to everyone. From that moment on, it seems that JESUS Christ will appear frequently to his faithful in the way he did after his resurrection before ascending to heaven. During the same period he will also suddenly come to take many just people to heaven through a holy death consoled by his visible presence.[425] These just are signified by the ripe wheat that the Son of man harvests with his sickle. But a still greater number of wicked people, signified by the grapes that his angel, not himself, will harvest from all the earth, will die by the sword in the most murderous wars that will be fought between the two cities of God and the devil: 'So the angel swung his sickle over the earth and gathered the vintage of the earth, and he threw it into the great wine press of the wrath of God, and blood flowed from the wine press, as high as a horse's bridle, for a distance of about two

422 Mt 24; Lk 17, 18, 21; Mk 13.

423 Acts 1: 11.

424 Rev 14: 14.

425 Mt 24: 42–51; 25: 1–46.

hundred miles.'[426] This will be followed by the new hymn which the just in heaven, harvested from the earth as ripe wheat, sing to the king: 'Great and amazing are your deeds, Lord God the Almighty! Just and true are your ways, King of the nations!'[427] The whole hymn is a celebration of the most wise and excellent order of Providence unfolded bit by bit in the course of the centuries. The bloody wars are associated with the seven scourges, indicated by the seven vessels containing the seven plagues called 'the last, for with them the wrath of God is ended'.[428] In fact, the breaking of the seventh vessel is followed by the fall of Babylon, and then the Son of man appears to his enemies 'with great power and majesty.'[429]

823. The first six plagues did not humble the power of evil organised on earth, despite the blow it had received and the fearfulness of the plagues. They were so terrible that the whole of nature is seen as suffering and disturbed by extraordinary planetary phenomena, particularly the sixth plague, of which a part will be 'a violent earthquake, such as had not occurred since people were upon the earth.'[430] This disturbance of all nature seems to be Christ's meaning when he says that people 'will faint from fear confused by the roaring of the sea and the waves.'[431] Nevertheless the infuriated power of evil will think only of uniting its forces more strongly to apply all its strength against the power of good: 'And I saw three foul spirits like frogs coming from the mouth of the dragon, from the mouth of the beast, and from the mouth of the false prophet.' (who is his minister) 'These are demonic spirits, performing signs, who go abroad to the kings of the whole world, to assemble them for battle on the great day of God the Almighty.'[432] This offensive and defensive alliance or league established through the delegates of the emperor, who is the beast, will bring the power of

[426] Rev 14: 19–20.

[427] Rev 15: 3.

[428] Rev 15: 1, 6.

[429] Lk 21: 27†.

[430] Rev 16: 18.

[431] Lk 21: 25–26.

[432] Rev 16: 13–14.

evil to its climax, to its most perfect united state and organisation; the psalms tell us in fact what happens as a result: 'The kings of the earth set themselves, and the rulers take counsel together, against the Lord and his anointed.'[433] Christ had permitted the devil to arouse successfully the terrible power of the kings of all the earth so that the glory of Christ's victory, which must follow the sound of the seventh trumpet, would be maximum.

824. Three chapters now follow, all describing the total defeat of the organised power of evil in the very formidable empire, whose capital city is called Babylon. This powerful city is described as a wanton woman with whom the kings sin and who sits on the beast. The beast is the wicked emperor who had already relentlessly persecuted the Church for three and a half years. The seven heads of the beast, as they are called, must apparently be the seven kings subject to his empire: five of them are contemporaries who will have already fallen (perhaps the emperor had despoiled them of their kingdoms) by the time the great confederation of princes is formed. The five kings are succeeded by a single king: either the kingdoms of the five had been entrusted to him or he is a new king, subject to the great emperor. This single king is followed by a seventh, who also lasts only for a short time, and when all these kings have been swept away, the beast alone rules. But he also ceases to reign: he is either conquered by other tributary powers or deposed by his own ministers and peoples, or he himself shrewdly lays down his command. Ten kings hold his empire and rule it as an aristocracy, as something held in common by them all: 'And the ten horns which you saw are ten kings, who have not yet received a kingdom: but shall receive power as kings, one hour after the beast. These have one plan.'[434] But the conspiracy concocted by the beast against Christ does not cease; on the contrary, the ten allied kings, aware that their enterprise needs a great captain, turn to the beast and once again place him at the head of their armies, giving him their power and authority.[435]

825. Christ however must conquer this formidable army of

[433] Ps 2: 2.

[434] Rev 17: 12–13†.

[435] Rev 17: 13.

the ten kings captained by a man of extraordinary military valour, and must take and burn the capital, Babylon. Before doing this, he appears to the faithful in the city and makes them leave so as to escape the massacre that must take place in it.[436] Indeed, he calls them to arms against that queen of iniquity: 'Render to her as she herself has rendered, and repay her double for her deeds; mix a double draught for her in the cup she mixed',[437] because this will be the time when a tunic will be sold to buy a sword.[438] At that time JESUS Christ will reveal to his servants all that is about to happen. And when in heaven they see the approaching triumph, greater than all the previous triumphs of their king, they will sing Alleluia with infinite joy: 'Then I heard what seemed to be the voice of a great multitude, like the sound of many waters and like the sound of mighty thunder peals, crying out, Alleluia!.'[439]

826. The conquering king will now appear, already indicated by the white horse that appeared to John when the first seal was broken. The royal power of Christ, the God-Man, that shone forth at the resurrection, is the same power that must shine forth at the end of the world and, as it were, at the conclusion of things:

> Then I saw heaven opened, and there was a white horse! Its rider is called Faithful and True, and in righteousness he judges and makes war. His eyes are like a flame of fire, and on his head are many diadems; and he has a name inscribed that no one knows but himself. He is clothed in a robe sprinkled with blood, and his name is called WORD OF GOD. And the armies of heaven, wearing fine linen, white and pure, were following him on white horses. From his mouth comes a sharp sword with which to strike down the nations, and he will rule them with a rod of iron; he will tread the wine press of the fury of the wrath of God the Almighty. On his robe and on his thigh he has a name inscribed: King of kings and Lord of lords.[440]

[436] Rev 18: 4.

[437] Rev 18: 6.

[438] Lk 22: 36.

[439] Rev 19: 6.

[440] Rev 19: 11–16.

This is the coming of the Son of God seen by everybody and announced by Christ: 'and they shall see the Son of man coming in the clouds of heaven with much power and majesty';[441] 'For as lightning comes out of the east and appears even into the west: so shall also the coming of the Son of Man be.'[442] It is the coming mentioned by John at the beginning of the book of Revelation: 'Look! He is coming with the clouds; every eye will see him, even those who pierced him; and on his account all the tribes of the earth will wail.'[443] He will appear at the head of the army of saints drawn up in battle against the allied armies led by the beast and by the kings subject to the beast: 'And (suddenly) the beast was captured' (perhaps without any need for a battle) 'and with it the false prophet who had performed in its presence the signs by which he deceived those who had received the mark of the beast and those who worshipped its image.'[444] But when the ten kings see they have been deceived, they will turn their hatred against Babylonia, put the people to the sword and burn the city.[445] The beast and his false prophet 'were thrown alive into the lake of fire that burns with sulphur.' (a temporal punishment, symbol of eternal punishment) 'And the rest were killed by the sword of the rider on the horse, the sword that came from his mouth; and all the birds were gorged with their flesh.'[446]

827. The devil has thus been defeated. After being confounded in his false wisdom, he wanted to meet Christ, confronting power with power. But the Christ, with every obstacle removed and as legitimate conqueror in every way, can now restore the kingdom of Israel, foretold by the prophets and about which the Apostles asked the risen Master whether he would restore it at that time. The Lord made no denial and confirmed that it would one day be restored: 'It is not for you to know the times or periods that the Father has set by his own

[441] Mt 24: 30†.

[442] Mt 24: 27†.

[443] Rev 1: 7.

[444] Rev 19: 30.

[445] Rev 18: 16.

[446] Rev 19: 20–21.

authority.'[447] This is the temporal reign of JESUS Christ, described in the tenth chapter of the book of Revelation. It begins with the expulsion of the dragon from the earth and his imprisonment in hell: 'Then I saw an angel coming down from heaven, holding in his hand the key to the bottomless pit and a great chain. He seized the dragon, that ancient serpent, who is the Devil and Satan, and bound him for a thousand years, and threw him into the pit, and locked and sealed it over him, so that he would deceive the nations no more, until the thousand years were ended.'[448] The dead saints now rise, perhaps the most perfect among them, to be judges with Christ and reign with him on earth for a thousand years: 'Then I saw thrones, and those seated on them were given authority to judge. I also saw the souls of those who had been beheaded for their testimony to Jesus and for the word of God. They had not worshipped the beast or its image and had not received its mark on their foreheads or their hands. They came to life and reigned with Christ a thousand years. The rest of the dead did not come to life until the thousand years were ended. This is the first resurrection.'[449] A psalm had already foretold that 'the wicked shall not rise again in judgment,' (that is, to judge) 'nor sinners in the council of the just.'[450] St. Paul had taught that this must be the order of the resurrection: first Christ, then those who are Christ's, who believed in his coming, and then comes the end, that is, the resurrection and condemnation of the others.[451] When Christ, the conquering king, emerged from the sepulchre, 'the tombs also were opened, and many bodies of the saints who had fallen asleep were raised. After his resurrection they came out of the tombs and entered the holy city and appeared to many'.[452] Similarly at his second coming as conquering king and judge of the world, the other dead saints who had either been martyred or by keeping to the path of perfection had emulated the martyrs,

447 Acts 1: 7.

448 Rev 20: 1–3.

449 Rev 20: 4–5.

450 Ps 1: 5.

451 1 Cor 15: 23–24.

452 Mt 27: 52–53.

[827]

must rise to pronounce judgment with Christ and reign over the earth. In fact, many highly regarded scholars consider it probable that the saints who rose after the resurrection of Christ died again. But as this is not defined by the Church, I do not accept it because after the Lord's resurrection the dead saints had already been admitted to the beatific vision, which is also indicated by Christ's promise to the thief: 'Today you will be with me in paradise.'[453] Consequently, if they rose, they rose in a glorified state, and their appearances demonstrated that their body had the gifts of a glorified body. In my opinion we cannot believe that death continued to have some dominion over a person who had attained the state of glory; for me, such a belief would detract from the power of the resurrection of JESUS Christ and would not conform to God's normal way of operating: 'for the gifts and the calling of God are irrevocable',[454] as divine Scripture often states. After the second coming of the Saviour the risen saints will not be continuously visible on earth but will appear here and there, just as Christ did during the forty days he remained with his disciples after the resurrection. And although some perfect, just people will die during the reign of a thousand years, they will, it seems, immediately rise again, if we take into account that difficult passage of the Apostle where he says: 'For the Lord himself, with a cry of command, with the archangel's call and with the sound of God's trumpet, will descend from heaven, and the dead in Christ will rise first. Then we who are alive, who are left,' (that is, those of us faithful who at the time will be alive) 'will be caught up in the clouds together with them to meet the Lord in the air.'[455] Here we see that the bodies of Christ and of the Saints will not be subject to gravity, just like weightless things, and will appear when and to whom they wish [*App*., no. 15].

828. During this period on earth Christ and his Saints will guide and counsel human beings, whom no spirit of error will seduce and who will form one excellent and perfectly constituted society. In this way the ideal of human society will be realised, made sublime by the intervention of God, as it was at the

453 Lk 23: 43.

454 Rom 11: 29.

455 1 Thess 4: 16–17.

beginning in the earthly paradise, and even better, because we will have with us a God-Man. It also seems that the capital of the universal and blessed kingdom will be Jerusalem, or rather Rome perhaps. Thus the prophecy of Zechariah and other prophets about Jerusalem will be totally fulfilled: the rebuilding of the city after the captivity was only a symbol that was a long way from the truth.

829. After the thousands years of holiness and happiness on earth have passed, we read that the dragon will be let loose for a little time. This, it seems, may be explained as follows. The false *wisdom* of the devil has been confounded by the wisdom of Christ, and the devil has consequently been cast down from heaven to earth. His blind and unjust *power* was also conquered by the just power of Christ, and he has been thrown from earth into the abyss. It seems that he now had nothing left with which to oppose God. However, it is not improbable that he found a new expedient, and this expedient, we must note, was hypocrisy. After a thousand year of infernal torments it is not absurd to think that this father of lies pretended he had repented and promised God that if he were freed from the abyss, he would not harm human beings again. God knew very well that the devil wanted him to believe in this repentance, but because God wished 1. that the father of lies suffer the ultimate humiliation of being convinced of the facts, of his hypocrisy and powerlessness for good; 2. that Christ also did not miss this final glory of having fully convinced the devil of his totally powerless obstinacy in evil; and 3. that his servants have an opportunity for new heroic acts of virtue, he granted the angel of darkness this final experiment. But after the experiment, the devil will be confounded by *foolishness*, *powerlessness* and incorrigible *evil*, three confusions that corresponded to the three divine attributes glorified in Christ: wisdom, power and holiness, all of which are themselves in the service of and grounded in the one attribute of his GOODNESS.

830. So the devil is freed from his chains and at once engages, with ever greater ardour, in his old trade of seducing people: 'When the thousand years are ended, Satan will be released from his prison

and will come out to deceive the nations at the four corners of the earth, Gog and Magog, in order to gather them for battle;

they are as numerous as the sands of the sea. They marched up over the breadth of the earth and surrounded the camp of the saints and the beloved city.'[456] The experiment helped another purpose. Humanity was totally holy; every help had been freely given it by Christ. Nevertheless, hardly had the demon been released than humanity was seduced. The clearest proofs that God had given humanity of his goodness, wisdom and power to keep it faithful to him no longer had any value; it still needed to be deeply convinced that without God it is nothing, that finite being could not bestow any moral and eudaimonological good on itself, and that all its good came from God alone and from Christ alone. How great the glory the infinite would derive from this! Hence the final event was fitting and necessary so that humanity might be fully instructed and humbled and, in this total humbling of itself and in the supreme glory it will give to God, might find the maximum, moral and eudaimonological good to which Christ wanted to raise it.

831. As for the perjured, sacrilegious devil, the only treatment left was justice. The war is now ended by God alone: 'And fire came down from God, out of heaven, and consumed them,' (those who were besieging the holy city) 'and the devil who had deceived them was thrown into the lake of fire and sulphur, where the beast and the false prophet were, and they will be tormented day and night forever and ever.'[457] When the devil had been locked in the abyss the first time, there was no mention of sulphur and fire. Hence his punishment has three levels, corresponding to his three defeats: 1st., expulsion from heaven, corresponding to the defeat of his false wisdom; 2nd., expulsion from earth and imprisonment in the abyss, corresponding to the second defeat of his proud power; and 3rd., eternal fire, corresponding to the third defeat of the hypocritical boasting of his goodness. Previous to these three defeats and three punishments, he was damned and punished for his original sin of pride. But his three reckless attempts tripled the bitterness of his eternal loss.

832. And now, after the judgement and condemnation of the devil, the solemn judgment of the human race takes place. At the sight of the judge's throne, heaven and earth dissolve, and

456 Rev 20: 7–9.

457 Rev 20: 9–10.

their place is taken by the dead;[458] the wicked also rise. In an instant the angels sent by Christ gather all peoples before him. The books are opened, and final sentence is pronounced on all human beings individually according to their merits. The heavenly Jerusalem is entirely built of living stones, dressed into perfect squares and prepared beforehand, each having infinite value. This spouse of the Lamb, without spot and wrinkle, clothed in festive raiment and of infinite beauty, the masterpiece of God's wisdom, goodness and power, the fruit of the created universe, the work of the ages, finally and fully justifies, exalts and glorifies divine Providence for ever beyond all human thought.

[458] Rev 20: 11–12.

[832]

Chapter 29

Continuation — The result of antagonism

833. I will summarise what has been said and make an observation about the result of the struggle between the finite and the infinite that I have described.

I said it is fitting to the divine attributes that God bring his creature to the greatest moral perfection and happiness.

I used three reasons to demonstrate this truth.

The first was deduced from the law *of extremes*, which God always follows in his operation.

The second came from the law of *maximum effect*. God could not procure the maximum effect in his creature if he did not urge his creature on to the summit of moral perfection and happiness, because a higher level of moral perfection is never equalled by the accumulation of levels of lesser perfection; degrees of moral perfection differ as species differ. Thus, in the same way that a thousand individual degrees of heat, if kept separate, do not, as we saw, produce the effect obtained by ten degrees acting together, so a lesser perfection in a thousand people is incomparably below the value of a greater perfection in only one person.

Finally, the third reason was deduced from the law of the *complete realisation of the various species*. A given essence is never fully realised if the summit of its perfection is not realised.

834. The maximum moral perfection in the intelligent creature consists in the creature's experiential and practical knowledge of 1. the Creator, 2. its own original nothingness, and 3. its total dependence on the Creator, from whom comes every good. This is the only way the creature has to attain the greatest possible knowledge of God who must by his essence embrace the whole of entity, that is, being as beginning and end, and therefore cause of all the being and perfection of things. To acknowledge one's own nothingness in comparison to Creator, who is essential good and the cause of all created good, is in fact the greatest possible act of humility and also the greatest possible act of adoration and praise.

But the only way the creature can know in a practical way the infinite greatness of God in comparison with itself is by an act of self-denial; it must in practice give prior place to the Creator and not to all the pleasant feelings it can obtain from its own limited excellence.

God therefore had to provide his creature with a suitable opportunity for renouncing itself so that it could extol the Creator more greatly. He provided this opportunity both for the angels and for human beings.

The angels, as purely spiritual and active beings, have naturally a feeling of excellence and superiority to us, and God gave them the opportunity to deny this feeling by adoring the humanity that he had deified, that is, the Christ.

We on the other hand, as composite and passive beings, have naturally the feeling of animal pleasure, and God gave us the occasion to deny this feeling by our abstaining from a fruit 'pleasant to the sight and good for food.'[459]

If both these kinds of creatures had obeyed, they would have given just obeisance to the Creator and thus grown in moral perfection.[460]

But the moral perfection they would have obtained could not be the greatest possible because the humble submission required of the angels was not an act sufficient to make them know in practice the total nothingness of angelic nature in comparison to the Creator. Similarly, the mortification demanded of human beings was not the full sacrifice of human nature in honour of the Creator; such mortification could not have given us full, practical and meritorious knowledge of the total nothingness of human nature compared to the Creator.

The angel did not have the opportunity to acknowledge in practice and meritoriously all the deficiency of its nature. To have this opportunity it had to see angelic nature cast down into the abyss of evil. Similarly human beings had no opportunity to acknowledge in practice and meritoriously all the deficiency of human nature; they had to see human nature infected by all the evil it could receive.

God could of course have made both the angel and the human

[459] Gen 2: 9.

[460] Cf. Aug., *De C. D.*, 19: 18.

being pass the test. But at this point his infinite goodness came into play, consulted his wisdom as it were, and they both asked: Can the angelic and the human creature produce a greater moral fruit by our allowing them to fall or by sustaining them?

The decision was:

1. A greater fruit would be obtained by allowing a portion of the angels to fall in order that the angelic nature, which is shared by those who had not fallen, might know itself experientially, that is, know all the evil its nature was capable of, and be able to humble itself totally before the Creator, acknowledging its total salvation from him by his gratuitous choice, and at the same time might acquire the merit of detesting and combating evil more actually than ever before. The moral perfection of the faithful angels, raised to the height of these sentiments, outweighed by far in God's scales the value of the salvation of all the lost angels.

2. A greater fruit would be obtained by allowing man to fall and in this way infect all his descendants, except one young girl, destined to be the mother of the Redeemer. The fall would be permitted in order that redeemed human nature might know in practice all the evil to which it is susceptible and into which it had freely fallen, and therefore had to extol the Creator as its sole hope and refuge, and source of every good.

835. Moreover, the redemption of human beings was not only a benefit for them but had its effect on the angels. The redemption of humanity immensely increased the angels' moral perfection and therefore their happiness, for many reasons:

First, the loss or salvation, the preservation or destruction of human nature became the motive for the struggle between the demons and God. Clearly then, the full defeat of the devil that I described in the previous chapter gave the good angels a new and more intense, experiential knowledge of the greatness, wisdom and goodness of God compared with the impotence, foolishness and wickedness of angelic nature. Therefore angelic nature had a tremendous reason for giving eternal praise to the Lord, humbling itself in the depths of its feeling, even to annihilating itself before the Lord.

836. Secondly, the good angels had the opportunity to exercise their zeal in the war against the devil and so become

participants in the divine victory as ministers and free second causes, and as such even more in the divine glory.

837. Thirdly, they could exercise their charity towards human beings, of whom they became guardians and defenders.

838. Fourthly, they could adore the humanity of Christ, serve it and also, through the reverence due to Christ, serve those who have Christ within them. This was an exercise of supernatural humility, in which a greater nature justly gave obeisance to an immensely smaller nature, because the Creator united himself to this smaller nature.

839. Fifthly, having put their faith in the words of God and believed in the mystery of the incarnation, they afterwards drew from this mystery a great depth of light and a wonderful increase of their wisdom. In such a great mystery they pondered the divine wisdom and goodness that shines there so brightly and limitlessly.

840. Sixthly and finally, the love and vision of JESUS Christ gave them an immense increase of happiness, as is written: in him 'angels long to look.'[461]

841. Thus, God disposed the whole of creation so that at the end the maximum quantity of moral perfection and beatitude would be accumulated in his intelligent creatures. But perfection and beatitude consist in the experiential, practical knowledge (that is, accompanied by the assent of the will, by love and by action) of the Creator. Such knowledge was possible only by comparing creatures to the Creator. In this comparison creatures appeared as NOTHING to themselves, and the Creator appeared as their ALL. The comparison could not therefore be perfectly made without the antagonism between the finite and the infinite.

842. I said that the knowledge of the Creator which perfected creatures could result only from the comparison that they made experientially between themselves and the Creator. The reason is that the only thing the creature can know through experience by means of perception is itself and what happens in itself. And whenever what happens in it is infinite, the creature as finite imposes a kind of limit on the event. Hence, the Scholastics' saying: *quidquid recipitur ad instar*

[461] 1 Pet 1: 12.

recipientis recipitur [whatever is received is received according to the manner of the receiver]. The creature therefore had to know within itself, through the experience it had of itself, what kind of greatness, power, wisdom and goodness the Creator had. On the one hand, it had to measure all its own deficiency and, on the other, the Creator's greatness, which was non-deficient. To do this, it had to use itself as a measure, reasoning more or less like this: 'My being is of such and such an amount, but it is totally deficient. Therefore the quantity of my being is nothing in comparison with the quantity of a being that is non-deficient.'

But how could the creature come to this conclusion through experience? Experience of a real annihilation is not possible: if the creature were annihilated, it would obtain no fruit from the annihilation because the creature no longer is. But God wishes that it gives, or rather that it itself draws the greatest fruit from the knowledge of its own original nothingness. The creature therefore could not acquire the intense, practical persuasion of its own nothingness if it did not experience its deficiency in all that it is formed for and to which it aspires; in fact it fails to obtain all it desires and sees itself as insufficient for fulfilling the very purpose for which it exists. Formed for justice and moral good, it had to experience their loss. Formed for enjoyment, it had to experience extreme suffering. Angelic nature, because simple, could not be destroyed without being annihilated. Human nature, because composite, could be destroyed, that is, dissolved, but not annihilated, because the soul, separated from the body, would still remain and be capable of intelligence; there would still be a subject, a subsistent person. Consequently, death had to be an experience accommodated to human nature.

843. Such extreme experiences by the creature of its own deficiency were not designed by the Creator to harm the creature, but on the contrary to give it its maximum good. Having totally failed, it had to be raised from the depths of wretchedness by the spontaneous and gratuitous goodness of the Creator, and borne directly to the apex of perfection and happiness. In this way, after knowing itself and its works, it might know the Creator and the works the Creator was carrying out in it.

844. In angelic nature these two kinds of knowledge were acquired simultaneously. While one part of the angels in which the angelic nature subsists experienced natural deficiency, the

other part, in which the same nature also subsists, were enlightened and sustained, experiencing in themselves who the Creator was, and at the same time seeing who they might have been in the fate of their companions.

845. But in human nature one of these kinds of knowledge succeeds the other. Human beings first transgressed, and then came their redemption and sanctification: first, death, and then their resurrection.

846. However, because my interest here is concerned more with human beings, there are two final works that God accomplishes in fallen humanity, and through these works makes it experience his goodness, wisdom and power:

1. The first, which is relative to moral evil, was to redeem us all from sin and sanctify us. This was achieved by the victory of Christ over sin, a victory that continues in his followers for all time until the end of the world. And because the most holy humanity of our Lord JESUS Christ together with the Word had conquered, and we together with his humanity were also victorious, God associated us with himself in the glory of this great victory. The victory however is not due to human valour or ability, but to God alone: it was God who in coming to the our aid led us back from sin and made us once more capable of works of justice. Hence St. Paul says: 'But now the justice of God has been manifested without the law,' (that is, not in virtue of the Mosaic law) 'although the law and the prophets bear witness to it. And the justice of God through faith in JESUS Christ' (that is, not through our trust in our own ability to do good, which failed) 'came into and on all those who believe in him, because there is no distinction; since all sinned and needed the glory of God' (that is, his gratuitous goodness in which his glory and the victory over the finite creature shine out); 'they are gratuitously justified, through the redemption which is in Christ JESUS.'[462]

847. 2. The second work of God, which concerns eudaimonological evil, was our salvation from destruction. It is Christ's victory over death which is fulfilled at the time of the final resurrection. The Apostle says: 'The last enemy to be destroyed is death. For "God has put all things in subjection under his feet."

[462] Rom 3: 21-24 [R].

But when it says, "All things are put in subjection," it is plain that this does not include the one who put all things in subjection under him. When all things are subjected to him, then the Son himself' (as man) 'will also be subjected to the one who put all things in subjection under him, so that God may be all in all.'[463] Note, the Apostle says that it was God who subjected all things to Christ, and at the end Christ himself as man will be subjected to God, acknowledged as the sole source of every good. Everything will end in the GLORY OF GOD ALONE, the purpose of the universe; and all the saints, the Head and the members, will be sanctified and blessed in so sublime a glory.

848. Divine Scripture celebrates Christ's victory over death in a very special way; the victory is decisive because with death humanity is also destroyed, which is the intention and fixed purpose of the enemy of good. If a work of God, such as humanity, had been destroyed, it would have dishonoured its author, as if anything he does could be destroyed by another power. Humanity, once destroyed, could no longer merit, nor praise the Creator, nor produce fruit for him. It is true that the soul remained immortal, but the soul on its own is not humanity, it is simply a kind of fragment of humanity, something left over after the destruction. In addition, the only thing left to the soul without its body and thus deprived of the instrument designed to present it with the real objects of its cognitions, is, by the nature of the soul, an immobile act of intuition of ideal being. As a result the soul cannot have any awareness or reflection or freedom unless aided from outside. Consequently, in this state it cannot, through its own means, know or celebrate its Maker. Hence in the psalm humanity cries from the depths: 'Will you show wonders to the dead? Or shall physicians raise [them] to life, and give praise to you? Shall any one in the sepulchre declare your mercy: and your truth in destruction? Shall your wonders be known in the dark, your justice in the land of forgetfulness?'[464] We see here that in the Scriptures death is often called darkness, the land of forgetfulness, because with death according to nature we would forget all the knowledge we acquired in life. Hence the Israelites sang with the feelings

[463] 1 Cor 15: 26–28.

[464] Ps 87: 11–13†.

proper to human nature: 'The heavens are the Lord's heavens, but the earth he has given to human beings. The dead do not praise the Lord, nor do any that go down into silence. But we will bless the Lord from this time on and forevermore.'[465] This means that we cannot naturally understand how we can live in heaven, which is the dwelling place of God (a pure spirit) and of the other pure spirits. Without our body, we would neither know nor praise God, and therefore we need an earthly dwelling. This was a great mystery for nature, impenetrable for all the Hebrews. After the revelation of this great mystery, Christ taught that the greatest act of charity was the giving of one's life.[466] Similarly, in ancient times the greatest act of faith and hope was the giving of one's life at the word of God; such was Abraham's sacrifice and Job's protestation, who said: 'Though he kill me, yet I will trust in him';[467] such also the psalmist's protestation: 'Because your steadfast love is better than life, my lips will praise you.'[468] The failure to understand how the soul could live an operative life without the body was the cause of the Sadducee's error. When refuting them, Christ did not explain the subsistence of the soul without the body, which would not have been sufficient; he convinces them with the word of God, who in divine Scripture is called the God of Abraham, Isaac and Jacob. This supposes that these patriarchs lived because God was not 'a God of the dead but of the living.'[469] In fact the Sadducee's objection concerned the *resurrection*, not the simple *subsistence of the soul*. Without knowledge of the former it was impossible to understand how the soul might live an operative life. Nor does Christ explain to the Sadducees how just souls, separated from their bodies, had to be compensated for the loss of corporeal life by being given a mysterious communication with the glorious flesh of Christ. The word of Scripture had to be sufficient for them to remove their error; they were not capable of more. But he did explain it to his disciples: he told them

465 Ps 115: 16–18.

466 Cf. Baruch 2: 16–18.

467 Job 13: 15.

468 Ps 63: 4.

469 Mt 22: 32.

[848]

that the bread he was to give them was his flesh which was to take the place of the life of the world,[470] and he told Martha that he was 'the resurrection and the life'.[471] In fact, just as there are two deaths, there are two resurrections. Before the believer recovers his body at the final resurrection, he first loses his earthly life, but at the very moment this happens, his soul is drawn into communication with the most sacred humanity of JESUS Christ who comes to take him on his deathbed, according to the words of the Gospel. Christ who unites the soul of the dead person to himself is also at this moment its *resurrection*, because he restores to the soul the *operative life* it otherwise would have lost, and he continues to be true *life* for it, as he never detaches himself from it throughout eternity. This explains why St. Paul speaks of a dwelling that the soul receives after the present life in place of the dwelling that its body previously had: 'For we know that if the earthly tent we live in is destroyed, we have a building from God, a house not made with hands, eternal in the heavens.'[472] This 'house' does the work of the body.

849. The defeat of *sin* therefore means the defeat of *hell*, and because the defeat of sin means that death is defeated, eternal life in paradise is ushered in, the final state of the human race.

Nevertheless, a part of the human race, like a part of the angels, is lost. This was the sad effect of the free will of the creature, but necessary for the greatest good, granted the law of wisdom, which requires the greatest effect to be obtained with the least means. If this evil had not been permitted by divine wisdom, the good attainable by angelic and human nature would not have been obtained in the state of loss, for the following reasons:

1. The reprobate are a continuous, experiential demonstration to the just of the nothingness of their nature and of the infinite goodness of God, who has chosen them.
2. They justify the superiority and just dominion of the saints faithful to God over the wicked unfaithful to God.
3. They give the just a patent experience of the deformity

[470] Jn 6: 52.

[471] Jn 11: 25.

[472] 2 Cor 5: 1.

of sin, a deformity that makes the beauty of virtue stand out before all intelligences.

4. Eternal justice uses proportionate and inevitable suffering to restore the balance between moral good and eudaimonological good, between moral evil and eudaimonological evil. This is a new experiential means by which the whole of divine greatness and holiness is perceived by the creature. The reprobate demonstrate therefore how sublime and insuperable this eternal justice is.

850. To understand these reasons, we must understand the first truth I established: every created intelligence needs to know through actual experience that the finite is defective and that the infinite is not defective in order that the knowledge possessed by created intelligence might be intense enough and effective enough to move it to great acts. This need comes from its *limitation*, which not even God can exclude without making created intelligence infinite, which is absurd. The intelligent creature therefore had to *perceive* the divine attributes, and perceive them with its own nature, whether this nature *in se* perceives or perceives in the creative act through which it subsists. Hence not even the blessed would fully and effectively know God's greatness, justice, goodness, wisdom and other attributes unless these were manifested in act in the effects produced in the creatures whom they see in God. Thus the Apostle explains the mystery of election and reprobation. He says that with the latter God wished 'TO SHOW his wrath and TO MAKE KNOWN his power', and with the former 'TO MAKE KNOWN the riches of his glory for the objects of mercy, which he has prepared beforehand for glory.'[473] And those to whom he wanted *to make known* his justice and mercy are the whole of angelic and human nature. Once these creatures knew his attributes, they could use this knowledge to glorify the Creator and thus increase their perfection and happiness, which are completed in this knowledge and praise. The kind of individuals in which these creatures attained this perfection and beatitude were those who, because they remained good, were called by St. Paul 'objects of mercy'. Moreover God could not have *made known* these attributes to the creature unless the attributes, of

[473] Rom 9: 22–23.

themselves, manifested their effects in the creature, not through any defect in God's power but through defect in the creature, through the limitation of the creature, who has no other way of knowing divine things. St. Paul again confirms this teaching with the authority of the Old Testament. In fact, the Old Testament clearly and repeatedly gives the reason for the plagues God sent against the Egyptians: in afflicting Pharaoh God wished to teach all peoples a great lesson so that they might know his power and learn to fear his name. Thus God orders Moses to say to Pharaoh: 'But this is why I have let you live: to show you my power, and to make my name resound through all the earth.'[474] Indeed God wanted the plagues to teach Pharaoh (if Pharaoh had not hardened his heart) why he was being justly afflicted by God. Hence God had Moses say to him: 'For this time I will send all my plagues upon you yourself, and upon your officials, and upon your people, so that you may know that there is no one like me in all the earth.'[475] Thus the whole Hebrew people had sensible experience for always singing the greatness of God demonstrated in the portents done in Egypt and in the desert and in the conquest of Canaan. The whole Christian world itself also extols God in the same way, when he manifests his attributes through punishments and blessings, all of which will be eternal matter for eternal praise by the comprehensors. I repeat, God had to reveal fully his justice and goodness in his external works in order that these two attributes might be so totally and effectively perceived that they stimulated the creature's spirit to respond with affections and works. This good comes also from the terrible justice that is eternally exercised in hell. St. Augustine, considering this truth, expressed an opinion that summarises all my thought: 'If everyone were saved, then what is owed to sin through justice WOULD REMAIN UNKNOWN; if no one were saved, then what grace bestowed would remain unknown.'*[476]

[474] Ex 9: 16.

[475] Ex 9: 14.

[476] *Ep*. 194: 5. — What he says previous to this also deserves to be read and is to the point: 'They think they believe that God respects persons. They believe that God takes no account of any previous merits but shows mercy to whom he wishes, calls whom he chooses to call and makes pious those whom

CHAPTER 30

Continuation. — Forces God brings together in the battle

851. The universe and all that happens in it depend on God as first cause.

But God obtains the events necessary for making his excellent, eternal plan a reality, for putting detail on it and giving it flesh, by acting sometimes as a positive cause and sometimes as a negative cause. As a positive cause he produces good; as a negative cause he excludes superfluity, permits the evil of culpable sin and determines the penal evil. Everything that happens in the universe, relative to his great purpose, is good or evil. The intermingling of goods and evils and the battle between them result not only in the most wonderful, complete victory of good over evil, but in both the triumph of God, who is the essential good, and in the final perfection of creatures, which becomes superabundant through knowledge of the triumph and lasts for ever. Hence Scripture says God has poured out his wisdom on all his works.[477]

852. I first of all discussed how wisdom directs divine operation when God operates as a *positive cause*, and I explained diverse laws of this operation. I next considered how the same wisdom disposes created natures when God acts as a *negative cause*, and discussed the kind of conflict that takes place between their deficient effects (evil consists in this deficiency) and their full, complete effects — good consists in this fullness

he wishes. They pay little attention to the fact that he punishes the damned who have merited punishment, and gives grace to the saved who have not merited it. The damned therefore cannot complain that they do not deserve their punishment, nor can the saved glory in themselves as having deserved his grace. Indeed there is no respect for persons where one and the same clay of damnation and offence is involved *so that those who have been saved might learn from the damned because the saved would also be subject to torment if grace did not come to their aid*'* (194: 4).

477 'He poured her out upon all his works, upon all the living according to his gift; he lavished her upon those who love him'* (Sir 1: 9–10). Wisdom is poured upon all God's works, but only those who love him possess it properly and use it to their great advantage.

and completeness. But the great depth and richness of the subject indicate that before continuing we should look again at some considerations that so far have not had sufficient attention; I mean the nature of the forces God bring together in the mortal battle between good and evil.

853. I said that God fights with his wisdom and does not show his power until after he has legitimately conquered with the peaceful weapons of reason. He displays his power so as to do justice to both the conqueror and the conquered, decreeing triumph for the former and pain for the latter. I must examine this truth more closely.

When I say that God does not fight the enemies of good with his power but with his wisdom, we may ask how wisdom alone can succeed against the real forces brought together by violent and wicked people.

The reply is: God arranges that the combat takes place only between second causes, giving both good and wicked causes their existence, their nature and forces, with equal impartiality. We saw that at the beginning he created natures, helped them all, gave intelligent natures freedom to do good or evil, and established universal laws that regulated both the natural and the supernatural orders to which all entia were to be equally subject; he kept the subordination and chain of causes constant and thus permitted them to operate. The creation of natures was certainly a work of his power, but no battle is involved here: his power simply produced and gave nature to beings who were then left to their free will and native forces. When some turned away from justice and were thus the first to engage in battle against justice and also against those who practised justice, he did not intervene (as he could have done) in favour of the latter by annihilating the former or by some other act of divine power. On the contrary he maintained the forces of both the wicked and the good: he left them to combat each other, and willed that victory should come as a spontaneous result from the valour of the combatants and the interplay of second causes.

854. But if this is the case, in what sense did I say that God conquered with his wisdom?

Divine power certainly drew contingent natures from nothing and maintained them and the laws proper to them, but it was *wisdom* that determined the *mode* and *order* of these natures. In regard to their *mode*, wisdom fixed their quantity, weight, number, the measure of species and individuals, their time, their space, etc. In regard to their *order*, it connected and mixed them, placing them in certain determined relationships and giving them a suitable disposition. But this *mode* and *order* according to which contingent natures had been chosen, arranged and distributed, had been determined and decreed by infinite wisdom. Divine wisdom foresaw everything, and at the beginning when it gave things their location, it laid down the seeds of all the future effects and the relationships and harmony to be formed between them so that at the end of time, it obtained the overall result of the greatest good, the most stupendous victory of good. Hence this victory was foreseen and determined from the very beginning by a totally simple act of wisdom that alone could determine it; the only thing God's power did was to make the combatants exist. The victory itself is solely an *order*, an order of substances and acts, not *substances* themselves or their acts as such.[478] Order is the object of wisdom; substances and acts are the object of power. Therefore, whenever Scripture says that all creatures always carry out the divine will, it attributes this great obedience to the power of the first creative act, which gave them their subsistence and order, and in the act gave the command, as it were, concerning all they had to carry out in the future, *quia ipse* DIXIT *et facta sunt* [because he SPOKE and they were made]; it is a pronouncement of the Word that gives them subsistence, *sunt* [they are]. *Ipse* MANDAVIT, *et creata sunt* [he COMMANDED and they were created] is the command, the act of wisdom that harmonises them. *Statuit ea in aeternum et in saeculum saeculi* [he established them for ever, and for all ages] (producing the substances), *PRAECEPTUM POSUIT* [HE LAID DOWN A LAW] (establishing fitting order among them), *et non praeteribit* [and it shall not pass away].[479]

855. To anyone prepared to think, it is clear how much the outcome of human things depends on the series and chain of events. Hence the common proverb: 'Make me a prophet and I

[478] Hence St. Thomas fittingly says that '*Fate* does not mean a disposition pertaining to the genus of quality but a disposition that arranges the *order*; and order *is not a substance* but a *relationship*'* (*S.T.*, I, q. 116, art. 2, ad 3).

[479] Ps 148: 5–6†.

will make you rich', and also the origin of the 'fate' of ancient popular belief, of poets and indeed of philosophers, the power of which was thought superior to Jupiter's. This error manifestly resulted from observation of the constant course of second causes which, we could say, the supreme Being respects as his first law and will. But uneducated minds took this as an indication that the course was independent of divine power. Muslims did not place fate in the unbreakable connection of second causes but in the necessity of individual events, and attributed this necessity to the decretive will of God. Thus they fell into the absurdity that every event happens in any case, whether human beings posit its cause or not, or even remove the cause. This renewed the sophism which the ancient philosophers fittingly called the *idler*, ἀργὸς λογος.[480] Minds subject to this attitude notice that events often happen despite human will and human providence to the contrary. As a result they consider nothing but this necessity without thinking that effects are always connected with their cause. Hence, if the effects are *fatal*, the cause must be *co-fatal*, as Chrysippus said.[481] In our day, the study of a very long history, like the life of humanity that has developed through several thousand years, has had a beneficial result: it has opened people's eyes to see much better the nature of the invincible force of the chain of countless causes. They have seen that this force produces effects that are often inevitable and often unforeseeable by the individual human being, but are very easily foreseen and prearranged by the first author of the chain. Consequently, today a school of *fatalistic historians* has emerged, falling again into the error of pagan fate.

856. However, although there is error and ignorance in such a system, it is nevertheless true that the overall outcome of events that are composed of a long, complicated series of causes and of effects which in turn become causes, is for the most part truly beyond the ability of individual human beings, and often beyond that of the masses, whose forecasts are valueless because they do not foresee things at a sufficient distance, nor correct by time or by their own means what happens unexpectedly or is

[480] Cicero calls it *ignava ratio* [ignorant reason].

[481] Cic., *De Fato*, 13.

not personally experienced. On the other hand divine wisdom has foreseen everything, including all the causes arranged from the beginning for the most sublime purpose, and makes the succession of things always unfold in accord with the purpose that it wills, namely the great, pre-determined victory.

857. Rightly then, all human beings, in all times, aware of their impotence relative to the final outcome of things, agree that a great, mysterious power stands above them, master of everything, dispenser of everything, whether it is called fate or deity, or by other names. They strongly felt the need for it and the fear of it, and they were religious. The impious motto of the epicureans, *primus in orbe Deos fecit timor* [it was fear that first made Gods in the world], is a striking argument for the existence of this hidden, immense, supraworld force on which all mortals, particularly the impious, confess to be dependent, despite themselves. Hence, when Thrasymedes, celebrating the feast of Neptune on the island of Pylos, offered the golden vase to Mentor so that he might pass it to Telemachus and drink in honour of Neptune, Homer has him say:

> … offer the cup of the sweet draft
> To your companion, in whom,
> It would seem, dwells fear of the gods,
> When every living thing needs gods.

This concept is continually repeated by all the most ancient authors. When the pagans were oppressed and had no refuge or strength to resist violent oppressors, they turned in supplication to the invisible being, controller of the world, and did so with the same spontaneity of nature with which the mind rises to God through the principle of integration.[482] Yet they did not think however that the chain of second causes had to be broken. Naturally, and as it were instinctively, they understood that the outcome of events depended totally on the arrangement and connections of the chain by a supreme mind in one way rather than another; only here did they find sufficient reason to explain why things were connected in a particular way rather than in another. Natural sense gave such importance to this first and necessary ordering of the things of the world by an eternal

[482] *NE*, 3: 1264–1273.

mind that it very often forgot the second causes on which, as such, the overall fortunate or unfortunate effect of the events that were desired or feared did not in any way depend. On the contrary, the effect depended totally on the *order of those causes*, and the order itself depended on the wisdom that had arranged the causes. Under this dispensation justice could not ultimately perish. Moreover, this intimate persuasion common to human beings, especially the unfortunate and ill-treated, is often expressed by poets, for example by Horace in these verses:

> Jupiter has sway over kings,
> Who in turn are feared by their own peoples.
> Resplendent with a magnificent triumph,
> He moves everything with a flicker of his eyebrow.*[483]

858. What is this movement of all things that Jupiter effects purely by a flicker of his eyebrow? All the movements of the world are indeed appropriately attributed to his eyebrow, that is, to his gaze, because the body's gaze represents the mind's gaze, that is, knowledge of things; and God initiates and guides things solely with his knowledge of them. Hence, according to the intimate sense of the Gentiles, it is not the power of Jupiter that breaks the series of causes, but the power that, once these causes are created, orders them in such an appropriate manner that justice not only does not perish but finally triumphs.

859. But we will gain a much better understanding of the extent of this silent, hidden strength of wisdom that arranges the order of causes if we consider that no single event occurs except as an effect of the total, very long and intricate series of causes that have prepared and arranged that order. On the other hand there are individual, passing events and accidents which considered in themselves are of no importance. Yet the whole of human happiness and unhappiness depends on them. Just one of these events is often sufficient to thwart all our plans, even our great plans; that one event is sufficient to destroy all our power, to make certain what is most unlikely, indeed to overturn the course of our life and, after changing the course of the life of one individual, alter the course of life of millions of others

[483] *Odyssey*, bk. 3, 1.

— in fact it is sufficient to change the fortune of nations. What can a human being do to resist these events that have been so well prepared and, as it were, secretly prepared? Who amongst us, in the event of death, can extend his or her life one single day? A great many accidents can at any moment cut short the course of our life, and accidents can be unforeseen. Nevertheless all these are in the hands of Him who had mentally ordered the series of causes and effects; for each of these, he prescribes the hour, minute and instant when it must happen; and obedient to his command, it does not fail. Horace says: 'One plants his saplings in rows on a larger property than another. One who is more noble in lineage comes to the field of Mars to share the honours. One who is better in customs and repute, and another who has a great number of followers, contend with others. Necessity, with equal law, draws the lot of death for both the highest and the lowest; in the large urn every name is contained and shaken up.'[484] Who can say how different the events of the whole world would have been if Julian had returned victorious from war instead of being killed by the Parthians? Or if Alexander had not been struck down by death in Babylonia before he had appointed a successor and arranged the government of his conquests? Of if Julius Caesar had lived long?

860. The very moment when we cease to live on earth is in the hands of the wisdom that orders events, but equally the preservation or extinction of nations depends solely on this wisdom. Who can give succession to a prince or take it from him? Does this depend on his will, on his courage, on the might of his armies? Even the destiny of empires is bound in great part to the succession or extinction of the reigning houses. What, for example, would Italy be at present if so many royal lineages had not become suddenly extinct? Only God, who disposes these things, knows.

861. What I say about human life and the duration of lineages can also be said about every great human enterprise. The order of events determines the point where an enterprise comes to an end, and the pagans had seen and admitted this. One of them said:

[484] *Odyssey*, bk.3: 1.

We and our works are doomed to death,
Whether Neptune, brought onto the land, defends our fleet
From the north winds, a kingly work,
Or whether the lake, for a long time infertile and fit for oars,
Now supports its neighbouring cities and feels the heavy plough,
Or whether the river, taught to flow in a more fitting channel,
Has changed its course which was so destructive to the produce.
MORTAL WORKS WILL PERISH.*[485]

862. All these events, the extinction of individuals, of family lines, the certain termination of the greatest human works within a time fixed from eternity by the chain of causes are simply examples. But it is equally true of every single event, great or small: each has the time decreed for it. We humans are only a means destined to execute these high decrees.

863. This truth, when applied, forms the sublime in Greek tragedies. They show us fate asserting itself with infallible outcome through a series of natural causes extraordinarily and inevitably bound together against all external appearance, contemptuous of all human power and despite all human prudence. But if the tragic poet used a contrivance to bring some God onto the stage, the good sense of the ancients reproved him because they wanted to see divine wisdom shining out in the play, in the wonderful connection of the events, not divine power arbitrarily introduced. Hence Horace's precept:

> Do not have God intervene unless some problem has arisen that calls for a solution,*[486]

clearly dictated by my principle of sufficient reason, that is, of the least means, which requires the direct intervention of God in the things of this world only because of the need for a good that cannot otherwise be obtained.

864. I wish to point out here that whenever tragedy solves a

[485] Horace, *De Arte poet.*

[486] Horace, *De Arte poet.*

problem in a natural way, which has not been foreseen by the wisest people and obstructed by all their might and prudence, the tragedy is always sublime, because understanding it is sublime. It is sublime to see with one's own eyes, as it were, human matters conducted by a supramundane power which although hidden, awesome and inevitable, is in no way violent. If moreover the event favours justice and virtue, opposing the injustice and vice that nearly prevail and triumph, then the tragedy is *probable* as well as appearing *sublime*. As I said, the law according to which causes are connected requires the final outcome of external events to harmonise with virtuous and just works in opposition to injustices and iniquities. The contrary to this (which is the exception) happens only when the law of the least means requires otherwise. The probable is in fact constituted by things that happen in the normal way, while the improbable is constituted by the abnormal and the exceptional. For this reason, every school of poetry that glorifies vice sins against the law of probability.

865. We must also note that divine wisdom has previously established an order not only for external events but for human thoughts and affections, and this order is another powerful weapon with which divine wisdom conquers and succeeds in making all things have the outcome it wants.

In fact, a single thought present in a mind, or not present at the due time, is sufficient to change the destinies of the entire world. We see that all the most famous conquerors were aware of being guided by some kind of fate. Caesar's destiny stands out in this regard: this very ambitious man forgot his own bravery and attributed his impressive successes to his destiny, to a kind of higher disposition; without this he could not explain to himself his victories or the course of his life. Attila, we know, was guided by some internal feeling. This barbarian-devastator protested that not he but something superior to him moved him to his enterprises, and he called himself the scourge of God. The terrible Nadir Shah, conqueror of India, made the same claim. And everybody knows how Napoleon, the most recent of famous captains, judged his successful enterprises. Amazed at events, he often declared that victory does not depend on man but rather on a fleeting moment, on a sudden thought that is not sought but comes totally of itself at the right instant, and without it all is lost. Like all his predecessors, he often mentioned his star in his warlike deeds, and frequently paid homage to the divinity. He felt and admitted the profound concept contained in the name given by Scripture to the supreme Being: 'the God of armies'.

866. But an instantaneous thought that comes and goes like lightning is not the only thing that can determine victory or defeat. Every determination we make depends on the sudden presence or sudden absence of thoughts; the coming or going of a thought is not under our control. When Joseph's brothers saw him coming in the distance, they said: 'Let us kill this dreamer and see if his dreams will help him'; they thought they had their brother's destiny in their hands and could freely turn into nothing what the dreams had forecast. But this did not happen because their thoughts, movements and the resulting persuasions of their spirit were not under their control, even though thoughts and persuasions are very intimate to us. In fact the thought of killing their brother quickly changed into the thought of selling him, which they considered the equivalent of their plan. In this way however they unknowingly cooperated in the verification of the dreams they contemned. On the other hand, if the brothers had not been persuaded that they could prevent the dreams coming true and had not tried to override them, Joseph would certainly not have become the viceroy of Egypt. But nevertheless, the brothers were free: they could certainly have killed him, or they could have sold him or ignored and dismissed the dreams. But they freely preferred the second course of action, less iniquitous than the first, because according to the series of their thoughts the second followed the first and was chosen; it would not have been chosen if it had not followed the first.

867. Constantine was a hostage of Galerius but obtained permission from the tyrant to return to his father, Constantine Chlorus. If Galerius, for whatever reason, had delayed one single day in granting the permission, or if the young hero had not suddenly had the thought of leaving that same evening when the permission of the Nicomedian court was granted, and if he had not had the horses killed at the stations he passed through, he would have been victim of the cruel, ambitious old man who the next day vainly wanted his prey pursued. Here we have a thought that did not come to Galerius, but did come to

Constantine. On such a small thing depended the triumph of the Cross, the peace of the Church, the removal of tyrants who were tearing humanity apart, the restoration of the Roman empire, the founding of Constantinople, the Council of Nicea, and the great works of the Fathers of the fourth century, in short, the destiny of the whole world; we ourselves are the offspring of that thought. Neither Constantine nor Galerius knew the immense and countless consequences of the unseen thought which at one instant Galerius did not have, and at another, Constantine had. These things could not therefore be objects of their choice. God however knew them thoroughly, and he alone had pre-chosen them. Very much to the point here is the passage in Job where he speaks about God: 'He changes the heart of the princes of the people of the earth, and deceives them that they walk in vain where there is no way. They shall grope as in the dark, and not in the light, and he shall make them stagger like men that are drunk.'*[487] God is said 'to deceive' the arrogant, wicked princes, meaning that he permits them to be deceived and confounded in their thoughts and counsels. We read the same in another place: 'The heart of the king is in the hands of the Lord and he moves it to what he wills.' This divine power over the thoughts of the great is likened by Scripture to God's power to send water down from the sky and make it descend from the mountains and spread it over the face of the earth.[488]

868. Hence, just as the rains and waters, divided into rivers, move and divide by natural causes predisposed by God, so the sequence of human thoughts and thoughts that come and go at certain determined moments are natural effects produced by natural causes (among which are included pure intelligences). But God had either established and ordered all these causes and effects at the beginning or brought them about later by the manifestation of his will. Therefore, if we bear in mind that all human operations without exception begin from thoughts, and

[487] Job 12: 16–25†. The whole of this fine part of Job deserves careful consideration relative to the discussion.

[488] 'The king's heart is a stream of water in the hand of the LORD; he turns it wherever he will'* (Prov 21: 1).

that without thoughts they cannot begin, we will clearly see that because God is the first organiser and disposer of thoughts, he alone has in his hands all human events and their certain outcomes.

869. Although I say that the sequence of human thoughts has its natural causes, sometimes plain to see, sometimes concealed, I do not say that the origin, the coming and going of thoughts in human minds, depends either solely on their natural connection and association or solely on the accidental sensations we receive from the objects that are around us and ordered by Providence. These causes certainly do have an immense influence on the movements of the human spirit, but besides these there are invisible beings, good and bad, who can concur in arousing and dispelling thoughts, as I have said. They also are second causes, ordered by God in accord with his indefectible plan, and they perform their actions throughout the whole universe according to the laws of their nature. This was the constant feeling of antiquity, including pagan antiquity, that attributed a genie to every human being. It is also confirmed by Christian tradition: Boethius wrote, 'The fatal sequence of events is in the course of being woven: fate is fulfilled through the ministry of some spirits working for divine Providence, or through the work of the soul, through the service of all nature, through the heavenly motion of the stars, through angelic power, or through the varying diligence of demons, either some of them or all of them.'[489] St. Thomas also teaches the same.[490]

870. Consequently, if God, within certain limits prescribed by wisdom, permits demons to arouse in human spirits thoughts and plans that are a temptation or serve evil, if he authorises his angels to place in human minds thoughts that invite those minds to good or directs them to a happy outcome in good works, he again makes no direct use of his power. It is still second causes that operate according to their own laws and a pre-established connection. At most, God does not exercise his imperious authority but the peaceful office of teacher and persuader.

[489] *De Consol.*, bk. 4, p. 6.

[490] *S.T.*, I, q. 96, art. 2.

871. But I must mention other weapons in addition to those of the wise connection of things and the interior operations in souls. One of these weapons used by divine wisdom in its battle to defeat evil and triumphantly conquer for good consists in the spontaneous effects that come from human malice, virtue and holiness.

872. Malice and iniquity are in themselves a deterioration of the nature and person of the wicked. Hence if the wicked freely choose these states, they debase and ruin themselves. Sinners are damaged and bring shame on themselves through the very fact of their sin. St. Augustine, speaking about the robber and the one who is robbed, rightly observes that the first does greater harm to himself than to the other, 'because the former suffers the damage of money, the latter of innocence.'[491]

873. After the moral evil that corrupts the most noble part of ourselves, we suffer penal evil through natural ways. The psalm says, 'See how they conceive evil, and are pregnant with mischief, and bring forth lies. They make a pit, digging it out, and fall into the hole that they have made.'[492] St. Augustine says we must not think 'that the peacefulness and ineffable light, which is God, draws from itself the means for punishing sins. On the contrary, it so orders sins that the very things that were pleasures for sinners are instruments of the Lord who punishes them.'[493] This is treated extensively both in Scripture which describes the natural evils joined to sins, and in the books of moral philosophers of every age, to which daily experience bears clear testimony. But, to avoid endless discussion, I will deal only with the subject of natural evils joined to sins.

874. First, sin blinds in varying degree those who commit it and love it. Not only does it banish supernatural light, it reduces natural light, in the following way. The things that we know and enrich our mind are not necessarily norms for its operation; only those items of knowledge we choose are norms and principles of its actions.

[491] Enarr. in ps. 7, 17.

[492] Ps 7: 14–15.

[493] Enarr. in ps. 7, 16.

If we operated according to all we know, if our action followed all the items of information we possess as norms, our operation would be right and just. But a wicked person who conceived a disordered affection chooses this as his guide. Therefore, he chooses as norm of his operations only the things he knows which second his passion either by justifying it or fostering it, or providing it with the means to satisfy itself. Thus the intelligence of the rebellious angel was darkened by his pride. He had great knowledge of both God and himself but took as norm of his operation only the knowledge of himself; he looked only at himself, at his own excellence. He thus turned his gaze away from God and the divine excellence, and vainly prided himself in overcoming the one whom he knew could not be overcome. Before the Flood the giants did the same, those notorious, wicked men whose memory has been preserved in all peoples. Their bold deeds are related in all mythologies; their defeat is told in Horace and Job. There is a truth always sensed, always admitted by all people, and therefore not unknown to them, that an inescapable power, a necessity, a fate, a God, the first cause, orderer of everything, rules over all human forces. However they did not take it as a norm of their operation, instead they limited their attention to their bodily power and their bold spirit; they blindly persuaded themselves they could fight God himself, and somehow succeed in the combat. But all the time they did not know that the author of nature had prepared the waters in which they would inevitably perish, drowned by their own arrogance. Scripture therefore rightly attributes their loss to their foolishness, that they gave no thought to the means God had of humbling them solely by the forces of nature, just as Scripture attributes Noah's salvation to his own wisdom: Noah took as norm of his operation the knowledge of the God who arranged, that is, had already arranged, all things from the beginning.[494]

[494] Wis 14; Sir 16. — We have seen that God wished to use his practice of humbling nature as sober instruction for the human race, teaching it to know him as far greater than nature. By means of this necessity God humbled the whole of nature even to the level of the nothingness from which it had come. However it was a supreme help to nature, that is, to the intelligences he had created, and results from the following psychological, or rather pneumalogical, law: 'When an intelligent spirit possesses goods exceeding its normal state, it is tempted to fix its intelligence and affection on them in such a way

[874]

875. There is then this natural difference between the good and the bad: the good are enlightened and guided by the all the truth they know; the bad espouse a small portion of the truth and willingly deprive themselves of the light of the other part, which they attack because it opposes their passions. This gives the good, whom Scripture calls *wise*, a huge advantage over the bad, who are called *foolish*. Hence, the bad, we are told, walk in darkness, stumble and fall, whereas the good walk in the light; they are prudent and masters of themselves, moving straight forward, certain of their purpose. It is also most appropriately written that the wicked person whose heart grows narrow because he limits it to the objects of his passions, also diminishes in intelligence: 'He that wants understanding thinks vain things, and the foolish, and erring man, thinks foolish things.'[495]

876. It adds that because the wicked trust in themselves, they cannot receive any special light from the fount of holiness; in fact they refuse to receive. On the other hand the good who trust in God have Providence at their side through the presence of the angels, who arouse fitting thoughts in them. God also himself directly enlightens them.

877. Therefore penal evils, to which the wicked are subject, derive from two sources: 1. from themselves as people who blind themselves, and 2. from the disposition of things and events that do not harmonise with their operation.

that it blinds itself to what is outside them and to what is superior to itself. In short, it ceases to pay attention to the greatness of the Creator from whom it receives everything.' This is why knowledge alone does not lead us to God; on the contrary, if it is not counterbalanced and informed by charity, it leads us away from him and we become proud. This observation is not mine, but St. Paul's; he notes that God had to use a doctrine that teaches and inculcates humility through FAITH, which was judged as foolishness, to oppose human KNOWLEDGE, which instilled nothing but pride and was considered wisdom: 'For since, in the wisdom of God, the world did not know God through wisdom,' (that is, through the speculations of philosophers and teachers proud of their knowledge) 'God decided, through the foolishness of our proclamation, to save those who believe'* (1 Cor 1: 21).

[495] Sir 16: 23†. — For the same reason, also St. Paul says that if the princes of this world had known Christ they would not have crucified him (1 Cor 2: 8). They did not know him because of the ignorance produced by sin, through the blindness of their passions.

878. Moreover, because the foundation of every vice is presumptuous confidence in its own strength, Scripture says: 'Let them be taken in their pride,'[496] and tells us that they will enter the trap by their own action.[497]

879. In regard to the domestic society of the wicked, we see a great many troubles: 'Panic and insolence will waste away riches; thus the house of the proud will be laid waste' (that is, the substance of the proud will be torn away). 'Whoever builds his house with other people's money is like one who gathers stones for the winter. An assembly of the wicked is like a bundle of tow, and their end is a blazing fire.'[498]

880. Relative to civil societies, we should note the misfortunes that come to them from injustice and iniquity: 'As the judge of the people is himself, so also are his ministers: and what manner of man the ruler of a city is, such also are they that dwell therein. An unwise king shall be the ruin of his people: and cities shall be inhabited through the prudence of the rulers... A kingdom is translated from one people to another, because of injustice, and wrongs, and injuries, and diverse deceits... God has overturned the thrones of proud princes, and has set up the meek in their stead. God has made the roots of proud nations to wither, and has planted the humble of these nations. The Lord has overthrown the lands of the Gentiles, and has destroyed them even to the foundation. He has made some of them to wither away, and has destroyed them, and has made the memory of them to cease from the earth.'[499]

881. As regards individuals, they are weakened by vice. Every vice brings with it infinite evils. It would take too much time to recount the diseases they produce: doctors have spoken about them, but still not sufficiently. All diseases can be reduced ultimately to sin as their universal cause.[500]

Wicked people are not happy because they are deeply disordered and an affliction to themselves. The peace and

[496] Ps 58: 13†.*

[497] 'In the transgression of the evil there is a snare'* (Prov 29: 6).

[498] Sir 21: 4, 8–9.

[499] Sir 10: 2–3, 8, 17–20†.

[500] On this matter, see Roselly de Lorgue, *La mort avant l'homme*.

consolations of the just greatly exceed all the talk and thought of those who have not experienced these comforts. Even if the wicked sometimes enjoy *external goods* and pleasures, they have no *satisfaction*.[501] Hence Scripture says that 'he will not enjoy his own riches'[502] and whatever he eats 'the belly of the wicked suffers want.'[503]

882. Furthermore, the just are given a light, an affection, a security, a supernatural confidence. This is the seed of their future total triumph. As the Apostle says: 'You reap whatever you sow. If you sow to your own flesh, you will reap corruption from the flesh; but if you sow to the Spirit, you will reap eternal life from the Spirit.'[504]

Therefore the constancy of the good never diminishes. The internal goods that they neither obtain nor lose through violence give them new strength of spirit which makes them content, and indomitable in their meekness. But the wicked, constantly exhausted by their laborious efforts, always laid low by their violent activity, lose their strength, become languid, and they themselves often admit this.[505]

883. Granted these things and also others that could be pointed out, we find verified the law that is imposed on the wicked and which I stated earlier: THEY CAN BEGIN BUT NOT FINISH (cf. 319). The wicked can certainly begin because if God did not allow them to begin, there would be no combat. However, they cannot finish because the outcome of what is undertaken is the only thing that matters, and God has reserved this to himself and his people. Temporary oppression and humiliation are not in fact the outcome: they are the path that precedes and leads to the outcome. Hence, 'the desire of the wicked comes to

[501] Cf. *SP*, bk. 4.

[502] Sir 14: 5.

[503] 'The righteous has enough to satisfy his appetite, but the belly of the wicked suffers want'* (Prov 13: 25).

[504] Gal 6: 8. Cf. *Saggio sulla Speranza*, bk. 3.

[505] 'Many times we said: "Will this present crisis be the last?", but it was always followed by others. This is because we always fall asleep after victory. *We pass suddenly from extreme energy to extreme weakness.*'* *Rapport de Louchet à la Convention Nationale le 26 vendémiaire, ann. 4 sur la situation de la République*.

nothing,'[506] and 'every product decays and ceases to exist, and the man who made it will pass away with it,'[507] and 'with him who fears the Lord, it will go well at the end.'[508] 'To fear the Lord is the root of wisdom,'[509] that is, knowledge of happiness; not to fear God is the fullness of stupidity because the wicked appear 'like the morning mist' (which gives no water) 'or like the dew that goes away early, like chaff that swirls from the threshing floor or like smoke from a window.'[510]

It must be remembered however that the deficiency of the wicked, which causes them to succumb unfailingly, originates solely from themselves. Having separated themselves from God, they refuse to enjoy the strengths and forces that he would have been ready to give them. God simply permits the separation they freely choose, and he permits it because he is moved by his infinite goodness that draws the maximum good from their evils towards the sum total of his creatures. Thus God said to Israel: 'Destruction is your own, O Israel; your help is only in me.'[511] Scripture is never tired of making us understand in a thousand ways that God is the source of goods; all evils happen because he stops providing goods to those who reject them.

'They have forsaken me, the fountain of living water, and dug out cisterns for themselves, cracked cisterns that can hold no water.'[512] 'You have forsaken the God that begot you, and have forgotten[513]

the Lord that created you. The Lord saw, and was moved to wrath: because his own sons and daughters provoked him. And he said: I will hide my face from them, and will consider what their last end shall be (*et considerabo novissima eorum*),' which is precisely the outcome that all wicked enterprises lacked. 'You

[506] Ps 112: 10.

[507] Sir 14: 19.

[508] Sir 1: 13.

[509] Ibid., 1: 20.

[510] Hos 13: 3.

[511] Hos 13: 9†.

[512] Jer 2: 13.

[513] Deut 32: 18–20†. 'The wicked forget God' means they do not take 'the knowledge they have of God as norm of their actions'; it is a lack of *practical knowledge*.

[883]

have ignored all my counsel and would have none of my reproof; I also will laugh at your calamity; I will mock when panic strikes you.'[514] God is simply a spectator, present at the defeat of the wicked; they perish of themselves without any need for him to suppress them, without any need of help. 'You abandoned me,' (thus God speaks to Roboam and the princes of Juda, when the Egyptian king was advancing on Jerusalem) 'so I have abandoned you to the hand of Shishak.'[515] God simply withdraws, remains inactive; his enemies are lost by their own action. The psalmist describes God who operates and ceases to operate in this way: 'These all look to you to give them their food in due season; when you give to them, they gather it up; when you open your hand, they are filled with good things. When you hide your face, they are dismayed; when you take away their breath, they die and return to their dust.'[516] Job describes the natural goods that God allows the wicked to have, then immediately turns to Him who ordered the series of second causes: 'Yet because their good things are not in their hand, may the counsel of the wicked be far from me.'[517] He at once describes the many accidents that God has permitted and that despoil them of their fleeting goods which God had previously left to them.

To sum up. Everywhere in Scripture goods come from God as *positive cause*; evils depend on God as *negative cause*: God permits but does not operate. This is sufficient for the creature to fall under the fascination of evils when left to his own strength, in which he trusted.

[514] Prov 1: 25–26.

[515] 2 Chron 12: 5.

[516] Ps 104: 27–29.

[517] Job 21: 16†.

[883]

CHAPTER 31

Eleventh consequence: the law of speed of operation

Wisdom is more mobile than any motion*
Wis 7: 24

884. The law of the least means governing the operation of wisdom prompted God both in the choice of the *entia* that were to make up creation so that it would be perfect, and in the choice of their *actions*. Consequently, his creative goodness could not attain its purpose without these two instruments: 1. entia chosen to fit the end, and connected harmoniously together; and 2. actions, predisposed and combined in a wonderful harmony for the same end.

885. We have seen that God, in creating entia and following this great principle, was guided by the laws of parsimony, connection, continuity, variety and excluded equality.

We have also seen that the great end essential to divine operation is to obtain the maximum good realised in his creature. In order to determine which *actions* had to be pre-established so that entia as causes could obtain this great end, I considered 1. the necessary unity of action of the first cause for fulfilling the divine purpose, 2. the diverse ways in which the first cause, by its operation and non-operation, obtains this end through second causes, 3. the nature of the end, expressed in the Scriptures as *divine glory*, and 4. the need for antagonism and a final victory of the power of good over evil, of infinite goodness over finite infirmity.

After seeing therefore not only which kind of entia but which actions had to be determined and established by the first cause if creation was to be directed to its final perfection and enriched by the greatest good, the only thing now remaining to be done is to observe the *manner* in which these actions had to play their part in the great drama. The manner is determined by three laws, which we must now examine: 1. the *law of speed*; 2. the *law of accumulation* and 3. the *law of seed*. I will begin with the first.

886. The law of the least means obviously implies and results in a *maximum speed of operation*. But to determine this concept and prevent it from being misunderstood, I must explain it.

887. The individual action of a brute ens that obeys necessity does not concern us here. As we have seen, the speed of action of a brute ens would always be determined by the force that produces the action (cf. 434–446). However, the force could be impeded to varying degree by external obstacles, and hence a smaller number of obstacles would mean a quicker and fuller operation of the force. The principle therefore that determines the maximum effect in such a case is 'the greatest ease of operation', and this is the greatest possible when the force meets no obstacle at all or the smallest possible obstacle.

888. But another element enters the calculation when many actions are connected together for one purpose. The sufficient reason for the mutual position of many agents is not in their individual natures but solely in the mind that give them order, (cf. 445). Hence the intended effect does not depend on the action of each but on the order of them all as a whole; it is now an intellectual purpose, not a purely physical purpose. Thus geometrical designs would not have a natural purpose or reason if there were no intellect that wished to use them to facilitate the connection of its thoughts. Similarly, a machine does not have a purely physical purpose that may be different from other physical effects; its value lies totally in giving to the intelligence that designed it the result the intelligence wanted when it built the machine. For example, a clock does not strike the hours for itself but for the craftsman who devised it so that he can accurately know the divisions of time. Nevertheless when many brute agents are skilfully connected together, each uses the energy it has, in so far as obstacles allow. Thus, energy is a determined quantity, and obstacles change or diminish its effect.

889. In the case of intellective, moral agents, we see that although their power is limited and determined, the quantity of power passing into an action is not determined. These agents have, as it were, a certain deposit of energy, upon which they draw or which they bring into action more or less as they will. Similarly the quantity of effect that a moral-intellective ens can produce is not determined in the same way as the quantity of

effect a brute ens can produce. In the moral-intellective ens, the quantity changes according to the degree of development of willed activity.

890. It follows first of all therefore that the effect of an individual brute force has no need whatsoever to be determined by an ordering wisdom; its determination is found in the nature of the immutable force that produces it. I say this because I have so far not succeeded in understanding Leibniz's thought when he claims that the laws of motion of bodies are in some way arbitrary. Perhaps my failure to understand him arises from my insufficient reflection on the matter. I confess that I would like to understand, if this were the case, because I would acquire a beautiful and important truth. But, as I said, I cannot so far accept it because I have not succeeded in understanding it. Even if his opinion were true, the law of speed I am discussing here would possibly be modified in its application, but it would still be true in itself.

891. Secondly, the effect that a mind wants from many brute entia or many cooperating forces, can vary in degree. Hence, wisdom is needed for determining the connection and cooperation between them so that the effect is maximum.

892. Thirdly, to draw the maximum effect from many cooperative moral-intellective entia in themselves or when mixed with brute entia, a double intervention of wisdom is necessary in order to 1. connect them in an appropriate way and 2. stimulate them to a greater quantity of action.

893. Granted this information, we can understand how one of the conditions for obtaining the greatest effect is *maximum speed of action* and therefore the greatest saving of time.

But to determine this greatest possible speed of action, the other conditions of the problem must be taken into account. If a part of a machine accelerated its motion more than it should, it would either break down, or the desired effect would not be obtained, or obtained in lesser degree.

The maximum speed of action therefore we are talking about must be an *harmonious* speed, verified in the complex whole and in the co-operation of the movements, and *producing the greatest effect*.

But if certain given entia and certain forces of the entia produce the same quantity of effect in shorter time, then clearly the *complex whole* of these entia and forces has operated with more speed in my sense, because this kind of speed is the speed I am discussing and is the law that divine wisdom, by its nature, constantly maintains in giving all things their measure of motion.

894. Mankind finds and values this law of the greatest speed and greatest possible saving of time in the most contrary things, for example in the fine arts, in mechanics, political enterprises, moral behaviour, human work and natural processes.

We enjoy the rapidity with which an epic or drama proceeds to its solution, the rapidity with which a story is told or a series of compelling arguments is driven home when well arranged by the speaker. The value of style is in brevity; there is beauty in an epigram, in a succinct motto, in a witticism. Nearly all sublime replies as well as humorous ones draw their impact from promptness and speed; these are always valued. Hence these diverse ways of using speech and thought attain the intended end: much is said in few words, and the mind that understands them is moved to perform new and rapid acts.

895. Napoleon said that his superiority over others depended solely on his greater speed of thought: others arrived at the same point, but he got there first. Not only his speed of thought but the speed with which he moved his armies contributed greatly to their victory in so many battles.

896. Again, why are we impressed by a slender, athletic person? Why is a good horse so much appreciated, and the same for railways and steamboats? They are highly valued for the speed with which they obtain the desired effect.

If a mill, a loom, a spinning-wheel uses the same energy as another mill, loom or spinning-wheel to produce in the same time more cloth, more drapery, more yarn, containing the same quantity and quality of material, it has more value. But its greatest value depends solely on producing the effect in less time.

We can honestly say that all great people became great by the speed with which they operated. They were great because they did very many and very great things in a short time, using the most decisive and most expeditious means.

897. Careful observation shows that this rapidity is the characteristic of the nations that are destined by Providence in their initial stages for a great mission in the world. Lucius Julius Florus says of the Romans: 'In the seven hundred years from

King Romulus to Caesar Augustus, the Roman people accomplished so many things in both peace and war that if the greatness of the empire is compared with its years, it seems that the time taken should have been much longer.'[518]

898. Similar to this rapidity that we have described is the rapidity exercised by Providence in the government of the world. But God's rapidity is much greater than every other rapidity. His Providence created all entia, placed them in an order and gave them an impulse such that this tremendous machine of the universe would produce the greatest fruit at the greatest possible speed, that is, in the least time possible.

But to determine more accurately this overall speed relative to the quantity of the product, one must always turn to the law of the least means on which the speed depends. If the same quantity of good could have been obtained from the world in two periods of time, one twice as long as the other, it was contrary to divine wisdom to choose the longer period because half of the movements and actions of the world during it would have been futile.

899. But when both the total product of good and the duration of the world vary, we come up against a very difficult problem concerning maxima and minima,. The time during which the means is applied is to be reckoned as lost, but what proportion does this loss have to the quantity of the product? In other words, granted for example that the world is allowed to last an extra century, how much must the total product increase to justify this extension in the eyes of wisdom? The basis for a solution to this very divine problem would, it seems to me, have to be the following.

Let us grant that the product of every ens and every act does not result only from the ens' operation but from its operating in harmony with the complex of other entia and other acts constituting the world. If an ens or an act were taken away from the world, but the world still produced the same or even more, then that ens and act are superfluous or harmful, and wisdom would not produce them. If that ens or act were added to the world and if, after all the goods, evils and consequences had been calculated, the world produced a greater net good, which

[518] *Epit. Rer. Rom.*, bk 1, Proem.

was the maximum obtainable in all possible combinations, then the ens or the act would have to be included in the world. This principle must be applied to all the acts that the world would perform in the extra century, considered in their overall composition.

900. It must noted that the principle of speed applied to the development of the immense, divine drama of the universe must not be sought in the physical or intellectual orders but in the moral order, which the other two serve as means.

In the order of moral goods we must distinguish, as it were, *substance* and *accident*. The first principle of every wise government is to tend to the *substantial good*, and not to waste its time promoting the accidents resulting in a reduction of substantial good.[519] Hence, a general, for example, who prefers to collect the spoils left behind on the field of battle rather than pursue the enemy and complete the rout, clearly loses precious time. His tactic sins gravely against the principle of maximum speed. In the government of the world, this principle of substance and accident is followed before every other principle. Providence applies the principle of speed to the substance of the desired effect and leaves the accidents to act in their own way, due to the limitation of creatures. Provided the substance rapidly increases and multiplies, it does not matter whether those advantages that can be considered as accidents are slow in eventuating or are lost.

901. Therefore we can only be struck by the extraordinary speed of moral development when we consider the great and substantial events that take place in human history and truly contain the summit of good. Events rapidly succeed one another: one is not complete before the other begins and follows closely on. None of the events wastes an instant of time in taking on a symmetry, so to speak, or acquiring a regular form. This is accidental, insignificant perfection which is often seen to be sacrificed by supreme Providence to make place for another substantial good to be produced in the world without loss of time.

902. If we look unbiasedly at the principal events of the moral

[519] In *The Philosophy of Politics* I posited this principle as the most general of political criteria. Cf. *SC*, 1–38 .

order and if what I am saying is understood, none of them seems to have that completion and regularity of accidents that our narrow, limited human mind would like to find. I will give a few examples.

The diffusion of the Gospel is a substantial event, and the speed of its diffusion to the furthest corners of the globe is quite astonishing, as in fact had been forecast.[520] It seems that even in Apostolic times nearly all nations had heard the good news. The divine Scriptures glorify God for this speed: 'His word runs swiftly,' as the psalm says,[521] and the preachers of the Gospel and the saints are 'like arrows in the hand of a warrior';[522] the warrior is the God-Man.

903. When deeply rooted idolatry had to be torn out, the quickest means was to call in the barbarians of the north and by their hand destroy the Roman empire, in whose political constitution and in the customs of the peoples that the abomination of idolatry had taken root. The evils that resulted from the invasion were virtually negligible accidents compared with the great good understood in the great plan. Mohammed's sword was also a rapid means for such a great purpose.

904. When the Christian world had to be cemented together out of individuals and form *Christianity*, the rapid means used by Providence was to raise up a Charlemagne and later a Gregory VII, in accord with eternal practice, of which it is written: 'The power of the earth is in the hand of God, and IN HIS TIME he will raise up a profitable ruler over it.'*[523] Later, came Peter the Hermit and other preachers of the Crusades. Many problems came with the use of all these great instruments, but they were accidents: wisdom discounted them and pressed forward.

905. God often uses the most striking punishments as a tremendous means for destroying the greatest obstacles to his purpose, thus suddenly changing the face of the earth for the better. Scripture always joins the attribute of rapidity to divine chastisements: in Leviticus God says to the Hebrews: 'I will

[520] Is 5: 26.

[521] Ps 147: 15.

[522] Ps 126: 4.

[523] Sir 10: 4†.

quickly visit you.'[524] Elsewhere he says: 'Beware lest perhaps your heart be deceived,... and you perish *quickly* from the excellent land, which the Lord will give you.[525] This is repeated many times.[526]

906. Whenever civil society, grown old and corrupt, is to be renewed, the supreme Provider does not dissolve it bit by bit, because this would be a waste of time. He shatters it violently, that is, permits it to be shattered. The French revolution, as Count de Maistre relates, swallowed up many centuries.

907. The rapidity of punishments is itself a mercy of the Lord. At the same time as punishments strike more harshly and instil a greater terror in people, they save many victims by the speed with which they pass. Scripture says that the persecution of sinners will be shortened for the sake of the elect.

908. Why was the life of the Lord on earth so short? — because the law of speed required the God-Man to fulfil his exalted mission in the shortest time possible. Not one single day of such a precious life was to be used more than necessary; indeed, not simply a day, not even the blink of an eye; every individual instant was counted.

909. For a similar reason God shortens the life of great people. It is enough that the mission given them is completed. Sometimes he does not allow them even to complete the task they are doing; granted that the work is well under way or has started and its success is assured, they are no longer necessary. Thomas Aquinas left his *Summa* incomplete; the perfection it lacked was accidental. His pen had already given to the world the whole substance of his great system that gave unity and wonderful order to the teaching of Christianity that had developed through twelve centuries. Thus St. Louis died in Africa, St. Gregory VII in exile, St. Augustine in Hippo besieged by the Vandals, St. Francis Xavier at the gates of China. Some sow, others reap.

[524] Lev 26: 16†.

[525] Deut 11: 16–17†.

[526] Deut 28: 20; Joshua 23: 16; Psalm 36: 2; Joel 3: 4. — In Deut 7: 10† we read that God is 'repaying forthwith them that hate him, so as to destroy them, without further delay immediately rendering to them what they deserve.'*

910. The enterprises, labours and works of people eminent for their sanctity can be so numerous that they seem beyond the strength of a mortal. But why oppress one individual with so much labour? Why such a great harvest and so few workers? The reply is the law of the least means, and particularly the law of speed of action. To produce many great people by second causes is time lost: time, in its rapid passage, produces those it can and destroys them. They are driven to operate well, fulfilling the counsel of God, 'in all your works be quick'.[527] Hence in Isaiah, even the angels are called *swift* ministers of God; that is why there is no harm in depicting them with wings.[528]

911. I repeat however, speed of action does not apply to individual events but to the complex of events; it is an harmonious speed. Sense itself also operates rapidly although blindly,[529] but the rapidity of wisdom is enlightened, it is rapidity related to the end.

The following is an example of the harmonious speed of operation by Providence. God promised the Hebrews he would *quickly* exterminate the Canaanite nations before them.[530] How is it then that he had previously said he would destroy those nations 'by little and little and by degrees'*?[531] Both are true: destroying them a little at a time fulfilled more quickly God's purpose of establishing the Hebrew people in the promised land. If the land, which was too large for the small number of Hebrews, had been cleared of its original inhabitants, the wild beasts would have deserted it,[532] leaving it to become forest. Therefore, after the Hebrews had multiplied they would have had to spend a greater amount of time cultivating it and making it burgeon. Hence he retained those anathematised nations almost as serfs of his people.

Moreover, in this way God's goodness extended also to the

[527] Sir 31: 27†.

[528] Is 18: 2†.

[529] For the *speed* of operation proper to sense and instinct, see *SP*, 345–370.

[530] 'You shall know therefore this day that the Lord your God himself will pass over before you, a devouring and consuming fire, to destroy and extirpate and bring them to nothing before your face *quickly*'* (Deut 9: 3†).

[531] Deut 7: 22†.

[532] Ibid.

other nations. These were so idolatrous and corrupt that their emendation by means of second causes would have required a very long time and also an effort that would have been fruitless. However, although the law of speed, by which God causes good to originate in humanity, required their destruction, he tolerated them for some time as an extra good, so that they would have no excuse. Indeed he foresaw they would harden their hearts even more, abuse his patience and thus merit the extermination that was required for the universal good of the earth and of his people. Some of them however, after learning the truth through contact with the Hebrews, gathered good mature wheat into the storehouse of the supreme Patron.[533]

912. I will give another example of the speed God employs to counter the blind speed of sense. The promptness and speed of human sensuality and ignorance likes to see the desired effect immediately. It has a certain impatience with waiting, as if it perceives nothing further that is important. Thus when the Hebrews saw Christ on the cross, they mockingly said: 'Come down from the cross'. But Christ did not come down, because he did not have the haste they had. Longsuffering is a great virtue of wise people, and Scripture celebrates magnificently God's *patience*, which shines brightly in the works of his mercy towards all mankind. This supreme patience is fully harmonious with and fitting to the supreme *speed* of the most wise operation.

913. The moral universe therefore does not amble; it hastens towards its ultimate solution, seizing and drawing into its fast-moving vortex the intellectual and physical universes. If such speed of movement were not a most brilliant ornament of the Almighty's work, the saints would not ask for it with their urgent prayers, nor would Christ have given the petition that all people throughout all the centuries continuously make: *adveniat regnum tuum* [may your kingdom come]. For the rest,

[533] 'For it was the Lord's doing to harden their hearts so that they would come against Israel in battle, in order that they might be utterly destroyed, and might receive no mercy, but be exterminated, just as the Lord had commanded Moses'* (Josh 11: 20). The meaning is: 'God permitted this because he knew that it was more advantageous to the universal good of humanity that those perverse nations should become obstinate and fight the Hebrews.'

the wonderful speed with which the canvas of the eternal plan unfolds is indicated in all those places of the divine Scriptures where it says that the day of the final judgment will come promptly and describes the day as if imminent: 'The great day of the Lord is near, near and hastening fast.'[534] Revelation tells us that JESUS revealed to John those things that 'must soon take place',[535] and at the end JESUS says: 'Surely I am coming soon', to which the Church replies: 'Amen. Come, Lord JESUS.'[536] The end of the universe comes as soon as possible.

[534] Zeph 1: 14.

[535] Rev 1: 1.

[536] Rev 22: 20.

[913]

CHAPTER 32

Twelfth consequence: the law of the accumulation of goods

The best man took the best, and gave the worse to the worse man*

Iliad, 14: 382

914. We now come to the second of the three laws that determine the quality of the manner in which those operations of the universe are carried out by which Providence obtains its end. I call it the *law of the accumulation of goods.*

915. Because I consider all I write as part of one sole work, I will not repeat here the discussion about the general maxims for judging an excellent government; such discussion pertains to the *Philosophy of Politics*. I will give only a few of the maxims found in that work supported by rather important demonstrations.

1. The governor of a mass of people is excellent when, without harm to anyone, his way of governing produces the greatest overall net good for the governed.

2. Perfect goodness of government gives priority to producing a quantity of greater good in the governed, in preference to the equal distribution of good (because here we are dealing with a good to which no individual has a right). Hence, if producing a good that is equally distributed should result in the reduction of the total sum, perfect goodness requires that the good accumulate rather than be distributed in equal amounts.[537]

Let us see whether this is the case in divine government. We will then know whether it is appropriate to infinite goodness to permit goods to be accumulated in some individuals, rather than to dispose things so that they are distributed equally.

916. First, it is certain that divine Providence strictly observes the laws of justice and supreme equity; these are the first elements of goodness and the foundation on which goodness

[537] *SP*, 581–628.

builds. All this clearly follows from what I said:

1. To produce its effects in the universe Providence follows *universal laws* by which all entia can obtain their good whenever they make suitable use of the laws.

2. Providence uses *universal means*, from which again everyone can equally draw profit. For example, the preaching of the Gospel is a universal, public means and is compared 'to a net which was thrown into the sea and gathered fish of every kind'[538] and to the seed that 'fell on rocky ground'.[539] Another universal means is the communication of grace to those who have certain predispositions, etc.

3. Providence uses *second causes*, which include those precisely that, as a result of varying use of universal laws and means, draw evil and good from these in different ways. For example, God exercises great patience with everybody, according to certain universal laws, but just as some sinners draw salvation from his patience, others draw a hardened heart; hence St. Augustine's opinion: 'Evil human hearts that make evil use of God's patience, become hardened.'*[540] Later I will discuss at greater length the justice and equity that God practises equally towards all human beings.

Granted therefore as most certain that the rights of justice and equity must above all be safeguarded, I return to the subject of goodness. The question is: 'Which is more appropriate to goodness: to have goods accumulate in some people or distributed to everybody in equal quantities? I replied that if the accumulation means that human nature acquires a greater net good, then accumulation must be preferred. But is this true in the case of government by Providence?

917. We will see that it is true, if we consider the way the goods are produced that Providence intends for its purpose.

How then are moral goods produced which are precisely the final goods intended by Providence and have eudaimonological goods attached to them? In what proportion do they increase?

Moral goods, especially those in the supernatural order, increase in the way that capital increases, by trading with it.

538 Mt 13: 47–49.

539 Ibid., 3–23.

540 *QQ. in Ex.*, bk. 2, q. 37.

Christ said this when he made the comparison between God dispensing his treasures and a rich man distributing his capital to different servants for them to trade with it.[541] The profit made by each servant varies according to the ability of each. One servant uses his one talent to make a profit of ten talents, while another servant makes a profit of only five with his one talent. Surely it is clear that to have a greater return, more money must be given to those who have more ability to trade?

In the case of the Gospel, this ability to trade with it as capital must lie in how well disposed people are to the Gospel, and also how they use their free will as foreseen by God. Generally speaking, and granted that all things are equal, it is fitting that God gives more goods and graces to those who not only have better dispositions for using them (both natural and supernatural dispositions) but will in fact use them better.

If however these natural and supernatural dispositions and the good use that will be made of the capital are themselves gifts of God, why does he not distribute these dispositions and good use equally?

917a. Once again the great law of the least means comes into play. We have seen that the gifts the Lord makes to created entia have necessarily a limited quantity, whatever this may be (cf. 480–485). We must therefore investigate whether it is more fitting for infinite goodness *to accumulate* or *to spare out* these dispositions and good use. An example may help. Let us suppose that one hundred units of disposition and good use are to be distributed, and that the capital to be distributed and traded with is also one hundred units. The capital is grace and primal moral good and, let us say, it can be doubled by each unit of disposition and good use. Let us now suppose two possible distributions: in the first, one unit of disposition and good use plus one unit of capital are given to each of a hundred individuals; in the second distribution, all one hundred units of disposition and good use plus the whole capital of one hundred units are accumulated in one individual only. Which of these two distributions will give a greater profit? Clearly the second. In the first, where one individual has only one unit of disposition and good use and only one unit of capital, the capital will be

[541] Lc 19: 12–24.

doubled, as we supposed, giving a profit of one unit of moral good. The total profit therefore for a hundred individuals is a hundred units of moral good. In the second, each unit of the one hundred units of capital will be increased a hundredfold by the one hundred units of disposition, giving a profit of a hundred times a hundred, that is, ten thousand. The accumulation of gifts therefore in the second distribution has exceeded the total obtained in the first by nine thousand nine hundred units of moral good. Hence if the maximum goodness of a liberal governor naturally seeks the most abundant fruit possible, it must accumulate the goods to be distributed, not share them out and thus waste them.

918. This very important truth, which explains so many apparent irregularities in the government of Providence, appears still clearer if we bear in mind that in the moral life of human beings the progress of good increases with much greater rapidity, for the following reasons:

1. Every new moral good gained increases the capital with which we are trading. Consequently, the trading is always renewed in proportion to the increased capital, and returns what business people call *compound interest*.

2. The dispositions and ability to trade, as well as the will to make good use of them, increase up to a certain amount. Hence, to know the accurate amount of the total profit, the increased capital must be multiplied by the increased ability.[542] But only God knows the number of times the trading is renewed and, so to speak, the capital turned over. In regard to ourselves, it is sufficient to have some understanding of the great rapidity with which holy people make their way.

919. In the parable of the talents it is understood that each talent would produce one other: five would produce five, two, two. Here there is an increase of only one transaction.[543] But in the parable of the pounds it is understood that each pound

[542] Anyone who has accompanied me so far would, I think, be interested in chapter three of Fr. Segneri's *Divoto di MARIA*. He uses a calculation similar to mine to show the unlimited sum of holiness accumulated in the Blessed Virgin at the end of her life.

[543] Mt 25: 14–23.

would produce ten and five.[544] Here the increase is obtained from repeated transactions.

920. The same conclusion can be drawn from another consideration, from the good diffused by a person in whom goods have accumulated. It is certain that if I enrich someone who has a great affection for his fellow human beings and is naturally generous, I will have done a greater good than if I had divided the same quantity of wealth among several people who were hard and stubborn of heart.

Leibniz, who saw this truth, drew an excellent principle from it for regulating generosity. In a letter to Arnaldus he says:

> If several people need help and assistance, but they cannot all be helped, that person must be preferred whose help results in a greater, final good.
>
> Consequently, where competing cases occur, and all other things being equal, the better person must be preferred, that is, the one who clearly has a greater love. The good we do to such a person multiplies in many others and, by helping that one person alone, many others are helped. Even generally speaking, granted all other things are equal, the person that must be preferred is the one in the better state. I will show that the help that can be given to one's neighbour follows the progression of multiplication and not the progression of addition.[545]
>
> In fact, if two numbers, one greater than the other, are multiplied by a third number, the multiplication adds more to the greater number than addition could have done. Thus, 5 multiplied by 2 gives 10, but a greater

[544] Lk 19: 12–20.

[545] Prior to Leibniz, Aristotle had seen something similar when he wrote that *commutative justice* follows arithmetical progression, while distributive justice follows *geometrical progression* (*Nicom*., bk 6, c. 6). This fine principle was later accepted by St. Thomas (*S.T.*, II-II, q. 61, art. 2). In fact good sense tells us that a reward must be given in proportion to merit, employment given in proportion to suitability, and benefits in proportion to goodness and to the aptitude to make good use of them, etc. Grotius incorrectly claims that this rule is not universal (*De S. B. et P.*, bk. 1, c. 1, §8) because there may be only one suitable person, and hence the employment must be given to that one person without comparison to others. But even when there is only one person suitable, it nevertheless always remains true in general that if there were another more suitable person, that person would be preferred.

> number, 10 for example, multiplied by 2 gives 20; similarly, 6 multiplied by 2 gives 12, but 12, a greater number than 6, multiplied by 2 gives 24. In the first case, 5 has increased by 15; in the second, 6 has increased by 18. Hence in total, more is gained by multiplying the greater number by the multiplier.
>
> This difference between addition and multiplication is also of great use in the case of justice, because to help is to multiply, just as to harm is to divide. The reason is this: a person who helps or is helped is an intelligent being. An intelligent being that uses what is given to it can apply everything to everybody, and this is to multiply or, as is said in Latin, *in se invicem ducere*.
>
> Suppose that someone has three degrees of wisdom and four of power. His total value will be twelve and not seven because each degree of his wisdom can activate all four degrees of his power.
>
> The same is true even in homogeneous things. A person who possesses a hundred thousand pounds is richer than a hundred people who each possess a thousand because the union of all the pounds makes their use more profitable. The first will gain while doing nothing, whereas the others will lose although working hard. When it is a question therefore of helping where the poverty is the same for all, it is better to prefer the wisest among the poor as the most favoured by God; where the wisdom is equal, preference is given to the one who has a greater disposition for it, because to be born with the aptitude or disposition for wisdom is a gift of fortune, that is, of God.
>
> Those who possess (still supposing all other things equal) must be preferred, as more favoured by fortune. On the other hand, when two people seek exemption from a fine, or whenever it is a case of loss or harm of some kind, the one who has committed a straightforward fault must be preferred to the one who has added deceit to evasion, or the one who is unhappy or unfortunate must be preferred to the first two.[546]

921. Leibniz required that in those who aspire to some benefit 'the poverty must be equal'. Relative to divine Providence, this condition, we should note, is verified in the most complete manner: human beings, prior to receiving gifts from God, do

546 Ep. Ad Arnaldum.

[921]

not exist; they are all equally nothing. This is a maximum poverty that ceases even to be poverty because besides the subject's lack of everything, there is no subject. Before we were created, God did not even have any subjects to whom to communicate his benefits. Consequently, when distributing his benefits, he could not be directed by some right that the subjects might have, nor by any reason of suitability pre-existing in them. In fact, he was most liberal in the distribution of his gifts, and his infinite goodness met no obstacle that might prevent him from dispensing them in a way they would be more fruitful. His gifts therefore were accumulated in some, because accumulation is the way of drawing the greatest fruit from them.

922. These considerations throw light on the gospel assertion: 'To all those who have, more will be given; but from those who have nothing, even what they have will be taken away.'*[547] In other words, God gives new graces and new gifts to those who are well disposed to use them well. But those who are not well disposed, even the graces and gifts they have and misuse will be taken from them. How then is it said that the gifts and graces taken from someone who has been unworthy and lazy in trading with them are given to another who is worthy and diligent? This procedure refers to the total, predetermined quantity of graces and gifts to be distributed. As I said, this quantity cannot be infinite, but is finite and measured by eternal wisdom (cf. 477–492). All that is required is that it be distributed here and there to human beings who will make the greatest use of it; not one single particle of it is lost or returns empty and sterile to the master.[548] The good of holiness therefore increases in some, decreases in others, without exceeding the final, pre-established total. Of course, the virtue and holiness of a human being, while on earth, can continually grow, but all these increases were calculated at the beginning by the great Arithmetician who made the world. If some people, by refusing or burying their talent, contribute to the diminution of their holiness, this is balanced by an increase of holiness in others because it cannot in fact be diminished. All this happens through the action of second causes. Nobody's powers are restricted or obstructed by the

[547] Lk 19: 26.

[548] Is 55: 11.

predetermination of the sum total of good; rather this total is calculated in harmony with the powers and use that the intelligent creatures to whom they are given will make of them. Someone might ask why give the talent in the first place to someone who will bury it? Why give the pound to someone who will wrap it unprofitably in a cloth? The answer is: mercy desires it this way. In fact, without this experience human beings, who learn from experience, would not be fully convinced about the evil disposition and ineptitude of those to whom no capital had been given to trade with. But when their laziness or folly has been shown as a fact, and when instruction has been given to human nature, and divine equity and benignity justified, the ill-bestowed money is taken from the inept servant and added to the possessions of those who have given good proof of their diligence.

923. Note, the smallest quantity possible is used in the experiment, that is, one talent, one pound, so that the lowest amount of capital would remain fruitless for the shortest time. Indeed, the fruit it can bear is, as I said, precisely the demonstration that a person who has no aptitude for managing a little matter has no aptitude for managing greater matters.

924. Some people are scandalised by the apparent obscurity of the divine Scriptures. They think certain truths could be more clearly and expressly stated. But Christ makes us note that also here God's excellent and most wise dispensation of his gifts shines out clearly. Christ had to announce the truths of salvation to people of many different dispositions, to the wicked and hard of heart, to those well disposed to receive these truths. Therefore he preferred to announce them in a general way, concealed under the veil of parables, so that well disposed people, meditating on them and asking for light from him, could come to understand them, while at the same time the truths remained hidden from those who were negligent, alienated and adverse to the truth. In other words, five talents were given to anyone who had the ability to increase them, and only one talent to anyone who did not have this ability; this act was completely just because it was equal for all. Indeed, even the veiled truth, hidden in parables, gives some light to minds, but we cannot come to the fullness of its light without effort. Thus, when Christ was questioned by

his disciples why he spoke in parables, he replied: 'To you it has been given to know the mysteries of the kingdom of heaven, but to them it has not been given. For to those who have, more will be given, and they will have an abundance; but from those who have nothing, even what they have will be taken away. The reason I speak to them in parables is that seeing they do not perceive, and hearing they do not listen, nor do they understand.'[549] In other words: 'You have the good disposition to draw profit from the truth. Having heard the parables, you search for their explanation, and this is given to you. But to them, who do not have this good disposition, the parables are nevertheless still given, just as to you, but without any explanation because they do not search for it; it would be a wasted light, and according to the law of wisdom nothing must be uselessly wasted.' Hence Christ adds: 'With them indeed is fulfilled the prophecy of Isaiah that says: "You shall indeed hear, but never understand, and you shall indeed see, but never perceive. For this people's heart has grown dull, and their ears are heavy of hearing, and their eyes they have close, lest they should perceive with their eyes, and hear with their ears, and understand with their heart and turn for me to heal them."'[550] Consequently, this placing of a veil over them and over many other evilly disposed people, and the words of Scripture whose meaning is sometimes also covered are wisdom that does not wish to waste the light. It is also mercy towards the wicked so that their sin is not increased and they might find some excuse in their ignorance, although blameworthy, like the excuse that Christ on the cross made for them to the Father: 'Father, forgive them; for they do not know what they are doing.'[551] We find this economy of Providence often mentioned in the Scriptures because

[549] Mt 13: 11–13.

[550] Is 6: 10 — Mt 13: 14–15. This argument concerning the economy that divine wisdom and goodness observe when speaking to us in an obscure way is dealt with by Houtteville, bk. 2, c. 1. According to him, the origin of the *literal* and *moral* meanings lie in God's intention that the prophecies be dictated in a rather enigmatic and parabolic style. He adds: 'God, who always follows ordinary paths, had disposed that the enigmatic style should be the genius of the nation' or, as I would say, of that age of humanity.

[551] Lk 23: 34. Cf. *CS*, 345–356.

[924]

the operation of wisdom is consistent with itself at all times. Thus in Exodus God speaks to the Israelite people who had sinned: 'I will send an angel before you... I will not go up among you, or I would consume you on the way, for you are a stiff-necked people.'[552] The abuse of greater and more excellent gifts of God would in fact have been a greater crime and deserving of greater punishment.

925. The same principle of accumulation is declared by Christ with another allegory: 'No one after lighting a lamp hides it under a jar, or puts it under a bed, but puts it on a lampstand, so that those who enter may see the light.'[553] The lampstand are those who have the appropriate dispositions for profitably receiving the light of grace, profitably for their own advantage and the advantage of others, 'so that those who enter may see the light.' Moreover, besides showing the path followed by the good, the light given to the Apostles and Saints also enlightens, that is, brings into the open, the iniquities of the wicked and thus justifies divine justice. Scripture therefore adds that 'nothing is hidden that will not be disclosed, nor is anything secret that will not become known and come to light.'[554] But the gift made by the Lord cannot shine forth to the good and bad unless those who receive it cooperate with it and through this cooperation become true lampstands. Hence, Christ says to his disciples: 'Then pay attention to how you listen,'[555] that is, be careful to listen to my words so that they bring forth fruit. He then strengthens them for doing this with the good that will result for them: 'For to those who have, more will be given; and from those who do not have, even what they seem to have will be taken away,'[556] that is, the proud illusion which makes them think they know, when in fact they are ignorant, will be removed; and in the end they will clearly see their own ignorance, precisely through the light that manifests everything.

926. Christ expresses the same thought when he says: 'The

552 Ex 33: 2–3.
553 Lk 8: 16.
554 Ibid., 17.
555 Ibid., 18.
556 Ibid., 18.

measure you give will be the measure you get, and still more will be given you.'[557] The measure with which we measure people and everything else is our affection, which is either right or wrong. If we measure them with an affection that conforms to the truth, the measure is just, but if we measure everything with an affection contrary to the truth, following passions blindly, the measure is unjust. Christ's judgment therefore conforms to St. Paul's: 'If you sow to your own flesh, you will reap corruption from the flesh; but if you sow to the Spirit, you will reap eternal life from the Spirit.'[558] Those who sow to the flesh are those who do not have, and lose what they think they have, that is, their flesh destined for corruption. Those who sow to the spirit have, and gain eternity. Hence again, Christ concludes 'to those who have will be given,'* that is, goods will accumulate in them in this life and the future life; 'and those who do not have, even what they have will be taken away from them,'* they will become poorer and poorer in this life and in the life to come.

927. When people say that 'gold makes gold' and 'one misfortune begets another', they are talking about an everyday fact, a true law of Providence. If they blame or malign Providence, they do so because they do not understand Providence's sublime reasons and are unable to raise their mind to the contemplation of them.

We must conclude therefore that irregularities and inequalities in the distribution of the goods of nature and of grace in no way detract from a sublime Providence — on the contrary, they demonstrate its wisdom and exquisite goodness.

928. But there is more. If the accumulation of goods is required by the law of wisdom and, granted that an infinite wisdom presides over the government of the universe, the accumulation must necessarily be maximum. Consequently, all the goods, gifts and graces that God had destined for the human race had to be united and accumulated in one single human being (because this is the greatest possible accumulation that can be conceived), and communicated from this one being to others, poorest and most wretched as they are. And so it was. This human being is Jesus Christ. The whole, entire

[557] Mk 4: 24.

[558] Gal 6: 8.

universe is suspended from this most simple point. True goods are found solely in him; all those who possess them possess them in him alone. Hence,

> he is the image of the invisible God,[559] the firstborn of all creation; for in him all things in heaven and on earth were created, things visible and invisible, whether thrones or dominions or rulers or powers — all things have been created through him and for him. He himself is before all things, and in him all things hold together. He is the head of the body, the church; he is the beginning, the firstborn from the dead, so that he might come to have first place in everything. For in him all the fullness of God was pleased to dwell, and through him God was pleased to reconcile to himself all things, whether on earth or in heaven, by making peace through the blood of his cross.[560]

929. But if the law of accumulation was completely executed in Christ, the same law is executed as far as possible in other human beings to whom Christ communicates from his fullness.

Consequently, in God's eyes one person or a few can contain and often do contain more good and have more value than an countless multitude. Infinite goodness always saves the greater good when two goods cannot be saved; it prefers to save the treasure contained in one or few rather than that contained in an immense number. Thus, if a corrupt society, many members of which deserved to be exterminated, were an instrument capable of producing just a few holy people, this production can be of such great value that it is fitting for divine goodness to preserve the entire society that produces such a precious, exquisite fruit, even if in appearance very limited. Here we see the reason why a few just people could have been enough to save the Pentopolis from final destruction[561] and why a few just people often preserve entire nations from extinction.

559 The term 'invisible God' excludes the error of the Platonists. They claimed that the divine reality could be perceived by natural intuition. But this reality is not known to us positively through nature but through JESUS Christ our Lord.

560 Col 1: 15–20. Cf. also 1 Cor 15, Rev 1.

561 Gen 18.

CHAPTER 33

Thirteenth consequence: the law of germ

930. The laws of *speed* and of the *accumulation of goods* demonstrate the way in which divine wisdom executes in the world the most general law of the least means and the particular laws derived from this law. But if we investigate *how* God brings about this speed and accumulation, we find another law, which I have called the law of *germ*. It will be the subject of this chapter.

931. I understand the *law of germ* as 'the decree of the Creator which ordained that goods begin in their minimum state, a state of self-containment and potency, and then evolve and become distinct through a movement proper to them'.

932. The law, considered this way, is seen as a legitimate consequence of the principle I have posited: 'God willed to draw from creatures all the good that they were able to give according to their nature. He did not posit another cause because this would have been superfluous whenever the cause was already in them' (cf. 511–513).

933. From this principle I deduced the necessity of second causes (cf. 514–521), because the principle presupposes them, stating simply: 'Leave second causes to do all they can'. This itself expresses the parsimony of divine intervention, and consequently also expresses, in addition to the existence of second causes, their freedom and opportunity to do all the good of which they might be capable.

934. The law of germ therefore simply states the way God draws the greatest good possible from second causes. It has three parts:

First part. God created beings in their intricate state.

Philo[562] thinks that at the beginning God created the fertilised germs of plants and animals (except man, whom he formed directly). These then developed into plants and animals, as

[562] See Philo's three sermons on Providence, published in Armenian, pp. 8–9. St. Augustine is of the same opinion; cf. *De Trinit*., 3: 13.

Genesis seems to teach.[563] Corresponding to this is the common opinion that the season when the world was created, or at least when the germs began movement, was spring.[564]

According to this economy, God positioned the germs of all things, or as St. Augustine calls them, the seminal reasons, at the beginning in such a way that they would develop on their own from their intricate, hidden state and thus be the causes of their own growth and perfection.

935. *Second part.* In their development the first germs produced other germs, and so on to infinity.

The development effected by continually new seeds and germs is more rapid than every other because it happens through continuous multiplication. Each germ produces, and in turn each production again produces. Mathematicians clearly see the marvellous rapidity with which the total of productions grows in this way, and in a short time exceeds calculation.

Nature's luxuriant richness in the production of vegetable and animal life must be attributed to this law. There is also a similar speed of production in the moral law.

936. *Third part.* The number of first germs was the lowest possible for the purpose.

We can see how at the start few were necessary because, as I said, they were constituted to produce or posit in being germs similar to themselves. Hence, it seems that at the beginning one germ alone was sufficient for every individual species of things. It is also probable that God observed this parsimony in creation.[565]

I trust that these few lines about the law of germ are sufficient.

563 Cf. *Catechesi*, 32.

564 '… when divine love
first moved those beautiful things'.
Dante, *Inf.*, 1: 39–40.
For Dante, as for Scripture, *beautiful things* are *par excellence* the stars.

565 In this chapter I have used *germ* rather than seed to avoid the problem of those things St. Augustine calls *seminum semina* [seeds of seeds], whose number cannot be limited solely to reasons, as I will explain elsewhere.

CHAPTER 34

The absolute measure of goods and evils

937. I have now come to the end of my task, which was to develop the law of the least means and show its wonderful fecundity, spawning as it were many particular laws contained virtually within it, and to apply it to justify the government of Providence. I am fully convinced that Providence has been totally justified, and greatly glorified; the arguments, it seems to me, are so clear that anyone who is still not satisfied must not have understood them.

I can therefore consider my task at an end. All that has been said makes an objection against the providence of the Creator no longer possible: all objections have in fact been overcome. But we should note that the justification of the divine government of the world, as I have explained it, is independent of its consequences: God had to follow the eternal law of the least means, whatever the subsequent effect was, and whatever absolute measure of good might have come through it, whether very great or very small. It is true that if the total good had had to be less than the total evil, there would be no sufficient reason for creation to exist, and hence it would never have existed. But if the total good were only a little greater than the evil, and moreover this good could not have been obtained by the law of the least means, nevertheless creation would still not have been in vain; it would have had its reason. Even though this good, little greater than the evil, would have been the maximum possible, more could not have been asked of wisdom and infinite goodness, because wisdom and infinite goodness are not in any way obliged to what is absurd, nor can they carry out or will the absurd, because to want a good greater than what is possible would be to want the absurd.

Nevertheless, we can have a reasonable curiosity about the final result of the excellent government of creation by the law of the least means: will the quantity of good obtained at the end be much greater or only a little greater than the quantity of evil which had to be allowed in order to obtain that good? I cannot end without answering this curiosity.

938. The result is in fact very consoling. Not only will the quantity of total good exceed that of evil but, relative to evil, it is an infinite quantity. If we apply the principles of mathematicians to the total, the quantity of evil is so minute that it could be completely ignored in the calculation. The happy result also gives us a new and unexpected way of freeing Providence from every censure. The evil, which seems so great to our very narrow way of thinking, is in fact so little relative to the infinite amount of good that after both the evil and the amount of good necessary to compensate for it have been subtracted, the remaining good is still infinite as it was before. Hence the universe gives a net fruit of infinite quantity.

This conclusion is drawn from the following arguments.

939. First, we have seen that evil is simply a *privation of good*, which is not an annihilation but only a diminution of good. Therefore *pure evil* cannot exist, that is, there cannot be evil alone — some good is always necessary, which contains the evil and is reduced by the evil.[565] Good however, which is something positive, can be *pure good* without admixture of any evil. This is to the advantage of the total good because the total of pure good must also have added to it all the good that is mixed with evil.

St. Thomas, the greatest of thinkers, notes that 'evil cannot be pure, without some good mixed with it, in a way corresponding to total good is not mixed with evil.'*[566]

Eight centuries earlier, St. Thomas' master had said: 'There is a nature in which there is no evil at all and no evil can be. But it is impossible for a nature to lack good. Hence not even the nature

565 St. Augustine fittingly calls evil *bonum diminutum* [diminished good]. However not every diminution of good is evil: the concept of evil refers to that diminution which breaks the *order* of good, not to the diminution that decreases only the *quantity*.

566 *S.T. Suppl.*, q. 69, art. 7, ad 9. — St. Thomas gives an excellent answer to those philosophers who claim to argue to the non-existence of God from the existence of evil: 'If there is evil, there is God. Evil cannot exist unless there is an order of good, precisely because evil is privation of this order. And the order of good would not be, if God were not' (*C.G.*, III, 71: 7).

of the devil, as nature, is evil; it was perversity that made it evil.'[567]

Pure evil therefore cannot exist. But good, whether pure or mixed, is in everything that is.

940. Moreover, there is not only and always a certain portion of good with evil (because there is an entity, a nature, and every entity, every nature is good), but there is also something good in the perverse act itself. No intelligent nature can ultimately desire anything if there is not some good in the thing. Hence, St. Thomas says that everyone who does evil *intendit bonum* [intends good],[568] and no intellectual being can wish evil as evil because evil is necessarily always *praeter intentionem agentis* [outside the intention of the agent].[569] Consequently this good, present in the wicked act, must also be added to the sum of good.

941. When evil occurs in an ens, especially moral evil, which is the greatest of all evils and is as it were grafted on to the good, it is not simply there, next to the good: on the contrary, a struggle breaks out between the good and the evil intermingled with each other. In this struggle the good is opposed to the evil and battles against it. This is the origin of pain and affliction. However, this activity that arises naturally in the good, which resists the evil, even though it does not succeed in expelling it, is itself something good, a new good originating from the presence of the evil. Consequently, every evil must grant to good, that is, to nature which as such is good, the opportunity to be able to exercise its natural activity. This ontological law applies to the evil that both animal being and intellectual being can experience. In animal being, the pain suffered is the effort nature makes to expel the evil; in intellectual being, moral evil is necessarily followed by the evil of affliction. In this treatise on Providence, the only evil that concerns us is that of moral-intellective beings (who are the only end worthy of an eternal wisdom and goodness). It is therefore sufficient to consider how the affliction immediately attached to evildoing restores

[567] St. Augustine, *D.C.D.*, 9: 13.

[568] *C.G.*, III, 71: [5].

[569] Ibid., III, 4: [2].

in another way the violated moral order, and does so despite the evildoer — this must certainly be a good. Moreover, when I say that moral evil occasions in the one accepting it an evil of affliction, I do not always mean a corporeal evil, although this is sometimes attached; I mean an interior, spiritual torment. It is indeed a certain fact of human nature 'that every disordered spirit,' as St. Augustine says, 'is a torment to itself'. But if this is the necessary and truly ontological effect of evil in every single individual, the effect must be much more in the case of the order that divine wisdom has established between many individuals: their order is such that their conflict ends in a greater affliction for the guilty and a great contentment for the upright. Thus the great man who, above all others, illustrated the justifications of Providence says:

> Unhappy people, as unhappy, do not enjoy peace because they are deprived of the tranquillity of the order that knows no disturbance. Nevertheless, as deservedly and justly unhappy, they cannot, in their unhappy state, break away from this order, not because they are joined to those who are happy but because they are separated from them by the law of the order... Those who sin are worse if they take pleasure in the harm done to justice. And if those who suffer (due to sin) do not emend their lives as a result of their suffering, they at least suffer through the loss of salvation. Furthermore, if justice and salvation are goods, and if it is right that a person grieves rather than rejoices over the loss of a good,... it is certainly more fitting that the unjust suffer in torment than that they take pleasure in an offence. Hence, just as rejoicing over a good that has been abandoned in sin is proof of an evil will, so grieving over a good lost in suffering is proof of a good nature. Indeed, those who grieve over the lost peace of their nature grieve precisely because they still have in them some remnants of peace, and these make nature a friend to itself.[570]

There is therefore more good in an evildoer who suffers than in an evildoer who rejoices. Moreover, because every evildoer

570 St. Augustine, *D.C.D.*, 19: 13.

[941]

suffers to some degree, there is no evil that does not bring with itself this good of punitive justice. Through such good the essential goodness of being shines out, because even when being forsakes its own individual order, it cannot break the universal order; on the contrary, it makes this order resplendent in another way. This is also another good to be added to the sum of goods.

942. Throughout this book we have seen the grandeur and great value of many other goods that God has drawn from permitting moral evil. We have seen how many greater goods God draws from the guilty when they convert, and how many goods he extracts if they become obdurate. St. Augustine says: 'These are called vessels of anger because God makes use even of them to make the riches of his glory known in the vessels of mercy,'[571] in both this life and the next. Those who suffer eternally as punishment for their injustice are also alive and are, so to speak, burning memorials. As a result the blessed have a more vivid knowledge of the gratuitous mercy shown them and of how great their happiness is; they love and praise God more, the God who has saved them from torment, from which they had no cause to be saved; they rejoice more greatly in God because they have seen what they could have suffered. This is due to a law that governs the knowledge intelligent of creatures: they need experience and comparison in order to be intensely affected by their knowledge. The same reason guided the Greeks, as Zenophon tells us, when they stood ready to fight the approaching Persian army: they swore not to rebuild the temples that had been demolished or burnt down by the barbarians so that the ruins could be seen by posterity as clear, eternal memorials of barbaric impiety. This information could certainly have been passed on to future generations in another way but it would be more impressive and effective if posterity could see the fact with their own eyes. Hence all the goods that God can draw from painful and moral evil in a thousand ways, including the evil that endures for eternity, must be added to the sum of good.

[571] Op. Imp. Contr. Iul., 1: 127.

943. In regard to eudaimonological evils, these fall either on the good or the wicked. They are indeed evils for the wicked because they deprive the wicked of the corruptible good they seek. Montaigne rightly said that 'reason can bring relief to other pains, but the pain of vice does not have this comfort.[572] Thus, *pleasures* must be distinguished from *satisfaction*, and the latter must be noted as more valuable than the former.[573] The wicked are never satisfied, but the good always are, amidst all the pains of this world. Hence, the eudaimonological evils of the good are not strictly speaking evils because what causes no discontent and is desirable is not evil. But if the good do not accept these evils willingly, it is because they, the good, are not totally good; they have some moral defect which must be purged by the evils. If however they willingly accept them, they make progress and have acquired a good that is immeasurably greater than the evil they suffer. Granted therefore that eudaimonological evils, relative to the good, are not evils, and relative to the wicked are evils but such that they restore and vindicate violated justice, then clearly this kind of evils contributes to the increase of the sum of good.

944. Furthermore, every evil is limited; there cannot be a *total evil*, precisely because, as we saw, there cannot be a *pure evil*. Evil is simply the diminution of the order in, and proper to, a finite nature. Consequently, it can do no harm except in a finite order and to a finite degree. On the other hand, there can be and there is a *total good*, which is God, and it can be possessed by the intelligent creature. The intelligent creature can of course rebel against God and in some fashion hate God, and it is true that this disorder has an infinite element in it, that is, it is infinite because one of the two terms of the relationship is infinite. But the object of the reprobate's hatred is at first and strictly speaking not God as such, because God as God cannot be hated by anyone, but God considered as punitive justice, in so far as this justice obstructs the corruptible good on which the reprobate have fixed their love. Thus, the precise object of their hatred is not

572 Bk. 3, c. 2.

573 *SP*, bk. 4.

strictly speaking infinite in the way that the love the Saints have is infinite.

945. Secondly, the wicked do not know God in the same way as the just who have been raised to the supernatural order. The just know God much more and in an infinitely more excellent way than the wretched. Hence, because love and hatred are proportionate to their objects in so far as these are known, the hatred of God, and therefore the moral evil of the wicked, can never be as great as the love of God, that is, as great as the moral good of the saints. The moral good of the saints must always be greater, and beyond all comparison, than the moral evil of the wicked.

The total *moral good* therefore is far greater than the total moral evil; and *eudaimonological good* corresponds exactly to moral good, to which the order of divine justice wills the eudaimonological good to be united.

946. We must also note that the simple absence of the supernatural order, that is, of the grace that makes us sharers in the divine nature (granted that human nature is not corrupt and the will is not depraved), does not strictly speaking have the concept of evil, because the supernatural order is not a constitutive element of our nature nor owed to it. Hence moral evil begins and ends in nature and stays within the limited confines of nature; everything supernatural and infinite is not subject to corruption. Of course, if this nature sins after having been raised to the supernatural order, the sin is infinitely greater than it would have been if humanity had not be raised to this order. But it is still true that when the supernatural order ceases through sin, it removes itself from the corruption, which the supernatural order itself cannot receive. Thus the corruption that remains is always confined within the sphere of nature, although the corruption retains a relationship to the infinite. On the other hand, the holy person joined to God and sharing in divine nature enjoys the supernatural order. Humanity is thus raised above itself to the infinite, and becomes as it were one with the infinite. Clearly therefore, the least supernatural good is immeasurably greater than all possible evil; supernatural good cannot in any way be measured against evil, which is inferior to nature. Consequently, there is more good in one human

being who is in the grace of God and enjoys God than there is evil in all the wicked and all the demons put together. The total of goods is therefore infinitely greater than the total of evils.

947. The same applies to eudaimonological good. The least of the saints enjoys more than all that the damned and demons together suffer because each saint enjoys the infinite and in an infinite order. This excess of eudaimonological good is indicated by divine Scripture where we read that 'no eye has seen, nor ear heard, nor the human heart conceived, what God has prepared for those who love him';[574] such expressions are not used anywhere else to describe the very bitter torments of the reprobate. It is also written that 'grace and mercy are for the elect of God. But the ungodly will have the corruption that they have thought'.[575] It says 'will have the corruption that they have thought' because wickedness begins with thought, that is, with the *practical esteem* of things, while the corruption, that is, the punishment, is proportioned to the thought of the ungodly because it comes to them as a consequence of their perversity commensurate with their thought. Elsewhere it is taught that the torments of the reprobate will be in proportion to their sinful enjoyments,[576] but it is not taught that the joy of the saints will be measured by what they have suffered but rather that their joy will exceed their present sufferings[577] and that their reward will be beyond compare and be worthy of almighty God.[578]

948. Moreover, those who are good will enjoy all things. St. Paul expressly states that the rich patrimony of the elect is made up of all things, in addition to the possession of God.[579] The wicked however will not be tormented by all things, but only by the things that are destined for their punishment. Furthermore, the good will not be simply lords of the universe;

[574] 1 Cor 2: 9.

[575] Wis 3: 9–10 [R].

[576] Rev 18.

[577] Rom 8: 18.

[578] 'I am your reward exceeding great'* (Gen 15: 1†).

[579] 1 Cor 3: 22–23.

everything will contribute to make them happy and rejoice. They will also be, and are already, judges of all things,[580] and helpers of God in his providential government.[581]

949. In addition, the reprobate are isolated from each other, each suffering on their own and with the pain that comes to them from their accomplices. On the other hand the good form one single, most intimately connected body; each one rejoices, and will rejoice in the common beatitude, such that the happiness of all will be reflected and multiplied a thousandfold in each individual. Hence in Scripture, God is called *most high*, principally because of the abundant goodness with which he defends and raises the good above the wicked.[582] Speaking about the final state reserved for his faithful, Scripture says: 'You have multiplied your wonderful works, O Lord my God: and in your thoughts there is no one like you';[583] in other words, no one can conceive the happiness God has prepared for the just.

950. Consequently, if a minimum degree of moral, eudaimonological and supernatural good in one creature exceeds the moral and eudaimonological evil in all angelic and human creatures, then the excess of the total good over the evil will be immense. We need simply to consider that in the elect supernatural good has accumulated tremendously, and whatever

[580] 1 Cor 2: 15. — The faculty of judging is proportionate to *merit* because it results from the degree of perfection with which the law if fulfilled. Therefore Niniveh, Tyre and Sidon, although reprobate, will condemn the generation that was deaf to Christ's words, because those cities were less wicked. Hence the more perfect will judge the less perfect. In the hierarchy of the saints each order will judge the lower orders and be judged by the higher orders. Only Christ, judged by no one, will judge all. As the source of merit, he is the judge who communicates judicial power in proportion to merits. Therefore the Fathers give to followers of the evangelical counsels a special power in the last judgment. The Venerable Bede says: 'The orders of the elect are two in the future judgment. One is of those who with the Lord will be judges; they are those mentioned in this place (Mt 19) who have left everything and followed him. The other is of those who are judged by the Lord. They have not left everything but charitably gave alms daily to Christ's poor from what they possessed. Hence they will hear the judgment: "Come, blessed of my Father, etc."'* (*Hom. In natali s. Bened.*).

[581] 1 Cor 2: 9.

[582] Ps 82: 19.

[583] Ps 39: 6†.

opinion we have about the number of those who are saved, they must be many, because Christ said that 'in my Father's house there are many dwelling places.'[584] Moreover, in the banqueting hall, not only had a second group been invited so that the empty places were filled — this group is the types I have spoken about — but a crowd of people of every kind, the blind, the lame, the poor and the maimed, found in the streets, had been forced to come in to fill the hall.[585] Again, the vastnass of the divine city is unlimited because it measures 1,628,000 cubic stadia,[586] built totally of living stones. We also read that God will reign over all peoples, and all will exult in him,[587] and that he will save human beings and even beasts — the latter can be understood as sinners likened to beasts.[588]

951. But by how much is the total good increased when Jesus Christ is also placed on the scales that measure the total good? What scale in fact can measure such a weight in which are hidden 'all the treasures of wisdom and knowledge'[589] and all the fullness of grace?[590] The archetype of exalted humanity is realised here: all the other saints are the realisation of the types or

584 Jn 14: 2. St. Augustine maintains that the number of those saved is less than those damned. Nevertheless, he applies to the former the promise made to Abraham: 'I will make your offspring as numerous as the stars of heaven and as the sand that is on the seashore' (Gen 22: 17), and continues: 'The holy and good faithful are indeed few compared with the many evil, but *in themselves they are many* because "the children of the desolate woman are more numerous than the children of the one who is married" (Gal 4: 27), and "many will come from east and west and will eat with Abraham and Isaac and Jacob in the kingdom of heaven" (Mt 8: 11). Moreover, God prepares for himself a numerous people that performs good works (Tit 2: 14), and in Revelation many thousands that no one can count are seen, from every tribe and tongue dressed in white robes and carrying palms of victory (Rev 7: 9)'* (*Ep.* 93 *ad Vincentium Rogat.*, n. 30).

585 Lk 14: 21–23.

586 Rev 21: 16 [one cubic stadium is about 6, 331, 625 cu. metres].

587 'Clap your hands, all you peoples; shout to God with loud songs of joy... God is king over the nations; God sits on his holy throne. The princes of the peoples gather as the people of the God of Abraham' (Ps 47: 1, 8–9).

588 Ps 36: 6.

589 Col 2: 3.

590 Ibid., 1: 19.

full species. They share in a part of the good which Christ possesses in fullness and has communicated to them, as it is written: 'From his fullness we have all received',[591] precisely in the way that the imperfect full species draws upon the complete-full species without diminishing it. We can therefore sum up as follows. First, Christ is God, and in comparison to God the world is nothing. Next, the humanity of Christ has the grace of the hypostatic union, which is infinite, whereas the finite, relative to the infinite, is nothing. Thirdly, the humanity of Christ possesses God by virtue of this union; hence the richness of his humanity is infinite, and the world is nothing in comparison with it.

From this richness, that is, from God, who is possessed by the humanity (a possession that consists in being possessed, which is the only way the finite can possess the infinite), the humanity can draw all it desires, not simply the beatific vision but a vision of maximum comprehension among all the visions that human nature can have. Hence all possible moral good is realised in Christ alone. To this immeasurable quantity of moral good corresponds a quantity of eudaimonological good: 'All mine are yours, and yours are mine',[592] and: 'Father, glorify me in your own presence with the glory that I had in your presence before the world existed.'[593]

952. But this is not sufficient for our purposes. What Christ possesses in all fullness, he divides among his own, except the incommunicable hypostatic union and everything that properly pertains to it. St. Thomas says that grace was given to Christ 'as to a kind of universal principle in the genus of beings who have grace'.[594] Hence the humanity of Christ receives from the divinity to which it is joined not only every grace as such but also all the immense mass he destined to be shared among human beings. Thus he says: 'For their sakes I sanctify myself, so that they also may be sanctified in truth,'*[595] as if to say: 'From the

[591] Jn 1: 16.

[592] Jn 17: 10.

[593] Jn 17: 5.

[594] *S.T.*, III, q. 7, art. 9.

[595] Jn 17: 19.

source of my divinity I transfer into my humanity the grace I intend to pour from the fullness of my humanity into the humanity of other human beings.'

Thus the habitual grace of Christ is, as it were, shared out and renewed in the saints in all possible ways, such that the composite whole of all the saints doubles in a certain manner the realisation of the archetype of humanity. In Christ however, the union of all graces and the inexhaustible font of divinity, which is his very person, render his grace immeasurably greater and make it his so that he is the master of graces, and it is in this that his *specific eminence* consists.

953. But we must also note that he gives every saint a kind of ability to communicate the received grace to others, similar to the communicative ability Christ has as proper to him and as master of grace. Hence the conversation, words and acts of all holy people impart a great blessing and great grace to all those who have contact with them and are disposed to receive grace. But this overflow of grace as it were, which in its excess is further divided, is proportionate to the measure of sanctity of the holy people from whom it comes. The grace is thus triplicated in a certain way in the composite whole of those with whom holy people share their own abundance. But this never prevents holy people who have received grace from other holy people obtaining still more grace directly from the font that is Christ, who dwells in the just throughout all time. What is written in the psalm is thus justified in the person of JESUS Christ: 'The mercies of the Lord I will sing for ever. I will show forth your truth with my mouth to generation and generation. For you have said: Mercy shall be built up for ever in the heavens' (that is, in just souls):[596] 'your truth shall be prepared in them. I have made a covenant with my elect: I have sworn to David my servant' (father of the Messiah): 'your seed' (the Messiah) 'will I settle for ever. And I will build up your throne' (in the saints) 'unto generation and generation.'[597]

954. Again, eudaimonological good in Christ corresponds to the holiness of Christ and the Saints. It is communicated from Christ to the thousands of his Saints:

[596] 1 Pet 1: 4.

[597] Ps 88: 2–5†.

> I will make him the firstborn, the highest of the kings of the earth. Forever I will keep my steadfast love for him, and my covenant with him will stand firm. I will establish his line forever, and his throne as long as the heavens endure. If his children forsake my law and do not walk according to my ordinances, if they violate my statutes and do not keep my commandments, then I will punish their transgression with the rod and their iniquity with scourges; but I will not remove from him my steadfast love, or be false to my faithfulness. I will not violate my covenant, or alter the word that went forth from my lips.[598]

These words demonstrate the certainty of the predestination of the elect, and the immovable security of the good that God from eternity has destined to draw from his creatures for an eternity that is to come.

955. Moreover, precisely because the good decreed by God endures eternally, the mass of good I have described above must be multiplied by the whole duration of eternity.

956. The absolute quantity of good therefore that God draws from his creature exceeds the quantity of evil by so great a degree that it is immeasurable, and cannot be conceived by the human intellect. This outcome is of great consolation to poor, suffering mortals like us, and greatly justifies Providence in the permission of evils. Indeed, it effectively invites all reasonable and upright people to proclaim ceaselessly the praises of Providence.

957. But even after thus praising God highly because he uses his infinite wisdom in the service of his goodness, and his goodness rejoices with everlasting exultation, our thoughts turn to those most unfortunate people who are lost and we feel pity for them as victims immolated for the universal good. We reason and ask ourselves: Is it true then that God has abandoned these individuals? Has he fatefully and inevitably sacrificed them to an eternal evil? How are they guilty of being lost through the execution of such a terrible decree? — In fact, to ask these questions indicates that everything that has already been said and fully answers them, has been virtually forgotten. However, it is to be expected that they may present themselves again to a weak

598 Ps 89: 27–35.

spirit and wavering mind, and be revived even after being solved. Despite the irrefutable reasons that have answered and settled these supreme questions, people unfortunately still return to them due to a kind of distraction or an almost irresistible instinct. They are guided not by a calm mind but by a perturbed spirit which always seems to see in lost companions an immense object of their sympathetic compassion. Taking account therefore of this great human weakness that is *persuaded* with difficulty, even though *reason* has no doubts, I will, in the next chapter, deal expressly with the providence that God uses towards all the individual intellective beings he has created.

[957]

Chapter 35
Providence relative to individuals

> It is written: 'Mercy and truth are the universal ways of the Lord.' Therefore his grace cannot be unjust, nor his justice cruel*
>
> St. Augustine, *D. C. D.*, 7: 27

958. The question concerning the overall *universal good* of all intelligent creatures differs greatly from the question concerning the *good of individuals*. The objection concerning the salvation of individuals usually arises from confusing the two questions. Solving the first is considered as solving the second.

The objection usually argues as follows: 'If obtaining the maximum overall good requires some intelligent creatures to be lost, they are lost by virtue of the decree that establishes the maximum good. Therefore their loss is necessary, which means they are lost without their fault.' But no reasoning could in any respect be more mistaken and weaker than this. Anyone who raises this objection is ignorant of divine operation.

I will first distinguish the two questions and then demonstrate that 1. their solution depends on totally diverse but not contradictory principles, and 2. far from contradicting each other, their particular solutions wonderfully accord with and help each other in proving the infinite perfection of God, the first, supreme cause of all things.

959. The question of overall good concerns the *end* of the government of the universe.

The question concerning the good of individuals concerns the *means*, because the good of individuals is a means for procuring the overall good, which in fact is the sum of the good of individuals.

960. The overall good is the object of *goodness*. In other words, a law of the supreme goodness of a government requires that it desire to obtain and does obtain maximum possible good.

The good of individuals, besides being the object of the goodness of a government, is also the object of *justice*, *equity* and of *what is fitting*. Individuals must be ordered to the universal good in a *manner* that does not injure any of their rights nor does any harm to what is fitting to them; the greatest possible goodness and consideration must be exercised towards them.

961. The *overall good* is governed by the law of the least means that I have explained, because this good alone is precisely 'the greatest good obtained by the least means'.

The *good of individuals* is governed by other laws that originate from the relationship of the individual with the government. These laws can be summarised as: 'Government must not cause individuals any evil. It must give them all that is their due and even more than is due, as much as possible.'

962. The question of the overall good therefore is solved by the decree to obtain 'the greatest good with the least means'. The question of the good of individuals is solved by establishing a *manner* of treating individuals so that they are helped rather than harmed and can thus contribute directly or indirectly to realising the overall good.

963. Hence we must reconcile the solutions of these two questions so that the end of the greatest good is certainly obtained by the least means, while at the same time individuals are respected and treated with all possible goodness and generosity. It is precisely this reconciliation, this most perfect accord, that shines out in the divine government of the world and makes God's government worthy of the eternal praises that all blessed intelligences render it. Let us see therefore with what ineffable goodness God has treated and treats every individual human being without obstructing the great end in view, but on the contrary procuring it.

964. God's operation would not be appropriate to supreme Being if it did not at the same time harmonise with all his divine attributes. To do so, it must satisfy three kinds of conditions:

1. The first kind: it must harmonise with the *intrinsic order of being*, an order found originally only in God. This condition is prior to every creature, is totally objective, governs creation, and is *ontologically necessary*.

2. The second kind arises from the *moral requirement of creatures*. It presupposes their existence, is founded on them (that is, on their relationship with their ideal types) as if they were its title to exist, and is *morally necessary*.

3. The third kind of conditions is founded solely on the *fullness of God's goodness*. The creature or its type has no title to this kind; it is something totally free. If we want to find a necessary reason for it in divine freedom that tends to what is excellent, we can call it *teletically necessary*.

965. The first condition reduces to the impossibility of God creating a being that lacks the intrinsic order proper to the being. Opposed to this condition would be:

1. A creation cut off from its end, or the end was not moral, because only *moral good* has essentially the concept of end. Hence those who imagined a universe where intelligent creatures were happy without being moral, would simply be imagining an absurdity. Happiness essentially requires moral good, which is the greatest and final good that any intelligence can enjoy.

2. A creation in which intelligent beings destined to final, ultimate good, that is, moral good, are not subject to the eternal law of justice — justice requires that happiness be joined to virtue, and unhappiness to vice. Therefore to imagine a creation where vice lacked a penalty is to imagine another absurdity. In creating it, God would destroy himself because he would destroy the intrinsic order of being in its most excellent part, the part that *rejoices* in an end. Compassion towards guilty people who suffer a just penalty is caused solely by the limitation of our minds, which cannot understand how close, necessary and immutable the bond is between fault and punishment. Perfect intelligence and perfect goodness are therefore obliged to prefer the union between penalty and vice rather than the happiness of the wicked, because such happiness is not a good but an objective evil.[599] In fact, when we say objective evil we are saying evil that takes place in God, but God is essentially object, where no evil can take place; in other words we are saying something absurd.

966. These objective, absolute and ontological conditions that prescribe what the intrinsic order of being must be if it is to be a suitable object of creation precede all other conditions; they are

[599] St. Augustine says the same when he nobly states: 'Nothing is more unhappy than the happiness of sinners which nourishes penal impunity and strengthens evil will like an internal enemy'* (*Ep*. 138: 14).

immutable and do not depend on any creature but on eternal truth. Divine goodness cannot do anything to our advantage if these conditions are not safeguarded, which moreover become conditions of our very happiness. Like every other intelligent being, we can enjoy happiness only through justice and on condition that all the laws of justice are applied. The conditions exist therefore prior to creation; they determine and qualify it, and both the providence governing the composite of creatures and the providence governing individual creatures equally depend on it.

967. The third condition, founded on infinite goodness, does not apply to the providence governing individuals because infinite goodness entails a tendency to produce the maximum overall good obtained by the minimum means. The condition's existence depends on the providence governing the whole, which is served by the parts, and I have spoken at length about this providence.

968. The second condition for divine operation is occasioned by the titles that the creature could have for asking something of the Creator. These titles are founded on the ideal types of the creature, and they are the only conditions that apply to the providence governing individuals.

969. But what do these titles allow the creature to claim from its Creator?

We must exclude what the creature could claim from the Creator by the title of a promise that the Creator has freely made to it. Such a promise pertains to the order of divine goodness, not to the order of justice or of equity, although once the promised is made, a title of justice comes into being. But what can the creature claim by a title that it itself possesses?

970. One word suffices for the answer: *nothing*. Everything the creature has, including existence and therefore any titles it could possess, are gifts from the Creator. The question therefore reduces to this: Did the Creator, when drawing the creature out of nothing, place in its nature some titles by which it can ask something from him?

971. We must distinguish two classes of things to which the creature's demand could extend: 1. that which pertains to *real* being, and 2. that which pertains to the *order of being*.

972. In regard to *real being*, no creature, as I said, has a right to

demand it for itself or to demand more of it or less of it, and the contrary is absurd. The very fact of thinking real being would suppose that the creature could have some right before it exists.

973. In regard to the *order of being*, being is physical, intellectual and moral. Physical being and intellectual being cannot have any right because right is a moral thing. If God chooses to create beings with a perfect physical order and a perfect intellectual order, this is in keeping with his perfections, and is one of the conditions of the first kind I have called *ontological*. But it cannot be the object of any *juridical demand* by the creature because in the physical and intellectual orders the creature is not moral, and hence has no rights. But in the moral order the creature can in some way demand the following conditions:

1. The law of justice shall be observed towards the creature, that is, that eudaimonological good shall be joined to ethical good, and eudaimonological evil to ethical evil.[600]

[600] The *ethical order* therefore also includes the *physical* and *intellectual order* because the well-ordered intellectual and physical part forms the major part of eudaimonological good. Note however that the balance between moral good and eudaimonological good can be obtained in several ways, and only one of them needs to be obtained for the law of justice to be safeguarded. For example, God can permit a physical evil to strike a just person who has given consent. This is what he did when he allowed Christ to be crucified, and thus restored the balance with a tremendous abundance of eudaimonological goods. These compensated for the evil suffered and corresponded to the merit of the one who suffered, as happened in the glory of Christ; it is sufficient that the balance between moral and eudaimonological good is maintained in the sum of all the perpetual series of goods and evils to which the human being is subject. The restoration of this balance between eudaimonological and moral good, despite some fleeting irregularities, is the task of omnipotence. Job therefore praised God's greatness precisely because God can so order things that the innocent person may suffer for a moment without God being unjust. This may seem absurd but is not so; it is merely extraordinary: 'If I summoned him and he answered me, I do not believe that he would listen to my voice. For he crushes me with a tempest, and multiplies my wounds without cause' (Job 9: 16–17), as if to say, he persecutes me without cause, that is, without fault, and to all appearances has not heard my voice. In fact however, he hears me because he reserves for me an abundant reward for all my evils; he is therefore just but in a way that is sublime and almost incomprehensible to those who look at appearances. Hence 'If strength is demanded, he is not strong: if equity of judgment, no man dare bear witness for me'* [Job 9: 19†]. This is the same as what Christ said to his disciples: 'Do not be afraid, little flock, for it is your Father's good pleasure to give you the kingdom'* (Lk 12: 32).

2. The creature shall not be created morally defective, nor defective in person, because *moral evil inherent in person* is greater than the good inherent in physical and intellectual existence that pertain to *nature*. Hence, if the creature had been created morally defective, it would have received from the Creator more evil than good, and the Creator would appear to be a being that does evil and not good.

3. After the creature has been created, the Creator shall not deprive it of moral good by using his omnipotence to produce in it the disorder of the moral evil of person, and this for the reason just given above.

4. Finally, the creature shall not be created disordered such that it was obliged to fall into moral evil through natural impotence, although it was good in person. If this happened, the creature's moral evil would have to be again imputed to the Creator as to the true author of the evil.

974. These demands can in some sense be called four rights that the moral-intellective creature has relative to the Creator. But strictly speaking, they are ontological conditions rather than rights. Before created nature demands these conditions in so far as it shares in the order of being, they are already desired and demanded by the order of being existing in God. Hence they cannot in any way be violated by the Creator; their violation would involve the destruction of being itself, that is, of God.

975. A fifth demand can be added to those already mentioned. Although it does not have the title of right, it is fitting and appropriate. The intellective creature, created upright by God in the moral order and capable of preserving this order, shall not be subjected to the necessity of sin by the invincible seduction or temptation of evil creatures. Even if this happened, neither the evil produced by the tempter nor the natural weakness of the tempted creature could in any way be imputed to God. This is repugnant to the very honour of God, who is the natural custodian and defender of his innocent creatures. This condition therefore pertains to the first, or has affinity to it.

976. All these conditions are totally fulfilled by God relative to individual human beings. Therefore no individual can complain to him; on the contrary, each must have the greatest gratitude for the nature they potentially received in their first father,

who came innocent from God's hands, established in the sublime state of the supernatural order, which was an infinite, gratuitous gift, not included in human nature or in its intrinsic order. If the first father sinned, the sin did not come from God — what came from God was the freedom and the power not to sin, and also the warning about the evil the first father would incur by sinning, a warning which itself was also a gift, not due to him but bestowed through goodness. But the bountiful largesse of divine goodness towards all the individuals of human nature did not stop there. On the contrary, there were a great many other beneficent, gratuitous providences that God disposed and still disposes for each member of the human race. I cannot list them all but a few will suffice for our purposes and I will treat them briefly. To the first we can add the others that follow on. Each of them alone would be enough to prove the truth of faith that God *omnes homines vult salvos* [desires everyone to be saved]).[601] He wills this with a most sincere, not a weak will, truly providing the means by which the human race, if it had used and were to use them, could be sanctified and become blessed in all its members. God made eternal salvation possible for all individual human beings by the following special providences:

977. *First providence*. After God had created and constituted the heads of the human race in a state of original justice, this state, as I have said, was to have passed by means of heredity into all their descendants if the first heads had not lost it through their own free will. Thus, in the first institution, all their individual descendants were given the certain and easy means to be always good and happy.

978. *Second providence*. It is also certain that after Adam's fall, God, although offended, did not in any way abandon human nature to itself but gratuitously promised disobedient man a Redeemer. The grace of salvation by *faith* was attached to this promise, which had to, and could, pass into the descendants. Once again a means was gratuitously given to every single human being to escape the universal catastrophe of their perdition. But they freely neglected this second mercy as well, and the fathers took little care to teach the children. The result

601 1 Tim 2: 4.

was that God had to use the exemplary punishment of the flood to destroy the corrupt generations who would have handed on to their descendants the vice-ridden, dangerous qualities they had contracted, but not the salutary qualities they had received from God. Nevertheless, up till the flood the *revelation* of the future Messiah could not be lost. It had been entrusted to the fathers who had lived so long that Noah had been a contemporary of those who had for many years conversed with Adam himself.

979. *Third providence*. Consequently, God made Noah head of the human race and consigned to him the precious deposit of the promise that contained FAITH, that is, the means of salvation destined again for all his individual descendants. Everyone without exception would have saved themselves, up to the time of the coming of the Messiah, according to the plan of divine goodness and long-suffering, if they had wanted to make use of that gift. But for the third time many, with their free will, rejected the proffered salvation and thus offended again against the infinite goodness that had wanted to save them all. Having abandoned God, they fell into idolatry and forsook the clear light of revelation and faith together with the grace annexed to them and, as St. Paul says, 'They became futile in their thinking, and their senseless minds were darkened.'*[602]

980. We learn from these facts that on three occasions God himself provided for the eternal salvation of all the individual members of the human race. The first time, when he created Adam innocent and upright in all his faculties, was an ontological-moral necessity, or if preferred, was justice. The second time was with the promise of the Redeemer; this was pure mercy because the evil of the human race had come from man, not from God. Nor was God obliged to add other gifts to undeserving human nature or to pardon his offender or to come to the help of his enemy. Consequently, man and his descendants were justly perishing through their own fault. The third time was a much greater mercy, when God restored the human race in the family of Noah.

But when, after all this, the human race had again freely perverted itself, what did God do?

[602] Rom 1: 21.

981. He found and used *other providences* by which he made eternal salvation possible for every individual human being.

The first and second perversions were man's work. God however, far from giving the human race the impulse for perversion, gave it all the means to avoid perversion. But because perversion had been chosen freely, he could not prevent it without doing some harm to his creature. What was he to prefer? After respecting all the moral demands of his creatures, after carrying out everything appropriate according to justice and equity, after providing superabundantly for them and being in a position to act with total freedom, the field was open to his goodness. God could choose, and owed it to himself to choose, what his infinite goodness demanded, and nothing appropriate to individuals could limit his goodness — his goodness was able to tend directly to its essential purpose, namely, to obtain the greatest good with the least means. From that moment, the lot of individuals became subordinate to the lot of the whole because even if some were lost for the good of the whole, this was due to their own corruption that had made them undeserving of every special provision. We thus have the reason for his permitting sin: it was God's goodness that decreed the permission, sin was permitted because only in this way did goodness remain free to obtain the excellent end that would have been obstructed if God had had regard for justice and equity towards individuals — such regard would have prevented the diffusion of his goodness as much as he desired. The book of Wisdom says the same: 'For even if we sin we are yours', that is, we have become your thing that you can dispose of as you wish, and then the book adds: 'knowing your power,'*[603] that is, we sense all the lordship you have acquired over us.

982. This certainly does not mean that God abandoned some individuals to their total and irreparable perdition, but simply that he divided his gifts among them according to the law of his goodness. He certainly did not use his goodness to damn them but to benefit them. As Sirach says: 'The compassion of man is toward his neighbour: but the mercy of God is

[603] Wis 15: 2.

upon ALL FLESH.'*[604] But the extent to which he did this varied because he owed nothing to anyone; he was the totally free master of his gifts. He distributed them with appropriate sublime wisdom so that the sinful human race might be ultimately disposed in all the beautiful gradation necessary for producing the greatest possible eudaimonological and moral good, in accord with the desire of his unlimited goodness.

983. God acquired this total freedom for sharing his gifts as a result of sin which made everyone equally undeserving of every gift. But sin also produced another result very fitting to divine government: the course of second causes that God had so wisely arranged could be allowed to proceed freely. Even if through the action of these causes some people died in their guilt or were left deprived of some of his gifts, there would be nothing unjust in this; they would have had all that is theirs, and universal goodness would have fully obtained its end, ordering also these accidents to this end in the manner we have seen. Thus, everything would have been carried out in accord with the law of the least means, without any extraordinary, direct action.

Let us see therefore the economy God used in the distribution of his gifts, and how, with a most equitable and beneficent judgment, he drew all varieties possible from the human species through the clever play of second causes.

984. As I have said, God determined to send into the world his Word that he might be incarnate and merit in all truth the title of SAVIOUR OF THE WORLD,[605] or, as St. Paul calls him, 'Saviour of all human beings'[606] which is the same as saying that for him every individual human being who has not refused his help could avoid eternal torments.

985. The law of second causes which, as I said, had to be

[604] Sir 18: 12†. All this part of Sirach deserves special attention. It points out that God is merciful to us all precisely because he sees us as damaged and as sinners: 'He has seen the presumption of their heart that it is wicked, and has known their end that it is evil.'* These words certainly do not mean that God condemns everybody. In fact the sacred text continues: 'Therefore he has filled up his mercy in their favour, and has shown them the way of justice'* (Sir 18: 10–11†).

[605] 1 Jn 4: 14.

[606] Cf. 1 Tim 4: 10. — Wisdom also calls God *omnium salvatorem* [saviour of all] (16: 7).

maintained by a universal providence, could have prevented some people from obtaining knowledge about the Redeemer and the benefit of the redemption coming to them.[607] Hence St. Alphonsus says: 'With his antecedent will God wills all to be saved. He has therefore given the universal means for saving all. These means however sometimes do not have their effect, either due to the will of those who do not wish to avail themselves of them or because others cannot avail themselves of them due to second causes (like the natural deaths of babies). But God is not obliged to hinder the course of second causes, because he had already disposed everything according to the just judgments of his general providence.'[608] What then did God do, to whom everyone of his creatures is dear?

986. Among those whose ability to profit from the universal benefit of the redemption had been prevented by the order of second causes, for example those to whom no knowledge about the Redeemer had come due to the negligence of their parents or who had died as babies without baptism, God distinguished two classes with supreme equity and mercy. One class consisted of those who had been stained only with *simple sin* (like original sin) and its necessary consequences.[609] The other class consisted of those who had burdened themselves with *fault*, that is, with grave sin freely committed by them.

987. These last, who sinned personally and freely when they could have not sinned and died in their sin, are most justly in the hands of supreme justice; they are those who are lost without being restored by the redemption because they did not want this. This also seems to be one of the conditions I have called ontological, from which God cannot exempt himself without opposing the order of being and destroying himself.

In the case of those of the first class, although not justified, God made them experience diverse effects of his gratuitous, generous mercy.

607 'Although he died for all, not all received the benefit of his death but only those to whom the merit of his passion is communicated'* (Council of Trent, Sess. 6, *De Iustific.*, c. 1.

608 *Del gran mezzo della preghiera*, p. 2, c. 1.

609 Note: these consequences can never impel us to the hatred of God or truth, but simply to some disorder in the love of creatures.

988. The culpable sin of the second group has its origin in their soul, in their free will. The sin of the first originates, strictly speaking, not in the soul but in the body, which is received in a damaged state through generation and inclines the soul to fault.[610]

The Redeemer wished to save the whole man, both *soul* and *body*. He had to effect therefore a *double regeneration*, the regeneration of the soul and that of the body.

Furthermore, because *simple sin*, which has its origin in the damaged body, was both universal and inevitable to the whole human race, such that no act of free will was involved, he ordained that all human beings, who did not freely sin, would be regenerated in body through the resurrection.

In the case of *culpable sin*, which comes from a free act of the soul, he ordained that it could be taken away only through a pure free act of the soul, but the soul must believe in and obey the Redeemer and, if able, receive baptismal cleansing in the new law.

Thus those who had only the sin originating in the body that has been condemned to death receive through the merit and virtue of Christ a better body in the final resurrection, so that the soul ceases to be harassed and inclined to sin. Consequently, although such people are not justified but always in debt due to sin committed in the present life, they are freed from sensible torments, and acquire a satisfying existence,[611] as a pure gift of the Redeemer. This is admirable equity and wonderful gentleness.

989. The justification of human beings therefore is certainly only one, and originates from faith in the Redeemer and from the baptism he instituted. But divine piety is so extensive that those who due to second causes had perhaps been unable to

610 Writing against the Pelagians, St. Augustine says: 'The origin of God's anger about the innocence of babies comes from the *share* in and *stain* of original sin'* (*Epist.*, 193: 4), where the words 'the share in and stain of sin' are used most appropriately. 'Share' expresses the relationship of the baby with Adam which involves the baby in the share of, as it were, inevitable decadency. 'Stain' expresses intrinsic uncleanness and also the moral wreck of the soul that constitutes original sin, the existence of which is denied by the Pelagians.

611 Cf. the appendix to the Italian edition of 1845, *Sulla condizione de' bambini morti senza battesimo*.

have this means of justification could be saved from the torments of sense and enjoy natural goods, granted they died immune from every personal fault. This was not because they merited salvation, but obtained it through the human and compassionate affection borne them by the God-Man who has received power over all his brothers and sisters according to the flesh.

990. How did Providence order these second causes through which knowledge about the Saviour reached many, while some died before it reached them? How does Providence pre-choose those who receive this knowledge and those who do not receive it? — As we have seen, Providence always operates according to the law of its essential goodness, which seeks the greater good. This greater good depends partly on the *remote dispositions* of people, and particularly on their natural awareness of their own deficiency. They are therefore ready to accept the help that might come to them from on high.

991. We must conclude therefore, together with many Fathers and doctors, that adult unbelievers, who have lived their lives totally in keeping with natural justice, would be helped by God. This seems more probable to me in so far as those who are clearly blameless in their life must certainly have been helped by some actual, providential grace, which disposes them to receive habitual, sanctifying grace.[612] Granted this, it seems certain that people who are favoured and protected by God in this way can no longer be abandoned without their fault. God never begins a work and leaves it imperfect, nor does he regret his gifts. This is all the more true if such people perform works of mercy towards their neighbour, and if they pray, stimulated and

[612] St. Thomas expressly taught that without God's grace no one can avoid all mortal sins (*S.T.*, II-I, q. 109, art. 8). On the other hand he accepted the hypothesis that the gift of salvation, even by miracle, would not be denied to anyone who has no knowledge of the Redeemer and lives according to the precepts of natural justice. He therefore clearly understands that such a person has been given either some internal, extra-natural help or some providential, external disposition that removed serious occasions of sin. Only in this way can the two seemingly opposite teachings be reconciled. However the Hebrews themselves and the proselytes of Judaism had a true faith and a grace proportionate to them. The same is true of pagans who believed in a future Messiah, which must have been a special grace in them.

moved by an impulse from above, as we read about Cornelius the centurion.[613]

992. If God does no injustice but rather exercises mercy to those individuals who through the limitation of second causes (however wisely ordered) have no or insufficient knowledge about the Redeemer, how much more to those who through his kind disposition hear the good news!

It seems certain that all those who lived before Christ and had the promise of a future redeemer communicated to them, and also those who could of themselves conceive the notion, the need and the hope for one, already had a principle of salvation; and if they cooperated with it could attain justification. Thus the Redeemer was called the 'expectation of the nations'. Moreover, although the more explicit revelation and the divine declarations had been entrusted to the Hebrew people, God was solicitous for the other nations; indeed he had created them that they might know him, give him glory and be saved.[614] Hence when the passage of time had caused the primitive tradition of a redeemer to become blurred among the pagans, God provided that the divine Scriptures should be translated into Greek and thus be communicated to them, and the enslaved Hebrew people should carry in their midst the light of the true God. He also provided a great number of other means by which knowledge of the promised redeemer was never obliterated even among the pagans. And when the Saviour appeared, we read that everywhere a rumour spread that some great person was to come at that time from heaven for the salvation of the earth.

993. We must believe even more readily that sufficient grace to believe is given to those to whom the Gospel is sufficiently

[613] Acts 10. — In many place of his works, St. Augustine distinguishes between on the one hand the graces that prepare a person for justification and on the other the grace of justification and those who follow this grace, for example in the passage: 'The Spirit breathes where he wills. But we must admit that he helps in one way without indwelling and in another way when indwelling. While still not indwelling, he helps people to become faithful; when indwelling, he helps them as already faithful'* (*Ep.*, 194: 18).

[614] God addresses his people thus: 'And the Lord has chosen you this day, to be his peculiar people, as he has spoken to you, and to keep all his commandments: And to make you higher than all nations *which he has created, to his own praise, and name, and glory*'* (Deut 26: 18–19†).

proclaimed under the law of grace. Christ's words, *qui vero non crediderit, condemnabitur* [the one who does not believe will be condemned],[615] clearly indicate a judicial sentence that presupposes fault — if they had not received the gospel word and with it the ability to believe it, they would not fall into this fault. Hence all who listen to the preaching of the Gospel are given *potestatem filios Dei fieri* [power to become children of God].[616] With this grace they can all come to baptism, or certainly conceive an effective desire for it.

994. Just as sin therefore abolishes all the conditions of the second kind, that is, the rights or demands of mere fittingness that the creature can have relative to the Creator, so when God begins to give freely to the sinful creature some actual grace that can dispose the creature for justification, he gives back to his creature, as it were, a title by which it can expect (if it does what it can) the completion of mercy, the gift of justifying grace. But this is only a kind of title of fittingness for divine operation.

995. What I mean is that justification gives the intelligent creature a juridical title. Indeed, it is certain that all those who have received, together with faith and baptism, the grace of justification, can never lack helps to eternal life without their fault. They are assured of salvation by the merits and prayer of Christ,[617] because, as St. Thomas notes, the smallest portion of grace is sufficient to conquer all temptations.[618] St. John says: 'Those who have been born of God do not sin'* [1 Jn 3: 8], that is, they are no longer subject to the need to sin. Therefore, the fulfilment of the divine precepts is not impossible for the justified if they pray, as the Council of Trent has expressly defined,[619] and they always have the grace to pray.

996. However, relative to those who fall into mortal fault after

615 Mk 16: 16.

616 Jn 1: 12.

617 Jn 17: 9, 19.

618 *S.T.*, III, q. 70, art. 4.

619 'If anyone says that the precepts of God are impossible for those justified and constituted under grace, let them be anathema.' 'God does not command the impossible, but by commanding moves us to do what we can and to ask for what we cannot, and he helps us so that we can'* (Sess. 6, *De iustif.*, can. 18, c. 9).

justification through faith and baptism, they are again stripped of all acquired titles to divine mercy, and thus return to the condition of those who are under the total control of divine goodness. Whether they are abandoned to justice or saved once again, divine goodness disposes them with all wisdom to the universal good. It does this mostly by means of second causes through which some of them, struck down by death after sin, perish. But if they are spared death, they are given space to repent because a perennial source of justice is open to them in the sacrament of penance, and also with prayer they can beg for the grace they need, even though they cannot merit it.[620] Natural forces themselves can also cause us to have a natural displeasure for our sins. Moreover, because sin does not cause Christian sinners to lose either the faith or the character, they can, if they wish, always repent, motivated by those truths of faith they believe; this could be called in a certain sense *ex motivo fidei*. Consequently, they can also conceive a desire to be justified, which brings them to a confessor. Moreover, it seems to me that when they have begun their confession, God confers the grace of supernatural attrition, if they did not already have it. This is required as preparation for the grace of the Sacrament because a grace that disposes the penitent for justification seems to be attached to the confession of sins as an integral part of the Sacrament. This certainly cannot be doubted for those who have come to confession, moved by a supernatural impulse of actual grace. Similarly, the prayer of Christian sinners has the advantage over the prayer of the non-Christian in that, as the gift of faith does not fail through the loss of grace, they can pray with the light of faith. In this case, in my opinion, the help derived from the perfective, actual grace of their prayer comes afterwards, if it has not preceded.

997. All these things lead us to the conclusion that if all the individuals composing the human race, but principally Christians, have the desire and the hope, they can always be saved, granted that there is no hardening of heart, as in those who no

[620] St. Augustine and St. Thomas agree in their teaching that 'God hears the prayer of the sinner which proceeds *from the good desire of nature*, out of pure mercy.' Cf. St. Aug., *In Jo.*, Tract. 83; St. Thomas, *S.T.*, II-II, q. 83, art. 16, and q. 178, art. 2, ad 1.

longer have the desire or have lost hope. Therefore no one can truly say: I want to but cannot. 'The salvation promised by this religion,' St. Augustine says, 'which is the only true religion that truthfully promises true salvation, has never been lacking for anybody who was worthy, and anyone who lacked salvation was not worthy.'*[621] These words, which the Saint never retracted, simply state that no one becomes worthy through the merits that come from themselves but from grace.[622]

[621] *Ep.*, 102, q. 2.

[622] *Retract.* 2: 31, and also in the book *De Praedestin. SS.*, c. 10: 'If we discuss and want to know in what way a person is worthy, some say by human will, but I say by grace or divine predestination.'*

CHAPTER 36
Conclusion

> Mercy and truth however unite together because it is written: 'Mercy and truth have met each other' (Ps 84: 11†). Hence, mercy does not hinder truth by which the deserving are punished, and truth does not hinder mercy by which the undeserving are saved'*
>
> St. Augustine, *ad Sixtum, ep.* 194

998. All that has been said leads to the conclusion that there is a *double providence*: the providence of universals and the providence of individuals, and each follows its own law.

The *providence of universals* follows the law of supreme goodness. If this is considered relative to the *way* it operates, it is called 'law of the least means', which I have discussed at great length in this book.

The law that follows the *providence of individuals* is that of supreme justice, equity, fittingness and conformity with the other divine attributes, which I discussed here at the end.

999. The reconciliation and *harmony of these two providences* and of their two laws constitutes the perfection of the government of the world.

The two providences and the two laws that guide them seem sometimes to contradict each other: *individual good* apparently clashes with *universal good*. Hence the perfection of the divine government of the world consists in observing everything that justice, fittingness and the divine attributes require in providing for each individual creature and at the same time ordering things in such proportions, relationships and correspondences that the good of individuals and the regard shown them do not in any way prevent the maximum universal good but are a very helpful means and the necessary elements for constituting it. Consequently, the universal good is supreme in all divine government, and everything serves it.

1000. Because there are two providences and the diverse laws that they follow, it seems possible to affirm opposing propositions concerning the providence by which supreme Being disposes human beings. On the contrary, the two providences truly accord in a wonderful way so that the divine governor, who in his operation harmonises the two laws, confirms in an unexpected and marvellous manner both series of propositions.

Concerning the providence of universals it is written: 'Will what is moulded say to the one who moulds it, "Why have you made me like this?" Has the potter no right over the clay, to make out of the same lump one object for special use and another for ordinary use?'[623] We can also apply here all those many passages where divine Scripture talks about the supreme predestination of human beings, which is simply the great decree of the maximum universal good.

Concerning the providence of individuals it is written: 'There will be anguish and distress for everyone who does evil, the Jew first and also the Greek, but glory and honour and peace for everyone who does good, the Jew first and also the Greek. For God shows no partiality.'[624] And again: 'Know that all lives are mine; the life of the parent as well as the life of the child is mine: it is only the person who sins that shall die.'[625] To this we can add all those passages where God is called a just and fair judge, and shows respectful reverence to all his individual creatures.

1001. The fullest reconciliation of the two providences was attained, as I said, through the permission of fault. Through fault human beings had freely renounced the providence of individuals and had therefore left the infinite goodness of God totally free to order individuals to the maximum universal good, partly by mercy and partly by justice. St. Paul says the same: 'For God has imprisoned all in disobedience' (by the permission of evil) 'so that he may be merciful to all. O the depth of the riches and wisdom and knowledge of God! How unsearchable are his judgments and how inscrutable his ways! For who has known the mind of the Lord? Or who has been his counsellor? Or who has given a gift to him, to receive a gift in

[623] Rom 9: 20–21.

[624] Rom 9: 9–11.

[625] Ezek 18: 4.

return? For from him and through him and to him are all things. To him be the glory forever. Amen.'[626]

With these words I conclude this work. Far from intending to scrutinise the deep secrets of God, I wished to demonstrate that they cannot in fact be scrutinised, and I indicated the noble laws God follows most faithfully in the government of the world; he alone understands their vastness and applies them. It was my hope and desire to help human beings to be silent before the excellent and most wise Provider, not censuring him or complaining, but each day loving, adoring and blessing ever more

> The Providence that governs the world
> With that counsel which conquers
> All created opinion before it plumbs the depths.[627]

[626] Rom 11: 32–36.

[627] Dante, *Par.* 11: 28–30.

[1001]

Appendix

1. (12)
[Leibniz's refutation of Bayle]

Pierre Bayle raised objections against providence, which he based on the existence of evils, but he concluded that they seemed insoluble and invincible. Leibniz, who defended divine providence, showed that Bayle could not avoid these difficulties because he was content to use specious language instead of logic.

Among the other very fine things Leibniz said on the matter, he distinguished the kinds of arguments that can be brought against a given truth. According to him they are two: 1. the *demonstrative* kind and 2. the *apparent and conjectural* kind. He pointed out that, whether reason or faith is used, a truth that is certain (for example the wisdom and goodness of God etc.) can be refuted only by *demonstrative* argument, not by *conjectural and apparent* argument. But no one has ever discovered or put forward a demonstrative argument against the divine attributes; on the contrary all the arguments put forward have the character of pure conjecture and appearance. The great man says:

> We do not need revealed faith to know that there is only one principle of everything, a perfectly good and sensible principle. Reason teaches us this with infallible proof. Consequently all the objections based on the course of things in which imperfections are seen are founded solely on false appearances. If we could understand universal harmony, we would see that what we are tempted to censure is inseparable from the plan that is most worthy of being chosen; in short, we would see and not merely believe that what God did is best.

From this he concludes that Bayle's claim that *reason* contradicts *faith* is invalid because, if Bayle's argument had any force, it would make reason contradict reason. Leibniz also wisely says (*Discours de la conformité de la foi avec la raison*, 28–29, 32):

> When reason is used to contradict an article of our faith, objections based on probability cannot cause any difficulty. Everybody agrees that mysteries are contrary to appearances and when seen solely from the point of view of reason, are not probable; it is enough that they contain no absurdity. Therefore they can be refuted only by demonstrations. This is certainly the way that holy Scripture must be understood when it warns us that human beings see God's wisdom as folly, and St. Paul notes that the Gospel of JESUS Christ is folly to the Greeks and a scandal to the Hebrews because basically one truth could not contradict another — the light of reason is no less a gift of God than that of revelation. Theologians who understand what they are doing have no difficulty in accepting that *the motives for credibility* justify once and for all the authority of holy Scripture when confronted with the tribunal of reason. Reason later surrenders to Scripture and sacrifices *all its probabilities* to it... One of the causes that could have had most influence in making Bayle think that it was impossible to answer the difficulties presented by reason against faith is that he seems to be asking that God be justified in a manner similar to that normally used to argue the case of someone accused before a judge. But he ignored the fact that in human tribunals, which do not always attain the truth, it is often necessary to decide according to clues and *probabilities*, and especially according to *presumptions* or *prejudices*, whereas it is agreed, as I observed, that mysteries are improbable,

although they are true. Indeed, the merit of faith is precisely to believe on the word of God that what is *improbable* is *true*. And in order to know what God's word is, there are *motives of credibility*, and these taken together form the most demonstrative proof.

2. (40)
[Dugald Stewart and the separation of reason from faith]

I must note here the great influence of the prejudice held from the earliest times by people who had always taken the greatest care to educate their reason. Dugald Stewart, in his preface to the first volume of the *Supplement to the Encyclopedia Britannica*, attributes to a passage of Melanchthon, and consequently to the Reformation, the opinion that the moral distinction between good and evil does not come from revelation but exists in itself! He later affirms that this teaching has also been profitable to Catholics. As proof he cites a passage from the work of Lampredi concerning the right of nature and of peoples. And finally he says that the Roman Church wanted to separate revelation from reason, setting these two in opposition to each other which, he states quite openly, is *the most pernicious heresy of that Church*.

We can say in the first place, with all truth and without fear of error, that Melanchthon's passage, which is merely five printed lines and very little known, and which Stewart did not take from Melanchthon's works but from Christian Meiners, could not have produced any noticeable change in the world's moral ideas. Secondly, it is extraordinary how he fails to see that in the passage he took from Lampredi he is quoting a place in Melchior Cano where this Catholic theologian refutes Luther not with a few lines and gratuitous assertions but at length and powerfully. One of Luther's most harmful errors was precisely that he divided reason from revelation, claiming that moral good and evil existed solely in so far as they were revealed (Melchior Cano, we must note, was a contemporary of Melanchthon and died in the same year). Is it possible to be blind in the presence of such a clear truth? Stewart himself admits that the teaching was not only the teaching of the first of the Protestants but was afterwards upheld for a long time by the Protestants. He also admits how in 1598 Daniel Hoffmann, professor of theology at Helmstadt university, still maintained, following Luther's lead, that philosophy is the mortal enemy of religion and that truth divides into two branches, philosophical truth and theological truth, so that what is true in philosophy can be false in theology. How then after all this can Stewart attribute this error to Catholics and give Melanchthon the merit of having enlightened the world? He does so, openly and without the least proof, with all the ease with which he asserts the teaching of a few, quickly forgotten sentences. Such an absurdity was never accepted by Catholics, and we could call the author's assertion a gratuitous and serious calumny if we did not rather attribute it to the incredible force of prejudice. Catholics always strongly rejected the absurdity of the innovators. It was condemned by the supreme Pastors of the Church, from Ockham, who was one of the first to uphold it, to Pomponazzi, who was condemned by Leo X in the fifth Council of the Lateran. All this was done before the errors of reform were spread by Luther and before Melanchthon removed the darkness over humanity with his few Latin sentences drawn from oblivion. Later on, Daniel Hoffmann was also condemned for the same reason.

If Melanchthon, following Luther, did not err in this, it means that he made one error less, precisely because he held to the Catholic opinion. Christianity is a wise religion. The Supreme Pontiffs who preside over it have always and necessarily been the defenders and promoters of wisdom. They knew that the Chair of truth could reign only in light. They encouraged this wisdom, this light, this truth, and invoked it against errors. They have widely diffused both it and religion throughout the world, and with these two have spread civilisation throughout the human race, together with all the good things of civilisation. For how long then will people, guided by the light of centuries, be so gullible as to believe the most obvious lies?

3. (60)
[Victor Cousin and the confusion between the Platonic and Christian systems]

The new philosophical school of Paris, which owes its life and growth to the rare genius of Victor Cousin when he re-instated Plato's ideas, certainly gives new dignity to philosophy, which had been debased in the world by the material and pedantic spirit of the sensists. I gladly pay public honour to the worthy translator of Plato and Proclus. However I cannot fail to note how he wrongly confuses the *Platonic system* with the *Christian system* relative to the truth. These systems are at an infinite distance from each other, as distant as an image is from the thing that is imaged, as the light that reveals things is from the things themselves, as the rays of the sun are from the sun from which

[*App*., 3]

they come. Plato, ignorant of Christianity, could do no more than see the reflected rays of the divinity and substitute them for the divinity, because he wished to give his pupils the absolute. His guide was *created light*, and with this he knew that God had to exist, but he did not perceive God himself. In short, although he could rise to the contemplation of the *abstract and common truth*, this truth is totally different from the *first, subsistent truth*. It is in fact very easy to confuse the first, subsistent truth with the abstract truth that shines in the human mind and that St. Thomas so acutely distinguishes. It is precisely in this distinction that the separation between the Christian and Platonic systems must be found; without this distinction, the two systems are confused.

Moreover, the natural light of our mind, sought so much with that sublimity of which great minds are capable, presents some totally divine characteristics, and extracts them from its origin, of which it reveals the trace and preserves the analogy. In fact this light shows itself to possess an eternal immutability, a power unconquerable by any force, even an infinite force, an obviousness from which all certainty draws its origin. We must admit that the first Fathers of the Church were themselves enchanted at first sight by these characteristics. What they said was the origin in our time of the Platonic school founded in the Tyrol by Frs. Ercolano and Filibert. Everyone knows the heresies that arose from Platonism. The Catholic Church fought against these heresies for a long time, precisely because that Church is something totally different from a sect of natural philosophy. Nevertheless, it is not difficult to acknowledge that the truth that shines naturally in our minds cannot be the object of Christianity, but only of a natural philosophy, if we consider that no matter how much richness philosophy manifests, we see it solely as a *pure rule of the mind*, an abstraction, and never as a *subsistent being*; and without this subsistence the principal characteristic is absent, that is, the essence of divinity.

To retort that the truth we see *shows itself* as subsistent is not valid. In this a case, the truth would not have a visible subsistence *in se* and inseparable from what we see; it would have a hidden subsistence which we discover by reasoning. Hence, this subsistent thing is not the light of truth that we see with our natural intuition but something which, although invisible, we discover when we argue that it must be joined to that light, similar to the way we prove that in bodies there must be, in addition to the accidents, a substance we do not see. Consequently, we do not see God naturally as a simple, subsistent being, nor do we see him through any likeness that can be found in creatures, nor in the light of natural truth. Hence, while we are on earth, we cannot ever know the mode of his existence, although we can certainly ascend to the fact that he exists by starting from external things and also from this internal, abstract truth.

4. (146)
[Materialism and the principles of reasoning]

Modern *materialism*, like the greatest errors of the spirit, has had a slow, concealed development. The universal attitude of minds towards it must be sought mainly (and surprisingly) in the 17th century. Even the spirit of people who otherwise have good intentions was somehow tainted with it for reasons it would take too long to develop. In connection with this and with my comments on the progress of Kant's thought, we should consider the passage in Pascal where clear traces of this materialism are easily recognised. Speaking about the impossibility of reason to prove the principles of reasoning, he says:

> This impossibility indicates simply the weakness of our reason but not the uncertainty of all our knowledge, as they (the Pyrrhonians) claim. Knowledge of the first principles, that there is, for example, *space*, *time*, *number*, *movement*, *matter*, is as solid as any of the knowledge our reasoning gives us. Reason must rest on this knowledge of intelligence and feeling, and find in it all it has to say. I feel that there are three dimensions in space and that numbers are infinite. Reason subsequently demonstrates that there are no two square numbers one of which is double the other.*
>
> *Pensées de Pascal*, 2nd part, art. 1.

We note here:

1. The tendency to use *space*, *time*, *movement*, *number*, *matter*, etc. as examples of the first principles of reason. The *necessity* of all these external, real things can never be proved in

the way that the *necessity* of the first principles is proved. External real things are first *data* that must not be confused with the first *principles* of reasoning.

2. To say that the knowledge of the supposed first principles is as solid in us as the consequences deduced from them by reasoning allows us to reply that both the principles and the consequences are equally uncertain; in short, such principles are only subjective.

3. To say that our inability to demonstrate the first *principles of reasoning* depends on the weakness of our reason and not on the nature of the principles themselves which possess an intuitive and hence undemonstrable truth, is a marked move towards Kantism. To concede that the inability to demonstrate these principles is a weakness of reason supposes that of their nature they can be demonstrated. But anything that of its nature can be demonstrated, yet is not in fact demonstrated, cannot be accepted as true, in which case the supreme principles of reason are gratuitously accepted and hence have only a gratuitous or subjective, not an objective, truth, which is Kant's opinion.

5. (186)
[The *Biblioteca Italiana*'s comment on evil as privation]

In an article about this work [*Theodicy*] in the *Biblioteca Italiana* (fasc 131), this teaching [that evil is simply a privation of good] is considered doubtful. It says: 'Such a definition,' (that evil is a privation of good) 'considered to be true, would have pleased the ancient Peripatetics because it seems to admit the negative principle — they admitted privation and non-existence. But it would not agree with the viewpoint of the Encyclopedists (cf. art. *Evil*), nor of the Englishman King whose treatise on evil received much praise.' It could be said that the Encyclopedia does not seem the most appropriate authority to quote, and in the case of the Peripatetics and Scholastics it could well be time to cease being contemptuous for once of what is not known. It could also be remarked that the *Biblioteca* contradicts what it said on the previous page where it claimed that I give too much importance to things already known, for instance the fact that I give the name 'cosmic law' to the principle of limitation of creatures considered as the cause of all their imperfections. But the *Biblioteca* fails to see that this principle, which it says everybody knows, is in fact only the very same privative principle that, according to the article, is so controversial. Nevertheless, the quotation from Leibniz that I put at the end of the essay could have called attention to this fact, because the quotation teaches precisely that both *limitation* and the *negative* or *privative principle* are the same: 'Once again we see here St. Augustine's opinion that the cause of evil is not from God but from nothing, that is, not from something positive but *privative, that is, from what I have called the limitation of creatures*.'*

But what is to be said about the authority of King and the Encyclopedia, which the *Biblioteca* quotes against my opinion? If King and the Encyclopedia had in fact said the error which is ascribed to them, they would not deserve to be quoted. But it has to be confessed in their defence that they said something quite different. I will quote the French starting from the point where the extract from the work of the Archbishop of Dublin, Dr. King, begins; it forms the article quoted by the Encyclopedia: 'The general system of the honourable archbishop of Dublin is the following: 1. All creatures are necessarily imperfect, and always at an infinite distance from the perfection of God. If a negative principle is accepted, like the privation of the Peripatetics, we could say that every created being is composed of existence and non-existence. It is a nothing in respect of both the perfections that it lacks and the perfections possessed by other beings. *This defect in the constitution of created beings, or as it can be called, this mixture of non-entity, is the necessary principle of all natural evils, and makes moral evil possible, as will be seen from what follows*, etc.'*

6. (242)
[The system of Pope, Shaftesbury and Bolingbroke and evils and good in the universe]

Pope's system, as well as Shaftesbury's and Bolingbroke's,

sought to justify divine Providence against the objection concerning evils. It differs greatly from the system I follow. When these authors said, as they certainly did, that 'evils are necessary for the order of the universe', they were considering the order only in its materiality and external appearance, and went no further, as if they were talking about some spectacle contemplated by our intellect. In short, they spoke about a *physical order* and found it excellent because governed by *general, constant laws*, obeyed by the largest star and the smallest atom. From this they saw that a wonderful regularity resulted.

But is this sufficient to defend Providence? Preservation of the laws of the universe and the obligatory order it presents to the intellect have no importance for us if these laws and order are not directed to our happiness. For example, we would consider it better, and rightly so, if the law of gravity were less constant when its fulfilment meant that we were buried under a mountain that had collapsed on us. In my system, evils are shown as necessary to the order of the universe, but in a different sense. I speak about a *moral order*. I say evils are necessary to bring about the greatest degree of virtue in humanity and the highest degree of happiness. The system of authors who consider *physical order* and forget the relationship between created things and the virtue and happiness of intelligent beings (which applies only to us) gives rise to their familiar dictum 'Everything is good.' In my system the existence of evil is not denied; on the contrary it is admitted as an evident, undeniable fact. I accept that 'the dictum *everything is good*, understood in an absolute sense and without the hope of a future, is simply an insult to the difficulties of life', as Voltaire says (*Préf. au Poème sur le désastre de Lisbonne*). We cannot say 'everything is good' in an absolute sense unless we do away with the idea of evil, as people do who consider things solely in themselves and not in relationship to intellectual, moral being, for which alone evil truly exists. For this reason, in my system, 'everything is good' changes to 'everything serves good', that is, everything concurs to produce the greatest sum of virtue and happiness in the human race. I agree therefore with Voltaire when he says in reference to the system of Pope and the other two authors: 'It is clear that their system undermines the very foundation of the Christian religion and explains nothing at all'* (*Dictionnaire* *philosophique*, art. *Bien*), but I leave it to him to reconcile himself with himself when he says elsewhere: 'Pope had said *everything is good* in a very acceptable sense, whereas nowadays they [his supporters] give it a meaning that can be attacked'* (*Préf. au Poème sur le désastre* etc.).

7. (374)
[Stanislaus Hosius on the residue of sin]

In 1551, the celebrated president of the Council of Trent, Stanislaus Hosius, wrote a compendium of the Catholic faith for the Synod of Petrikov. In this fine work he clearly explains this teaching about the residue of sins that remains after the Sacrament of Penance has been received (*Confessio catholicae fidei christiana, etc.*, c. 48). He writes: 'It is not solely punishment that remains after the fault has been forgiven. The fault is not so totally abolished through penance that no residue of it remains for which punishment is due.'* He demonstrates this with the example of David. Although the prophet Nathan had told him that the Lord had taken away his sin, he continued to ask God 'that he will cancel his iniquity and cleanse him of it more fully'. This was due to the residue of the sin that, although forgiven, still remained in him: 'St. Chrysostom says that (David) does not consider the wound cured enough (*In Ps. 50,* Hom. 2). He prays rather that the scar be healed and his pristine comeliness restored.'* The learned Cardinal continues: 'In baptism we see that after the guilt of the original sin has been forgiven, the residue of that sin nevertheless remains, that is, the *fomes* of concupiscence, which has to be mortified by pious exercises for the whole of one's life. The same happens in the sacrament of penance. A kind of *fomes* remains, a certain residue of sin, which must be cleansed by healthy satisfaction. Moreover, when past sin has become habit, that is, it has taken deeper root, the necessary cleansing is greater and longer. We can indeed be quickly cleansed, St. Bernard says (*Serm. De Coen. Dom.*), but much must be cured if we are to be healed.'* The Cardinal confirms this teaching by many testimonies taken from St. Augustine (*De blasph*, in S.S.), St. Basil (Hom. *De poenit.*), St. Gregory of

Nyssa (Orat. *Non esse dolendum ob eorum obitum qui in fide decesserunt*), Origen (*In Levit*., c. 8), St. Cyprian (Serm. *De eleemoysn.*) and from many others. Hosius calls these scars 'residue of a previous fault *quibus poena debetur* [for which punishment is due]. Although they do not have the *concept of fault* because free will does not will them, they retain the *concept of sin*, both habitual and venial, because the will retains a disordered attachment which sometimes it does not advert to, and cannot in any case immediately reject.

8. (374)
[Cardinal Hosius on satisfaction for sin]

Again Hosius, an authoritative interpreter of the Council of Trent, of which he was president, explains the doctrine of temporal punishment for which the debt remains after the reception of sacramental absolution: 'Satisfaction is made for temporal punishment through fasting, alms, prayer and other pious exercises of the spiritual life. But these practices do not make satisfaction for eternal punishment, which by the sacrament or the desire for the sacrament is forgiven together with the fault. Temporal punishment, as the sacred writings teach, is not always totally forgiven (as it is in baptism) for those who through lack of gratitude for the grace of God that they have received have saddened the Holy Spirit and not feared to violate God's temple.'

After using authoritative testimonies to corroborate this necessity of penal exercises, he continues: 'This satisfaction however is not made in order to expiate fault or eternal punishment; it is to be attributed solely to Christ. Only he was made a propitiation for our sins, and not only for ours but for those of the whole world (1 Jn 2: 2). Only he by dying destroyed death; through death he abundantly satisfied our sins; through death he reconciled us to his heavenly Father. Therefore I am not at the moment speaking about this satisfaction but about the satisfaction that above all consists in those fruits of penance that Christ, in the name of justice, deemed worthy (Mt 6): fasting, prayer and alms, whether received by us or enjoined on us through our parish priests and ministers of the Sacraments. When this is done with faith and charity, the causes of sin are removed, the remains of sin are healed, and temporal punishment is either taken away or mitigated. Finally, good example is given.'* This takes nothing away from Christ's merit; rather it pertains to his supreme goodness to make us all capable of making part satisfaction through ourselves because the ability to give this satisfaction through ourselves pertains to the excellence of the moral state. In doing this we imitate Christ and follow the Redeemer in the work itself of Redemption. 'Christ made abundant satisfaction for our sins, suffered greatly for us and underwent death. But he did not suffer or make satisfaction for us in order that we might not suffer and do nothing for our sins after we had once fallen from the grace that we had obtained through baptism after dying with him (1 Pet 2). On the contrary he gave us an example to follow in his footsteps: just as he took up his cross after assuming our flesh and was truly immune from every sin, we also, stained by so many sins, should take up our cross. This is what he counsels: "If any want to become my followers, let them deny themselves and take up their cross and follow me" (Mt 16: 24).

'When Gregory is explaining Samuel's words to Saul, "See, what has remained is set before you" (1 Sam 9: 24), he says "has remained" because Christ did not make up for everything we have. He certainly redeemed us all through his cross but what remained was the necessity for those to undergo crucifixion who trusted in their redemption and in reigning with him (Bk. 4, *in lib. Reg.*, c. 4). The man who had seen this residue said: "If we suffer with him we shall reign with him," as if to say, "Christ's satisfaction has value only for those who fill up what remained." Hence blessed Peter the apostle says: "Christ also suffered for you, leaving you an example, so that you should follow in his steps" (1 Pet 2: 21). Also Paul: "I complete in my body what is lacking in the passion of Christ."' Nevertheless the penal satisfaction we give to divine justice has no value except through the merits of Christ alone, and through his grace. 'Someone may retort: "What has the cross of Christ brought me if I have to continuously carry my own cross, as if his is not sufficient?" His cross has brought you a great deal. Our cross would have no use whatsoever nor would we gain any fruit from it if Christ's cross had not preceded; whatever value our cross has comes by merit of his. In the same way, the usefulness of our satisfaction for sins would avail nothing if Christ's satisfaction had not preceded. Through his death and blood those things become efficacious that, pleasing to God, are performed by us in satisfaction for our sins. Therefore whatever our satisfaction does for us, it does so by the virtue, merit and efficacy of Christ's passion. His passion is the source and foundation of all our good works; they are no more ours than his, who lives in us and works in us, Christ himself, because "apart from me," he says, "you can do nothing"' (Jn 15: 5).

9. (389)
[Moral and Meritorious Freedom]

Moral freedom, which we are discussing, must be distinguished from *meritorious freedom*, which is a source of merit. *Meritorious freedom*, which I also call *bilateral freedom*, is simply a branch of moral freedom. Some modern thinkers restrict 'freedom' solely to meritorious freedom. But I see no need for the meaning of 'freedom' to be arbitrarily restricted in this way, contrary to ancient and common use — to claim this would be a question of words. Domenico Viva rightly says (*Propositio* 3, Jans. 18):

> It is a question of meaning whether a will free only from coercion is to be called absolutely free. Many affirm, and St. Thomas agrees (*De Potentia*, q. 10, art. 2, ad 5): 'God loves himself freely with his will, although he necessarily loves himself. According to Scotus (*Quodlib*., 6), the Divine Will necessarily wills its goodness, yet in willing it is free.' In the same sense they teach *passim* that the Holy Spirit proceeds freely from the Father and the Son, and that the blessed love God.*
>
> It is certain that the act with which God loves himself and with which the blessed love God is holy and therefore truly moral, although not free. In this case therefore I call *moral* the freedom that is necessary for constituting a *morally good* act. This freedom is not always *meritorious freedom*; the latter must be immune not only from all coercion

> but from all necessity. *Merit* is a form of moral good but although it contains a large amount of moral goodness, is not every moral good, because there is a moral good that is not merit, like the love with which God loves himself and the blessed love God.

But we must not confuse *moral freedom*, as I call it here, with spontaneity. Spontaneity has a much broader meaning. It does not express a power but a *mode of operation* of various powers. Real being (instinct, in this case) also operates with spontaneity but there is nothing moral in the action. Again, intellective being operates with spontaneity but its operation is not moral.

1. *Moral freedom* is a principle that is internal to the operator; it is not an external cause that moves the operator. In this sense St. John Damascene defines what is free: 'A spontaneous action is an action whose principle and cause is contained in the one who acts'* (*De fide ortodoxa*, bk. 2, c. 24). This is not sufficient to constitute meritorious freedom. Although the cause of the love that God bears to himself is certainly not outside God but rather is God himself, this love does not have the freedom that is meritorious freedom, although its freedom is essentially a holy and moral freedom.

2. Moral freedom is not every internal principle of an operative being. Strictly speaking it is the internal principle that constitutes the being as moral; it is the tendency to common good, to every good, to every entity (because *ens et bonum convertitur* [ens and good are interchangeable]) and therefore to all being. This tendency is the first act which posits in being the power to act with moral goodness, which elsewhere I have called *moral instinct*. This teaching however will become much clearer with my explanation in the text.

10. (397)
[The possibility of error and sin]

It is just as difficult to explain the possibility of *error* in an intelligent being as it is in a moral being. I have shown that two faculties must be distinguished in human understanding: 1. *pure knowledge* and 2. *affirmation* and persuasion. Error occurs not in the former but in the latter, which for the most part is subject to the human will (cf. *NE*, 3: 1245–1362; *CS*, 26–29; *Sistema di Filosofia*, 71). The faculty of *pure knowledge as such* is produced in us by ideal being; the *faculty of persuasion* is produced by *real being when connected to the faculty of knowledge*. The little work of Giuseppe Ferrari, *De l'erreur* (Paris, 1840) deserves to be read because it presents the difficulty philosophers encounter when explaining how error can arise in an intelligent being. But he wrongly believes that he sees a contradiction when I say that human beings, due to the *necessity of operating*, must make *practical judgments* even when they are not speculatively certain about a matter, and these judgments are sometimes erroneous without their fault. He says that despite this I condemn idolatry, materialism, etc. According to him I am not coherent if I do not excuse also these errors that are due to necessity of operating. But his own intelligent insight can see by itself that 1. idolatry, materialism, etc. are not *practical judgments* but true speculative errors that are not necessary for operating; 2. the *necessity of operation* that I am discussing does not concern the *mode* of operation but the operation itself. For example, if I want to preserve my life I need to eat, but this necessity certainly does not oblige me to eat bread rather than fruit or meat. Thus, granted that human beings need a religion, it in no way follows that they are necessitated to take on an erroneous, absurd religion, like idolatry. Idolatry would never have arisen in the world if voluntary vices had not darkened human intelligences or, to use my own expression, had not moved their *persuasion* to assent to falsehood.

A difficulty similar to that of explaining the possibility of *error* is the difficulty of explaining the possibility of *sin*, which is precisely the difficulty I undertook to unravel.

11. (457)
[Continuity and Gradation relative to Species]

It is to Leibniz's great credit that he deduced the concept of a polyps from the law of continuity and predicted their discovery: 'I consider the force of the principle of continuity to be such that I would not be surprised if some entities were found that relative to diverse properties, for example relative to nutrition and multiplication, could be considered equally as either vegetables or animals. Indeed, I am convinced that such entia must exist and that natural history may one day discover them.' But in my opinion Monsieur Leibniz proposed the law of continuity in too general a way. He proposed it as a gradation among entia. It must however be restricted to each *species* (there is nevertheless another law which I call the 'restrictedness of species', which I will discuss elsewhere). No gradation in fact exists between one species and another; there is only a jump. Thus, between brute matter and feeling, and between feeling and intelligence there is a distance that cannot be crossed. Moreover, between contingent nature and necessary being, there is infinity.

Leibniz might have been led to extend the law of continuity too far for the reason that species had not been well classified by philosophers. Animals, for example, are divided by naturalists into many species but strictly speaking they constitute only one species. The same applies to vegetables and minerals. The species that are called species of animals, vegetables and minerals are simply gradations within the same species; they should be called *generations* or *families* instead of species. I must make another observation. Is the continuity within the same species perfect? This cannot be determined by experiment. Reasoning demonstrates that it would be absurd if continuity meant that there is an infinitely small distance between one class of entia and another of the same species; an infinite small difference does not exist in nature because in nature the infinitely small does not exist. If however the law of continuity means that the differences are as small as they can be, the law acquires a meaning that is not absurd, and this is precisely how I understand it. In fact it is not difficult for us to understand that all possible classes of animals exist. But because every animal, in order to be what it is, requires certain conditions, such as the fusion of many feelings into one, the absence of internal pain, harmonious individuality and the preservative, reproductive cycle of functions, then clearly not every aggregate of atoms can constitute an animal, that is, an appropriate organisation; only certain determined aggregates can do this when wisely assembled. Consequently, among these kinds of aggregates there can certainly be a gradation but not in the sense that situated between one aggregate and another there is no possibility of other aggregates of atoms that are unsuitable for constituting either an animal or a suitably organised animal seed. In this latter sense the species of created entia can constitute a continuous chain, that is, no possible species can be inserted between them. But I will discuss this at greater length in *Cosmology*, if God grants me life and the necessary freedom to publish it. Although there will always be infinity between the contingent and the necessary, this does not break the chain if the chain is formed of links that are possible in reality — among possible things the contingent does not approach the point of attaining the necessary.

12. (476)
[Possible Worlds and the Least Action for the Greatest Good]

Leibniz's optimism cannot be accepted in the general way he expressed it. But let us imagine that in all the possible worlds the good that is in fact obtained was not obtained by the least quantity of action. In this case divine wisdom would give all these worlds second place to those in which the good could be obtained with the least quantity of action; this is a law essential to wise operation. Hence the world where the *minimum quantity of action* is used to obtain the good is *better* than all those where this law is not observed. Indeed all the other worlds are defective and therefore not suitable for being created by God: after all, *Dei perfecta sunt opera* [the works of God are perfect] (Deut 32, 4). We can therefore apply here Valla's argument about Providence, taken up so wisely by Leibniz. For the sake of brevity I will use the words with which Fontenelle summarised it in his eulogy of Leibniz:

> In a dialogue of Lorenzo Valla the author pretends that Sextus, son of Tarquinius the Proud, goes to Delphi to consult the oracle about his destiny. Apollo predicts that he will violate Lucrezia. Sextus complains about the prediction. Apollo replies that it is not his (Apollo's) fault; he simply divines it: Jupiter has regulated everything and

> Sextus must make his complaint to him. The dialogue ends here, where we see that Valla saves God's foreknowledge at the cost of his goodness. But not Leibniz. According to his system, he continues what Valla has pretended. Sextus goes to Dodona and takes Jupiter to task about the crime to which he is destined. Jupiter replies that it is enough that he does not go to Rome, but Sextus says clearly that he will not give up his hope of the kingdom, and departs. After his departure, the high priest Theodorus asks Jupiter why he didn't give Sextus another will. Jupiter sends Theodorus to Athens to consult Minerva, who introduces him into the palace of destinies where all the possible universes from the worst to the best are presented on tablets. In the best universe Theodorus sees Sextus' crime, from which comes Roman freedom, a government rich in virtue and an empire that helps a great part of the human race. Theodorus can only hiss his disapproval.

If instead of saying that the pictures in the palace of destinies displayed the worst and the best universes, he had said they displayed the universes where the law of the least means is not observed and those where it is observed and that Sextus' crime, or other similar crimes, was among the latter, the pretended case is most apt for explaining my thought. However, it must be noted that Sextus was in fact *free* to go or not go to Rome. Hence his crime was free. Jupiter did not will it but permitted it for the greater good that had to come from it.

13. (529)
[God's *scientia media* (middle knowledge)]

In all this discussion, indeed in the whole of this book, use is made of a *scientia media* [*middle knowledge*]. I am following the example of the Fathers of the Church who always had recourse to this knowledge when discussing the ways of Providence. Hence I think it best to explain the sense in which this kind of knowledge must, it seems to me, be admitted in God. The question is: How can God know future events? He cannot know them in their reality because this does not yet exist, nor in their immediate causes because these, being free, are not

[*App*., 13]

determined to one effect alone, nor in the decrees God gives them because God does not make a decree for things that have never existed nor will exist. He knows them in his wisdom. God, as Scripture tells us, does nothing without infinite wisdom: *omnia in sapientia fecisti* [in wisdom you have made them all] (Ps 104: 24); granted an hypothesis, he knows what his wisdom must decree. In my opinion, the law of wisdom is the law of the 'least means', the law that disposes everything so that a maximum good is obtained. For example, granted the hypothesis that Christ's gospel had in fact been preached to the inhabitants of Tyre and Sidon, God knows in this new occurrence of things whether the law of the least means would have required those people to convert or not upon hearing the gospel. If the law of wisdom required this, God knows he would have decreed it and that it would have happened.

But how could God know that the greatest possible good obtainable in keeping with the hypothesis would have required the conversion of those people? He would know by calculating all the other circumstances of the universe, among which would be the disposition of those people and also the *natural gratitude* I alluded to in the previous footnote [135]; after being humbled by their own disorders and because their conscience was not at rest, this gratitude would have led them to consider the light and aid offered them a great benefit. The fact that they might be corrupt, even more corrupt perhaps than the Hebrews, is not an obstacle. God could still give them the grace of conversion, which he did not give the Hebrews. He would do this not because the people of Tyre and Sidon had a natural disposition to receive the gospel light as a great benefit and therefore merited the grace of conversion, but because the grace received in the dispositions would have borne greater fruit as soon as the dispositions had been informed and elevated by grace. This grace therefore would always have been a totally gratuitous gift; it would have been given to the undeserving, probably to a people who because of their sins were more undeserving than the Hebrew people. But even so, it would still have borne its fruit, a fruit respectively maximum, while the conversion of Corozain and Bethsaida would not have given a respectively maximum fruit. Thus, at the final day it will be possible to compare the people of the two Phoenician cities with the Hebrews; the former will be a cause of shame to the latter and condemn them, not through the inhabitants' absolute goodness but through their better natural disposition to receive and make the gospel grace bear fruit in them, if it had been given.

In this sense we can distinguish in God a knowledge midway between the knowledge of *simple intelligence* and the *knowledge of vision*. In exactly the same way therefore, we can distinguish a middle knowledge between a *simple antecedent will* and a *consequent will*, and say with Leibniz:

> The object of the *primal antecedent will* is each good and each evil in itself, excluding all combinations of these, and tends to promote every good and prevent every evil. The *middle will* refers to the combinations, that is, when some good is joined to an evil. In this case the will has some tendency to this combination if the good exceeds the evil. But the decretory and *final will* results from the consideration of all the goods and evils involved in the deliberation; it results from a total combination.
>
> *Théod.*, 2: 119.

It is not necessary, I am sure, to tell the reader that these dispositions of several kinds of knowledge and several kinds of will have no place at all in God; they are solely in our way of conceiving things. In God however there is only one most simple knowledge and one most simple will. If anyone should object that God does not need knowledge of future events, this knowledge nevertheless helps to explain somehow the ways of divine wisdom, and the explanation is not false because it corresponds in God to the result that is the object of his decrees.

14. (548)
[St. Augustine on the necessity of sin and freedom from it]

We must note that according to the mind of St. Augustine and the feeling of the Catholic Church all necessity of sinning ceases in those who are in the grace of God or who turn to this grace; the exception are moral imperfections and venial sins, which no one can totally avoid. St. Augustine speaks about this unfortunate necessity of sinning for no other reason than to give glory to the grace of JESUS Christ, which alone frees us from the need. Hence, in the same number [*Op. imperf. contra Iul.*, 1: 105] he says: 'Only the grace of God through JESUS Christ our Lord brings freedom from all sins whether original or moral, and those that have been committed or will be committed. In him we are regenerated, and from him we have learnt to pray not only "Forgive us our debts", that is, because we have sinned, but also "Do not lead us into temptation", that is, lest we sin.'* — It is a pure calumny of the Jansenists to have attributed to St. Augustine the teaching that human beings in the present state of fallen nature operate always according to which of the two pleasures in them prevails, without the intervention of their free will. If this were true, all sin without exception would be necessary because, once the freedom *from necessity* is destroyed, the only freedom left would be freedom *from coercion*. St. Augustine teaches very clearly that 1. grace can be lost by sin; 2. those who are in grace but sin, always sin freely because in those who are in grace there is no necessity at all to sin; 3. in the state of fallen and unredeemed nature there are two species of sins: necessary sins and free sins (faults). Hence, in his reply to Pelagius who was accusing him of the same calumny as the Jansenists (an extraordinary thing!), that is, that he did not accept free sins in fallen man, he says: 'I grant that in human beings there are sins which are committed *not out of necessity* but by the will, and these are straightforward sins; *hence there is freedom to abstain from them*. There are also sins arising from the necessity of ignorance' (moral imperfections) 'or from the necessity of affections. The human race' (before receiving grace or after the loss of grace) 'is full of these kinds of sins, which are not only sins but *punishment for sins*. How can you say that sin is found neither in my definitions nor in behaviour?'* (ibid.).

15. (601)
[Existence of Spirits without Corporeal Matter]

St. Thomas notes that 'because the ancients did not form an accurate concept of intellective power (*ignorantes vim intelligendi*) nor distinguish between FEELING and INTELLECT, they judged there was nothing in the world except what fell under sense and imagination. And because only the body falls under the imagination, they thought that there was no other body than ens' (*S.T.*, I, q. 50, art. 1). Aristotle discusses this crude manner of the ancients' view in book 4 of the Physics. Among the Hebrews, the same view also explains the Sadducees' error in denying spirits. But even when the error was corrected, the human mind had great difficulty in conceiving the existence of intelligent substances totally separate from corporeal matter. This in turn resulted in a second error, the error of those who conceived God as the soul of the world. But because this opinion was excluded by the light of faith, there was a third opinion according to which all spirits except God were clothed with some sort of body.

This idea is found in Origen; about it St. Thomas says: 'But this' (giving God a body) 'contradicts Catholic faith, which makes God exalted above all things, as Psalm 8: 2 says: "You have set your glory above the heavens."* Although Origen rejected this opinion about God, he held the same opinion as others about other spirits. In this matter, as in many other things, he was mistaken by following the opinions of the ancient philosophers' (Orig., Περὶ ἀρχῶν, bk. 1, c. 6). Also St. Augustine, as St. Thomas notes, 'uses the opinion of the Platonists without asserting it,'* and said that demons might be like animals clothed with ethereal bodies (*Epp.*, bk. 1, ep. 9). — *Super Genes. ad litt.*, bk. 3, c. 10). Later Pope St. Gregory called angels, perhaps metaphorically (as St. Thomas thinks), a reasoning animal (Homily 10, *De Epiphan.*). St. John Damascene 'wrote that the angels are called incorporeal and immaterial relative to us but compared to God are corporeal and material' (*Ortodox. Fidei*, bk. 2, c. 3). Finally, in the 12th century, St. Bernard wrote: 'Just as we attribute immortality to God alone, so only to him do we attribute incorporeity. The nature of incorporeity has no need of the support of a corporeal instrument, neither through itself nor through others' (*Super Cant.*, Serm. 6).

We see just how difficult it is for us to conceive a pure spirit that subsists without any corporeal vestiture. I will demonstrate in the appropriate place that angels, although pure spirits, have a kind of contact of action with bodies (St. Thomas, *S.T.*, I, q. 51, art. 1).

[*App.*, 15]

16. (751)
[Knowledge proper to the Angels]

What I said about the human being applies also to angelic nature. I argued that the human being could not have been taught to know the wisdom and goodness of God if this wisdom and goodness had not been revealed in creation, which is a complex of signs by which we can come to know the supreme goodness and wisdom in their creative act. I said that by means of these signs we rise to the concept of the Creator's essential wisdom and goodness while we are in this life. But when we are taken up to see the Creator himself, we perceive the same creative act that is the divine essence, and in this act contemplate directly the creative wisdom. Consequently, the knowledge of God that the blessed have completes that of viators, and the object of both kinds of knowledge is the same: creation. However, viators contemplate it in its term distinct from God, whereas the blessed contemplate it in its principle which is God himself.

The same, it seems to me, must be said about angelic knowledge, but with this difference: we who on our way know corporeal things through passive feelings produced in us by the action of bodies; the angels know bodies through active feelings produced by their own action on bodies. In this way bodies can be *signs* of higher cognitions for us and the angels, and the means of communication between us and the angels. Again, just as sensations and images are the *species* that make us know bodies, so *active feelings* are the *species*, so to speak, proper to angels. According to the opinion that I prefer, these *active feelings* are inserted into angelic nature and created with it in a way similar to the *fundamental feeling*: this feeling, with which human beings feel their own body, is innate, that is, inserted in human nature and created with it. This is the way I explain angelic knowledge *per species innatas* [through innate species], by means of which, St. Thomas says, *cognoscunt res in propria natura* [they know things in their proper nature] (*S.T.*, I, q. 58, art. 7). Granted this opinion, we can distinguish in the creation of the angels the creation of their subjective reality, relative to order but not to time. This reality is perhaps indicated in the first verse of Genesis by the word *caelum* [heaven]: *In principio creavit Deus* coelum *et terram* [In the beginning God created the *heavens* and the earth] (1: 1), that is, he created the heavenly nature (angelic) and the terrestrial (the human world) by the communication of intellective light, or by the object that informs angelic minds. This communication can be indicated on the first day of creation, of which it is said: *Fiat lux et facta est lux* [Let there be light and there was light] (Gen 1: 3). St. Augustine says that this passage states: *Lux qua angelica mens formata est* [The light by which the angelic mind was formed] (*De Gen. ad litt.*, 4, n. 50). If the work of creation is distinguished into six days, so we can fittingly understand that six activities or active feelings, in other words six *angelic perceptions*, followed subsequently in the angels, which corresponds to the knowledge St. Augustine called *vespertina* [evening]. We see therefore how true it is that the angels *non accipiunt cognitionem a rebus* [do not receive knowledge from things] (St. Thomas, *S.T.*, I, q. 80, art. 6) because they act on corporeal things, and are not passive to them, as we are.

This does not mean that they are creators of bodies. God is the only creator both of the angels and of their activities, and also of the term of these natural activities, which bodies are. In the same way, God is the author of the fundamental feeling proper to the human being and to space, although space is the term of the fundamental feeling. The angels' *morning knowledge* is that through which they know things *secundum quod sunt in verbo* [in so far as things are in the word], and through this knowledge they see things in the creative act, in the divine essence. Hence, such knowledge pertains to the angels who are blessed, and in it they are passive. St. Augustine says: 'The angelic mind *adheres with pure charity to the word of God.* Thus, after it has been created with the order with which it precedes the rest, it sees in the word of God the things to be done before they are done'* (*De Gen. ad litt.*, 4: 49). St. Augustine causes no problem here when he says that the angelic mind *illo ordine creata est ut praecedat cetera* [is created with the order with which it precedes the rest] because he is not speaking here of the order of time but the order of reason as we see from what he says next (*De Gen. ad litt.*, 5: 51–55).

[*App.*, 16]

17. (827)
[The Resurrection of the Just][(1)]

(1). The reader should note the following:

1. It is an error to hold that after the resurrection the just will enjoy corporeal pleasures. This was the heresy of the Millenarians, which was strongly refuted by St. Jerome and condemned by the Church. Jesus Christ has expressly stated: 'For when they rise from the dead, they neither marry nor are given in marriage, but are like angels [of God] in heaven'[1] (Mk 12: 25).

2. It would also be mistaken to believe that the just who have risen lived with an animal life. This is excluded by Christ's words and by the state of glorified bodies, which St. Paul calls *spiritual* (1 Cor 15: 44).

3. For the same reason it would be a mistake to think that earthly and material goods were goods for the just, and would abound as a reward of their virtue. The spiritualised body has neither use for these goods nor are they appropriate to it. As St. Paul says: 'For the kingdom of God is not food and drink'[2] (Rom 14: 17).

4. Another error would be to believe that the just would first rise to animal life and then, after some time, pass to glorious life. This would be contrary to the express witness of the divine Scriptures (Jn 5; 1 Cor 15; Mt 22; 25; Dan 12) that the just will rise glorious.

5. A fifth error would be to believe that the universal, solemn judgment of the good and wicked will not take place at the same time. But the Scriptures teach otherwise (Dan 12; Mt 23; 25; Jn 5; 12).

6. It would be an error to think that bodies will take a significant period of time to rise, because certainly the bodies of the just will rise in the twinkling of an eye, as St. Paul teaches: 'In a moment, in the twinkling of an eye, at the last trumpet. For the trumpet will sound, and the dead will be raised imperishable, and we will be changed'[3] (1 Cor 15: 52).

7. Finally it would be an error to believe that the Mosaic law will be restored to power in a thousand years, as some

(1) Because the Latin quotations in this long appendix are many, a superscript number has been used in place of the asterisk to facilitate reference to the Latin in the Original Language References section.

falsely imagine. This law, because figurative, was fulfilled and made void with the truth of the new law of grace.

(2). The refutation of these errors however still leaves the question concerning the time of the resurrection of the just, which the Church has not defined. St. Jerome, who did not follow the opinion of those who thought the resurrection of the just would take place more than a thousand years before the resurrection of the reprobate, says: 'Although we do not follow it, we do not condemn it because many Churchmen and martyrs said the same. Let each abound in good sense and let all things be reserved to the Lord's judgment (Jer 19).'[4] Some theologians hold that a serious difficulty about this opinion can be found in the Scriptures which clearly state that the just will rise *in novissimo die* [on the last day] (Job 19: 25; Jn 6: 44; 11: 24). In Scripture however the word 'day' is often used as a synonym of time; St. Augustine says: 'It is obvious that the Scriptures usually use *day* or *hour* also for *time*'[5] (*Ep*. 197: 2). Hence we often read 'on that day' (Ezek 38: 10, 18–19; 39: 8, 12–13) for 'at that time', as the context clearly shows. This is because Scripture uses undetermined time to express time that is often determined. In other places facts are narrated which we are told will happen 'on the last day' but it is clear that they cannot happen in the last twenty-four hours of the world. Thus Jeremiah, when prophesying the return of the Hebrews from slavery, and more accurately their conversion to the Gospel, of which the return was a symbol, says: 'In the latter days you will understand this,'[6] (30: 24) and immediately adds, 'At that time, says the Lord, I will be the God of all the families of Israel, and they shall be my people'[7] (31: 1). Here, 'at that time' clearly expresses in different words exactly what 'in the latter days' means in the immediately preceding phrase. Hosea also declares that the Hebrews will be converted on the last day: 'They shall come in awe to the Lord and to his goodness in the latter days'[8] (Hos 3: 5). Moreover the time when the Hebrews enter the Church and rekindle their cooled fervour in the world will certainly not be the last day of the universe.

(3). Micah uses the same phrase to indicate the time of the Messiah's coming and the propagation of the Gospel: 'In days to come the mountain of the Lord's house shall be established as the highest of the mountains, and shall be raised up above the hills. Peoples shall stream to it'[9] (Mic 4: 1). Here we see that the Prophet understands 'days to come' as the last age of the world, which is that of the Messiah and embraces the time stretching from his coming until the universal judgment. Hence the Fathers normally divide the whole duration of the world into seven ages. These seem to be symbolised in the six days of creation and in the seventh which not unsuitably would mean the time of the law of grace when Christ has given his *peace* to humanity; he allows even those here on earth who have this peace to enjoy a certain rest, which is a foretaste of heaven. The same peace also seems to be signified appropriately by the eighth day, which is the day of the Lord. The Fathers therefore took it to mean the ultimate perfection: 'Many psalms,' says St. Ambrose, 'are written for the eighth day… The eighth day is the perfection of our hope; similarly, the eighth is the sum of virtues'[10] (*In Lk*, bk. 1, c. 6). This explains why St. John calls the time of grace not only the last day but the 'last hour': 'Children, it is the last hour! As you have heard that antichrist is coming, so now many antichrists have come. From this we know that it is the last hour'[11] (1 Jn 2: 18); here the word 'hour' is used to mean a longer, undetermined time.

St. Augustine also writes very much to the point to Hesychius: 'But a time of a thousand years, if their end were the end of the world, could be called the very last universal time or "the last day" because it is written: "For a thousand years in your sight are like yesterday" (Ps 90: 4). Anything therefore done for a thousand years could be said to be done in the last time or on the *last day*. I repeat: in this matter we must often say: Let us consider how many years ago John the Evangelist said: "It is the last hour" (1 Jn 2: 18). If we were alive at that time and heard this, how many years would we think would pass, or would we not rather hope that the Lord was coming when John was still alive? He did not say: it is the last time, the last year or month or day, but "It is the last hour". See how long this hour is! But it was not a lie because hour must be understood as meaning time'[12] (*Ep*., 199: 17).

(4). In the brevity of a footnote I certainly cannot explain the many and serious reasons that have made me prefer before all others the interpretation I have given of this difficult place in

Revelation. I will simply make a few observations. St. Paul speaks of the *last trumpet* and says that when it makes its first sound the *dead* will rise *incorrupt*, that is, the just, but says nothing about the others. In fact he had said: 'But each in his own order: Christ the first fruits' (Christ will rise first), 'then at his coming those who belong to Christ'[13] (1 Cor 15: 23). A little later he says: 'We will all rise' (good and wicked) 'but we will not all be changed'[14] (only the good will be changed into the glorious state); then still speaking about these same people: 'in a moment, in the twinkling of an eye, at the last trumpet. For the trumpet will sound, and the dead will be raised imperishable, and we will be changed'[15] (1 Cor 15: 51-52). The last trumpet is the seventh, as we learn from St. John (Didymus ap. Hier. *Ep. Ad Minerium et Alex*; Oecumenius; Theophylactus). — But St. John clearly says that this trumpet of the seventh angel extends its sound not just for one day only but for many days: *in diebus vocis septimi angeli* (Rev 10: 7). Nevertheless St. Paul says that the elect will rise at the first sound of the trumpet: *canet enim tuba et mortui resurgent*, and its sound will continue for many days, that is, for a long time. This tells us that the just rise a long time before the final judgment.

(5). St. John calls this resurrection of the just the *consummation of the mystery of God* and, agreeing completely with St. Paul, adds that the consummation of this mystery must take place at the start of the trumpet's sound: 'But in the days when the seventh angel is to blow his trumpet, the mystery of God will be fulfilled, as he announced to his servants the prophets'[16] (Rev 10: 7). To indicate that the glorified bodies will no longer be subject to the law of time, he says: *Quia tempus non erit amplius* [Because time will be no more] (ibid. 6). It is true that St. Paul's words, *mortui resurgent incorrupti* [the dead will rise incorrupt], are applied by some to all the dead, including the reprobate, but it seems to me the context requires the opposite. Estius says: 'To this we must add that Scripture always accepts that the incorruption applies to the good and never attributes it to the reprobate, only to the elect. Therefore the commentary of those who interpret this place as meaning all the dead, even the wicked, whom they say will be incorrupt because they could not die, seems to me of little probability'[17] (In h. l.), and the words that follow, *et nos immutabimur* [and we shall be changed] cause no problem. St. Paul distinguishes between the elect who will be dead at the coming of Christ and those who will be alive (1 Thess 4) and says that both will be glorified: 'We who are alive, who are left until the coming of the Lord, will by no means precede those who have fallen asleep'[18] (1 Thess 4: 15).

This passage caused some authors (particularly the Greeks) to think that the just living on earth at the coming of Christ would not die but pass from life to glory. They based themselves on the reading of many codices that read: 'We do not all die but we will all be changed.'[19] Although St. Thomas does not exclude this reading, he says: 'Those codes that read "We do not all die but we will all be changed" could be read as: the dead will rise incorrupt, that is, in a state of incorruption, and we who are alive, even though we do not rise because we do not die, will nevertheless be changed from a state of corruption into incorruption. This seems to agree with what 1 Thess. 4 says: "We who are alive, who are left, will be taken up together with them, etc." Thus, in both places the Apostle numbers himself with the living'[20] (In h. l.). But no one need be exempt from death because the passages of St. Paul can be explained in the way that St. Augustine explains them in his work *De baptism. Parv.*, bk. 2, c. 31: 'At the end some are granted not to feel death because of a sudden change'[21] (cf. *Retract.* 2: 33; *Ep.* 193, 9–11). Some Greek interpreters have observed that according to the quoted reading St. Paul does not in fact say that those alive at the time of the coming of Christ 'will not die' but that they 'will not sleep', which means they will not remain dead for any length of time; for example, Oecumenius says: 'But some say that the Apostle said: "We will not sleep a long death as if corruption and dissolution were necessary,"' and later: 'The phrase "we will not sleep" must be taken to mean that we will not sleep with a lasting sleep so that a sepulchre, corruption and dissolution are necessary, but those who are still alive will undergo only a short death.'[22]

The part of St. John's Gospel where Christ says that the dead will hear the voice of the Son of God could perhaps mean that the seventh angel of the book of Revelation is Christ, in the way that the previous angels symbolised popes and bishops (an archangel could in fact represent Christ, and serve him as the ambassador and nuncio of his will, as we can see from St. Paul in 1 Thess 4: 15 where the trumpet is also called *tuba Dei* [God's trumpet] as if it were larger than the previous ones). Moreover, in this same place of St. John, Christ speaks distinctly about the resurrection of the good. This resurrection has a spiritual beginning, when they rise from the death of sin by receiving grace, which is the seed of the future resurrection of the body. Hence the general resurrection of the just (this *mysterium Dei* [mystery of God]) began with the preaching of Christ, who gave life back to their souls, and it will be consummated in the resurrection of their bodies: 'Very truly, I tell you, the hour is coming, and is now here, when the dead will hear the voice of the Son of God, and those who hear will live'[23] (Jn 5: 25). It says 'those who hear' because only the good, who accept and keep Christ's word, are being spoken about. The phrase, 'the hour is coming', indicates the future resurrection of the body. It is followed by 'and is now here' to indicate the resurrection of souls, which is the seed and title of that future resurrection of the body and was begun with the first coming of Christ. Later, speaking about the resurrection of all people, both good and wicked, Christ says: 'Do not be astonished at this' (he is alluding to what he had said before about his power to give resurrection also to the body, but is now extending this power to give resurrection to all people without distinction, not simply the good); 'for the hour is coming when all who are in their graves will hear his voice and will come out — those who have done good, to the resurrection of life, and those who have done evil, to the resurrection of condemnation'[24] (Jn 5: 28–29). We need not deduce from this that the resurrection of the good and of the wicked is simultaneous but only that both are done by the power of the voice of the Son of God. According to St. John, his voice, indicated by the seventh trumpet, sounds for a long time.

We also need to consider those places where Christ predicts the last things to come (Mt 24; 26: 1; Mk 13; Lk 21). These clearly mention a coming of the Son of man prior to the last judgment by some time. We read first that the Gospel will have been preached to all nations: 'until the times of the Gentiles are fulfilled'[25] (Lk 21: 24), and: 'And this gospel of the kingdom will be proclaimed throughout the world, as a testimony to all the nations'[26] (Mt 24: 14). Next there will be signs in the heavens:

[*App.*, 17]

'Then they will see the Son of Man coming in a cloud with power and great glory'[27] (Lk 21: 27; Mt 24: 30; Mk 13: 26). This coming in the cloud corresponds to the coming that St. John describes in Revelation: 'I looked, and there was a white cloud, and seated on the cloud was one like the Son of Man'[28] (Rev 14: 14).

The Gospel also tell us that after this coming of the Son of man in a cloud, the redemption of the just *is near*, that is, their resurrection: 'Now when these things begin to take place, stand up and raise your heads, because your redemption is drawing near'[29] (Lk 21: 28); hence, some time must pass before the end of the world. This resurrection is expressed more clearly in St. Matthew and St. Mark: the former says: 'And he will send out his angels with a loud trumpet call, and they will gather his elect from the four winds, from one end of heaven to the other'[30] (Mt 24: 31); the latter says: 'Then he will send out the angels, and gather his elect from the four winds, from the ends of the earth to the ends of heaven'[31] (Mk 13: 27), where only the just are mentioned, but nothing about the resurrection of the wicked. It seems also that the just will fill the space between heaven and earth, suspended glorified in the air. All this is in perfect agreement with what we read in Revelation: 'They came to life and reigned with Christ a thousand years'[32] (Rev 20: 4), which is the consummation of the previously mentioned 'mystery of God': 'in the days of the seventh angel when he blows his trumpet' (Rev 10: 7). In St. Luke, Christ, after speaking about the coming of the Son of man, warns his disciples that the kingdom of God *is near*: 'So also, when you see these things taking place, you know that the kingdom of God is near'[33] (Lk 21: 31). The other two Evangelists also mention the same warning: 'So also, when you see these things taking place, you know that it is near, at the very gates'[34] (Mk 13: 29) and: 'So also, when you see all these things, you know that he it is near, at the very gates'[35] (Mt 24: 33). This coming of the Saviour is like the leaves of the fig tree: they show that the fruit is close to being ripe (Mt 24: 32; Mk 13: 28; Lk 21: 29–30) and hence it is not yet the end of things. St. Augustine acknowledges that these places of the Gospel are certainly speaking about a coming of the Son of man long before the judgment (*Ep.* 199: 41–45). After discussing St. Luke 21: 27–31, he argues: 'When it says: "when you see these things taking place", the only things we could understand are those mentioned above. But the words contain also these others: "Then they will see the Son of Man coming in a cloud with power and great glory." Therefore even when this is seen, it will not be the kingdom of God but the kingdom will be near'[36] (n. 43). He then points out that both St. Mark and St. Matthew follow the same order in the narration: they give the coming of the Son of God the same position in the order, that is, a certain time before the end of the world: 'We see that the other two Evangelists also follow this order,'[37] and after quoting the relevant places, he repeats the above observation: 'The words "When you see these things taking place" can only mean surely the things mentioned above? But the words also contain these others: "Then they will see the Son of Man coming in a cloud with power and great glory; and then he will send out the angels, and gather his elect." It will not be the end therefore but the end will be near'[38] (n. 43).

Someone might object: surely it is possible that the words, 'When you see these things taking place' do not refer to everything mentioned above but only to some of them, and therefore the coming of the Son of man can be excluded? This is impossible because St. Matthew expressly says: 'All these things' and hence also includes the coming of Christ already mentioned. In the words of St. Augustine: 'Do all the things mentioned above have to be understood where Christ said: "When you see these things taking place" or only some of them, that is, can we exclude: "Then they will see the Son of Man coming, etc."? It will indeed be the end, although not close at hand. But Matthew made clear that nothing can be excluded; everything that has been said must be accepted: "When you see these things taking place". In fact immediately after saying: "And the powers of heaven will be moved", Christ says that "the Son of man will appear in heaven and all the peoples of the earth will mourn. They will see the Son of Man coming on the clouds of heaven in great power and glory, and he will send his angels with a trumpet and a loud voice, and they will gather his elect from the four winds, from the furthest parts of the heavens to their remotest bounds. Learn a parable from the fig tree. When its branches are young and leaves appear, you know that summer is near. So you, when you see *all these things*, know that it is near at the gates.'"[39] St. Augustine, guided by these considerations, says that the coming of Christ described in these places can be understood in two ways: either of his mystical coming, in the way that he continuously comes in his Church, or of his manifest coming, with that body with which he sits at the right of the Father (n. 41). However he adds: 'But it is difficult to judge which of these two is to be chosen';[40] he admits that the second is more obvious: 'The more immediate sense is that when people have heard and read "And then they will see the Son of Man coming in a cloud with power and great glory", they will preferably accept the coming which is not through the Church but in Christ's own person, when he will come to judge the living and the dead'[41] (n. 42). This is the common opinion of commentators; they are persuaded by the words 'then they will see' and by the whole context of the discourse.

I therefore conclude this long footnote with the wise counsel of this great Father: 'But these things' (the things that concern Christ's mystical, daily coming, excluding those few passages that obviously refer to his manifest, bodily coming) 'must not be rashly presented so that a valid contradiction occurs; particularly because among those who do not treat the holy Scriptures as improbable, the obscurity of divine discourses of this kind (by which God wishes to exercise our understanding) can have not only more effect on one person than on another, but be such that one person sometimes understands more, the other less'[42] (n. 45). I hope that the opinion I have given will be understood with this same spirit of moderation, because I am fully aware that there are other interpretations of these particular texts. Whether the interpretation I have preferred seems the most coherent, I willingly leave to the judgment of wise people.

Original Language References

Title page: Ἀγαθὸς ἦν, ἀγαθῷ δὲ οὐδεὶς περὶ οὐδενὸς οὐδέποτε ἐγγὶγνεται φθόνος

Quotations in numbered Paragraphs:

184. *Sicut aberrandi causa meta non ponitur, sic nec natura mali in mundo existit.*

Mala quae nulla sua natura subsistent, a Domino non creantur.

185. *Per Verbum omnipotens Deus omnia condidit unus*
A quo natura est nulla creata mali:
Et quod non fecit dives sapientia Verbi,
Non habet in rerum conditione locum.
Nulla igitur vitiis substantia, nullaque vita est,
Quae vegetet corpus, materiamque suam.
Sed cum libertas discedit ab ordine recto,
Nec servant proprium quae bona sunt modulum
In culpa et vitio est vagus in contraria motus,
Fitque malum veram deseruisse viam.

188 (title). *Omnis creatura certis suae naturae circumscripta est limitibus.*

339. *Ac, dum prima novis adolescit frondibus aetas*
Parcendum teneris: et dum se laetus ad auras
Palmes agit laxis per purum immissus habenis
Ipsa acies nondum falcis tentanda.

348 (title). *Ego sapientia... quando praeparabat caelos, aderam; quando certa lege et gyro vallabat abyssos; quando aethera firmabat sursum et librabat fontes aquarum quando circumdabat mari terminum suam, et legem ponebat aquis, ne transirent fines suos; quando appendebat fundamenta terrae: cum eo eram cuncta componens, et delectabar per singulos dies, ludens coram eo omni tempore, ludens in orbe terrarum: et deliciae meae, esse cum filiis hominum.*

374. *O felix culpa quae talem ac tantum meruit habere Redemptorem!*

417 (title). *Sapiens operator perficit opus suum breviori via qua potest.*

465. *Causas rerum naturalium non plures admitti debere, quam quae et verae sint et earum phaenomenis explicandis sufficient.*

Effectuum naturalium eiusdem generis eaedem assignandae sunt causae, quatenus fieri potest, ut descensus lapidum in Europa et in America, reflexionis lucis in terra et in planetis.

476. *Deus satius duxit de malis bona facere, quam nulla mala esse permittere.*

535. *In his quae providentia debite reguntur non debet esse aliquid frustra.*

538. *Iam non amplius in aeternum ex te fructum quisquam manducet.*

548. *peccandi necessitas unde abstinere liberum non est, illius peccati* POENA *est, a quo abstinere liberum fuit, quando nullum pondus necessitates urgebat.*

550. *ut iudex punit eos qui legem praetereunt,* NON EIS INFERENS DE SE IPSO MALUM, *sed in id quod elegerunt eos expellens, ad complendam summam miseriarum.*

560. *Nec obdurat Deus impertiendo malitiam, sed non impertiendo misericordiam.*

588. *Cuivis potest accidere, quod cuiquam potest.*

Exstat ut in mediis turris aprica casis.

Quantus Eryx, et quantus Athos, gaudetque nivali
Vertice se attollens pater Apenninus ad auras.

594 (title). *Ad divinam providentiam pertinet, ut gradus entium qui possibiles sunt adimpleantur.*

612. *vae autem homini illi per quem scandalum venit.*

617 (title). *Particularia sunt propter naturam universalem; cuius signum est, quod in his in quibus potest natura universalis conservari per unum individuum, non sunt multa individua unius speciei.*

632. *In substantiis autem materia est propter formam;* PER HANC ENIM PARTICIPAT DIVINAM BONITATEM, PROPTER QUAM OMNIA FACT SUNT.

Ex quo patet, quod particularia sunt PROPTER NATURAM

UNIVERSALEM: cuius signum est, quod in his in quibus potest natura universalis conservari per unum individuum, non sunt multa individua unius speciei.

635. *Vos et Cyclopea saxa*
Experti, revocate animos, maestumque timore
Mittite: forsan et haec olim meminisse iuvabit.

642 (title). *Et cum sit una, omnia potest; et in se permanens omnia innovat.*

658. *conclusit Deus omnia in incredulitate; ut OMNIUM MISEREATUR.*

672. *UT INNOTESCAT PRINCIPATIBUS ET POTESTATIBUS in coelestibus per Ecclesiam MULTIFORMIS SAPIENTIA DEI.*

UT OSTENDERET in saeculis supervenientibus ABUNDANTES DIVITIAS GRATIAE SUAE.

739. *Proinde, etsi non interim laetiore nunc, veruntamen potentiore gratia indigent isti.*

776. *nunc autem et viderunt et oderunt, et me et Patrem meum.*

850. *Si omnis homo liberaretur, utique LATERET quid peccatis per iustitiam debeatur: si nemo, quid gratia largiretur.*

857. *Regum timendorum in proprios greges,*
Reges in ipsos imperium est Iovis
Clari giganteo triumpho
Cuncta supercilio moventis.

861. *Debemur morti nos, nostraque sive receptus*
Terra Neptunus classes aquilonibus arcet,
Regis opus, sterilisque diu palus aptaque remis
Vicinas urbes alit, et grave sentit aratrum:
Seu cursum mutavit iniquum frugibus amnis
Doctus iter melius: MORTALIA FACTA PERIBUNT.

863. *Nec Deus intersit nisi dignus vindice modus*
Inciderit.

867. *Qui immutat cor principum populi terrae et decipit eos ut frustra incedant per invium. Palpabunt quasi in tenebris et non in luce, et errare eos faciet quasi ebrios.*

872. *cum ille patiatur damnum pecuniae, iste innocentiae.*

875. *Qui minoratur corde, cogitat inania, et vir imprudens et errans, cogitat stulta.*

884 (title). *Omnibus enim mobilibus mobilior est sapientia.*

904. *In manu Dei potestas terrae, et utilem rectorem suscitabit* IN TEMPUS *super eam.*

910. *in omnibus operibus tuis esto velox.*

911. *paulatim atque per partes.*

914 (title) ’Εσθλὰ μὲν εσθλὸς ἔδυνε, χέρεια δὲ χεὶρονι δοσκον.

916. *Mala corda hominum, patientia Dei male utendo, durescunt.*

922. *Omni habenti dabitur et abundabit: ab eo autem qui non habet, et quod habet auferetur ab eo.*

926. *qui enim habet, dabitur illi.*

et qui non habet, etiam quod habet auferetur ab eo.

939. *Malum non potest esse purum absque commixtione boni; sicut bonum summum est absque commixtione mali.*

952. *Et pro eis ego sanctifico meipsum, ut sint et ipsi sanctificati in veritate.*

958 (title). *Cum enim scriptum sit: ‘Universae viae Domini misericordia et veritas’, nec iniusta eius gratia, nec crudelis esse potest iustitia.*

979. *Evanuerunt in cogitationibus suis, et obscuratum est insipiens cor eorum.*

981. *Etenim si peccaverimus tui sumus, scientes magnitudinem tuam.*

995. *Omnis qui natus est ex Deo peccatum non facit.*

997. *Salus religionis huius per quam solam veram salus vera veraciterque promittitur, nulli unquam defuit; qui dignus fuit, et cui defuit, dignus non fuit.*

998 (title). *Quae tamen misericordia.*

Quotations in Footnotes:

75. Peccatum non transit in posteros a primo parente per modum demeriti, quasi ipse omnibus mortem meruerit et infectionem peccati, sed per modum traductionis consequentis traductionem naturae: non enim unius personae actus toti naturae mereri vel demereri potest, nisi limites humanae naturae trascendat, ut patet in Christo, qui Deus et homo est, unde a Christo nascimur filii gratiae, non per carnis traductionem sed per meritum actionis. Ab Adam vero nascimur filii irae per propagationem, non per demeritum.

76. *Nulla res quae est in inferiori gradu naturae, potest appetere superioris naturae gradum, quia esse si transferretur in gradum superioris naturae... iam ipsum non esst. Sed in hoc imaginatio decipitur: quia enim homo appetit esse in altiori gradu quantum ad aliqua accidentalia, quae possunt crescere absque corruptione subiecti; aestimat quod possit appetere altiorem gradum naturae, in quem pervenire non posset, nisi esse desineret.*

77. *Quasi pannus menstruatae universae iustitiae nostrae.*

82. *Sunt iusti atque sapientes et* OPERA EORUM IN MANU DEI.

84. *Abscondam faciem meam ab eis, et considerabo novissima eorum.*

89. *On y verra sans doute avec intérêt, qu'en ne considérant même dans les principes éternels de la raison, de la justice et de l'humanité que les chances heureuses qui leur sont constamment attachées; il y a un grand avantage à suivre ces principes, et de graves inconvéniens à s'en écarter: leurs chances, comme celles qui sont favorables aux lotteries, finissent toujours par prévaloir au milieu des oscillations du hasard. Je désire que les réflexions répandues dans cet essai, puissant mériter l'attention des philosophes et la diriger vers un objet si digne de les occuper.*

91. *Ce n'est donc point parcequ'il se glorifie de sa raison que l'homme s'égare, mais parcequ'il se méprend sur sa nature en s'attribuant ce qui n'est pas à lui.* DANS SON ORGUEIL, IL CONFOND LA CAPACITÉ DE CONNOÎTRE, AVEC LA PUISSANCE DE PRODUIRE. *Il oublie que son intelligence, purement passive à l'origine, naît et se développe à l'aide des vérités qu'on lui donne, et qu'elle a reçu. Doué du pouvoir de combiner les vérités primitives et d'en tirer des conséquences, pouvoir borné comme toute action d'un être fini, il cherche en soi la certitude ou la dernière raison des choses, et ne l'y trouvant pas, il commence à douter. Les vérités se retirent, la nuit se fait; au milieu de cette nuit, il cesse de se reconnoître lui-même, seul et fier de sa solitude, il essaie de créer; il remue d'obscurs souvenirs,*

et croit peupler d'êtres réels son entendement désert, parcequ' il évoque des fantômes. Mais bientôt détrompé, las de ce vain labeur, il ferme les yeux et s'assoupit dans des ténèbres éternelles.

96. *Cum Deus sit ipsa essentia bonitatis, decuit ipsum summo modo se creatures communicare, quod in opere Incarnationis impletum fuisse credendum est.*

Ea [enim] quae ex sola Dei voluntate proveniunt supra omne debitum creaturae, nobis innotescere non possunt, nisi quatenus in sacra Scriptura traduntur, per quam divina voluntas [nobis] innotescit.

102. *Harum (rerum) vero electio penes mentem nostram est, nam ipsa (mens) actionis fons est et origo.*

105. *Tria tantum in homine reperimus, id est corpus et animam et voluntatem. Nam ut corpori anima data est; ita et potestas utrique utendi se ut vellet, indulta est.*

112. *N'avançons pas que les Abeilles, ainsi que tous les Animaux, sont de pure machines, des horloges, des métiers, etc. Une Ame tient probablement à la machine: elle en sent les mouvements: elle se plaît à ces mouvements; elle reçoit par la machine des impressions agréables ou déplaisantes, et c'est cette sensibilité qui est le grand et l'unique mobile de l'Animal.*

113. *Mirari satis non possumus, quod naturae effectus conspirent semper cum generalissimo canone metaphisico, qui nobis dictat: 'Naturam nihil facere frustra, semper agere per viam brevissimam, quae possunt fieri per pauca, nunquam natura fieri per plura.'*

127. *Non enim hoc est ex insufficientia divinae virtutis, sed ex immensitate bonitatis ipsius, per quam suam similitudinem rebus communicare voluit, non solum quantum ad hoc quod essent, sed etiam quantum ad hoc quod aliorum causae essent: his enim duobus modis creaturae communiter omnes divinam similitudinem consequuntur, ut supra ostensum est. Per hoc etiam decor ordinis in rebus creatis apparet.*

128. *faciet quaecumque volui, et prosperabitur in his, ad quae misi illud.*

133. *Gratias Domino Deo nostro, qui contra ista mala misit nobis adiutorium singulare. Quo enim non tolleret,*

quem non involveret, in quod profundum non demergeret fluvius iste horrendae nequitiae generis humani, nisi crux Christi in tanta velut mole auctoritatis eminentius firmiusque figeretur, cuius apprehenso robore, stabiles essemus, ne male suadentium, vel in mala impellentium tam vasto mundi huius gurgite abrepti sorberemur? In ista enim colluvie morum pessimarum et veteris perditae disciplinae, maxime venire ac subvenire debuit caelestis auctoritas.

138. Videte enim vocationem vestram, fratres, quia non multi sapientes secundum carnem, non multi potentes, non multi nobiles: sed quae stulta sunt mundi, elegit Deus, ut confundat sapientes: et infirma mundi elegit Deus, ut confundat fortia: et ignobilia mundi, et contemptibilia elegit Deus, et ea quae non sunt, ut ea quae sunt destrueret: ut non glorietur omnis caro *in conspectus eius.*

141. In his quae providentia debite reguuntur, non debet esse aliquid frustra. Cum igitur manifestum sit causas aliquas esse contingentes, ex eo quod impediri possunt ut non producant suos effectus, patet quod contra rationem providentiae esset, quod omnia ex necessitate contingerent.

150. Peccavit quidem opus Dei, id est angelus vel homo; sed opere suo peccaverunt, non opere Dei: ipsi sunt enim bonum opus Dei; peccatum vero eorum, malum opus ipsorum est, non Dei.

153. Sic providentur naturales effectus, ut etiam causae naturales ad illos naturales effectus ordinentur, sine quibus illi effectus non provenirent.

159. Numquid propter te derelinquetur terra, et transferentur rupes de loco suo?

167. Quem… Graeci nomine ornamenti appellavere, eum nos a perfecta absolutaque elegantia, mundum.

181. Inter cetera, propter quae mirabile divini artifcis ingenium est, hoc quoque existimo, quod in tanta copia rerum nunquam in idem incidit; etiam quae similia videntur, cum contuleris, diversa sunt; tot facit genera foliorum, nullum non sua proprietate signatum; tot animalia, nulli similitudo cum altero convenit.

198. *Sed si duo perfecte similia sunt in se possibilia, quod inficiatus non est Leibnitius, cum non potuerit videre haud esse in se pugnantia, nonne potest Deus ex his unum pro temino suae actionis eligere?*

217. *Cognitio singularium non pertinet ad perfectionem animae intellectivae secundum cognitionem speculativam. Pertinet tamen ad perfectionem eius secundum cognitionem practicam, quae non perficitur absque cognitione singularium in quibus est operatio, ut dicitur in VI Ethicorum.*

257. *Tu signaculum similitudinis, plenus sapientia, et perfectus decore.*

In die illa, dicit Dominus exercituum, Assumam te Zorobabel fili Salathiel serve meus, dicit Dominus, et ponam te quasi signaculum, quia te elegi, dicit Dominus exercituum.

258. *Creatio active significata significat actionem divinam, quae est eius essentia cum relatione ad creaturam. Sed relatio in Deo ad creaturam non est realis, sed secundum rationem tantum.*

261. *Si aequalitas omnimoda esset in rebus, non esset nisi unum bonum creatum. Gradus autem bonitatis superior est, ut aliquid sit bonum, quod non posit deficere a bonitate. Inferior autem eo est, quod potest a bonitate deficere. Utrumque igitur gradum bonitatis perfectio universi requirit. Ad providentiam autem gubernantis pertinet, perfectionem in rebus gubernatis conservare, non autem eam minuere. Igitur non pertinet ad divinam providentiam, ut omnino excludat a rebus potentiam deficiendi a bono. Hanc autem potentiam sequitur malum: quia quod potest deficere, quandoque deficit; et ipse defectus boni malum est.... Non est igitur ad divinam providentiam pertinens, ut omnino malum a gubernatis prohibeat.*

269. *Caritas autem est quae unit nos Deo, qui est ultimus finis humanae mentis.*

271. *Intellectus creatus non videt divinam essentiam secundum modum ipius essentiae, sed secundum modum proprium, qui finitus est.*

274. *Non est necessarium quod sciens causam, sciat omnes eius*

effectus, nisi causam comprehendat, quod non competit intellectui creato; et ideo unusquisque videntium Deum per essentiam, tanto plura in eius essentia conspicit, quanto clarius divinam essentiam intuetur et inde est quod de his potest unus alium instruere, et sic scientia angelorum et animarum sanctarum potest augeri usque ad diem iudicii; sicut et alia quae ad praemium accidentale pertinent, sed ulterius non proficient: quia tunc erit ultimus status rerum, et in illo statu possibile est quod omnes omnia cognoscant quae Deus scientia visionis novit.

Non omnes omnia vident in essentia divina, sed anima Christi ibi plane videbit omnia, sicut et nunc videt. Alii autem videbunt ibi plura vel pauciora secundum gradum quo Deum cognoscent, et sic anima Christi de his que prae aliis videt in verbo, omnes alias illuminabit. Unde dicitur Apocalypsi 21 quod 'claritas Dei illuminabit civitatem Hierusalem et lucerna eius est agnus'. Et similiter alii superiores illuminabunt inferiores, non quidem nova illuminatione, ut scientia inferiorum per hoc augeatur, sed quadam continuatione illuminationis sicut si intelligatur quod sol quiescens illuminat aerem; et ideo dicitur Danieli 12 quod qui ad iustitiam erudiunt plurimos, fulgebunt quasi stellae in perpetuas aeternitates.

275. Res autem quaelibet est intelligibilis secundum id quod habet de actu, non secundum id quod habet de potentia ut patet in 9 Metaphysicorum.

278. Putas ne Deus e vicino ego sum, dicit Dominus? et non Deus de longe? Si occultabitur vir in absconditis; et ego non videbo eum, dicit Dominus? Numquid non caelum et terram ego impleo, dicit Dominus?

300. Et tu Domine deridebis eos: ad nihilum deduces omnes gentes.

324. Significatur potentia impetusque horribilis hostium ut saepe alias exercitus numerosi, omnia instar fluvii inundantes, fluminibus comparantur, velut… Simili imagine, ad adumbrandum irruentem graecorum exercitum usus est Virgilius…

327. Ad brevitatem viam quam sapiens operator observat; pertinet quod non faciat per multa quod sufficienter potest fieri per unum. Et ideo convenientissimum fuit, quod per unum hominem omnes alii salvarentur.

389. *Postquam te invenerint omnia, quae praedicta sunt, novissimo tempore reverteris ad Dominum Deum tuum, et audies vocem eius. Quia Deus misericors, Dominus Deus tuus est. Non dimittet te, nec omnino delebit, neque obliviscetur pacti, in quo iuravit Patribus tuis.*

476. *Quod autem personarum acceptorem Deum se credere existimant, si credant quod sine ullis praecedentibus meritis, cuius vult miseretur, et quos dignatur vocat, et quem vult religiosum facit: parum adtendunt, quod debita reddatur poena damnato, indebita gratia liberato, ut nec ille se indignum queratur, nec dignum se iste glorietur, atque ibi potius acceptionem nullam fieri personarum, ubi una eademque massa damnationis et offensionis involvit* ut liberatus de non liberato discat, quod etiam sibi supplicium convenire, nisi gratia subveniret.

477. *Et effudit illam super omnia opera sua, et super omnem carnem secundum datum suum, et praebuit illam diligentibus se.*

478. *Fatum dicitur dispositio non quae est in genere qualitatis, sed secundum quod dispositio designat ordinem, qui non est substantia sed relatio.*

488. *Sicut divisiones aquarum, ita cor regis in manu Domini, quocumque voluerit inclinabit illud.*

494. *Nam quia in Dei sapientia, non cognovit mundus per sapientiam Deum: placuit Deo per stultitiam praedicationis salvos facere credentes.*

496. *Comprehenduntur in superbia sua.*

497. *Peccantem virum iniquum involvet laqueus; et iustus laudabit atque gaudebit.*

503. *Iustus comedit et replet animam suam: venter autem impiorum insaturabilis.*

505. *Combien de fois n'avons nous pas dit: 'La crise actuelle sera la dernière? et toujours il en est survenu de nouvelles. La raison de cela est que nous nous endormons toujours après la victoire: Nous passons brusquement de l'extrême energie à l'extrême foiblesse.*

526. *reddens odientibus se statim, ita ut disperdat eos, et ultra non differat, protinus eis restituens quod merentur.*

530. *scies ergo hodie quod Dominus Deus tuus ipse transibit ante te, ignis devorans atque consumens, qui conterat eos et deleat atque disperdat ante faciem tuam velociter.*

533. *Domini enim sententia fuerat ut indurarentur corda eorum et pugnarent contra Israel, et caderent, et non mererentur ullam clementiam, ac perirent, sicut praeceperat Dominus Moysi.*

579. *Ego merces tua magna nimis.*

581. *Duo sunt ordines electorum in iudicio futuri: unus iudicantium cum Domino, de quibus hoc loco memorat qui reliquerunt omnia et secuti sunt illum; alius iudicatorum a Domino, qui non quidem omnia sua pariter reliquerunt, sed de his tamen quae habebant quotidianas dare eleemosynas Christi pauperibus curabant, unde et audituri sunt in iudicio: 'Venite benedicti Patris mei, etc.'*

585. *Idem quippe fideles sancti et boni, et in comparatione plurium malorum pauci sunt, et per se ipsi multi sunt: quia 'multi filii desertae magis quam eius quae habet virum'; et 'Multi ab Oriente et Occidente venient et recumbent cum Abraham, Isaac et Iacob in regno caelorum'; et quia exhibet sibi Deus populum abundantem aemulatorem bonorum operum in Apocalypsi, ex omni tribu et lingua in stolis albis palmisque victricibus.*

588. *Omnes gentes plaudite manibus: iubilate Deo in voce exultationis… Regnabit Deus super gentes: Deus sedet super sedem sanctam suam…. Principes populorum congregati sunt cum Deo Abraham.*

600. *Nihil est infelicius felicitate peccantium qua poenalis nutritur impuritas et mala voluntas velut hostis interior roboratur.*

601. *si fortitudo quaeritur, robustissimus est, si aequitas iudicii, nemo audet pro me testimonium dicere.*

Nolite timere pusillus grex, quia complacuit Patri vestro dare vobis regnum.

605. *Vidit praesumptionem cordis eorum quoniam mala est, et cognovit subversionem illorum quoniam nequam est.*

Ideo adimplevit propitiationem suam in illis, et ostendit eis viam aequitatis.

608. *Verum, etsi ille pro omnibus mortuus est, non omnes tamen mortis eius beneficium recipiunt, sed ii dumtaxat, quibus meritum passionis eius communicatur.*

611. *Unde igitur ira Dei super innocentiam parvuli, nisi originalis sorte et sorte peccati?*

614. *Spiritus ubi vult spirat: sed, quod fatendum est, aliter adiuvat nondum inhabitans, aliter inhabitans. Nam nondum inhabitans adiutat ut sint fideles, inhabitans, adiuvat iam fideles.*

615. *Et Dominus elegit te hodie, ut sis ei populus peculiaris, sicut locutus est tibi, et custodias omnia praecepta illius et faciat te excelsiorem cunctis gentibus quas creavit in laudem et nomen et gloriam suam.*

620. *Si quis dixerit Dei praecepta homini etiam iustificato et sub gratia constituto esse ad observandum impossibilia, anathema sit. Deus impossibilia non iubet, sed iubendo movet et facere quod possis, et petere quod non possis, et adiuvat ut possis.*

621. *Orationem peccatoris ex bono naturae desiderio procedentem Deus audit, ex pura misericordia.*

623. *Si discutiatur et quaeratur unde quisque sit dignus, non desunt qui dicant voluntate humana: nos autem dicimus gratia vel praedestinatione divina.*

Quotations in the Appendix

No. 1. *Cette impuissance, ne conclut autre chose que la foiblesse de notre raison, mais non pas l'incertitude de toutes nos connoissances, comm'ils (les pyrrhoniens) le prétendent: car la connoissance des premiers principes, comme, par exemple, qu'il y a espace, temps, mouvement, nombre, matière, est aussi ferme qu'aucune de celles que nos raisonnmements nous donnent. Et c'est sur ces connoissances d'intelligence et de sentiment, qu'il faut que la raison s'appuie, et qu'elle fonde tout son discours. Je sens qu'il y a trois dimensions dans l'espace, et que les nombres sont infinits; et la raison démontre ensuite qu'il n'y a point deux nombres carrés, dont l'un soit double de l'autre.*

No. 5. *Et huc redit sancti Augustini sententia quod causa mali non sit a Deo, sed a nihilo, hoc est non a positivo, sed a privativo, hoc est ab illa quam diximus, limitatione creaturorum.*

Voici l'idée générale du système de l'illustre archevêque de Dublin. 1. Toutes les creatures sont nécessairement imparfaites, et toujours infinement éloignées de la perfection de Dieu; si l'on admettoit un principe négatif, tel que la privation des péripatéticiens, on pourroit dire que chaque être créé est composé d'existence et de non-existence; c'est un rien tant par rapport aux perfections qui lui manquent, qu'à l'égard de celles que les autres êtres possèdent: ce défaut ou, comme on peut l'appeler, ce mélange de non-entité, dans la constitution des êtres créés, est le principe nécessaire de tous les maux naturels, et rend le mal moral possible, come il paroîtra par la suite, etc.

No. 6. *Il est clair que leur système sape la religion chrétienne par ses fondements, et n'explique rien du tout.*

Pope avait dit tout est bien en un sens qui était très-recevable, et ils le disent aujourd'hui en un sens qui peut être combattu.

No. 7. *Neque vero poena tantum remanet, dimissa culpa, verum et ipsa culpa non ita per poenitentiam aboletur ut non illius aliquae maneant reliquiae quibus poena debetur.*

Non satis habet curatum esse vulnus ait Chrysostomus, etiam cicatricem sanari, pristinum etiam decorem restitui petit.

Quod fieri videmus in baptismo, ut remisso originalis peccati reatu, reliquiae tamen eius maneant, fomes ille concupiscentiae, quem tota vita piis exercitiis oportet mortificare: hoc et in poenitentiae sacramento evenit. Manent, quasi fomes quidam, quaedam reliquiae peccati, quas purgare satisfactione salubri necesse est: cum praesertim praeteritum peccatum in consuetudinem abiit, quod quanto fixerat radices altius, tanto maiore et longiore purgatione opus habet. Nam lavari quidem cito possumus, dicit Bernardus, ad sanandum vero opus est curatione multa.

No. 8. *Fit autem satisfactio per ieiunia, eleemosynas, orationes et alia pia spirtualis vitae exercitia; non quidem pro poena aeterna, quae vel sacramento, vel sacramenti voto una cum culpa remittitur, verum pro poena temporali, quae ut sacrae literae docent, non tota semper, ut in baptismo fit, dimittitur illis, qui gratiae Dei quam acceperunt, ingrati, Spiritum sanctum contristaverunt, et templum Dei violare non sunt veriti.*

Fit autem huiusmodi satisfactio non ad culpam vel poenam aeternam expiandam, haec enim satisfactio soli Christo tribuenda est. Solus ille factus est propitiatio pro peccatis nostris, non pro nostris tantum, verum et totius mundi. Solus ille mortem moriendo destruxit, per eam pro peccatis nostris abiunde satisfecit, per eam Patri suo celesti nos reconciliavit. Non de hac itaque satisfactione nunc loquimur; sed de ea quae in iis maxime poenitentiae fructibus consistit, quos iustitiae nomine Christus dignatur, in ieiunio, oratione, et eleemosyna sive a nobis ea suscepta, sive per parochos nostros Sacramentorumque dispensatores nobis iniuncta sit; quae cum ex fide et charitate peragitur, peccatorum causas exscindit, peccati reliquiis medetur, ac temporalem poenam vel tollit, vel mitigat: denique et in exemplum adhibetur.

Est quidem ita, quod Christus pro peccatis nobis abiunde satisfecit, pro nobis tot cruciatus, ac mortem etiam ipsam perferendo. Sed num ideo passus est, num ideo satisfecit, ut nos iam nihil patiamur, nihil faciamus pro peccatis nostris, posteaquam semel a gratia illa exciderimus, quam illi commortui, per baptismum consequuti fueramus? Quin ille nobis exemplum dedit potius, ut eius vestigia sequamur, ut sicut ipse tulit crucem suam, carnem nostram indutus, verum ab omni peccato prorsus immunis, ita et nos tot peccatis contaminati, tollamus et ipsi crucem nostram. Hoc est quod nos admonet dicens: 'Si quis vult venire post me abneget semetipsum, et tollat crucem suam, et sequatur me.' Explicans illa verba Samuelis ad Saulem Gregorius: 'Ecce quod remansit, pone ante te.' 'Remansit quidem, inquit, quia non omnia nostra Christus explevit. Per crucem quidem suam omnes redemit: sed remansit, ut qui redimi et regnare cum eo nititur, crucifigatur.' Hoc profecto residuum viderat, qui dicebat: 'Si compatimur et conregnabimus.' Quasi dicat: 'Quod explevit Christus non valet, nisi ei, qui id quod remansit, adimplet.' Hinc beatus Petrus apostolus dicit: 'Christus passus est pro nobis, vobis relinquens exemplum ut sequamini vestigia eius.' Hinc Paulus ait: 'Adimpleo ea, quae desunt passionum Christi in corpore meo.'

Dicit hic aliquis: 'Quid ergo mihi contulit crux Christi, si nihilominus opus est assidue portare me crucem propriam, quasi illa non suffecerit?' Multum adeo contulit. Nullus enim esset nostrae crucis usus, neque fructum ex ea caperemus ullum, nisi Christi crux praecessisset, cuius merito valet nostra crux, quicquid valet. Ad eumdem modum et satisfactionis nostrae pro peccatis nulla esset prorsus utilitas, nisi Christi satisfactio praecessisset, per cuius mortem et sanguinem efficacia redduntur, et Deo grata, quae fiunt a nobis in satifactionem pro peccatis nostris. Quod ergo prodest nobis nostra satisfactio, non aliter prodest, nisi virtute, merito, et afficacia Christi passionis, quae fons et fundamentum est omnium bonorum operum nostrorum, quae iam non nostra magis sunt, quam eius qui vivit in nobis, qui operatur in nobis, Christi, quia 'sine me, inquit, nihil potestis facere.'

No. 9. *Quaestio est de voce, num voluntas solum libera a coactione, dicenda sit absolute libera: multi affimant, et in hac acceptione D. Thomas dicit: 'Deus sua voluntate libere amat seipsum, licet de [necessitate amet seipsum; et Scotus: 'Voluntas Divina] necesario vult bonitatem suam et tamen in volendo est libera', et in eodem sensu docent passim Spiritum Sanctum libere procedere a Patre et Filio, ac beatos Deum amare.*

Sponte id fieri dicitur, cuius principium et causam continet is qui agit.

No. 14. *A peccatis omnibus sive originalibus, sive moralibus, vel quae facta sunt, vel ne fiant, non liberat nisi gratia Dei per Iesum Christum Dominum nostrum, in quo regenerati sumus, et a quo didicimus orando dicere non solum Dimitte nobis debita nostra, id est quia peccavimus; verum etiam, Ne nos inferas in tentationem, id est ne peccemus.*

Cum igitur et illa fateamur in hominibus esse peccata quae committuntur non necessitate, sed voluntate, quae tantummodo peccata sunt, unde ab eis liberum est abstinere; et peccatis de ignorantiae vel affectionum necessitate venientibus, quae iam non solum peccata, verum etiam poena sunt peccatorum, plenum sit genus humanum: quomodo dicis definitionibus nostris peccatum nec in moribus inveniri?

No. 15. *Elevata est magnificentia tua super caelos.*

non asserendo sed opinione Platonicorum utens.

No. 16. *Mens vero angelica, pura charitate inhaerens verbo dei, postea quam illo ordine creata est ut praecederet cetera, prius ea vidit in verbo Dei facienda, quam facta sunt.*

No. 17. [1] *Cum enim a mortuis resurrexerunt, neque nubent, neque nubentur, sed sunt Sicut Angeli [Dei] in Coelis.*

[2] *Non est enim regnum Dei esca et potus.*

[3] *In momento, in ictu oculi, in novissima tuba; canet enim tuba, et mortui resurgent incorrupti, et nos immutabimur.*

[4] *Licet non sequamur, tamen damnare non possumus, quia multi ecclesiasticorum virorum et martyres ista dixerunt, et unusquisque in suo sensu abundet, et Domini cuncta iudicio reservantur.*

[5] *Omitto dicere quemadmodum soleant Scripturae diem vel horam, etiam pro tempore ponere.*

[6] *In novissimo dierum intelligetis ea.*

[7] *In tempore illo, dicit Dominus: Ero Deus universis cognationbus Israel, et ipsi erunt mihi in populum.*

[8] *Et pavebunt ad Dominum et ad bonm eius, in novissimo dierum.*

[9] *Et erit: in novissimo dierum erit mons domus Domini praeparatus in vertice montium et sublimis super colles: et fluent ad eum populi.*

[10] *Pro octava enim multi inscribuntur psalmi… Sicut enim spei nostrae octava perfectio est, ita octava summa virtutum est.*

[11] *Filioli, novissima hora est: et sicut audistis quia antichristus venit; et nunc antichristi multi facti sunt: unde scimus quia novissima hora est.*

[12] *Sed et mille annorum tempus, si eorum finis esset*

saeculi finis, posset universum dici novissimum tempus, vel etiam novissimus dies, quia scriptum sest: 'Mille anni ante oculos tuos tanquam dies unus', ut quidquid per eosdem mille annos gereretur, novissimo tempore vel novissimo die diceretur geri. Iterum enim dico quod in hac causa saepe dicendum est: Consideremus ante quam multos annos dixerit beatus Iohannes Evangelista, 'Novissima hora est.' Nam si tunc essemus, hoc audito, quando crederemus tot annos postea transituros, ac non potius ipso adhuc Iohanne in corpore constituto, Dominum speraremus esse venturum? Neque enim dixit, Novissimum tempus est, aut novissimus annus, aut mensis, aut dies, sed 'Novissima hora est'. Et ecce ista hora quam longa est: nec tamen est ille mentitus, sed utique intelligendus est horam pro tempore posuisse.

[13] *Unusquisque in suo ordine, primitiae Christus: Deinde ii qui sunt Christi, qui in adventu eius crediderunt.*

[14] *Omnes quidem resurgemus, sed non omnes immutabimur.*

[15] *In momento, in ictu oculi, in novissima tuba: canet enim tuba, et mortui resurgent incorrupti: et nos immutabimur.*

[16] *Sed in diebus vocis septimi angeli cum coeperit tuba canere, consummabitur mysterium Dei, sicut evangelizavit per sanctos suos prophetas.*

[17] *Quibus accedit quod incorruptionem Scriptura semper accipit in bono: nec usquam reprobis eam attribuit, sed solis electis: ut proinde commentarius eorum qui partem hanc de omnibus mortuis interpretantur, etiam malis, quos incorruptos fore dicunt, quia mori non poterunt, nobis parum probabilis videatur.*

[18] *Nos qui vivimus, qui residui sumus in adventum Domini, non praeveniemus eos qui dormierunt.*

[19] *Non omnes quidem morimur sed omnes immutabimur.*

[20] *Posset tamen etiam secundum illos qui habent: 'Non omnes quidem morimur sed omnes immutabimur' legi sic: Mortui resurgent incorrupti, id est ad statum incorruptionis: et nos qui vivimus, licet non resurgamus, quia non morimur, tamen immutabimur de statu corruptionis*

in incorruptionem. Et videtur consonare iis quae dicit 1 Thess. 4: 'Nos qui vivimus, qui relinquimur, simul rapiemur cum illis, etc.', ut sic et ibi et hic connumeret se vivis.

[21] *Hoc quibusdam in fine largietur, ut mortem repentina commutatione non sentiant.*

[22] *Alii vero dicunt Apostolum dixisse: 'Non dormiemus de longa morte, quasi corruptione ac dissolutione opus sit.' Istud 'non omnes dormiemus', hoc modo oportet accipere, quod non dormiemus diuturna dormitione, ut opus sit sepulcro ac solutione ad corruptionem: sed brevem mortem sustinebunt qui tunc reperientur.*

[23] *Amen, Amen dico vobis, quia venit hora, et nunc est, quando mortui audient vocem Filii Dei: et qui audierint, vivent.*

[24] *Nolite mirari hoc quia venit hora, in qua omnes qui in monumentis sunt, audient vocem Filii Dei; et procedent qui bona fecerunt, in resurrectionem vitae: qui vero male egerunt, in resurrectionem iudicii.*

[25] *Donec impleatur tempora nationum.*

[26] *Et praedicabitur hoc Evangelium regni in universo orbe, in testimonium omnibus gentibus.*

[27] *Et tunc videbunt Filium hominis venientem in nube cum potestate magna et maiestate.*

[28] *Et vidi, et ecce nubem candidam et super nubem sedentem similem Filio hominis.*

[29] *His autem fieri incipientibus, respicite et levate capita vestra: quoniam appropinquat redemptio vestra.*

[30] *Et mittet angelos suos cum tuba et voce magna: et congregabunt electos eius a quatuor ventis, a summis caelorum usque ad terminos eorum.*

[31] *Et tunc mittet angelos suos, et congregabit electos suos a quatuor ventis a summo terrae usque at summum caeli.*

[32] *Et vixerunt, et regnaverunt cum Christo mille annis.*

[33] *Ita et vos cum videritis haec fieri, scitote quia prope est regnum Dei.*

[34] *Sic et vos cum videritis haec fieri, scitote quod in proximo sit in ostiis.*

[35] *Ita et vos cum videritis haec omnia fieri, scitote quia prope est in ianuis.*

[36] *Cum ergo dicit, 'Cum videritis haec fieri', quae intelligere poterimus, nisi ea quae supra commemorata sunt? In his est autem etiam quod ait, 'Et tunc videbunt Filium hominis venientem in nube cum potestate magna et maiestate.' Proinde etiam hoc cum visum fuerit, non iam erit regnum Dei, sed prope erit.*

[37] *Hunc ordinem videmus et duos alios Evengelistas tenere.*

[38] *Quid est 'Cum videritis haec fieri', nisi ea qua supra dixit? In quibus est etiam illud quod ait: 'Et tunc videbunt Filium hominis venientem in nubibus cum virtute multa et gloria: et tunc mittet angelos suos et congregabit electos suos.' Non itaque tunc erit finis, sed tunc erit in proximo.*

[39] *An dicendum est, non omnia, quae supra commemorata sunt esse intelligenda, ubi ait, 'Cum videritis haec fieri', sed aliqua eorum hoc videlicet excepto quod dictum est, 'Et tunc videbunt Filium hominis venientem, etc.?' Ipse quippe finis erit, non tunc proximus erit. Sed Matthaeus aperuit, nullis exceptis esse accipiendum quod positum est, 'Cum videritis haec fieri. "Nam et apud ipsum cum dictum esset, Et virtutes caelorum movebuntur"; Et tunc apparebit, inquit, signum Filii hominis in caelo et tunc plangent omnes tribus terrae. Et videbunt Filium hominis venientem in nubibus caeli in virtute multa et maiestate: et mittet angelos suos cum tuba et voce magna, et congregabunt electos eius a quatuor ventis, a summis caelorum usque ad terminos eorum. Ab arbore autem fici discite parabolam. Cum iam ramus eius tener fuerit, et folia nata, scitis, quia prope est aestas: ita et vos cum videritis haec omnia, scitote quia prope est in ianuis.'*

[40] *Sed horum duorum quid hic potius eligendum sit, iudicare difficile est.*

[41] *Promptior quidem sensus est, ut quisque cum audierit vel legerit: 'Et tunc videbunt Filium hominis venientem in nube cum potestate magna et maiestate', ipsum prorsus accipiat eius adventum, non per Ecclesiam, sed per se ipsum, quando venturus est ad vivos et mortuos iudicandos.*

[42] *Sed haec non sunt temere pollicenda, ne aliquid occurrat quod valide contradicat, praesertim quia in talibus divinorum eloquiorum obscuritatibus, quibus nostras intelligentias Deo placuit exercere, non solum alius alio movetur acutius eorum, qui Scripturas sanctas non improbabiliter tractant; sed etiam quilibet unus illorum, aliquando minus, aliquando melius intelligit.*

Index of Biblical References

Numbers in italic indicate footnote numbers and, if applicable, where the quotation is found in the text. Bible references are from RSV (Common Bible)

Index of Persons

Numbers in roman indicate paragraphs or, where stated, the appendix (app.); numbers in italic indicate footnotes

General Index

Numbers in roman indicate paragraphs or, where stated, the appendix (app.); numbers in italic indicate footnotes